LITERACIES

W. W. NORTON & COMPANY   NEW YORK LONDON

LITERACIES

READING, WRITING, INTERPRETATION

TERENCE BRUNK
RUTGERS UNIVERSITY

SUZANNE DIAMOND
RUTGERS UNIVERSITY

PRISCILLA PERKINS
ROOSEVELT UNIVERSITY

KEN SMITH
INDIANA UNIVERSITY SOUTH BEND

Copyright © 1997 by W. W. Norton & Company, Inc.
All rights reserved. Printed in the United States of America.

The text of this book is composed in Electra
with the display set in Optima.
Composition by Maple-Vail Composition Services.
Manufacturing by The Maple-Vail Book Manufacturing Group.
Book design by JoAnne Metsch.
Cover illustration: *Pablo Picasso* by Robert Sulkin.

Library of Congress Cataloging-in-Publication Data
Literacies : reading, writing, interpretation / Terence Brunk . . . [et.
    al.].
        p.   cm.
    ISBN 0-393-97043-4 (pbk.)
    1. College readers.   2. English language—Rhetoric.   I. Brunk,
Terence.
PE1417.L62   1996
808′.0427—dc20   96-17093
                                                                        Rev.

W. W. Norton & Company, Inc., 500 Fifth Avenue, New York, N.Y. 10110
http://web.wwnorton.com
W. W. Norton & Company Ltd., 10 Coptic Street, London WC1A 1PU

2 3 4 5 6 7 8 9 0

CONTENTS

PREFACE

As the editors of this book, we look at reading and writing as conversational processes. People "listen" to what texts say, discuss with other readers the meanings they find, and "talk back" to those texts by writing (and revising) their responses to the ideas they encounter. The readings we chose for *Literacies* represent many different ways of interpreting experience and the world. As you look through these pages, you will find the research of anthropologists next to short stories about family life, or a philosopher's theories about gender next to an essay that explores the social connection between words and diseases. The writers in this book speak different specialized languages, but by tracing the terms and ideas that are important to each reading, applying these ideas to new texts and contexts, and considering what these concepts say about the lives we live, active readers can make these texts "speak" to each other in illuminating, sometimes startling ways. The study questions, assignments, and invitations to write give students and teachers some of the tools they need to begin thinking about their own "literacies" in new and empowering ways.

Appropriately, this book is itself the result of many ongoing conversations: among ourselves (often over hundreds of miles), with other teachers, and, perhaps most importantly, with the countless students who have read these texts with us and shared, both in class discussions and in writing, their diverse, always growing interpretations. Like the rest of us, our students bring their experiences and commitments with them when they read and write. We believe this book offers strategies to help students put the lives they have led in the service of making new knowledge—academic, personal, and social. We have much to learn from what they say and write.

The four of us originally developed *Literacies* while we were all teaching in the Rutgers University Writing Program. As members of one of the Writing Program's textbook committees, we needed to replace a text which did not sufficiently challenge students to develop meaningful reading, writing, and interpretive skills. When we could not find the kind of book we sought, we began to construct such a book ourselves. We owe a particular debt to Ken Smith, whose reputation for sound pedagogical judgment lent weight to the project in the days before many teachers and program administrators had had a chance to judge *Literacies* for themselves. While he was a course coordinator and a writing program associate director at Rutgers, Ken maintained close communication with the Rutgers Writing Program administration, successfully articulating at all stages our shared vision of the ways in which the new textbook would enhance writing instruction for Rutgers students. Since that first edition, a second and revised edition of *Literacies* has been used, not only at Rutgers but in different institutional settings and in different parts of the United States.

We have many friends in the Rutgers University Writing Program whom we wish to thank: Carol Allen, Hugh English, Nancy Glazer, Katie Hogan, Priti Joshi, April Lidinsky, Ann Rea, Laura Sebastian-Coleman, Dawn Skorczewski, Susan Welsh, Mike Williamson, and Matthew Wilson are only some of the people whose feedback and encouragement have contributed to the project. We especially wish to thank Kurt Spellmeyer, our partner in many formative conversations about reading, writing, and pedagogy.

During her time at Rutgers, Marilyn Rye raised issues about reading and writing that we have tried to build upon in this book. We have adapted the flexible and dynamic Invitations to Write that Lou Kelly developed at the University of Iowa and wish to thank her for giving us permission to introduce them in this new context. Carl Klaus gave us helpful advice when we needed it. Our reviewers—including Nancy Barry, Luther College; Alexander Friedlander, Drexel University; Thomas Miller, University of Arizona; and Linda H. Peterson, Yale University—kept us aware of the needs of teachers and students working in a variety of writing settings. We appreciate their thoughtful honesty. Finally, we wish to thank Libby Miles for her work on the biographical sketches and our friends at Norton: Allen Clawson, for his efforts in bringing Norton and *Literacies* together; Marian Johnson, for her skilled manuscript editing; Kate Lovelady, for her work on permissions; Diane O'Connor, for attending to production; and Carol Hollar-Zwick, our editor, for her ability to keep our conversations focused while still hearing and responding to the productive differences among our ideas about the project.

TERENCE BRUNK
SUZANNE DIAMOND
PRISCILLA PERKINS
KEN SMITH

INTRODUCTION

READING, RATIFICATION, AND RISK

You take a chance when you read. You risk an encounter with another person's ideas and experiences, and you may not be the same when you are finished. Paying close attention to someone's words is an act of respect and a form of inquiry, a way of taking the world seriously. When you think about the ways a writer's words relate to what you know of the world, you take your own ideas and experiences seriously too. There is no telling where that inquiry might lead and whose ideas might be challenged in the process. Everything is up for grabs, then, when you think about what you read, and that is the power, and the risk, of the encounter. Reading like that can change a person.

As you read the first paragraph, you may have questioned what we said, and rightly so. You may have thought of other kinds of reading you know well—reading a novel for pleasure, for example, enjoying the suspense and the lively characters, or reading a magazine or nonfiction book to learn something new about a favorite pastime, or reading a manual to learn how to make a useful repair. There are many reasons for reading and as many ways to read, and you undoubtedly have made several of them a regular part of your life. Since this is a textbook, and you have probably been assigned to read it, you may have read that first paragraph in yet another way. How, you might ask yourself now, are you accustomed to reading textbooks? If your experience is like ours, you may feel that schools have sometimes taught you to accept textbooks as storehouses of approved and authoritative information, neatly arranged and ready to be learned. As textbook writers, we invite you to read this textbook much differently than that. Read *Literacies* as openly and contentiously as you can.

If you used your reading experience to challenge what we said in the first paragraph, then you were reading our words for something other than authoritative information. Instead, you may have started to ask yourself what relations you could find between another person's understanding, presented in the paragraph, and your own. If so, then you were beginning to explain and explore and evaluate one body of ideas and experience—ours—in light of another—yours. Whenever you take that step as a reader, you prepare yourself to become a more powerful thinker, a person who can shape new insights from an encounter with someone else's perspective. This book is about becoming that kind of reader—and making that kind of reading work for you as a writer.

Along the way to those goals, even readers who scrutinize rather than faithfully accept a textbook's authority face another barrier. We are thinking now of a trait of human psychology that Dean Barnlund, a writer in *Literacies*, describes in his essay "Communication in a Global Village." Barnlund mentions "how powerfully human beings are drawn to those who hold the same beliefs and how sharply they are repelled by those who do not." Although Barnlund talks generally about communication in his essay, we can apply his idea to the act of reading. He says that this common psychological trait "converts many human encounters into rituals of ratification, [with] each person looking to the other only to obtain endorsement and applause for his own beliefs." Some people read this way all the time. They seek out books and articles that support their opinions, or they look into a text only until they know where the writer "stands" on an issue. There is no true inquiry, no risk of encounter, in those reading practices. If we approach reading as a "ritual of ratification," an opportunity for "endorsement and applause," where we want the writer to confirm what we already believe, then our wish will probably come true. When we read to ratify, our ideas will remain unchanged.

Yet good readers probably begin, more often than not, with something like ratification. As people read, they may find it much easier to recognize something they share with a writer than to sort out their differences. As members of a community, for example, as citizens, readers may want to affirm shared values, for the sake of stability or solidarity, for the sake of continuity and an orderly life. Furthermore, if you have ever been persuaded temporarily by a powerful argument, or if you have ever "lost yourself in a book," you probably know that good readers, even when they resist ratification, still have to read a text closely and openly enough to risk being swayed by what it says, as Robert Scholes, another *Literacies* writer, points out. But good readers, he believes, do not stop there. Having submitted for a while to someone else's meanings in a text, they step back, reconsider from their own perspective, and find ways to evaluate based on what they bring to the reading and what they know of the world. After having temporarily "surrendered," good readers use their critical skills to "recover" their own integrity and shape their own meanings, Scholes says, which may now be broader and more powerful because they will incorporate elements of both persons' perspectives. In that way, readers who inquire and establish connections between what they know and what they read create an opportunity for a new understanding of themselves and others. Good readers abandon the safety of ratification and risk an encounter with another person's ideas and experiences in exchange for the opportunities of new thinking and growth. This back-and-forth process, with its exchange of meanings and its possibilities for new ones, is interpretation. Let's look at a detailed example of the process.

THE VILLAGERS AND THE ANTHROPOLOGIST

You may wonder how serious we are when we invite you to challenge what you read in this book. Many of the writers in *Literacies* are experts in their particular fields, and students of ours have sometimes asked whether they really have the authority to question what the experts have written. But many of the readings in this book show how important it is for individuals to reflect on, and when necessary, challenge the beliefs of others. You may know from your own experience the difference such an act can sometimes make for a person or for a wider group or community. One writer in particular, Nancy Scheper-Hughes, shows how even the seemingly unequal exchange between an expert anthropologist and the people she studies can teach both sides something they hadn't expected when they truly risk an encounter with the other's ideas and experiences. In fact, experts in several fields like anthropology have drawn on the views of outsiders in recent years to refresh their thinking about how societies work. In an exchange of ideas, locating an outsider's point of view can sometimes provoke a breakthrough.

As valuable as it is, this can be very challenging or even disturbing, as Scheper-Hughes shows in her essay "The Anthropological Looking Glass." Scheper-Hughes points out that anthropologists' books are ordinarily "shielded" from responses by nonexperts, especially responses by the people they study and write about. Often anthropologists haven't written in the language spoken by the people they study, so their subjects haven't been able to dispute or even add to what the anthropologists say about their society. Accustomed to having their authority shielded in this way, anthropologists can find it "most unsettling" when their subjects do speak back, as in the case of Scheper-Hughes's own research in a village in western Ireland. After living in and studying the village of Ballybran for a year, Scheper-Hughes wrote a book called *Saints, Scholars, and Schizophrenics*. In her book she argued that the whole region around Ballybran was sinking slowly under the weight of stifling social customs that cause mental illness in an alarming number of the inhabitants. When the book was published in 1979, many villagers read it avidly, saw how their way of life was portrayed, and came to their own angry conclusions about the book's value and truthfulness. They disputed the book, though quietly, in their customary ways. More importantly, perhaps, they used the book. One man was so pleased to see some of his witty sayings quoted there that he memorized them so he could say them again—a very curious example of ratification, perhaps. One group began to examine the difficult social problems the book revealed, and one woman reported that she and her friend were able to discuss common problems as they never could before. "A great burden has been lifted," that villager said.

All of this new thinking was made possible by working back and forth between Scheper-Hughes's anthropological perspective and what she calls the "common sense world" of the village. As the village readers considered these two perspectives, their ideas about their own lives came up for fresh thought and discussion—that is, for the benefits and risks of revision. Spurred on by the outsider's view of their society, some of the villagers made an inquiry and started to undo the limits of ratification. As they reconsidered their common-sense world, they composed a new understanding that corresponded to their own contexts and desires and their new, wider perspective. By reading the anthropology text, the villagers were able to read their experience again, freshly. When they encountered this outsider's voice, written in an unfamiliar, specialized language, they discovered that they had to examine their own lives in order to read the anthropology. They discovered that experience can be read—that is, reinterpreted rather than merely ratified—just as a book can be. They also had a chance to discover one of the important aspects of *Literacies*—the opportunities for revision that are created when we bring different social voices together. If the villagers of Ballybran came to see reading as a risky chance for crossing boundaries, as a valuable chance for revision, then they made the experience of reading part of their own process of change and growth. They also proved something very important: when mere ratification stops, the authority to interpret can belong to anyone—villagers, college students, anthropologists—who dares to use it.

That last statement helps to explain one more trait of the villagers' encounter with Scheper-Hughes. In her essay, she reflects on the angry reception her book met in Ballybran. She reports that some of her friends and acquaintances were wounded by her portrayal of their village life and her assessment of its weaknesses and broke off their friendships with her. Some strongly questioned her right to publish their private ways to the world. Through their replies to her book, she began to reconsider the purposes and methods of anthropology. She asked herself what she hoped to accomplish by writing an account that was critical of its subject's ways. Even though the villagers would seem to have no right to question the expert on her field of expertise, question her they did, and she found herself startled by their inquiries. As she reflected on their views of anthropology in general and on her work in particular, she began to revise her understanding of her field's ethical obligations to the people being studied. By challenging the anthropologist and perhaps even changing her, the villagers of Ballybran started to change the field of anthropology.

LITERACIES

We have kept in mind the interpretive encounter between Nancy Scheper-Hughes and the people of Ballybran as we have written and revised the materials for this book. Our title, *Literacies*, introduces some of the opportunities you may encounter as you write your essays. We chose this name to acknowledge the many types of essays and stories in these pages, the many kinds of specialist writers represented here, and the specialized kinds of language and knowledge used to compose these readings. In the late twentieth century, it is not possible to assume that there is one general sort of literacy that suits all experiences, all audiences, and all occasions. Our society is made up of many social voices, many kinds of expertise, many contexts and languages, and we believe that a reading anthology that includes many of those voices offers a more realistic sense of the complex lives we are all leading. Furthermore, our world of contesting social voices offers special opportunities for a person to go beyond ratification to shape her own meanings. Each person can try out some of the ways of interpreting used by these different social voices— learning from any of them, rather than ratifying one of them. Your course's sequence of writing assignments will ask you to explore those possibilities throughout the semester, working through a variety of perspectives as you write and revise, just as the people of Ballybran and their visiting anthropologist did.

This book invites you to be a reader and writer who questions boundaries, who uses the knowledge and the literacies you already possess to grapple with other literacies, who dares to speak within and across academic fields and areas of experience, and who composes essays that go beyond ratification. In order to do that, you will need to study what it means to bring another person's language into a conversation with your own. This means much more than quoting an author to "back up" or "prove" your point—we recognize that as ratification. While you might hear someone refer to the conversational writing process as "quoting" (since it does involve placing someone else's words in quotation marks in your paper), "quoting" itself is not an adequate explanation of the process of bringing together literacies that are strangers to each other. When you turn to the readings in *Literacies*, you will find many voices to work with, and at first they might be very strange in each other's company. But that strangeness is your chance to see your subject freshly, just as it was for Nancy Scheper-Hughes's friends and acquaintances in the Irish village and for Scheper-Hughes herself. These diverse literacies have the power to make things visible in a new way. Use that power as a partner in your work this semester. As you read, as you participate in class discussions, and as you write your drafts and revisions, bring these voices into the conversation. Let their words, their terms, their phrases and sentences, and their ideas and experiences aid and influence you as you revise your ideas. Make the specific language of another person part of the back-and-forth process of interpretation. Readers and writers who know how to do that can find ways to develop their ideas almost anywhere. They take advantage of the diversity we find in a world of competing literacies.

RESOURCES OF THE BOOK

The forty-three writers in *Literacies* represent a wide range of academic disciplines, kinds of writing, and bodies of cultural experience. We chose them not just for their variety but also because of the ways they approach writing and interpretation. In their essays, short stories, letters, and interviews, these writers consider diverse perspectives and think critically with the help of distinctive tools of analysis that they have found useful in their diverse contexts. In doing so, they provide us with a set of critical tools—special concepts or terms for thinking about the meaning of experiences and the work of academic disciplines. As active readers, you and the other members of your class can use those tools this semester. These texts are not provided for you to ratify, but to use both in your writing class discussions and in the essays that you will go on to write.

READING QUESTIONS

Each of the readings is accompanied by four sets of questions designed to help with the back-and-forth work of interpretation. The Before Reading questions build on the knowledge that you, as a reader, bring to new texts; they are meant to help you connect your knowledge to what the text says. Because this knowledge is often quite diverse, the Before Reading questions may invite you to explore such things as common experiences, preconceptions about a subject, important terms, or historical background. For example, before you read "Chosen People," Stuart Ewen's history of the consumer in American life, we invite you to reflect on times when you have cared about the image you present to others. Ewen puzzles over the love Americans have for presenting certain images of themselves, so your insights may help you to evaluate his theory. We also ask your thoughts about the terms "consumer" and "middle class"—two terms that are vital to Ewen's discussion. Finally, we ask you to discuss some ways of reacting to a piece of advertising, a question Ewen also addresses in his essay. In all of these cases, you don't have to wait for Ewen to speak. Even before you have heard his theory, you can activate some of your relevant knowledge and experience; you can speak and write, first. Then, when you read Ewen's essay, you can see how he addresses, perhaps even responds to, your ideas about the subject. And having prepared some of your own ideas and experiences ahead of time, you will be less tempted merely to ratify the words of the expert. You will be ready to make reading into more of a dialogue between you and the writer.

Each *Literacies* text is followed by three other kinds of questions: Active Reading, Reading in New Contexts, and Draft One / Draft Two questions. Because we've tried to choose dynamic readings, the essays in this book invite active reading. The writers all share a commitment to seeing their topics from more than one perspective, rather than dictating a dogmatic monologue about them. In the readings, something develops, something changes contexts, something is looked at in light of new terms, fresh examples, different perspectives. When you read with that dynamic quality in mind, you can trace those new terms, examples, perspectives within each text, and when you find them you can begin to deepen your understanding of the writer's thinking. Instead of discovering a single main idea, for example, you may see a series of linked ideas that rely on each other and on important examples to complete a line of thought, and you may need to return to several points in the text and examine what has been brought up there, what has changed, what is new. The Active Reading questions point out some ways to begin that task. After Shirley Brice Heath's study of the literacy practices of a small, isolated community called Trackton, for example, one of the Active Reading questions asks you to compare the ways the community trains children for reading and writing in Trackton and the ways the training prepares children for new situations outside of the community. By looking at their literacy skills in two contexts, then, you have a chance to understand something new—about literacy? about Trackton? about poverty or isolation?—that would be harder to pin down without the difference in perspective. Because all of the writers in *Literacies* use varying examples, terms, contexts, and perspectives to give richness to their thinking and writing, you can practice the same kinds of analysis as you read each selection.

Reading in New Contexts questions invite you to continue the process of active reading by applying a text's special concepts or terms to another *Literacies* reading. Good readers practice this trait almost automatically—perhaps you already pick up the ways of talking and thinking you encounter and try out new ideas in other contexts. The Reading in New Contexts questions ask you to practice this process. We select one or more terms or ideas for each question and suggest a context in which to apply them. In "The Social Power of Expert Healers," for example, Howard Brody creates three terms for looking at the imbalance of power between physicians and patients. If you work with his definitions of these terms—owned power, aimed power, and shared power—and you apply them to other unequal social relationships, you will clarify his meaning and prepare yourself to evaluate the terms as ideas. If you can confidently apply and evaluate ideas and terms in new contexts by the end of the semester, you will have accomplished something very important in your writing course.

Draft One / Draft Two questions ask you to practice all of the interpretive skills contained in the other sets of questions while working through a process of rethinking and revision. Whether these questions call directly on personal experience or not, all of the Draft One / Draft Two sets ask you to work with more than one perspective as you write and revise. Draft One questions introduce a problem or topic and suggest some ways of shaping a response, while Draft Two questions introduce a different perspective into the discussion and call for a revision of your first response in light of that new perspective. Together, these questions invite you to compose an essay that uses multiple perspectives much the way many *Literacies* readings do. You will need to work on these paired questions over several days or even a couple of weeks in order to have time to read and reread the texts, to reflect on your prior knowledge of the topics, and to work back and forth between the different perspectives you encounter as you write and revise. One of the sets of questions following Victor Seidler's essay is typical: The Draft One question works with Seidler's idea that our society's ways of defining men's social roles are damaging to men, asking you to evaluate that idea in light of your own experience. To complete the Draft Two question, you will need to extend and revise your work by incorporating the men's experiences described in another *Literacies* reading. By the time you complete the project, you will have evaluated Seidler's idea from at least two perspectives, in successive drafts, which means you will be in a good position to explain your judgment of its merit.

INVITATIONS TO WRITE

The Invitations to Write come in two varieties. The first set of Invitations addresses common aspects of reading, writing, and revising, and invites you to describe and make decisions about the way you approach assignments. These Invitations suggest ways to be more strategic about how you shape interpretations or revise them for an audience. The second set addresses error in grammar, punctuation, and spelling. These Invitations introduce a more systematic approach to error than you might already be using. Since most writers make a few mistakes repeatedly, with some guidance they can compile a personal handbook of their most common error patterns and use the handbook to search out those patterns, spot those errors, and fix them. In time, writers who take a systematic approach to their own patterns of error can hand in papers that are free of anything that will distract a reader from the ideas they contain.

Both sets of Invitations are opportunities for you to write informally about your interpretive and composing practices and to reflect how your practices are serving you now. Taken in that spirit, they create occasions for you to consider how to make the most of your writing course.

ASSIGNMENT SEQUENCES

Following the readings, you will find a collection of sequenced writing assignments, or sequences, designed to offer opportunities for extended intellectual projects. While most Draft One / Draft Two questions invite you to draft and revise with two or three perspectives in mind, in a sequence you will stay with a topic for several weeks, encountering three or more readings and a variety of perspectives, concepts, and bodies of experience which you will use in a series of class discussions and essays. Whether your teacher selects one or two of the twelve sequences in *Literacies* or provides others, you will find that there is a great advantage to staying with a topic for several reading and writing assignments. You have a lengthy opportunity to reread, resee, and comprehend ideas as you apply them in new contexts. Extended work with a set of ideas resembles the work you will be doing in your academic major and in your career, so the interpretive challenges you face in the sequences have a special realistic value.

MLA AND APA CITATIONS AND BIOGRAPHICAL SKETCHES

Literacies includes a brief guide to MLA and APA citation. Refer to this guide for the basic requirements for giving credit when you quote, paraphrase, or draw information from a source, including the readings in this book. If you use the guide to make accurate citations for the passages you quote from *Literacies*, you will become accustomed to one of these two styles of citation and will be prepared to use a fuller version when you write longer research essays for other courses. While composing citations is the most mechanical aspect of learning to quote from sources, it is an important tool for making other readers and writers your partners as you develop ideas. When you quote, you point to something meaningful; when you discuss what you quote, you involve yourself with the ideas and experiences of others and explore the relations you find there. When your teacher or classmates respond to a draft you have written, they will be better able to involve themselves in your thinking and give useful feedback if they can refer to the passages from which you have taken your quotations. In your writing class, as in other academic and professional fields, referring accurately to source materials helps everyone work together to consider new problems in the light of old understandings.

Finally, *Literacies* concludes with biographical sketches of the people who wrote the book's essays, stories, and interviews. The sketches provide basic background about the authors and the names of a few of their other works, so you can read and study further, if you wish.

CONCLUSION

In *Literacies* we offer a series of reading and writing practices that support the process of interpretation. In your writing course use the different elements of this book to become more strategic about your work as a reader and writer. Make several of the book's suggested reading and writing practices your own, and use them whenever you need to come to an understanding, to shape an interpretation, of complex and conflicting materials. Make sure that your regular interpretive practices activate the best elements of your own judgment and experience. Make other writers partners in your thinking by quoting them and discussing what you quote. Make it your project this semester to better understand the process that gives an idea merit. You can risk an encounter with the ideas and experiences of others, using what you bring to a reading to involve yourself in the writer's concerns, and working out a new position for yourself as a result. You can make knowledge, not just recall it; you can combine ideas and examples in fresh and interesting ways, not just repeat the combinations that others have made. You can speak and write with a new authority about the meaning of your own experience and the experience of others.

INVITATIONS TO READ AND WRITE

On the following pages, you will find a number of "Invitations" to write about some common aspects of the reading and writing process. The Invitations ask you to reflect on your own approach to the problems of reading, writing, and revising and to try some new strategies that you may find helpful. Use the Invitations on your own or with your teacher's guidance, but adapt them to your own circumstances. Focus your energies on the parts of the Invitations that you find most relevant to your reading and writing task. When you sit down with one of them, write informally, as if you were talking on paper, about what you find there. With these ideas and questions, we invite you to become more aware of the choices you can make as an interpreter.*

---

* Invitations to Write were first composed by Lou Kelly for her students at the University of Iowa's Writing Lab. She also coined the term "talking on paper." We have borrowed several of her pedagogical principles in these Invitations, most of which were first composed for students at Rutgers University, New Brunswick, by Ken Smith and Dawn Skorczewski. The Invitations from Rutgers have been revised and reprinted here with their permission. We are also indebted to Lou Kelly for the model we follow here in the Invitations that address a systematic approach to error, including the personal handbook.

In brief, the Invitations focus on the following aspects of the reading and writing process:

1. **Reading Actively** opens up the conversation with a series of active ways to mark up the text of a new reading.
2. **What Does This Have to Do with My Life?** offers tools for making meaningful connections with what you read.
3. **Taking a Second Look at the Reading** suggests strategies for the essential act of rereading.
4. **Getting Started on an Essay** calls for writing informally about the possibilities you see as you begin writing.
5. **What Is the Assignment Really Asking?** proposes some ways of becoming a skillful reader of assignment questions.
6. **What Do the Teacher's Comments Mean?** shows how to make your teacher's suggestions count as you write and revise.
7. **Asking Your Own Questions** invites you to become your own best reader.
8. **Organizing, or Making Relations Clear** explores practical ideas for shaping an essay.
9. **Checking Your Progress** asks you to reflect at midcourse on the progress you are making toward your course goals.

The following four Invitations introduce a systematic approach to copyreading your work:

10. **How Do You Deal with Error?** calls for an inventory and evaluation of your own copyreading practices.
11. **Tracking a Pattern of Error** offers a strategy for learning to recognize and control one of your common errors.
12. **Reviewing . . . in Your Own Words** asks you to take stock of the new copyreading work you have done.
13. **Using Your Personal Handbook to Copyread a New Draft** puts your new copyreading strategy to use on a new piece of writing.

INVITATION 1

Reading Actively: How to Mark a Text

Reading a text for the first time can be a challenge for any reader. When you encounter a new reading, you open yourself to the writer's words and ideas, insights and prejudices, as well as to kinds of language and forms of writing that might be unfamiliar to you. The newness of these reading experiences can make a text difficult to understand. But every time you pick up something to read, you have an opportunity to read actively—to work with the words on the page to develop your own understanding.

Developing your own understanding involves more than just being able to take notes that summarize an author's main ideas, even though taking notes can be a useful part of active reading. You begin to make a reading your own when you respond to it by adding your own words to the material on the page. Adding your voice to the author's creates a fuller conversation between the two of you, the kind of conversation that makes new meaning—not just summary—possible. Active readers have usually developed several ways of marking the things they read in order to record their part of that conversation. That's how they begin to speak up about what they are reading.

Try some of the following ways of marking a text, of recording your part of the conversation, and of making the reading your own. Also, invent other ways of marking a text, to suit your own needs.

- Mark any passages that call to mind or help you think about personal experience. Comment on the connections you see there.
- Mark concepts or statements that remind you of other things you've read. Comment on the ways these passages confirm, challenge, or otherwise relate to ideas and events you've encountered in other texts.
- Mark passages that seem especially right or wrong to you. Comment on the reasons for your strong reactions. What ideas and experiences do you bring to these passages, and how do they influence your response? Even if you are not sure, record all of your strong first responses to a reading— your "gut reactions."
- Mark the writer's main terms as they are used throughout the text, especially when the writer defines the terms. Be alert to and comment on the different ways the writer uses each term, including the ways he or she provides different perspectives on a term.
- Mark any unusual word choices or phrases. Comment on why they seem unusual and on the effect these have on you as you read.
- Mark any unfamiliar words. Decide whether it would be disruptive or helpful to look them up as you make a first reading. Use a college dictionary and jot down the definition that seems closest to the way the word is used in the text. Revise the definition, in your own words, based on the way the word is used in the text.

- Mark any major transitions you notice with the letter "T". These might come between a section of storytelling and a section of discussion, between a passage of ideas and a passage of examples, or any other place where a text changes somehow. Return to these transitions when you want to think about how a text is organized to develop an idea or accomplish the writer's other goals. Mark words like "but" or "however" as clues to transitions.
- Mark any difficult sections that you wish to return to later and clarify. Comment on the problem in understanding you face in these sections, and, later, record your best answer to that problem. You might also try putting the passage into your own words.
- Mark places where you see interesting connections between the author's ideas and the examples the author provides. Comment on the relations between the two, and write down any questions they bring to mind.

INVITATION 2

What Does This Have to Do with My Life?

Write about one of these two perspectives:

1. Sometimes a reading or writing assignment seems to be merely academic. That is, it seems to relate only to the world of the college or university, never touching the life you know outside of school. But assignments are more rewarding if you can look past that impression and *make* a connection with the life you have lived or the life you hope to live.

It's good for a person's morale to be able to connect schoolwork and life experience, but that's not the end of it. When you make those connections, you can start to use the knowledge and experience you bring with you to deepen the value of the schoolwork. You can use your worldly knowledge to illuminate the specialized knowledge of the academy.

Here are some questions that might help you do that. Write informally about several of these—see what connections you can make and explore:

- Are there any passages in the reading that you, because of your life experience, are especially able to understand and appreciate? Write about one of those passages and show how it relates to your experience.

- What specialized terms does the writer use to discuss this topic? Do you know of any events or facts that help explain one of those terms or reveal its usefulness? Do you know of any event or facts that challenge or contradict the writer's understanding of those terms? Write about these.
- Have you experienced or witnessed anything that the writer's academic knowledge doesn't take into account? Write about one or more of those events, and tell how to change the academic knowledge to take them into account.

2. How does the reading illuminate my life?

You may feel, on the other hand, that the reading says more about your life than your life says about the reading. In that case, explore those links as you write informally about one or more of these questions:

- Choose a passage from the reading, and tell what it helps explain about an experience you have known. After you have said as much as you can, consider this: does the passage exhaust the meaning of the experience, or is there more to be said? What other idea or theory would help you account for the experience you have in mind?
- Would a person who accepted this writer's ideas choose the same paths in life that you have chosen or that you have seen others choose? How would the ideas from this reading alter your life or the life of someone you know well?
- Are the writer's ideas useful to a person in a certain profession? What difference would these ideas make for someone practicing that profession?

INVITATION 3

Taking a Second Look at the Reading

When you prepare to write your next essay, you should turn back to the *Literacies* readings to refresh your memory and generate ideas. As you reread, you will probably notice new ideas or examples or even contradictions in a writer's thoughts. You will almost certainly find quotations you would like to consider. You may even be surprised at how differently a reading strikes you the second time around.

You have a great advantage when you reread. You already know, in a general way, what the reading has to offer. As you make your way through a second time, you can work more strategically with the material. Many writers clarify their thoughts and find material for their writing by rereading, but often they use different reading strategies as they do this. They return to the reading with something new they want to accomplish. With a second reading, you can start to make the reading your own.

Try one or more of these things when you reread:

- Make a short list of questions you would like to answer as you read, and take notes about them as you go.
- Make a list of terms or concepts you would like to examine, and identify passages where the writer works with them.
- Write down an idea you would like to test against the experiences described in the reading. As you finish a portion of the narrative, take notes about the relations you see developing between idea and experience.
- Try reading the paragraphs out of order. Instead of starting with the first paragraph, as you did when you first read it, turn, for example, to a part of the reading that confuses you or a part that you haven't thought about yet. Write about what you find there.
- If you really want to take a fresh look at something, read it backward. Try reading the last paragraph or page, then summarizing it. Then read and summarize the previous paragraph or page, and so on. What do you see differently in the reading when you begin by thinking about where it ends up?

INVITATION 4

Getting Started on an Essay

Choose some ideas or difficult passages in your current reading or writing assignment. Write as much as you can about them—ask questions, sum up the arguments in the readings, plan your argument (if you are this far along), or spin out ideas and possibilities. Don't worry about writing polished paragraphs just yet. Instead, try out the tools and materials you have before you and see how you might use them to compose an essay. If you have no idea where to begin, try writing in detail about something you do not understand. You need to start thinking and talking, taking a first step. Pick up your pen or turn on the computer and begin writing.

INVITATION 5

What Is the Assignment Really Asking?

Perhaps this would be a good time to look closely at your current writing assignment. Whether the assignment comes from your teacher or from *Literacies*, it is good strategy to read and reread it. When you are just starting an essay or trying to revise one, looking back at the assignment can help you take a fresh look at the work to be done.

As you read an assignment, you should probably mark it up, right on the page itself. You can, of course, write down your first thoughts about the assignment, but you can make your mark in other ways too. For example, you can put a box around the part of the assignment that you find most important. You can underline the concepts or terms you plan to grapple with in your essay. You can mark each of the assignment's tasks with a number, in order to make sure that each one finds its way into your thinking and your draft. Whatever strategy you take, your words, marks, or numbers will remind you of how you are interpreting the assignment itself.

Here are some other things you might find useful to do:

- If you haven't addressed part of the assignment yet, copy that part on another sheet and write informally about it. What ideas and examples can you offer, tentatively, in response?
- If the assignment calls for you to quote from a reading, find and copy down two or three promising quotations on another sheet. (Include the page number for each quotation.) What can you say, tentatively, about the quotations? Tell why each one is important for the issues you are considering in this assignment.
- If the assignment invites you to draw on the insights of your personal experience, make a list of particular experiences that are relevant. Write informally about one or two of these experiences.
- How many different tasks does the assignment ask you to carry out? What parts of your draft or notes or outline address each of those tasks? Is anything missing?
- Does your draft fulfill the mechanical aspects of the assignment, such as length, number of sources, use of MLA or APA style, and so forth?

These are different ways of returning to the assignment sheet for guidance in writing or revising your essay. Think and write about the ones that would help you continue your work at this moment.

INVITATION 6

What Do the Teacher's Comments Mean?

Your teacher's comments on your essay probably include some specific suggestions about how to improve it. If your teacher comments on a rough draft, you can try out the suggestions or answer the teacher's questions as you revise. The teacher may also ask you to apply comments from one essay as you write your next essay. Sometimes the teacher's suggestions are easy to apply, but sometimes you may wonder how to follow his or her advice. Take some time to study the comments, to look for patterns among them, and to explain the comments to yourself by putting them into your own words. Try one or more of these:

- Look through the teacher's comments on your most recent essay. In your own words, write down what the teacher suggested or asked you to think about. Be thorough when you do this—if the teacher said three things, talk about each of them rather than bunching them together. If you find it difficult to explain what your teacher is saying to you, copy down a sentence or two of the teacher's comments and then try to say in a few sentences what the teacher might mean.
- Group the comments into categories. Does your teacher mention anything about reading, for example? organizing? developing your ideas? using quotations? copyreading? What do the categories tell you about the advice your teacher is giving?
- If your teacher has commented on a few essays by now, talk about the comments on each of them. Are there any ideas or types of comments that appear on more than one of your essays?
- After you have reviewed the comments and explained some of them in your own words, write informally about how you can apply those suggestions to the essay you're working on now.

INVITATION 7

Asking Your Own Questions

You've probably noticed that your teacher asks questions about your essays rather than merely correcting them. Teachers do this because they believe that writing a good essay is like having a conversation, and the questions keep the back-and-forth conversation going between a writer and a reader.

As a writer you also have a kind of conversation with the writers you read as well as with the teacher and other members of your class. In this back-and-forth exchange, with the help of good questions, you refine your understanding of the reading and relate it to what you already know about the world.

Most professional writers have other people read their drafts and ask questions. They also learn to ask the questions themselves, so they do not depend entirely on other readers for feedback. Learning how to ask those questions for your own drafts is an important goal for this course.

- What kinds of questions help a writer revise? Recall a few questions that have helped you make an essay stronger, and think about the kinds of questions they were. How might a reader think of more of these questions?
- What different purposes do the questions serve? Are some useful early in the process of writing an essay, while others might be useful later on?

You might want to write informally about the things we've just asked. Or you may want to turn to your own essay and ask some questions yourself, in the margin, as an aid to your own revision. Compare the questions you and your other readers have written to see whether there are any patterns there.

You will strengthen your independence as a writer if you do as professional writers do—use feedback from other readers, but also ask the questions that will help you develop your ideas further on your own.

INVITATION 8

Organizing, or Making Relations Clear

Often college students come to question what they learned about organizing an essay earlier in their school careers. As writers take on more demanding college assignments, standard organizing models like the five-paragraph theme, sometimes taught in high school, no longer seem adequate to the complexity of the material. Even a more flexible technique, such as working from an outline, can fall apart as the ideas and examples continue to evolve. During this course, you may have discovered that your familiar understanding of how to organize an essay no longer meets your needs.

Concepts of organization often fail a writer when they are arbitrary. The old-fashioned five-paragraph theme organizes all material in the same way, whether the material fits the five-part pattern or not. Some outlines are no more than a checklist of topics and fail, as a result, to develop any relations between the topics. This kind of outline often leads to an essay containing a series of more or less unrelated paragraphs set out in arbitrary order. From experiences like these, a writer discovers that good organization is not so much the order of an essay's elements as the relations it establishes between them.

Whether those elements are quotations or examples you are thinking of using, terms that help you talk about a topic, ideas that you have, stories you wish to tell, or even paragraphs you have already drafted, you need to develop the relations among them in order to shape your point and organize your essay. Here are some ways to establish those relations during the process of writing your essay.

Take a few minutes to make a list of the elements you have at hand for your essay, and then choose a pair to write about. Write informally about some of the relations you see between the two elements you have chosen.

If you have any trouble getting started, try one or more of these ways of inventing new ideas about relations:

- Tell a story in which the two elements play a part.
- Tell what one element helps you understand about the other element. Talk about any special words or phrases from one that you want to use when you discuss the other.
- Tell what you can add to the essay if you talk about these two elements together, or if you talk about one element in light of the other.
- Write about similarities you see between the two elements; then write about differences.
- Write about any cause and effect relations you see between the two elements.

As you return to other pairs of elements and write informally about the relations you see between them, some of those relations will become increasingly important to you, and you will be able to decide which elements belong together. As that happens, some possible organizational patterns will emerge. Your growing sense of the relations you want to discuss will give your essay an organization, and not an arbitrary one. A reader will follow your linked ideas and examples with greater awareness of the argument you are making.

INVITATION 9

Checking Your Progress

Turn to this Invitation after you have been working in the course for several weeks, a time when you may also be writing for your other classes. How has it been going? What parts of your work in class and at home have helped you to progress toward some of your goals?

What are your goals at this point in your writing course? What would you like to continue working on? What would you like to work on in a different way?

How do you feel about your reading now? Are there certain approaches to reading that are becoming more fruitful? Have you altered your approach to reading in any way?

How do you feel about your writing now? Are you doing new things now as you write? Are certain practices working for you? Are you becoming a different sort of writer?

What part of the class's activities would you like to talk over with the teacher? Have you visited the teacher during office hours? What questions would you ask the teacher if you could?

Have you considered visiting the Writing Center, in order to have another person read your work? What questions would you ask a reader there?

Write informally about any of these questions or other things that are on your mind. Take stock of the semester so far, tell your teacher about it, and explain where you want to go from here and how you plan to get there.

A Systematic Approach to Error

In your writing class, your teacher will explain the course's goals for matters of "formal correctness" and give you ways to achieve those goals. Formal correctness refers to the conventions of grammar, spelling, and usage upheld in colleges and universities as well as in publishing, broadcasting, business, and other fields in which writing plays a central role.

The more familiar you become with these conventions, also known as "standard edited English," the more flexible you will be as a writer. Outside of your writing class, you will make your own decisions about when and how to use these conventions. You will decide for yourself how much time to spend copyreading a final draft of a research essay or business report, and you will judge which copyreading strategies work best for you. The more comfortable you become with the conventions of formal correctness in your writing class, the better position you will be in to make choices about your writing later on.

It is true that formal correctness is not always essential to clear written communication. In our experience, however, students want to be able to follow its conventions when they address certain audiences, including professors and employers. In these cases, writers consider anything that fails to fulfill these conventions as an error. Most writers can identify and correct some of their errors, but find other errors frustrating, often because the conventions that govern them seem illogical or abstract—and they frequently are. Yet even fairly straightforward errors can be difficult to overcome when writers do not understand the patterned character of error. We have found that many students approach error haphazardly, when a systematic approach to this patterned problem can give much better results.

In the pages that follow, you will find four Invitations that introduce you to a systematic approach to error. On those pages, we invite you to examine your usual ways of dealing with error and to work with one or more readers to develop a personal handbook to the errors you make most often. We suggest ways to use that guide as an aid in copyreading your essays during the remainder of the course. If you compile and update a handbook to the patterns of error that are most common in your writing, you will be able to use it to learn how to spot and fix those errors effectively. While this work begins with the help of a teacher, Writing Center tutor, or other reader who understands patterned error, it allows you, in time, to become an independent copyreader of your own work.

INVITATION 10

How Do *You* Deal with Error?

You will more easily learn to control your errors if you think about, and describe in detail, how you already deal with errors in your writing. Write informally about as many of the following questions as you can:

When you look for errors in your essay, what do you do? And when do you do it? as you are writing? after you have written a paragraph? after you finish the essay? at some other time?

What errors are you most concerned about? What errors do you usually find?

How do you fix the errors you find? Do you consult reference books or get help from someone else? What do you do when you aren't certain about a possible error?

What is the most difficult or uncertain part of this whole process for you? What parts of the process already satisfy you?

Is there anything else you would like to mention about your approach to error?

Be thorough here, so you and your teacher can make good judgments about your current practices and about ways for you to copyread more effectively.

INVITATION 11

Tracking a Pattern of Error

To learn to copyread more effectively, begin with your own patterns of error. Most writers eventually discover that they make the same few errors repeatedly, rather than making dozens of different kinds of errors. Once a writer knows the patterns of her own errors, she can learn how to look systematically for those particular ones. This approach can give a writer much more control over the formal correctness of a finished essay.

Begin by asking your teacher, a Writing Center tutor, or another reader to point out one or two of your most common patterns of error, errors that show up repeatedly in your drafts. Prepare a sheet of paper for each pattern, a place to record what you know about that kind of error. Give the error a name, either an everyday name like "-ING words" or a grammatical term like "Gerunds," and use that name as the title of the sheet. Write down examples of the error from your own essays. (In most cases, you should copy down complete sentences, so you can think about the error's context.) Next, underline the problem and write a corrected version. Briefly explain any tips you know for spotting and fixing the error. (Some patterns, for example, always occur in the same part of a sentence, and others occur near particular words or types of words. These clues can help you locate the problem in your papers.) Because these patterns are sometimes hard to explain or even to see, you will probably need to work with someone, at least briefly, as you prepare most of these reference sheets.

Keep these sheets in a folder where you write, and review them when you copyread your essays. Add other sheets as the semester continues, until you have a personal handbook to your main patterns of error. You will need to be very serious about using the sheets as you copyread, but if you do you will make good progress. By preparing and updating your personal handbook with the teacher or tutor or on your own, and by drawing on it as a regular part of your copyreading process, you should be able to spot and fix the errors much more effectively by the end of the semester. By strategic effort, you will come to control the patterns of error.

INVITATION 12

Reviewing . . . in Your Own Words

After you have worked on a pattern of error with your teacher, a tutor, or another reader, you should probably review what you have discovered, in order to make sure that you have really made this new knowledge your own. Take a few minutes to talk on paper about the pattern of error you have learned to find and fix. The following questions may help, and adding to or changing them to fit your situation may also be useful.

What pattern of error have you worked on? What tips help you find it? How do you go about fixing it? Give a few examples of the error and its correction—use your new sheet, if you wish, but do not simply recopy it. Try to come up with at least one new example on your own. Use your own words to explain what to do, so that you will be better able to remember and understand how to approach this error.

INVITATION 13

Using Your Personal Handbook to Copyread a New Draft

With your teacher, your tutor, or another reader, you have discussed how to find a pattern of error that seems to be a habit for you. Identifying a habit is the first step toward breaking it, but you also need practice in spotting and fixing the error. Review your personal handbook and other notes you have made about your error, and then look for that error in your new draft. Be especially alert to the clues or tips you have recorded, since these will help you know where to look for the error. If you find that you have made the error, correct it, but also copy the particular sentence on a blank sheet. If you detect any other errors, make a note of them on a separate page as well. Review these notes later, or discuss them with one of your readers; then add them to your personal handbook.

If you find no errors in your new piece of writing, it may mean that you have broken the habit, or it may mean that you still have trouble spotting the error. If you suspect that you are making errors but not finding them, carefully review your personal handbook again to decide what you're supposed to be looking for. You might also try reading your essay aloud, to help you hear the error. Be strategic. No matter what approach you take, tell yourself what you're trying to find before you start looking.

THE
READINGS

BEFORE READING MAYA ANGELOU

1. Looking back on your childhood, think of some games you played, people you pretended to be, or television characters you identified with. How have these experiences prepared you for your role(s) as a man or woman? as a member of a certain socioeconomic class? as a member of a particular race or ethnic group?

2. List some of the names, nicknames, even titles ("Dr.," "Boss," "Young Lady," "Young Man," etc.) that you have been known by or that you have used to address other people. How do you decide what an appropriate form of address is? How do the forms of address you use indicate your status in relation to other people?

3. Write informally about one or two of your own childhood experiences, perhaps a time when you felt you were blamed for something you didn't do. When you were writing these autobiographical accounts, what choices did you make in order to promote certain interpretations of your experience and discourage others? How aware were you of these choices while you were making them? Based on your observations, list some questions you think you should ask of other autobiographical texts, like " 'Mary.' "

"MARY"

Recently a white woman from Texas, who would quickly describe herself as a liberal, asked me about my hometown. When I told her that in Stamps my grandmother had owned the only Negro general merchandise store since the turn of the century, she exclaimed, "Why, you were a debutante." Ridiculous and even ludicrous. But Negro girls in small Southern towns, whether poverty-stricken or just munching along on a few of life's necessities, were given as extensive and irrelevant preparations for adulthood as rich white girls shown in magazines. Admittedly the training was not the same. While white girls learned to waltz and sit gracefully with a tea cup balanced on their knees, we were lagging behind, learning the mid-Victorian values with very little money to indulge them. (Come and see Edna Lomax spending the money she made picking cotton on five balls of ecru tatting thread. Her fingers are bound to snag the work and she'll have to repeat the stitches time and time again. But she knows that when she buys the thread.)

    We were required to embroider and I had trunkfuls of colorful dish-towels, pillowcases, runners and handkerchiefs to my credit. I mastered the art of crocheting and tatting, and there was a lifetime's supply of

From *I Know Why the Caged Bird Sings* (1970).

dainty doilies that would never be used in sacheted dresser drawers. It went without saying that all girls could iron and wash, but the finer touches around the home, like setting a table with real silver, baking roasts and cooking vegetables without meat, had to be learned elsewhere. Usually at the source of those habits. During my tenth year, a white woman's kitchen became my finishing school.

Mrs. Viola Cullinan was a plump woman who lived in a three-bedroom house somewhere behind the post office. She was singularly unattractive until she smiled, and then the lines around her eyes and mouth which made her look perpetually dirty disappeared, and her face looked like the mask of an impish elf. She usually rested her smile until late afternoon when her women friends dropped in and Miss Glory, the cook, served them cold drinks on the closed-in porch.

The exactness of her house was inhuman. This glass went here and only here. That cup had its place and it was an act of impudent rebellion to place it anywhere else. At twelve o'clock the table was set. At 12:15 Mrs. Cullinan sat down to dinner (whether her husband had arrived or not). At 12:16 Miss Glory brought out the food.

It took me a week to learn the difference between a salad plate, a bread plate and a dessert plate.

Mrs. Cullinan kept up the tradition of her wealthy parents. She was from Virginia. Miss Glory, who was a descendant of slaves that had worked for the Cullinans, told me her history. She had married beneath her (according to Miss Glory). Her husband's family hadn't had their money very long and what they had "didn't 'mount to much."

As ugly as she was, I thought privately, she was lucky to get a husband above or beneath her station. But Miss Glory wouldn't let me say a thing against her mistress. She was very patient with me, however, over the housework. She explained the dishware, silverware and servants' bells. The large round bowl in which soup was served wasn't a soup bowl, it was a tureen. There were goblets, sherbet glasses, ice-cream glasses, wine glasses, green glass coffee cups with matching saucers, and water glasses. I had a glass to drink from, and it sat with Miss Glory's on a separate shelf from the others. Soup spoons, gravy boat, butter knives, salad forks and carving platter were additions to my vocabulary and in fact almost represented a new language. I was fascinated with the novelty, with the fluttering Mrs. Cullinan and her Alice-in-Wonderland house.

Her husband remains, in my memory, undefined. I lumped him with all the other white men that I had ever seen and tried not to see.

On our way home one evening, Miss Glory told me that Mrs. Cullinan couldn't have children. She said that she was too delicate-boned. It was hard to imagine bones at all under those layers of fat. Miss Glory went on to say that the doctor had taken out all her lady organs. I reasoned that a pig's organs included the lungs, heart and liver, so if Mrs. Cullinan was walking around without those essentials, it explained why she drank alcohol out of unmarked bottles. She was keeping herself embalmed.

When I spoke to Bailey[1] about it, he agreed that I was right, but he also informed me that Mr. Cullinan had two daughters by a colored lady and that I knew them very well. He added that the girls were the spitting image of their father. I was unable to remember what he looked like, although I had just left him a few hours before, but I thought of the Coleman girls. They were very light-skinned and certainly didn't look very much like their mother (no one ever mentioned Mr. Coleman).

My pity for Mrs. Cullinan preceded me the next morning like the Cheshire cat's smile. Those girls, who could have been her daughters, were beautiful. They didn't have to straighten their hair. Even when they were caught in the rain, their braids still hung down straight like tamed snakes. Their mouths were pouty little cupid's bows. Mrs. Cullinan didn't know what she missed. Or maybe she did. Poor Mrs. Cullinan.

For weeks after, I arrived early, left late and tried very hard to make up for her barrenness. If she had had her own children, she wouldn't have had to ask me to run a thousand errands from her back door to the back door of her friends. Poor old Mrs. Cullinan.

Then one evening Miss Glory told me to serve the ladies on the porch. After I set the tray down and turned toward the kitchen, one of the women asked, "What's your name, girl?" It was the speckled-faced one. Mrs. Cullinan said, "She doesn't talk much. Her name's Margaret."

"Is she dumb?"

"No. As I understand it, she can talk when she wants to but she's usually quiet as a little mouse. Aren't you, Margaret?"

I smiled at her. Poor thing. No organs and couldn't even pronounce my name correctly.[2]

"She's a sweet little thing, though."

"Well, that may be, but the name's too long. I'd never bother myself. I'd call her Mary if I was you."

I fumed into the kitchen. That horrible woman would never have the chance to call me Mary because if I was starving I'd never work for

1. Bailey is Angelou's brother [*Editors*].
2. Angelou's name as a child was Marguerite Johnson [*Editors*].

her. I decided I wouldn't pee on her if her heart was on fire. Giggles drifted in off the porch and into Miss Glory's pots. I wondered what they could be laughing about.

Whitefolks were so strange. Could they be talking about me? Everybody knew that they stuck together better than the Negroes did. It was possible that Mrs. Cullinan had friends in St. Louis who heard about a girl from Stamps being in court and wrote to tell her. Maybe she knew about Mr. Freeman.[3]

My lunch was in my mouth a second time and I went outside and relieved myself on the bed of four-o'clocks. Miss Glory thought I might be coming down with something and told me to go on home, that Momma would give me some herb tea, and she'd explain to her mistress.

I realized how foolish I was being before I reached the pond. Of course Mrs. Cullinan didn't know. Otherwise she wouldn't have given me the two nice dresses that Momma cut down, and she certainly wouldn't have called me a "sweet little thing." My stomach felt fine, and I didn't mention anything to Momma.

That evening I decided to write a poem on being white, fat, old and without children. It was going to be a tragic ballad. I would have to watch her carefully to capture the essence of her loneliness and pain.

The very next day, she called me by the wrong name. Miss Glory and I were washing up the lunch dishes when Mrs. Cullinan came to the doorway. "Mary?"

Miss Glory asked, "Who?"

Mrs. Cullinan, sagging a little, knew and I knew. "I want Mary to go down to Mrs. Randall's and take her some soup. She's not been feeling well for a few days."

Miss Glory's face was a wonder to see. "You mean Margaret, ma'am. Her name's Margaret."

"That's too long. She's Mary from now on. Heat that soup from last night and put it in the china tureen and, Mary, I want you to carry it carefully."

Every person I knew had a hellish horror of being "called out of his name." It was a dangerous practice to call a Negro anything that could be loosely construed as insulting because of the centuries of their having been called niggers, jigs, dinges, blackbirds, crows, boots and spooks.

Miss Glory had a fleeting second of feeling sorry for me. Then as

3. Angelou had been raped by a Mr. Freeman, and she had testified in court against him [*Editors*].

she handed me the hot tureen she said, "Don't mind, don't pay that no mind. Sticks and stones may break your bones, but words . . . You know, I been working for her for twenty years."

She held the back door open for me. "Twenty years. I wasn't much older than you. My name used to be Hallelujah. That's what Ma named me, but my mistress give me 'Glory,' and it stuck. I likes it better too."

I was in the little path that ran behind the houses when Miss Glory shouted, "It's shorter too."

For a few seconds it was a tossup over whether I would laugh (imagine being named Hallelujah) or cry (imagine letting some white woman rename you for her convenience). My anger saved me from either outburst. I had to quit the job, but the problem was going to be how to do it. Momma wouldn't allow me to quit for just any reason.

"She's a peach. That woman is a real peach." Mrs. Randall's maid was talking as she took the soup from me, and I wondered what her name used to be and what she answered to now.

For a week I looked into Mrs. Cullinan's face as she called me Mary. She ignored my coming late and leaving early. Miss Glory was a little annoyed because I had begun to leave egg yolk on the dishes and wasn't putting much heart in polishing the silver. I hoped that she would complain to our boss, but she didn't.

Then Bailey solved my dilemma. He had me describe the contents of the cupboard and the particular plates she liked best. Her favorite piece was a casserole shaped like a fish and the green glass coffee cups. I kept his instructions in mind, so on the next day when Miss Glory was hanging out clothes and I had again been told to serve the old biddies on the porch, I dropped the empty serving tray. When I heard Mrs. Cullinan scream, "Mary!" I picked up the casserole and two of the green glass cups in readiness. As she rounded the kitchen door I let them fall on the tiled floor.

I could never absolutely describe to Bailey what happened next, because each time I got to the part where she fell on the floor and screwed up her ugly face to cry, we burst out laughing. She actually wobbled around on the floor and picked up shards of the cups and cried, "Oh, Momma. Oh, dear Gawd. It's Momma's china from Virginia. Oh, Momma, I sorry."

Miss Glory came running in from the yard and the women from the porch crowded around. Miss Glory was almost as broken up as her mistress. "You mean to say she broke our Virginia dishes? What we gone do?"

Mrs. Cullinan cried louder, "That clumsy nigger. Clumsy little black nigger."

Old speckled-face leaned down and asked, "Who did it, Viola? Was it Mary? Who did it?"

Everything was happening so fast I can't remember whether her action preceded her words, but I know that Mrs. Cullinan said, "Her name's Margaret, goddamn it, her name's Margaret." And she threw a wedge of the broken plate at me. It could have been the hysteria which put her aim off, but the flying crockery caught Miss Glory right over her ear and she started screaming.

I left the front door wide open so all the neighbors could hear.

Mrs. Cullinan was right about one thing. My name wasn't Mary.

ACTIVE READING

1. Find several places in Angelou's essay where you believe her views about herself or other characters change. What specific clues does Angelou provide to signal these changes? What knowledge do you bring to the reading to help you interpret these clues?

2. List as many images of the Cullinan house as you can find. What do the details Angelou provides suggest about the people who live, work, and visit there? Discuss the different reactions the inhabitants, employees, and guests have to the house and to some of the objects it contains.

3. What direct and indirect information does the text give you about the moral values of Mrs. Cullinan and her friends? How do you think their view of themselves would relate to your view of them? How do you account for any difference between what they seem to think of themselves and the way you see them act?

READING IN NEW CONTEXTS

1. Locate two or three moments in the text where Angelou seems to be speaking as an adult looking back on an experience rather than as a child in the midst of that experience. How do these passages prompt

you to view the events of the reading in certain ways? Use your new understanding of the "shape" an adult author can give to a text about past experience to consider Rodriguez's or Sanders's discussions of their childhoods.

2. How does Miss Glory's attitude toward name-changing affect your perception of her? Angelou's perception of her? How might Anzaldúa's or Bettelheim's attempts to explain "complicity" help you reexamine Miss Glory's attitude?

3. At which points in the text does Angelou seem to gain or lose power? Why? Examine how Angelou's experiences of power and powerlessness might extend Brody's ideas of power beyond the context of what he calls "expert healers."

DRAFT ONE / DRAFT TWO

1. *Draft One:* Looking back at your responses to Before Reading #2, discuss how your own experiences with naming contribute to your interpretation of Marguerite's actions. (You might also want to consider her later decision to change her name from Marguerite Johnson to Maya Angelou.)

Draft Two: How might you use Angelou's experience with names to reconsider Kingston's thoughts about her nameless aunt, or Fienup-Riordan's desire for an "authentic" Yup'ik name? Use your insights from Draft One to reassess the significance of names or naming in one of these other readings.

2. *Draft One:* What characteristics do you associate with a "family" community? Reread " 'Mary' " and note the information it provides about the Johnson (Angelou) and Cullinan families. Use your response to this information to develop your own theory of what a family community should be like.

Draft Two: How do families relate to the larger social communities in which they exist? Consider how the Johnson and Cullinan families relate to each other and to the larger community. Revise your theory of the family from Draft One into a theory of the village or town community. You might find some of Kingston's or Bellah's ideas helpful for writing this essay.

BEFORE READING GLORIA ANZALDÚA

1. Anzaldúa, a Chicana woman, writes about feeling "invisible" in mainstream culture. Think of one or two times when you felt that you were not being "seen" by people around you. How did you act in these situations? Why?

2. Anzaldúa's text is a letter, one addressed to people she may not know personally. What are some of the reasons people use letters to communicate? List the various styles, tones, methods of organization, and word choices you have used in letters. Why do you write different kinds of letters in different ways?

3. Some Christian traditions use the phrase "speaking in tongues" to describe the unintelligible proclamations made by a speaker believed to be "possessed" by the spirit of God. What words or ideas come to mind when you see the phrase "speaking in tongues"? What expectations about Anzaldúa's text does her use of this phrase in her title raise for you?

4. Briefly describe the kinds of writing you have been asked to do in high school and college: essays, term papers, reports, and so forth. How do you characterize academic writing? What do you think the goals of academic writing are?

GLORIA ANZALDÚA

SPEAKING IN TONGUES:
A LETTER TO 3RD WORLD
WOMEN WRITERS

21 mayo 80

Dear mujeres de color, companions in writing—

I sit here naked in the sun, typewriter against my knee trying to visualize you. Black woman huddles over a desk in the fifth floor of some New York tenement. Sitting on a porch in south Texas, a Chicana fanning away mosquitos and the hot air, trying to arouse the smouldering embers of writing. Indian woman walking to school or work lamenting the lack of time to weave writing into your life. Asian American, lesbian, single mother, tugged in all directions by children, lover or ex-husband, and the writing.

It is not easy writing this letter. It began as a poem, a long poem. I tried to turn it into an essay but the result was wooden, cold. I have not yet unlearned the esoteric bullshit and pseudo-intellectualizing that school brainwashed into my writing.

How to begin again. How to approximate the intimacy and immediacy I want. What form? A letter, of course.

From *This Bridge Called My Back: Writings by Radical Women of Color* (1981). Originally written for *Words in Our Pockets* (Bootlegger: San Francisco), the Feminist Writers' Guild Handbook.

My dear *hermanas,* the dangers we face as women writers of color are not the same as those of white women though we have many in common. We don't have as much to lose—we never had any privileges. I wanted to call the dangers "obstacles" but that would be a kind of lying. We can't *transcend* the dangers, can't rise above them. We must go through them and hope we won't have to repeat the performance.

Unlikely to be friends of people in high literary places, the beginning woman of color is invisible both in the white male mainstream world and in the white women's feminist world, though in the latter this is gradually changing. The *lesbian* of color is not only invisible, she doesn't even exist. Our speech, too, is inaudible. We speak in tongues like the outcast and the insane.

Because white eyes do not want to know us, they do not bother to learn our language, the language which reflects us, our culture, our spirit. The schools we attended or didn't attend did not give us the skills for writing nor the confidence that we were correct in using our class and ethnic languages. I, for one, became adept at, and majored in English to spite, to show up, the arrogant racist teachers who thought all Chicano children were dumb and dirty. And Spanish was not taught in grade school. And Spanish was not required in High School. And though now I write my poems in Spanish as well as English I feel the rip-off of my native tongue.

I *lack imagination* you say

No. I lack language.
The language to clarify
my resistance to the literate.
Words are a war to me.
They threaten my family.

To gain the word
to describe the loss
I risk losing everything.
I may create a monster
the word's length and body
swelling up colorful and thrilling
looming over my *mother,* characterized.
Her voice in the distance

unintelligible illiterate.
These are the monster's words.[1]

CHERRÍE MORAGA

Who gave us permission to perform the act of writing? Why does writing seem so unnatural for me? I'll do anything to postpone it—empty the trash, answer the telephone. The voice recurs in me: *Who am I, a poor Chicanita from the sticks, to think I could write?* How dare I even considered becoming a writer as I stooped over the tomato fields bending, bending under the hot sun, hands broadened and calloused, not fit to hold the quill, numbed into an animal stupor by the heat.

How hard it is for us to *think* we can choose to become writers, much less *feel* and *believe* that we can. What have we to contribute, to give? Our own expectations condition us. Does not our class, our culture as well as the white man tell us writing is not for women such as us?

The white man speaks: *Perhaps if you scrape the dark off of your face. Maybe if you bleach your bones. Stop speaking in tongues, stop writing left-handed. Don't cultivate your colored skins nor tongues of fire if you want to make it in a right-handed world.*

> "Man, like all the other animals, fears and is repelled by that which he does not understand, and mere difference is apt to connote something malign."[2]

I think, yes, perhaps if we go to the university. Perhaps if we become male-women or as middleclass as we can. Perhaps if we give up loving women, we will be worthy of having something to say worth saying. They convince us that we must cultivate art for art's sake. Bow down to the sacred bull, form. Put frames and metaframes around the writing. Achieve distance in order to win the coveted title "literary writer" or "professional writer." Above all do not be simple, direct, nor immediate.

Why do they fight us? Because they think we are dangerous beasts? Why *are* we dangerous beasts? Because we shake and often break the white's comfortable stereotypic images they have of us: the Black domestic, the lumbering nanny with twelve babies sucking her tits, the slant-

1. Cherríe Moraga's poem "It's the Poverty," from *Loving in the War Years*, an unpublished book of poems.
2. Alice Walker, editor, "What White Publishers Won't Print," *I Love Myself When I Am Laughing—A Zora Neale Hurston Reader* (New York: The Feminist Press, 1979), p. 169.

eyed Chinese with her expert hand—"They know how to treat a man in bed," the flat-faced Chicana or Indian, passively lying on her back, being fucked by the Man *a la* La Chingada.

The Third World woman revolts: *We revoke, we erase your white male imprint. When you come knocking on our doors with your rubber stamps to brand our faces with DUMB, HYSTERICAL, PASSIVE PUTA, PER- VERT, when you come with your branding irons to burn MY PROPERTY on our buttocks, we will vomit the guilt, self-denial and race-hatred you have force-fed into us right back into your mouth. We are done being cush- ions for your projected fears. We are tired of being your sacrificial lambs and scapegoats.*

I can write this and yet I realize that many of us women of color who have strung degrees, credentials and published books around our necks like pearls that we hang onto for dear life are in danger of contributing to the invisibility of our sister-writers. "La Vendida," the sell-out.

The danger of selling out one's own ideologies. For the Third World woman, who has, at best, one foot in the feminist literary world, the temp- tation is great to adopt the current feeling-fads and theory fads, the latest half truths in political thought, the half-digested new age psychological axioms that are preached by the white feminist establishment. Its follow- ers are notorious for "adopting" women of color as their "cause" while still expecting us to adapt to *their* expectations and *their* language.

How dare we get out of our colored faces. How dare we reveal the human flesh underneath and bleed red blood like the white folks. It takes tremendous energy and courage not to acquiesce, not to capitulate to a definition of feminism that still renders most of us invisible. Even as I write this I am disturbed that I am the only Third World woman writer in this handbook.[3] Over and over I have found myself to be the only Third World woman at readings, workshops, and meetings.

We cannot allow ourselves to be tokenized. We must make our own writing and that of Third World women the first priority. We cannot edu- cate white women and take them by the hand. Most of us are willing to help but we can't do the white woman's homework for her. That's an energy drain. More times than she cares to remember, Nellie Wong, Asian American feminist writer, has been called by white women wanting a list of Asian American women who can give readings or workshops. We are in danger of being reduced to purveyors of resource lists.

Coming face to face with one's limitations. There are only so many

---

3. Anzaldúa is referring to the original publication of the essay [*Editors*].

things I can do in one day. Luisah Teish addressing a group of predominantly white feminist writers had this to say of Third World women's experience:

> "If you are not caught in the maze that (we) are in, it's very difficult to explain to you the hours in the day we do not have. And the hours that we do not have are hours that are translated into survival skills and money. And when one of those hours is taken away it means an hour not that we don't have to lie back and stare at the ceiling or an hour that we don't have to talk to a friend. For me it's a loaf of bread."

> Understand.
> My family is poor.
> Poor. I can't afford
> a new ribbon. The risk
> of this one is enough
> to keep me moving
> through it, accountable.
> The repetition like my mother's
> stories retold, *each* time
> reveals more particulars
> gains more familiarity.

> You can't get me in your car so fast.[4]

> CHERRÍE MORAGA

"Complacency is a far more dangerous attitude than outrage."[5]

NAOMI LITTLEBEAR

Why am I compelled to write? Because the writing saves me from this complacency I fear. Because I have no choice. Because I must keep the spirit of my revolt and myself alive. Because the world I create in the writing compensates for what the real world does not give me. By writing I put order in the world, give it a handle so I can grasp it. I write because life does not appease my appetites and hunger. I write to record what others erase when I speak, to rewrite the stories others have miswritten about me, about you. To become more intimate with myself and you. To discover myself, to preserve myself, to make myself, to achieve self-

4. Moraga, *ibid.*
5. Naomi Littlebear, *The Dark of the Moon* (Portland: Olive Press, 1977), p. 36.

autonomy. To dispell the myths that I am a mad prophet or a poor suffering soul. To convince myself that I am worthy and that what I have to say is not a pile of shit. To show that I *can* and that I *will* write, never mind their admonitions to the contrary. And I will write about the unmentionables, never mind the outraged gasp of the censor and the audience. Finally I write because I'm scared of writing but I'm more scared of not writing.

Why should I try to justify why I write? Do I need to justify being Chicana, being woman? You might as well ask me to try to justify why I'm alive.

The act of writing is the act of making soul, alchemy. It is the quest for the self, for the center of the self, which we women of color have come to think as "other"—the dark, the feminine. Didn't we start writing to reconcile this other within us? We knew we were different, set apart, exiled from what is considered "normal," white-right. And as we internalized this exile, we came to see the alien within us and too often, as a result, we split apart from ourselves and each other. Forever after we have been in search of that self, that "other" and each other. And we return, in widening spirals and never to the same childhood place where it happened, first in our families, with our mothers, with our fathers. The writing is a tool for piercing that mystery but it also shields us, gives a margin of distance, helps us survive. And those that don't survive? The waste of ourselves: so much meat thrown at the feet of madness or fate or the state.

24 mayo 80

It is dark and damp and has been raining all day. I love days like this. As I lie in bed I am able to delve inward. Perhaps today I will write from that deep core. As I grope for words and a voice to speak of writing, I stare at my brown hand clenching the pen and think of you thousands of miles away clutching your pen. You are not alone.

> Pen, I feel right at home in your ink doing a pirouette, stirring the cobwebs, leaving my signature on the window panes. Pen, how could I ever have feared you. You're quite house-broken but it's your wildness I am in love with. I'll have to get rid of you when you start being predictable, when you stop chasing dustdevils. The more you outwit me the more I love you. It's when I'm tired or have had too much caffeine or wine that you get past my defenses and you say more than what I had intended. You surprise me, shock me into knowing some part of me I'd kept secret even from myself.—Journal entry.

In the kitchen Maria and Cherríe's voices falling on these pages. I can see Cherríe going about in her terry cloth wrap, barefoot washing the dishes, shaking out the tablecloth, vacuuming. Deriving a certain pleasure watching her perform those simple tasks, I am thinking *they lied, there is no separation between life and writing.*

The danger in writing is not fusing our personal experience and world view with the social reality we live in, with our inner life, our history, our economics, and our vision. What validates us as human beings validates us as writers. What matters to us is the relationships that are important to us whether with our self or others. We must use what is important to us to get to the writing. *No topic is too trivial.* The danger is in being too universal and humanitarian and invoking the eternal to the sacrifice of the particular and the feminine and the specific historical moment.

The problem is to focus, to concentrate. The body distracts, sabotages with a hundred ruses, a cup of coffee, pencils to sharpen. The solution is to anchor the body to a cigarette or some other ritual. And who has time or energy to write after nurturing husband or lover, children, and often an outside job? The problems seem insurmountable and they are, but they cease being insurmountable once we make up our mind that whether married or childrened or working outside jobs we are going to make time for the writing.

Forget the room of one's own—write in the kitchen, lock yourself up in the bathroom. Write on the bus or the welfare line, on the job or during meals, between sleeping or waking. I write while sitting on the john. No long stretches at the typewriter unless you're wealthy or have a patron—you may not even own a typewriter. While you wash the floor or clothes listen to the words chanting in your body. When you're depressed, angry, hurt, when compassion and love possess you. When you cannot help but write.

Distractions all—that I spring on myself when I'm so deep into the writing when I'm almost at that place, that dark cellar where some "thing" is liable to jump up and pounce on me. The ways I subvert the writing are many. The way I don't tap the well nor learn how to make the windmill turn.

Eating is my main distraction. Getting up to eat an apple danish. That I've been off sugar for three years is not a deterrent nor that I have to put on a coat, find the keys and go out into the San Francisco fog to get it. Getting up to light incense, to put a record on, to go for a walk— anything just to put off the writing.

Returning after I've stuffed myself. Writing paragraphs on pieces of paper, adding to the puzzle on the floor, to the confusion on my desk making completion far away and perfection impossible.

26 mayo 80

Dear mujeres de color, I feel heavy and tired and there is a buzz in my head—too many beers last night. But I must finish this letter. My bribe: to take myself out to pizza.

So I cut and paste and line the floor with my bits of paper. My life strewn on the floor in bits and pieces and I try to make some order out of it working against time, psyching myself up with decaffeinated coffee, trying to fill in the gaps.

Leslie, my housemate, comes in, gets on hands and knees to read my fragments on the floor and says, "It's good, Gloria." And I think: *I don't have to go back to Texas, to my family of land, mesquites, cactus, rattlesnakes and roadrunners. My family, this community of writers. How could I have lived and survived so long without it. And I remember the isolation, re-live the pain again.*

"To assess the damage is a dangerous act,"[6] writes Cherríe Moraga. To stop there is even more dangerous.

It's too easy, blaming it all on the white man or white feminists or society or on our parents. What we say and what we do ultimately comes back to us, so let us own our responsibility, place it in our own hands and carry it with dignity and strength. No one's going to do my shitwork, I pick up after myself.

It makes perfect sense to me now how I resisted the act of writing, the commitment to writing. To write is to confront one's demons, look them in the face and live to write about them. Fear acts like a magnet; it draws the demons out of the closet and into the ink in our pens.

The tiger riding our backs (writing) never lets us alone. *Why aren't you riding, writing, writing?* It asks constantly till we begin to feel we're vampires sucking the blood out of too fresh an experience; that we are sucking life's blood to feed the pen. Writing is the most daring thing I have ever done and the most dangerous. Nellie Wong calls writing "the three-eyed demon shrieking the truth."[7]

6. Cherríe Moraga's essay, see "La Güera."
7. Nellie Wong, "Flows from the Dark of Monsters and Demons: Notes on Writing," *Radical Woman Pamphlet* (San Francisco, 1979).

Writing is dangerous because we are afraid of what the writing reveals: the fears, the angers, the strengths of a woman under a triple or quadruple oppression. Yet in that very act lies our survival because a woman who writes has power. And a woman with power is feared.

> What did it mean for a black woman to be an artist in our grandmother's time? It is a question with an answer cruel enough to stop the blood.[8]
>
> ALICE WALKER

I have never seen so much power in the ability to move and transform others as from that of the writing of women of color.

In the San Francisco area, where I now live, none can stir the audience with their craft and truthsaying, as do Cherríe Moraga (Chicana), Genny Lim (Asian American), and Luisah Teish (Black). With women like these, the loneliness of writing and the sense of powerlessness can be dispelled. We can walk among each other talking of our writing, reading to each other. And more and more when I'm alone, though still in communion with each other, the writing possesses me and propels me to leap into a timeless, spaceless no-place where I forget myself and feel I am the universe. *This* is power.

It's not on paper that you create but in your innards, in the gut and out of living tissue—*organic writing* I call it. A poem works for me *not* when it says what I want it to say and *not* when it evokes what I want it to. It works when the subject I started out with metamorphoses alchemically into a different one, one that has been discovered, or uncovered, by the poem. It works when it surprises me, when it says something I have repressed or pretended not to know. The meaning and worth of my writing is measured by how much *I* put myself on the line and how much nakedness I achieve.

> Audre said we need to speak up. Speak loud, speak unsettling things and be dangerous and just fuck, hell, let it out and let everybody hear whether they want to or not.[9]
>
> KATHY KENDALL

8. Alice Walker, "In Search of Our Mothers' Gardens: The Creativity of Black Women in the South," *MS*, May 1974, p. 60.
9. Letter from Kathy Kendall, March 10, 1980, concerning a writer's workshop given by Audre Lorde, Adrienne Rich, and Meridel LeSueur.

I say mujer magica, empty yourself. Shock yourself into new ways of perceiving the world, shock your readers into the same. Stop the chatter inside their heads.

Your skin must be sensitive enough for the lightest kiss and thick enough to ward off the sneers. If you are going to spit in the eye of the world, make sure your back is to the wind. Write of what most links us with life, the sensation of the body, the images seen by the eye, the expansion of the psyche in tranquility: moments of high intensity, its movement, sounds, thoughts. *Even though we go hungry we are not impoverished of experiences.*

> I think many of us have been fooled by the mass media, by society's conditioning that our lives must be lived in great explosions, by "falling in love," by being "swept off our feet," and by the sorcery of magic genies that will fulfill our every wish, our every childhood longing. Wishes, dreams, and fantasies are important parts of our creative lives. They are the steps a writer integrates into her craft. They are the spectrum of resources to reach the truth, the heart of things, the immediacy and the impact of human conflict.[10]
>
> NELLIE WONG

Many have a way with words. They label themselves seers but they will not see. Many have the gift of tongue but nothing to say. Do not listen to them. Many who have words and tongue have no ear, they cannot listen and they will not hear.

There is no need for words to fester in our minds. They germinate in the open mouth of the barefoot child in the midst of restive crowds. They wither in ivory towers and in college classrooms.

Throw away abstraction and the academic learning, the rules, the map and compass. Feel your way without blinders. To touch more people, the personal realities and the social must be evoked—not through rhetoric but through blood and pus and sweat.

Write with your eyes like painters, with your ears like musicians, with your feet like dancers. You are the truthsayer with quill and torch. Write with your tongues of fire. Don't let the pen banish you from yourself. Don't let the ink coagulate in your pens. Don't let the censor snuff out the spark, nor the gags muffle your voice. Put your shit on the paper.

10. Nellie Wong, *ibid.*

We are not reconciled to the oppressors who whet their howl on our grief. We are not reconciled.

Find the muse within you. The voice that lies buried under you, dig it up. Do not fake it, try to sell it for a handclap or your name in print.

Love,
Gloria

ACTIVE READING

1. Locate the points in Anzaldúa's text where she describes being or becoming naked. For each of these passages, try to determine the different values that are associated with "nakedness" by Anzaldúa and by mainstream culture. How do ideas of nakedness change throughout the essay?

2. Anzaldúa's text includes quotations from many sources. Working with two or three examples from her letter, write or talk about some of the different ways Anzaldúa uses quotation. Why do you feel she uses these quotations the way she does?

3. Choose two or three passages from Anzaldúa's letter where you feel she is "speaking in tongues." What aspects of these passages led you to select them? How does viewing these passages as examples of speaking in tongues affect the way you understand them? Consider how you might revise your response to Before Reading #3 after discussing these passages.

READING IN NEW CONTEXTS

1. What does Cherríe Moraga mean when she writes "to assess the damage is a dangerous act"(18)? At what points do you see Anzaldúa going beyond "damage assessment" to a new form of analysis? Apply the idea of damage assessment to Baldwin's or Durham's essays.

2. Consider how Brody or another writer defines "power" or discusses the ethical problems associated with exercising "power." Use these ideas to explore notions of power and oppression in two or three passages from Anzaldúa's letter. How do Brody's notions need to be adapted to fit Anzaldúa's context?

3. Locate two or three places where you feel Anzaldúa is "writing for effect": making astonishing claims or using surprising language to elicit particular responses from her readers. Why do you think she chooses to write for effect at these points? How might your reaction to these passages in Anzaldúa's letter give you a way of working with similar moments in a reading by Rich or Kozol?

DRAFT ONE / DRAFT TWO

1. *Draft One*: Respond to Anzaldúa's letter with a letter of your own. In your letter, explain how your emotional reactions to Anzaldúa's text shape your response to some of her ideas.

   Draft Two: Anzaldúa claims that "[Writing] works when it surprises me, when it says something I have repressed or pretended not to know" (19). Find one or two passages in your letter from Draft One that you suspect might contain some surprising or repressed thoughts, thoughts you weren't aware of when writing the letter. Explore or build upon those thoughts as you revise your letter.

2. *Draft One*: List some of the skills you hope to develop as a student. How well do these skills match up with the goals of academic writing you identified in Before Reading #4? Discuss the ways your own academic writing helps or hinders you in developing your desired skills.

   Draft Two: Locate two or three places in Anzaldúa's letter where you feel her writing is academic and two or three other places where you feel it is not. (It might help to note some of the reasons you define these sections as academic or nonacademic.) How does her movement between these styles affect your thoughts about her text? How do the experiences and problems you described in Draft One contribute to your response?

BEFORE READING MARGARET ATWOOD

1. List some of the kinds of stories you are familiar with. Why do people tell stories? What stories do you tell or listen to, and what value do those stories have?

2. What everyday forms of self-expression do you use? What do you want people to know or think about you when you use them? Discuss the factors that influence how and when you express aspects of yourself.

3. Think about the kinds of writing you do in this course, other courses, and outside of college. What role does self-expression play in the writing you do? Consider how your written self-expression relates to the kinds of self-expression you discussed in Before Reading #2.

4. What types of audiences have you been a part of? Based on your experience, what would you say makes a group of people an "audience"? How are audiences shaped by what they read, see, or attend? How is the work of writers, speakers, or other performers (musicians, athletes, etc.) shaped by their audiences?

MARGARET ATWOOD

AN END TO AUDIENCE?

I have been asked here presumably because I am story-teller and you wish to know something about the state of story-telling, either in this country or in this decade or both. So I don't see how I can do worse than by beginning with a few stories.

Here we find ourselves immediately at the heart of the problem; for how am I to know what kind of stories you wish to hear? Do you wish to hear stories about John and Mary, two perfectly well-adjusted people who have a mature relationship, a nice house, two and a half children, a dog and some hobbies that they share? Or do you wish to hear stories about John and Mary being devoured by a great white shark? Perhaps you would like to know about the day John wakes up and notices that Mary has turned into a great white shark, in which case we will quickly realize that we are in the middle of a modern psychological novel and change the subject at once. Or perhaps you would rather hear, in a liberationist mode, about the day Mary wakes up and notices that John has *always* been a great white shark and she'd better make some speedy decisions about her own priori-

From *Second Words: Selected Critical Prose* (1982). Atwood presented this essay, which has been edited for presentation here, as an address at Dalhousie University in 1980.

ties. But I would insult your intelligences by supposing that you all want to hear the same kinds of stories, and this is the clue to the marketing problems facing almost all publishers today. As a story-teller then, all I can do is to tell the kinds of stories I wish to tell or think I ought to tell and hope that someone or other will want to listen to them, which is, and has been for some time, the plight of the writer in a post-romantic society.

You will notice that I'm calling myself a story-teller rather than a novelist. This notion got put into my head by an interviewer who recently asked me, How do you distinguish between story-telling and literary art? I don't, I said. Literary art is simply the means by which the story-teller feels he or she can most efficiently tell a particular story. By story-telling, we obviously don't mean just the plot. Think of a simple joke; now think of the same joke told, first well and then badly. It's the timing, isn't it? And the gestures, the embellishments, the tangents, the occasion, the expression on the face of the teller, and whether you like him or not. Literary critics talking about fiction may call these things style, voice and narrative technique and so forth, but you can trace them all back to that moment when the tribe or the family is sitting around the fire or the dinner table and the story-teller decides to add something, leave something out or vary the order of telling in order to make the story a little better. Writing on the page is after all just a notation, and all literature, like all music, is oral by nature.

Neither of my parents are writers, but both of them are very good story-tellers; and since they're both from Nova Scotia, I'd like to illustrate one kind of story by giving you a couple of samples of the kind of thing I used to hear around the dinner table when I was growing up. Anyone from rural Nova Scotia is well-steeped in what we now call the oral tradition but which they didn't call anything of the sort. Sometimes they called these stories "yarns"; sometimes they didn't call them anything. They were just things that had once happened.

For instance, there was the ingenious man who lived down around the South Shore and built a circular barn for his cows. The cows spent the night facing outwards, with their rear ends all facing inwards towards the centre of the circle, which made mucking out the barn more efficient. Each cow had its own door, and the doors, equidistant around the perimeter of the circle, were worked by a central pulley. Every morning people would gather from miles around to watch the cows being let out of the barn. At the sound of a horn, the doors would all fly upwards at once, and the cows, urged on by little boys with switches, would squirt out of the barn like drops from a lemon. Or so my father said. As for my mother, one of the most memorable events in her life was the day the hellfire-

and-brimstone preacher at the Woodville United Church got too carried away. During one especially thunderous phrase his false teeth shot from his mouth; but he reached up with his hand, caught them, re-inserted them and continued on without missing a beat. "The pew shook," said my mother, stressing the fact that my grandfather was very strict about behaviour in church: to laugh would be certain death.

These are true stories and there are many more like them; everyone knows stories like that, and they are one point of beginning for a novelist. Another point of beginning would go something like this:

On his way home from the war with Troy, Odysseus made a side trip to the land of the dead. Near a grove sacred to Persephone, he dug a trench, as he had been instructed to do, and let it fill with blood from a sacrificed ram and a black ewe. Attracted by the smell of the blood, many ghosts crowded around the trench, including those of Odysseus' own mother and several of his friends. But he would not let them drink until the ghost he had been waiting for appeared, the ghost of Teiresias, who had been both man and woman and was thus very wise and able to fore-tell the future. He drank from the trench and instructed Odysseus; after that many of the ghosts drank, and the blood made them substantial and gave them voices, so that Odysseus was able to converse with them.

Anyone listening to these stories can tell at once that they are of quite different sorts. We think of the first kind as "real" or "true," and of the second kind as "imaginary," "fabulous" or "mythological." Yet you have only my word for it that the first stories are true, and no proof at all that the second one is not. Put both kinds together and you have, for instance, James Joyce.

Why do people tell stories, "real" stories or "made up" stories, and why do people listen to them? Nobody knows, but it seems to be some-thing that the human race has always done. At this point we could all hug ourselves and conclude that therefore the human race will always do it, and we need not bother our heads any more about the matter. But my central message to you tonight is that authorship as we know it, literature as we know it, is in serious danger of becoming extinct. If this is so, and I will present my evidence in due time, we had better start wondering whether we think authors and stories, poetry and fiction, are a good thing or a bad thing. And if they are a good thing, what are they good *for*?

Let me proceed in an oblique way by telling you a few more stories.

I was recently at a University in the United States, on one of those jaunts that includes a poetry reading, lunch with everyone who teaches Women's Studies, and a few hours spent with Creative Writing classes in poetry. I have nothing against universities or creative writing classes; I have attended the former and taught the latter. But something odd was going on. The creative writing class was pervaded by an unnatural calm. A student would read his poem, which had been Xeroxed and passed around in advance. There would be a few ruminative noises. Then the other members of the class would speak, hushed and reverent, in tones that recalled a Quaker prayer meeting. They said things like this: "I think you could do without that colon." "Maybe you could break that line after the word 'language.' " "I like it, it works for me." "It works for me too, except for the place where he rhymes 'spastic' with 'plastic.' "

Finally I could stand it no longer. "Why am I here?" I said. "What do you want me to talk to you about? What do you want to ask me? This is just a roundabout way of saying, Why are *you* here? What kind of activity do you think writing poetry is, and why do you do it? Where do you see yourselves going with it after you've finished with this class? Who's out there listening to you, and where are you going to publish? Do you see your audience as other poets who will admire the placement of your colons, or do you envisage a more general readership? Talking of reading, what do you read? Do you care enough about poetry to say, ever, that you think someone's poem is *terrible?*"

Well, it quickly became evident that I had stepped way over the line that separates decorum from bad taste in creative writing classes such as these. One was not, it appears, supposed to question the *raison d'être* of such classes. One was not supposed to discourage the students. One was supposed to radiate the air of genteel encouragement appropriate to, say, physiotherapists, or people who teach recreational ceramics. The role of the poet in her society was not to be examined. The goal of the class was to keep its enrolled and fee-paying students from quitting in despair, to give them all passing grades so as not to discourage next year's crop, and, with luck, to teach the student to turn out poems publishable in the kinds of little magazines favoured by the instructor. None of this was said. It was all implicit. I had done a bad thing, I had fiddled with the underpinnings of a delicately balanced structure, and the students, although mute during official time, were eager to talk afterwards. I spent an uneasy night at the Holiday Inn, plagued by dreams of a time in the future when all writing would be done by creative writing students, for creative writing students; though my waking self has been aware for some time that between the activity known as creative writing and writing itself there is no necessary connection.

•   •   •

A friend of mine told me once that when she'd been in France a man, upon hearing she was a writer, commented, "It is an honourable profession." In Canada we don't—even now—think of writing as an honourable profession. We don't think of it as a profession at all. We think of it, still, as something called "expressing yourself." I'm sure you've all heard the one about the writer and the brain surgeon who met at a cocktail party. "So you write," said the brain surgeon. "Isn't that interesting. I've always wanted to write. When I retire and have the time I'm going to be a writer." "What a coincidence," said the writer, "because when I retire I'm going to be a brain surgeon."

Deep down inside, most people think that writing is something anyone can do, really, because after all it's only expressing yourself. Well, it's probably true that anyone can write. Anyone can play the piano too, but doing it well is another thing. If writing is merely and only self-expression, then all the philistine reactions to it I've been caricaturing above would be, in my opinion, quite justified.

Readers and critics both are still addicted to the concept of self-expression, the writer as a kind of spider, spinning out his entire work from within. This view depends on a solopsism, the idea that we are all self-enclosed monads, with an inside and an outside, and that nothing from the outside ever gets in. It goes hand in hand with that garland of clichés, the one with which women writers in particular are frequently decorated, the notion that everything you write *must* be based on personal experience. *Must*, because those making this assumption have no belief in the imagination, and are such literalists that they will not invest interest in anything they do not suppose to be "true." Of course all writing is based on personal experience, but personal experience is experience—wherever it comes from—that you identify with, *imagine* if you like, so that it becomes personal to you. If your mother dies and you don't feel a thing, is this death a personal experience? "If a clod be washed away by the sea, Europe is the less," said John Donne; or, to paraphrase him as Adrienne Rich does, "Every woman's death diminishes me."

We like to think of writing as merely personal, merely self-expression, and hopefully neurotic, because it lets us off the hook. If that's all it is, if it is not a true view of the world or, Heaven forefend, of a human nature of which we ourselves partake, we don't have to pay any serious attention to it. I happen to believe that at its best writing is considerably more and other than mere self-expression. But what more, what other?

Earlier this summer I was with another group of apprentice writers. They were taking a summer course and many of them were quite earnest and advanced. "Why do you want to write?" I asked them, being by this time very curious about the answers. The first man, an ex-policeman, said he wrote in order to entertain people and to leave a record of himself behind. I did not question why one would want to do either of these things. There were some versions of the self-expression motif, elaborated in the direction of Jungian depth therapy; one does encounter, from time to time, the view that writing is somehow good for the writer, like vitamin pills or primal screaming. One man hinted that writing might have what he called a "political" function.

"What about," said I, "the desire for revenge and the wish to be important?" Blushes all around. Again, I had mentioned something you weren't supposed to. But if one is answering the question, "Why do you want to be a writer?" rather than the one I asked, then such petty motivations cannot be overlooked, because there's a little of that in every young writer when he envisages himself as a future, successful writer.

The question I actually asked was, "Why do you want to write?" and I believe the two questions are quite different. To think of *being a writer* is to imagine oneself as a noun, a thing called a writer; it is to imagine oneself playing a certain kind of role, being treated in a certain kind of way by society. It is to see one's body in a special dress, relating to other bodies as a social entity. *Being a writer* is signing your name in bookstores and making a horse's ass of yourself on TV talk shows and giving speeches like this one. It is concerned with versions of the self; it is *self* centred, and it has nothing much to do with writing, except insofar as it provides you with material.

To think of writing, on the other hand, is to think of a verb. Writing itself is a process, an activity which moves in time and through time, and it is self-less. I don't mean that it thereby makes the writer unselfish; on the contrary, a writer these days has to be selfish to the point of ruth-lessness, if only—at the lowest level—to be able to seize the time neces-sary to write from all those who are clamouring for it. But writing is self-less in the same way that skiing is, or making love. How can you take part intensely in such an involving polyaesthetic activity and still be thinking about yourself? In writing, your attention is focused not on the self but on the thing being made, the thing being seen, and let us not forget that *poet* means *maker* and *seer* means *one who sees*.

•   •   •

Reading is also a process and it also changes you. You aren't the same person after you've read a particular book as you were before, and you will read the next book, unless both are Harlequin Romances, in a slightly different way. When you read a book, it matters how old you are and when you read it and whether you are male or female, or from Canada or India. There is no such thing as a truly universal literature, partly because there are no truly universal readers. It is my contention that the process of reading is part of the process of writing, the necessary completion without which writing can hardly be said to exist.

• • •

The ideal reader, for a serious writer, is intelligent, capable of feeling, possessed of a moral sense, a lover of language, and very demanding. By *demanding*, I don't mean picky. Above all, such a reader will know what kind of book you are writing and will not expect you, as so many critics do, to be writing the book she would write if she were you; nor will the ideal reader expect a romance to be a satire, or a tragedy to be a comedy. There was a noticeable decline in the level of hockey-playing when the league was expanded to include audiences uneducated enough in the sport to think it was cute to throw rolls of toilet paper onto the ice.

"Well," I said to the summer students, "you've said some things I wouldn't disagree with, but I'll go a little farther. Here is what I believe about what you all say you want to do. I believe that poetry is the heart of the language, the activity through which language is renewed and kept alive. I believe that fiction writing is the guardian of the moral and ethical sense of the community. Especially now that organized religion is scattered and in disarray, and politicians have, Lord knows, lost their credibility, fiction is one of the few forms left through which we may examine our society not in its particular but in its typical aspects; through which we can see ourselves and the ways in which we behave towards each other, through which we can see others and judge them and ourselves."

Writing is a craft, true, and discussions of the position of colons and the rhyming of *plastic* and *spastic* have some place in it. You cannot be a concert pianist without having first learned the scales, you cannot throw a porcelain vase without having put in a good number of hours at the wheel. But writing is also a vocation. By *vocation* I mean a lifetime pursuit to which you feel called. There is a big difference between a doctor who goes into medicine because he wants to cure people and one who goes into it because that's where he thinks the money is. They may both be able to fix your broken leg, technically just as well; but there is a difference. Under the right conditions, the first may turn into Norman Bethune.[1] The second never will. If you want to be a writer, you should

---

1. Canadian doctor who provided medical aid to Mao Zedong's army during the Chinese struggle against the Japanese in World War II [*Editors*].

go into the largest library you can find and stand there contemplating the books that have been written. Then you should ask yourself, "Do I really have anything to add?" If you have the arrogance or the humility to say yes, you will know you have the vocation.

Writing is also a profession, and, at its best, an honourable one. It has been made honourable by those who have already been members of it.

• • •

Writing can also be an art, and one of the reasons that so many writers dodge this on television talk shows is that art is hard to define or describe. Money is easier to talk about, so we talk about money. Nevertheless, art happens. It happens when you have the craft and the vocation and are waiting for something else, something extra, or maybe not waiting; in any case it happens. It's the extra rabbit coming out of the hat, the one you didn't put there. It's Odysseus standing by the blood-filled trench, except that the blood is his own. It is bringing the dead to life and giving voices to those who lack them so that they may speak for themselves. It is not "expressing yourself." It is opening yourself, discarding your *self*, so that the language and the world may be evoked through you. *Evocation* is quite different from *expression*. Because we are so fixated on the latter, we forget that writing also does the former. Maybe the writer *expresses*; but *evocation*, calling up, is what writing does for the reader. Writing is also a kind of sooth-saying, a truth-telling. It is a naming of the world, a reverse incarnation: the flesh becoming word. It's also a witnessing. *Come with me*, the writer is saying to the reader. *There is a story I have to tell you, there is something you need to know.* The writer is both an eye-witness and an I-witness, the one to whom personal experience happens and the one who makes experience personal for others. The writer *bears witness*. Bearing witness is not the same as self-expression.

There's something compulsive about the act of writing. All writers play Ancient Mariner at times to the reader's Wedding Guest, hoping that they are holding the reader with their glittering eye, at least long enough so he'll turn the next page. The tale the Mariner tells is partly about himself, true, but it's partly about the universe and partly about something the Wedding Guest needs to know; or at least, that's what the story tells us.

Jacob, so one of the stories goes, wrestled with an angel all night, neither prevailing against the other; and he would not let go until the angel blessed him. *What is your name?* said the angel, unable to give the blessing until the name was spoken. When the angel gave the blessing, it was not for Jacob alone but for his people. There is not a writer alive who would fail to interpret this story as a parable of his own relationship with his art. The encounter with language is a struggle in which each side is equally active, for what writer has not felt the language taking him over at times, blocking him at others? We all hope for the blessing; we all hope finally to be able to speak our names. And, we hope that if we receive the blessing it will not be for ourselves alone.

I notice that I've just used the word "hope" three times, which may surprise some of you, since I doubt that there's a writer in Canada who is asked more often, "Why are you so pessimistic?" I will dodge the question of whether or not the media bunnies (both male and female, and not to be confused with serious journalists) who ask this question lead lives that can be called real in most senses of the word. What I usually say to them is, *What you think is pessimistic depends very largely on what you believe is out there in the world.* I myself think that compared to reality I'm a reincarnation of Anne of Green Gables, but that's beside the point. I think that the world consists of Hell, Purgatory, Middle Earth, Limbo, Paradise and Heaven. Most of them are here with us in this room tonight. It is the duty of the writer not to turn down a visit to any of them if it's offered. Some people only live in a couple of these places but nobody lives in just one. I suspect that the people who ask the question want books to transport them to Paradise, as some compensation for being stuck in Purgatory or Limbo: the band-aid theory of literature. But back to hope. Writing, no matter what its subject, is an act of faith; the primary faith being that someone out there will read the results. I believe it's also an act of hope, the hope that things can be better than they are. If the writer is very lucky and manages to live long enough, I think it can also be an act of charity. It takes a lot to see what is there, both without flinching or turning away and without bitterness. The world exists; the writer testifies. She cannot deny anything human.

So, I said to the summer students. Are you up to it?

Time will tell whether they are or not, but even if they are, they still may not become writers; or if they do, they may become writers of quite another kind. I said earlier that literature as we know it is in serious danger of becoming extinct, and now that I've told you all the good things it does I will frighten you by telling you why.

Writer and audience are Siamese twins. Kill one and you run the risk of killing the other. Try to separate them, and you may simply have two dead half-people. By "audience," I don't necessarily mean a mass audience.

• • •

It has always been one function of the artist to speak the forbidden, to speak out, especially in times of political repression. People risk imprisonment and torture because they know there are other people who are hungry for what they have to say. Inhabitants of concentration camps during the second world war jeopardized their already slim chances of survival by keeping diaries; why? Because there was a story that they felt impelled to tell, that they felt the rest of us *had* to know. Amnesty International today works the same way: all it does is tell stories. It makes *the story* known. Such stories have a moral force, a moral authority which is undeniable. The book of Job begins with a series of catastrophes, but for each there is a survivor. Story-telling at its most drastic is the story of the disaster which is the world; it is done by Job's messengers, whom God saved alive because someone had to tell the story. *I only am escaped alone to tell thee:* When a story, "true" or not, begins like this, we must listen.

• • •

In any totalitarian takeover, whether from the left or the right, writers, singers and journalists are the first to be suppressed. After that come the union leaders and the lawyers and judges. The aim of all such suppression is to silence *the voice*, abolish the word, so that the only voices and words left are those of the ones in power. Elsewhere, the word itself is thought to have power; that's why so much trouble is taken to silence it.

Nothing to worry about here, you say. We live in a free society. Anyone can say anything. The word is not an issue here; you don't get killed for social and political criticism, and anyway novels and poetry are just a few artists *expressing themselves*. Nobody takes them seriously. It won't happen here.

Well, perhaps. But there's more than one way to skin a cat.

• • •

I've implied that the writer functions in his or her society as a kind of soothsayer, a truth teller; that writing is not mere self-expression but a view of society and the world at large, and that the novel is a moral instrument. *Moral* implies political, and traditionally the novel has been used not only as a vehicle for social commentary but as a vehicle for political commentary as well. The novelist, at any rate, still sees a connection between politics and the moral sense, even if politicians gave that up some time ago. By "political" I mean having to do with power: who's got it, who wants it, how it operates; in a word, who's allowed to do what to whom, who gets what from whom, who gets away with it and how.

But we're facing these days an increasing pressure on the novel. I'll be careful when I use the word "censorship," because real censorship stops a book before it's even been published. Let us say "suppression." The suppression is of two kinds. One has to do with the yanking of books out of schools and libraries, and is usually motivated by religious objections to depictions of sexual activity. I happen to find this stance pornographic, for the following reason. Pornography is a presentation of sex in isolation from the matrix which surrounds it in real life; it is therefore exaggerated, distorted and untrue. To select the sexual bits from a novel like *The Diviners* and to discard the rest is simply to duplicate what pornographers themselves are doing. It would take a very salacious mind indeed to find *The Diviners*, or indeed the works by Alice Munro, myself and others which have been put through this particular centrifuge, unduly arousing. You have to wade through too much other stuff. Literary writers are easy targets; they don't shoot off your kneecaps. It's a lot safer to villify them than it is to take on the real pornographers.

(The Bible, of course, contains blasphemy, torture, rape, sodomy, orgies, murder, lying and lots of other unpleasant things. It also contains the Sermon on the Mount, which would mean a lot less without its setting. Its setting is the world as it is, human nature as it is. Christ consorted with publicans and sinners, not just because they were more of a challenge but because there were more of them; he didn't have too much use for holier-than-thous. Incidentally, the Bible itself has more than once appeared on lists of banned books.)

Nevertheless, I don't think writers can scream very hard about their books being removed from schools. The students should do the screaming if they want the books, and a system in which parents were not allowed to protest about what their children are being taught would be a fascist dictatorship. The only way to fight this trend is by counterprotest, and it remains to be seen whether enough people feel strongly enough about the corollary to free speech, free reading, to make this effective. But libraries are another matter. Libraries are for adults, and no one has the right to remove anything from them without the consent of the community at large.

The other kind of suppression is semi-political and is, in my view, more dangerous. There are two cases before the courts right now on which I can't comment. Suffice it to say that if the plaintiffs win them the effect will be to scare publishers away from anything with serious political comment. In fact these cases, although they have not yet been decided, are already having this effect. The novel takes as its province the whole of life. Removal of the right to comment on politics will gut it.

If you think Canada is really a country dedicated to democracy and the principle of free speech, remember the War Measures Act. Remember the letters to the editor. Remember how few people spoke out. We are a timorous country, and we do tend to believe that what those in authority do *must*, somehow, be justified.

What we're facing, then, is a literary world split between the huge entertainment-package blockbusters written by "elements" and deemed both money-making and politically innocuous by the powers that be, and a kind of publishing underground to which the rest of us will be banished. The literary audience, which has never been a mass one, will either content itself with the literary equivalent of Muzak—writing to suck your thumb by—or it will stop reading altogether. Some bright soul will put together a mail-order operation, perhaps. As for the writers, they will either become "elements" or they will fulfill my nightmares about the creative writing students. They will stop writing for readers *out there* and write only for readers *in here*, cosy members of an in-group composed largely of other writers and split into factions or "schools" depending on who your friends are and whether you spell I with a capital I or a small one. This tendency will merely support the average serious reader's impression that such writing has nothing to say to *him*. This is already happening to poetry, though in Canada, which as we all know is a cultural backwater, it hasn't happened quite as thoroughly yet.

You may have thought I was going to say something about Canadian novels, and how we all ought to read them because, although nasty-tasting, they are good for us because they tell us about ourselves. I didn't do that because I think the problem is far larger than Canada; although the trends I've outlined will be reflected in Canada too, if they continue unchecked. Of course in entertainment packages it doesn't matter a hoot whether the "element" is Canadian or not, and the citizenship of great white sharks is irrelevant. But in serious literature there is always a voice, and there is no such thing as a voice without a language and without an accent. All true namings have an accent, and accents are local. This does not make the naming of their world less true, however, but more true.

•　　•　　•

A country or a community which does not take serious literature seriously will lose it. *So what?* say the Members of Parliament, the same ones who object to the creeps in long underwear. *All we want is a good read. A*

murder mystery, a spy thriller, something that keeps you turning the pages.
I don't have the time to read anyway.

Well, try this. It could well be argued that the advent of the printed word coincided with the advent of democracy as we know it; that the book is the only form that allows the reader not only to participate but to review, to re-view what's being presented. With a book you can turn back the pages. You can't do that with a television set. Can democracy function at all without a literate public, one with a moral sense and well-developed critical faculties? Can democracy run on entertainment packages alone?

And in whose interest is it that participatory democracy continue to function anyway, even in the imperfect way that it does? Not that of governments, which would like to see a combination of bureaucracy and oligarchy, with the emphasis on the bureaucracy. Not that of big business, which would like a quiescent labour market stuffed to senility with entertainment packages. Canada could easily pass legislation that would protect the book industry we now so tenuously have. Quotas on paperback racks, like the radio quotas that have done so well for the record industry; a system of accredited bookstores, like the ones in, dare I mention it, Quebec. It wouldn't be difficult, but who cares enough to make it happen?

I will leave such questions with you, since you are, after all, the audience. It will not be by the writers, who are too few in number to have any influence at the polls, but by the audience itself that such questions will ultimately be answered.

ACTIVE READING

1. What do you think Atwood means when she defines writing as a "selfless" process? Locate two or three passages in her essay that you suspect demonstrate "selflessness." In what ways are these passages selfless? How do your discussions of these passages clarify your understanding of selfless writing? What new questions do they raise?

2. Atwood begins her essay by imagining different stories to tell; she concludes by leaving her audience with a series of questions to ponder and, perhaps, to act upon. How do these and other sections of Atwood's

essay give you a sense of why she feels people tell stories? Based on your observations about Atwood, how might you revise your thoughts from Before Reading #1?

READING IN NEW CONTEXTS

1. What relationship does Atwood see between reading and writing? How do you respond to her ideas about this relationship? Explore your thoughts by reflecting on your own experience of reading and writing about another essay in this class.

2. What do you think Atwood gains or loses by breaking the unspoken rules of the writing class she visits? How might breaking unspoken rules help clarify what those rules are? Use your observations about this incident to explore another text, perhaps the one by Scheper-Hughes or Anzaldúa, in which someone uses verbal or written language to violate unspoken rules. How does what you learn from these violations compare to what the writer learns?

DRAFT ONE / DRAFT TWO

1. *Draft One:* Choose a text by Kingston, Durham, or another writer who grounds his or her essay in personal experience. Working with two or three examples from the text, examine the role the writer's imagination seems to play in his or her use of personal experience. Based on your findings, discuss Atwood's claim that the imagination is a type of personal experience.

   Draft Two: Look over the essays you have written so far in this course. In which parts of these essays did you most rely on your imagination (you might consider your introductions, choices of quotations, connections between readings, interpretations of passages, or other elements of your essays)? Compose your own theory of the role your imagination plays in your nonfiction writing.

2. *Draft One:* How do you respond to Atwood's concluding questions about the relationship between democracy and the people's willingness and ability to work with the printed word? Use your observations about Atwood to reconsider your response to the discussions of literacy offered

by Heath or Fishman. Develop your own theory of the role literacy should play in society.

Draft Two: Consider some of the indirect means of suppression or censorship of books Atwood mentions in her essay. How might Atwood's observations help you understand Anzaldúa's claims about the difficulties faced by writers who choose to experiment with less familiar forms of writing? How might your discussion of Anzaldúa lead you to revise your theory of literacy from Draft One?

BEFORE READING JAMES BALDWIN

1. According to your experiences or observations, how do people use religion?

2. Discuss a local institution you know of that fails to carry out some of its social purposes. Why does it fail? What are the consequences for you or someone you know when an institution on which you rely fails you?

3. Investigate race relations in the United States in the middle part of this century (the years Baldwin describes in his essay). Consult a reference book and note some of the trends and historical events relating to matters of race.

JAMES   BALDWIN

DOWN AT THE CROSS

> Take up the White Man's burden—
> Ye dare not stoop to less—
> Nor call too loud on Freedom
> To cloak your weariness;
> By all ye cry or whisper,
> By all ye leave or do,
> The silent, sullen peoples
> Shall weigh your Gods and you.
>
> —KIPLING

> Down at the cross where my Saviour died,
> Down where for cleansing from sin I cried,
> There to my heart was the blood applied,
> Singing glory to His name!
>
> —HYMN

I underwent, during the summer that I became fourteen, a prolonged religious crisis. I use the word "religious" in the common, and arbitrary,

Originally published in *The New Yorker* as "Letter from a Region in My Mind," November 17, 1962. Collected in *The Fire Next Time* (1963).

sense, meaning that I then discovered God, His saints and angels, and His blazing Hell. And since I had been born in a Christian nation, I accepted this Deity as the only one. I supposed Him to exist only within the walls of a church—in fact, of *our* church—and I also supposed that God and safety were synonymous. The word "safety" brings us to the real meaning of the word "religious" as we use it. Therefore, to state it in another, more accurate way, I became, during my fourteenth year, for the first time in my life, afraid—afraid of the evil within me and afraid of the evil without. What I saw around me that summer in Harlem was what I had always seen; nothing had changed. But now, without any warning, the whores and pimps and racketeers on the Avenue had become a personal menace. It had not before occurred to me that I could become one of them, but now I realized that we had been produced by the same circumstances. Many of my comrades were clearly headed for the Avenue, and my father said that I was headed that way, too. My friends began to drink and smoke, and embarked—at first avid, then groaning—on their sexual careers. Girls, only slightly older than I was, who sang in the choir or taught Sunday school, the children of holy parents, underwent, before my eyes, their incredible metamorphosis, of which the most bewildering aspect was not their budding breasts or their rounding behinds but something deeper and more subtle, in their eyes, their heat, their odor, and the inflection of their voices. Like the strangers on the Avenue, they became, in the twinkling of an eye, unutterably different and fantastically *present.* Owing to the way I had been raised, the abrupt discomfort that all this aroused in me and the fact that I had no idea what my voice or my mind or my body was likely to do next caused me to consider myself one of the most depraved people on earth. Matters were not helped by the fact that these holy girls seemed rather to enjoy my terrified lapses, our grim, guilty, tormented experiments, which were at once as chill and joyless as the Russian steppes and hotter, by far, than all the fires of Hell.

Yet there was something deeper than these changes, and less definable, that frightened me. It was real in both the boys and the girls, but it was, somehow, more vivid in the boys. In the case of the girls, one watched them turning into matrons before they had become women. They began to manifest a curious and really rather terrifying single-mindedness. It is hard to say exactly how this was conveyed: something implacable in the set of the lips, something farseeing (seeing what?) in the eyes, some new and crushing determination in the walk, something peremptory in the voice. They did not tease us, the boys, any more; they reprimanded us sharply, saying, "You better be thinking about your soul!"

For the girls also saw the evidence on the Avenue, knew what the price would be, for them, of one misstep, knew that they had to be protected and that we were the only protection there was. They understood that they must act as God's decoys, saving the souls of the boys for Jesus and binding the bodies of the boys in marriage. For this was the beginning of our burning time, and "It is better," said St. Paul—who elsewhere, with a most unusual and stunning exactness, described himself as a "wretched man"—"to marry than to burn." And I began to feel in the boys a curious, wary, bewildered despair, as though they were now settling in for the long, hard winter of life. I did not know then what it was that I was reacting to; I put it to myself that they were letting themselves go. In the same way that the girls were destined to gain as much weight as their mothers, the boys, it was clear, would rise no higher than their fathers. School began to reveal itself, therefore, as a child's game that one could not win, and boys dropped out of school and went to work. My father wanted me to do the same. I refused, even though I no longer had any illusions about what an education could do for me; I had already encountered too many college-graduate handymen. My friends were now "downtown," busy, as they put it, "fighting the man." They began to care less about the way they looked, the way they dressed, the things they did; presently, one found them in twos and threes and fours, in a hallway, sharing a jug of wine or a bottle of whisky, talking, cursing, fighting, sometimes weeping: lost, and unable to say what it was that oppressed them, except that they knew it was "the man"—the white man. And there seemed to be no way whatever to remove this cloud that stood between them and the sun, between them and love and life and power, between them and whatever it was that they wanted. One did not have to be very bright to realize how little one could do to change one's situation; one did not have to be abnormally sensitive to be worn down to a cutting edge by the incessant and gratuitous humiliation and danger one encountered every working day, all day long. The humiliation did not apply merely to working days, or workers; I was thirteen and was crossing Fifth Avenue on my way to the Forty-second Street library, and the cop in the middle of the street muttered as I passed him, "Why don't you niggers stay uptown where you belong?" When I was ten, and didn't look, certainly, any older, two policemen amused themselves with me by frisking me, making comic (and terrifying) speculations concerning my ancestry and probable sexual prowess, and for good measure, leaving me flat on my back in one of Harlem's empty lots. Just before and then during the Second World War, many of my friends fled into the service, all to be changed there, and rarely for the better, many to be ruined, and many to die. Others fled to other states and cities—that is, to other ghettos. Some went on wine or whisky or the needle, and are still on it. And others, like me, fled into the church.

For the wages of sin were visible everywhere, in every wine-stained and urine-splashed hallway, in every clanging ambulance bell, in every scar on the faces of the pimps and their whores, in every helpless, new-born baby being brought into this danger, in every knife and pistol fight on the Avenue, and in every disastrous bulletin: a cousin, mother of six, suddenly gone mad, the children parcelled out here and there; an inde-structible aunt rewarded for years of hard labor by a slow, agonizing death in a terrible small room; someone's bright son blown into eternity by his own hand; another turned robber and carried off to jail. It was a summer of dreadful speculations and discoveries, of which these were not the worst. Crime became real, for example—for the first time—not as a possi-bility but as *the* possibility. One would never defeat one's circumstances by working and saving one's pennies; one would never, by working, acquire that many pennies, and, besides, the social treatment accorded even the most successful Negroes proved that one needed, in order to be free, something more than a bank account. One needed a handle, a lever, a means of inspiring fear. It was absolutely clear that the police would whip you and take you in as long as they could get away with it, and that everyone else—housewives, taxi-drivers, elevator boys, dishwashers, bartenders, lawyers, judges, doctors, and grocers—would never, by the operation of any generous human feeling, cease to use you as an outlet for his frustrations and hostilities. Neither civilized reason nor Christian love would cause any of those people to treat you as they presumably wanted to be treated; only the fear of your power to retaliate would cause them to do that, or to seem to do it, which was (and is) good enough. There appears to be a vast amount of confusion on this point, but I do not know many Negroes who are eager to be "accepted" by white people, still less to be loved by them; they, the blacks, simply don't wish to be beaten over the head by the whites every instant of our brief passage on this planet. White people in this country will have quite enough to do in learning how to accept and love themselves and each other, and when they have achieved this—which will not be tomorrow and may very well be never—the Negro problem will no longer exist, for it will no longer be needed.

People more advantageously placed than we in Harlem were, and are, will no doubt find the psychology and the view of human nature sketched above dismal and shocking in the extreme. But the Negro's experience of the white world cannot possibly create in him any respect for the standards by which the white world claims to live. His own condition is overwhelming proof that white people do not live by these standards. Negro servants have been smuggling odds and ends out of white homes for generations, and white people have been delighted to have them do it, because it has assuaged a dim guilt and testified to the intrinsic superiority of white people. Even the most doltish and servile Negro could scarcely fail to be impressed by the disparity between his situation and that of the people for whom he worked; Negroes who were neither doltish nor servile did not feel that they were doing anything wrong when they robbed white people. In spite of the Puritan-Yankee equation of virtue with well-being, Negroes had excellent reasons for doubting that money was made or kept by any very striking adherence to the Christian virtues; it certainly did not work that way for black Christians. In any case, white people, who had robbed black people of their liberty and who profited by this theft every hour that they lived, had no moral ground on which to stand. They had the judges, the juries, the shotguns, the law—in a word, power. But it was a criminal power, to be feared but not respected, and to be outwitted in any way whatever. And those virtues preached but not practiced by the white world were merely another means of holding Negroes in subjection.

It turned out, then, that summer, that the moral barriers that I had supposed to exist between me and the dangers of a criminal career were so tenuous as to be nearly nonexistent. I certainly could not discover any principled reason for not becoming a criminal, and it is not my poor, God-fearing parents who are to be indicted for the lack but this society. I was icily determined—more determined, really, than I then knew—never to make my peace with the ghetto but to die and go to Hell before I would let any white man spit on me, before I would accept my "place" in this republic. I did not intend to allow the white people of this country to tell me who I was, and limit me that way, and polish me off that way. And yet, of course, at the same time, I *was* being spat on and defined and described and limited, and could have been polished off with no effort whatever. Every Negro boy—in my situation during those years, at least— who reaches this point realizes, at once, profoundly, because he wants to live, that he stands in great peril and must find, with speed, a "thing," a gimmick, to lift him out, to start him on his way. *And it does not matter what the gimmick is.* It was this last realization that terrified me and— since it revealed that the door opened on so many dangers—helped to hurl me into the church. And, by an unforeseeable paradox, it was my career in the church that turned out, precisely, to be my gimmick.

For when I tried to assess my capabilities, I realized that I had almost none. In order to achieve the life I wanted, I had been dealt, it seemed to me, the worst possible hand. I could not become a prizefighter—many of us tried but very few succeeded. I could not sing. I could not dance. I had been well conditioned by the world in which I grew up, so I did not yet dare take the idea of becoming a writer seriously. The only other possibility seemed to involve my becoming one of the sordid people on the Avenue, who were not really as sordid as I then imagined but who frightened me terribly, both because I did not want to live that life and because of what they made me feel. Everything inflamed me, and that was bad enough, but I myself had also become a source of fire and temptation. I had been far too well raised, alas, to suppose that any of the extremely explicit overtures made to me that summer, sometimes by boys and girls but also, more alarmingly, by older men and women, had anything to do with my attractiveness. On the contrary, since the Harlem idea of seduction is, to put it mildly, blunt, whatever these people saw in me merely confirmed my sense of my depravity.

It is certainly sad that the awakening of one's senses should lead to such a merciless judgment of oneself—to say nothing of the time and anguish one spends in the effort to arrive at any other—but it is also inevitable that a literal attempt to mortify the flesh should be made among black people like those with whom I grew up. Negroes in this country—and Negroes do not, strictly or legally speaking, exist in any other—are taught really to despise themselves from the moment their eyes open on the world. This world is white and they are black. White people hold the power, which means that they are superior to blacks (intrinsically, that is: God decreed it so), and the world has innumerable ways of making this difference known and felt and feared. Long before the Negro child perceives this difference, and even longer before he understands it, he has begun to react to it, he has begun to be controlled by it. Every effort made by the child's elders to prepare him for a fate from which they cannot protect him causes him secretly, in terror, to begin to await, without knowing that he is doing so, his mysterious and inexorable punishment. He must be "good" not only in order to please his parents and not only to avoid being punished by them; behind their authority stands another, nameless and impersonal, infinitely harder to please, and bottomlessly cruel. And this filters into the child's consciousness through his parents' tone of voice as he is being exhorted, punished, or loved; in the sudden, uncontrollable note of fear heard in his mother's or his father's voice when he has strayed beyond some particular boundary. He does not know what the boundary is, and he can get no explanation of it, which is frightening enough, but the fear he hears in the voices of his elders is more frightening still. The fear that I heard in my father's voice, for example, when he realized that I really *believed* I could do anything a white boy could do, and had every intention of proving it, was not at all like the fear I heard when one of us was ill or had fallen down the stairs or strayed too far from the house. It was another fear, a fear that the child, in challenging the white world's assumptions, was putting himself in the path of destruction. A child cannot, thank Heaven, know how vast and how merciless is the nature of power, with what unbelievable cruelty people treat each other. He reacts to the fear in his parents' voices because his parents hold up the world for him and he has no protection without them. I defended myself, as I imagined, against the fear my father made me feel by remembering that he was very old-fashioned. Also, I prided myself on the fact that I already knew how to outwit him. To defend oneself against a fear is simply to insure that one will, one day, be conquered by it; fears must be faced. As for one's wits, it is just not true that one can live by them—not, that is, if one wishes really to live. That summer, in any case, all the fears with which I had grown up, and which were now a part of me and controlled my vision of the world, rose up like a wall between the world and me, and drove me into the church.

As I look back, everything I did seems curiously deliberate, though it certainly did not seem deliberate then. For example, I did not join the church of which my father was a member and in which he preached. My best friend in school, who attended a different church, had already "surrendered his life to the Lord," and he was very anxious about my soul's salvation. (I wasn't, but any human attention was better than none.) One Saturday afternoon, he took me to his church. There were no services that day, and the church was empty, except for some women cleaning and some other women praying. My friend took me into the back room to meet his pastor—a woman. There she sat, in her robes, smiling, an extremely proud and handsome woman, with Africa, Europe, and the America of the American Indian blended in her face. She was perhaps forty-five or fifty at this time, and in our world she was a very celebrated woman. My friend was about to introduce me when she looked at me and smiled and said, "Whose little boy are you?" Now this, unbelievably, was precisely the phrase used by pimps and racketeers on the Avenue when they suggested, both humorously and intensely, that I "hang out" with them. Perhaps part of the terror they had caused me to feel came from the fact that I unquestionably wanted to be *somebody's* little boy. I was so frightened, and at the mercy of so many conundrums, that inevitably, that summer, *someone* would have taken me over; one doesn't, in Harlem, long remain standing on any auction block. It was my good luck—perhaps—that I found myself in the church racket instead of some other, and surrendered to a spiritual seduction long before I came to any carnal knowledge. For when the pastor asked me, with that marvellous smile, "Whose little boy are you?" my heart replied at once, "Why, yours."

The summer wore on, and things got worse. I became more guilty and more frightened, and kept all this bottled up inside me, and naturally, inescapably, one night, when this woman had finished preaching, everything came roaring, screaming, crying out, and I fell to the ground before the altar. It was the strangest sensation I have ever had in my life—up to that time, or since. I had not known that it was going to happen, or that it could happen. One moment I was on my feet, singing and clapping and, at the same time, working out in my head the plot of a play I was working on then; the next moment, with no transition, no sensation of falling, I was on my back, with the lights beating down into my face and all the vertical saints above me. I did not know what I was doing down so low, or how I had got there. And the anguish that filled me cannot be described. It moved in me like one of those floods that devastate counties, tearing everything down, tearing children from their parents and lovers from each other, and making everything an unrecognizable waste. All I really remember is the pain, the unspeakable pain; it was as though I were yelling up to Heaven and Heaven would not hear me. And if Heaven would not hear me, if love could not descend from Heaven—to wash me, to make me clean—then utter disaster was my portion. Yes, it does indeed mean something—something unspeakable—to be born, in a white country, an Anglo-Teutonic, antisexual country, black. You very soon, without knowing it, give up all hope of communion. Black people, mainly, look down or look up but do not look at each other, not at you, and white people, mainly, look away. And the universe is simply a sounding drum; there is no way, no way whatever, so it seemed then and has sometimes seemed since, to get through a life, to love your wife and children, or your friends, or your mother and father, or to be loved. The universe, which is not merely the stars and the moon and the planets, flowers, grass, and trees, but *other people*, has evolved no terms for your existence, has made no room for you, and if love will not swing wide the gates, no other power will or can. And if one despairs—as who has not?—of human love,

God's love alone is left. But God—and I felt this even then, so long ago, on that tremendous floor, unwillingly—is white. And if His love was so great, and if He loved all His children, why were we, the blacks, cast down so far? Why? In spite of all I said thereafter, I found no answer on the floor—not *that* answer, anyway—and I was on the floor all night. Over me, to bring me "through," the saints sang and rejoiced and prayed. And in the morning, when they raised me, they told me that I was "saved."

Well, indeed I was, in a way, for I was utterly drained and exhausted, and released, for the first time, from all my guilty torment. I was aware then only of my relief. For many years, I could not ask myself why human relief had to be achieved in a fashion at once so pagan and so desperate— in a fashion at once so unspeakably old and so unutterably new. And by the time I was able to ask myself this question, I was also able to see that the principles governing the rites and customs of the churches in which I grew up did not differ from the principles governing the rites and cus- toms of other churches, white. The principles were Blindness, Loneliness, and Terror, the first principle necessarily and actively cultivated in order to deny the two others. I would love to believe that the principles were Faith, Hope, and Charity, but this is clearly not so for most Christians, or for what we call the Christian world.

I was saved. But at the same time, out of a deep, adolescent cunning I do not pretend to understand, I realized immediately that I could not remain in the church merely as another worshipper. I would have to give myself something to do, in order not to be too bored and find myself among all the wretched unsaved of the Avenue. And I don't doubt that I also intended to best my father on his own ground. Anyway, very shortly after I joined the church, I became a preacher—a Young Minister—and I remained in the pulpit for more than three years. My youth quickly made me a much bigger drawing card than my father. I pushed this advantage ruthlessly, for it was the most effective means I had found of breaking his hold over me. That was the most frightening time of my life, and quite the most dishonest, and the resulting hysteria lent great passion to my sermons—for a while. I relished the attention and the relative immunity from punishment that my new status gave me, and I relished, above all, the sudden right to privacy. It had to be recognized, after all, that I was still a schoolboy, with my schoolwork to do, and I was also expected to prepare at least one sermon a week. During what we may call my heyday, I preached much more often than that. This meant that there were hours and even whole days when I could not be interrupted—not even by my father. I had immobilized him. It took rather more time for me to realize that I had also immobilized myself, and had escaped from nothing whatever.

The church was very exciting. It took a long time for me to disengage myself from this excitement, and on the blindest, most visceral level, I never really have, and never will. There is no music like that music, no drama like the drama of the saints rejoicing, the sinners moaning, the tambourines racing, and all those voices coming together and crying holy unto the Lord. There is still, for me, no pathos quite like the pathos of those multicolored, worn, somehow triumphant and transfigured faces, speaking from the depths of a visible, tangible, continuing despair of the goodness of the Lord. I have never seen anything to equal the fire and excitement that sometimes, without warning, fill a church, causing the church, as Leadbelly and so many others have testified, to "rock." Nothing that has happened to me since equals the power and the glory that I sometimes felt when, in the middle of a sermon, I knew that I was some-how, by some miracle, really carrying, as they said, "the Word"—when the church and I were one. Their pain and their joy were mine, and mine were theirs—they surrendered their pain and joy to me, I surrendered mine to them—and their cries of "Amen!" and "Hallelujah!" and "Yes, Lord!" and "Praise His name!" and "Preach it, brother!" sustained and whipped on my solos until we all became equal, wringing wet, singing and dancing, in anguish and rejoicing, at the foot of the altar. It was, for a long time, in spite of—or, not inconceivably, because of—the shabbi-ness of my motives, my only sustenance, my meat and drink. I rushed home from school, to the church, to the altar, to be alone there, to com-mune with Jesus, my dearest Friend, who would never fail me, who knew all the secrets of my heart. Perhaps He did, but I didn't, and the bargain we struck, actually, down there at the foot of the cross, was that He would never let me find out.

He failed His bargain. He was a much better Man than I took Him for. It happened, as things do, imperceptibly, in many ways at once. I date it—the slow crumbling of my faith, the pulverization of my fortress— from the time, about a year after I had begun to preach, when I began to read again. I justified this desire by the fact that I was still in school, and I began, fatally, with Dostoevsky. By this time, I was in a high school that was predominantly Jewish. This meant that I was surrounded by people who were, by definition, beyond any hope of salvation, who laughed at the tracts and leaflets I brought to school, and who pointed out that the Gospels had been written long after the death of Christ. This might not have been so distressing if it had not forced me to read the tracts and leaflets myself, for they were indeed, unless one believed their message already, impossible to believe. I remember feeling dimly that there was a kind of blackmail in it. People, I felt, ought to love the Lord *because* they loved Him, and not because they were afraid of going to Hell. I was forced, reluctantly, to realize that the Bible itself had been written by men, and translated by men out of languages I could not read, and I was already, without quite admitting it to myself, terribly involved with the effort of putting words on paper. Of course, I had the rebuttal ready: These men had all been operating under divine inspiration. *Had* they? *All* of them? And I also knew by now, alas, far more about divine inspiration than I dared admit, for I knew how I worked myself up into my own visions, and how frequently—indeed, incessantly—the visions God granted to me differed from the visions He granted to my father. I did not understand the dreams I had at night, but I knew that they were not holy. For that matter, I knew that my waking hours were far from holy. I spent most of my time in a state of repentance for things I had vividly desired to do but had not done. The fact that I was dealing with Jews brought the whole question of color, which I had been desperately avoiding, into the terrified center of my mind. I realized that the Bible had been written by white men. I knew that, according to many Christians, I was a descendant of Ham, who had been cursed, and that I was therefore predestined to be a slave. This had nothing to do with anything I was, or contained, or could become; my fate had been sealed forever, from the beginning of time. And it seemed, indeed, when one looked out over Christendom, that this was what Christendom effectively believed. It was certainly the way it behaved. I remembered the Italian priests and bishops blessing Italian boys who were on their way to Ethiopia.

Again, the Jewish boys in high school were troubling because I could find no point of connection between them and the Jewish pawnbrokers and landlords and grocerystore owners in Harlem. I knew that these people were Jews—God knows I was told it often enough—but I thought of them only as white. Jews, as such, until I got to high school, were all incarcerated in the Old Testament, and their names were Abraham, Moses, Daniel, Ezekiel, and Job, and Shadrach, Meshach, and Abednego. It was bewildering to find them so many miles and centuries out of Egypt, and so far from the fiery furnace. My best friend in high school was a Jew. He came to our house once, and afterward my father asked, as he asked about everyone, "Is he a Christian?"—by which he meant "Is he saved?" I really do not know whether my answer came out of innocence or venom, but I said coldly, "No. He's Jewish." My father slammed me across the face with his great palm, and in that moment everything flooded back—all the hatred and all the fear, and the depth of a merciless resolve to kill my father rather than allow my father to kill me—and I knew that all those sermons and tears and all that repentance and rejoicing had changed nothing. I wondered if I was expected to be glad that a friend of mine, or anyone, was to be tormented forever in Hell, and I also thought, suddenly, of the Jews in another Christian nation, Germany. They were not so far from the fiery furnace after all, and my best friend might have been one of them. I told my father, "He's a better Christian than you are," and walked out of the house. The battle between us was in the open, but that was all right; it was almost a relief. A more deadly struggle had begun.

Being in the pulpit was like being in the theater; I was behind the scenes and knew how the illusion was worked. I knew the other ministers and knew the quality of their lives. And I don't mean to suggest by this the "Elmer Gantry" sort of hypocrisy concerning sensuality; it was a deeper, deadlier, and more subtle hypocrisy than that, and a little honest sensuality, or a lot, would have been like water in an extremely bitter desert. I knew how to work on a congregation until the last dime was surrendered—it was not very hard to do—and I knew where the money for "the Lord's work" went. I knew, though I did not wish to know it, that I had no respect for the people with whom I worked. I could not have said it then, but I also knew that if I continued I would soon have no respect for myself. And the fact that I was "the young Brother Baldwin" increased my value with those same pimps and racketeers who had helped to stampede me into the church in the first place. They still saw the little boy they intended to take over. They were waiting for me to come to my senses and realize that I was in a very lucrative business. They knew that I did not yet realize this, and also that I had not yet begun to suspect where my own needs, *coming up* (they were very patient), could drive me. They themselves did know the score, and they knew that the odds were in their favor. And, really, I knew it, too. I was even lonelier and more vulnerable than I had been before. And the blood of the Lamb had not cleansed me in any way whatever. I was just as black as I had been the day that I was born. Therefore, when I faced a congregation, it began to take all the strength I had not to stammer, not to curse, not to tell them to throw away their Bibles and get off their knees and go home and organize, for example, a rent strike. When I watched all the children, their copper, brown, and beige faces staring up at me as I taught Sunday school, I felt that I was committing a crime in talking about the gentle Jesus, in telling them to reconcile themselves to their misery on earth in order to gain the crown of eternal life. Were only Negroes to gain this crown? Was Heaven, then, to be merely another ghetto? Perhaps I might have been able to reconcile myself even to this if I had been able to believe that there was any loving-kindness to be found in the haven I represented. But I had been in the pulpit too long and I had seen too many monstrous things. I don't refer merely to the glaring fact that the minister eventually acquires houses and Cadillacs while the faithful continue to scrub floors and drop their dimes and quarters and dollars into the plate. I really mean that there was no love in the church. It was a mask for hatred and self-hatred and despair. The transfiguring power of the Holy Ghost ended when the service ended, and salvation stopped at the church door. When we were told to love everybody, I had thought that that meant *everybody*. But no. It applied only to those who believed as we did, and it did not apply to white people at all. I was told by a minister, for example, that I should never, on any public conveyance, under any circumstances, rise and give my seat to a white woman. White men never rose for Negro women. Well, that was true enough, in the main—I saw his point. But what was the point, the purpose, of *my* salvation if it did not permit me to behave with love toward others, no matter how they behaved toward me? What others did was their responsibility, for which they would answer when the judgment trumpet sounded. But what *I* did was *my* responsibility, and I would have to answer, too—unless, of course, there was also in Heaven a special dispensation for the benighted black, who was not to be judged in the same way as other human beings, or angels. It probably occurred to me around this time that the vision people hold of the world to come is but a reflection, with predictable wishful distortions, of the world in which they live. And this did not apply only to Negroes, who were no more "simple" or "spontaneous" or "Christian" than anybody else—who were merely more oppressed. In the same way that we, for white people, were the descendants of Ham, and were cursed forever, white people were, for us, the descendants of Cain. And the passion with which we loved the Lord was a measure of how deeply we feared and distrusted and, in the end, hated almost all strangers, always, and avoided and despised ourselves.

But I cannot leave it at that; there is more to it than that. In spite of everything, there was in the life I fled a zest and a joy and a capacity for facing and surviving disaster that are very moving and very rare. Perhaps we were, all of us—pimps, whores, racketeers, church members, and children—bound together by the nature of our oppression, the specific and peculiar complex of risks we had to run; if so, within these limits we sometimes achieved with each other a freedom that was close to love. I remember, anyway, church suppers and outings, and, later, after I left the church, rent and waistline parties where rage and sorrow sat in the darkness and did not stir, and we ate and drank and talked and laughed and danced and forgot all about "the man." We had the liquor, the chicken, the music, and each other, and had no need to pretend to be what we were not. This is the freedom that one hears in some gospel songs, for example, and in jazz. In all jazz, and especially in the blues, there is something tart and ironic, authoritative and double-edged. White Americans seem to feel that happy songs are *happy* and sad songs are *sad*, and that, God help us, is exactly the way most white Americans sing them— sounding, in both cases, so helplessly, defenselessly fatuous that one dare not speculate on the temperature of the deep freeze from which issue their brave and sexless little voices. Only people who have been "down the line," as the song puts it, know what this music is about. I think it was Big Bill Broonzy who used to sing "I Feel So Good," a really joyful song about a man who is on his way to the railroad station to meet his girl. She's coming home. It is the singer's incredibly moving exuberance that makes one realize how leaden the time must have been while she was gone. There is no guarantee that she will stay this time, either, as the singer clearly knows, and, in fact, she has not yet actually arrived. Tonight, or tomorrow, or within the next five minutes, he may very well be singing "Lonesome in My Bedroom," or insisting, "Ain't we, ain't we, going to make it all right? Well, if we don't today, we will tomorrow night." White Americans do not understand the depths out of which such an ironic tenacity comes, but they suspect that the force is sensual, and they are terrified of sensuality and do not any longer understand it. The word "sensual" is not intended to bring to mind quivering dusky maidens or priapic black studs. I am referring to something much simpler and much less fanciful. To be sensual, I think, is to respect and rejoice in the force of life, of life itself, and to be *present* in all that one does, from the effort of loving to the breaking of bread. It will be a great day for America, incidentally, when we begin to eat bread again, instead of the blasphemous and tasteless foam rubber that we have substituted for it. And I am not being frivolous now, either. Something very sinister happens to the people of a country when they begin to distrust their own reactions as deeply as they do here, and become as joyless as they have become. It is this individual uncertainty on the part of white American men and women, this inability to renew themselves at the fountain of their own lives, that makes the discussion, let alone elucidation, of any conundrum—that is, any reality—so supremely difficult. The person who distrusts himself has no touchstone for reality—for this touchstone can be only oneself. Such a person interposes between himself and reality nothing less than a labyrinth of attitudes. And these attitudes, furthermore, though the person is usually unaware of it (is unaware of so much!), are historical and public attitudes. They do not relate to the present any more than they relate to the person. Therefore, whatever white people do not know about Negroes reveals, precisely and inexorably, what they do not know about themselves.

White Christians have also forgotten several elementary historical details. They have forgotten that the religion that is now identified with their virtue and their power—"God is on our side," says Dr. Verwoerd—came out of a rocky piece of ground in what is now known as the Middle East before color was invented, and that in order for the Christian church to be established, Christ had to be put to death, by Rome, and that the real architect of the Christian church was not the disreputable, sun-baked Hebrew who gave it his name but the mercilessly fanatical and self-righteous Saint Paul. The energy that was buried with the rise of the Christian nations must come back into the world; nothing can prevent it. Many of us, I think, both long to see this happen and are terrified of it, for though this transformation contains the hope of liberation, it also imposes a necessity for great change. But in order to deal with the untapped and dormant force of the previously subjugated, in order to survive as a human, moving, moral weight in the world, America and all the Western nations will be forced to reexamine themselves and release themselves from many things that are now taken to be sacred, and to discard nearly all the assumptions that have been used to justify their lives and their anguish and their crimes so long.

"The white man's Heaven," sings a Black Muslim minister, "is the black man's Hell." One may object—possibly—that this puts the matter somewhat too simply, but the song is true, and it has been true for as long as white men have ruled the world. The Africans put it another way: When the white man came to Africa, the white man had the Bible and the African had the land, but now it is the white man who is being, reluctantly and bloodily, separated from the land, and the African who is still attempting to digest or to vomit up the Bible. The struggle, therefore, that now begins in the world is extremely complex, involving the historical role of Christianity in the realm of power—that is, politics—and in the realm of morals. In the realm of power, Christianity has operated with an unmitigated arrogance and cruelty—necessarily, since a religion ordinarily imposes on those who have discovered the true faith the spiritual duty of liberating the infidels. This particular true faith, moreover, is more deeply concerned about the soul than it is about the body, to which fact the flesh (and the corpses) of countless infidels bears witness. It goes without saying, then, that whoever questions the authority of the true faith also contests the right of the nations that hold this faith to rule over him— contests, in short, their title to his land. The spreading of the Gospel, regardless of the motives or the integrity or the heroism of some of the missionaries, was an absolutely indispensable justification for the planting of the flag. Priests and nuns and schoolteachers helped to protect and sanctify the power that was so ruthlessly being used by people who were indeed seeking a city, but not one in the heavens, and one to be made, very definitely, by captive hands. The Christian church itself—again, as distinguished from some of its ministers—sanctified and rejoiced in the conquests of the flag, and encouraged, if it did not formulate, the belief that conquest, with the resulting relative well-being of the Western populations, was proof of the favor of God. God had come a long way from the desert—but then so had Allah, though in a very different direction. God, going north, and rising on the wings of power, had become white, and Allah, out of power, and on the dark side of Heaven, had become— for all practical purposes, anyway—black. Thus, in the realm of morals the role of Christianity has been, at best, ambivalent. Even leaving out of account the remarkable arrogance that assumed that the ways and morals of others were inferior to those of Christians, and that they therefore had every right, and could use any means, to change them, the collision between cultures—and the schizophrenia in the mind of Christendom— had rendered the domain of morals as chartless as the sea once was, and as treacherous as the sea still is. It is not too much to say that whoever wishes to become a truly moral human being (and let us not ask whether or not this is possible; I think we must *believe* that it is possible) must first divorce himself from all the prohibitions, crimes, and hypocrisies of the Christian church. If the concept of God has any validity or any use, it can only be to make us larger, freer, and more loving. If God cannot do this, then it is time we got rid of Him.

ACTIVE READING

1. What does Baldwin mean by "gimmick" (45)? Explain how the term applies to several groups and individuals in the essay.

2. Find several passages where you can distinguish between what Baldwin understands as a teenager and what he understands later, as he writes this essay. What do you make of the differences you find there?

3. Baldwin writes about the desire for "safety" (42) as well as the desire for "communion" (48). In the context of his experiences growing up, what do these two terms mean, and what do they have to do with each other?

4. In his final paragraph, Baldwin discusses how "the realm of power" (55) influences broad historical events. Work out a definition of that phrase, and then locate several events in Baldwin's early life where he found himself within that realm on a local level. How does the "realm of power" work in everyday life?

READING IN NEW CONTEXTS

1. Baldwin writes about a "labyrinth of attitudes" (55) that helps him explain some of the workings of racism. Prepare a definition of that phrase based on Baldwin's use of it, and then consider another *Literacies* text in which someone's life is influenced by a similar labyrinth. What does the second text add to your understanding of the term?

2. "The collision of cultures . . . ," says Baldwin, "had rendered the domain of morals as chartless as the sea once was" (56). Make a study of the way two or three individuals or communities respond to that dilemma in other texts, such as Fienup-Riordan or Anzaldúa.

3. At one point, Baldwin says that some people of his community "achieved with each other a freedom that was close to love" (53). What do you think he means by "love," if the example he offers here is only "close to love"? How do those ideas of "love" and "close to love" compare to the ideas of community described in Rich or Bellah?

DRAFT ONE/DRAFT TWO

1. *Draft One*: Baldwin suggests that people may have the ability to "renew themselves at the fountain of their own lives" (54). For Draft One, use his text and another *Literacies* text to explain how that process of renewal might work.

Draft Two: For Draft Two, consider another text from *Literacies* that you feel makes a social criticism of one kind or another. Explore the relations you see between social criticism and the process of renewal you have considered in Draft One.

2. *Draft One:* Describe your relationship with a particular social institution, such as school or a religious group, during adolescence. How did the complications of adolescence and the goals and practices of the social institution interact with each other?

Draft Two: Compare your findings in Draft One with the experience of adolescence and church that Baldwin describes. Based on the similarities and differences between your experiences and Baldwin's, analyze how social institutions work for people of that age, between childhood and adulthood.

BEFORE READING DEAN BARNLUND

1. Consider television, movies, magazines, books, and other sources for your knowledge of other cultures. How do your different sources tend to portray other cultures? How do such portrayals shape your level of interest in other cultures?

2. How do you interact with people from cultures, religions, or backgrounds different from your own? Drawing on your own experience, discuss some of the problems that arise when you try to communicate across these differences. How do you work to overcome these problems?

3. Describe what you would expect everyday life to be like in a "village." Where do your ideas about villages come from? What advantages and disadvantages do you see to looking at the world community as a "global village"?

4. List some of the meanings the word "neighbor" has for you. How do you decide who your neighbors are? What characteristics do you expect to find in your neighbors?

DEAN   BARNLUND

COMMUNICATION
IN A GLOBAL VILLAGE

> Nearing Autumn's close.
> My neighbor—
> How does he live, I wonder?
>
> — BASHŌ

These lines, written by one of the most cherished of *haiku* poets, express a
timeless and universal curiosity in one's fellow man. When they were written, nearly three hundred years ago, the word "neighbor" referred to people very much like one's self—similar in dress, in diet, in custom, in
language—who happened to live next door. Today relatively few people
are surrounded by neighbors who are cultural replicas of themselves.
Tomorrow we can expect to spend most of our lives in the company of
neighbors who will speak in a different tongue, seek different values, move
at a different pace, and interact according to a different script. Within no
longer than a decade or two the probability of spending part of one's life in
a foreign culture will exceed the probability a hundred years ago of ever
leaving the town in which one was born. As our world is transformed our
neighbors increasingly will be people whose life styles contrast sharply
with our own.

From *Public and Private Self in Japan and the United States* (1975).

The technological feasibility of such a global village is no longer in doubt. Only the precise date of its attainment is uncertain. The means already exist: in telecommunication systems linking the world by satellite, in aircraft capable of moving people faster than the speed of sound, in computers which can disgorge facts more rapidly than men can formulate their questions. The methods for bringing people closer physically and electronically are clearly at hand. What is in doubt is whether the erosion of cultural boundaries through technology will bring the realization of a dream or a nightmare. Will a global village be a mere collection or a true community of men? Will its residents be neighbors capable of respecting and utilizing their differences, or clusters of strangers living in ghettos and united only in their antipathies for others?

Can we generate the new cultural attitudes required by our technological virtuosity? History is not very reassuring here. It has taken centuries to learn how to live harmoniously in the family, the tribe, the city state, and the nation. Each new stretching of human sensitivity and loyalty has taken generations to become firmly assimilated in the human psyche. And now we are forced into a quantum leap from the mutual suspicion and hostility that have marked the past relations between peoples into a world in which mutual respect and comprehension are requisite.

Even events of recent decades provide little basis for optimism. Increasing physical proximity has brought no millennium in human relations. If anything, it has appeared to intensify the divisions among people rather than to create a broader intimacy. Every new reduction in physical distance has made us more painfully aware of the psychic distance that divides people and has increased alarm over real or imagined differences. If today people occasionally choke on what seem to be indigestible differences between rich and poor, male and female, specialist and nonspecialist within cultures, what will happen tomorrow when people must assimilate and cope with still greater contrasts in life styles? Wider access to more people will be a doubtful victory if human beings find they have nothing to say to one another or cannot stand to listen to each other.

Time and space have long cushioned intercultural encounters, confining them to touristic exchanges. But this insulation is rapidly wearing thin. In the world of tomorrow we can expect to live — not merely vacation — in societies which seek different values and abide by different codes. There we will be surrounded by foreigners for long periods of time, working with others in the closest possible relationships. If people currently show little tolerance or talent for encounters with alien cultures, how can they learn to deal with constant and inescapable coexistence?

The temptation is to retreat to some pious hope or talismanic formula to carry us into the new age. "Meanwhile," as Edwin Reischauer reminds us, "we fail to do what we ourselves must do if 'one world' is ever to be achieved, and that is to develop the education, the skills and the attitudes that men must have if they are to build and maintain such a world. The time is short, and the needs are great. The task faces all men. But it is on the shoulders of people living in the strong countries of the world, such as Japan and the United States, that this burden falls with special weight and urgency."[1]

Anyone who has truly struggled to comprehend another person—even those closest and most like himself—will appreciate the immensity of the challenge of intercultural communication. A greater exchange of people between nations, needed as that may be, carries with it no guarantee of increased cultural empathy; experience in other lands often does little but aggravate existing prejudices. Studying guidebooks or memorizing polite phrases similarly fails to explain differences in cultural perspectives. Programs of cultural enrichment, while they contribute to curiosity about other ways of life, do not cultivate the skills to function effectively in the cultures studied. Even concentrated exposure to a foreign language, valuable as it is, provides access to only one of the many codes that regulate daily affairs; human understanding is by no means guaranteed because conversants share the same dictionary. (Within the United States, where people inhabit a common territory and possess a common language, mutuality of meaning among Mexican-Americans, White-Americans, Black-Americans, Indian-Americans—to say nothing of old and young, poor and rich, pro-establishment and anti-establishment cultures—is a sporadic and unreliable occurrence.) Useful as all these measures are for enlarging appreciation of diverse cultures, they fall short of what is needed for a global village to survive.

What seems most critical is to find ways of gaining entrance into the assumptive world of another culture, to identify the norms that govern face-to-face relations, and to equip people to function within a social system that is foreign but no longer incomprehensible. Without this kind of insight people are condemned to remain outsiders no matter how long they live in another country. Its institutions and its customs will be interpreted inevitably from the premises and through the medium of their own

1. Reischauer, Edwin. *Man and His Shrinking World.* Tokyo: Asahi Press, 1971, pp. 34–5.

culture. Whether they notice something or overlook it, respect or ridicule it, express or conceal their reaction will be dictated by the logic of their own rather than the alien culture.

There are, of course, shelves and shelves of books on the cultures of the world. They cover the history, religion, political thought, music, sculpture, and industry of many nations. And they make fascinating and provocative reading. But only in the vaguest way do they suggest what it is that really distinguishes the behavior of a Samoan, a Congolese, a Japanese or an American. Rarely do the descriptions of a political structure or religious faith explain precisely when and why certain topics are avoided or why specific gestures carry such radically different meanings according to the context in which they appear.

When former President Nixon and former Premier Sato met to discuss a growing problem concerning trade in textiles between Japan and the United States, Premier Sato announced that since they were on such good terms with each other that the deliberations would be "three parts talk and seven parts 'haragei'."[2] Translated literally, "haragei" means to communicate through the belly, that is to feel out intuitively rather than verbally state the precise position of each person.

Subscribing to this strategy—one that governs many interpersonal exchanges in his culture—Premier Sato conveyed without verbal elaboration his comprehension of the plight of American textile firms threatened by accelerating exports of Japanese fabrics to the United States. President Nixon—similarly abiding by norms that govern interaction within his culture—took this comprehension of the American position to mean that new export quotas would be forthcoming shortly.

During the next few weeks both were shocked at the consequences of their meeting: Nixon was infuriated to learn that the new policies he expected were not forthcoming, and Sato was upset to find that he had unwittingly triggered a new wave of hostility toward his country. If prominent officials, surrounded by foreign advisers, can commit such grievous communicative blunders, the plight of the ordinary citizen may be suggested. Such intercultural collisions, forced upon the public consciousness by the grave consequences they carry and the extensive publicity they receive, only hint at the wider and more frequent confusions and hostilities that disrupt the negotiations of lesser officials, business executives, professionals and even visitors in foreign countries.

2. Kunihiro, Masao, "U.S.-Japan Communications," in Henry Rosovsky (Ed.), *Discord in the Pacific*, Washington, D.C.: Columbia Books, 1972, p. 167.

Every culture expresses its purposes and conducts its affairs through the medium of communication. Cultures exist primarily to create and preserve common systems of symbols by which their members can assign and exchange meanings. Unhappily, the distinctive rules that govern these symbol systems are far from obvious. About some of these codes, such as language, we have extensive knowledge. About others, such as gestures and facial codes, we have only rudimentary knowledge. On many others—rules governing topical appropriateness, customs regulating physical contact, time and space codes, strategies for the management of conflict—we have almost no systematic knowledge. To crash another culture with only the vaguest notion of its underlying dynamics reflects not only a provincial naïvete but a dangerous form of cultural arrogance.

It is differences in meaning, far more than mere differences in vocabulary, that isolate cultures, and that cause them to regard each other as strange or even barbaric. It is not too surprising that many cultures refer to themselves as "The People," relegating all other human beings to a subhuman form of life. To the person who drinks blood, the eating of meat is repulsive. Someone who conveys respect by standing is upset by someone who conveys it by sitting down; both may regard kneeling as absurd. Burying the dead may prompt tears in one society, smiles in another, and dancing in a third. If spitting on the street makes sense to some, it will appear bizarre that others carry their spit in their pocket; neither may quite appreciate someone who spits to express gratitude. The bullfight that constitutes an almost religious ritual for some seems a cruel and inhumane way of destroying a defenseless animal to others. Although staring is acceptable social behavior in some cultures, in others it is a thoughtless invasion of privacy. Privacy, itself, is without universal meaning.

Note that none of these acts involves an insurmountable linguistic challenge. The words that describe these acts—eating, spitting, showing respect, fighting, burying, and staring—are quite translatable into most languages. The issue is more conceptual than linguistic; each society places events in its own cultural frame and it is these frames that bestow the unique meaning and differentiated response they produce.

As we move or are driven toward a global village and increasingly frequent cultural contact, we need more than simply greater factual knowledge of each other. We need, more specifically, to identify what might be called the "rulebooks of meaning" that distinguish one culture from another. For to grasp the way in which other cultures perceive the world, and the assumptions and values that are the foundation of these perceptions, is to gain access to the experience of other human beings.

Access to the world view and the communicative style of other cultures may not only enlarge our own way of experiencing the world but enable us to maintain constructive relationships with societies that operate according to a different logic than our own.

SOURCES OF MEANING

To survive, psychologically as well as physically, human beings must inhabit a world that is relatively free of ambiguity and reasonably predictable. Some sort of structure must be placed upon the endless profusion of incoming signals. The infant, born into a world of flashing, hissing, moving images, soon learns to adapt by resolving this chaos into toys and tables, dogs and parents. Even adults who have had their vision or hearing restored through surgery describe the world as a frightening and sometimes unbearable experience; only after days of effort are they able to transform blurs and noises into meaningful and therefore manageable experiences.

It is commonplace to talk as if the world "has" meaning, to ask what "is" the meaning of a phrase, a gesture, a painting, a contract. Yet when thought about, it is clear that events are devoid of meaning until someone assigns it to them. There is no appropriate response to a bow or a handshake, a shout or a whisper, until it is interpreted. A drop of water and the color red have no meaning, they simply exist. The aim of human perception is to make the world intelligible so that it can be managed successfully; the attribution of meaning is a prerequisite to and preparation for action.[3]

People are never passive receivers, merely absorbing events of obvious significance, but are active in assigning meaning to sensation. What any event acquires in the way of meaning appears to reflect a transaction between what is there to be seen or heard, and what the interpreter brings to it in the way of past experience and prevailing motive. Thus the attribution of meaning is always a creative process by which the raw data of sensation are transformed to fit the aims of the observer.

The diversity of reactions that can be triggered by a single experience—meeting a stranger, negotiating a contract, attending a textile conference—is immense. Each observer is forced to see it through his own eyes, interpret it in the light of his own values, fit it to the requirements

3. For a fuller description of the process of assigning and communicating meaning, see Dean Barnlund, "A Transactional Model of Human Communication," in J. Akin and A. Goldberg (Eds.), *Language Behavior*, The Hague: Mouton, 1970.

of his own circumstances. As a consequence, every object and message is seen by every observer from a somewhat different perspective. Each person will note some features and neglect others. Each will accept some relations among the facts and deny others. Each will arrive at some conclusion, tentative or certain, as the sounds and forms resolve into a "temple" or "barn," a "compliment" or "insult."

Provide a group of people with a set of photographs, even quite simple and ordinary photographs, and note how diverse are the meanings they provoke. Afterward they will recall and forget different pictures; they will also assign quite distinctive meanings to those they do remember. Some will recall the mood of a picture, others the actions; some the appearance and others the attitudes of persons portrayed. Often the observers cannot agree upon even the most "objective" details—the number of people, the precise location and identity of simple objects. A difference in frame of mind—fatigue, hunger, excitement, anger—will change dramatically what they report they have "seen."

It should not be surprising that people raised in different families, exposed to different events, praised and punished for different reasons, should come to view the world so differently. As George Kelly has noted, people see the world through templates which force them to construe events in unique ways. These patterns or grids which we fit over the realities of the world are cut from our own experience and values, and they predispose us to certain interpretations. Industrialist and farmer do not see the "same" land; husband and wife do not plan for the "same" child; doctor and patient do not discuss the "same" disease; borrower and creditor do not negotiate the "same" mortgage; daughter and daughter-in-law do not react to the "same" mother.

The world each person creates for himself is a distinctive world, not the same world others occupy. Each fashions from every incident whatever meanings fit his own private biases. These biases, taken together, constitute what has been called the "assumptive world of the individual." The world each person gets inside his head is the only world he knows. And it is this symbolic world, not the real world, that he talks about, argues about, laughs about, fights about.

INTERPERSONAL ENCOUNTERS

Every communication, interpersonal or intercultural, is a transaction between these private worlds. As people talk they search for symbols that will enable them to share their experience and converge upon a common meaning. This process, often long and sometimes painful, makes it possible finally to reconcile apparent or real differences between them. Various words are used to describe this moment. When it involves an integration of facts or ideas, it is usually called an "agreement"; when it involves sharing a mood or feeling, it is referred to as "empathy" or "rapport." But "understanding" is a broad enough term to cover both possibilities; in either case it identifies the achievement of a common meaning.

• • •

It would be reasonable to expect that individuals who approach reality similarly might understand each other easily, and laboratory research confirms this conclusion: people with similar perceptual styles attract one another, understand each other better, work more efficiently together and with greater satisfaction than those whose perceptual orientations differ. . . . Research done by Donn Byrne and replicated by the author demonstrates how powerfully human beings are drawn to those who hold the same beliefs and how sharply they are repelled by those who do not.[4]

Subjects in these experiments were given questionnaires requesting their opinions on twenty-six topics. After completing the forms, each was asked to rank the thirteen most important and least important topics. Later each person was given four forms, ostensibly filled out by people in another group but actually filled out to show varying degrees of agreement with their own answers, and invited to choose among them with regard to their attractiveness as associates. The results were clear: people most preferred to talk with those whose attitudes duplicated their own exactly, next chose those who agreed with them on all important issues, next chose those with similar views on unimportant issues, and finally and reluctantly chose those who disagreed with them completely. It appears that most people most of the time find satisfying relationships easiest to achieve with someone who shares their own hierarchy of beliefs. This, of course, converts many human encounters into rituals of ratification, each person looking to the other only to obtain endorsement and applause for his own beliefs. It is, however, what is often meant by "interpersonal understanding."

• • •

It must be emphasized that perceptual orientations, systems of belief, and communicative styles do not exist or operate independently. They overlap

---

4. Byrne, Donn, "Interpersonal Attraction and Attitude Similarity," *Journal of Abnormal and Social Psychology*, 62, 1961.

and affect each other. They combine in complex ways to determine behavior. What a person says is influenced by what he believes and what he believes, in turn, by what he sees. His perceptions and beliefs are themselves partly a product of his manner of communicating with others.

• • •

There is an underlying narcissistic bias in human societies that draws similar people together. Each seeks to find in the other a reflection of himself, someone who views the world as he does, who interprets it as he does, and who expresses himself in a similar way. It is not surprising, then, that artists should be drawn to artists, radicals to radicals, Jews to Jews — or Japanese to Japanese and Americans to Americans.

The opposite seems equally true: people tend to avoid those who challenge their assumptions, who dismiss their beliefs, and who communicate in strange and unintelligible ways. When one reviews history, whether he examines crises within or between cultures, he finds people have consistently shielded themselves, segregated themselves, even fortified themselves, against wide differences in modes of perception or expression. (In many cases, indeed, have persecuted and conquered the infidel and afterwards substituted their own cultural ways for the offending ones.) Intercultural defensiveness appears to be only a counterpart of interpersonal defensiveness in the face of uncomprehended or incomprehensible differences.

INTERCULTURAL ENCOUNTERS

Every culture attempts to create a "universe of discourse" for its members, a way in which people can interpret their experience and convey it to one another. Without a common system of codifying sensations, life would be absurd and all efforts to share meanings doomed to failure. This universe of discourse — one of the most precious of all cultural legacies — is transmitted to each generation in part consciously and in part unconsciously. Parents and teachers give explicit instruction in it by praising or criticizing certain ways of dressing, of thinking, of gesturing, of responding to the acts of others. But the most significant aspects of any cultural code may be conveyed implicitly, not by rule or lesson but through modelling behavior. The child is surrounded by others who, through the mere consistency of their actions as males and females, mothers and fathers, salesclerks and policemen, display what is appropriate behavior. Thus the grammar of any culture is sent and received largely unconsciously, making one's own cultural assumptions and biases difficult to recognize. They seem so obviously right that they require no explanation.

In *The Open and Closed Mind,* Milton Rokeach poses the problem of cultural understanding in its simplest form, but one that can readily demonstrate the complications of communication between cultures. It is called the "Denny Doodlebug Problem." Readers are given all the rules that govern his culture: Denny is an animal that always faces North, and can move only by jumping; he can jump large distances or small distances, but can change direction only after jumping four times in any direction; he can jump North, South, East or West, but not diagonally. Upon concluding a jump his master places some food three feet directly West of him. Surveying the situation, Denny concludes he must jump four times to reach the food. No more or less. And he is right. All the reader has to do is to explain the circumstances that make his conclusion correct.[5]

The large majority of people who attempt this problem fail to solve it, despite the fact that they are given all the rules that control behavior in this culture. If there is difficulty in getting inside the simplistic world of Denny Doodlebug—where the cultural code has already been broken and handed to us—imagine the complexity of comprehending behavior in societies whose codes have not yet been deciphered. And where even those who obey these codes are only vaguely aware and can rarely describe the underlying sources of their own actions.

If two people, both of whom spring from a single culture, must often shout to be heard across the void that separates their private worlds, one can begin to appreciate the distance to be overcome when people of different cultural identities attempt to talk. Even with the most patient dedication to seeking a common terminology, it is surprising that people of alien cultures are able to hear each other at all. And the peoples of Japan and the United States would appear to constitute a particularly dramatic test of the ability to cross an intercultural divide. Consider the disparity between them.

Here is Japan, a tiny island nation with a minimum of resources, buffeted by periodic disasters, overcrowded with people, isolated by physical fact and cultural choice, nurtured in Shinto and Buddhist religions, permeated by a deep respect for nature, non-materialist in philosophy, intuitive in thought, hierarchical in social structure. Eschewing the

5. Rokeach, Milton. *The Open and Closed Mind.* New York: Basic Books, 1960. (Denny has just completed his first jump to the East.)

explicit, the monumental, the bold and boisterous, it expresses its sensuality in the form of impeccable gardens, simple rural temples, asymmetrical flower arrangements, a theatre unparalleled for containment of feeling, an art and literature remarkable for their delicacy, and crafts noted for their honest and earthy character. Its people, among the most homogeneous of men, are modest and apologetic in manner, communicate in an ambiguous and evocative language, are engrossed in interpersonal rituals and prefer inner serenity to influencing others. They occupy unpretentious buildings of wood and paper and live in cities laid out as casually as farm villages. Suddenly from these rice paddies emerges an industrial giant, surpassing rival nations with decades of industrial experience, greater resources, and a larger reserve of technicians. Its labor, working longer, harder, and more frantically than any in the world, builds the earth's largest city, constructs some of its ugliest buildings, promotes the most garish and insistent advertising anywhere, and pollutes its air and water beyond the imagination.

And here is the United States, an immense country, sparsely settled, richly endowed, tied through waves of immigrants to the heritage of Europe, yet forced to subdue nature and find fresh solutions to the problems of survival. Steeped in the Judeo-Christian tradition, schooled in European abstract and analytic thought, it is materialist and experimental in outlook, philosophically pragmatic, politically equalitarian, economically competitive, its raw individualism sometimes tempered by a humanitarian concern for others. Its cities are studies in geometry along whose avenues rise shafts of steel and glass subdivided into separate cubicles for separate activities and separate people. Its popular arts are characterized by the hugeness of Cinemascope, the spontaneity of jazz, the earthy loudness of rock; in its fine arts the experimental, striking and monumental often stifle the more subtle revelation. The people, a smorgasbord of races, religions, dialects and nationalities, are turned expressively outward, impatient with rituals and rules, casual and flippant, gifted in logic and argument, approachable and direct yet given to flamboyant and exaggerated assertion. They are curious about one another, open and helpful, yet display a missionary zeal for changing one another. Suddenly this nation whose power and confidence have placed it in a dominant position in the world intellectually and politically, whose style of life has permeated the planet, finds itself uncertain of its direction, doubts its own premises and values, questions its motives and materialism, and engages in an orgy of self criticism.

It is when people nurtured in such different psychological worlds meet that differences in cultural perspectives and communicative codes may sabotage efforts to understand one another. Repeated collisions between a foreigner and the members of a contrasting culture often produce what is called "culture shock." It is a feeling of helplessness, even of terror or anger, that accompanies working in an alien society. One feels trapped in an absurd and indecipherable nightmare.

It is as if some hostile leprechaun had gotten into the works and as a cosmic caper rewired the connections that hold society together. Not only do the actions of others no longer make sense, but it is impossible even to express one's own intentions clearly. "Yes" comes out meaning "No." A wave of the hand means "come," or it may mean "go." Formality may be regarded as childish, or as a devious form of flattery. Statements of fact may be heard as statements of conceit. Arriving early, or arriving late, embarrasses or impresses. "Suggestions" may be treated as "ultimatums," or precisely the opposite. Failure to stand at the proper moment, or failure to sit, may be insulting. The compliment intended to express gratitude instead conveys a sense of distance. A smile signifies disappointment rather than pleasure.

If the crises that follow such intercultural encounters are sufficiently dramatic or the communicants unusually sensitive, they may recognize the source of their trouble. If there is patience and constructive intention the confusion can sometimes be clarified. But more often the foreigner, without knowing it, leaves behind him a trail of frustration, mistrust, and even hatred *of which he is totally unaware*. Neither he nor his associates recognize that their difficulty springs from sources deep within the rhetoric of their own societies. Each sees himself as acting in ways that are thoroughly sensible, honest and considerate. And—given the rules governing his own universe of discourse—each is. Unfortunately, there are few cultural universals, and the degree of overlap in communicative codes is always less than perfect. Experience can be transmitted with fidelity only when the unique properties of each code are recognized and respected, or where the motivation and means exist to bring them into some sort of alignment.

THE COLLECTIVE UNCONSCIOUS

Among the greatest insights of this modern age are two that bear a curious affinity to each other. The first, evolving from the efforts of psychologists, particularly Sigmund Freud, revealed the existence of an "individual unconscious." The acts of human beings were found to spring from motives of which they were often vaguely or completely unaware. Their unique perceptions of events arose not from the facts outside their skins but from unrecognized assumptions inside them. When, through intensive analysis, they obtained some insight into these assumptions, they became free to develop other ways of seeing and acting which contributed to their greater flexibility in coping with reality.

The second of these generative ideas, flowing from the work of anthropologists, particularly Margaret Mead and Ruth Benedict, postulated a parallel idea in the existence of a "cultural unconscious." Students of primitive cultures began to see that there was nothing divine or absolute about cultural norms. Every society had its own way of viewing the universe, and each developed from its premises a coherent set of rules of behavior. Each tended to be blindly committed to its own style of life and regarded all others as evil. The fortunate person who was able to master the art of living in foreign cultures often learned that his own mode of life was only one among many. With this insight he became free to choose from among cultural values those that seemed to best fit his peculiar circumstances.

Cultural norms so completely surround people, so permeate thought and action, that few ever recognize the assumptions on which their lives and their sanity rest. As one observer put it, if birds were suddenly endowed with scientific curiosity they might examine many things, but the sky itself would be overlooked as a suitable subject; if fish were to become curious about the world, it would never occur to them to begin by investigating water. For birds and fish would take the sky and sea for granted, unaware of their profound influence because they comprise the medium for every act. Human beings, in a similar way, occupy a symbolic universe governed by codes that are unconsciously acquired and automatically employed. So much so that they rarely notice that the ways they interpret and talk about events are distinctively different from the ways people conduct their affairs in other cultures.

As long as people remain blind to the sources of their meanings, they are imprisoned within them. These cultural frames of reference are no less confining simply because they cannot be seen or touched. Whether it is an individual neurosis that keeps an individual out of contact with his neighbors, or a collective neurosis that separates neighbors of different cultures, both are forms of blindness that limit what can be experienced and what can be learned from others.

It would seem that everywhere people would desire to break out of the boundaries of their own experiential worlds. Their ability to react sensitively to a wider spectrum of events and peoples requires an overcoming of such cultural parochialism. But, in fact, few attain this broader vision. Some, of course, have little opportunity for wider cultural experience, though this condition should change as the movement of people accelerates. Others do not try to widen their experience because they prefer the old and familiar, seek from their affairs only further confirmation of the correctness of their own values. Still others recoil from such experiences because they feel it dangerous to probe too deeply into the personal or cultural unconscious. Exposure may reveal how tenuous and arbitrary many cultural norms are; such exposure might force people to acquire new bases for interpreting events. And even for the many who do seek actively to enlarge the variety of human beings with whom they are capable of communicating there are still difficulties.

Cultural myopia persists not merely because of inertia and habit, but chiefly because it is so difficult to overcome. One acquires a personality and a culture in childhood, long before he is capable of comprehending either of them. To survive, each persons masters the perceptual orientations, cognitive biases, and communicative habits of his own culture. But once mastered, objective assessment of these same processes is awkward since the same mechanisms that are being evaluated must be used in making the evaluations. Once a child learns Japanese or English or Navaho, the categories and grammar of each language predispose him to perceive and think in certain ways, and discourage him from doing so in other ways. When he attempts to discover why he sees or thinks as he does, he uses the same techniques he is trying to identify. Once one becomes an Indian, an Ibo, or a Frenchman—or even a priest or scientist—it is difficult to extricate oneself from that mooring long enough to find out what one truly is or wants.

Fortunately, there may be a way around this paradox. Or promise of a way around it. It is to expose the culturally distinctive ways various peoples construe events and seek to identify the conventions that connect what is seen with what is thought with what is said. Once this cultural grammar is assimilated and the rules that govern the exchange of meanings are known, they can be shared and learned by those who choose to work and live in alien cultures.

When people within a culture face an insurmountable problem they turn to friends, neighbors, associates, for help. To them they explain their predicament, often in distinctive personal ways. Through talking it out, however, there often emerge new ways of looking at the problem, fresh incentive to attack it, and alternative solutions to it. This sort of interpersonal exploration is often successful within a culture for people share at least the same communicative style even if they do not agree completely in their perceptions or beliefs.

When people communicate between cultures, where communicative rules as well as the substance of experience differs, the problems multiply. But so, too, do the number of interpretations and alternatives. If it is true that the more people differ the harder it is for them to understand each other, it is equally true that the more they differ the more they have to teach and learn from each other. To do so, of course, there must be mutual respect and sufficient curiosity to overcome the frustrations that occur as they flounder from one misunderstanding to another. Yet the task of coming to grips with differences in communicative styles—between or within cultures—is prerequisite to all other types of mutuality.

ACTIVE READING

1. How does Barnlund define "neighbors" in "Sources of Meaning" and one or two other sections of his essay? How do the roles of neighbors change from one section to the next? Revise your response to Before Reading #4 with these questions in mind.

2. Barnlund uses several phrases, like "the assumptive world" (63), that help explain how our attitudes toward life are shaped by culture. Find two or three other phrases from his essay that also help explain how our views are shaped. How do these phrases differ from each other in meaning? Why do you think Barnlund develops new terms throughout his essay?

3. Define for yourself the notions of an individual's "private world" and a culture's "universe of discourse." Use your definitions to examine Barnlund's claim that communication patterns between individuals can teach groups of people how to communicate across cultural differences.

READING IN NEW CONTEXTS

1. Barnlund writes that "It is differences in meaning, far more than mere differences in vocabulary, that isolate cultures" (65). Choose a text by Tan, de Saint Victor, or another writer who seems to address problems in cross-cultural communication. How do distinctions between meaning and vocabulary operate in the second text? What strategies can you develop for overcoming or working around these distinctions in the text you are writing about?

2. Barnlund suggests that "cultures exist primarily to create and preserve common systems of symbols" (65). Evaluate Barnlund's claim by examining a "common system of symbols" in a second reading, perhaps one by Walker or Baldwin. What cultural symbols do you find in the second reading? How do people in the second text preserve, challenge, or revise those symbols?

3. According to Barnlund, "It would seem that everywhere people would desire to break out of the boundaries of their own experiential worlds" (74). What happens when you apply this claim to people in the Mac-Leod or Fishman readings? Use one of these texts to develop your own theory about how people decide if and when to move beyond their own experiential worlds.

DRAFT ONE/DRAFT TWO

1. *Draft One:* Barnlund claims we need to "inhabit a world that is relatively free of ambiguity" (66). Examine how Rich or another writer copes with ambiguous evidence or signals. How do you think this writer feels about life in an ambiguous world?

   Draft Two: List some examples of ambiguity you have experienced yourself. What new questions about ambiguity do your experiences raise for your discussion in Draft One? Revise your analysis from Draft One to account for your own experiences of ambiguity.

2. *Draft One:* How hopeful is Barnlund that the people of the world will find ways to communicate effectively with each other? How hopeful are you? Write informally about one or two recent world events. How

do these events affect your optimism or concern about the prospects of communication in the global village?

Draft Two: Reread your response to Before Reading #3. Then look at a text by Durham or another writer concerned about his or her place in society. How do you think this second author feels about the idea of the "global village"? How might his or her ideas lead you to revise your arguments from Draft One?

BEFORE READING ROBERT BELLAH ET AL.

1. Write about some of the choices you have made between belonging to a group or community and striking out on your own. Tell what was at stake in the choices.

2. To what degree do different groups you are affiliated with each have a special language or way of talking? Give some examples, and explain why these differences in language are trivial or important.

3. Define "private life" and "public life." Do these terms complement or oppose each other? Discuss some examples to show what you mean.

4. Discuss some of the ways a group you are affiliated with uses its history or heritage to guide its actions. Describe one or two specific examples of this process, and evaluate the results.

ROBERT BELLAH ET AL.

COMMUNITY, COMMITMENT, AND INDIVIDUALITY

Les Newman, very much a middle-class American, has found a home in the church, one that allows him to take a critical view of the environing society. He says that "American society is becoming very self-oriented, or very individual-oriented: what's in it for me, how much do I get out of it, am I getting everything I'm entitled to in my life? It is tearing down a lot that is right about the country. People don't look at the repercussions of their individual actions outside of themselves."

For this evangelical Baptist, reared in the South, just graduated from a well-known business school, and now working as an executive in the California suburbs, such sweeping criticism becomes more specific in characterizing his fellow-alumni. Most of them "felt they didn't need God, didn't need religion. There was a strong impression in business school, the self-made individual, being able to do it all yourself if you just work hard enough and think hard enough, and not having to rely on other people." It is precisely because such self-made individuals don't appreciate their need for God that they don't appreciate their need for other people, Les Newman observes. He experiences both needs in the

From *Habits of the Heart* (1985). Bellah's co-authors on this essay are Richard Madsen, William Sullivan, Ann Swidler, and Steven Tipton.

active life of his church congregation. Its members aren't "the standard go-to-church-Sunday-morning people" who practice "a ritual as opposed to a lifestyle." For them religion is more than just saying "Here's a set of morals to live by and here's this great example of 2,000 years ago." The heart of their shared life and teaching "is that Jesus Christ is a person. He's alive today, to relate to today. He works in your life today, and you can talk to Him through the week in prayer." Church for this believer, therefore, "isn't just a place, it's a family" that has given him the closest friends he has. Despite leaving home, moving to California, and entering the competitive world of business, he has found a new family-like anchor for his life, a new bond to other people through the shared celebration of a "personal relationship with Jesus Christ."

In this traditional Christian view, what connects one self to another is the objectively given reality of their creation as God's children and God's own continuing presence in the world in Jesus Christ. This reality is one each person freely accepts, thus establishing the bonds of the Christian congregation while affirming individual identity. Reflecting on this process of self-integration, the Baptist businessman testifies, "I got my personal Christian relationship with Jesus and that has sort of been the ongoing thing that has tied together a whole bunch of different things. That relationship with Christ has changed me somewhat as an individual when it comes to my outlook on the world. He is the person who has steadied my emotion. Before, I was kind of unstable, and I've had some pretty good lows, and now I find that doesn't happen. It has strengthened my commitment in my marriage, and it's had a great deal of impact on the way I relate to other people at work. My life is such a combination of disjointed events. My childhood was just a whole series of moves." Relating oneself to Christ, even in the disjointed course of social uprooting and cultural conflict, yields an experience of the self's integrity.

His church community has helped Les Newman find a language and a set of practices that have strengthened his marriage, aided him in dealing with his work situation, and given him a more coherent sense of self, as well as providing him with some critical distance from the environing society. Ted Oster . . . has no such community and seems much more at ease in the first language of modern individualism, a language he uses to explain most of what goes on around him. Yet when pressed to explain why he remains in a long marriage, his several attempts to do so in cost / benefit terms finally break down. His happiness with his wife comes from "proceeding through all these stages of life together. . . . It makes life meaningful and gives me the opportunity to share with somebody, have an anchor, if you will, and understand where I am. That for me is a real relationship." Here Ted Oster seems to be groping for words that could express his marriage as a community of memory and hope, a place where he is not empty, but which essentially defines who he is. It is as though he had to invent a second language out of the failing fragments of his usual first language.

Although we did not see it in the case of Ted Oster, and only tentatively in the case of Les Newman, communities of memory, though often embedded in family experiences, are an important way in which individuals are led into public life. Angelo Donatello, a successful small businessman who has become a civic leader in a suburb of Boston, tells how a reluctant concern for the ethnic heritage rooted in his family finally led him into public life: "One of the important things that got me into politics was that I was a confused individual. I came from a real old-fashioned Italian family in East Boston. We spoke both languages at home, but I was more Americanized than my brothers or sisters, so to speak. We were forgetting our heritage—that meant becoming more free, more liberal, being able to express myself differently. Thirteen or fourteen years ago, there was a group of people in town who talked about forming a chapter of the Sons of Italy. I would not have been one of the first ones to propose such a thing. My wife was Irish—I was one of the first ones in my family to marry out. But I went to these meetings. Before I had gotten into this I had forgotten my heritage." What catalyzed Angelo's involvement was the unexpected appearance of prejudice when the group tried to buy a piece of land for the Sons of Italy hall. In fighting the opposition, which seemed to focus on the belief that Italians are drunken and rowdy, Angelo became involved with the town government. Remembering his heritage involved accepting his origins, including painful memories of prejudice and discrimination that his earlier efforts at "Americanization" had attempted to deny.

The experience of ethnic prejudice helped Angelo see that there is more to life than leaving behind the past, becoming successful on his own, and expressing himself freely. But as he became more involved with the community he had tried to forget—more active, that is, in the Sons of Italy—he also became more involved with his town. Elected a selectman, he saw it his duty to represent not only Italian-Americans but also the welfare of the town as a whole. Abandoning one kind of individualism, he was led toward a civic individualism that entailed care for the affairs of his community in both the narrower and wider senses. While leaving behind "Americanization," he became American.

Marra James provides an interesting contrast to Angelo Donatello.

Born in a small town in West Virginia, she has lived for some years in a Southern California suburb, where she has become active in a variety of causes focussing around environmental issues such as saving wild land from development. Marra was raised in the Catholic church and was active in her parish when she first came to California. She does not go to church anymore as she has gone beyond what she calls "structural religion." Yet she has carried a sensitivity to ritual over into her new concerns. She dates her involvement in the environmental movement from the celebration of the first Earth Day at a local college, and she was, when interviewed some ten years later, actively planning the local tenth anniversary celebration.

Marra has a strong and explicit understanding of the importance of community: "Many people feel empty and don't know why they feel empty. The reason is we are all social animals and we must live and interact and work together in community to become fulfilled." But she sees serious impediments to the realization of community in America: "Most people have been sold a bill of goods by our system. I call it the Three C's: cash, convenience, consumerism. It's getting worse. The reason you don't feel a part of it is that nobody is a part of it. Loneliness is a national feeling." But Marra has not reacted to this realization with despair. She is intensely active and returns to the fray whether she wins or loses. In her years as city council member and chair of a county planning commission, she has suffered plenty of defeats. "I sometimes describe myself as a rubber ball," she says. "I've been pushed down sometimes to where I've almost been pressed flat, but I've always been able to bounce back." For Marra, politics is a worthwhile educational endeavor, win or lose, perhaps especially when you lose.

Marra James is remarkable in the scope with which she defines her community: "I feel very much a part of the whole—of history. I live in a spectrum that includes the whole world. I'm a part of all of it. For what I do impacts the whole. So if I'm going to be wasteful, misuse resources—that will impact the whole world." Marra identifies herself as a moderate Republican, but her politics go beyond any such label. For her, the "whole world" is a community of memory and hope and entails practices of commitment that she assiduously carries out. Undoubtedly, there has been involvement in many communities along the way, each one important in constituting her as the person she is—her family, the church, the network of her fellow environmental activists. In trying to give substance to what is as yet an aspiration by defining her community as the whole world, she runs the risk of becoming detached from any concrete community of memory.

Finally, let us consider the example of Cecilia Dougherty, in whose life a series of communities of memory have played a part in leading to her present political commitment in ways even clearer than in the case of Marra James. Cecilia lives in a part of Santa Monica whose landscape is shaped by shade trees, schools, and churches. She . . . is an active member of the Campaign for Economic Democracy. At present she works for a local attorney involved in progressive causes, and in addition serves as an elected official of city government. Despite these rather daunting commitments, Cecilia is the single mother of four teenagers, her husband having died several years ago, an event that was for her at once traumatic and transformative.

Cecilia Dougherty began her political activism in her forties following the great break caused in the continuity of her life by her husband's death. She started out by working on the congressional campaign of a local candidate, in part because his opponent supported many things she opposed, but also to try out her capacities to engage in political life on her own. Cecilia had begun to think about taking more public initiative while her husband was living.

The critical event was meeting a colleague of her husband, a woman of their age, who told Cecilia that having heard good things about her from her husband, she was eager to learn more about her. Cecilia says that she began, "I have four children . . ." but the woman persisted, saying, "Wait just a minute. I didn't ask about your children, I asked about you. Where are *you* coming from?" At this Cecilia was stunned. "I mean, my role was a housewife and I didn't quite grasp what she was really talking about." But the woman told her: "I'm not talking about your identity as Greg's wife. I'm concerned with your identity as a human being, as a person, and as an individual, and as a woman." She invited Cecilia to join a consciousness-raising group, "a turning point in my life, a real change for me."

Once into the consciousness-raising group, Cecilia Dougherty experienced herself as waking up as if from a sleep, reaching back to hopes and aspirations she had had as a girl, before becoming a wife and mother. Cecilia rediscovered that she had wanted to become a teacher, and at first thought about going to college to fulfill that dream. She was already working as a clerk for a labor union, however, and she decided to tailor her educational aspirations around that. "I decided that I would work with what I had already." Whatever earlier "gut feelings" Cecilia may have discovered in consciousness raising, her decision to build on the past, on what she "had already," is characteristic of the way she has acted on her new sense of freedom and efficacy.

In fact, for all their importance as catalysts, contact with feminist consciousness raising and discovering her identity "as a person and as an individual" have not been the determining factors in Cecilia Dougherty's activist commitments. Rather, as she describes it, the new sense of efficacy that she learned from consciousness raising in a real sense returned her to earlier commitments and an identification with the cause of the dignity of working people that was deeply rooted in her family's experience. Her sense of purpose in political involvement is not based simply on radical individualism but grounded in the continuity of generations: "I want to see the have-nots have power that reflects their numbers, and I want to protect the future of my children and my grandchildren. I feel a historical family responsibility for continuing to be working for progressive causes."

When Cecilia was asked to explain her commitment to activism, she responded, characteristically, with the story of how her ideals of self developed through the experience of her family. That is, she employed a "second language" that organizes life by reference to certain ideals of character—virtues such as courage and honor—and commitments to institutions that are seen as embodiments of those values. For example, Cecilia's feminism is in part emulation of her mother in a different context. Her mother was an Italian immigrant who married at eighteen and did not go to college, but became the first woman in her county to be elected chair of the state Democratic Central Committee. "So," commented Cecilia, "she made me realize a commitment at a very early age. By eight years old, I was working in party headquarters, licking stamps and answering the phone."

But the paradigmatic event that gave Cecilia a deep sense of identity with the labor movement and its goals of a more just and inclusive society involved her father. When Cecilia was fourteen, her father, an Irish Catholic immigrant working for an energy corporation, went on strike. This was shortly after World War II. Cecilia vividly recalls the weeks of the strike, especially the union solidarity that got the family through it. "We went every night to the town where the union hall was," she recounted, "for dinner in the soup kitchen kind of thing, and my mother would help cook." However, the decisive event occurred six weeks into the strike, when her father was arrested on charges of throwing rocks at strike-breakers.

The shock was that Cecilia's father, "who'd been such a good citizen: so honest, and so conscientious, the American-way type person," should be not only arrested, but attacked in court as a communist and rabble-rouser. The revelation of the low tactics of the corporation's lawyers had a strong impact on her, resulting in a sense of moral outrage that continues to frame her political concerns. She was also deeply impressed by her father's courage and sense of honor under attack by the "company attorneys, with their suits and everything." Most of all, she was impressed by the strength of the solidarity in the labor movement. "I realized then the value of the union and how we were utterly dependent on the union for our very sustenance."

Thus when Cecilia Dougherty returned to politics in the Democratic party, and when she decided to become heavily involved in local activism, she could, and did, draw upon a considerable heritage. She describes her transition from working wife and mother to her present, much more public involvements not so much as a choice—in the sense that one might choose to take up painting versus taking up bowling—but as a response to part of her identity, as fulfilling a responsibility to which her life, her heritage, and her beliefs have called her.

Asked what she sees her activism achieving, Cecilia responded by saying that she hopes to "bring people away from concern only about their own lives, to a sense of much, much broader, greater responsibility. It sounds very grandiose! Probably the most I'm going to be able to do is sustain and build better community in Santa Monica, you know, and that's certainly a life's work." The image of community contained in Cecilia's account of the strike is quite different from the association of like-minded individuals advocated by others we talked to.

The fundamental contrasts between Cecilia Dougherty's self-understanding and the first language of modern individualism can be narrowed to three. First, Cecilia articulates her sense of self by reference to a narrative illustrative of long-term commitments rather than desires and feelings. While she sees certain breaks with her past as crucial "turning points" in her life, she interprets the resulting freedom as an opportunity for new commitments, often "working from what I had already." Thus, unlike the radical individualistic notion of a life course based on leaving home in order to become a free self, Cecilia's self-image is rooted in a concept of the virtues that make an admirable life, especially those exemplified in the lives of her mother and father. This is the second contrast: that her sense of self is rooted in virtues that define a worthwhile life and have been passed on and modeled by others who have shared that tradition, not in a contentless freedom attained by leaving concrete commitments behind.

The third distinguishing feature of Cecilia's "second language" is her notion that community means a solidarity based on a responsibility to care for others because that is essential to living a good life. She describes her solidarity with working people and "the have-nots" as an expression of a concern for human dignity, the violation of which sparked her first anger at the abuse of power. This sense of a community of solidarity recalls the classical civic contrast between the private person who thinks first of himself alone and the citizen who knows himself to be a participant in a form of life through which his own identity is fulfilled. The civic vision is quite different from the image of a gathering of like-minded individuals whose union depends entirely on their spontaneous interest. Indeed, thinking about this contrast tends to confirm Tocqueville's claim that public order and trust cannot spring from individual spontaneity alone, but require the kind of cultivation that only active civic life can provide.

The lived source of the civic language in Cecilia Dougherty's life is not hard to identify: it was her and her parents' lifelong commitments to the labor movement. It was probably reinforced by a similar emphasis on solidarity in the Catholicism she shared with parents and husband. It is this that she has been able to expand into a general concern for "economic democracy."[1]

It is characteristic of Cecilia Dougherty and the others we have just considered that they define themselves through their commitments to a variety of communities rather than through the pursuit of radical autonomy. Yet Cecilia, like the others, exhibits a high degree of self-determination and efficacy. She exemplifies a form of individualism that is fulfilled *in* community rather than against it. Conformism, the nemesis of American individualism, does not seem to be a problem for Cecilia and the others. Their involvement in practices of commitment makes them able to resist pressures to conform. On occasion, they show great resilience in so doing, as when Marra James bounces back after being "pressed flat." Our examples suggest that Tocqueville was probably right in believing that it was isolation, not social involvement, that led to conformism and the larger danger of authoritarian manipulation.

There are authoritarian groups in the United States, sometimes devoted to destructive ends. What makes them different from genuine communities is the shallowness and distortion of their memory and the narrowness of what they hope for. A radically isolating individualism is not a defense against such coercive groups. On the contrary, the loneli-

---

1. Cecilia Dougherty might be surprised to know that the early-twentieth-century Catholic social thinker Monsignor John A. Ryan, author of *Distributive Justice* (New York, 1927), was already using the term "economic democracy."

ness that results from isolation may precipitate the "hunger for authority" on which such groups feed.

Sometimes Americans make a rather sharp dichotomy between private and public life. Viewing one's primary task as "finding oneself" in autonomous self-reliance, separating oneself not only from one's parents but also from those larger communities and traditions that constitute one's past, leads to the notion that it is in oneself, perhaps in relation to a few intimate others, that fulfillment is to be found. Individualism of this sort often implies a negative view of public life. The impersonal forces of the economic and political worlds are what the individual needs protection against. In this perspective, even occupation, which has been so central to the identity of Americans in the past, becomes instrumental—not a good in itself, but only a means to the attainment of a rich and satisfying private life. But on the basis of what we have seen in our observation of middle-class American life, it would seem that this quest for purely private fulfillment is illusory: it often ends in emptiness instead. On the other hand, we found many people . . . for whom private fulfillment and public involvement are not antithetical. These people evince an individualism that is not empty but is full of content drawn from an active identification with communities and traditions. Perhaps the notion that private life and public life are at odds is incorrect. Perhaps they are so deeply involved with each other that the impoverishment of one entails the impoverishment of the other. Parker Palmer is probably right when he says that "in a healthy society the private and the public are not mutually exclusive, not in competition with each other. They are, instead, two halves of a whole, two poles of a paradox. They work together dialectically, helping to create and nurture one another."[2]

Certainly this dialectical relationship is clear where public life degenerates into violence and fear. One cannot live a rich private life in a state of siege, mistrusting all strangers and turning one's home into an armed camp. A minimum of public decency and civility is a precondition for a fulfilling private life. On the other hand, public involvement is often difficult and demanding. To engage successfully in the public world, one needs personal strength and the support of family and friends. A rewarding private life is one of the preconditions for a healthy public life.

For all their doubts about the public sphere, Americans are more engaged in voluntary associations and civic organizations than the citizens

2. Parker J. Palmer, *The Company of Strangers: Christians and the Renewal of America's Public Life* (New York: Crossroad, 1981), p. 31.

of most other industrial nations. In spite of all the difficulties, many Americans feel they must "get involved." In public life as in private, we can discern the habits of the heart that sustain individualism and commitment, as well as what makes them problematic.

ACTIVE READING

1. Bellah notices certain tensions, dichotomies, or even contradictions in the lives of the people he studies. Find several of these and discuss them. What role do these tensions ordinarily play in people's lives?

2. Use details from the lives of several of Bellah's subjects to help describe and define a "community of memory and hope" (81). Are you as satisfied with this kind of community as a social value as Bellah seems to be? Discuss your reactions.

3. Find several passages in this essay where a person manages to "take a critical view of the environing society" (79). Use the passages to address these questions: What makes it possible for an individual to take a critical view? What is the social value of criticism?

4. Compile a list of phrases and sentences from different parts of the essay that show a person "[inventing] a second language out of the failing fragments of his usual first language" (81). How does the process work?

READING IN NEW CONTEXTS

1. Explain what Bellah means by a "frame" (85) and apply that idea to one or more *Literacies* texts that describe acts of resistance or protest, such as Anzaldúa or hooks & West. How is a frame created, and what role does it play in social criticism?

2. Use several of Bellah's terms to evaluate the quality of life in a community you know well. What particular aspects of that community's customs and circumstances does Bellah help you appreciate or challenge?

3. Apply your ideas about the "community of memory and hope" from Active Reading #2 to the community represented in another *Literacies*

text, such as MacLeod or Baldwin. What does Bellah's phrase suggest about that other community?

4. Use Bellah's ideas about creating a second language and your work on Active Reading #4 to analyze the ideas and events in another *Literacies* text, such as Tan, Rosaldo, or Rich. Based on the evidence of these readings, what role does language play in a person's sense of self?

DRAFT ONE/DRAFT TWO

1. *Draft One:* Choose another text that explores the relations between an individual and a wider community, such as Heath, Fishman, or Kingston. Use several of Bellah's main terms or ideas to explore the events of the other text. Which details of the narrative would Bellah find important, and why? What does Bellah help you explain in this other text?

   Draft Two: For Draft Two, consider the concluding paragraphs of Bellah's essay in light of the most troubling aspects of the other text. What events or ideas in the other text most successfully challenge Bellah's argument about the proper relation of public and private life, of individual and community? Extend Bellah's theory to meet these challenges, or replace it with a theory of your own.

2. *Draft One:* Arrange to interview a person from the community you wrote about in Reading in New Contexts #2. Compose interview questions that explore some of Bellah's concepts of community and individuality, as well as your own. After the interview, write a draft that narrates some of that person's important biographical events and decisions in light of Bellah's major concepts.

   Draft Two: Test Bellah's ideas about critical distance against some of your own recent experiences as a reader and writer evaluating personal knowledge. For a new draft, recall the experience of reading and rereading Bellah's essay, and review the writing you have done for Draft One and Reading in New Contexts #2 about a community you know well. Use quotations from Bellah and from your two writings, along with your recent experiences as a reader and writer, to compose an essay in which you explain and evaluate Bellah's ideas about critical distance.

BEFORE READING BRUNO BETTELHEIM

1. How have you learned about the Holocaust? Based on what you have read, seen, or been told, discuss what you think some of the ignored lessons of the Holocaust might be.

2. How do you cope with emotionally difficult situations? Looking back at one or two stressful experiences, discuss the differences between coping strategies that helped you resolve a situation and ones which served some other purpose(s). With the help of hindsight, explain what those other purposes might have been.

3. How do the different kinds of endings (for instance, happy, tragic, unre-solved) of books and movies affect your responses to them? Working with a specific example or two, offer a theory about the relationship between such endings and the ways they encourage their readers or viewers to perceive the world.

BRUNO BETTELHEIM

THE IGNORED LESSON
OF ANNE FRANK

When the world first learned about the Nazi concentration and death camps, most civilized people felt the horrors committed in them to be so uncanny as to be unbelievable. It came as a severe shock that supposedly civilized nations could stoop to such inhuman acts. The implication that modern man has such inadequate control over his cruel and destructive proclivities was felt as a threat to our views of ourselves and our humanity. Three different psychological mechanisms were most frequently used for dealing with the appalling revelation of what had gone on in the camps:

(1) its applicability to man in general was denied by asserting—contrary to evidence—that the acts of torture and mass murder were committed by a small group of insane or perverted persons;

(2) the truth of the reports was denied by declaring them vastly exaggerated and ascribing them to propaganda (this originated with the German government, which called all reports on terror in the camps "horror propaganda"—*Greuelpropaganda*);

(3) the reports were believed, but the knowledge of the horror repressed as soon as possible.

All three mechanisms could be seen at work after liberation of those

From *Surviving and Other Essays* (1952).

prisoners remaining. At first, after the discovery of the camps and their death-dealing, a wave of extreme outrage swept the Allied nations. It was soon followed by a general repression of the discovery in people's minds. Possibly this reaction was due to something more than the blow dealt to modern man's narcissism by the realization that cruelty is still rampant among men. Also present may have been the dim but extremely threatening realization that the modern state now has available the means for changing personality, and for destroying millions it deems undesirable. The ideas that in our day a people's personalities might be changed against their will by the state, and that other populations might be wholly or partially exterminated, are so fearful that one tries to free oneself of them and their impact by defensive denial, or by repression.

The extraordinary world-wide success of the book, play, and movie *The Diary of Anne Frank* suggests the power of the desire to counteract the realization of the personality-destroying and murderous nature of the camps by concentrating all attention on what is experienced as a demonstration that private and intimate life can continue to flourish even under the direct persecution by the most ruthless totalitarian system. And this although Anne Frank's fate demonstrates how efforts at disregarding in private life what goes on around one in society can hasten one's own destruction.

What concerns me here is not what actually happened to the Frank family, how they tried—and failed—to survive their terrible ordeal. It would be very wrong to take apart so humane and moving a story, which aroused so much well-merited compassion for gentle Anne Frank and her tragic fate. What is at issue is the universal and uncritical response to her diary and to the play and movie based on it, and what this reaction tells about our attempts to cope with the feelings her fate—used by us to serve as a symbol of a most human reaction to Nazi terror—arouses in us. I believe that the world-wide acclaim given her story cannot be explained unless we recognize in it our wish to forget the gas chambers, and our effort to do so by glorifying the ability to retreat into an extremely private, gentle, sensitive world, and there to cling as much as possible to what have been one's usual daily attitudes and activities, although surrounded by a maelstrom apt to engulf one at any moment.

The Frank family's attitude that life could be carried on as before may well have been what led to their destruction. By eulogizing how they lived in their hiding place while neglecting to examine first whether it was a reasonable or an effective choice, we are able to ignore the crucial lesson of their story—that such an attitude can be fatal in extreme circumstances.

While the Franks were making their preparations for going passively into hiding, thousands of other Jews in Holland (as elsewhere in Europe) were trying to escape to the free world, in order to survive and / or fight. Others who could not escape went underground—into hiding—each family member with, for example, a different gentile family. We gather from the diary, however, that the chief desire of the Frank family was to continue living as nearly as possible in the same fashion to which they had been accustomed in happier times.

Little Anne, too, wanted only to go on with life as usual, and what else could she have done but fall in with the pattern her parents created for her existence? But hers was not a necessary fate, much less a heroic one; it was a terrible but also a senseless fate. Anne had a good chance to survive, as did many Jewish children in Holland. But she would have had to leave her parents and go to live with a gentile Dutch family, posing as their own child, something her parents would have had to arrange for her.

Everyone who recognized the obvious knew that the hardest way to go underground was to do it as a family; to hide out together made detection by the SS most likely; and when detected, everybody was doomed. By hiding singly, even when one got caught, the others had a chance to survive. The Franks, with their excellent connections among gentile Dutch families, might well have been able to hide out singly, each with a different family. But instead, the main principle of their planning was continuing their beloved family life—an understandable desire, but highly unrealistic in those times. Choosing any other course would have meant not merely giving up living together, but also realizing the full measure of the danger to their lives.

The Franks were unable to accept that going on living as a family as they had done before the Nazi invasion of Holland was no longer a desirable way of life, much as they loved each other; in fact, for them and others like them, it was most dangerous behavior. But even given their wish not to separate, they failed to make appropriate preparations for what was likely to happen.

There is little doubt that the Franks, who were able to provide themselves with so much while arranging for going into hiding, and even while hiding, could have provided themselves with some weapons had they wished. Had they had a gun, Mr. Frank could have shot down at least one or two of the "green police" who came for them. There was no surplus of such police, and the loss of an SS with every Jew arrested would have noticeably hindered the functioning of the police state. Even a butcher knife, which they certainly could have taken with them into hiding, could have been used by them in self-defense. The fate of the Franks wouldn't have been very different, because they all died anyway except for Anne's father. But they could have sold their lives for a high price, instead of walking to their death. Still, although one must assume that Mr. Frank would have fought courageously, as we know he did when a soldier in the first World War, it is not everybody who can plan to kill those who are bent on killing him, although many who would not be ready to contemplate doing so would be willing to kill those who are bent on murdering not only them but also their wives and little daughters.

An entirely different matter would have been planning for escape in case of discovery. The Franks' hiding place had only one entrance; it did not have any other exit. Despite this fact, during their many months of hiding, they did not try to devise one. Nor did they make other plans for escape, such as that one of the family members—as likely as not Mr. Frank—would try to detain the police in the narrow entrance way—maybe even fight them, as suggested above—thus giving other members of the family a chance to escape, either by reaching the roofs of adjacent houses, or down a ladder into the alley behind the house in which they were living.

Any of this would have required recognizing and accepting the desperate straits in which they found themselves, and concentrating on how best to cope with them. This was quite possible to do, even under the terrible conditions in which the Jews found themselves after the Nazi occupation of Holland. It can be seen from many other accounts, for example from the story of Marga Minco, a girl of about Anne Frank's age who lived to tell about it. Her parents had planned that when the police should come for them, the father would try to detain them by arguing and fighting with them, to give the wife and daughter a chance to escape through a rear door. Unfortunately it did not quite work out this way, and both parents got killed. But their short-lived resistance permitted their daughter to make her escape as planned and to reach a Dutch family who saved her.[1]

This is not mentioned as a criticism that the Frank family did not plan or behave along similar lines. A family has every right to arrange their life as they wish or think best, and to take the risks they want to take. My point is not to criticize what the Franks did, but only the universal admiration of their way of coping, or rather of not coping. The story of little Marga who survived, every bit as touching, remains totally neglected by comparison.

1. Marga Minco, *Bitter Herbs* (New York: Oxford University Press), 1960.

Many Jews—unlike the Franks, who through listening to British radio news were better informed than most—had no detailed knowledge of the extermination camps. Thus it was easier for them to make themselves believe that complete compliance with even the most outrageously debilitating and degrading Nazi orders might offer a chance for survival. But neither tremendous anxiety that inhibits clear thinking and with it well-planned and determined action, nor ignorance about what happened to those who responded with passive waiting for being rounded up for their extermination, can explain the reaction of audiences to the play and movie retelling Anne's story, which are all about such waiting that results finally in destruction.

I think it is the fictitious ending that explains the enormous success of this play and movie. At the conclusion we hear Anne's voice from the beyond, saying, "In spite of everything, I still believe that people are really good at heart." This improbable sentiment is supposedly from a girl who had been starved to death, had watched her sister meet the same fate before she did, knew that her mother had been murdered, and had watched untold thousands of adults and children being killed. This statement is not justified by anything Anne actually told her diary.

Going on with intimate family living, no matter how dangerous it might be to survival, was fatal to all too many during the Nazi regime. And if all men are good, then indeed we can all go on with living our lives as we have been accustomed to in times of undisturbed safety and can afford to forget about Auschwitz. But Anne, her sister, her mother, may well have died because her parents could not get themselves to believe in Auschwitz.

While play and movie are ostensibly about Nazi persecution and destruction, in actuality what we watch is the way that, despite this terror, lovable people manage to continue living their satisfying intimate lives with each other. The heroine grows from a child into a young adult as normally as any other girl would, despite the most abnormal conditions of all other aspects of her existence, and that of her family. Thus the play reassures us that despite the destructiveness of Nazi racism and tyranny in general, it is possible to disregard it in one's private life much of the time, even if one is Jewish.

True, the ending happens just as the Franks and their friends had feared all along: their hiding place is discovered, and they are carried away to their doom. But the fictitious declaration of faith in the goodness of all men which concludes the play falsely reassures us since it impresses on us that in the combat between Nazi terror and continuance of intimate family living the latter wins out, since Anne has the last word. This is simply contrary to fact, because it was she who got killed. Her seeming survival through her moving statement about the goodness of men releases us effectively of the need to cope with the problems Auschwitz presents. That is why we are so relieved by her statement. It explains why millions loved play and movie, because while it confronts us with the fact that Auschwitz existed it encourages us at the same time to ignore any of its implications. If all men are good at heart, there never really was an Auschwitz; nor is there any possibility that it may recur.

The desire of Anne Frank's parents not to interrupt their intimate family living, and their inability to plan more effectively for their survival, reflect the failure of all too many others faced with the threat of Nazi terror. It is a failure that deserves close examination because of the inherent warnings it contains for us, the living.

Submission to the threatening power of the Nazi state often led both to the disintegration of what had once seemed well-integrated personalities and to a return to an immature disregard for the dangers of reality. Those Jews who submitted passively to Nazi persecution came to depend on primitive and infantile thought processes: wishful thinking and disregard for the possibility of death. Many persuaded themselves that they, out of all the others, would be spared. Many more simply disbelieved in the possibility of their own death. Not believing in it, they did not take what seemed to them desperate precautions, such as giving up everything to hide out singly; or trying to escape even if it meant risking their lives in doing so; or preparing to fight for their lives when no escape was possible and death had become an immediate possibility. It is true that defending their lives in active combat before they were rounded up to be transported into the camps might have hastened their deaths, and so, up to a point, they were protecting themselves by "rolling with the punches" of the enemy.

But the longer one rolls with the punches dealt not by the normal vagaries of life, but by one's eventual executioner, the more likely it becomes that one will no longer have the strength to resist when death becomes imminent. This is particularly true if yielding to the enemy is accompanied not by a commensurate strengthening of the personality, but by an inner disintegration. We can observe such a process among the Franks, who bickered with each other over trifles, instead of supporting each other's ability to resist the demoralizing impact of their living conditions.

Those who faced up to the announced intentions of the Nazis prepared for the worst as a real and imminent possibility. It meant risking one's life for a self-chosen purpose, but in doing so, creating at least a small chance for saving one's own life or those of others, or both. When Jews in Germany were restricted to their homes, those who did not succumb to inertia took the new restrictions as a warning that it was high time to go underground, join the resistance movement, provide themselves with forged papers, and so on, if they had not done so long ago. Many of them survived.

Some distant relatives of mine may furnish an example. Early in the war, a young man living in a small Hungarian town banded together with a number of other Jews to prepare against a German invasion. As soon as the Nazis imposed curfews on the Jews, his group left for Budapest—because the bigger capital city with its greater anonymity offered chances for escaping detection. Similar groups from other towns converged in Budapest and joined forces. From among themselves they selected typically "Aryan" looking men who equipped themselves with false papers and immediately joined the Hungarian SS. These spies were then able to warn of impending persecution and raids.

Many of these groups survived intact. Furthermore, they had also equipped themselves with small arms, so that if they were detected, they could put up enough of a fight for the majority to escape while a few would die fighting to make the escape possible. A few of the Jews who had joined the SS were discovered and immediately shot, probably a death preferable to one in the gas chambers. But most of even these Jews survived, hiding within the SS until liberation.

Compare these arrangements not just to the Franks' selection of a hiding place that was basically a trap without an outlet but with Mr. Frank's teaching typically academic high-school subjects to his children rather than how to make a getaway: a token of his inability to face the seriousness of the threat of death. Teaching high-school subjects had, of course, its constructive aspects. It relieved the ever-present anxiety about their fate to some degree by concentrating on different matters, and by implication it encouraged hope for a future in which such knowledge would be useful. In this sense such teaching was purposeful, but it was erroneous in that it took the place of much more pertinent teaching and planning: how best to try to escape when detected.

Unfortunately the Franks were by no means the only ones who, out of anxiety, became unable to contemplate their true situation and with it to plan accordingly. Anxiety, and the wish to counteract it by clinging to each other, and to reduce its sting by continuing as much as possible with their usual way of life incapacitated many, particularly when survival plans required changing radically old ways of living that they cherished, and which had become their only source of satisfaction.

My young relative, for example, was unable to persuade other members of his family to go with him when he left the small town where he had lived with them. Three times, at tremendous risk to himself, he returned to plead with his relatives, pointing out first the growing persecution of the Jews, and later the fact that transport to the gas chambers had already begun. He could not convince these Jews to leave their homes and break up their families to go singly into hiding.

As their desperation mounted, they clung more determinedly to their old living arrangements and to each other, became less able to consider giving up the possessions they had accumulated through hard work over a lifetime. The more severely their freedom to act was reduced, and what little they were still permitted to do restricted by insensible and degrading regulations imposed by the Nazis, the more did they become unable to contemplate independent action. Their life energies drained out of them, sapped by their ever-greater anxiety. The less they found strength in themselves, the more they held on to the little that was left of what had given them security in the past—their old surroundings, their customary way of life, their possessions—all these seemed to give their lives some permanency, offer some symbols of security. Only what had once been symbols of security now endangered life, since they were excuses for avoiding change. On each successive visit the young man found his relatives more incapacitated, less willing or able to take his advice, more frozen into inactivity, and with it further along the way to the crematoria where, in fact, they all died.

Levin renders a detailed account of the desperate but fruitless efforts made by small Jewish groups determined to survive to try to save the rest. She tells how messengers were "sent into the provinces to warn Jews that deportation meant death, but their warnings were ignored because most Jews refused to contemplate their own annihilation."[2] I believe the reason for such refusal has to be found in their inability to take action. If we are certain that we are helpless to protect ourselves against the danger of destruction, we cannot contemplate it. We can consider the danger only as long as we believe there are ways to protect ourselves, to fight back, to escape. If we are convinced none of this is possible for us, then there is

2. Nora Levin, *The Holocaust* (New York: Thomas Y. Crowell, 1968).

no point in thinking about the danger; on the contrary, it is best to refuse to do so.

As a prisoner in Buchenwald, I talked to hundreds of German Jewish prisoners who were brought there as part of the huge pogrom in the wake of the murder of vom Rath in the fall of 1938. I asked them why they had not left Germany, given the utterly degrading conditions they had been subjected to. Their answer was: How could we leave? It would have meant giving up our homes, our work, our sources of income. Having been deprived by Nazi persecution and degradation of much of their self-respect, they had become unable to give up what still gave them a semblance of it: their earthly belongings. But instead of using possessions, they became captivated by them, and this possession by earthly goods became the fatal mask for their possession by anxiety, fear, and denial.

How the investment of personal property with one's life energy could make people die bit by bit was illustrated throughout the Nazi persecution of the Jews. At the time of the first boycott of Jewish stores, the chief external goal of the Nazis was to acquire the possessions of the Jews. They even let Jews take some things out of the country at that time if they would leave the bulk of their property behind. For a long time the intention of the Nazis, and the goal of their first discriminatory laws, was to force undesirable minorities, including Jews, into emigration.

Although the extermination policy was in line with the inner logic of Nazi racial ideology, one may wonder whether the idea that millions of Jews (and other foreign nationals) could be submitted to extermination did not partially result from seeing the degree of degradation Jews accepted without fighting back. When no violent resistance occurred, persecution of the Jews worsened, slow step by slow step.

Many Jews who on the invasion of Poland were able to survey their situation and draw the right conclusions survived the Second World War. As the Germans approached, they left everything behind and fled to Russia, much as they distrusted and disliked the Soviet system. But there, while badly treated, they could at least survive. Those who stayed on in Poland believing they could go on with life-as-before sealed their fate. Thus in the deepest sense the walk to the gas chamber was only the last consequence of these Jews' inability to comprehend what was in store; it was the final step of surrender to the death instinct, which might also be called the principle of inertia. The first step was taken long before arrival at the death camp.

We can find a dramatic demonstration of how far the surrender to inertia can be carried, and the wish not to know because knowing would create unbearable anxiety, in an experience of Olga Lengyel.[3] She reports that although she and her fellow prisoners lived just a few hundred yards from the crematoria and the gas chambers and knew what they were for, most prisoners denied knowledge of them for months. If they had grasped their true situation, it might have helped them save either the lives they themselves were fated to lose, or the lives of others.

When Mrs. Lengyel's fellow prisoners were selected to be sent to the gas chambers, they did not try to break away from the group, as she successfully did. Worse, the first time she tried to escape the gas chambers, some of the other selected prisoners told the supervisors that she was trying to get away. Mrs. Lengyel desperately asks the question: How was it possible that people denied the existence of the gas chambers when all day long they saw the crematoria burning and smelled the odor of burning flesh? Why did they prefer ignoring the exterminations to fighting for their very own lives? She can offer no explanation, only the observation that they resented anyone who tried to save himself from the common fate, because they lacked enough courage to risk action themselves. I believe they did it because they had given up their will to live and permitted their death tendencies to engulf them. As a result, such prisoners were in the thrall of the murdering SS not only physically but also psychologically, while this was not true for those prisoners who still had a grip on life.

Some prisoners even began to serve their executioners, to help speed the death of their own kind. Then things had progressed beyond simple inertia to the death instinct running rampant. Those who tried to serve their executioners in what were once their civilian capacities were merely continuing life as usual and thereby opening the door to their death.

For example, Mrs. Lengyel speaks of Dr. Mengele, SS physician at Auschwitz, as a typical example of the "business as usual" attitude that enabled some prisoners, and certainly the SS, to retain whatever balance they could despite what they were doing. She describes how Dr. Mengele took all correct medical precautions during childbirth, rigorously observing all aseptic principles, cutting the umbilical cord with greatest care, etc. But only half an hour later he sent mother and infant to be burned in the crematorium.

Having made his choice, Dr. Mengele and others like him had to delude themselves to be able to live with themselves and their experience.

3. Olga Lengyel, *Five Chimneys: The Story of Auschwitz* (Chicago: Ziff-Davis, 1947).

Only one personal document on the subject has come to my attention, that of Dr. Nyiszli, a prisoner serving as "research physician" at Auschwitz.[4] How Dr. Nyiszli deluded himself can be seen, for example, in the way he repeatedly refers to himself as working in Auschwitz as a physician, although he worked as the assistant of a criminal murderer. He speaks of the Institute for Race, Biological and Anthropological Investigation as "one of the most qualified medical centers of the Third Reich," although it was devoted to proving falsehoods. That Nyiszli was a doctor didn't alter the fact that he—like any of the prisoner foremen who served the SS better than some SS were willing to serve it—was a participant in the crimes of the SS. How could he do it and live with himself?

The answer is: by taking pride in his professional skills, irrespective of the purpose they served. Dr. Nyiszli and Dr. Mengele were only two among hundreds of other—and far more prominent—physicians who participated in the Nazis' murderous pseudo-scientific human experiments. It was the peculiar pride of these men in their professional skill and knowledge, without regard for moral implications, that made them so dangerous. Although the concentration camps and crematoria are no longer here, this kind of pride still remains with us; it is characteristic of a modern society in which fascination with technical competence has dulled concern for human feelings. Auschwitz is gone, but so long as this attitude persists, we shall not be safe from cruel indifference to life at the core.

I have met many Jews as well as gentile anti-Nazis, similar to the activist group in Hungary described earlier, who survived in Nazi Germany and in the occupied countries. These people realized that when a world goes to pieces and inhumanity reigns supreme, man cannot go on living his private life as he was wont to do, and would like to do; he cannot, as the loving head of a family, keep the family living together peacefully, undisturbed by the surrounding world; nor can he continue to take pride in his profession or possessions, when either will deprive him of his humanity, if not also of his life. In such times, one must radically reevaluate all of what one has done, believed in, and stood for in order to know how to act. In short, one has to take a stand on the new reality—a firm stand, not one of retirement into an even more private world.

If today, Negroes in Africa march against the guns of a police that

4. Miklos Nyiszli, *Auschwitz: A Doctor's Eyewitness Account* (New York: Frederick Fell, 1960).

defends *apartheid*—even if hundreds of dissenters are shot down and tens of thousands rounded up in camps—their fight will sooner or later assure them of a chance for liberty and equality. Millions of the Jews of Europe who did not or could not escape in time or go underground as many thousands did, could at least have died fighting as some did in the Warsaw ghetto at the end, instead of passively waiting to be rounded up for their own extermination.

ACTIVE READING

1. Bettelheim stresses that his purpose in writing is not to criticize the Frank family's actions. Collect and comment on passages that show what Bettelheim *is* trying to do in his essay, if he is not criticizing the Franks.

2. What does "survival" mean at different points in Bettelheim's argument? Consider how this concept changes when he applies it to individuals, families, and communities. How does Bettelheim relate certain kinds of survival to other kinds?

3. What kinds of knowledge have you developed out of your own experiences of psychological strain? (Your response to Before Reading #2 may help here.) Explain how your knowledge could complicate Bettelheim's arguments about the Franks. As you do this, keep in mind how the differences between your experiences and the Franks' might shape your interpretation of their story.

READING IN NEW CONTEXTS

1. Bettelheim outlines some "psychological mechanisms" he believes people use when faced with information that threatens "our views of ourselves and our humanity" (91). How might your knowledge of these mechanisms help you interpret another text (for instance, Baldwin, Garson, or Rich) in which someone tries to cope with threatening information? What does the second text tell you about these psychological mechanisms that Bettelheim himself does not say?

2. Writing analytically—even critically—about events like the Holocaust can feel extremely risky, perhaps even sacrilegious. Show how you see Bettelheim dealing with the tension between his desire to make what he thinks is an important argument, on the one hand, and his desire to respect his subject matter, on the other. How does his approach to a socially risky subject compare to Durham's or el-Saadawi's?

3. Bettelheim, Barnlund, and Weeks all write in different ways about social "uncertainty." Look for moments in Bettelheim's essay where he uses observations about individuals in order to make arguments about people in general. Then discuss some moments in Barnlund's or Weeks's essays where the writer makes general observations in order to guide individuals' actions. From your perspective, what are some specific advantages and disadvantages of each writer's approach?

DRAFT ONE / DRAFT TWO

1. *Draft One:* Bettelheim suggests that attachment to possessions or professional identity can shield people from crucially important truths. Use Bettelheim's theories to help you explore the effects of such attachments on a community you belong to.

   Draft Two: How do the ideas of hooks & West, Brody, or Bellah modify your own understanding of the relationship between community life and materialism (or professionalism)? With the help of one of these essays, revise the analysis of your own community that you started in Draft One.

2. *Draft One:* According to Bettelheim, the Holocaust teaches us that the state has the power to change people's personalities. Working closely with Bettelheim's text, begin by listing some of the other powers the state has. Then discuss what Bettelheim believes are powers belonging to the individual. What relationship do you see between the powers of the state and the powers of the individual?

   Draft Two: Use the theories of individual power offered by Brody or Lorde to revise and extend your first draft. What do these writers help you to say about the relationship between emotion and individual power, either in Bettelheim's text or in your own life?

BEFORE READING FRANK BLACK ELK

1. What ideas do you have about Native American religions or spiritual traditions? Where do your ideas come from? Discuss how these ideas relate to what you know of other religious belief systems.

2. Define what "progress" means to you. What signs of progress have you encountered or heard about in your community or workplace? How has progress made your life easier or more difficult?

3. Whom would you expect to be an expert on Marxism? on Native American culture? Consider the kinds of experience or training you feel would make someone an expert on these topics. What would you expect these experts to think about their areas of expertise? Why?

4. Look up "dogma" in a good dictionary. Under what circumstances, or about what issues, do you feel dogmatic beliefs might be appropriate or inappropriate? What leads you to think that such beliefs are appropriate or inappropriate?

FRANK   BLACK   ELK

OBSERVATIONS
ON MARXISM AND
LAKOTA TRADITION

I

I have been asked to make some observations concerning the relationship between Marxism and the spiritual traditions of the Native Peoples of this hemisphere. First, allow me to say that I am no Marxist scholar. I suppose my understanding of the subject is the result of what has been popularly projected to me, often enough by people calling themselves Marxists or Marxist-Leninists. I assume that what they've passed along to me is an accurate enough summary of the main points of their tradition. Second, allow me to say that no individual can hope to accurately address the range of spiritual tradition indigenous to the Americas. There are a great number of cultures among Native People, each with its own infinitely complex spirituality. To do justice to the subject, representatives of each tradition would be necessary.

Of course, this is impossible in the context of a book such as that which has been proposed to me. Coverage of just the question of spirituality would require volumes, if done in full, and then the balance of the subjects to be covered would remain, requiring additional volumes. Obviously, few people would possess the time and energy to read such a lengthy work and so it is impractical.

From *Marxism and Native Americans,* edited by Ward Churchill (1983).

Of necessity, then, I will restrict the bulk of my observations to the traditions of my own people, the Lakota people. I am not a spiritual leader or an "expert," even in this. Spiritual leadership is the role of the tribal elders, for the most part, and I am young. I have, nonetheless, been fortunate enough to have benefited from the wisdom and knowledge of my uncle, Wallace Black Elk, my aunt, Grace Black Elk, and various other elders. I know enough to speak in generalities, which is what is needed here.

Finally, my limited focus upon the Lakota traditions is not as potentially misleading as it may appear at first glance. I believe that, despite their great differences in some very important ways, most spiritual traditions of the Americas share certain central values and understandings. This is, in a way, the same as that the various factions of the Christian Church hold certain core features in common, despite other dissimilarities. This is not to say that I believe that all native spirituality sprang from a single source as the Christian religion is reputed to have, nor even that I believe Christianity is the product of a given source.

Along with Vine Deloria, Jr., in his book *God Is Red*, I feel that spiritual traditions were probably born of and continued by such things as the geography from which they sprang; they are *truly* indigenous to certain areas and are the only forms of spirituality appropriate to those areas. In any event, an understanding of the Lakota tradition in its possible relationship to the Marxist tradition should prove helpful to those seeking to understand similar relationships between Marxism and other natural spiritual traditions.

II

My first impressions of Marxism came through hearing statements such as "religion is the opiate of the people." Since Europeans often have considered Native spirituality as being "religion," such statements were confusing to me. I asked several people for an explanation of this and, in each case, I received essentially the same answer. Yes, by religion, spirituality was being referred to; spirituality or religion is one of the ways the "ruling class" subverts the revolutionary energies of the people. By promising a glorious "afterlife" or "heaven" to those who stay in line during their lives on earth, and by threatening a horrible and eternal afterlife called "hell" to those who do not stay in line, the ruling class is able to maintain its position of social power by frightening the people away from revolting and taking power for themselves. The church is obviously associated with the ruling class and helps to define what staying in line means.

This description of religion obviously served to describe the Christian Church, an institution which has nothing at all to do with the traditional spirituality of the Lakota people. I pointed this out to each of the individuals who were explaining the various negative social effects of religion to me, in hopes that this would cause them to consider that my people's "religion" was not addressed by their analysis. But it did not. In each case, it was asserted (with various twists, according to the speaker) that, while religious forms tend to vary from culture to culture, or even within a given culture, the net social result of all religions is essentially the same: the people are "drugged" by religious "superstition" to the point of not reaching their full potential as human beings.

But, I asked, have you really examined all the spiritual traditions of all the different cultures on earth in order to reach this conclusion? Well, no, was the general reply, that would be much too lengthy and complicated an understanding. Besides, there's really no need, it has been dialectically determined that this is the social result of religion. Instead of wasting large amounts of time and energy analyzing what it already understands to be a socially negative condition, Marxism wisely devotes its resources to the understanding of a positive social vision which can overcome religion and ruling classes in general.

Usually, I tried one last time. But traditional Lakota spirituality could not serve the social purposes you describe, I insisted, again and again. The Lakota have never had a ruling class; leaders serve by consensus of the people. The Lakota have never been concerned with heaven and hell. The Lakota have never even had need for a church, at least not in the sense that Christianity has a church. Wouldn't it be wise for Marxists to take a look at traditional Lakota spirituality, in its own right, and see if it weren't something other than the religious "opiate" condemned by Marxism.

But my informants would have none of this. They were sorry, of course, perhaps even a bit embarrassed, to have to explain to me that what I was saying, while perhaps true as far as it went, didn't really matter. The problem, as they saw it, was that religion possessed socially useful attributes at certain, rather primitive levels of social organization. History shows that, as societies develop, religion assumes less and less useful social characteristics, becomes more and more socially repressive as a means to continue its existence (once the real need for it has passed) until finally it assumes a role as one of the most reactionary social forces. So, even if Lakota spirituality seems to retain certain superficially appealing characteristics now, as Lakota culture goes through its inevitable evolution "into the twentieth century," this same spirituality will just become like a dead weight around the neck of the people, a weight always attempting to pull them down into the mire of primitive superstition.

Finally, one individual (gently) explained to me that, while he was thrilled to see me standing up for the sovereignty and self-determination of my people—as a Third Worlder—I had to be constantly alert to the dangers of "glamorizing" my heritage and traditions. After all, he cautioned, it is absolutely essential to a "correct" understanding of the situation that one bear in mind that traditional Lakota and other indigenous spiritual forms of this hemisphere are aspects of *stone age culture*, and, of course, no sane human being would consciously advocate a return to life in the stone age. One must be realistic, one must carefully separate "advanced" ideas from "backward" ideas; a "new age" is dawning. What was done to the Indians was genocide, was horrible, but it's past; the duty of all Indians now is to leave the past behind and move on into the future, a new social order is emerging and Indians should take an equal place in that order.

That tore it. The guy sounded just like the headmaster at the old boarding school I was sent to after being kidnapped from my parents by the Bureau of Indian Affairs. Although you can be assured my old headmaster was hardly trying to convert me to a belief in Marxism, both he and the Marxist were equally sure that they possessed the "keys" to solving the problems of Native People. They were also, despite their prepackaged "solutions," equally and completely ignorant of the people they figured to "help." And they were equally disinterested in doing anything at all to overcome that little matter of abject ignorance.

"Listen, my friend," I said, "the *only* social order I have the least bit of interest in joining is an independent Lakota Nation, the same independent Lakota Nation *you* folks guaranteed us you wouldn't mess around with before *you* started coming up with better ideas of how *we* should live our lives."

"Frank," he replied (laughing, of course), "you're a hopeless romantic."

"Romantic," I retorted (getting really hot at his too smug amusement), "refers to Rome. I, in case it hasn't dawned on you, am an Oglala Lakota. You will kindly keep your racist bullshit in your mouth."

"Let's cut this Indian crap . . ."

But, I was already walking away rapidly. He was lucky I didn't put serious pressure on his jaw with my fist. Maybe if, as always, he hadn't been forty pounds and four inches bigger than me, I would have. And so it goes. . . .

Anyway, at that point, Marxism and I experienced a decided parting of the ways. Officially. Unofficially I remained intrigued by the "liberation" rhetoric of Marxism and the obvious willingness of at least some Marxists to put their all on the line in efforts to resist oppression and to overturn the status quo. Anyone possessing any familiarity at all with the contemporary colonial conditions imposed on Native Peoples throughout the Americas by the status quo, should be able to readily understand the appeal for me that comes with the idea of overturning it. I kept my eyes open, but I was (and remain) wary.

III

I can't say that I've exactly been obsessed with thinking about Marxism since I first investigated it. But, as I said, certain aspects of it retained a sort of natural appeal. So, I considered the problems which had turned up in my discussions with Marxists, at least from time to time. Basically, I came up with what I think are a couple of major points.

First, it seems Marxists are hung up on exactly the same ideas of "progress" and "development" that are the guiding motives of those they seek to overthrow. They have this idea that Lakotas are (or, at least, were) a primitive people in relation to Europe. Any rational person would have to ask what's so "primitive" about a people which managed to maintain a perpetually democratic way of life, which shared all social power equitably between both sexes and various age groups, which considered war essentially a sport rather than an excuse to indulge in the wanton slaughter of masses of people, which killed game only for food rather than as a "sport," which managed to occupy its environment for thousands and thousands of years without substantially altering it (that is to say, destroying it). That same rational person would have to ask why any sane individual would not choose to live that way if the chance were available, or aspire towards such an existence if the chance wasn't immediate.

That same rational person would then have to ask what's so "advanced" about a culture which generates authoritarianism and dictatorship as a social norm, which deprives its women, its ethnic minorities, its elders and its youth of any true social power, which engages in the most lethal warfare on a regular basis and has left perhaps a half billion mangled bodies in its wake during this century alone, which is eliminating entire species of plant and animal life forever and without real concern, and which has utterly devastated the environment of this continent in approximately two centuries. Finally, that same rational person would have to ask what sort of lunatic would *choose* to switch from the first way of life to the second.

The answer, of course, is probably even a lunatic wouldn't choose anything that crazy. The real question is why people trapped in the second way of life don't *really* start seeking ways to get over into the first one. The answer is, perhaps, simply that they don't know how. And, they're so used to pretending to have all the answers (that attitude seems to be inbred within the second way of life) that they're afraid to admit they no longer know how. So they—Christians, Capitalists, Communists, Fascists, the whole range of "ists" and "isms" making up Euro culture—demand that we Native People all become a part of their insanity and fear.

Our way of life was and is possible only because of the values and attitudes instilled in us by our spirituality, our spiritual traditions. The difference between Native spirituality here and the Christian form which dominates Europe can be measured in the difference between the two ways of life.

But things are not quite this simple. The European put down of Native peoples is more complex. They call us primitive, but as we've seen, there's no obvious rational reason for this. And Europeans pride themselves on their rationality. So there must be a less obvious reason. This seems to be that Europeans have decided, generally speaking, that our primitiveness lies in the fact that we (like most of the world) are "underdeveloped." Now, it's not immediately clear what is meant by this either. Clearly, Europeans generally don't know enough about the subtleties—or even the crudities—of our cultures to have any idea as to the state of our "development" in those terms. So the answer must lie in some superficial area which is immediately visible, even to a total outsider.

This leads me back to the "comrade's" observation that my people, the Lakota people, were a *stone age* culture before the whites came here. But how is that? Is there something stoney about our governmental forms or our medicine or our emotions, art, or food? What is this stone age by which Euros define our culture? Well, it seems that our weapons and tools were made of stone, a material utilized in its more or less natural state. Thus we are a primitive people. No more questions to ask about us in that. Thus too, are we underdeveloped. No further questions there either.

It can even be quantified. Let's see now, the stone age occurred in *Europe* about 10,000 years or so before Euros went sailing off to "discover" stone using peoples on the other side of the Atlantic. It follows, through some preoccupation or dementia, that the people stumbled upon by a group of thoroughly lost Italian and Spanish sailors must have been 10,000 years behind Europe; after all, they didn't even possess muskets and steel swords with which to civilize savages. Gee, what retards.

Now, none of these "enlightened" Europeans ever got around to asking the savages whether there might, in fact, be a *reason* why the Natives fancied using stone tools and such. After all, no one could rightly expect an underdeveloped, primitive savage to *reason* about much of anything. Such an assessment, on purely material terms, was clearly borne out by the Aztec, Inca and Mayan (among other) cities "discovered" almost immediately by the conquistadores. And so, it has become a tradition in Europe to view virtually everyone else as underdeveloped, backward and retarded. Which isn't to say that Euros ever had much reason for such odd behavior, just that they were and are rather greedy folks on the whole, and possessed of the weapons (pure and simple) to enforce their peculiar standard of measure on anyone who happened to be nearby.

It's the peculiarity of the standard of measure here which strikes me as being most important. It's all a matter of the "will" and ability to accumulate material; the standard also indicates a need to constantly arrange and rearrange material. The standard of measure seems to me to be that the more compulsive a culture can become in terms of gathering up and rearranging material, the more "advanced" it is considered to be. The more relaxed, at peace, and willing to leave material things (beyond real needs) alone a culture can be shown to be, the more "backward" it is considered. Now, such "logic" is rather odd, to say the least.

A hundred years ago a great Lakota spiritual leader, *Tatonka Yatonka*, the Sitting Bull, observed of whites that, "the love of possessions is a disease with them." My hunch is that, as usual, the savage hit the nail squarely on the head. Of course, Sitting Bull didn't know much about the psychoanalytic theories of Sigmund Freud, and neither do I, but it would seem that Freud and the Bull were in total agreement on at least some things: that there is a certain neurotic behavior characterized by a driving compulsion to gather up material and play with it and that it's an obsessive preoccupation with purely physical accumulation and arrangement. The name of this particular disease or disorder of the mind, Freud termed *anal retention.*

Perhaps Freud considered this to be a disease indicating an "advanced" mental state. I'm not really sure about that. But it would seem quite possible, given the standard of measure it likes to foist off on other peoples, and which is really just the reflection of its own cultural value structure, that somewhere in the course of its "development" the whole of Europe got stuck in the adolescent and retentive stage.

Perhaps if some deep thinker can sit me down and prove to me that the Lakota were and are culturally deprived because of their marked inability to indulge in spectacular material displays like World War II, I would be prompted to change my analysis of all this. But I consider the probability of anyone really wanting to attempt to present such a case to be a bit low. Likewise, if someone could show me how plastic Barbie Dolls, TV Dinners, Porsche 911s, punk rock, double olympic sized swimming pools constructed for the officers in Saigon, Cam Rahn Bay and Danang, napalm and cluster bombs, lakes of asphalt called parking lots and all the rest of the vast array of lethal and useless European material *really* benefits my cultural essence one iota, I might reconsider. But again, I doubt very much that anyone wants to tackle such an absurdity.

I mean, *consider* the implications of a tradition which compels its people to march across half a continent, engage in a major war to steal the land from my people, engage in genocide in order to preserve their conquest, and all primarily so they can dig gold out of a small portion of that land, transport it back across the continent, and *bury* it again at Ft. Knox! The virulence of the disease Sitting Bull spoke of is truly staggering.

And, lest Marxists think they've somehow evaded this critique simply because capitalism held and holds power during the periods I'm talking about, let me remind you that it was a "hard core" Marxist who so smugly informed me that I needed to very carefully become "realistic," to *join* the insanity without "romantic" resistance, and get ready for the "new order" coming up. No matter what mud the capitalists might wish to sling at the memory of Karl Marx, they can never deny he was a good European: he transported the Puritan ideal of heaven in the next life through productive work in this one into an idealism proclaiming heaven is attainable on earth through the *same* productive work.

I've heard it said that Marx's greatest "achievement" was to completely secularize Christian dogma. I don't know if this evaluation is correct. However, I'm certain he accomplished this, and that it was a major theoretical turning point in European history. He set out to demolish the opium of Europe's people, and I'd calculate he succeeded. Whatever spirituality remained in Christendom died with Marx. The anal retentive complex which had always been sputtering in the Euro psyche became concretized as "dialectical materialism"; materialism has thus *become* the European religion.

The upshot of all this is that, as a non-European, an outsider, I have trouble differentiating between Marxists, Capitalists, and all the other "ists." Just like I've never really been able to unscramble all the theological fine points which distinguish the various denominations of the Christian religion. All Christians say essentially the same thing to me: "Become Christian." All the materialists have their own, essentially similar, message: "Get with the program, become a materialist." They are *all* proselytizers; that is, seeking to gain recruits, more recruits. All of them want me to change; none of them care to support who I am. A European is a European is a European.

Christians, Capitalists, Marxists; all any of them really want from me is my identity as a Lakota, as an "other." All any of them really want of the Lakota is their identity as a people, as something "other" than the understanding (or misunderstanding) of Europe. I, and my people, are just so much more *material* to be accumulated and rearranged into something we weren't and never wanted to be.

At this point, having thought the matter over, I arrived at a monumentally "romantic" conclusion. On a theoretical level, as well as a personal level, Marxism and I were necessarily going our separate ways. I may ultimately become fodder material for another European power group vying for more things to play with, but not by *choice*, thanks. And as to the "unrealism" of my decision to attempt to participate in the continuation of Lakota traditions, values, and non-materialist spirituality, I will quote one of the Marxists who did (and still does, in a way) attract me, "Be realistic, demand the impossible." I believe Dany Cohn-Bendit said that. And anyway, the impossible, ain't.

Despite my disenchantment with Marxism and with the general potential for European culture to provide anything like solutions to the global problems it has created, I was intrigued when asked to prepare this paper. I decided to back up and study in a bit more depth, to read some of the Marxist literature beyond the "fundamentals" I'd earlier waded through. Much of what I attempted, although I thought I understood Marxism to be intended as a "working class" theory, was couched in a language which rendered it thoroughly unintelligible (much like Marx himself). I don't know that I understood all I read; I don't know that it's an issue one way or the other. Obfuscation is an aspect of intellectual "gamesmanship"; what I'm concerned with are practical realities. I doubt that I ever became proficient in "the meaning of Marcuse," if that matters to anyone.

Two of the books I read during this preparation period did grip my attention, however; at least in certain sections. These were *Unorthodox Marxism* by Michael Albert and Robin Hahnel (South End Press, Boston, 1978) and *Alienation* by Bertell Ollman (Cambridge University Press, 1971). The parts which really got me excited were the sections where the authors describe the Marxist idea of *dialectics*, which both books bring out in remarkably similar fashion, and the meaning of which I'd never been quite clear on before. As Albert and Hahnel in particular note, Marxists are often to be heard referring to dialectics this and dialectical that, but more often than not, they—never mind the rest of us "uniniti-ated" types—don't really seem to have a handle on what this somewhat mystical word is supposed to mean; it seems to usually be just another of the eternal string of left wing buzz words. So it was a revelation to read some reasonably articulate definition of the famous dialectic. I was also quite taken with some aspects of Ollman's alienation theory too, but I'll get to that later.

Now, if I may take the liberty to do so, I'd like to briefly lay out what it was that struck me about the above authors' descriptions of how dialec-tics work. All of them seem to agree that it is a *relational* means of con-ceiving reality. That is to say that any aspect of reality must be viewed as related, by virtue of existing at all, to all other aspects of reality. Nothing can be truly understood except in relation to everything else. Thus, the universe can be understood as a total of all its parts, but the understanding of any of the parts does not produce an understanding of the universe. In fact, unless the interaction of the universe is understood, a true under-standing of any single part within it can never really be arrived at. Like I said, dialectics would seem to be—by design—a completely relational way of thinking; in other words, a view in which all things are relations.

Dialectics seems to be held out by Marxists as the foundation of all Marxian philosophy, the way of thinking which distinguishes Marxism from other European philosophies. Marxists pride themselves in being able to achieve a more total view of circumstances than can their opposi-tion, which tends to think in terms of more simplistic linear systems, like cause and effect. Up to this point, I have to wholeheartedly agree with the Marxist theory, at least in principle. But I wonder how many Marxists have ever heard, much less understood, the word, *Metakuyeayasi?*

As I understand it, Christians close their prayers with the word "amen," the meaning of which originally meant "all men," or some such.

The term seems rather limited in its intended application (one might even term it "human chauvinist" in its implications) and clearly sexist in its structure, but that's the Christian church for you. The Lakota, on the other hand, close, open, and often punctuate their prayers with the word *Metakuyeayasi*, a generally accepted translation of which is "all relations." And anyone thinking "all relations" is referring simply to fathers, mothers, cousins and brothers, is less than ignorant of the Lakota. These human relations are, of course, included. But, in the same sense, so are the four legged animals, the animals which crawl and swim and fly, the plants, the mountains, lakes, plains, rivers, the sky and sun, stars, moon, the four directions . . . in short, everything. Everything in the universe is related within the tradition of Lakota spirituality; everything is relational, and can only be understood in that way.

The basis for this understanding on the part of traditional Lakota culture is its spirituality. The relationality of the universe is a spiritual proposition, a force so complex and so powerful that it creates a sense of wonder and impotence in any sane human who truly considers it. Only through the devotion of the better part of a lifetime of intensive study under the supervision of an array of seasoned teachers who have also devoted their lives to a lifetime of study can one hope to begin to fathom this complexity and power which we call *Tunkashila*, the Grandfather, the Universe, the Great Mystery. This is why our tribal elders are necessarily our spiritual leaders, our teachers: only they have had sufficient time to gain the knowledge which allows even a limited understanding of the Great Mystery of the Relations.

It may be a somewhat jolting announcement to make to doctrinaire Marxists who are convinced otherwise by the memorization of some "revolutionary" tract or other, but Lakota spirituality is—in perhaps the only translational terms comprehensible to Marxists—the pursuit of a true understanding of the dialectical nature of the universe. That, and to conform our lives to living relationally, as a relation among relations; *not* at the expense of our relations. Rather than being "an opiate" to the Lakota people, the traditional Lakota spirituality, our religion as it were, actually constitutes a stimulant, a social agent requiring a perpetual pursuit of dialectical knowledge and action. This, it seems to me, is what Marxists are always *saying* they're about. *Metakuyeayasi*, on the other hand, is the conceptual essence of Lakota spirituality, a spirituality which is the practical essence of Lakota life itself.

It also seems to me, the problem here is not merely one of a one-sided intercultural ignorance. Rather, as Albert and Hahnel point out in

Unorthodox Marxism, even the "heavyweight" Marxist theorists seem at a loss to define the difference between how their "dialectics" works and how the more complex systems of linear logic work. I believe this is true because Marxism, at least in the form available in this country today, doesn't work through a dialectical system of thought at all. It *does* work through the same logical systems as the "bourgeois" theorists it says it opposes; it takes a linear, cause and effect, route to understanding problems and proposing solutions, rather than a truly relational approach.

So, when Marxists come upon a culture which functions on the basis of *truly* dialectical understanding and thought, they don't understand it, they don't recognize it, they condemn their own avowed means to reason as being "primitive" and "underdeveloped." As my Marxist acquaintances would say, the magnitude of the "contradiction" here is overwhelming. And so it goes. . . .

It seems entirely reasonable to me that, if Marxists had ever *really* been functioning on the basis of dialectics, they would have been interested in finding out enough about Lakota culture to discover whatever the exact relationship between the tradition and theirs might be. They didn't. But if they had, I'm confident they would (with some astonishment, no doubt) have discovered what I've noted above. Of course, since they have always been prone to dismiss Lakota culture as backward, *before* they investigated its true nature, there's no way they could make the subsequent discovery. Perhaps even if they had engaged in some serious attempts at investigation they would *still* not have understood the significance of what they were seeing, because I'm hardly convinced they yet understand or practice dialectical reasoning.

If Marxists had ever come close to comprehending the universe in anything remotely resembling a truly relational sense, it seems utterly inconceivable that they could engage in perpetuating the arrogance of logic through which Europe has assigned humanity a mystical place of inherent superiority among living things. It seems equally impossible that a relational world view could accommodate the rather stupid notion that the universe was somehow designed as the playground for human exploitation. Such examples could be continued at great length.

In any event, the question must be posed: if Marxism has been completely unable to discover the certain, rather obvious, commonality noted above between themselves and a Native tradition, what else has their "advanced learning" managed to miss? This is not an idle question. If Marxists truly believe dialectics is the most sophisticated "mode of reason" ever discovered by humanity (and, of course, this discovery is held to have been made in Europe—the way Europe "discovered" America), then they are hardly in a position to condemn a culture which functions on that basis as something to be "transcended" out of hand.

Rather than being condemned as "primitive," such cultures must be considered—if Marxist definition is not to be flatly self-contradictory—as "advanced" in terms of their "modes of reason." Europe pales to retardation by comparison. The simple fact is that the Lakota possessed a fully functional lifeway based in dialectical knowledge thousands of years before Marx, and it remains in matured effect while Marx's descendents are still attempting to actualize their dialectical rhetoric. We have *much* to teach our proto-dialectical friends.

ACTIVE READING

1. What relationship does Black Elk see between "religion" and "spirituality"? What distinctions does he make between these words? Look over several passages in which one or both of these words appear. How does he use these terms to clarify his ideas about Marxism?

2. Choose three or four sections in which Black Elk reacts to what someone else has written or said. When does he react as an expert, and when does he grant that role to someone else? How does his movement in and out of the expert role affect your response to his arguments?

3. Review the passages in which Black Elk develops his understanding of the dialectic. How does dialectical logic differ from the other kinds of logic to which Black Elk refers in his essay? How dialectical do his own arguments seem to be?

READING IN NEW CONTEXTS

1. Locate several passages in which Black Elk uses ideas of reason or rationality. When does he view reason positively, and when does he view it negatively? Use your observations about Seidler, Rich, or another writer whose work highlights the tension between rationality and irrationality to examine the role of reason in Black Elk's essay.

2. How would you describe Black Elk's overall feelings about Marxism? How do they relate to el-Saadawi's thoughts about Islam or Rosaldo's feelings about mainstream anthropology? Use the notion of dialectical thinking to help you examine these writers' relationships to the institutions or theories they write about.

3. Choose another *Literacies* text, perhaps by Heker, Baldwin, or Fishman, in which you feel someone's beliefs might interfere with that person's ability to make good choices for him- or herself. How does the debate between Black Elk and his Marxist informants about the role of Lakota tradition help you examine the person from the second reading?

DRAFT ONE / DRAFT TWO

1. *Draft One:* Find several places where Black Elk represents spoken words without quotation marks. What tones or emotions do these passages suggest? How do they make you feel about the speaker? Discuss the role you think such passages play in Black Elk's arguments.

   Draft Two: Select several passages from Kozol, Scheper-Hughes, or another *Literacies* author who uses quotation marks to indicate spoken words. How do these direct quotations make you feel about the speaker and what he or she says? How might your feelings differ if the author used indirect quotation or paraphrase instead of direct quotation? Using the second text and your ideas from Draft One, develop your own theory about the ways writers decide when and how to represent speech.

2. *Draft One:* How might Black Elk's observations about Marxism lead you to revise your response to Before Reading #2? Based on your responses, write an essay examining how Marxist goals and values might help or hinder your own community.

   Draft Two: Choose Rodriguez, Fishman, or another *Literacies* author you believe addresses the issue of community. How would this author respond to your ideas from Draft One? Why do you think she or he would respond that way?

BEFORE READING HOWARD BRODY

1. How interested would you expect to be in an essay written by a medical doctor? Talk about the kinds of subject matter and language you might look for in this sort of text.

2. Discuss the social factors that influence the relationship a patient has with his or her physician. Where does your own knowledge about patient/doctor relationships come from?

3. Who are some of the people or groups whose advice you take seriously? Do you consider these people experts in a particular area of knowledge or field of experience? What does the word "expert" mean to you? Where do experts get their authority?

HOWARD   BRODY,   M. D.

THE SOCIAL POWER
OF EXPERT HEALERS

I wish to argue that the physician's social power (and, to a lesser extent, cultural power) derives not only from physicianhood per se but also from membership in a particular social class, that of the affluent, professionally trained expert. I will suggest further that some ethical analyses in medicine will be flawed or incomplete unless this source of power (and of the abuse of power) is taken into account.

THE CASE OF OPAL

Opal, now two and a half, suffers from microcephaly, extreme developmental delay, grand mal seizure disorder, regurgitation with aspiration (partially corrected by surgery), feeding by jejunostomy tube, and recurrent respiratory infections requiring eight to ten hospitalizations a year. She was delivered by emergency cesarean section at four weeks past her due date. Her teenage mother was a heavy user of drugs throughout the pregnancy; her father (unmarried) also used drugs and was in prison by the time Opal was born. Opal's mother had had only sporadic prenatal care and showed up at the hospital in labor, initially unsure of her due

From *The Healer's Body* (1992).

date. The fetal monitor showed loss of fetal heart tones requiring emergency cesarean section.

Opal was in the nursery for six weeks and required respirator support. She also developed her seizure and reflux problems at that time. (Microcephaly did not become evident until Opal was eight months of age.) Her teenage mother initially took her home and cared for her with the help of the maternal grandmother. After a short time, the mother dropped Opal off at grandmother's house with a request to "take care of her for a while while I get a break." She stayed away three weeks. Finally, the grandmother suggested that she assume legal custody of Opal; the mother and the father (contacted in prison) both agreed. Grandmother now takes care of Opal full-time; Opal's mother comes by to visit once a week or so.

The grandmother lives in a farmhouse in a rather isolated area. The house belongs to her male companion, who is a truck driver; he occasionally helps out by taking care of Opal for short periods. Opal also has an uncle in his early twenties who is seldom seen; once he came home for a while with a broken leg (suffered in a fight over drugs) and demanded that his mother take care of him while he was disabled. Income for Opal and the grandmother consists primarily of Social Security, state Crippled Children's funds, and Aid to Dependent Children. These cover most medical care but still leave grandmother with many unpaid bills. For example, as the previous summer was unusually hot, Opal had great difficulty with perspiration and secretions, and the grandmother and her male companion installed air conditioning in the house; they were unable to get the welfare grant for the added utility expenses and currently are in arrears to the power company for seven hundred dollars.

Grandmother spends almost her entire day taking care of Opal, who needs fairly constant attention for clearing secretions in her throat, feeding her, and administering range-of-motion exercises prescribed by the physical therapist. There are some school programs for handicapped children Opal's age, but the grandmother has not utilized them; she claims that Opal's frequent infections have made this impossible but also admits that she thinks she can take care of Opal better than anyone else can.

The primary physician and other members of the crippled children's team who make occasional home visits as well as see Opal in the hospital have noted that they consider the grandmother to be pathologically attached to Opal. The grandmother has virtually no interests or human contacts outside of Opal's care. She is totally unwilling to engage in any discussion of Opal's poor long-term prognosis, saying, "She won't die until I die." Although she generally uses denial to avoid the subject, she has said specifically on several occasions that if Opal did die she would not want to go on living herself. Dealing with these issues is also complicated by distrust toward the hospital and toward at least some caregivers. The grandmother has contacted a lawyer to discuss whether "mistakes" made by the physician who did the cesarean section caused any of Opal's problems (highly unlikely). During one hospitalization, Opal suffered a burn on the hand from the efforts of an inexperienced phlebotomist to warm the extremity before blood drawing, and this incident has also led grandmother to threaten the hospital with legal action. She does, however, seem to trust the primary-care pediatrician and the crippled children's team.

That group is now meeting in their weekly family assessment conference. They wish to try to intervene to do something about grandmother's clinging relationship with Opal, thinking in part that Opal could benefit from some school programs and that the grandmother could also benefit from giving up some of Opal's care and finding other interests. They hypothesize that this clinging relationship is meeting some deeply felt needs of the grandmother. She seems to feel guilty for having been unable to control her daughter better during the pregnancy, to keep her off drugs and get her to accept regular prenatal care. (Hence, presumably, the displaced anger in trying to blame the obstetrician.) Moreover, Opal, despite her inability to do any of the things that a normal two-year-old would, is in many ways, the perfect child. She will remain forever in a totally dependent status and will never challenge the grandmother's authority or control. ("Opal is the only kid in the family the grandmother knows will never do drugs," is how one of the team members put it.)

The discussion among the medical staff turns to mechanisms to accomplish the desired changes. One person suggests that legal pressure could be applied if there is a school program that could benefit Opal and the grandmother refuses to cooperate. "Is it illegal not to send a two-year-old to school?" another wonders. And a third says, "Look, we have a kid that is being well cared for and a grandmother who is happy. Who are we to mess with this?"

POWER, INTERESTS, AND EXPERTS

There are a variety of ways to approach this case ethically. Surely it could be asked what the plans ought to be if Opal suffers a crisis, is hospitalized, and questions of aggressive life-prolonging treatment come up. More to the point now, should the staff intervene regarding school placement and the overly clinging relationship between the child and the grandmother?

Both these issues will no doubt be addressed first by asking what would be in Opal's "best interests." Does grandmother reflect Opal's best interests in her decisions? Or is she so preoccupied with her own interests that she is a poor surrogate decision-maker for Opal? Is it in Opal's interests to be deprived of the training and stimulation that the school could provide? What about the additional infections she would be exposed to at school? Or the risk of upsetting the major caregiving relationship in Opal's life—perhaps the only thing that stands between Opal and the back ward of a state hospital?

How should the team resolve disputes about what is truly in Opal's interest? I have argued that the term *best interests*, if not actually meaningless, is at least extremely difficult to specify with any operational precision (Brody 1988). As Humpty Dumpty would have it, the question is not what the term means, but who is to be master. I suggest that almost any effort to state what would be in Opal's best interests is really a disguised way to promote some specific *adult* agenda, which entails a variety of value judgments about how "good" people ought to lead their lives.[1]

One such agenda is that of the particular social class and subculture to which Opal's family belongs. This is a way of life shaped by chronic financial inadequacy, uncertain employment, and constant battles with social bureaucracies designed by the middle class to treat the lower class as adversaries.[2] This way of life is further shaped by the relative inability to control one's environment or plan for the future and by the pervasive

1. This assertion must of course be qualified. It could be determined to be contrary to Opal's best interests right now to cause her such sensations as pain and hunger. But these basic and obvious interests of all sentient beings say little about the important decisions that must be made about Opal's care.

2. I am indebted to Leonard Fleck for pointing out the peculiar injustice of the bureaucracy Americans have created as a result of a patchwork of health-care entitlement programs. Many of those who lack health insurance in the United States are among the working poor and therefore pay taxes. These taxes go to support systems like Medicaid, which hire staff to make sure that only those truly eligible get benefits. Therefore, the working poor effectively pay taxes to make sure that they are excluded from the health-care system. Likewise, private insurance companies hire extra staff to make sure that only those eligible receive benefits; and that practice adds to the cost of private insurance, helping to price insurance out of the market for the smaller companies that employ most of the working poor. Some have calculated that Americans could pay for health care for all citizens now excluded from coverage if they saved the money they now spend on administering this crazy quilt of systems (Himmelstein and Woolhandler 1986).

temptation of alcohol and other drugs as escapes from this grim realization. In this setting, certain kinds of human relationships make sense which would be dysfunctional in a middle-class world. And an infant like Opal may indeed have a value that would be unthinkable in a social world that prizes good looks, mental proficiency, and accomplishments. According to this agenda, the decisions involving Opal ought to be made by those who are of her world and who have the closest family and emotional ties.

A quite different agenda is that of the upper-middle-class, professionally trained healers, or "experts." This is the group to which the physicians and the crippled children's team belong. They are committed to a worldview that prizes specialized, scientifically based knowledge and the dividing up of all human experience into problems for which one must consult the correct expert if one is to have any chance of being happy.[3]

Moreover, if these experts have psychological training, then of course they know the motives and intentions of the average citizen better than he does; and if he is so impertinent as to reject their advice, they can state precisely which mental pathology is responsible for his aberrant behavior. According to this agenda, what is best for Opal is what this group of experts says is best, and indirectly it is whatever creates the greatest chance of future employment for all members of the expert class, including special-education teachers, physical therapists, social workers, family counselors, and of course physicians.[4]

A quite different agenda would be that of the conservative group which has become increasingly vocal in U.S. politics during the 1980s. Their reaction to Opal's case would be one of disgust for all family members, whom they would censure as unemployed junkies ripping off the welfare system and having sex outside of marriage. Presumably this group

3. A caricature of this view is that the ideal citizen is one who on getting up in the morning immediately checks whether any of the American Cancer Society's seven early warning signs of cancer has appeared overnight, runs the precise number of miles at precisely the target pulse rate that his sports medicine specialist has recommended after his graded exercise electrocardiogram, and then phones his nutritionist to see how much fiber he should eat for breakfast.
4. My analysis here draws heavily on Lasch 1979 and to a lesser extent on Freidson 1970; see also Illich 1976. On the irony of a society that is increasingly preoccupied with its health and as a result feels a decreased sense of well-being, see Barsky 1988. No doubt this paragraph in the text presents a vicious caricature of "experts"; but since many of my readers, like me, are among them, it is wise occasionally to remind ourselves how foolish we can look to those who do not share our comfortable presuppositions.

would favor using any medical technology to keep Opal alive regardless of her prognosis; fight against using tax dollars to create any supportive services to aid her when she is well; call for locking up both her parents for as many years as possible; and blame the grandmother for her failure to discipline her daughter properly and teach her the proper values.[5]

Each of these three agendas has a different status within American society. The third has managed to rise several notches during the 1980s, with the success of a federal administration committed to it. But for our purposes the most important agenda is the second one. If anyone in the United States runs afoul of administrative or legal rules—particularly within the school or court systems—it is this agenda which is most likely to be forcibly imposed by the state apparatus. It is this class of experts which is likely to decide who should go to jail, who should be committed to a mental hospital, who should be enrolled in this or that school program, and for how long, and what counts as having achieved benefit from being there; and judges, teachers, and school boards are likely to acquiesce in whatever course of action the experts suggest.

Of course, all this has been heard before. It has become the stock criticism against medicine more generally and psychiatry particularly (Szasz 1974). The argument goes that these disciplines have almost no scientific credence but function simply as a means of social control imposed by the ruling class for its own benefit. To these critics, the Chief of Medicine is correct in assessing the real Aesculapian power of the physician as very limited. They contend that social power is the primary element of physician power and that the myth of Aesculapian power is used as a smoke screen lest the lower classes catch on.

This line of criticism may seem trite and simplistic, but it is also occasionally on target. Numerous examples could be given; for now it may be sufficient to consider the question of psychiatric testimony regarding the future potential of criminals for violence. It seems difficult to dispute that there is hardly any scientific basis for making confident pre-

---

5. William B. Weil, in commenting to me on this case, has suggested that there is a fourth agenda, one of rights of the disabled. I would argue that that agenda is actually a hybrid, adopting sanctity-of-life elements from the third agenda and elements of liberal do-gooderism from the second. A common observation in the wake of the Baby Doe controversies in the early 1980s is that the movement for the rights of the disabled, previously a creature of the political left (because it advocated reallocating tax revenues to aid a self-proclaimed minority group), had suddenly made an uneasy alliance with the conservative right in espousing a sanctity-of-life ethic for the treatment of seriously deformed newborns.

diction of future violent behavior. Rather, there seems to have arisen an unholy alliance between the courts and certain psychiatrists. The courts benefit by passing off difficult decisions about length of sentence and the sort of facility to which prisoners should be sent; they get to pretend that these decisions derive from objective criteria instead of from irreducibly subjective judgments for which the judges themselves would be held accountable. A few psychiatrists, who have made a career out of giving such testimony, would find their income and prestige in jeopardy were the lack of scientific validity for their conclusions ever discussed. A larger group of psychiatrists, who may have genuine sympathy for individual prisoners or patients and want to view themselves as aiding them, offer testimony of low potential for violence altruistically; and so they too, though for better motives, acquire an interest in obscuring the scientific basis of their predictions. The rest of us, who can be relied upon most of the time not to want to know what really goes on in courtrooms or in prisons, are inclined to leave this unholy alliance to its own devices and not to question it.[6]

Yet focusing on these examples of the use of pseudo-Aesculapian power for social control will obscure the more subtle message of the Chief of Medicine story about the fine line between the use and the abuse of physician power. It is one thing for people to view themselves as victims of the abuse of power by physicians and other powerful groups in society; it is another for them to view themselves as active collaborators in that abuse of power. But ultimately the public must acknowledge their role, as the more thoughtful critics of physician power make clear.

As Lasch (1979) has eloquently stated, we Americans seem to have become, as a society, profoundly uncomfortable with and estranged from a set of functions and behaviors that our forebears viewed as natural and manageable. We have adopted an ideology of personal happiness which holds that life consists of a series of snares to be avoided and problems to be solved, and that only by getting the advice and aid of specialist experts can we solve those problems in such a way as to assure happiness. I view this as an ideology rather than a rational belief because the more experts we consult, the more unhappy we get. But of course we tell ourselves, in that case, that we went to the wrong experts or did not properly follow their advice: ideology always wins out over facts.

The power of this ideology can be seen in that efforts to reject it

6. For representative views on psychiatrists' predictions of violent behavior, see Peszke 1975; Ewing 1983; Monahan 1984; Chiswick 1985.

end up re-creating it in a different form. Many in American society view physicians as too powerful and call for a return of power over one's health to the individual. Among some groups involved in holistic cancer self-help for instance, it is an article of faith that cancer is easily preventable and curable and that physicians have a selfish interest in avoiding and suppressing these preventive and curative measures in order to make more money off cancer sufferers. But the movements dedicated to overturning the power of the expert healers—notably the so-called holistic or alternative medicine movement—tend to re-create the structure of the system they reject. People appear to become every bit as dependent on the counsel of these "alternative" experts as they were on that of the more traditional healers.

It is doubtful that we can replace this ideology with another, less dysfunctional and less neurotic one. It is therefore especially important to see how it feeds the temptation to abuse the power of the class of experts either for social control or for the personal gain of the expert class. *Personal gain* must here be construed as including the expansion of employment opportunities for like-minded experts by systematically expanding the number of experts that must be consulted before a "problem" can be declared "solved."

The difficulty of doing away with this ideology, however, can itself be used as a rationalization to avoid change, even where individual experts can make small modifications for the better. This difficulty requires a hard look at how physicians might abuse power in this fashion and what can be done to avoid that abuse.

ABUSES OF EXPERT POWER

The abuses of power attached to membership in the expert class cut across all guidelines for judging the responsible use of power. Owned power becomes a problem when the role of the expert and the need to consult experts over every detail of day-to-day living are taken for granted. It is easy for the physician to deny under these circumstances that she has any such power since the self-image of the expert healer is to be helpful, not manipulative for selfish ends.[7] But power that is unrecognized is hard to channel into responsible uses.

7. "The elite cannot truly be thought of as men who are merely 'doing their duty.' In considerable part they are the ones who determine their duty, as well as the duties of other men. They do not merely follow orders; they give orders. They are not merely bureaucrats; they command bureaucracies. They may try to disguise these facts from

Similarly, aimed power is resisted so long as the self-image of benevolent helper remains untarnished. If the power tends both to respond to the needs and desires of individuals and to cement the social authority of the expert class, the first aim of the power may be confused with the total aim. Justifications for the use of power will be offered which miss the problematic features of the case but sound superficially compelling. Worse, alternative strategies may be denounced in the name of the individual autonomy they are supposed to promote. Since the public willingly complies with the expert ideology, refusal by the expert to accept the assigned role could be seen as a violation of the autonomy of the client or patient and as an attempt to impose a new ideology on them out of paternalistic arrogance: "we know better than they do what they really need."[8]

Shared power is difficult to achieve so long as the physician occupies this expert role.[9] To empower the patient might, in some ways at least, threaten the social hegemony of the expert class and put experts out of their jobs. Despite this pull, most experts genuinely want to be helpful and see an overdependence as unhelpful to their clients. But the more subtle problem is that even given the urge to empower, the ideology may be so strong that the empowerment itself becomes a reinforcement of helpless dependence. It may, in the end, seem as if one can get power only by going to the right expert and following his advice precisely; one cannot get power simply by choosing to exercise it. In an age when people pay lots of money to attend seminars that purport to teach assertiveness and self-esteem, this danger seems real.

I [have] argued [elsewhere] that some abuses of power might be called playing God. The expert may be tempted to use the power attached

---

others and from themselves by appealing to traditions of which they imagine themselves to be the instruments, but there are many traditions, and they must choose which ones they will serve. And now they face decisions for which there simply are no traditions" (Ladd 1981, citing Mills 1959).

8. An oft-cited example of this phenomenon is the clash between the modern physician, who has been trained to believe in patient autonomy, and the old-fashioned patient, who expects and indeed values paternalistic treatment from the doctor. To the extent that one can autonomously choose to be treated paternalistically, the physician's efforts to promote the patient's autonomy can themselves be denounced as unwarranted paternalism.

9. Ladd (1981) indicates that the sharing of power is a useful antidote to the possible abuses of social and political power by physicians. He fails to address, however, the problem of sharing when the power has been rendered culturally invisible. In this regard, shared power requires owned power as a prior condition.

to his role not simply to carry out his role functions and assist those who seek his aid but to try to redesign the world—often by rewarding the "good" and punishing the "bad." Of course, if the power were appropriately aimed and owned, the expert would have to take explicit responsibility for doing this—and by implication would have to defend publicly his judgments as to who the good and the bad are and what gives him the right to decide their fate. The net result is that some patients get approved for disability or other benefits while others get turned down; some needy persons have opportunities and assistance opened up to them while others face a brick wall of bureaucratic inertia. No expert has to own responsibility for making any value-laden judgments because each of these acts can be justified in terms of the professional judgments within a particular field of expertise.

The challenge for physicians (and other experts) is to find ways to make their patients feel genuinely more powerful to control their own lives and health; to be more aware of the actual ends of their social and cultural power, not only the ends that bear the most benign interpretation; and to be willing to accept responsibility for the use of power with a realistic understanding of all its facets.

THE RABKIN EXPLOSION

It is of little use to analyze the power of the healing experts in our society if the only conclusion is that the experts are bad people (or else that the society is bad). A further case study may help at this point to illustrate how complex the issues around power and expertise can be.

This case comes from an unusual source. People are by now used to the idea that books and articles on medical ethics might present controversial cases, which become the subject of heated debate. But it is a bit out of the ordinary for controversial cases to arise in literature and medicine journals.[10] Nevertheless, the growing field of literature and medicine now has one "hot" case study to its credit, and it may prove instructive here.

David Barnard, a professor of medical humanities trained in religion and psychology, contributed a case study which he titled, "A Case of

---

10. "Literature and medicine" refers to an emerging field within the medical humanities. Professors of literature have turned to the study of medical themes, teaching various works of fiction that portray medical themes and examining how language is used within the practice of medicine itself. The journal *Literature and Medicine* is the primary compendium of work in this field.

Amyotrophic Lateral Sclerosis" (Barnard 1986). As a participant-observer, he followed "Dr. Valerie Walsh" in a series of visits with "Mr. and Mrs. Baker." Mr. Baker was seventy-seven when he developed progressive weakness and was diagnosed as having ALS. Mrs. Baker, seventy-three, became his caretaker in spite of her own medical problems of angina, diabetes, and arthritis. Dr. Walsh came to bond closely with the Bakers, who were in turn deeply and openly grateful for the care that she provided. But she also struggled with two ongoing problems. The first was her desire to clarify Mr. Baker's wishes regarding intensity of medical treatment, particularly the eventual question of intubation and mechanical ventilation. The signals given by both Bakers strongly suggested their desire to hold onto hope and not to face the grim prognosis. The second was the Bakers' insistence on remaining in their own home, at some distance from needed social and nursing services, and their resistance to efforts to place aides or other workers in the home following an unfortunate incident with an uncaring person. These limitations conflicted with Dr. Walsh's desire to provide the best care possible for Mr. Baker and to spare the strain on Mrs. Baker's health.

Eventually, after months of home visits that left Dr. Walsh feeling both isolated and frustrated, she was able to get Mr. Baker to articulate his desire not to receive mechanical ventilation; she also was able to arrange for a health aide to visit the home to help with the most burdensome physical chores. Within a month, however, Mrs. Baker was dead of a sudden heart attack. Mr. Baker then had to be placed in a nursing home, where he died six weeks later.

When the case study was solicited for the journal *Literature and Medicine*, the issue editor, Joanne Trautmann Banks, had some questions about the case history format. To what extent was the study an "objective" account of events, and to what extent was it fiction? With this in mind, she requested a commentary from an authority on narrative theory, Eric Rabkin. Rabkin's commentary (1986) is perhaps most notable for violating one of the norms of commentaries in scholarly journals: it is markedly uncivil, even angry.[11] He concluded that Barnard had elected to ignore the needs of the Bakers in order to write a manuscript that glorified the caring physician; that Dr. Walsh had been driven more by a need to

11. An example of the tone that runs throughout the article is an early sentence, "I must stress that I personally believe Barnard and Walsh in no *conscious* way acted to harm the Bakers" (Rabkin 1986, p. 43; emphasis in original). In context, this sentence can best be interpreted as saying: not only did they do evil things, but they were also too stupid to know what they were doing.

see herself as a hero-martyr than by a realistic appraisal of the Bakers' needs; and that between them Barnard and Walsh had lied to Mr. Baker about his disease and its prognosis and probably hastened Mrs. Baker's death.

Not unnaturally, given his background, Rabkin chose to analyze Barnard's text as a piece of fiction, and indeed Rabkin offered much internal evidence to justify that way of looking at the material. His analysis led him to conclude that Barnard was too self-effacing as narrator; if he was actually present in the home during some of the highly emotional exchanges he described, then his being there was a part of the narrative, and it was not honest to act as if he were merely the reader's window onto events. Rabkin also identified a number of passages that hinted at Dr. Walsh's personal needs—to do battle against a dread disease; to protect Mr. Baker from demoralizing news by being the sole judge of what he was ready to hear and when; to keep other potential team helpers out of the case while complaining that she was left to deal with the Bakers all by herself; and especially to accept the frequent and forceful expressions of gratitude and praise bestowed on her by the Bakers.

Rabkin suggested that two things should have been done. First, Mr. Baker should have been confronted earlier with his poor prognosis so that open planning could have taken place; and second, Dr. Walsh should have insisted on getting the Bakers to move closer to the center of the city, where more services were close at hand. Banks thus felt obligated to call for another commentary on the ethics of these recommendations, and that was supplied by David H. Smith (1986). Smith faulted Rabkin for ethical inconsistency. Presumably the need to tell Mr. Baker the truth was rooted in respect for his autonomy. How, then, could Rabkin recommend violating Mr. Baker's autonomy by forcing him to leave the home that meant so much to him and his wife?[12]

These are the basic facts of the case and the central issues in the

---

12. Smith's commentary on patient autonomy seems correct as far as it goes; but it also appears to be a cheap shot in the context of the case. It seems reasonable that a more active confrontation with the Bakers, focused on the eventual need for additional home services and the threats to Mrs. Baker's own health, would have caused them to revise their initial views on accepting help or even on moving (after all, they did eventually accept an aide, after saying consistently that they would refuse). And in turn, insisting on being more forthright about Mr. Baker's actual prognosis would seem to be a vital element in this process of confrontation. Although Rabkin openly admitted his lack of clinical experience and skills, his recommendations nevertheless seem to have a clinical cohesion which Smith fails to recognize.

controversy that erupted around its publication. What light can the case shed on the question of experts' power?

An interesting role reversal developed in this controversy. Walsh is the physician, and Barnard seems to have accepted the role of the physician's apologist. It would therefore seem natural for them to impose their own views on the Bakers, paying scant attention to what the Bakers themselves say they want. And Rabkin, as defender of the patient against the power of the experts, might have been expected to call the expects to task. But the reality of the case is quite different. Dr. Walsh is the one who seems to be listening to the Bakers, telling them what they want to hear, backing off when they indicate they do not wish to deal with certain issues, and supporting their oft-stated wish to remain in their own home. It is Rabkin, by contrast, who urges Dr. Walsh to push her expert opinion of the matter onto the Bakers and force them to move to a more convenient location for sending a crowd of like-minded experts into the Baker home to take care of them. This observation by itself does not establish who is right and who is wrong (if anyone is either). But it does suggest that things may be muddier than they first appear. Taking sides with or against the experts is not enough to assure moral purity.

What should have been done in this case? Rabkin's telling observations suggest that Dr. Walsh's course was not driven by the most appropriate needs. But neither is it clear that Rabkin's suggestions are wise: people cannot be forced to move, accept home services, or face a harsh prognosis squarely.

It is always much easier to be wise or creative in retrospect in such cases. What would have happened, though, if Dr. Walsh had paid more attention to her own conflicts about the Bakers earlier in the course of treatment? She was defending their rights and their privacy, she was having their praise and gratitude heaped on her, yet she still felt frustrated and fearful that things would not go well. This led to her increasing isolation from her medical team. What if she had seen this isolation and had decided to get the team more involved and to consult other physicians as to what her own feelings meant?[13]

Through this consultation, Dr. Walsh may have learned more about

---

13. A family physician found herself taking care of a close friend during a terminal illness. This physician feared that the personal ties could lead her to mistakes in judgment, but she did not use that as an excuse to withdraw. Instead she made special efforts to consult regularly with her colleagues to be sure that her management of the case was reviewed regularly by more impartial observers. I am grateful to Elizabeth Alexander, M.D., for this illustration.

her own psychological needs and how they were influencing her treatment decisions. In addition, she might have evolved a positive plan for confronting the Bakers with the difficult care issues. Ideally, the confrontation would lead each faction—the Bakers and the healing experts—to own the part of the problem that only they could solve.

Dr. Walsh might have arranged for some colleagues on her medical team to accompany her on a home visit to make a less biased assessment of the home situation and of Mr. Baker's present and future needs. If after that visit no new plans could be formulated, the next step might be to return to the Bakers' home and tell them something like the following:

"Our team is frustrated. We are getting mixed messages about you and your situation and don't know how to interpret them.

"On the one hand, we know that you love each other, that you value your home life and your privacy, that Mrs. Baker is dedicated and unselfish in providing care, and that Mr. Baker has shown great emotional strength in coming to grips with a serious disease. These are all very important, and it ought to be our job as a health-care team to support and reinforce them.

"On the other hand, we know that a good deal of help is available for families in situations like yours, and we are puzzled as to why we have not been able to get you linked up with such help. We have heard Mrs. Baker express her own frustration with how things are going, and we know that she fears that her own health will be affected by the strain. And we are not sure that we have yet had a frank discussion about what Mr. Baker's future needs are going to be.

"We are frustrated because we have these two sets of messages—one saying that things are going well and the other that things are going badly. Until we get our own problem solved, we are afraid we will not provide for you the high-quality care you deserve. Can you help us work toward a resolution?"

If this approach seems like a reasonable alternative to the trap Dr. Walsh sensed herself falling into, it may be because the message is a complicated mix of owned power and owned powerlessness. The powerlessness is admitted: the health team cannot remake the Baker family into their image of the ideal client and cannot force the Bakers to place a higher value on receiving certain sorts of technical assistance than on remaining together in their own home without outside interference. The team cannot even get a clear idea of what the problem is without their participation. The power is stated more subtly: there is a clear threat that if the Bakers do not discuss these matters and in the process talk about things that they have heretofore been unwilling to talk about, assistance will be withdrawn at some level. But this threatened use of power does not seem inappropriate, for professionals should be able to avoid giving care under circumstances in which they feel strongly that they cannot do a good job.[14]

If this team conference approach to the Baker's situation represents an ethically superior alternative to what actually occurred, then why was it not done or even considered? One hypothesis is that the three parties— Mr. Baker, Mrs. Baker, and Dr. Walsh—were locked in a serious but unrealized power struggle. Indeed, one might conclude that all three were guilty of the unowned, unaimed, and unshared use of the power that they possessed, thereby producing a tangle of cross-purposes.[15]

Dr. Walsh never examined the types of power she did and did not possess in relation to the Bakers. For example, she agonized over her power to destroy Mr. Baker's hope by being too candid in discussing the prognosis of ALS, but she paid scant attention to the power she was assuming by taking it upon herself to decide how much he wanted to hear and when. She worried about an eventual bad outcome and several times

14. Of course, if professionals claimed that they could do a good job only in those circumstances where they were given enough control unilaterally to define both the problem and the solution in their own terms, then professional help would be too much of a threat to individual autonomy for American society to tolerate. My assumption, by contrast, is that professionals define respect for individual autonomy as part of what it means to do a good job: and that the conclusion, "I can't do a good job in this case," is reached only after extensive dialogue with the would-be client.

15. I here omit the fourth party, Barnard, from consideration. For one thing, Rabkin has already given him sufficient grief to render him an unappealing target for further criticism. For another, Barnard's lapse was primarily in the area of owned power, in that he tried to efface himself as the narrator rather than acknowledge and reveal the role he played in the unfolding of the case. He portrayed himself at the start of his article (Barnard 1986) as a "participant-observer" but then went on to write as all observer and no participant. It is perhaps revealing that Barnard's purported misstatement of the issues found an echo in the editorial comments of the issue editor of the journal. Rabkin took Barnard to task for calling his article, "A Case of Amyotrophic Lateral Sclerosis," as if this locution would guarantee the scientific objectivity of what followed—and as if what really mattered was Mr. Baker's disease, not Mr. Baker. In her brief editorial note that introduced the series of three articles, Joanne Trautmann Banks used the title, "A Controversy about Clinical Form." This again runs the risk of leaving out the human dimension of the account in favor of a comfortable scholarly analysis. If we are to take Rabkin seriously (even to disagree with him), the controversy is not over clinical form; it is over whether some professionals abused the people they were supposed to be helping.

referred to the Bakers as a "time bomb," but continued to make her routine home visits without asking whether they might be reinforcing the impression that no additional help was needed. She paid no attention to the potential for a power struggle between her and Mrs. Baker that was inherent in a female physician's making house calls.

Without having examined the power issues, Dr. Walsh could never be sure what she was trying to do with her power. How much was aimed at doing battle with ALS, which had killed a previous patient of hers just before she met the Bakers? How much was aimed at keeping up her own hopes, in the guise of keeping up Mr. Baker's hopes? (When she finally did bring up the subject of mechanical ventilation, Mr. Baker responded promptly and thoughtfully, with appropriate sadness; there was no clue from that exchange that the subject could not have been safely broached six months earlier.) How much was aimed at maintaining herself in the role of sole caregiver, the only one who could meet the needs of the Bakers?

Power is almost impossible to share when one does not know that one has it and does not know what one is doing with it. Therefore Dr. Walsh lost opportunities to empower the Bakers through her visits and her care. This failure assured that any power the Bakers exercised themselves had as much chance of being in conflict as in collusion with Dr. Walsh's power. The Bakers were in a bind: they were quite socially isolated and needed the comfort that Dr. Walsh's visits provided. They could not bring the power struggle out in the open without threatening that relationship. And so on the surface, all of Dr. Walsh's efforts were met with expressions of praise and gratitude, but no one looked critically at those statements to see what issues might lie concealed below them.

The Bakers, on their side, had similar problems with power. Mr. Baker seems to have become quite absorbed in his illness. His calm resignation in the face of weakness and loss of independence was commendable. But there is almost no hint, in the passages recorded by Barnard, of any real concern for the toll the illness must be taking on Mrs. Baker. At one point Mrs. Baker complains bitterly that her husband is not trying to help himself. His reaction is to defend his efforts: it's not that he isn't trying, but his muscles simply will not respond. Any reaction from him like, "I know how hard it is on her, and I worry about her health," is absent from the record. Neither wishes to admit that Mr. Baker is going to die soon. This means they cannot address the subject of what life will be like for Mrs. Baker after he is gone—whether she will be able to function well or whether his illness will have taken such toll on her that she will have to go into a nursing home. There is thus a sense in which Mr. Baker's power to cope with his illness is being directed against his wife, not just against the effects of the ALS.

Mrs. Baker's efforts to use her power mirror Dr. Walsh's. Mrs. Baker also has a strong need to be seen as the sole caregiver, even at the cost of being the hero-martyr. At one point she proclaims, pointing at her husband, "I'm going to get ten more years out of this if it kills me!" (Barnard 1986, p. 29). This statement is a tragic foreshadowing of the actual outcome of the case. Mrs. Baker also has a strong need to buoy her own hopes by not facing the serious prognosis of ALS. A statement by Mr. Baker that suggests resignation and acceptance is likely to be followed by an aggressively optimistic interruption from his wife. In retrospect, when Dr. Walsh withheld frank discussions about prognosis because she felt that her patient was not ready to hear them, we may wonder whether it was actually Mrs. Baker she was protecting. It is thus possible that Mrs. Baker used her power to maintain control and sustain her own sense of her role instead of trying to achieve the best outcomes for Mr. Baker and meet his real needs. This also made it inevitable that Mrs. Baker would become locked in a power struggle with Dr. Walsh.[16]

The way all parties used their power at cross-purposes makes it understandable why a better resolution was not reached—and why the outcome of the case might have been the best that could *practically* have been achieved. Still, when it comes to the appropriate use of power, the professional must assume a deeper responsibility than the client. It is perfectly excusable for the Bakers to be unclear on what their power consisted of and how it was being employed; it is less excusable for Dr. Walsh. My analysis suggests that all three guidelines on the responsible use of power would need to be consulted to avoid this sort of outcome in future cases.

The analysis suggests a further clue. If Dr. Walsh went wrong, it may be due in part to an inappropriate and unrealized *self-preoccupation*. She

---

16. A revealing statement by Dr. Walsh, toward the end of the case, is, "I feel like I have no control over what's happening right now. I'm completely dependent on [Mrs. Baker], and she's doing an *excellent* job" (Barnard 1986, p. 40). An undercurrent in this passage is that Dr. Walsh thinks that she herself should have control and feels badly for not having it. (The obvious rejoinder is: the caregiver who is actually in the home should be the central figure, and the doctor should not feel threatened in her role by the strength and power of the caregiver.) Although Dr. Walsh implies that she resents Mrs. Baker's power, she lauds her work, thereby mirroring the praise and gratitude that the Bakers feel obliged to heap on Dr. Walsh at every opportunity.

may have been too wrapped up in her needs to vanquish the disease, decide what should be told to the patient, and see herself as a certain kind of compassionate physician. Thus an important character trait for physicians to cultivate would be a way of avoiding, or at least identifying, self-preoccupation.

REFERENCES

Barnard, D. 1986. A case of amyotrophic lateral sclerosis. *Literature and Medicine* 5:27–42.

Barsky, A. J. 1988. The paradox of health. *New England Journal of Medicine* 318:414–18.

Brody, B. A. 1988. Ethical questions raised by the persistent vegetative state. *Hastings Center Report* 18 (1):33–37.

Chiswick, D. 1985. Use and abuse of psychiatric testimony. *British Medical Journal* 290:975–77.

Ewing, C. P. 1983. "Dr. Death" and the case for an ethical ban on psychiatric and psychological predictions of dangerousness in capital sentencing proceedings. *American Journal of Law and Medicine* 8:407–28.

Freidson, E. 1970. *Profession of medicine: A study of the sociology of applied knowledge.* New York: Harper and Row.

Himmelstein, D. U., and Woolhandler, S. 1986. Cost without benefit: Administrative waste in U.S. health care. *New England Journal of Medicine* 314:441–45.

Illich, I. 1976. *Medical nemesis: The expropriation of health.* New York: Pantheon.

Ladd, J. 1981. Physicians and society: Tribulations of power and responsibility. In *The law-medicine relation: A philosophical exploration,* edited by S. F. Spicker, J. M. Healey, and H. T. Englehardt. Boston: Reidel.

Lasch, C. 1979. *The culture of narcissism.* New York: Norton.

Mills, C. W. 1959. *The causes of World War Three.* New York: Simon and Schuster.

Monahan, J. 1984. The prediction of violent behavior: Toward a second generation of theory and policy. *American Journal of Psychiatry* 141:10–15.

Peszke, M. A. 1975. Is dangerousness an issue for physicians in emergency commitment? *American Journal of Psychiatry* 132:825–28.

Rabkin, E. 1986. A case of self defense. *Literature and Medicine* 5:43–53.

Smith, D. H. 1986. The limits of narrative. *Literature and Medicine* 5:54–57.

Szasz, T. S. 1974. *The myth of mental illness.* New York: Harper and Row.

ACTIVE READING

1. This text features many everyday words and phrases whose meanings Brody reshapes for somewhat specialized purposes. Make a list of some of these terms, and, for each one, explain how Brody's context changes their significance for you.

2. In one footnote, Brody mentions the difficulty of sharing power "when the power has been rendered culturally invisible" (129). Which passages in his essay help you to explain how power becomes "culturally invisible"? Find some passages that show Brody or his subjects making power "visible."

3. Brody's essay combines stories about patients and medical professionals with analysis of the power each party holds. Pick a two- or three-page section of his essay, and mark those passages which work mostly to tell you the story of a particular patient and his or her doctor. Then (perhaps using a different-colored pen) mark those passages which work mostly to analyze or interpret the story Brody is telling. What do the analytical passages tell you that the story parts do not?

READING IN NEW CONTEXTS

1. Brody introduces the concepts of "owned," "aimed," and "shared" power without explicitly defining them. Locate passages in his essay that allow you to define these terms. What relationship do you see among these three kinds of power? Use one or more of these concepts to reinterpret a power relationship in another *Literacies* text you have read this semester.

2. Brody notes "an ideology of personal happiness" (127) in contemporary culture. Working with Brody's comments and with another text that examines personal happiness—Walker, de Saint Victor, and Gilmore are some options—try to explain what is "ideological" about this commonplace idea.

3. The idea of acting in another person's "best interests" is more complicated, says Brody, than people usually admit. How does Brody's discussion of this idea shape your response to Scheper-Hughes, Rodriguez, or another *Literacies* essay in which certain people speak or act for other people?

DRAFT ONE / DRAFT TWO

1. *Draft One:* Use your own experience of an illness or injury that required medical attention as the starting point for a reading of Brody's essay from a *patient's* point of view. In your essay, explain which of his terms are relevant to your own experience and why.

   Draft Two: Working with your first draft and another *Literacies* essay that treats "experts" and "subjects," develop a theory of how power works in unequal relationships. In each of the relationships you analyze, how does the distribution of power affect each party's feelings about that relationship?

2. *Draft One:* Of the many ways to interpret Dr. Walsh's story, one might be that she is a weak or even a bad doctor, while another might focus on cultural expectations about doctors that discourage Dr. Walsh from making effective choices. Use Brody's distinction between personal failure, on the one hand, and disabling cultural expectations, on the other, to write about a time when you tried hard to do something but couldn't. Which of Brody's ideas are useful for analyzing your own experience of "failure"?

   Draft Two: Baldwin, Gilmore, and Kozol also tell stories of apparent failure in the face of powerful cultural forces. How do Brody's and your own insights help you interpret the cultural meaning of failure in one or more of these texts?

BEFORE READING BARBARA CHRISTIAN

1. Discuss an activity—maybe a hobby or a field of study—that is important to you but that your family or friends have complained about. What objections have they raised about your participation in this activity? How have you answered those objections?

2. Based on your own experience or on your knowledge about other writers, what kinds of obstacles do writers tend to face as they go about their work? Discuss some ways of addressing these obstacles.

3. Read the subtitle of Christian's essay. What do you expect her essay to be about? What circumstances do you do your own work "in the midst of," and how do these circumstances affect what you accomplish?

BARBARA CHRISTIAN

BLACK FEMINIST PROCESS:
IN THE MIDST OF . . .

I am sprawling at the low table I work at, surrounded by books and plants, a pad and pencil in front of me. Brow knit, sometimes muttering, sometimes reading or staring out the window, I am engrossed. My 10-year-old daughter touches me.

"Come play a game," she implores.

"I'm working," ending the discussion, I think. Her skeptical face bends down.

"You're not teaching," she retorts, "You're just reading a story."

I see an image from Foucault's "Fantasia of the Library," at the center of which is a European male reader, surrounded by books, which comment on books, his posture rapt. Not too long ago I'd read Marcelle Thiebaux's commentary on Foucault's "Fantasia," in which she proposed replacing the male reader with a woman reader. She reminds us that her reader would occupy a different space; her reading would be seen as time away from her main work. Interruptions would be normal and she would likely be reinterpreting the book she is reading without even being aware of it, reinventing herself in the midst of patriarchal discourse, as to who she is supposed to be.

From *Black Feminist Criticism: Perspectives on Black Women Writers* (1985).

Quite true, I think, but most of my black sisters *and* brothers would not even have gotten in the library, or if some of them did, like the parlour maid in *Jane Eyre*, they'd be dusting the books. *Their* libraries in Alexandria and elsewhere had been burnt long ago in the wake of conquest and slavery.

Not wishing to prolong the discussion by reminding my daughter that 100 years ago, I would not even have been conceived of as a reader, might in fact have been killed for trying, I notice the Nancy Drew book she has in her hand, her finger still tucked in her place. She's probably solved the mystery already.

"Why are you reading?" she presses.

I know the words that come to my mind—"If I don't save my own life, who will?"—are triggered by the Walker essay I'd been reading and the book under her arm. I dodge her question.

"That would involve a long discussion. I'm working."

But her comment has set my mind on a different track. She knows it, sees the shift, and pulls out her now-constant refrain.

"I'm old enough to know." As indeed she is.

I remember as a young girl in the Caribbean gobbling up Nancy Drew books, involved in the adventures of this intrepid white teenage girl, who solved mysteries, risked danger, was central to her world. I know their pull for a young girl—the need to see oneself as engaging the dangerous world in a fiction protective enough to imagine it, the need to figure out the world, the need to win. And I remember the privileges of Nancy's world—pretty, intelligent, well taken care of, white, American, she had winning allies. What girl actually lives in that universe? What black girl protagonist competed with her? My daughter has read about Harriet Tubman, Mary McLeod Bethune; she has even met Rosa Parks. Historical personages, they are still too awesome for her.

Alice Walker notes in her essay that when Toni Morrison was asked why she wrote the books she did, she replied because she wanted to read them. And Marcelle Thiebaux makes the same comment in the *lit crit* language of our day: "The only possible library for a woman is one invented by herself, writing herself or her own discourse into it."

My daughter is waiting for an answer. If I'd been reading a how-to manual, a history book, or even a cookbook, she'd have accepted the answer about work.

Leaving momentous questions aside, I respond: "I enjoy it."

Abandoned for the moment by her friends, having solved the Nancy

Drew mystery, she sees a long boring afternoon ahead. She asks one of her whoppers:

"What good does it do?" Knowing that the reading will turn into writing, she looks at the low table, books, pen, and pencil: "What *are* you doing?"

A good question, I think. But she is not finished. Knowing she's got me in the grip of a conversation, she rallies:

"Why is it that you write mostly about black women's books? You read lots of other books. Is it because you like what they say best?"

Art is not flattery, I think, trying to remember if I'd read that in the Walker essay.

What my daughter was asking is not a new question. It's one I often ask myself. What is a literary critic, a black woman critic, a black feminist literary critic, a black feminist social literary critic? The adjectives mount up, defining, qualifying, the activity. How does one distinguish them? The need to articulate a theory, to categorize the activities is a good part of the activity itself to the point where I wonder how we ever get around to doing anything else. What do these categories tell anyone about my method? Do I do formalist criticism, operative or expressive criticism, mimetic or structuralist criticism (to use the categories I'd noted in a paper by a feminist colleague of mine)? I'm irked, weighed down by Foucault's library as tiers of books written on epistemology, ontology, and technique peer down at me. Can one theorize effectively about an evolving process? Are the labels informative or primarily a way of nipping the question in the bud? What are the philosophical assumptions behind my praxis? I think how the articulation of a theory is a gathering place, sometimes a point of rest as the process rushes on, insisting that you follow. I can see myself trying to explain those tiers of books to my daughter as her little foot taps the floor.

"Well, first of all," I say, having decided to be serious, "I'm a reader," stressing my activeness, as I try to turn her comment "You're just reading" on its head. As I state that simple fact, I think of the many analyses of the critic's role that bypass reading and move immediately to the critic's role as performer, as writer. I continue, "Reading is itself an involved activity. It's a response to some person's thoughts, and language, even possibly their heart."

When I read something that engages me, my reaction is visceral: I sweat, get excited, exalted or irritated, scribble on the edges of the paper, talk aloud to the unseen writer or to myself. Like the Ancient Mariner, I waylay every person in my path, "Have you read this? What about this, this, or this?" This reaction is no news to my daughter. She and her friends get that way about Michael Jackson, TV shows, stickers, possibly even Judy Blume. But that response, of course, is not so much the accepted critical mode, despite Barthes's *plaisir*. It's too suspect, too subjective, not grounded in reality.

Still, when I read much literary criticism today, I wonder if the critic has read the book, since so often the text is but an occasion for espousing his or her philosophical point of view—revolutionary black, feminist, or socialist program. The least we owe the writer, I think, is an acknowledgment of her labor. After all, writing is intentional, is at bottom, work.

I pause, trying to be as clear as possible to Najuma in my description of what I am doing.

"Right now," I say, "I'm listening to the voice, the many voices created by Alice Walker in this book and looking at the way she's using words to make these voices seem alive, so you believe them." (Aha, I think, formalist criticism, expressive criticism, operative criticism.) My daughter does not know these referents.

"Why," she inquires, "so you can write something?" She is now focused on the pencil and pad, which may take my attention away from her.

I try again, this time using a comparison. "Everybody wants to be understood by somebody. If you want somebody to know you, who you are, what you think and feel, you've got to say something. But if nobody indicates they heard you, then it's almost as if you never said anything at all. African people are wise when they say 'speech is knowledge.' "

My last sentence tells me my teaching instinct has been aroused. I'm now intent on her understanding of this point, the Nancy Drew book still in my mind.

"If black women don't say who they are, other people will and say it badly for them," I say, as I remember Audre Lorde's poem about the deadly consequences of silence. "Silence is hardly golden," I continue. "If other black women don't answer back, who will? When we speak and answer back we validate our experiences. We say we *are* important, if only to ourselves." Too hard for her, I think, but she's followed me.

"Like when you and your friends talk on the phone about how politicians don't understand what it means to be a mother?" she quips. "Then, why don't you just call Alice Walker on the phone and tell her what you think about her book?"

She has seen Alice. She's flesh and blood—a pretty brown-skinned woman with a soft voice. But I'm not finished.

"I am a black woman, which means that when I read I have a particular stance. Because it's clear to me that black people, black women, women, poor people, despite our marvelous resilience, are often prevented from being all they can be, I am also a black feminist critic."

I think of literary criticism as a head detaching itself from the rest of a body, claiming subjectivity only in one part of the brain. "Everybody has a point of view about life and about the world, whether they admit it or not," I continue.

"Then," she ventures, "why do you have all these other books around you?" (questioning my definite point of view). "And why can't you just tell Alice Walker what you think?"

While she's talking, she notices, on the low table, Paule Marshall's essay "Poets in the Kitchen." Seeing that our discussion is getting her nowhere, she changes the subject.

"Isn't it funny," she says, "that whenever your friends come over, whether you're cooking or not, you all end up in the kitchen?"

"That's what Paule is talking about." I shift back to our original conversation. "That's why I need all these other books. She's telling us how she learned about language and storytelling from her mother and her mother's friends talking in the kitchen" (rather than just in Foucault's library or Rochester's drawing room, I think).

"Are your friends poets too?" she smiles, amused by the thought. "They're in the kitchen because they're used to it," says Najuma as her face shows that she's begun thinking about the delights of food.

Yes, I think, but it's also because communities revolve around food and warmth, at least until they generate enough surplus to have women or blacks or some other group do it for them and they can retire to the library. (Ah, Marxist criticism?)

"That's true, Najuma, sometimes, we are forced to be there. But even then, human beings often make an opportunity out of a constraint. If we don't recognize what we're doing, the value of what we are doing . . . ? That's part of what a writer does. And as a critic (I now use the ponderous word), I call attention to the form, show how it comes out of a history, a tradition, how the writer uses it. If we and others don't understand Paule's form, that it *is* a form, we can't even hear what she's saying or how meaningful it is."

My being from the Caribbean helps me to recognize that people invent their own forms. I think of Ellison's discussion of the mask Afro-

Americans use, of Elaine Showalter's analysis of the double-voiced discourse of women. But I've lost her—my daughter's face puckers. Wondering if interrupting me has been worth it, she looks out the window.

Of course, I think, following my own train of thought, it's even more complicated than that. For in illuminating her kitchen poets, Paule is also calling attention to the constraints imposed on them. In denying her expression as art, those who control the society can continue their cultural hegemony. What's published or seen as central has so much to do with the cultural reproduction of the powerful.

But Najuma has interrupted my thoughts. Intently she asks: "Why do you write it down, why not just tell Alice about her book?" Writing, she knows, is even more private than reading, which separates her from me and has many times landed her in bed before she wanted to go.

I smile. Barthes's comment "Writing is precisely that which exceeds speech" comes to mind. I pause. "Well," I say, again searching for a clear way out. "Writing is another way of ordering your thoughts. You write things differently from the way you say them, if only because you can look back at what you write, at what other people have written, and can look forward to what you may write. A blank piece of paper is an invitation to find out what you think, know, feel, to consciously make connection."

Medium criticism, I think. Is she going to ask about tape recorders or TV shows? No, I've lost her. But if she had asked, I'd remind her that tape recordings are transcribed and edited; even TV shows, as instant as they seem, are based on scripts.

Seeing her perplexity, I try again. "Sometimes," I say, "I haven't the slightest idea what I'm thinking. There's so much rushing through my mind. Don't you feel that way sometimes?" I ask as I look at her stare out the window. "Writing helps to form that chaos (I change the word), all that energy."

I can see she's heard me.

"But what good is it besides knowing a little better what you are thinking. Who cares?"

"Hmm," I mutter, "if you don't care, who will?" But I refrain from this flippant comment and decide to take a leap. "Najuma, do you know why you worry about your kinky hair? Why there are so many poor people in this rich country? Why your friends sometimes tease you about reading too much?"

She pauses, then surprises me: "For the same reason, my school wasn't sure that a jazz class, instead of classical music, would be good music training," she says, imitating a grown-up's voice.

She does notice things; I feel triumphant: "And that has to do with ideas," I continue, "and how they affect consciousness." Does she know the meaning of that word? I use it so often; do I know what it means? "People *do* things, one of which might be writing, to help themselves and other people ask questions about who they are, who they might be, what kind of world they want to create, to remind ourselves that we do create the world." (I am now being carried away by my own rhetoric.) "I teach too, go to conferences, support organizations I believe in, am a mother," I emphasize, as I begin to worry about whether I've exalted writing too much.

But the writing point holds her: "So," she says, "writers tell people what to do?"

My mind winces. "Well, not so much as they ask questions, try to express reality as they see it, feel it, push against what exists, imagine possibilities, see things that might not yet exist," I say, as I think of Wilson Harris's discourse on vision as a historical dimension.

"Anyway," she says, clearly wanting to end this too serious conversation, "I know what a critic is, because I saw it in the newspaper. You say what's good and what's bad," she says in triumph, knowing that I will finally agree with her.

"Literature is not a horse race," I mutter, as I remember Doris Lessing's response to such a statement. Foucault's library looms again.

Calmly I state: "First you've got to know what it *is* you're reading. What the writer, the person speaking, is doing, which may be unfamiliar since no two of us are, fortunately, alike. Remember how you told me that I didn't understand your way of dressing, that it had a way of its own?" (I see her combining colors I wouldn't even dream of, but when I calm down, they certainly do make their own statement.)

"Then, how do you judge what's good or bad," she says, "since everybody has their own way?"

From the past, I hear R. P. Blackmur's words, "the critic will impose the excellence of something he understands on something he doesn't understand." All those texts from Plato and Aristotle through Northrop Frye, the rationalist critics, the structuralists begin to fall on me. I relax by breathing deeply.

"You play the piano," I remind her. "Sometimes, something you're learning doesn't sound quite right at first, until you begin to see the way it's put together, how it works, what it's trying to do. Then you hear it, something new perhaps, something you just didn't know about before. It sounds beautiful. Writing is like that too. It's got its own workings. At least you need to understand the workings before you can say whether it's done well, which is not the same, I think, as whether you like it or not." I think of the Latin American writers whose work I find beautiful but whose tradition I know little about.

"There's no absolute way to tell what's good or bad," I continue, wondering how I got into this conversation. "I try to hear a writer's voice, or more precisely the one she's gotten on the page in comparison to the one she might have in her head. Then I try to situate that in a tradition that has evolved some approximate ways of how that gets written down best." My thoughts go faster than my speech. I think the best writers are often the ones that break the tradition to continue it. Baraka's comment on art, "hunting is not those heads on the wall," though male, is true.

"In any case," I emphasize, as she retreats to the kitchen, this conversation having become too heavy for her, "every critic knows one thing—writing is a complex activity. That's one of the reasons, I suppose, why we too must write." By now, I'm talking to myself. "And oh, how we write, as we invent our own vocabularies of mystification. Sometimes, things ought to be switched around and writers should get a chance to judge us."

Munching an apple, Najuma passes through the room, sweetly ending the conversation: "It sounds to me like too much work. Why don't you get involved with the airlines, so we can travel free." For her, traveling is the most pleasurable activity humankind has invented. "Or if that's too much, try gardening," she continues, compromising on my fetish for plants. "At least you'd look like you're having fun," she concludes as she turns to her collection of airline flyers.

"But I do have fun doing this," I respond, though, humbled again by the terror of the blank page in front of me, it's a mystery to me why.

ACTIVE READING

1. Trace some of Christian's definitions of reading and writing. How do these definitions change at different stages in her essay? How do your own ideas about reading and writing influence the way you respond to her various definitions?

2. Throughout this essay, Christian alternates between recounting her conversation with Najuma and commenting on this conversation. How

does her tone change as she shifts between her "writing voice" and her "speaking voice"? How do these different styles of writing influence your interpretation of her arguments?

3. Christian makes a point of telling Najuma that she is not simply an academic, but a mother, too. Which passages in her essay help you understand why the connection between these two activities is important to Christian?

READING IN NEW CONTEXTS

1. Christian frequently refers to other writers and other texts. How does her use of quotation fit into her theories about reading and writing as social activities? Look at a *Literacies* essay whose writer seems to use quotation in a very different way (you might try Clifford, Kozol, or Shanley). Keeping in mind the differences between Christian's and the other writer's practices, what can you say about any similarities you find?

2. Wondering where her own work fits into the field of literary criticism, Christian asks herself, "Are the labels informative or primarily a way of nipping the question in the bud?" (145). After you compose your own answers to the question Christian raises, examine what Black Elk and Scheper-Hughes do with labels in their texts. In these texts, what questions might be in danger of being "nipped in the bud"? How do these writers confront that danger?

3. What connections do you see between Christian's gender and her professional identity? From what you can tell, is the relationship more obvious in Christian's case than it is in Fienup-Riordan's or Seidler's? Explain how you think that relationship contributes to each writer's work.

DRAFT ONE / DRAFT TWO

1. *Draft One:* Look again at your response to Before Reading #3. How does your own way of thinking about and dealing with interruption relate to Christian's strategies? What does this tell you about the kinds of work that each of you does?

Draft Two: Working with Christian and another writer (such as Fienup-Riordan, Rosaldo, or de Saint Victor) whose thoughts are influenced by the distractions he or she encounters, speculate about some ways in which your work for this class could be enriched, not just interrupted, by the people and events around you. What specific connections can you make between your current reading and the environment within which you read?

2. *Draft One:* Christian thinks to herself that "the best writers are often the ones that break the tradition to continue it" (150). Which traditions of literary scholarship might Christian be breaking in her essay? What traditions might she be trying to preserve by doing so? What kinds of information would you need in order to give complete answers to these questions?

Draft Two: Look at a pair of essays by a more traditional and a less traditional writer (try Atwood and Anzaldúa or Gilmore and Rosaldo). What traditions seem to be important to the two writers you study? How does the second writer "break the tradition to continue it"? What effects do these tradition-breaking strategies have on your reading of his or her text?

BEFORE READING JAMES CLIFFORD

1. What do tourists and the people who live and work in tourist areas each receive from the experience of tourism, and what do they give in return?

2. Clifford is an ethnographer, an anthropologist who writes descriptions of other cultures. In this essay, he is also an American tourist taking a vacation in another country. How do you expect his different roles to influence the experience of travel he describes here?

3. Take a few minutes to look over Clifford's unusual arrangement of sentences and paragraphs. What patterns do you see? Speculate about the kinds of work those patterns will require of you as a reader.

4. Look up the Chiapas region of Mexico at the library, and find out what has been happening there in the 1990s, since Clifford wrote his essay. You might begin your search with the index to a major newspaper, such as the *New York Times*.

JAMES CLIFFORD

INCIDENTS OF TOURISM IN CHIAPAS & YUCATAN

Notes in memory of Michel Leiris, 1901–1990

Arrival.

Leaving Mexico City, our plane flies close to volcanoes. Then, under a low sky in the streets of San Cristóbal de las Casas. Scattered smiles. What there is to see.

[falling on; as, an *incident* ray]

Dusk, wandering around. Impressions of San Cristóbal. Streets full of accelerating cars close to narrow sidewalks. Anxiety. Constantly watching out for a tired, three-year-old. Ben's disoriented, dragged through a noisy labyrinth. Wants to run. But where?

City coming to life. People moving in all directions.

Clatter of bells from a church somewhere in the dark. People's indifference to us, a relief. Only the other tourists, looking away, seem displeased by our presence, as we are by theirs.

Originally published in *Sulfur* (Fall 1991).

155

Glances into bright doorways, color coded rooms. Each a side altar, small collection, museum, Cornell box, universe, store.

Beyond the tourist experience: Explorer? Writer? Pilgrim? Scientist? Aesthete? Ecologist? Initiate? Poet? Politico? All the established routes/roots.

Available.

•

Collection.

Tourist "herds" in buses. Safe in their literal bubble.
Taking pictures, buying postcards.
We think we can speak (English) freely without being understood.
Safety of food consumed, streets walked on, sheets slept in.
The somehow inspiring colors of walls and houses.
Pleasures of ignorance. The nameless plants. Displeased by Muzak.
Invisible birds crying in the palms at the Zócalo.
Rolling drums and a cacophonous school band.

•

Incident.

Since Ben is in no shape for a restaurant, we decide to have dinner served in our hotel room. It's old fashioned and chilly, but with a fireplace that we were told could be used. Dinner beside a roaring blaze! However Judith's a little embarrassed to ask someone to lay the fire since today the weather in San Cristóbal turned warm. I prevail. We're tourists. So what if we want a fire on a warm night? The cozy atmosphere will be nice.

Two telephone calls. Finally a man appears with a half dozen sticks and a gas can. Glum, none of the usual banter. He douses the wood, throws on a match, watches a minute and leaves. The fire flares, fades. (We've paid 3,000 pesos—$1.25.) I look everywhere for paper to revive the flames, but none is to be found (the hotel staff are endlessly tidying up). Should we complain? (But for $1.25?) And we probably shouldn't have asked anyway. Still, the room *is* chilly. (A fire wouldn't have helped much.) And how could he bring just six sticks? (Is wood so hard to come by here?) Our cozy fire's only contribution to the room's atmosphere is a strong odor of gas.

Outside, crowds of people stroll in the warm evening. We're famished. More delays. Dinner comes at last, and it's delicious. The wine tastes good. We go to sleep.

•

Through a Doorway.

Photographs strictly forbidden, by order of the Indian municipal government.

"The San Loranzo [Zinacantán] church is remarkable mainly for its saints, many of whom wear Zinacanteco robes. It also has a wooden cross, twenty feet tall, swathed in blue cloth and decked with streamers like the ones on the Indians' hats. When we come out, copal smoke is billowing from the chapel door and the men who were drinking have gone inside. Three musicians on a bench to the right of the altar are playing a harp, a violin, and a guitar. The instruments, like the alcohol, are homemade; they produce a reedy, off-key dirge of fathomless sadness. Three other men in full regalia dance slowly, swaying to the maudlin songs. Hats and bottles are on the table, and behind those you see a dark Christ wreathed in arum lilies, chrysanthemums, and clouds of incense."

— RONALD WRIGHT, *Time among the Maya: Travels in Belize, Guatemala, and Mexico,* 1989

When we visit the church of San Lorenzo, a basketball tournament is in progress outside. Bright uniforms and a squawking loudspeaker.

•

Apprentice traveller.

For Ben, every day is a series of arbitrary moves. He's jerked from place to place, a lot of different faces, things, sounds. He works to invent routes and routines. Visits to a favorite place atop the Zócalo bandstand, retreats to the hotel room and a small collection of toys.

Ben shouts across the street to a grim looking soldier (helmet, automatic rifle) who's guarding a bank. White gloved fingers on the gun barrel ripple. A grin spreads beneath the reflecting sunglasses.

Collecting pats on the head.

A local boy plays with cheap plastic cars, a cowboy, an Indian. Ben contributes his matchbox rocketmobile. Things are set up, knocked down. A trade negotiated.

•

Incident.

Ben and I explore the hotel's long halls. On the third floor, a passage leads up to the roof. Suddenly the whole city of San Cristóbal is visible. A full 360° ringed by mountains. Immense, variegated dome of sky—an area of intense blue here, rain laden clouds there. Light filtering in at the edges. Exhilarating. We count all the churches.

Later, I remember what Mary Pratt, writing on the history of travel literature, calls the "monarch of all I survey scene." From a hilltop, promontory, balcony . . . the "whole" is grasped, usually as a natural (unpopulated) landscape. On our hotel roof, everything that made us feel strangers down in the streets (language, looks, gestures, fear of being cheated, of falling ill, of seeming stupid) is gone. Replaced by an expanded range of sight, a feeling of centrality.

Isn't some moment of power, of emptying/opening, part of any "good trip"?

•

We fly to Yucatan.

•

Incident.

Obligatory contretemps with *taxista* at Cancún Airport. We bargain him down to the going rate. Hey, no hard feelings. In the course of a pleasant conversation it emerges that our driver is a school teacher. Salary hasn't gone up in ten years. *No importa.* Our job is to make you feel welcome. His wife sells Fuller Brush products. He drives a dilapidated cab. The governments of Latin America are all corrupt, he says, with plenty of help from the USA. What counts is to be honest, to sleep well at night. My wife always has to wake me; I sleep too well.

Forty minutes down the coast to our resort, La Posada del Capitán Lafitte. (Its billboard features a pirate with eye patch.) At the end of a long bumpy driveway, stucco cabins and a perfect white beach.

•

Resort.

Idyllic community. No money openly changes hands. "Sign, Sign, Sign. Pay, Pay, Pay!" laughs the young man taking us to our *cabaña*. The poolside bar seems to be always open. Empty pockets. Bare feet. We relax. Every morning a couple of guys sweep the sand, clearing the debris thrown up by the waves.

Perfect white beach.

First night: a "floor show." The emcee, a waiter with pretty good English, asks us to be patient, to wait just "five Mexican minutes!" The manager's wife who operates the gift shop and a couple of waiters dance in costume, *típico*, beer bottles balanced on heads. (They seem to be having fun.) Music is provided by a trio of guitarists. Then a *piñada* for the kids, candy flying, balloons popping. Ben wild with excitement. Finally, an elimination broom dance. Young and old. Family ambiance. We drop our skepticism (It's a tourist trap, phoney, too windy, drinks expensive . . .) and begin to feel at home.

By breakfast the next day everybody seems to know "Ben."

Unlike the international tourist scene at San Cristóbal, every guest at the Posada Capitán Lafitte speaks North American English. We have all booked our *cabañas* through the same 800 number in Colorado. No averted looks. We are here to have fun with people just like us.

•

Virtuous tourists.

Adjoining the Posada Lafitte, another ideal community—"Kai Luum." There the guests rough it, in tents along the beach (covered by thatch canopies). Eco-tourism. Meals taken together in a big tent, sand floor. "Save the tortugas." "Honor system" bar. Diving shop. Adult castaways in athletic communion with nature. No kids under 16.

We visit Kai Luum for Thanksgiving dinner. (Children OK this once.) Turkey with all the trimmings. Lantern lit and festive. The waiters are silent, anonymous. At Kai Luum the "staff" are young North American men and women who stop for a moment at our table to chat. But the lack of any contact, even brief, with the non-White people working here feels oppressive . . . after the very friendly scene at Lafitte.

The Posada Capitán Lafitte and Kai Luum were founded together and still share some facilities. But the former is owned and managed by Mexicans, the latter by North Americans. The waiters, cleaners, beach sweepers, at both places are largely (Yucatec) Mayans.

How many different homes away from home are there in the tourist universe? "Authentic" San Cristóbal; the hotel scene at Cancún ("Miami Beach gone wild," someone called it). Kai Luum, Lafitte . . . Are some of these places less exploitative than others? Could we choose to be good tourists? Staying at the smaller establishments? Locally owned? (But what hierarchies of class, race, or ethnicity are hidden by the word "local"?) Worth a try perhaps.

With help from the Colorado 800 number (serving both Lafitte and Kai Luum) we have selected the "good" community, the one best suited to our liberal, family values. But our choice was based on a short paragraph in the guide book. And without Ben we would probably have picked Kai Luum!

•

Voice.

"That the native does not like the tourist is not hard to explain. . . . Every native would like to find a way out, every native would like a rest, every native would like a tour. But some natives—most natives in the world— cannot go anywhere. They are too poor. They are too poor to go anywhere. They are too poor to escape the reality of their lives; and they are too poor to live properly in the place where they live, which is the very place you, the tourist, want to go—so when the natives see you, the tourist, they envy you, they envy your ability to leave your own banality and boredom, they envy your ability to turn their own banality and boredom into a source of pleasure for yourself."

—JAMAICA KINCAID,
A Small Place, 1988

•

Ruin.

In travel guides and publicity, "Maya" is almost always attached to the adjective "ancient." Ancientmaya.

"The ground was entirely new; there were no guide-books or guides; the whole was a virgin soil. We could not see yards before us, and never knew what we would stumble upon next. At one time we stopped to cut away branches and vines which concealed the face of a monument, and then to dig around and bring to light a fragment, a sculptured corner of which protruded from the earth. I leaned over with breathless anxiety while the Indians worked, and an eye, an ear, a foot, or a hand was disentombed; and when a machete rang against the chiselled stone, I pushed the Indians away, and cleared out the loose earth with my hands."
— JOHN L. STEPHENS, *Incidents of Travel in Central America:*
Chiapas and Yucatan, 1841

Cobá. Fabulous stone stairs rising up through trees, strewn with the small, bright-colored bodies of tourists. Tallest pyramid in Yucatan. Halfway up, a cigarette butt squashed against old rock. Then a view of *la selva,* distant lakes, electricity pylons, some mysterious bumps in the surrounding green—structures of a Mayan city.

Twelve stories up, and still no overview. Forest. At the more famous ruins (Tulum, Chichen Itza, Palenque) you get a "map" at ground level. Here, only a few patches of green have been scraped off. No way to know where you are in the large city. No way at Cobá to step back, or up. In a proper ruin you magically experience the space of another civilization and time. You expand to fill the blanks left by (produced by) excavation.

Here, we find indifferent forest. Faceless.

•

The desire.

To excavate and complete. Establish names. Redeem the lost city.

Watch out for kids! Some nasty speed bumps on the straight road to Cobá almost bring us to a halt in a couple of Indian settlements.

"No doubt there were men living in Yucatan and its adjacent areas before the Mayan occupation of that space. They took sustenance from the land and their labors and when the Mayan civilization came they contributed their labor and allegiance to it and when the Mayan civilization was broken they continued to live there, as indeed they do now, centuries later. But it was the Mayan civilization that occupied that space, and so effectively that the mark of the occupation has outlasted the civilization. The present inhabitants hardly occupy it, and are largely indifferent to its former occupation. But there are others who come there to locate and study the old sites, to clear away the vegetation and debris from them, and to rename those whose old names have been lost. The old occupation still asserts itself even though the force of its assertion is now in contrast to the surrounding desolation."

—WILLIAM BRONK, *The New World*, 1974

Atop the smallest excavated pyramid at Cobá, a stone house. Ben takes possession, asks us in, kicks us out.

According to the guide book, Cobá is a preferred place for "independent travellers," hardy souls looking for real exploration. There's a luxury hotel nearby, belonging to a Club Med chain of "Archaeological Villas." Full library (ask concierge for key). Also a sophisticated gift shop selling artistic reproductions of Maya glyphs, "quality" Indian crafts. Gourmet restaurant.

"I leaned over with breathless anxiety while the Indians worked, and an eye, an ear, a foot, or a hand was disentombed. . . ."

•

Sophisticated travellers.

". . . when a machete rang against the chiselled stone, I pushed the Indians away, and cleared out the loose earth with my hands."

Judith (who studies Mayan linguistics) talks in Spanish with Luis, a waiter at the Posada Capitán Lafitte. A Mayan, he was emcee at the evening "floor show." They discuss Yucatec. Judith recognizes words and sounds that are reminiscent of Tzotzil (the language she works on in San Cristóbal). Luis wants his children to speak Yucatec, but his wife is not a Mayan. How? Visits to grandparents and other kin? Or . . . ?

The waiters are all young men, living away from their families (5 days a month home leave). They have Mexican first names (Luis, Manuel, Ricardo . . .) and Mayan last names. At Lafitte they study English with an elderly "regular" (guest/employee) from the States. Pay is low, compared with the earnings of a full-time taxi driver. But room and board are provided. With English, there's a prospect of mobility to a higher paid job. Maybe in Cancún.

The young men are travelers—part of the same transnational economy that made it possible for us to get from New York to highland Chiapas in less than 24 hours, that built the straight road to Cobá, that ensured our pleasant sojourn on this bit of pure coast. Different travelers—intersecting routes/roots—we spend some amiable time together. But the Mayans living at the Posada del Capitán Lafitte are working. We're on holiday. They go home for vacation. We go abroad. Everyone dresses casually. But their flowered shirts are uniforms.

The Mayans in the dining room have first hand knowledge of our language and culture. We know little of theirs.

Judith's "expertise" begins to emerge in conversations with our fellow guests. They're surprised to hear that the waiters and cooks are Indians speaking Yucatec to one another. (Yet it sounds very different from Spanish.) And they're fascinated to learn there are thirty living Mayan languages with millions of speakers.

We begin to feel different, with superior knowledge (morality?). Our fellow guests are just "tourists." (But some have been in the area much longer and more often than we have . . .) Isn't this sense of a special experience, sensibility, or knowledge an essential part of any good trip? The sophisticated traveller's "other" is the tourist.

And the distinction is a routine production.

•

Incident.

We hover in unclenched fetal positions over throngs of fish. Every imaginable color. No language for this but cliché. Voyeurs gazing. They notice us, hide sideways in the fire-coral. Sounds of heavy breathing. And a kind of participation. As we float the fish slide off, according to the same wave. Enormous, blatant strangers. (During a shower, we might have taken shelter together, without words.)

•

Incident.

Airplane travel: heavily disciplined and anesthetized. Little individuality or interaction. Why are these people, this collection, traveling north from Mexico? Hard to read who's who. Some dress up, others down (like me) for a flight. Signs of class? The poorest aren't here. At least that's obvious. "We" cross borders with travel agents, "they" use *coyotes.*

The tourist, political refugee, anthropologist, picture bride, journalist, grandchild, missionary, technician, *opère,* diplomat, poet, scholar, soldier of fortune, physician, athlete, cook, student, sales rep . . . each in a numbered seat.

And hitting the runway, our brakes take hold. The entire molded plastic environment vibrates uncontrollably.

Lucid moment of fear, of homecoming.

ACTIVE READING

1. What objects and incidents catch Clifford's attention as an anthropologist? Which catch his attention as a tourist? How do you distinguish between the two roles?

2. What does Clifford mean by an ideal or idyllic community? What does he mean by an authentic community? Discuss several details or incidents that suggest important similarities or differences between the two types of community.

3. Find a section where Clifford reports on a conversation without using quotation marks. How does he indicate the difference between his own voice and the voice of the other speaker, or the difference between his

voice or thoughts during the conversation and his later reflections? How does he show his attitude in direct and indirect ways?

READING IN NEW CONTEXTS

1. Tell about a time when you saw a meeting of two cultures that gave you a feeling of ambivalence. Compare the reasons for your ambivalence with some of the reasons for Clifford's mixed feelings in this essay.

2. Choose two or three of the terms Clifford uses toward the end of his essay, such as "distinction," "routine production," "uniforms," "discipline," or others that interest you. Use these terms to help explain some of the events in the early and middle parts of the essay.

3. Apply your discussion of ideal and authentic communities, from Active Reading #2, to another *Literacies* text, such as the short story by Alice Walker. Reconsider Clifford's ideas and experiences with the help of what you find there.

4. Compare Clifford's account of several tourist experiences, including the rooftop panorama of San Cristóbal, to the understanding about perception you find in another *Literacies* reading, such as Scholes, Barnlund, or Rosaldo.

DRAFT ONE / DRAFT TWO

1. *Draft One:* Tell a story from your own experience that helps explain how a specialist and a nonspecialist look at the same event. What can you say about expertise and perception, based on that story and on the ideas and events of Clifford's essay?

   Draft Two: Develop Draft One further with materials from a *Literacies* reading that was not written by an anthropologist, such as Scholes, Brody, or Durham. What happens to the ideas you have generated about perception and expertise when you relate them to another academic discipline or area of experience?

2. *Draft One:* Assemble both some anecdotes from your experience and some quotations from several readings on a topic of importance to you.

Over several days, compose sentences and paragraphs to serve as relating and organizing material for the collection of quotations and anecdotes. Continue working on this project until you have a full draft, written, if you wish, in an experimental form.

Draft Two: By yourself or with the advice of classmates, return to your draft and challenge yourself to say more about different parts of it. Accomplish this by rereading and revising, but also assemble a few more anecdotes and quotations to include in the essay. Work these materials into a new draft. In a postscript (a P.S.) to your essay, describe how this composing process differs from the way you usually write. What do you make of the difference in the process and in the results?

BEFORE READING JIMMIE DURHAM

1. How do you react when something you're reading contains words or phrases in an unfamiliar language? How do you figure out what these words might mean? Why do you think an author might choose to write in more than one language?

2. When writing in the first person, how do you decide when to use "I" and when to use "we"? How do you respond to these pronouns in texts you are reading? What are the implications of using one word rather than the other?

3. List a few commemorative holidays (for example, Martin Luther King Jr. Day) or historical events that have a personal significance for you. Why are these days or events important to you? What beliefs or values do you associate with them?

4. Who do you think "Those Dead Guys for a Hundred Years" might be? What expectations about the tones, topics, and purposes of Durham's essay does this title raise for you? Why does it raise these expectations?

JIMMIE DURHAM

THOSE DEAD GUYS
FOR A HUNDRED YEARS

I want you to hear these words. Now I am speaking to you about our lives.

That is the way we begin speeches in Cherokee, and then we say what we would like to see happen, with a simple statement that begins with "I want," as in "I want us to go to Washington and tell them just what's going on down here." The way white people exhort in their speeches—such as "we should . . ." or "we must . . ."—sounds to us not only arrogant but devious. Is this guy trying to hide from us his own thoughts? Then why speak? (They often do speak only for the purpose of hiding their thoughts.)

I want us to have an Eloheh Ga ghusdunh di at Dhotsua's old Ghadjiya in Goingsnake District, because it is now 1984, exactly one hundred years since the Allotment Act when our first new century of trouble began, and also when Dhotsua started the Nighthawk and told us that the U.S. government had no power to allot Cherokee land. "We follow the Bright Path of the One Who Allots each plant and animal and Cherokee and whites to their proper places."

Dhotsua died fighting. Before him, before 1884, hundreds of brave Otashtys and Beloved Women died fighting. They walked a straight path

From *I Tell You Now,* edited by Brian Swann and Arnold Krupat (1987).

and they won our lives for us and I have got to tell you that when I ride this New York subway I practically hate them. How the hell did they do it? Could they always find the money for the Con Edison bill or did they eat in the dark?

Sequoyah invented writing, marched on Washington, became the Uku of Arkansas and Texas, and then split for Mexico to make a treaty with Santana. "He was never known to make a foolish move."

But I did, and my brother did, and Larry Red Shirt sure did.

Now here is what happened that makes me call for the combined fires of the Council of Everything, and why I also ask my uncles to prepare for me an Ado dhlunh hi so di so that I can change myself: in 1984 I became forty-four years old, which is the average life span for an Indian man.

Is it a good thing to write about your own troubles and worries? Paul Smith, a Comanche guy with a weird history, said, "In this century the story of any Indian is a typical Indian story, no matter how different." Which means to me that in this allotted century of lives in dispersed parcels we are still the people, with a common thread.

I remember Greg Zephier with his bad heart, joking about turning forty-four and how we all laughed. But last year my brother died a month before his forty-fifth birthday. He was working as a farm laborer in Louisiana and just conked out. It was very hard for me, because we had been on the outs with each other for a few years. Just that month I had finally figured out some things about him and figured out that I really liked him. It was in my mind to come home in November and he and I would go fishing and I would explain to him how I liked him.

He was not happy that year he died; everything was going wrong. But he liked being outside all the time, and he told me how he liked seeing a wild pig in the fields once in a while. The guy who owned the farm or one of his sons would sometimes shoot the pigs and would roast them up. My brother was not invited and they never offered him a pig to take home. I am glad of that, because I can imagine my brother trying to lift a dead pig into the trunk of his car all by himself, or trying to clean it all by himself way over there in Louisiana.

My first memory of him is also my first memory of my father. We were in a creek back home, swimming and running around. None of us had any clothes on, and my mother was also there but I think she had on her dress. My father made a little millwheel in the creek with sticks and magnolia leaves. It really worked.

When we were little we were very thin and not growing well. I had

had rickets and my brother had something or other. But we were happy, with our sisters and dozens of cousins, and our parents, aunts and uncles, great-aunts and great-uncles, and two grandparents, and yellow jackets coming up out of the ground to sting us, and diamond-back turtles. My brother and I were like twins and went everywhere with our arms around each other's shoulders. We slept in the same bed until I left home. As teenagers we often had the same girlfriends. When we were twelve or so we had to go to the doctor because we were not developing right. Some hormone trouble. We had to dissolve bitter yellow pills under our tongues, and he would spit his out, so he stayed little and thin until he was about eighteen. People would call him Midget. In the family we called him Geronimo because he was so wild and because he admired Geronimo so much. He used to tell people that he was part Apache. I would say, "Me, too!" and he would say, "No, you're not, you're part coon." Once he told some people that I was a dog, but that was only because we were hunting ducks without a license and he was protecting me.

He was my best teacher when we were little because I was selfish and did not like anybody. He was generous and liked everybody, so he would interpret their mysterious actions to me and also ran interference between me and my mother. Once I tried to kill him with a hoe and almost succeeded, which scared us both. My brother was especially kind to me the rest of the day because he knew how I must have been feeling, to almost kill my brother. So we developed some secret bird whistles to signal each other in school if we got in trouble.

In the third grade I pulled a knife on another kid and the teacher took my knife away. The next day, after a family meeting over supper, my brother went as an official delegate from our family of woodcarvers and told the teacher that I had to have my knife back. She gave me and the knife into his custody.

Just a couple of months before he died he told my mother that he had always been afraid of everything, and that was why his life was so bad.

My father is called Son in his family because he is the oldest. He had three brothers and three sisters. One sister died young and the brother next to him died next, at forty-four. My father really took it hard, and I thought I understood. Only I wanted to say, "Your sons and daughters and grandchildren are with you." When he would look at me it was like part-way he was seeing a stranger, even an intruder, and partway seeing his brother instead of me. I did not understand until my brother died. For us, history is always personal. (I remember the Trail of Tears and Sequoyah's efforts as though I had been there.) History is directly involved with our families and our generations; tied with sacred white cotton string to the sweet and intense memories of our brother or sister is the desperate and intense hope of each generation to change this history.

I knew all along that in my parents' generation, as in their parents' generation and in mine so far, the history begun in 1884 has been bad for Cherokee people. It was bad before. What period in human history could be worse than 1784–1884 for the Cherokees? In the 1680s we were first invaded by European armies and settlers, so 1684 to 1784 was pretty bad, all right. Two epidemics of smallpox in that time, each wiping out fully half of the population.

But I could not know with my heart what the hope and desperation means to each of us for our own individual lives when the history wastes and lays down in stupid sugar cane fields our own brothers.

You think that they have finally killed you, because part of your life is the plans for redemption, and you cannot do it without all those people, especially brothers, who will give you the courage of their own returning to the battle.

A great Otashty Wahya has fallen dead in the sugar cane fields. An average Cherokee guy died at the average Indian male life span.

And I am forty-four in 1984, the close of a century, so either way I think about dying. Something is wrong with my stomach and my guts—they don't work. There is something painfully wrong with my throat, behind my Adam's apple. I don't want to go to the doctor because either he will tell me things I do not want to hear or he will say, "It is nothing that cannot be fixed up for a few hundred dollars," which I don't have.

In 1972 I joined the American Indian Movement and for the next eight years gave my life to it. Then it kind of all fell apart and left me feeling bad. Then last year my brother died, and this year I turned forty-four with some "physical problems," as the doctor says.

So that is why I want my uncles to give me the ceremony of Ado dhlunh hi so di. I need a change. I need to be changed like the old men change Tsola. But those uncles, my grandmother's brothers, are all dead, and my grandfather's brothers.

My uncle Jesse was in those old days about nine feet tall. He was extremely thin and wore overalls with a blue serge coat and a John B. Stetson hat, along with whatever shoes he had—sometimes hightop black tennis shoes. He did not always wear shoes. Uncle Jesse's eyes were fierce black but he was very kind. He gave my brother and me whiskey and told us about women. His shotgun was part of his eyes. He made sweat-lodges and taught us to go hungry and to use tobacco. For ceremonies he said you could use Camels but no other cigarettes. Camels could be changed into Tsola, medicine tobacco, and when we went fishing we had to spit tobacco juice into the water and on the bait as an offering. He and Tom and Doc were crazy old guys. They were not alcoholic, I guess, but pretty drunk.

Doc had something to do with my grandfather's death, long before I was born, and people did not speak to him. They said he had been drunk. But my father took me to see him where he lived back in the woods.

This year 1984 is the last of a century that has been different from those before it, which means that next year something even weirder will probably start up. Does anyone know where we have been since the Allotment Act? Now this is how the last hundred years was different: the Allotment Act was the first time they made a legislation affecting all Indians— the first time they completely ignored the treaties and acted as though we were some subminority to be legislated. In their hateful system, then, it was only natural that the first piece of legislation should say that we had to own land privately instead of communally, that we, in other words, had to begin being someone other than ourselves. The mere concept of parcels of owned land is an insult to Cherokees. Spiritually, it is like what if we were in power and we told the whites, "This guy Jesus was a stupid, filthy no-good and you have to get rid of all those churches and Bibles, and you Jews have to obey our laws and un-obey your own laws." Talking about it is impossible; in our own language the possessive pronouns can only be used for things that you can physically give to another person, such as "my woodcarving," "my basket."

Communally, and that means physically, that piece of legislation broke us up. Once they got the idea, though, they really kept piling it on. This has been the century of legislation: 1924, 1934, 1954, etc. So we all got confused. Do we have the right to be ourselves without U.S. permission, in spite of U.S. death-and-poison spells?

Hna quu huh? It did something else, too, na? 1884 invented Indians. Before, we were strictly Cherokees or Sioux or Apaches. When they legislated that we were all "Indians" and homeless, they lumped us all together, and this century has seen us trying to pull all those fingers into a fist.

They are not as smart as they think they are. Aren't they like the bear who got beat by a mouse? We know very well that if you put death-words on someone's corn, that kernel could wind up in your own soup. They put death-words on us but we are the corn they cannot swallow.

This is the century where we began to be Indians, as well as Cherokees or whatever. I have never believed that for a minute, no matter how much I say it, or listen to other guys' speeches. My brother never once believed that we would all pull together into a fist. Larry Red Shirt didn't believe it.

Of course, we know our sorrows and we know our fears better than we know our families. The betrayals and little dishonesties are bushels of kernels of poison corn, but do we know where we are going?

Now I want to say things you may have heard me preach about before, but the words are not empty. I know your brother died last year, or your daughter. It has never been truer than now that your daughter is my daughter, my brother is your brother.

I am not trying to get you to join my movement. I want an Eloheh Ga ghusdunh di where everyone shows up. Because Charlene La Pointe just showed me that those battered Sioux women in that shelter she runs on the Rosebud Reservation are my sisters turning to face an old century, then turning to face a new one, and Donna Thunder Hawk and Charon Asetoyer and Phyllis Young just showed me something.

So now I see the lives and hearts of those uncles, and my mother and father, through my brother and his grandson. I am the uncle, I must be the uncle now.

I want us to meet at Dhotsua's Ghadjia, whatever the hell happened to it; they turned it into a stompground or burned it down, but we can find it. Hna Quu, dini yotli! Alia liga! Wait, now. I didn't get finished yet. I just remembered something else.

HOW COME HE WROTE IT LIKE THAT?

So here's what happened: I showed the piece to a woman who is a good critic and she had a lot of criticisms and I agree with all of them. So then I wrote to Brian Swann and Arnold Krupat and told them I wanted to make some revisions, but I guess I didn't really want to because this is a last-minute addition. It is almost 1986, two years after the first writing.

In the first place, didn't he notice that the title is too close to *One Hundred Years of Solitude,* and anyway, wasn't the Allotment Act passed in 1887 or something? Yes, it was, and I can offer no explanation for why we always think it was 1884. Maybe that just *seems* right to us.

Then she said she didn't like the ending at all. "You're *still* being selfish; tell us *what* Donna Thunder Hawk, Charon Asetoyer, and Phyllis

Young showed you." "Just leave out the part about preaching; it does sound preachy and we know you can write better than that."

That one guy said that the piece seemed to be written in several voices, no clear style, and that it seemed to be telescoped, as though I had written it in a hurry without taking time to develop the different ideas.

For one thing, my father died this year. But at least he died on a fishing trip with two of my nephews. So when I went back to revise it, all the stories had changed.

But here is the real thing: I absolutely do not want to communicate anything to you. Another woman I showed it to said that I always seem to hold something back, that we never get to see inside, even in my poetry.

So you're probably saying if he doesn't want to communicate, why does he write? Here is the real truth: I absolutely hate this country. Not just the government, but the culture, the group of people called Americans. The country. I hate the country. I HATE AMERICA.

Now, if you ever come to my house I'll invite you in and act pleasant, and we might even become close friends. My hatred is really not as absolute as I need it to be. Why wouldn't I hate this country? Because you are a nice person? Because it makes you feel bad for me to hate this country? You want me to be properly indignant about "injustices" and still be on the side of you and your friends who are also "trying to bring about some changes in this country"?

Don't ask a white man to walk a mile in your moccasins because he'll steal them and the mile, too. Only, just try standing in my shoes for a minute. The *fact* of the U.S. is destructive to Indian country. Every piece of progress, social or material, is more destruction to Indian country. I'm not even going to bother to develop that idea, but why don't you just think about it—until the sun rises (that means all night long)?

Here is what I don't understand: how come so many Indians don't seem to (or at least don't admit it) hate this country? Simple—we hate ourselves and each other instead, and now there we all are, out there trying to impress the white folks with our one thing or another.

I do not want to entertain you in any sense of the word. I would hate it if you all came to understand me. And I'd really hate it if I wrote something like those "sensitive and honest" novels some black writers are doing, so that any white person with a few bucks could spend a quiet evening being entertained by our sorrows, and gaining in power by "a better understanding" of our predicament, our dreams.

Where am I supposed to go, and what am I supposed to do? Some folks say, "Why don't you go back home and live with your own people and those woods you claim to love so much?" In the first place, those woods are destroyed. In the second place, I am a human in the world in this century, just like you. It doesn't matter to me that there are contradictions that are irresolvable, because they *are* irresolvable. To be an Indian writer today means being on no path, contradicting yourself at every turn, so at least I want to face that condition and not "act nice," pretending it isn't true.

Anyway, I'm not sure I like Indians all that much, either. Our intelligentsia, the writers and artists, are such a bunch of stuck-up, apolitical, money-grubbing, and flaky ripoff artists, and our political leaders are usually crooks and pretentious bastards or either somebody's puppets. Our regular folks are usually drunk or bad-mouthing their neighbors. Do you know that out on the res we have just as much child abuse and wife-beating as the rest of the country? Alienated, man; this is definitely not the old days. The people that work in offices, they're the worst: petty, banal, officious, completely distrusting and cynical, and they always have that self-righteous superior attitude and they're always incompetent. Our elders are all off being gurus to some white weirdos and talking about how some big earthquake or flood is going to solve all our problems.

I didn't give up hope; *I* been hanging in. But those other guys. Walking around, AIM-lessly. There is a whole crowd of professional Indians, now; folks who wouldn't lift a finger if they weren't paid to but come off all concerned about our condition. They know they'd be out of a job if we ever got our act together and changed the condition.

Let's see, what else. That's all I have to say right now, except like I said, hna quu, dini yotli! And I guess I'll throw in a couple of poems here. Oh yeah, I meant to say that the reason I used several voices, or styles, is that I wanted to experiment with mixing different Cherokee speech patterns as a way of showing confusion and the fight for some clarity within that confusion. I'm sorry if it didn't work out right. Anyway, here are the poems. One thing, though—I wrote the first part of this piece as though I were writing to Indian people, with one half of my brain; with the other half of my brain I was writing to the white folks, because who reads all these things? The white folks.

If we read—now here is a subtle point—if we read, we read like the white folks. We become like the white folks for the duration of the reading; that is, we read passively, to be entertained instead of to be motivated to organize to take back our land and all of our rights, no bullshit and no stopgap measures. But anyway, how many Indians are reading this? A few of my fellow writers. But maybe, a couple of college students who need to see how crazy it got. So here are the poems.

GUY FINDS TWO DEERSKINS IN MANHATTAN!

Dateline Manhattan Island, April 22, 1984
A man claiming to be an American Indian
Discovered two deerskins today, on a trash heap
At 108th and Columbus Avenue.
The guy said he had no knowledge concerning
The origin of the skins or who placed them on
The trash heap.

"The hair is thick and shaggy, like northern deer
Have, so I don't think they were brought here
From Oklahoma, Texas, or Arkansas," he said.

"Immediately upon discovery I consulted
a wise woman from Brazil, who said that I
Should try to tan them," he claimed.

The Brazilian woman, who may also be at least
Part Indian, stated that she gave no such advice.
According to her the guy is always finding
Dead animals or remnants and bringing them to
Her apartment, which is furnished with a hammock
And purple walls.
"He believes that the coyote spirit leads him to
Things like that," she said in an interview.

The guy later denied her version of the story.
"I have no idea what's going on in Manhattan," he claimed.
"But obviously many animals lived here at one time.
And there were some Puerto Rican dudes hanging out
Close by so I wasn't sure if I should take
The skins or not. It was Easter Sunday and
Those guys would think I was nuts."

In the week previous to this incident a near-by
Church burned to the ground, and on Good Friday
(April 20) Russell Means of the American Indian Movement

Spoke at a meeting on Columbus Avenue near 107th.
Means has no known connection to the
Guy who found the deerskins.

I AM ONE OF THOSE INDIANS

I am one of those Indians that fly around.
When we fall off cliffs we yell AIIEEE!
And keep zooming, never hit dust or bounce
From boulders. (Hi na?)

I am one of those Indians you may see flying
Around the Empire State Building in late Spring evenings.
But we are not steel workers or high walkers,
And our flying does not come from being bucked
From the backs of rodeo broncos.

The Bureau of Indian Affairs assigned me this special job
As part of the Termination Act of 1954.
(Their Acts come in the fours; 1884 was the
Allottment Act, 1924 the Citizenship Act, 1934 the
Re-organization Act, and in 1984 I turned 44, to
Which I reply, Nunh gi! Nunh gi! Nunh gi!
Nunh gi!)

Ancestral graves and my specific gravity were all
Terminated in '54 and I act accordingly. I act
like a flapping Redskin. We are not stars or birds
or ghosts; more like flying peeping toms. I am
One of those Indians that fly around witnessing
prophetic novas in burnt-out toasters.
(Ka, ni, hi na?)

ACTIVE READING

1. Trace Durham's references to people and events in Cherokee history.
   What ideas do you find in each reference? How do these ideas change
   throughout the essay? How do you explain these changes?

2. List as many appearances of the word "hate" as you can find in Durham's essay. Using several examples from the text, describe the different attitudes or feelings Durham expresses with this word. How do these meanings affect your response to his essay?

3. What roles do "uncles" play for Durham? How does his own relationship to the role of "uncle" change? Explain why this change might be important to the concerns he raises in the essay.

4. Read over the "How Come He Wrote It Like That?" section, and choose two or three passages that seem important to you. How do these passages change the way you look at Durham's stories about his family in the first half of the essay? What purpose do these stories serve?

5. Briefly define what you think a "speech pattern" is. In your view, which passages of Durham's essay contain "Cherokee speech patterns" (176)? What makes you think so? How do these speech patterns work?

READING IN NEW CONTEXTS

1. What kind(s) of reader(s) does Durham envision for his essay? Adapt ideas about audience from Atwood, Lorde, or another *Literacies* author to help you describe the relationship(s) Durham tries to establish with his readers. How do his efforts affect you as a reader?

2. What "irresolvable contradictions" do you see Durham living and working with? How do they affect the way he writes his essay? Use your observations to examine the role played by contradiction in a text by Rosaldo, Baldwin, or Shanley.

3. How would you describe Durham's use of Cherokee history? How does it differ from the uses of the past suggested by Fienup-Riordan, Black Elk, or hooks & West? How might Durham's arguments encourage these writers to reconsider their ideas?

DRAFT ONE / DRAFT TWO

1. *Draft One:* How do the people in Durham's family stories and poems relate to where they live? How can you tell? Examine how Durham's ideas about place or setting affect your understanding of his essay.

Draft Two: Choose a text by MacLeod, Christian, Walker, or another *Literacies* writer for whom setting is important. What role does setting play in the text you selected? How do your observations from Draft One help you examine that role?

2. *Draft One:* Make a list of your goals when you prepare to revise an essay you have written. Write informally about some of the revision methods you use to achieve those goals. (You might want to look over your work from earlier in the semester for ideas.) Which methods work best for you? Why?

Draft Two: What criteria does Durham use when deciding if or how to revise sections of his essay? How does he respond to his own suggestions for revision and to suggestions made by others? How might Durham's ideas about revision challenge some of your observations from Draft One?

BEFORE READING STUART EWEN

1. Describe some times in everyday life when you care about the image you present to others. What values motivate you at these times?

2. How do you define the words "consumer" and "middle class"? Are they the same? What values and practices do you associate with each of them?

3. Find a piece of advertising presented as a letter. What image does the letter give of its intended reader? How does it accomplish this? How do you respond to this image?

CHOSEN PEOPLE

It's not what you own, it's what people think you own.

> —Company motto of Faux Systems,
> makers of the Cellular Phoney,
> an imitation car phone that
> looks like the real thing

MARKS OF DISTINCTION

A personalized letter arrives by mail. It has the *feel* of quality, written on heavy-weight, cream-colored, linen stationery, embossed at the top in gold:

Dear Mr. ———:

Because you are a highly valued American Express© Card member, I am inviting you to apply for the Gold Card at this time.

I believe you've earned this invitation. You've worked hard and have been recognized for your efforts. And nothing is more satisfying than achieving your own personal goals.

From *All Consuming Images* (1988).

Now it's time for you to carry the card that symbolizes your achievement—the Gold Card.

Only a select group will ever carry the Gold Card. So it instantly identifies you as someone special—one who expects an added measure of courtesy and personal attention. . . .

The Gold Card says more about you than anything you can buy with it. We think it's time you joined the select group who carry it.

Sincerely, . . .

An accompanying color brochure, adding sumptuous visions to laudatory words, invites Mr. ——— to "Come into your element." Opening up the richly coated stock of the brochure, he finds the following scenario:

The close of a fine meal.

The presentation of the bill.

And you take out the Gold Card©.

It is a gesture that speaks volumes.

It says you are someone special—whose style of living requires very special privileges.

Someone whose financial credentials rank among the nation's highest.

Someone who appreciates—indeed, has come to expect—an extra measure of courtesy and personal attention.

In fact, the Gold Card in your name says more about you than almost anything you can buy with it.

American Express "membership" has already placed you above the throng. Now, the gift of Gold will distinguish you even more.

The promise of "unspoken prestige" that runs through this elegant packet of junk mail is one representative specimen of a promise that is repeated endlessly across the landscape of American consumer culture: *You will be seen. You will be noticed. The symbols you display, your most valuable possessions, will permit you to stand apart from the crowd. You will be noteworthy and honored. You will be someone. You will have "joined the select group."* Only the faint remnant of perforations—at the top and bottom edges of the personalized letter—suggests that this promise of individual identity is being made, simultaneously, to a mass of others.

This highly individuated notion of personal distinction—marked by the compulsory consumption of images—stands at the heart of the "American Dream." To a certain extent, this continuous offer of personal distinction may indicate an epic crisis of identity that lurks within the inner lives of many Americans. Nonetheless, the promise is also an essential part of the way of life that is anxiously pursued by people who are now, or wish to become, part of the great American "middle class." This vision of status is offered to us by mail, it is reiterated by advertising; it is fed by the style industries; it is reinforced and mythologized in the publicized biographies—fact or fiction—of "folk heroes" and celebrities. According to the dream, this privileged existence is open to anyone who really wants it. Those who do not believe in the dream, do not deserve it. Those who do believe, but have not yet achieved it, must try harder. The Gold Card, which "says more about you than anything you can buy with it," is but one step in the right direction.

This dream resonates through much of American social history. To a large extent it has left its imprint on the aspirations and discontents of people and cultures around the world. The notion that each individual has fair access to status and recognition, and therefore can escape the anonymity and conditions of the common lot, has shaped the meaning and understanding of American *democracy*.

·   ·   ·

In the United States, by the 1830s, even budding cities of the recently settled West boasted an up-and-coming merchant middle class. Historian Edward Pessen notes that these parvenus "went to great pains to match the lavish living of the older upper classes of the eastern cities, succeeding to a large degree." As might be expected, the conspicuous consumption of luxuries provided these people with much desired marks of position: "Many of them lived in 'villas.' Expensive furniture, overloaded tables, fancy dress for dinner, extravagant entertainment, elegant carriages, ornate cotillions led by dancing masters imported from the East, characterized merchant life in the 'frontier towns.' "[1]

Yet it was not merchants alone who were surrounding themselves with the trappings of luxury. A growing market in cheap *luxury* items

1. Edward Pessen, *Jacksonian America* (1969), p. 53.

allowed others to purchase the symbolic accoutrements of status. Historian Alan Dawley writes that in Lynn, Massachusetts, in 1870, there was a class of "white-collar employees who earned only subsistence salaries and who called their condition 'genteel poverty.' " Though their holdings were small, their vocations and their sense of "pride lay in the prestige of being close to the social elite." These people lived close to the economic edge, and their "ability to get along well in economic terms" (their "competence," it was called) was very limited; their patterns of consumption and style "imitated the more commanding presence and sumptuous raiment of the upper middle classes."[2] Counting clerks and schoolteachers among their ranks, these "white-collar employees" anxiously strove to assemble a stylistic affinity to wealth.

If factory industrialism was producing icons of material abundance for some, it was bringing misery into the lives of many others. As Dawley puts it, "wealth and poverty were increasing apace." As some people assumed the mass-produced mantle of improved circumstances, the "wealth" of the industrial workers was, for the most part, "measured negatively by the goods they needed but did not have."[3] Critics and defenders of the factory system acknowledged the widespread immiserization that accompanied the expansion of factory industrialism, the social costs that coincided with the middle-class "delight in the unreal."

The tension between surface and substance, intrinsic to nineteenth-century industrialism, was evident in a critique published in the *Fourth Annual Report* of the Massachusetts Bureau of Labor, in 1873:

> Those who look beneath the surface of things, with unprejudiced eyes, are painfully conscious that wealth, though year by year still on the increase, goes now into fewer hands; that the results of industry are very unequally divided; that the advantages which machinery and division of labor bring, have been altogether in favor of capital and against labor, and that these evils are dangerously increasing from year to year.[4]

• • •

The emerging colossus of factory capitalism was giving rise to two contrasting perceptions of social reality. In 1847, *Scientific American*, a journal of science, technology, and invention, articulated one perspective

2. Alan Dawley, *Class and Community* (1976), pp. 151, 171.
3. Ibid., p. 149.
4. Ibid., p. 150.

when it described factory industrialism as producing the accoutrements of a "democracy," one "which invites every man to enhance his own comfort and status." Equating democracy with consumption, the magazine contended that the unfolding world of mass-produced objects was providing "the vehicle for the pursuit of happiness." Mass production, according to this outlook, was investing individuals with tools of identity, marks of their personhood.

For those laboring in many of the factories, however, industrial conditions systematically trampled upon their individuality and personhood. Many of the factory workers were migrants from premodern cultures of agriculture and handcrafts. Individuals whose work patterns were rooted in the more "irregular and undisciplined" structures of preindustrial labor were now being subjected to the monotonous discipline of machinery, and strict work rules were designed to rid them of preindustrial habits, memories, and temperaments.[5] Remuneration for work of this kind was most often low, a mere subsistence.

Out of these two conflicting ways of seeing and experiencing the new industrial reality, there emerged two distinct ways of apprehending the very question of *status* and *class*. By the mid-nineteenth century, both of these contending outlooks were being articulated. One way of comprehending class focused on the social relations of power which dominated and shaped the modern, industrial mode of *production*. The other outlook—which has left an indelible imprint on the meaning of style in contemporary American society—gave rise to a notion of class defined, almost exclusively, by patterns of *consumption*.

For those whose definition of class was drawn from the social relations of production, the nineteenth century highlighted a growing and irreconcilable conflict between those who profited from the increasingly mechanized and consolidated means of production, and those whose lives, labors, and energies were being consumed in service of this new industrial apparatus. As artisan craft and small-scale manufacture fell to an emerging economy of larger scale, more and more people were being drawn into the ranks of the industrial working class. For this growing population of factory workers, industrialism was creating a downward spiral of poverty, and a meager subsistence which only compounded the degraded conditions and exploitation that they faced at the workplace. While the captains of industry were surrounding themselves with the trap-

5. See title essay in Herbert Gutman, *Work, Culture, and Society in Industrializing America* (1977).

pings of status and wealth, the elements of style were of little consequence to the swelling numbers of factory operatives.

This was a working class very similar to the *proletariat*, described by Karl Marx and Frederick Engels during the same period. Writing in 1848, they depicted the modern working class as a "class of laborers who live so long as they find work and who find work only so long as their labor increases capital." Selling themselves "piecemeal," like a "commodity," their lives became more and more "exposed to all the vicissitudes of competition, to all the fluctuations of the market." The modern worker, they maintained, has become "an appendage of the machine, and it is only the most simple, most monotonous, and most easily acquired knack, that is required of him." The final indignity of his class position was that "as the repulsiveness of the work increases, the wage decreases."[6]

In mid-nineteenth-century America the gap between rich and poor was widening, and the wealth being accrued in factory capitalism was inextricably linked to the impoverishment of those whose labor was being drawn into its sphere of influence. *Class position* was part of the social relations of power that were emerging. *Class identity* was not a matter of individual choice, but of the position one inhabits in relation to the forces of production. This conception of *class*, elucidated by Marx and Engels, but shared by diverse others, encouraged people to look at groups of people not in terms of the individual claims they made for themselves, but in terms of where they stood within the *objective relations* of power. Such a consciousness of objective relations would, they believed, eventually give rise to a collective, revolutionary consciousness (and activity) among the expanding, international ranks of exploited workers.[7]

Such ideas spread in the United States, as well, during the rise of industrial and, then, corporate capitalism. Yet alongside this, another approach to the question of *class*—one resting on a flimsy, if seductive,

---

6. Karl Marx and Frederick Engels, *The Communist Manifesto* (1848), pp. 15–16.

7. For many living in the United States, or Western Europe, such an understanding of class may appear outdated, yet in many respects these insights into class continue to be relevant, if unappreciated. In today's, world, where transnational corporations dominate a global market economy, multitudes in Southeast Asia, Latin America, and elsewhere are—like the nineteenth-century proletarians of Europe and the United States—being forcibly separated from traditional modes of survival; being drawn into the orbit of factory production; being paid bare subsistence wages. Within the "developed" economies of the West, the "competition" offered by these miserably paid workers of the Third World has driven down wages and benefits; the gap separating rich and poor has widened once again.

foundation of appearances—was also taking hold. Within a society where, as Oliver Wendell Holmes had argued, inexpensively produced images were becoming more important than objects, it was increasingly possible to avoid dealing with objective relations. By the middle of the nineteenth century, the expanding market in appearances was helping to feed a notion of class defined primarily in *consumptive* rather than productive terms, highlighting individual, above common, identity. The idea of an American "middle class," constructed out of images, attitudes, acquisitions, and style, was emerging.

In eighteenth-century Europe, argues historian Karen Halttunen, "the term *middling class* referred to people who occupied a static social position between the extremes of peasantry and aristocracy, a position believed to offer only modest opportunities for advancement." In the teeming urban world of nineteenth-century America, however, "middle class" began to take on a new and volatile meaning, one which assumed that more and more people were engaged "in a passage from a lower to a higher social status."[8]

In an urban industrial world, where traditional hierarchical patterns of work and family life were disintegrating, and where new promises of economic opportunity were fueling the imagination, many people "imagined themselves on a social escalator to greater wealth and prestige."[9] At the heart of this mobile dream, argues Eric Foner, lay the republican "middle class goal of economic independence . . . the opportunity to quit the wage earning class."[10]

For the most part, Halttunen maintains, this middle class "lived suspended between the facts of their present social position and the promise, which they took for granted, of their economic future. In reality," she continues, "the middle-class escalator was at least as likely to go down as up. Whether rising or falling, however, middle-class Americans were defined as men in social motion, men of no fixed status." This condition of flux, she adds, "was believed to include a vast majority of Americans who were neither very wealthy nor very poor."[11]

This middle-class commitment to the ideal of social mobility was fed by the expanding market in appearances that characterized nineteenth-century industrial life. Mass-produced fashions, furniture, and other sym-

8. Karen Halttunen, *Confidence Men and Painted Women* (1982), p. 29.
9. Ibid., p. 29.
10. Eric Foner, *Free Soil, Free Labor, Free Men* (1970), pp. 16–17.
11. Halttunen, *Confidence Men and Painted Women*, p. 29.

bolic accoutrements of a privileged station were anxiously assembled by those who strove to avoid what one mid-nineteenth-century advice writer called the *"shame of being thought poor."*[12] An industry of advice literature began to emerge, offering would-be *arrivés* the proper behavioral techniques and etiquette by which they might complete their projects of pretension.

The obsession with appearances ran deep within this new middle-class life and affected the most minute details of existence. Proper attention to current fashions was complemented by intricate instructions on how to position one's hands or head, and how to move about in a proper "genteel" manner. Middle-class homes were marked by front rooms, parlors, adorned with overstuffed furniture, pianos, and other recognized symbols of prosperity. Back rooms, where people retreated from the primacy of display, were more plainly furnished.

The priority of facades was becoming a characteristic feature of American middle-class life. *Godey's Lady's Book*, a magazine which itself served as a middle-class guidepost in the mid-nineteenth century, bemoaned the extent to which pretense had become a cardinal element of middle-class behavior:

> The exterior of life is but a masquerade, in which we dress ourselves in the finest fashions of society, use a language suited to the characters we assume;—with smiling faces, mask aching hearts; address accents of kindness to our enemies, and often those of coldness to our friends. The part once assumed must be acted out, no matter at what expense of truth and feeling.[13]

• • •

Industrial-, corporate-, and finance-capitalists of the nineteenth century also assumed style as palpable evidence of their power. The artifacts with which these people surrounded themselves were, for the most part, handmade, intricately crafted, constructed of rare and expensive materials, often one of a kind. While social critics and jealous defenders of aristocratic taste decried the garish displays of the robber barons, these capitalists had, in a very real sense, inherited the prerogatives of now-fallen elites.

The nineteenth-century mass-produced style, which gave shape to a democratized, "middle class" existence, was different. It was composed

12. Ibid., p. 64.
13. Ibid., p. 66.

primarily of *kitsch*: cheap, mass-produced imitations of elite style. The ornate bric-a-brac described by Egon Friedell, or the ready-to-wear fashions that became increasingly available from the 1870s onward, were pale imitations of elite styles and were notable for their shoddiness.

Yet more important than its formal obeisance to the values of elites, this "middle class" pretension was more a social mask, claiming a power that was not there, than it was an achievement of real social power. The stylish ephemera of the new "middle class" existence was more of a symbolic fringe benefit, a *cultural wage*, which permitted its recipients to identify with the interests of the upper classes, while occupying a relationship to power that was more akin to that of the working classes. In its symbolic identification with power, this "middle class" performed, and continues to perform, a political function; it effects divisions among people who otherwise might identify with one another.

The ironic position of this middle class, committed at once to democratic mobility and to the imagery of entrenched elites, was captured succinctly by the mid-nineteenth-century social reformer Orestes Brownson. "The middle class," he wrote, "is always a firm champion of equality when it concerns humbling a class above it, but it is its inveterate foe when it concerns elevating a class below it."[14]

Writing in 1873, Ira Steward—a weaver and leader in the Massachusetts movement for an eight-hour workday—offered a prescient description and analysis of this emerging "middle class" and its consciousness; his words seem even more trenchant today. In powerful contrast with a notion of class rooted in the social relations of power, Steward depicted a growing "class" of people whose fragile identity was wedded to the consumption of goods, and whose troubled consciousness was enforced by a thin veil of appearances.

In his essay "Poverty," included in the 1873 report of the Massachusetts Bureau of Labor, Steward made a striking and unexpected detour from a discussion of pauperized wage laborers, and focused on the lives, conditions, and psychology of what he called the "middle class." The section deserves quotation at length:

> But has not the middle class its poverty—a poverty that should excite the most anxiety, and the most searching inquiry. . . .
> They are a large majority of the people, and their poverty is gener-

14. Foner, *Free Soil*, p. 23.

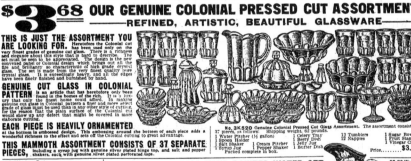

This page from the 1908 Sears Roebuck catalog is cluttered with "pressed cut glass" bric-a-brac—part of the early-twentieth-century, middle-class identity kit.

ally carefully concealed.[15] All who have barely enough to keep up appearances are just the ones to cover up the fact that they have nothing more. They are ranked among the middle classes; and their power to cover up their poverty, is made to argue that they are not poor.

The middle classes have the strongest motives for never making any parade or public complaint of their poverty. To advertise one's self destitute, is to be without credit, that tides so many in safety—to their standing in society—over the shallow places where ready resources fail. To be without credit and without resources, is to be dependent upon charity whenever employment fails, or sickness prevents employment, and to depend upon charity is an advertisement of one's destitution and poverty that the public is very slow to forget. . . .

To betray or confess the secrets of one's destitution, is also regarded, in some measure, as a sign of incapacity; for, as the world goes, the poor man is an unsuccessful man.

To dispel any evidence of their indigence, Steward observed, these "middle class" poor participate in a continuous effort to erect the semblance of substantiality; to construct a stylish imago in order to maintain a claim to social position; to secure those promotions which are available to "white collar" employees; to qualify for credit. All of this scurrying for position, Steward noted, made access to credit all the more imperative:

The poverty that publishes or argues one's incapacity, closes many a door to more profitable or advantageous situations or promotions. The more expensive and superior style of living adopted by the middle classes, must therefore be considered in the light of an *investment*, made from the soundest considerations of expediency—considering their risks and their chances—and from motives even of self preservation, rather than from the mere desire for self indulgence, or because the middle classes are not poor. Very few of them are saving money. Many of them are in debt; and all they can earn for years, is, in many cases, mortgaged to pay such debt,—"debt that increases the load of the future, with the burden which the present cannot bear."[16]

In the masquerade of elegance that shaped the lives of these "genteel" poor, Steward found pathos. In the haunted eyes of these people,

15. Most probably Steward's reference to the "majority," here, does not include blacks or immigrants, whose combined numbers were large, and who performed the most menial and low-paid work.

16. Ira Steward, "Poverty," Massachusetts Statistics of Labor, House Document 173, pp. 412–14.

the core of insecurity overwhelmed the surface of prosperity. In "the faces of thousands of well-dressed, intelligent, and well-appearing people," Steward perceived the "unmistakable signs of their incessant anxiety and struggles to get on in life, and to obtain in addition to a mere subsistence, a standing in society."[17]

• • •

These discussions of the "middle class" and its anxieties have a remarkably current ring to them. They point to the emergence of a consumer society, filled with mass-produced status symbols, in which judgment about a person is not based on what one *does* within society, but rather upon what one *has*. Such an understanding of class has moved away from the conception rooted in the social relations of power, and toward a notion based, for the most part, on income and credit. "Middle class" status was becoming something founded purely on one's ability to purchase, construct, and present a viable social self. While this modern idea of class invested more and more people with the iconography of status, it also tended to mask the relations of power that prevailed within society.

In the late nineteenth century, when Ira Steward was writing, the ability to assemble a "middle class" identity was still limited to a white, primarily Anglo-American population. Working-class people, largely white immigrants and blacks, had little access to the goods or necessary income to make this social presentation of self possible. In the twentieth century, with the growth of vast consumer industries and, for many, improved income, times of prosperity have been marked by increasing numbers of people entering the orbit of "middle class" existence. With these developments, Steward's prescient characterization of a "middle class" existence, shaped by the acquisition and display of stylish goods, has provided the predominant definition of class and aspiration in American society. The term *middle class*, like the term *consumer*,

17. Ibid., pp. 412–14. Ira Steward understood that this "middle class" performed an important political function in American society, erecting a buffer zone between extremes of wealth and poverty. "If men have nothing but a bare living," Steward observed, "they are in a condition to believe, at any critical moment, that they have something to gain from public disorder." Thus, the middle class's identification with the interests of the status quo forged an important alliance between them and the rich, one which might lead to agitation and rebellion among the pauperized classes. The conservative proclivities of an indebted middle class, noted by Steward in the 1870s, have been an important feature of the U.S. in the 1980s, where credit has been extended to millions and where an increasingly in-debt middle class proudly emerged as foot soldiers for Reaganism.

has become, for the most part, an appellation of citizenship.

This development reached its height in the twenty years after the end of World War II, when a period of economic boom drew unprecedented numbers into the ranks of the middle class. In the process, and with the assistance of anticommunist ideology, the alternative definition of class began to ebb in the public vernacular. Although many still lived in severe poverty, the most visible representation of social life depicted the "increased bunching of Americans around the middle-income levels, the increased blurring of occupational distinctions, and the increased adoption of middle-class living styles by families of diverse occupational background."[18] By the late 1950s, *Fortune* magazine asserted, nearly all Americans had the option of "choosing a whole style of life":

> A skilled mechanic who earns $7,500 after taxes may choose to continue living in "working class" style, meanwhile saving sizable sums for his children's college education; or he may choose to live like a junior executive in his own $17,000 suburban house; or he may choose to live in a city apartment house otherwise occupied by business and professional men. When the American "masses" have options of this breadth, . . . it is scarcely an exaggeration to suggest that we have arrived at a landmark in all the history of human freedoms.[19]

•   •   •

What was coming to fruition, for unprecedented numbers of people, was a society in which mass-produced, stylized goods were functioning as an intricate system of personal certification, an "identity kit." As Joan Kron has argued in *Home-Psych*, her book on the psychology of interior design, the utility of such "middle class" certification was inextricably linked to the growing anonymity of modern life:

> As more and more people leave the protection of closely knit communities and move into neighborhoods of strangers, the house becomes a credential as well as a haven. Just as we need the intimate relationships that a house can shelter, we need the respect and esteem provided by a home we create in our own image. And we must forgive ourselves for caring about the opinions of others and trying to influence them. . . . We all use material things to stand for us. That's the system.[20]

18. Editors of *Fortune, Markets of the Sixties* (1958), pp. 116–17.
19. Ibid., p. 90.
20. Joan Kron, *Home-Psych: The Social Psychology of Home and Decoration* (1983), p. 263.

Within the so-called yuppie (young urban professional) culture of the 1980s, we find the ultimate expression of such a "middle class" ideal, as well as its inherent anxieties. Amid a declining standard of living for many, these young professionals—many of whom are employed by the new "information industries"—scramble to surround themselves with the ever-changing "latest" in designer clothing, consumer electronics, and other commodified symbols of the *good life*. As they frenetically pursue this semiotic world of objects, they perform a role written for them, by Ira Steward, more than one hundred years before. Life is a tightening snare of credit and debt; all connection to society, or to social responsibility, is forsworn in favor of individual acquisition and display; stress and stress-induced conditions are endemic; *loneliness* and *emptiness* are common in their accounts of everyday life. In their ongoing presentation of self, it is essential that one's inner self, one's inner feelings, remain masked. This pose is well expressed by a 1984 television commercial for Dry Idea deodorant. "Never answer the phone on the first ring," begins the first in a series of instructions:

Never say, "I'll be right over."

Don't ever let 'em see you sweat.

It doesn't matter how anxious you are. . . . Never let 'em know you're anxious.

That's what *Dry Idea* is all about.

Such instructions are a common legacy of twentieth-century American life. In 1933—following a decade in which consumer industries had flourished, and in which mass-produced goods had extended their influence over the lives of many Americans—sociologist Robert Lynd commented dryly upon the rise of the *commodity self*. Discussing the "people as consumers," Lynd's words indicate the extent to which the tension between inner self and outer image had become a routine fixture in everyday life:

The process of growing up and of effective adult living consists in adjusting one's individual tensions by weighting them with values sufficiently congruous with the accepted values of society and at the same time with the urgent personal needs of the individual to enable him *to present some socially tolerable semblance of an integrated front in the business of living. Within each of us this exciting drama is played out in our every waking and sleeping hour until the end of the picture.*[21]

21. Robert S. Lynd, "The People as Consumers," Report to the President's Research Committee on Social Trends, *Recent Social Trends in the United States* (1933), pp. 866–67, emphasis added.

ACTIVE READING

1. Ewen's American Express brochure mentions "a gesture that speaks volumes" (184). Make a list of a few other gestures that speak in Ewen's essay, and use them to talk about some ways that meaning is carried in actions or objects, as well as in words.

2. How many different kinds of consumption does Ewen discuss? Find examples of each kind, and explain the relations Ewen sees among the different kinds.

3. What is a "commodity self," according to Ewen (196)? What other kinds of selves does Ewen describe in this essay? How do they differ from a commodity self?

READING IN NEW CONTEXTS

1. Find two or three advertisements for household products that make an appeal to the customer's image. Compare their persuasive strategies to those of the Sears Roebuck catalog page in Ewen's text (192), and explain how the advertisements support or challenge Ewen's account of American consumer values.

2. Ewen says that some people "construct" or "assemble" their identities. What other words, especially verbs, does he use to describe how people acquire their identities? Test these words against one or two other *Literacies* readings, such as Baldwin, Gilmore, or MacLeod, and tell what the words reveal about identity in the United States or elsewhere.

3. How do material objects help people form identities in the texts by Kingston and Walker? Explain how these texts confirm or challenge Ewen's ideas about things and identity.

DRAFT ONE / DRAFT TWO

1. *Draft One:* Tell the story of an event that has been important in shaping your sense of yourself, your identity. Then explain how the story shows your identity both as a product of your society and as something of your own making.

Draft Two: Use ideas and examples from the readings by Ewen and either Gilmore or Rich to revise Draft One. In your new version, explain some of the consequences of thinking of your identity as a product of society and of thinking of it as something of your own making.

1. *Draft One:* Pick out the person you find most admirable in the other *Literacies* texts you have read this semester, and compose a theory of identity for that person. Just as Ewen has used phrases such as "commodity self," "surface and substance," and "tools of identity," coin your own terms as you compose your theory.

Draft Two: Develop Draft One further by adding several detailed examples from the life of someone you admire, a person you know well. If necessary, interview that person to gather more information for your paper. Use these two individuals to test your terms and theory about the identity of an admirable person.

BEFORE READING ANN FIENUP-RIORDAN

1. Discuss some ideas you've heard about how humans should interact with the natural environment. What problems do you see with each of these ideas? Which historical human community do you believe has had the best understanding of nature? How can you tell?

2. Think of a book or movie that represents an encounter between two cultures. Describe it briefly, and then speculate about how members of each culture would react to the ways the movie or book portrays their people.

3. Explore some reasons why a community might want to understand its own history. What resources would you expect it to use, and what common barriers might it face?

4. Think about the idea of owning property. Where do your beliefs about property ownership come from? Explain any connection you see between these beliefs and your ideas about the environment or community history.

ANN FIENUP-RIORDAN

YUP'IK LIVES
AND HOW WE SEE THEM

THE IDEOLOGY OF SUBSISTENCE

In descriptions of the coastal Yup'ik Eskimos, as well as of other Eskimo groups, their ability to survive in a frigid and inhospitable environment has often been emphasized to the exclusion of a comprehensive account of the value system that makes such survival meaningful. In fact, by idealizing their survival ability, we emphasize that aspect of their way of life most comprehensible within our own cultural system. Small wonder the students of Malthus and Darwin are continually drawn to the contemplation of the life ways of the inhabitants of the Arctic, whose cultural adaptation seems to epitomize the necessary fit between natural constraints and human response.

Yet a close look at the value system and ritual exchanges that characterize their elegantly efficient, traditional technology reveals less common-sense environmental determinism than cultural imagination. Certainly the fact that the traditional distributions of seal meat serve to feed the aged and the needy cannot be denied. In fact, the periodic random distribution of the products of the chase may well be ecologically required, something on the order of give now so that in your turn you

From *Eskimo Essays* (1990).

may receive and so survive. Yet how this redistribution is accomplished, through an exchange of gifts between male cousins or between married women who are not related, is culturally determined and not nearly as preordained as one might suppose.

As the whole of symbolic anthropology is definitely an interpretive endeavor, and as the bulk of my work as an anthropologist has been directed toward this interpretation, I would like to relay in narrative fashion the experiences that taught me the significance of traditional and contemporary systems of exchange. I say *experiences* instead of *evidence* because anthropologists, just like other humans, are notorious for finding what they are looking for. I am under no illusion that what I "saw" while in the field was not at least partially a product of what I sought.

Further, and more important, I hope that by speaking through my own experiences I may help introduce the reader to a cultural logic that is difficult to convey through abstractions alone (such as, "the traditional Yup'ik Eskimos respected animals; they believed these animals had souls"). Thus, I take the tack of the seasoned hunter who requires the attention of the uninitiated while I tell a story of what it means to subsist.

In 1974 I was working in Anchorage, without experience of bush Alaska and without wish or desire to seek out such experience. I was studying anthropology and going off to investigate the mainland Chinese, and that was that. Then I was hired by the Nelson Islanders under a grant from the Alaska Humanities Forum to see what I could locate pertaining to the history and archaeology of pottery production in western Alaska. Whatever information I was able to find I was asked to take to Nelson Island in the spring of 1975. At that time I was to make a trip to Toksook Bay, the location of the Nelson Island School of Design, a production pottery that had recently been constructed in the village as a means of encouraging local industry and employment.

When I arrived on Nelson Island, I was initially impressed with how modern and Western the village of Toksook Bay seemed. It had electricity and running water, and most of the people I met during the first few days spoke English. Maybe they had once been exotic, but they certainly were not any more.

While I stayed in the village, I slept in the pottery workshop on an old army cot brought down from the National Guard armory. Every morning at about 7:30, with no knock or courteous inquiry as to whether I was presentable, several older village men would come into the building, turn up the stove, turn on the coffee pot, and take their places on the benches along the wall. From the back room where I had my cot, I could hear them talking slowly, softly. One might begin to mend an *uluaq*,[1] while another continued an ivory carving that he had started a few days before. Later during the morning, and again after the midday meal, younger men would drift into the pottery workshop, stand around, and silently watch what the older men were doing. No one paid any attention to me, although several of the older men were interested in the pictures I had brought of traditional Eskimo pottery from other parts of the Arctic. Also, no one paid any attention to the new pottery wheels and equipment that filled the workshop area.

At first I was bewildered by this apparent apathy in the face of government largesse. Community Enterprise Development Corporation had put up a substantial amount of money for the facility. Why were the old men here? Why was no one making pottery? I soon found that no one was making pottery because they were too busy doing everything else. It was spring, seal hunting was about to begin, and what little pottery production had taken place during the winter was at a standstill. Wages could not lure workers into the pottery. Hunting came first.

That old men gathered in the warmest communal space available (the community hall had no heat) was no surprise. In their youth most of them had lived together in the traditional *qasgiq*, or men's house. What better use to make of this new building, which had quickly proved itself incapable of housing Western industry as a design school. So the old men had taken over. Before I left the village, several snow machines were also moved in for repair, and there was talk by one village elder of using the building to cover the construction of a new boat.

The upshot of finding that my bedroom was in the modern version of the traditional men's house was that I didn't spend much time in it. Rather, I visited the houses and talked to the women. They said that I had come at the best time of the year, that the seal parties were about to begin.

Seal parties? What were they? I'd never read about seal parties. I'd never even heard of them. Well, my new friends told me, seal parties were given when the men and boys of the village brought home the first seals of the season. They were very exciting and lots of fun, as not only was the meat and blubber of every man's first-caught seal given away, but lots of other things as well. I was intrigued and waited eagerly for the parties to commence.

---

1. An *uluaq* is a woman's traditional semilunar knife set in a handle opposite the arc-shaped edge. It is also sometimes referred to as *ulu* in English from the Iñupiaq name for this type of knife (Jacobson 1984:391).

They began the next day—three parties in a row. I was just up and having a cup of tea when a little girl ran in the door and said to come quick. There, right next door, a woman was standing in her porch throwing Pampers and packs of gum into the waiting hands of a large group of women. I joined the fun and followed the group to the next house for a repetition of the event. I noticed that not all the same women attended, but other women joined the group. I asked about this later and was told that when a woman gives her seal party, her relatives could not attend; only her nonrelatives received the gift of meat.

By this time I was extremely excited. Here was a distribution of goods through which social relations were articulated. My interest in anthropology had originally been in the study of kinship systems. Also, I was convinced that one could not learn much about people's social relations simply by asking them genealogical questions such as "Who is your sister?" or "Who is your cousin?" Rather, to learn anything important about kinship, one must see it in action and witness what it means to be a sister or mother. The seal party provided a wonderful window into how the people of Nelson Island still thought about and acted out their ideas of what it meant to be related.

I found out later that while the explicit rule was that only nonrelatives attend one's seal party, in fact only sisters, mothers, mothers-in-law,

FIGURE 1. A seal party in the village of Toksook Bay, 1981 (Courtesy Don Doll, S.J.).

FIGURE 2. The presentation of gifts during the men's and women's exchange dance *(Kevgiruaq)*, Toksook Bay, 1979.

and parallel cousins were excluded. More important, the hostess of the seal party normally "gave away" the privilege of throwing the gifts to an older woman, who in her turn singled out one individual in the audience to receive a special gift. These women were usually cross-cousins, the mothers of children who would be, or had already been, married. Also, it was significant that what they gave each other was raw meat, for the gift of raw meat was traditionally the exchange that marked the marriage relationship between a man and a woman. Thus, the seal-party exchange paralleled the marriage exchange. During the event a woman gave away the products of the hunt of her husband and sons, the symbolic proof of their potency, not just to anybody, but to women who could eventually give their daughters to the hosting family as brides.

Much more might be said on the metaphorical marriage between cross-cousins that the seal party represents. What is important is that, as I found later on, the seal party is not an isolated relic of traditional culture but rather is part of an annual cycle of ritual distribution. Pieces of this cycle are no longer practiced, but other parts are still alive and well and still express coastal villagers' attitudes toward their land and their lives.

The immediate counterpart of the seal party on Nelson Island is the men's and women's exchange dance *(Kevgiruaq)*, in which men and women are said to fight through the dance. This sequence takes a slightly different form in the lower Yukon villages of Emmonak and Alakanuk, but the message is comparable. On the first night of the exchange dance, all the women in the village pair up as married couples, one woman taking the part of the husband and the other the part of the wife. Then, together, the women dance a multitude of gifts into the community hall and on the following morning give them out to the men of the village. The men perform for the women on the following evening, and the next morning the women receive gifts in their turn. The entire sequence of dances and gift-giving takes hours and hours, as everyone in the commu-

FIGURE 3. Mark John playing the part of wife during the men's and women's exchange dance, Toksook Bay, 1979.

nity has a turn on the dance floor. As each mock married couple comes out to dance, they are greeted by much laughing and teasing from the audience. The particular dance that is performed is always the same, but each couple vies with the others to make its rendition particularly hilarious. Young men put mop ends on their heads for hair. Fur parkas are turned inside out to imitate age and senility, and fake muscles are pushed into the dresses of the women who are playing the role of husband.

Even if one knew nothing about Yup'ik cultural configurations, the exchange dance would still be a splendid and exuberant performance to behold. Seen in the light of the seal party, its eloquence becomes apparent. Whereas in the seal party gifts are thrown out the doors of the individual houses, in the exchange dance gifts are danced in the door of the community hall. In the seal party these gifts consist of strips of cloth and bits of string, in fact bits and pieces of every conceivable household commodity. In the exchange dance, whole cloth is given, whole skeins of yarn, and sometimes quilts or bedspreads made from the very bits of cloth given away during the seal party. The length of cloth that a woman receives in the exchange dance she usually tears into strips for her seal party distribution. With the strips of cloth that she has collected from the various seal parties she has attended, she fabricates a quilted cover that she will then give away during the next year's exchange dance. If all that was required was a cover for the bed, the Yup'ik people have certainly taken a circuitous route to ensure its provision. In fact, after all the giving and receiving has been accomplished, no one is much the richer or poorer in material goods. Their world view, their whole cultural mode of being, has, however, been put on stage along with the dancers, acted out, and so reestablished and reaffirmed.

Social relations are also articulated in the dance. When I asked women how their dance partners were related to them, they said to me simply, "They are my relatives." In itself this was certainly an acceptable answer, but these so-called relatives were, in fact, the same persons who had been designated as nonrelatives at the seal parties! Cross-cousins who had stood on opposite sides as host and guest in one event joined together to host the entire community as a "married couple." As with the cycling of goods between the two events, relatives seemed to be cycling as well. Instead of a moral on the order of "never the twain shall meet," the Yup'ik celebrations seemed to imply that always that which is separated (socially, physically, and, as we shall see, metaphysically) will in the end be reunited.

As this ideological program is somewhat abstruse, let me detail a few more experiences to show how this point of view pervades village life today. In the spring of 1978 I made a visit to Nelson Island while I was pregnant with my first child. I was, of course, quite proud of my condition and sure that with the proper food and exercise the pregnancy and birth would go well. My Yup'ik friends, however, were not so blasé and proceeded to teach me an elaborate set of dos and don'ts that still accompanies pregnancy and childbirth in the village. I was to sleep with my head toward the door. As soon as I got up every morning, I was to run outside as fast as I could. Only then might I come in, sit down, and drink tea. In fact, any time during the day that I left the house I was to do it quickly without stopping in the doorway. If I were to pause in my exiting, the baby was sure to get stuck during delivery.

This series of prescriptions draws an obvious parallel between the womb in which the unborn baby lives and the house in which the expectant mother resides. Analogically, the throwing of gifts out of the house through the doorway at the time of the seal party is comparable to their birth. Analogous relationships exist between the progress of the souls of the human dead and the return of gifts into the community hall at the time of the exchange dance. In fact, imagery of birth and rebirth pervaded the system of symbols and meanings that was beginning to become apparent. The finality of death was everywhere averted, in both action and ideal.

Another anecdote will help make the significance of this cultural framework clear. During the time I lived on Nelson Island I had hoped in my heart of hearts that someone would give me a real Yup'ik name. No one ever did. They gave me a nickname that translated loosely as "big piece of fat." But that was as close to a traditional name as I got. Certainly I had asked about naming procedures, just as I had asked about pregnancy taboos, but with little solid response. I was made to feel acutely nosey. And, in fact, part of the message of this story is how little progress one can make in understanding the coastal Yup'ik people if one confines oneself to information acquired through a questionnaire approach. It certainly never worked for me, and in fact my best friends used to lie to me, in a good-natured way, to show me how foolish and misguided my occasional bouts of verbal curiosity were. Watching and listening, however, were different matters. And so it was with my understanding of the significance of naming.

Although I had never been given a name, when I returned to the village with my newborn daughter in the fall of 1978, she was immediately named. The older woman who had been my real teacher while I had lived on the island had had a cousin. That man had drowned not three weeks before. No sooner had my daughter and I come into the village than she came to where we were staying and gave my daughter the name of her dead cousin. Then, in every house in which we visited, people would ask me what my daughter's name was. When I told them, they would laugh and say such things as "Oh, he's come back a *kass'aq* [white person]!" or "He always did want to learn English!" or "To think now he has red hair!"

All this verbal play on the baby's name was a kind way of welcoming my daughter into their midst. But, as important, these endearments were wonderfully explicit expressions of the belief that in the newborn child the soul of the recently dead is born again. In the Yup'ik world, no one ever finally passes away out of existence. Rather, through the naming process, the essence of being human is passed on from one generation to the next.

This cycling of human souls is especially interesting when considered in light of the traditional belief that the souls of the seals must be cared for by the successful hunger in order that they, too, will be born again. Seals as well as other animals and fish are believed to give themselves to men voluntarily. A seal, for instance, is said to sense, and in fact to see, the merits of a hunter. If the hunter is seen to be "awake" to the rules of the proper relationship between humans and animals, and between humans and humans, then the seal will allow the hunter's harpoon or bullet to kill it. When the seal is hit, if the seal is likewise awake, its soul will retract to its bladder. Although its body will die and so provide life to humans, its soul will stay alive and await return to the sea. In fact, traditionally, the coastal Yup'ik Eskimos held a Bladder Festival every winter. At the Bladder Festival the bladders of the seals caught during the year along with the bladders of other animals were inflated, hung at the back of the men's house, and feasted and entertained for five days. Then, on the fifth day, each family took the bladders of the animals they had killed to the sea and pushed them down through a hole in the ice so that the souls of the seals might be born again.

Through these events the circle is completed. Not only do goods cycle, as do the seasons, but human and animal souls likewise are continually in motion. The birth of a baby is the rebirth of a member of its grandparental generation. The death of the seal means life to the village. The same people and the same seals have been on this earth from the beginning, continually cycling and recycling through life and death. Through this generational cycling, a life-celebrating system is put for-

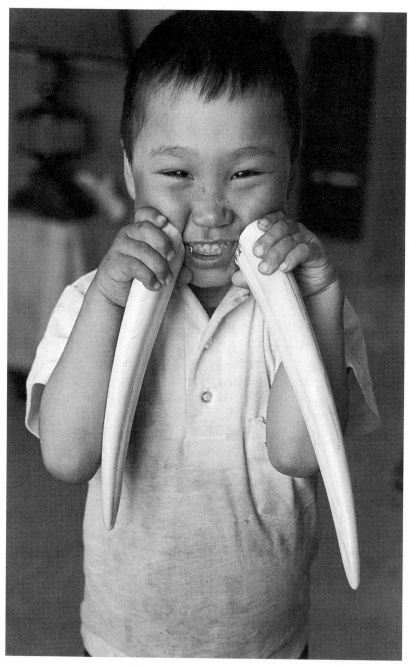

FIGURE 4. Fritzie Nevak with walrus ivory, Toksook Bay (Courtesy Don Doll, S.J.).

ward. The coastal Yup'ik Eskimos are not simply surviving on the resources of their environment but are living in a highly structured relationship to them. This relationship is important to comprehend, not as an exercise in Eskimo esoterica, but as the key to why they act and feel the way they do.

In light of the current subsistence debate,[2] the focus of present cultural consciousness on the coast and an issue that is not likely to be quickly resolved, one final anecdote is worth relating. In the spring of 1979 I revisited Nelson Island. It had been a good spring, and numerous seals and walrus had been taken. But Alaska Department of Fish and Game officials had unfortunately found several walrus carcasses at Cape Vancouver. Head hunters had taken the valuable ivory and left the rest of the meat to rot. Nelson Islanders accused Nunivak Islanders of the infraction and vice versa. Talking to an old man about the incident, I played devil's advocate and queried, "What difference does it make who killed them? Dead is dead and nothing can bring them back now, can it?" That I should have been so cavalier even now amazes me. The old man never lifted his eyes from the bench. "No," he said, "if they had been properly cared for they would have been able to return. Now they are gone forever."

Can these experiences help you to see the significance, in Yup'ik eyes, of the threat of an oil spill or game mismanagement? Although active shamanism and the celebration of the Bladder Festival are no more, too many embodiments of the traditional cosmology remain to be casually

---

2. Since the passage of the Alaska Native Claims Settlement Act (ANCSA) in 1971, regulatory control over land and sea resources has become as big an issue as landownership and the closely related issue of the retention of subsistence hunting and fishing as priority activities. The d(2) section of ANCSA mandated legislation passed in 1980 as the Alaska National Interest Land Conservation Act (ANILCA). Although ANILCA is nearly 450 pages long, it sets down only general guidelines for the U.S. Fish and Wildlife Service to follow in managing land. The Fish and Wildlife Service has begun to implement broad provisions of the bill, and its regulations will ultimately determine the bill's success or failure. As they say on the delta, "You can't eat a regulation"; but, what's worse, regulations can make it so you can't eat, period.

Legislative actions and administration policies have already begun to tie the concept of subsistence use as a priority activity into the fabric of management—for example, the issuing at a reduced fee of resident permits to hunt musk oxen on Nelson Island. Yet the villagers' continuing concern is that when resources dwindle and competition from other users increases, the political process will undercut their subsistence rights. As political battles in Alaska have made abundantly clear, their fears are justified.

catalogued as superstition or to allow the scientific attitude toward species extinction to hold sway. Even the youngest child is still instructed in a code of etiquette toward natural surroundings that is as important as any code of etiquette toward other human beings (see also Nelson 1977). Given this cultural framework, it is possible but altogether inappropriate to reduce subsistence activities to mere survival techniques and their significance to the conquest of calories. Their pursuit is not simply a means to an end but an end in itself.

In what little literature exists on western Alaska, authors often comment that, even given alternatives, living off the land is still the preferred pattern. This preference is explicable only if being a hunter has intrinsic value. What Richard Nelson says of the Iñupiat is equally true of the coastal Yup'ik Eskimos: "One of the things that continually amazes me when I go back there is that people are still out there hunting, dedicated—sometimes almost passionately dedicated—to continuing this way of life" (quoted in Schiller 1981:16).

Small wonder the words of the Nelson Island elders were echoed by their children and more sophisticated contemporaries during testimony in Bethel in the spring of 1981 on the repeal of the subsistence legislation. Everywhere the emphasis was on the real kinship between the people and their environment. Stewardship, not to mention ownership, of resources is taken with a grain of salt, as the real power is not in people, but in the continuing relationship between humans and the natural world on which they depend.

ROBERT REDFORD, APANUUGPAK, AND THE INVENTION OF TRADITION

A project is currently under way to produce a full-length feature film in the western Alaska village of Toksook Bay on Nelson Island. The screenplay, appropriately enough, focuses on a traditional hero—Apanuugpak—and epic tales of bow-and-arrow warfare that are still very much a part of the oral tradition of the Yup'ik Eskimos who make Nelson Island their home. There are, however, discrepancies between Yup'ik history as it can be read from oral tradition and as both the scriptwriter and the people of Toksook Bay choose to present it in the film. These discrepancies relate to both the making and the marketing of tradition, on Nelson Island and beyond.

The current rethinking of ethnographic inquiry has focused on the need for anthropological writing to reflect the dialogic character of ethnographic interaction. It follows that the dialogic character of other native/non-native encounters also merits scrutiny. Far from reducing the ethnographic enterprise to fiction, the current reevaluation of the role of the ethnographer lends support to the development of a more critical view of situations of cross-cultural exchange already under way.

My acquaintance with the Apanuugpak film project began in the summer of 1985, when I was living at Toksook Bay working on an oral history project sponsored by the Toksook Bay City Council, a project intended to help villagers record their history.[3] While sharing tea and conversation with friends, I was told that Robert Redford was coming to Toksook to play the part of the famous warrior Apanuugpak in a film that was to be made on Nelson Island in the near future. People proudly announced that this film would soon air on one of the fourteen cable channels that had recently been made available in the community. A standing joke soon developed. Every time we heard a plane pass over (which was often), friends teased that I should hurry and put on lipstick, dress up, and run over to the airport. There I would be the first to greet Mr. Redford, take the part of Mrs. Apanuugpak, and what a fine film that would be!

The apparently farfetched juxtaposition of Robert Redford and Apanuugpak that provided the material for so many jokes that summer had a factual basis and already a very interesting history. The idea for a film based on the Apanuugpak stories was the brainchild of Dave Hunsaker, a Juneau playwright who first came to Nelson Island in 1984 seeking support for a play he had written entitled *Inuit Antigone*. This play was an English adaptation of Sophocles' Greek drama into an Eskimolike genre. Hunsaker was searching for native actors for the production. He met with the Toksook Bay City Council and received their approval of his project with two conditions. The first was that the title of the production be changed from *Inuit* to *Yup'ik Antigone*. The second was that the play be performed in the Yup'ik language.

Yup'ik Antigone was well received from Bethel to New York City and eventually all the way to Greece. The farther the troop traveled from home, the more exotic they appeared. The critical acclaim given to the play was simultaneously refreshing and revealing. The most impressive

---

3. As of fall 1989, this project was still under way. It has involved primarily a group of Nelson Island men and women working to record traditional narratives and oral history from the oldest living Nelson Islanders. Some of these accounts are now being transcribed into Yup'ik and translated into English for use by students in the local elementary and high schools.

feature of *Yup'ik Antigone* was not the success of its international debut but the local enthusiasm it engendered. Applause was loudest closest to home. Nelson Islanders clearly enjoyed their introduction to Sophocles. The local production in the village high school was the first masked performance on the island since the missionaries' suppression of indigenous ceremony forty years before. Village elders both approved of and admired the dramatic staging, which shared elements with their traditional performance style.

Although the local enthusiasm *Yup'ik Antigone* elicited is commendable, it was not a factor in the response of the non-native audience. In the final analysis, the rave reviews the play received are telling examples of our Western objectification of culture and the fact that we are for the most part willing to take the other only on our terms—that is, translated through the Greeks. The play was constructed on the flawed assumption of a fundamental similarity between the Yup'ik Eskimos and the ancient Greeks. The face-to-face parent/child confrontations central to Sophocles' *Antigone* illustrate how different these two views of the world are. The Yup'ik pattern of conflict resolution prescribes both diffusion and extreme care in order not to injure the "mind" of the offender (Fienup-Riordan 1986a). One actor later commented on how embarrassed he was by so much "scolding" in the production. Another observer pointed out that a Yup'ik translation of an Italian sex comedy, with all its banter and innuendo, would have been culturally more appropriate than this translation of a Greek tragedy. While bestowing their applause, most of the audience persisted in using the Yup'ik people to define themselves and then concluded that they had witnessed a cultural universal.

Although supportive of *Yup'ik Antigone* and the sympathy it generated for Eskimo people, Nelson Islanders criticized its conflation of Yup'ik and Greek tradition. Villagers maintained that if Hunsaker wanted to produce a really fine play, he should forsake Greek drama and look to Yup'ik oral tradition. Hunsaker was receptive, and soon after *Yup'ik Antigone* completed its foreign tour, he visited Nelson Island to start work on a new production.

The stories that emerged as best suited for such a transformation were those concerning Apanuugpak, the famous warrior-hero of Nelson Island. Dealing as they do with the period of bow-and-arrow warfare in Yup'ik oral tradition, they are full of action and adventure and seemed ideally suited to the production Hunsaker and his Yup'ik coworkers had in mind. In Yup'ik narrative tradition, the Apanuugpak stories form but one set within a larger group of stories concerning the period of bow-and-arrow warfare in western Alaska during the seventeenth and eighteenth centuries. These stories can be divided roughly into four major sets, each pertaining to a different group of regional confrontations. They include the longstanding dispute between the people of Pastolik, at the mouth of the Yukon Delta, and the coastal people around Hooper Bay; the hostility separating the inhabitants of the lower coast and those of modern Quinhagak; confrontations between the lower Kuskokwim Eskimos (*Aglurmiut*) and the people of the middle Kuskokwim living near modern Kalskag; and, finally, the historic animosity between the people of the Kuskokwim drainage and the residents of Nunivak Island.

Aside from scattered references (Michael 1967:281; Nelson 1899:327–330), nineteenth-century explorers and ethnographers largely ignored evidence of Eskimo warfare, content to foster the stereotype of Eskimos as never hostile, not to mention warlike. Not until recently have the details of their bloody feuds and battles come into focus for outside investigators (Burch 1974; Burch and Correll 1972; Fienup-Riordan 1984; VanStone 1967; VanStone and Goddard 1981). For the local population these dramatic orations have been a staple of narrative tradition for at least 150 years and probably much longer. The turn-of-the-century Moravian missionary John Kilbuck was among the first to record accounts of all the major confrontations (Fienup-Riordan 1988:32–34, 43–50, 390–392). Moreover, contemporary oral accounts still exist concerning specific battles won and lost in all four of these major "wars" (for example, Fienup-Riordan 1986b:359–365).

Within this elaborate oral tradition stories of the exploits of the warrior-hero Apanuugpak, defender of Nelson Island, are told up and down the coast of western Alaska from Dillingham in the south all the way to Nelson Island and beyond. Depending on where the stories are recorded, Apanuugpak is depicted as a villain or a hero. In the Togiak area he is said to have been so powerful that no warrior could stand up to him. To protect themselves the Togiak people employed a powerful shaman to put a curse on Apanuugpak. As a result, on his return from a raid in the Togiak area, it is said that he was turned into a rock, which can still be seen when sailing along the coast.

For the people of Nelson Island, however, Apanuugpak is the embodiment of all that is powerful and cunning in a warrior. From his infancy, he is said to have been trained by his grandfather to be tough and strong. Stories recount the strict regimen of his youth, the storyteller often opposing this upbringing to the easy time young people have today. According to oral accounts, his grandfather would wake him up early every morning and have him run to the top of Nelson Island. On his return he would be given only one drop of water from the tip of the feather of a snowy owl to quench his thirst. Similarly, he was taken down to the beach every day and told to roll naked over mussel shells to toughen both his body and his mind.

Along with numerous stories concerning the rigors of Apanuugpak's training, other tales recount his exploits. In all these Apanuugpak emerges victorious by virtue of superior strength, courage, and ingenuity. The hallmark of his cunning is the mussel-shell armor that he wore under his parka, which rendered useless the arrows of his enemies. This "secret weapon" so annoyed his antagonists that, in one account, an opponent is said to have cried out in frustration, "Where in tarnation can we hit this Apanuugpak so that the arrow head can find its deadly mark?" To this, Apanuugpak answered, "Your arrows do not hit my body. Rather they land on the beaches at Engel'umiut!", referring enigmatically to the mussel shells that protected him (Billy Lincoln, Jan. 26, 1987, NI).

Significantly, the Yup'ik Eskimos categorize the Apanuugpak stories as historical narratives *(qanemcit)* rather than mythical tales *(qulirat)*. Whereas the narratives are grounded in the experience of a particular person, whether that person is living or dead, the tales are part of the experience of ancient ancestors and never involve particular individuals definitely believed to have existed. In the 1980s the Yup'ik people became more interested in recording and transcribing, although not necessarily translating, both literary genres.

This interest is part of a growing general self-consciousness in western Alaska brought on by intense efforts at cultural conversion, including new and often commercial interests in their traditional dances, carving, and storytelling. During the last decade Nelson Island has been the focus of a great deal of attention from outside writers, photographers, filmmakers, ornithologists, fish biologists, archaeologists, bureaucrats, and cultural anthropologists. Public hearings, held on an almost weekly basis, regularly confront villagers with the responsibility of reacting to proposed developments and changes in the regulatory systems that increasingly constrain their lives. In the face of this massive and unprecedented inquiry, some Nelson Islanders may view their past as inadequate to vindicate present positions. As a result, many are in the process of inventing a new past to meet the situation. At least some view Hunsaker's project as a vehicle for such re-creation. For both natives and non-natives, the dramatization of history becomes a viable mechanism for distancing oneself from the distress of the current political situation, albeit in different ways.

As the project gained momentum during the winter of 1985, Hunsaker spent several weeks on Nelson Island listening to English glosses on a multitude of different versions of the Apanuugpak stories. To reduce confusion the village council advised him to work with only one village elder (Billy Lincoln) and to develop his script primarily from Lincoln's version of the narratives in Yup'ik. A translator accompanied him, and through him Hunsaker heard the tales. Hunsaker was also able to ask Billy Lincoln questions about what he had heard, and he made notes. No detailed transcriptions or translations were made of the interviews. Although the film was to be based on the oral traditions, it was not intended to be a precise enactment of them.

Notes in hand, Hunsaker returned to Juneau, where he wrote a screenplay entitled *Winter Warrior*. He created a storyboard for the film, scene by scene. Several months later, Hunsaker took this picture sequence back to Nelson Island for review. Again he visited Billy Lincoln, to whom he showed the drawings. Through an interpreter Lincoln approved the script. The process was one of negotiation, not simple acceptance, as exemplified by one proposed scene that Hunsaker agreed to strike early in the going. Significantly, the scene depicted Apanuugpak's opponent confronting him with a gun. Here Hunsaker was attempting a commentary on the devastation and imbalance of power wrought by Alaska natives' acquisition of elements of Western technology. However, given the fact that oral tradition places Apanuugpak before the arrival of the first *kass'aq*, or white man, in western Alaska, Lincoln found the gun unacceptable.

The screenplay takes on a new dimension from the point of view of what the scriptwriter omitted and what Nelson Islanders chose to represent tradition. Just as Lincoln required the deletion of the gun scene because of its misleading reference to the period of historic contact, Hunsaker balked at including evidence of cold-blooded murder on the part of his hero. Rather, Apanuugpak's escalating lust for blood needed to appear consistently motivated by his obsession with revenge. For example, in traditional accounts of Apanuugpak's confrontation with an unarmed Bristol Bay native, Apanuugpak routinely dispatches the man for no reason more obvious than the fact of the encounter. In order not to jeopardize audience sympathy for the warrior-hero by the appearance of unmotivated violence, Hunsaker changed the story and let the man live.

Responding differently than he did to the scene with the gun, Lincoln accepted this explanation and approved the change. Clearly, history was viewed as neither totally sacred nor wholly profane but in specific instances open to alteration.

Given the current reflexive mood in anthropology, Hunsaker's dismissal of the perils of translation seems somewhat suspect. Admittedly his intent to collaborate, to make himself the vehicle for a Yup'ik story, is in line with the noblest recent attempts to do away with the power relationship inherent in traditional ethnographic/native relations. Moreover, the ability of film in general and Hunsaker's film in particular to employ traditional dramatic forms, including dance scenes and shamanic performances, has intriguing advantages over discursive ethnography.

The creation of film, like the creations of the written word, can empower a community by manipulating knowledge, but it can also be impoverishing. We cannot dismiss the irony that the film is based on stories no longer familiar to young people on Nelson Island, in part because they are so fully engaged by the movie channel on local cable television. Like ethnography, film might document oral tradition while contributing to its demise, as it is part of a cultural context in which oral literature rarely survives. Like the ethnographers criticized by Clifford (1983) and Rosaldo (1986), the filmmaker has confined to private conversation discussion of the circumstances that shaped his knowledge. In public-relations descriptions of the project, he depicted the story he created out of his encounters with Lincoln as a mirror image of the memory of the tradition bearer himself, thereby validating his creation as authentic and historically accurate. The first page of the screenplay precisely dates the historical drama as occurring in 1650. In the venerable tradition of anthropological realism, Hunsaker asks his audience to view his creation as a "true outline" (Rosaldo 1986:93).

Just as the ethnographer might adopt the trappings of ethnographic authority and proceed under the assumption that one can apprehend native life in unmediated fashion, the filmmaker strikes a collaborative pose that creates the illusion of the direct apprehension of historically and culturally distant acts and meanings. One possible response to this ploy by the anthropologist well versed in Yup'ik oral tradition is to dismiss the film as a variety of Western humanism artfully dressed in traditional Yup'ik fur clothing—a film that tells us more about the meaning people seek to see in their own history than about Yup'ik history itself. Even more interesting than the disjunction between "authentic" oral tradition and "inauthentic" cinematic representation, however, is the creative inter-

FIGURE 5. Apanuugpak's village: the film set constructed in 1985 on Nelson Island.

change enacted between filmmaker and Nelson Islanders, each re-creating themselves in terms of the history of the other.[4]

After undergoing the review process on Nelson Island, Hunsaker's next step was to submit his script to the Script Development/Film Laboratory Workshop of the Sundance Institute. Robert Redford founded the institute in 1980 to support and encourage films by independent filmmakers that reflect the richness and diversity of American life. Hunsaker's script was one of nine chosen for detailed review from among more than six hundred entries. At Sundance, a number of nationally known directors and scriptwriters gave the script a thorough critique and helped Hunsaker bring the Yup'ik narrative in line with Western dramatic concepts. At Sundance Hunsaker also had the opportunity to test special effects in filming scenes involving shamanic activity. During this period, Hunsaker remarked that he was especially impressed by the techniques employed by the Japanese cinematographer Akira Kurosawa and hoped to achieve the visual look of Kurosawa's films in his own finished product.

4. Anthropologists continue to debate the extent to which writing and for that matter filmmaking are inevitable corruptions (for example, Derrida 1973, 1974; Ong 1977, 1982). Although something may be sacrificed in such textualization, what is lost is not the power of a culture to re-create itself, which is at issue here (for example, Sahlins 1985; Wagner 1975).

During the summer before Hunsaker approached Robert Redford's Sundance organization, I was living at Toksook, working on their oral history project and waiting to become Mrs. Apanuugpak. Along with enjoying the joking and storytelling that were a part of that period, I was both surprised and delighted when, at the end of July and the close of the summer fishing season, the people of Toksook began building the set for the Apanuugpak film. Two dozen men and boys were employed in the construction of four sod houses, located on a point of land half a mile down the coast from the modern village. Pits were dug and driftwood hauled to the site. Within a week, the wooden skeletons of three of the houses had been completed and were ready to receive the grass insulating mats that women had been busy weaving back in the village. I visited the site every day and was impressed with how much people were enjoying the work. Older men boasted that they had seen nothing like this since their youth, and, clearly, for everyone under forty years of age this was a new and exhilarating experience.

Lincoln acted as foreman in the work. As the sod houses neared completion, he began directing work on the large *qasgiq*, or communal men's house, which formed the center of the new "old" community. This *qasgiq*, I was told, would never be left to rot as in times past. Instead, after the completion of the film, it would be preserved as a "permanent replica" and used as a shelter for the valuable gut parkas, wooden masks, and other artifacts that would also be produced for and used in *Winter Warrior*. This "living museum" would then function for western Alaska as a tourist attraction comparable to colonial Williamsburg.[5] Here Nelson Islanders' enjoyment in recreating their past is somewhat reminiscent of the pleasurable sentiments expressed by Kwakiutl natives involved in Edward Curtis's famous fictive reconstruction *In the Land of the War Canoes* (1914).

As much as I felt the immediate excitement engendered by the building project, I was particularly interested in rumors that were circulating concerning a celebration villagers planned to hold when they completed the *qasgiq*. I was told that traditionally the building or refurbishing of a men's house in late summer or early fall was marked by an *Ingulaq*, later referred to by the missionaries as a berry festival. This celebration was

5. A science fiction magazine published a story about Nelson Island. In it a man awakens in a traditional Eskimo village, dresses himself in fur clothing, and leaves the sod house to walk down the beach. His destination, however, is not a kayak but the modern village of Toksook Bay. He had paid cash to experience the past. His time was up and he was returning home.

FIGURE 6. The unfinished *qasgiq*, Toksook Bay in the background.

characterized by slow ceremonial dancing, also known as *ingulaq*, as well as the presentation of and feasting upon bowls of *akutaq*, a festive mixture of berries, oil, and snow. Islanders had not held such a performance for more than forty years and greatly anticipated the impending celebration.

Suddenly, two weeks later, both the construction of the old village and the plans for the *Ingulaq* were called to a halt. Apparently there had been a misunderstanding about the film's funding. Although the filmmaker had promised to pay workers if and when the film was funded, as yet no backers had been found and villagers had begun construction on the site without the filmmaker's knowledge. When the anticipated paychecks did not arrive, disgruntled workers refused to continue what they had begun spontaneously with such goodwill.

I was disappointed, as were many other people in the village. The turn of events was not without its irony. Here were men and women working to re-create a model of a bygone age, which they firmly maintained was more valuable to them than anything money could buy and representative of a way of life they held superior to modern cash-driven society. Nevertheless, without the promised paychecks, they would stop work rather than continue it for its own sake. They had come to place a price on their priceless heritage, which their actions, if not their words, treated as a commodity.

After my summer in Toksook, I continued to monitor the progress of the film project. Not until the fall of 1986 did I have the opportunity to read a draft of the script. What I read was far removed from Apanuugpak narratives I had heard on Nelson Island. I was reminded that the script was an adaptation for a commercial film, not an attempt at documentary, and that Hunsaker had based his work on the Apanuugpak stories with no intention of merely restating them.

In brief, the screenplay that I read in the fall of 1986 developed as follows. A young man (Apanuugpak) is being educated in the rules for right action by his grandfather. Although talented, he is presented as naive and immature. A neighboring group soon visits his village and seeks its support in a territorial struggle. Apanuugpak is troubled by this overture, having asserted in an earlier confrontation, "The waters don't belong to anybody" (Hunsaker 1986:11). Moreover, in a fight he accidentally causes the death of the headstrong brother of the chief of the visiting group. To atone for this sin, Apanuugpak leaves the village to seek spiritual renewal. However, during his quest he is captured by a witch-woman who keeps him a prisoner and through daily copulation gradually saps his strength. Fortunately, Apanuugpak is rescued from this predicament by a young woman he subsequently marries. The couple lives happily for a brief time. Yet trouble is already brewing. The feud that began with the accidental killing of the chief's brother escalates into warfare between the two groups, and in the course of the next four dozen scenes, forty-one additional individuals are dispatched on screen and reference is made to numerous others killed off screen. As the killing escalates, so does Apanuugpak's obsession with revenge. Finally, returning to his village to find all its inhabitants, including his grandfather, burned alive in the *qasgiq* (this disaster constitutes the previous scene), Apanuugpak realizes that war is wrong. He then confronts his enemies and declares that weapons are for killing animals, not human beings. Presumably he then rejoins his wife, through whom he begins to rebuild his shattered world.

The cinematographic "present," like its ethnographic counterpart, is given as one step removed from the contemporary world. In the film's closing scene, a young Yup'ik woman views with concern the photograph of her boyfriend, who has the face of Apanuugpak and is dressed in a National Guard uniform. The scene is set in a village on Nelson Island in the 1940s, a period during which the rights and duties of citizenship were introduced in quick succession in the coastal communities of western Alaska. This scene brings the film full circle. The film opened with a scene in which the villagers were gathered in a wood-frame community hall. There the voice and person of Lincoln were introduced, and in turn introduced the life and times of Apanuugpak. Thus, the entire film is framed as a narration concerning the distant past told in the immediate past. In this story within a story the other is represented not altogether accurately but as a trope for a cultural possibility other than our own. The filmmaker's decision to remove his message is new neither to ethnographic nor to cinematic representation. However, it is significant that Hunsaker's predecessors, including both Curtis and Robert Flaherty (*Nanook of the North*) used no such framing scenes. True to the period in which they worked, they were more content with the fiction of realism and less self-conscious in their use of material.

It is noteworthy that another recent attempt at indigenous dramatic representation in western Alaska was framed in a similar way. The play, produced by the village of Chevak (located less than one hundred miles up the coast from Nelson Island), was performed statewide. The main body of the play was a re-creation of the traditional Bladder Festival; five days of feasts were collapsed into an intense three-hour performance that included audience participation. As in *Winter Warrior*, an element of tradition was taken as the focus, in this case a ceremonial enactment of the belief in an endless cycle of birth and rebirth of human and animal souls. Also like *Winter Warrior*, the play was framed in the present, once removed. In the opening scene a "Brooks Brothers" native moves forward to the sound of disco music and takes a long pull from a flask of whiskey drawn out of a leather briefcase.

From the beginning, the Chevak players neatly juxtaposed the material success of this native Everyman to his spiritual decline; however, the spirits of his past engage him in the Bladder Festival, through which he is reborn along with the souls of the animals. It is perhaps appropriate that the ceremony that traditionally had the power to re-create the past in the future was chosen to represent tradition itself in the present. The Chevak production, just like Hunsaker's, looks to the past to supply the concrete symbolic forms that Western social symbolism has failed to provide. Apparently ethnography is not alone in its propensity to turn to "other times, other customs" (Sahlins 1985:32) to more clearly understand its own.

To return to *Winter Warrior*, the script as summarized here is both carefully developed and dramatically successful by Western standards. Fast paced, it clearly works as an adventure story. To achieve the dramatic force that is its strong point, however, the screenplay has moved far from the Nelson Island oral traditions and Yup'ik dramatic style on which it was based.

This shift is telling. First of all, in oral accounts Apanuugpak was born into warfare and from his earliest youth was trained as a virtual "killing machine." Although the filmmaker heard stories about Apanuugpak's early years, at least in reference, he did not use them because they were not part of Lincoln's account. This omission highlights the problems associated with using Lincoln as sole tradition bearer. Lincoln was born and raised north of Nelson Island, not on Nelson Island proper. Although he knew the stories of Apanuugpak's childhood, they may not have been part of his personal repertoire and consequently part of what he felt he had a right to communicate.

Second, in his screenplay Hunsaker adds substantially to the traditional stories of Apanuugpak's adult years. In Nelson Island oral tradition these narratives all revolve around the battles Apanuugpak fought and won and the tricks he played on his enemies. There are no stories of whom or how he married. However, at the end of his life, he is seen surrounded by his grandsons telling stories in the *qasgiq*. Thus the witch-woman scenes, as well as the subplot of Apanuugpak's twofold "salvation" by the woman who becomes his wife, are dramatic inventions. A more troublesome alteration concerns Apanuugpak's social role. As a warrior (*anguyaq*), Apanuugpak occupied a social position distinct from that of either a great hunter (*nukalpiaq*) or a shaman (*angalkuq*). In Yup'ik oral tradition, warriors are viewed as men apart, hunters of men rather than men who are hunters in either the animal or spirit worlds. In the screenplay these categories are collapsed, and Apanuugpak is presented as the quintessential embodiment of all three.

Third, in the screenplay Apanuugpak is depicted as the unwitting cause of the onset of warfare. He is also presented as the sadder but wiser restorer of the peace through his ultimate recognition of the evils inherent in warfare. This message is, in fact, a critical part of the meaning of the film and is epitomized in Apanuugpak's dramatic concluding statement: "Weapons are meant for killing animals, not humans." Here Hunsaker is using Yup'ik oral tradition to state what he considers a universal truth: War is wrong and through war a man risks losing his soul. Whatever the merits of this statement, it is ironic that Yup'ik stories celebrating the preeminent war hero of their past should be used as its vehicle.

In the final analysis, Hunsaker's most significant revision is the invention of the beginning and end of warfare and the placement of these accomplishments in the hands of a single human being, however famous. Yup'ik oral tradition does, in fact, have an explanation for the beginning and the end of warfare in general, as well as specific wars. For example, in perhaps the best-known account of the beginning and end of the Yukon Delta/coastal conflict, an unskilled hunter from Pastolik who had married into the village of Hooper Bay killed his hunting companions one after the other and claimed their catch as his own. When the people of Hooper Bay discovered his crime, he fled north to Pastolik. There he sowed the seeds of distrust among the Yukon Eskimos, who subsequently took the offensive against their coastal neighbors. Many battles took place during the ensuing years. However, during a period of extreme food shortage, a man from the Yukon and a man from Hooper Bay formed an unlikely partnership out on the ice while stalking a seal. They shared their catch and consequently saved each other's lives. From that time on the hostilities between the Yukon and coastal areas began to subside (Fienup-Riordan 1986b:38, 359–65).

This complete rendition of the beginning and end of the famous Yukon Delta/coastal conflict is revealing in several respects. It begins in theft and the refusal to cooperate; it ends in food-sharing and trading. Whereas the original conflict divides a group united by marriage, the resolution brings about the rapprochement of two originally distinct regional groups. In addition, the breach pivots around the food quest and a conflict over resources in one region. Although it does not originate as a boundary dispute, in the intervening war episodes men are depicted as defending a range or a site or a kill (Fienup-Riordan 1984:76–77).

Nelson Islanders have their own account concerning the end of wars (Fienup-Riordan 1983:247). In brief, two survivors approached their enemies seeking revenge after their own village had been destroyed. As they drew closer in their kayaks, they broke the spears they had intended to kill with and instead used them to beat the sides of their kayaks like drums. Then the women of the opposing village walked down to the shore to meet them and, standing in front of their men, began to dance. So it is said, from that time forward, Yup'ik people have never fought with bows and arrows but rather through the dance. Anyone who has seen Yup'ik dancing will know that this is indeed still the case!

Although Hunsaker had viewed Yup'ik dance, he had neither asked for nor received this origin story. He was likewise unaware of the cycle of narratives recounting the beginning and ending of warfare. His invention of such a sequence was thus not based on a considered rejection of these narratives but on limited information. Although sensitive to known issues, he was not told enough to realize his omission. What the narratives had in common was the motif of an endless cosmological cycling between birth and rebirth. In the traditional accounts of warfare, the primary issue was not death but rather in what manner life would be maintained in perpetuity. For Hunsaker, as for Sophocles before him, the inevitability of death becomes focal. On the contrary, within Yup'ik cosmology the narratives depicting warfare are about death's impossibility not its finality. This divergence in part explains the differences between Hunsaker's and Lincoln's views regarding the motivation and meaning behind Apanuugpak's acts of violence.

Finally, in replacing traditional accounts of the beginning and end of warfare, Hunsaker also transformed the traditional and contemporary Yup'ik concepts of territoriality. In the beginning of *Winter Warrior*, Apanuugpak exclaims, "The waters do not belong to anyone." This sentiment is brought full circle when, in the final scene of the film, the young woman views with concern the portrait of her boyfriend in his National Guard uniform. Here, along with the message "war is wrong," Hunsaker attempts to make the point that with the emergence of the modern nation-state in western Alaska, the same "foreign" issues of landownership and water rights that brought on the wars of the past are resurfacing in the present.

In fact, the traditional Yup'ik Eskimos possessed a well-developed sense of territory; however, rights to land and water use were not based on, or reduced to, possession of a particular site by an individual or group at any one point in time. Rather the concept of ownership was relational; a man had a right, and in fact an obligation, to use a site because of his relationship to previous generations of people who had a defined relationship to the species taken at that same place. In other words, a man had a right to use a site not because he owned the land but because his grandparent (by name and by birth) hunted there and had a relationship with the animals of that area. A man was his grandfather incarnate, and therefore the animals that gave themselves to him were those that gave themselves to his grandfather. A man's right to resource extraction was thus relational rather than possessive. In this sense ownership was and continues to be tied to defined territories insofar as these reflect social boundaries. This traditional understanding of territoriality does not correspond to the capitalist notion of property that the scriptwriter has the Yup'ik people reject.

In the fall of 1986 I discussed with the scriptwriter the differences between his screenplay and Yup'ik history as I understood it, arguing for changes in his script that would bring it closer to the form and meaning of Yup'ik oral tradition. His answer was simple and straightforward: We were talking about two different films. From my point of view the interchange was less than satisfactory as, like the native on whom the anthropologist relies, I was put in the uncomfortable position of being asked to give information without the requisite power to control its subsequent use. Within the context of our differences, however, two issues of broad significance emerged that merit consideration here.

It should be clear that Hunsaker and I hold different views of what is important about Nelson Island. As in *Yup'ik Antigone*, in *Winter Warrior* the scriptwriter chose to focus on the universality of the human condition. This is a venerable theme in the Western tradition, and much of anthropology has been framed as an attempt to speak to this issue. My chief concern, however, is that Yup'ik Eskimos in general, and Nelson Islanders in particular, have a unique way of looking at and acting in the world. From my perspective it makes no sense to override significant and instructive differences between the seventeenth-century Yup'ik Eskimos and contemporary American culture to present the ways in which Yup'ik people were in essentials "just like us" (Fienup-Riordan 1985:9).

The dialogue between Hunsaker and me was further constrained by the fact that we have different agendas. Both of us must have the support of our peers for our work to succeed. On the one hand, to find backing for his film, Hunsaker had to convince the Sundance Institute that his script had broad dramatic appeal, not that his facts were correct. On the other hand, I must convince research agencies that there is something special but not necessarily of universal appeal about the Yup'ik people that merits detailed inquiry.

Along with and related to the different practical constraints on our work, Hunsaker and I hold very different views about the meaning of history and tradition. When Hunsaker visited Nelson Island to discuss *Winter Warrior*, in addition to gathering Apanuugpak stories, he kept his ears open to the current state of affairs. The years during which he visited Nelson Island brought dramatic challenges to the political and cultural integrity of the region. Numerous state and federal agencies had become increasingly involved in the management and regulation of the fish and game on which Nelson Islanders depend for their livelihood. New regulations challenged the islanders' ability to freely harvest the geese, halibut, herring, and musk oxen that, among other species, inhabit the area. In addition, outside pressure on these resources had also escalated. At the same time that they were feeling increased pressure on these resources, their right to the use and "ownership" of ancestral lands was threatened by the approach of 1991, when village and regional corporation land becomes transferrable under the 1971 Alaska Native Claims Settlement Act.

In the context of this political situation Hunsaker carried out his "fieldwork" on Nelson Island. Perhaps not surprisingly, native suspicion and resentment of current non-native forms of regulation colored his interviews and history lessons. Nelson Islanders told him that in the past no one had specific rights over the land or the resources, and no one could restrict another's use. In fact, this is not an accurate presentation of the past, as already indicated. However, this was the view of Yup'ik history that Hunsaker took home with him, and he developed his script based on this history. Thus the "tradition" on which Hunsaker's screenplay rests, and that may well appear to be old, is quite recent in origin and has in fact been intentionally invented by Nelson Islanders to establish continuity between their present political position and a suitable historic past. Although they desire free use of their land "as in the past," unrestricted movement and unregulated access to resources were not a part of the nineteenth-century Yup'ik way of life.

The phenomenon of "invented traditions" is not unique to Nelson Island. Hobsbawm and Ranger (1983) make it the subject of detailed inquiry. Invented tradition, as distinguished from noninvented tradition and custom, is said to be a set of practices governed by accepted rules and of a symbolic nature that seeks to inculcate certain values implying continuity with the past. Insofar as there is reference to a historic past, Hobsbawm and Ranger note, the continuity with it is largely fictitious. Moreover, this phenomenon may in part be attributed to the contrast between the constant innovation of the modern world and the attempt to find some part of it invariant. Thus, increasingly, old materials (like the Apanuugpak stories or the Bladder Festival) are used to construct invented traditions of a novel type to establish a people's legitimacy through history.

Furthermore, Hobsbawm and Ranger (1983:8) distinguish between the adaptability of genuine traditions and the "invention of tradition." They contend that where old ways are alive, traditions need be neither revived nor invented. Where they are invented, it is often not because the old ways are no longer available or viable, but because those ways are deliberately not used or adapted. In the case of *Winter Warrior*, a double invention is in process, with Hunsaker inventing a trope for the condition of modern man based on a tradition of nonownership and an absence of territorial concepts that the people of Nelson Island have themselves invented to validate their contemporary relationship to the land. Hunsaker moves from the misinterpretation of tradition to its "invention" in his claim that the people of Nelson Island regard his screenplay as acceptable history. He already has a strong following for his project.

Hunsaker vacillates between naturalizing the Yup'ik as paragons of simplicity and virtue and historicizing them as victims of Western imperialism. Nowhere is he encumbered by the specificity of Yup'ik concepts of space, time, or personhood. He has responded instead to their contemporary plea for the severing of a connection with a white man's world they view as having gone awry. Hunsaker was told essentially, "We have always been a peaceful people living in harmony with our land. Boundaries have been imposed from without, and the constraint is unacceptable." In fact, the nineteenth-century Yupiit were preoccupied with the creation of boundaries and passages in a world perceived as formless without them (Fienup-Riordan 1987). Today the Yupiit are intent on breaking externally imposed constraints and are doing so in the name of tradition.

Hunsaker was finally forced to face the claim that his "invention" conflicts with other traditions still adhered to on Nelson Island. There was danger that the bow-and-arrow wars of the past were to be fought again in the regional newspaper, the *Tundra Drums*. An exchange of letters (Hunsaker 1987; Oscar 1987) concerning the use of explicit sexual imagery in the witch-woman scene undercut local support for the project. This "paper war" was doubly ironic in that the stated goals of the film project are "to advance public understanding of a little known traditional American culture" (Hunsaker 1986) and to be as "authentic" and historically accurate as possible. However, filmmakers (just like anthropologists), whatever else their objectives, are engaged in the process of "inventing traditions" inasmuch as they "contribute, consciously or not, to the creation, dismantling, and restructuring of the images of the past" (Hobsbawm and Ranger 1983:8).

Moreover, the push for the film is forcing more and more Nelson Islanders to expand their concept of what is and is not marketable within their own world. As in the case of the aborted construction of the old village, their oral traditions have begun to take on market value. Whereas they still value the oral traditions for what they can teach about proper living, Nelson Islanders are recognizing the monetary value they have in the contemporary world. Also, for the younger generation, the prospect of being an actor, not just a viewer, in a movie drama draws them toward what for many is the clearing-house if not the creator of Western reality—the media.

The younger villagers are the ones most interested in acting in the film. These would-be actors are the same generation of men and women made inactive in their own culture in part by the unreality of American television. In the 1940s Nelson Islanders were more in touch with their own past than with the national present in which they were nominally included. Today, that historical reality as constructed in myth and story has dimmed to the point where its preservation on the silver screen represents true re-creation.

To date, the community continues to support the film project over the voices of individual dissidents. Among villagers, however, support remains contingent on the filmmaker's ability to find funding for his project. Although their realities are not identical, the interests of the Nelson Islanders and the filmmaker in the film overlap, and they are not at odds. Nelson Islanders are not replacing their version of history with Hunsaker's, and they retain a measure of ironic distance from cinematic concessions to Western audiences in the name of profit.

Nevertheless, winning on Hunsaker's terms may be a form of losing if stories once told to provide moral guidance and to preserve tradition become equated with monetary gain. In the film project's relationship with the community, money has talked in the past and will again in the future. Although the filming will be done in the native language, the fact that the actors will be paid in cash, in the language of venture capitalism, elicits local support for the project. Whatever Hunsaker's view of his creation and its worth, Nelson Islanders are currently content to view it as a finite resource to be harvested if and when it arrives, in contrast to the infinitely renewable resources they harvested in the past.

Beyond the invention and reevaluation of history, the question arises concerning the extent to which the collection of Yup'ik artifacts and oral tradition constitutes an invention of heritage—by the filmmaker or by anthropologists in general. By his own admission, Hunsaker's selective recording and organization of Yup'ik material is an act of creation. Although finding support within the community, the impetus for making the film comes not only from within Nelson Island but from without. The farther away the film moves, the greater the interest it elicits. The product will be an ethnic display, not an act of Eskimo self-representation.

Just as the historicism of the nineteenth century and the belief that it was necessary to collect before it was "too late" made possible the ethnological collecting associated with the "museum movement" (Cole 1985:48; Dominguez 1986:549), so the social and political climate in Alaska enables the cinematographic invention of a new Yup'ik tradition. Similarly, the collections of Eskimo artifacts and the Eskimos themselves were and remain objects of interest not because of their intrinsic value but because of their perceived contribution to our understanding of our own history. The value of *Winter Warrior* will lie not in its "true" representation of the Yup'ik Eskimos, the proverbial "others," but in the degree to which it can be read as a referential index of ourselves.

At its best *Winter Warrior* may rise above the accusation of cultural imperialism. Just as cultural order is not immediately given but constantly achieved through the process of negotiation between symbolic structures and historical circumstances, a film is a marriage between script and actors, who in this case will be Yup'ik Eskimos acting in their own language in their own time and place. Although the city council has given permission to the filmmaker to pursue his project, they do not view their agreement as writ in stone but as contingent on continued goodwill and agreement on essentials between the filmmaker and the community. The filmmaker has developed a script that both he and they view as open to alteration as they begin to play it out in the filming process. Thus, the community feels in control of the production, to the credit of all concerned.

In the enthusiasm of Nelson Islanders to use their history to talk about their present, the distinction between "authentic," lived culture and "inauthentic" invented tradition loses its force. Rather the screenplay may be viewed as performing the role of mediator in Wagner's (1986) sense, insofar as its negotiation of cultural conceptions results in a re-creation of them. *Winter Warrior* as presently conceived will not represent the traditional Yup'ik way of life any more accurately or inaccurately than *Road Warrior* represents modern American culture. Rather, like *Road Warrior*, *Winter Warrior* will re-present it, complete with strategic omissions and additions. Although the film may provoke the purist, it is valid in its own right. In the best anthropological tradition, the text that is the film is more than description (accurate or inaccurate) of the Yup'ik past. Rather it embodies an act of translation, of re-creation, where both Yup'ik and non-Yup'ik audiences may learn something about themselves by means of the other.

Limits exist in our ability to apprehend the other. This point has been made in myriad ways, from Sahlins's (1976) dictum that no ethnography exists without ethnology to Wagner's (1975) exegesis on the invention of culture to Clifford and Marcus's (1986) grim conclusion that constructed truths are made possible only by lies of exclusion. Accepting these limits to its own enterprise, anthropology cannot fairly condemn the filmmaker, who faces challenges similar to those of ethnographic writing, including problems of narrative and focus, of editing, and of reflexivity.

As in the case of ethnography, although we can recognize the limits of the cinematographic enterprise, we do not have to reject it in toto. With ethnography's own authority in question, anthropology's chief use is not in standing up for the accurate representation of the pure culture of the past but in clarifying the significance of action in the present. The question of the differences between the ethnographic and cinematographic enterprise appears to be a reinvention of the Mead-Freeman debate in a colder clime.[6] Following Clifford's (1986) analysis of this debate, I would argue that if anthropology's response is dismissal on the grounds of inaccuracy or inauthenticity, it misses the point of the attempt to depict the Yup'ik past so as to provide a moral lesson for the present. Just as Mead went to Samoa and Hunsaker to Nelson Island, the Yup'ik Eskimos are visiting another time within their own world to frame a present as both inherited and in the process of being reinvented.

6. Whereas Margaret Mead (1928) selectively described aspects of Samoan culture to demonstrate that the stressful adolescence of American teenagers was not a universal phenomenon, Derek Freeman (1983) marshaled examples of Samoan anxiety and violence to show where Mead's conclusions were wrong. Freeman's criticism talked past the value of Mead's initial enterprise and ignored the fact that his account of the "real" Samoa was as much a framed construction determined by his point of view as Mead's had been before him.

REFERENCES

Burch, Ernest S., Jr. 1974. "Eskimo Warfare in Northwest Alaska." *Anthropological Papers of the University of Alaska* 16(2):1–14.
Burch, Ernest S., Jr., and Thomas C. Correll. 1972. "Alliance and Conflict: Inter-regional Relations in North Alaska." In *Alliance in Eskimo Society*, ed. Lee Guemple, pp. 17–39. Seattle: University of Washington Press.
Clifford, James. 1983. "On Ethnographic Authority." *Representation* 1(2):118–146.
Clifford, James, and George E. Marcus, eds. 1986. *Writing Culture: The Poetics and Politics of Ethnography*. Berkeley: University of California Press.
Cole, Douglas. 1985. *Captured Heritage: The Scramble for Northwest Coast Artifacts*. Seattle: University of Washington Press.
Derrida, Jacques. 1973. *Speech and Phenomena*. Evanston, Ill.: Northwestern University Press.
———. 1974. *Of Grammatology*. Baltimore: Johns Hopkins University Press.
Dominguez, Virginia R. 1986. "The Marketing of Heritage." *American Ethnologist* 13(3):546–555.

Fienup-Riordan, Ann. 1977–1987. Transcripts and translations of interviews with Yup'ik elders. Tapes 1–99. Unpublished manuscript compiled for the Nelson Island Oral History Project. Prepared with the support of the Alaska Humanities Forum, Anchorage.

———. 1983. *The Nelson Island Eskimo*. Anchorage: Alaska Pacific University Press.

———. 1984. "Regional Groups on the Yukon-Kuskokwim Delta." *The Central Yupik Eskimos*, ed. Ernest S. Burch, Jr., supplementary issue of *Etudes/Inuit/Studies* 8:63–93.

———. 1985. "The Uses and Abuses of Anthropology in Alaska." Distinguished Humanist Address. Alaska Humanities Forum, Anchorage, Feb.

———. 1986a. "The Real People: The Concept of Personhood among the Yup'ik Eskimos of Western Alaska." *Etudes/Inuit/Studies* 10(1–2):261–270.

———. 1986b. *When Our Bad Season Comes: A Cultural Account of Subsistence Harvesting and Harvest Disruption on the Yukon Delta*. Monograph Series 1. Aurora: Alaska Anthropological Association.

———. 1987. "The Mask: The Eye of the Dance." *Arctic Anthropology* 24(2):40–55.

———, ed. 1988. *The Yup'ik Eskimos as Described in the Travel Journals and Ethnographic Accounts of John and Edith Kilbuck, 1885–1900*. Kingston, Ont.: Limestone Press.

Freeman, Derek. 1983. *Margaret Mead and Samoa: The Making and Unmaking of an Anthropological Myth*. Cambridge: Harvard University Press.

Hobsbawm, Eric and Terence Ranger, eds. 1983. *The Invention of Tradition*. Cambridge: Cambridge University Press.

Hunsaker, Dave. 1986. *Winter Warrior*. Dancing Bear Productions, Juneau.

———. 1987. "Letter to John Oscar." *Tundra Drums* (Bethel, Alaska) 15(43):2, 23.

Jacobson, Steven A. 1984. *Yup'ik Eskimo Dictionary*. Fairbanks: Alaska Native Language Center, University of Alaska.

Mead, Margaret. 1928. *Coming of Age in Samoa*. New York: Morrow Quill.

Michael, Henry N., ed. 1967. *Lieutenant Zagoskin's Travels in Russian America, 1842–1844*. Toronto: University of Toronto Press.

Nelson, Edward W. 1899. *The Eskimo about Bering Strait*. Bureau of American Ethnology Annual Report for 1896–1897, vol. 18, no. 1. Washington, D.C.: Smithsonian Institution. (Reprinted 1983.)

Nelson, Richard K. 1977. *Shadow of the Hunter*. Chicago: University of Chicago Press.

NI = Nelson Island Oral History Project, Toksook Bay, Nelson Island, Alaska. Interviews taped between 1985 and 1989.

Ong, Walter J. 1977. *Interfaces of the Word*. Ithaca, N.Y.: Cornell University Press.

————. 1982. *Orality and Literacy*. London: Methuen.

Oscar, John. 1987. "Letter to Dave Hunsaker." *Tundra Drums* (Bethel, Alaska) 15(42):2.

Rosaldo, Renato. 1986. "From the Door of His Tent: The Fieldworker and the Inquisitor." In *Writing Culture*, ed. James Clifford and George E. Marcus. Berkeley: University of California Press.

Sahlins, Marshall. 1976. *Culture and Practical Reason*. Chicago: University of Chicago Press.

————. 1985. *Islands of History*. Chicago: University of Chicago Press.

Schiller, Paula. 1981. "Shadow of the Hunter." *Tundra Times* (Anchorage) 17(15):16.

VanStone, James W. 1967. *Eskimos of the Nushagak River: An Ethnographic History*. Seattle: University of Washington Press.

VanStone, James W., and Ives Goddard. 1981. "Territorial Groups of West-Central Alaska before 1898." In *Handbook of North American Indians*, vol. 6: *Subarctic*, ed. June Helm, pp. 556–561. Washington, D.C.: Smithsonian Institution.

Wagner, Roy. 1975. *The Invention of Culture*. Chicago: University of Chicago Press.

————. 1986. *Symbols That Stand for Themselves*. Chicago: University of Chicago Press.

ACTIVE READING

1. In her first section, "The Ideology of Subsistence," Fienup-Riordan chooses to write a narrative rather than a more traditional ethnographic description, yet she continues to use some special terms from anthropology. Pick a few passages where she uses narrative as well as anthropological language, and discuss the role that each kind of description plays as she constructs her portrait of the Yup'ik Eskimos.

2. Early in "The Ideology of Subsistence," Fienup-Riordan mentions "cultural imagination," but she does not define it in much detail. Find several passages in this piece that are examples of cultural imagination, and compose a detailed definition of the term.

3. In her second section, "Robert Redford, Apanuugpak, and the Invention of Tradition," Fienup-Riordan mentions three different accounts

of the end of Yup'ik warfare: that of the filmmaker, one from Yup'ik oral tradition, and one that is specific to Nelson Islanders. What does each account suggest about the values of those who have proposed it? Use details from this second section to help you discuss the roles of history and myth in each account.

4. At the beginning of "Robert Redford," Fienup-Riordan discusses "the dialogic character of . . . native/non-native encounters" (213). After looking up "dialogic" in a dictionary, trace the meaning of this concept through several incidents in her essay. Put together an expanded definition of Fienup-Riordan's phrase.

READING IN NEW CONTEXTS

1. Fienup-Riordan describes "the rules of proper relationship" (209) as a central element of Yup'ik Eskimo culture. Looking at Kingston, Clifford, or another *Literacies* text, use Fienup-Riordan's explanation of such rules to interpret the relationships you find there.

2. Use Fienup-Riordan's story about Yup'ik naming customs to speculate about the significance of names for both the Nelson Islanders and for Fienup-Riordan herself. Which of your observations help you say more about another *Literacies* text (such as Angelou, Kingston, or Walker) that focuses on the importance of names?

3. In her second section, the author mentions "the circumstances that shaped . . . knowledge" (218). Make a catalog of as many of those circumstances as you can find in her essays, and explain (perhaps with the help of Barnlund or Bettelheim) how you think the process of shaping knowledge works.

4. Based on your reading of the second section, what are the benefits and dangers of what Fienup-Riordan calls "invented tradition" (228)? Use your understanding of this concept to help you comment on the uses of tradition in a text such as Bellah's or Walker's.

DRAFT ONE/DRAFT TWO

1. *Draft One*: With the help of Fienup-Riordan's ideas about "relational" and "possessive" property rights, expand upon the analysis of ownership

that you began in Before Reading #4. How do the beliefs of the Yup'ik contribute to your own understanding of what it means to own something?

Draft Two: Use ideas from Draft One to explore the relationship between ownership and community life in Bellah, hooks & West, or MacLeod. How does this relationship differ in the new context?

2. *Draft One:* How do Fienup-Riordan's experiences support her theory that her encounters with the Yup'ik are a "creative interchange" through which she and her subjects "each [recreate] themselves in terms of the history of the other" (218–19)? Describe what you think are the requirements for that creative interchange.

Draft Two: Turn to another *Literacies* text and discuss whether the parties there manage to "[recreate] themselves in terms of the history of the other." What does that other text help you add to Draft One? What does it allow you to say about the meeting of different cultural groups?

BEFORE READING ANDREA R. FISHMAN

1. What do you recall about the process of becoming literate? Has your relation to your literacy skills changed at any time? Why or why not?

2. How should society resolve conflicts that arise between a family's values and the values of the public school system?

3. Describe some aspects of your education that have reinforced common customs and beliefs and others that have challenged them. What have these reinforcements and challenges contributed to your education?

A N D R E A   R.   F I S H M A N

BECOMING LITERATE:
A LESSON FROM THE AMISH

One clear, frost-edged January Sunday night, two families gathered for supper and an evening's entertainment. One family—mine—consisted of a lawyer, a teacher, and their twelve-year-old son; the other family—the Fishers—consisted of Eli and Anna, a dairy farmer and his wife, and their five children, ranging in age from six to seventeen. After supper in the Fisher's large farm kitchen—warmed by a wood stove and redolent of the fragrances of chicken corn soup, homemade bread, and freshly baked apples—the table was cleared and an additional smaller one set up to accommodate games of Scrabble, double Dutch solitaire, and dominoes. As most of us began to play, adults and children randomly mixed, Eli Fisher, Sr., settled into his brown leather recliner with the newspaper, while six-year-old Eli, Jr., plopped on the corner of the couch nearest his father with a book.

Fifteen or twenty minutes later, I heard Eli, Sr., ask his son, "Where are your new books?" referring to a set of outgrown Walt Disney books we had brought for little Eli and his seven-year-old brother, Amos. Eli, Jr., pointed to a stack of brightly colored volumes on the floor, from which

From *The Right to Literacy*, by Andrea A. Lunsford, Helene Moglen, and James Slevin (1990).

his father chose *Lambert, the Sheepish Lion*. As Eli, Jr., climbed onto the arm of the recliner and snuggled against his father, Eli, Sr., began reading the book out loud in a voice so commandingly dramatic that soon everyone was listening to the story, instead of playing their separate games. Broadly portraying the roles of both Lambert and his lioness mother and laughing heartily at the antics of the cub who preferred cavorting with the sheep to stalking with the lions, Eli held his enlarged audience throughout the rest of the story.

As most of us returned to our games when he finished reading, Eli, Sr., asked of anyone and everyone, "Where's the *Dairy?*" Daniel, the Fishers' teenage son, left his game and walked toward his father. "It's in here," he said, rummaging through the newspapers and magazines in the rack beside the couch until he found a thick newsletter called *Dairy World*, published by the Independent Buyers Association, to which Eli belonged.

Eli leafed through the publication, standing and walking toward the wood stove as he did. Leaning against the wall, he began reading aloud without preface. All conversation stopped as everyone once again attended to Eli's loudly expressive reading voice, which said:

> A farmer was driving his wagon down the road. On the back was a sign which read: "Experimental Vehicle. Runs on oats and hay. Do not step in exhaust."

Everyone laughed, including Eli, Sr., who then read the remaining jokes on the humor page to his attentive audience. All our games forgotten, we shared the best and the worst riddles and jokes we could remember until it was time for bed.

Occasions like this one occur in many homes and have recently attracted the interest of family literacy researchers (Heath; Taylor; Wells). The scene at the Fishers could have been the scene in any home where parents value reading and writing and want their children to value them as well. It would not be surprising if Eli and Anna, like other literacy-oriented parents, read bedtime stories to their children, helped with their homework, and encouraged them to attain high school diplomas, if not college degrees. But Eli and Anna do none of these things: they read no bedtime stories, they are annoyed if their children bring schoolwork home, and they expect their children to go only as far in school as they did themselves, as far as the eighth grade.

So, although Eli and Anna appeared on that Sunday night to be ideal pro-literacy parents, they may not be, according to commonly described standards, and one significant factor may account for their variations from the supposed ideal: Eli and Anna are not mainstream Americans but are Old Order Amish, raising their family according to Old Order tradition and belief. The Sunday night gathering I just described took place by the light of gas lamps in a house without radio, stereo, television, or any other electrical contrivance. Bedtime in that house is more often marked by singing or silence than by reading. Schoolwork rarely enters there because household, field, and barn chores matter more. And the Fisher children's studying is done in a one-room, eight-grade, Old Order school taught by an Old Order woman who attended the same kind of school herself. So while Eli, Jr., like his siblings, is learning the necessity and the value of literacy, what literacy means to him and the ways in which he learns it may differ in both obvious and subtle ways from what it means and how it's transmitted to many mainstream children, just as Eli's world differs from theirs, both obviously and subtly.

As suggested earlier, Eli, Jr., lives in a house replete with print, from the kitchen bulletin board to the built-in bookcases in the playroom to the tables and magazine rack in the living room. There are children's classics and children's magazines. There are local newspapers, shoppers' guides, and other adult periodicals. And there are books of children's Bible stories, copies of the King James Version of the Bible, and other inspirational volumes, none of which mark the Fishers' home as notably different from that of many other Christian Americans.

Yet there are differences, easily overlooked by a casual observer but central to the life of the family and to their definition of literacy. One almost invisible difference is the sources of these materials. Eli and Anna attempt to carefully control the reading material that enters their home. Anna buys books primarily from a local Christian bookstore and from an Amish-operated dry goods store, both of which she trusts not to stock objectionable material. When she sees potentially interesting books in other places—in the drugstore, in the book and card shop, or at a yard sale—she uses the publisher's name as a guide to acceptable content. Relatives and friends close to the family also supply appropriate titles both as gifts and as recommendations, which Anna trusts and often chooses to follow up.

Another, slightly more visible difference comes in the form of books and periodicals around the Fisher house that would not be found in many mainstream, farm, or Christian homes. Along with the local newspaper in the rack beside the couch are issues of *Die Botschaft*, which describes itself as "A Weekly Newspaper Serving Old Order Amish Communities

Everywhere." On the desk is a copy of *The Amish Directory*, which alphabetically lists all the Amish living in Pennsylvania and Maryland by nuclear family groups, giving crucial address and other information, along with maps of the eighty-seven church districts included.

On top of the breakfront in the sitting area are copies of songbooks, all in German: some for children, some for adults, and one—the *Ausbund*—for everyone, for this is the church hymnal, a collection of hymns written by tortured and imprisoned sixteenth-century Anabaptists about their experiences and their faith. Kept with these songbooks is a German edition of the Bible and a copy of the *Martyrs Mirror*, an oversized, weighty tome full of graphic descriptions in English of the tortured deaths of early Anabaptists, each illustrated by a black-and-white woodcut print.

Despite what may seem to be the esoteric nature of these texts, none remain in their special places gathering dust, for all are used regularly, each reinforcing in a characteristic way the Amish definition of literacy and each facilitating the image Eli, Jr., has of himself as literate.

Because singing is central to Amish religious observance and expression, the songbooks are used frequently by all members of the family. Because singing requires knowing what is in the text and because Amish singing, which is unaccompanied and highly stylized, requires knowing how to interpret the text exactly as everyone else does, the songbooks represent a kind of reading particularly important to the community, a kind that must be mastered to be considered literate. Yet because singing may mean holding the text and following the words as they appear or it may mean holding the text and following the words from memory or from others' rendition, children of Eli's age and younger all participate, appearing and feeling as literate as anyone else.

Functioning similarly are the German Bible and the *Martyrs Mirror*. Though only the older Fishers read that Bible, they do so regularly and then share what they've read with their children. It is the older Fishers, too, who read the *Martyrs Mirror*, but that text Eli, Sr., usually reads aloud during family devotions, so that Anna and all the children, regardless of age, participate similarly through his oral presentations.

While it may seem easier to accept such variant definitions of reading in shared communal situations like these, the participation of Eli, Jr., was equally welcome and equally effective in shared individual reading. When individual oral reading was clearly text-bound, as it is during family devotions, Eli was always enabled to participate in ways similar to his brothers' and sisters', making him a reader like them. When all the Fishers took turns reading the Bible aloud, for example, someone would read

Eli's verse aloud slowly, pausing every few words, so that he could repeat what was said and thereby take his turn in the rotation.

When the older children were assigned Bible verses or *Ausbund* hymn stanzas to memorize, Eli was assigned the same one as Amos, the sibling closest in age. Their assignment would be shorter and contain less complex vocabulary than the one the older children got, yet Amos and Eli would also practice their verse together, as the older children did, and would take their turns reciting, as the older children did, making Eli again able to participate along with everyone else.

Because oral reading as modeled by Eli, Sr., is often imitated by the others, Eli, Jr., always shared his books by telling what he saw or knew about them. No one ever told him that telling isn't the same as reading, even though they may look alike, so Eli always seemed like a reader to others and felt like a reader himself. When everyone else sat reading or playing reading-involved games in the living room after supper or on Sunday afternoons, Eli did the same, to no one's surprise, to everyone's delight, and with universal, though often tacit, welcome and approval. When the other children received books as birthday and Christmas presents, Eli received them too. And when he realized at age six that both of his brothers had magazine subscriptions of their own, Eli asked for and got one as well. Eli never saw his own reading as anything other than real; he did not see it as make-believe or bogus, and neither did anyone else. So, despite the fact that before he went to school Eli, Jr., could not read according to some definitions, he always could according to his family's and his own.

Just as all the Fishers read, so they all write, and just as Eli was enabled to define reading in a way that made him an Amish reader, so he could define writing in a way that made him an Amish writer. Letter writing has always been a primary family activity and one central to the Amish community. Anna writes weekly to *Die Botschaft*, acting as the scribe from her district. She, Eli, Sr., and sixteen-year-old Sarah all participate in circle letters, and the next three children all write with some regularity to cousins in other Amish settlements.

Yet, no matter who is writing to whom, their letters follow the same consistently modeled Amish format, beginning with "Greetings . . . ," moving to recent weather conditions, then to family and community news of note, and ending with a good-bye and often a philosophical or religious thought. I've never seen anyone in the community instructed to write this way, but in the Fisher family, letters received and even letters written are often read out loud, and though this oral sharing is done for informative rather than instructive purposes, it provides an implicit model for everyone to follow.

With all the other family members writing letters, reading them out loud, and orally sharing those they have received, Eli, Jr., wanted to write and receive letters, too, and no one said he couldn't. When he was very young, he dictated his messages to Sarah and drew pictures to accompany what she wrote down for him. Then, even before he started school, Eli began copying the dictated messages Sarah recorded, so that the letters would be in his own hand, as the drawings were.

Other forms of writing also occur in the Fisher household for everyone to see and use. Greeting cards, grocery lists, bulletin board reminders, and bedtime notes from children to absent parents were all part of Eli's life to some extent, and his preschool writing and drawing always adorned the refrigerator, along with the school papers of his brothers and sisters.

In addition, the Fishers played writing-involved games—including Scrabble and Boggle—in which everyone participated, as the family revised the rules to suit their cooperative social model and their definition of literacy. In any game at the Fishers, the oldest person or persons playing may assist the younger ones. No question of fairness arises unless only some players go unaided. Older players, too, may receive help from other players or from onlookers. Score is always kept, and, while some moves are ruled illegal, age or aid received neither bars nor assures a winner. Eli, Jr., therefore, has always played these games as well as anyone else.

Obviously, Eli, Jr., learned a great deal about literacy from all these preschool experiences, but what he learned went far beyond academic readiness lessons. More important, Eli learned that literacy is a force in the world—his world—and it is a force that imparts power to all who wield it. He could see for himself that reading and writing enable people as old as his parents and as young as his siblings to fully participate in the world in which they live. In fact, it might have seemed to him that, to be an Amish man, one must read and write, and to be a Fisher, one must read and write as well.

So, even before the age of six, Eli began to recognize and acquire the power of literacy, using it to affiliate himself with the larger Amish world and to identify himself as Amish, a Fisher, a boy, and Eli Fisher, Jr. However, what enabled Eli to recognize all these ways of defining and asserting himself through literacy was neither direct instruction nor insistence from someone else. Rather, it was the ability that all children have long before they can read and write print text, the ability, as Friere puts it, "to read the world." "It is possible," Friere asserts, "to view objects and experiences as texts, words, and letters, and to see the growing awareness of the world as a kind of reading, through which the self learns and changes" (6). Eli, Jr., clearly illustrates this understanding of how children perceive and comprehend the seemingly invisible text of their lives. What he came to understand and accept this way were the definition and the role of print literacy as his society and culture both consciously and tacitly transmit them.

When Eli, Jr., began school, therefore, he was both academically and socially ready to begin. To smooth the transition from home to school, Eli's teacher—like most in Old Order schools—held a "preschool day" in the spring preceding his entry to first grade. On that day, Eli and Mary, the two prospective first-graders in Meadow Brook School, came to be initiated as "scholars." Verna, their teacher, had moved the two current first-graders to other seats, clearing the two desks immediately in front of hers for the newcomers; all that day Mary and Eli sat in the first-grade seats, had "classes," and did seatwork like all the other children. They seemed to know they were expected to follow the rules, to do what they saw others doing, to practice being "scholars," and Verna reinforced that notion, treating those two almost as she would anyone else.

To begin one lesson, for example, "Let's talk about bunnies," she instructed, nodding her head toward the two littlest children, indicating that they should stand beside her desk. She then showed them pictures of rabbits, with the word *bunnies* and the number depicted indicated in word and numeral on each picture. After going through the pictures, saying, "three bunnies," "four bunnies," and having the children repeat after her, Verna asked three questions and got three choral answers.

"Do bunnies like carrots?" she asked.
"Yes," the two children answered together.
"Do they like lettuce?"
"Yes."
"Do they sometimes get in Mother's garden?"
"Yes."

Were it not for some enthusiastic head nodding, Eli, Jr., and Mary could have been fully matriculated students.

When she was ready to assign seatwork, Verna gave the preschoolers pictures of bunnies to color and asked, "What do we do first? Color or write our names?"

"Write our names," the pair chorused, having practiced that skill earlier in the day.

"Yes, we always write our names first. Go back to your desk, write your name, then color the picture. Do nothing on the back of the paper." And the children did exactly that, doing "what we do" precisely "the way we do it."

Verna also conducted what she called a reading class for the two preschoolers, during which they sat, and she held an open picture book facing them. Talking about the pictures, Verna made simple statements identifying different aspects of and actions in the illustrations. After each statement Verna paused, and the children repeated exactly what she had said. The oral text accompanying one picture said:

Sally is eating chips and watching TV.
Sally has a red fish.
Sally has spilled the chips.

After "reading" the text this way, the children answered questions about it.

"What does Sally have?" Verna asked.
"A fish," they replied.
"What color is her fish?"
"Red."
"Did Sally spill the chips?"
"Yes."
"Did the cat eat the chips?"
"Yes."

While the content of this lesson seems incongruous, I know, its form and conduct fit the Meadow Brook model perfectly. Precise recall and yeses are all that the questions demand. Even the last question, while not covered in the "reading," requires recognition of only what happens in the picture.

What happened in Meadow Brook School that day—and what would happen in the eight school years to follow—reinforced, extended, and rarely contradicted what Eli already knew about literacy. Reading and writing at school allowed him to further affiliate and identify himself with and within his social group. While his teacher occasionally gave direct instructions, those instructions tended to be for activities never before seen or experienced: otherwise, Eli and Mary knew to follow the behavioral and attitudinal lead of the older children and to look to them for assistance and support, just as they looked to the teacher. In other words, reading the school world came as naturally to these children as reading the world anywhere else, and the message in both texts was emphatically the same.

Most important here, however, may be the remarkable substantive coherence that Meadow Brook School provided, a coherence that precluded any conflict over what, how, or even whether to read and write. Eli's experience as a Fisher had taught him that reading comes in many forms—secular and religious, silent and oral, individual and communal—and they all count. Through his at-home experience, Eli had also learned which other, more specific, less obvious abilities count as reading in his world. He had learned to value at least four significant abilities: (1) the ability to select and manage texts, to be able to find his mother's letter in *Die Botschaft* or to find a particular verse in the Bible; (2) the ability to empathize with people in texts and to discern the implicit lessons their experiences teach: to empathize with Lambert the lion, who taught the possibility of peaceful coexistence, and to empathize with the Anabaptist martyrs, who taught the rightness of dying for one's faith; (3) the ability to accurately recall what was read, to remember stories, riddles, and jokes or to memorize Bible and hymn verses; and (4) the ability to synthesize what is read in a single text with what is already known or to synthesize information across texts in Amish-appropriate ways.

When Eli got to school, he found a similar definition of reading in operation. He and Mary were helped to select and manage text. Their attention was directed toward what mattered in the text and away from what did not. They were helped to discover the single right answer to every question. They had only to recall information without interpreting or extending it in any significant way. And they were expected to empathize with the people in Verna's lunchtime oral reading without questioning or hypothesizing about what had happened or what would happen next.

Similarly, before Eli went to school, he knew what counted as writing in his world, just as he knew what counted as reading. He learned at home that being able to write means being able to encode, to copy, to follow format, to choose content, and to list. And, when he arrived at school, this same definition, these same abilities, were all that mattered there, too.

While the dimensions of reading and writing that count at Meadow Brook and elsewhere in Eli's life seem little different from those that count in mainstream situations—a terrifying fact, I would suggest—it is important to recognize that several mainstream-valued skills are com-

pletely absent from the Amish world as I've experienced it. Critical reading—individual analysis and interpretation—of the sort considered
particularly important by most people who are mainstream-educated or
mainstream educators is not valued by the Amish because of its potentially divisive, counterproductive power.

Literary appreciation, too, is both irrelevant and absent because
the study of text-as-object is moot. How a writer enables a reader to empathize with his characters doesn't matter; only the ability to empathize
matters. Text, whether biblical or secular, is perceived not as an object
but as a force acting in the world, and it is the impact of that force that
counts.

When it comes to writing, the existing Amish definition also differs
in what is absent, rather than what is present. While grammar, spelling,
and punctuation do count for the Old Order, they do so only to the extent
that word order, words, and punctuation must allow readers to read—
that is, to recognize and make sense of their reading. If a reader readily
understands the intention of an adjective used as an adverb, a singular
verb following a plural noun, a sentence fragment, or a compound verb
containing a misplaced comma, the Amish do not see these as errors
warranting attention, despite the fact that an outside reader may.

Equally irrelevant in Old Order schools is the third-person formal
essay—the ominous five-paragraph theme—so prevalent in mainstream
classrooms. Amish children never learn to write this kind of composition,
not because they are not college-bound but because the third-person-
singular point of view assumed by an individual writer is foreign to this
first-person-plural society; thesis statements, topic sentences, and concepts
like coherence, unity, and emphasis are similarly alien.

One final distinction separates the Amish definition of literacy from
that of many mainstream definitions: the absence of originality as a desirable feature. Not only do community constraints limit the number of
appropriate topics and forms an Amish writer may use, but original
approaches to or applications of those topics and forms is implicitly discouraged by the similarity of models and assignments and by the absence
of fiction as an appropriate personal genre. All aspects of community life
reward uniformity; while writing provides an outlet for individual expression and identification, singular creativity stays within community norms.

For Eli Fisher, Jr., then, the definition of literacy he learned at home
was consistent with the one he found at school, though it differed in
several important ways from those of most MLA members, for example.

Yet for Eli, as for Friere, "deciphering the word flowed naturally from reading the immediate world" (7). From reading his world, this six-year-old derived a complete implicit definition that told him what literacy is and whether literacy matters. I can't help but wonder, however, what would have happened had Eli gone to school and been told, explicitly or through more powerful behaviors, that he really didn't know what counted as reading and writing, that his reading and writing were not real but other unknown or alien varieties were. What would have happened had his quiet imitative behavior made him invisible in the classroom or, worse yet, made his teacher assume that he was withdrawn, problematic, or less than bright? What if his work were devalued because it was obviously copied or just unoriginal? What if he had been called on to perform individually in front of the class, to stand up and stand out? Or what if he had been asked to discuss private issues in public? Or to evaluate what he read?

Had any of these things happened, I suspect that Eli would have had to make some difficult choices that would have amounted to choosing between what he had learned and learned to value at home and what he seemed expected to learn at school. To conform to his teacher's demands and values, he would have had to devalue or disavow those of his parents—a demand that public schools seem to make frequently of children from cultural or socioeconomic groups differing from those of their teachers or their schools, a demand that seems unfair, uncalled for, and unnecessary, not to mention counterproductive and destructive.

Eli Fisher's experience suggests, therefore, that those of us who deal with children unlike ourselves need to see our classrooms and our students differently from the way we may have seen them in the past. We need to realize that students, even first-graders, have been reading the world—if not the word—for at least five, six, or seven years; they come to school not devoid of knowledge and values but with a clear sense of what their world demands and requires, including what, whether, and how to read and write, though their understandings may differ significantly from our own. We need to realize that our role may not be to prepare our students to enter mainstream society but, rather, to help them see what mainstream society offers and what it takes away, what they may gain by assimilating and what they may lose in that process. Through understanding their worlds, their definitions of literacy, and their dilemmas, not only will we better help them make important literacy-related decisions, but we will better help ourselves to do the same.

WORKS CITED

Freire, Paulo. "The Importance of the Act of Reading." *Journal of Education* Winter 1983: 5–10.
Heath, Shirley Brice. *Ways with Words: Language, Life, and Work in Communities and Classrooms.* Cambridge: Cambridge UP, 1983.
Taylor, Denny. *Family Literacy.* Portsmouth: Heinemann, 1983.
Wells, Gordon. *The Meaning Makers.* Portsmouth: Heinemann, 1986.

ACTIVE READING

1. Find several passages suggesting that literacy is more than just the ability to decode marks on a page. Use those passages to compose a broader definition of literacy.

2. Fishman says that a society "both consciously and tacitly transmit[s]" (245) information to its children. Look up "tacit" in a college dictionary, and then find several passages where the Fisher family tacitly teaches something to its children. How do these tacit lessons shape their conception of literacy?

3. Find several passages where Fishman implies that she is drawn to the values and practices of both the Old Order Amish and "mainstream educators." What conflicts does that create for her, and where and how does she resolve them?

READING IN NEW CONTEXTS

1. Interview a few people of different ages and occupations about their experiences with errors in punctuation, grammar, and spelling. Based on the interviews, your own experience, and the Fishman essay, define error and discuss its social consequences.

2. According to Fishman, Eli Jr. "learned that literacy . . . is a force that imparts power to all who wield it" (244). Use examples from Fishman and from another *Literacies* text about reading and writing, such as Christian or Heath, to explain the force or power of literacy.

3. Paulo Freire, a prominent educator, sees a person's "growing awareness of the world as a kind of reading, through which the self learns and changes" (245). Test this idea against another *Literacies* narrative, such as Baldwin, Kingston, Heker, or Angelou.

4. Choose several terms from a *Literacies* text devoted to "individual analysis and interpretation," such as Rich, Scholes, or Bettelheim. Use the terms to explain what the people Fishman calls "mainstream educators" value and how they differ from the Old Order Amish.

DRAFT ONE / DRAFT TWO

1. *Draft One:* What relations do you see between the forms of reading and writing practiced by the Old Order Amish, such as the letter or the recitation of Bible verses, and their social values? Compose a draft in which you examine several of these forms or genres and explain how they serve the community in what Fishman might call "Amish-appropriate ways" (247).

   Draft Two: Turn to the *Literacies* text you consider most unlike the forms and genres you have addressed in Draft One. Name the forms of that text, such as narrative, letter, or poem, and describe their traits. Use that text to extend the discussion you began in Draft One of the connections between form or genre, social context, and conceptions of literacy.

2. *Draft One:* Tell a story of some important part of your own education, and then discuss how the values implicit in your experience resemble or differ from the educational values of both the Old Order Amish and Fishman's mainstream educators.

   Draft Two: Reconsider the story you told in Draft One in light of the ideas about the Amish and mainstream educators you developed in Reading in New Contexts #4. Use these ideas to clarify where you stand among these conflicting educational values.

BEFORE READING BARBARA GARSON

1. Talk about one of your first paying jobs. Why did you take it? What did you expect to gain from the experience? In what ways were your expectations fulfilled or not fulfilled?

2. What are the most significant challenges and difficulties facing American workers right now? How does the situation of American workers compare to those of workers in other parts of the world? In your answers to these questions, consider where your knowledge about workers in both the United States and other countries comes from.

3. How does your identity as a worker differ from your identity as a consumer? As you discuss the needs and priorities that go with each role, pay special attention to any conflicts that you notice. Where do those conflicts come from, and what do you do about them?

BARBARA GARSON

McDONALD'S—
WE DO IT ALL FOR YOU

JASON PRATT

"They called us the Green Machine," says Jason Pratt, recently retired McDonald's griddleman, " 'cause the crew had green uniforms then. And that's what it is, a machine. You don't have to know how to cook, you don't have to know how to think. There's a procedure for everything and you just follow the procedures."

"Like?" I asked. I was interviewing Jason in the Pizza Hut across from his old McDonald's.

"Like, uh," the wiry teenager searched for a way to describe the all-encompassing procedures. "O.K., we'll start you off on something simple. You're on the ten-in-one grill, ten patties in a pound. Your basic burger. The guy on the bin calls, 'Six hamburgers.' So you lay your six pieces of meat on the grill and set the timer." Before my eyes Jason conjures up the gleaming, mechanized McDonald's kitchen. "Beep-beep, beep-beep, beep-beep. That's the beeper to sear 'em. It goes off in twenty seconds. Sup, sup, sup, sup, sup, sup." He presses each of the six patties down on the sizzling grill with an imaginary silver disk. "Now you turn off the sear beeper, put the buns in the oven, set the oven timer and then the next

From *The Electronic Sweatshop* (1988).

beeper is to turn the meat. This one goes beep-beep-beep, beep-beep-beep. So you turn your patties, and then you drop your re-cons on the meat, t-con, t-con, t-con." Here Jason takes two imaginary handfuls of reconstituted onions out of water and sets them out, two blops at a time, on top of the six patties he's arranged in two neat rows on our grill. "Now the bun oven buzzes [there are over a half dozen different timers with distinct beeps and buzzes in a McDonald's kitchen]. "This one turns itself off when you open the oven door so you just take out your crowns, line 'em up and give 'em each a squirt of mustard and a squirt of ketchup." With mustard in his right hand and ketchup in his left, Jason wields the dispensers like a pair of six-shooters up and down the lines of buns. Each dispenser has two triggers. One fires the premeasured squirt for ten-in-ones—the second is set for quarter-pounders.

"Now," says Jason, slowing down, "now you get to put on the pickles. Two if they're regular, three if they're small. That's the creative part. Then the lettuce, then you ask for a cheese count ('cheese on four please'). Finally the last beep goes off and you lay your burger on the crowns."

"On the *crown* of the buns?" I ask, unable to visualize. "On top?"

"Yeah, you dress 'em upside down. Put 'em in the box upside down too. They flip 'em over when they serve 'em."

"Oh, I think I see."

"Then scoop up the heels [the bun bottoms] which are on top of the bun warmer, take the heels with one hand and push the tray out from underneath and they land (plip) one on each burger, right on top of the re-cons, neat and perfect. [The official time allotted by Hamburger Central, the McDonald's headquarters in Oak Brook, Ill, is ninety seconds to prepare and serve a burger.] It's like I told you. The procedures make the burgers. You don't have to know a thing."

McDonald's employs 500,000 teenagers at any one time. Most don't stay long. About 8 million Americans—7 per cent of our labor force—have worked at McDonald's and moved on.[1] Jason is not a typical ex-employee. In fact, Jason is a legend among the teenagers at the three McDonald's outlets in his suburban area. It seems he was so fast at the griddle (or

---

1. These statistics come from John F. Love, *McDonald's Behind the Goldenn Arches* (New York: Bantam, 1986). Additional background information in this chapter comes from Ray Kroc and Robert Anderson, *Grinding It Out* (Chicago: Contemporary Books, 1977), and Max Boas and Steve Chain, *Big Mac* (New York: Dutton, 1976).

maybe just fast talking) that he'd been taken back three times by two different managers after quitting.

But Jason became a real legend in his last stint at McDonald's. He'd been sent out the back door with the garbage, but instead of coming back in he got into a car with two friends and just drove away. That's the part the local teenagers love to tell. "No fight with the manager or anything . . . just drove away and never came back. . . . I don't think they'd give him a job again."

"I would never go back to McDonald's," says Jason. "Not even as a manager." Jason is enrolled at the local junior college. "I'd like to run a real restaurant someday, but I'm taking data processing to fall back on." He's had many part-time jobs, the highest-paid at a hospital ($4.00 an hour), but that didn't last, and now dishwashing (at the $3.35 minimum). "Same as McDonald's. But I would never go back there. You're a complete robot."

"It seems like you can improvise a little with the onions," I suggested. "They're not premeasured." Indeed, the reconstituted onion shreds grabbed out of a container by the unscientific-looking wet handful struck me as oddly out of character in the McDonald's kitchen.

"There's supposed to be twelve onion bits per patty," Jason informed me. "They spot check."

"Oh come on."

"You think I'm kiddin'. They lift your heels and they say, 'You got too many onions.' It's portion control."

"Is there any freedom anywhere in the process?" I asked.

"Lettuce. They'll leave you alone as long as it's neat."

"So lettuce is freedom; pickles is judgment?"

"Yeah but you don't have time to play around with your pickles. They're never gonna say just six pickles except on the disk. [Each store has video disks to train the crew for each of about twenty work stations, like fries, register, lobby, quarter-pounder grill.] What you'll hear in real life is 'twelve and six on a turn-lay.' The first number is your hamburgers, the second is your Big Macs. On a turn-lay means you lay the first twelve, then you put down the second batch after you turn the first. So you got twenty-four burgers on the grill, in shifts. It's what they call a production mode. And remember you also got your fillets, your McNuggets. . . ."

"Wait, slow down." By then I was losing track of the patties on our imaginary grill. "I don't understand this turn-lay thing."

"Don't worry, you don't have to understand. You follow the beepers, you follow the buzzers and you turn your meat as fast as you can. It's like I told you, to work at McDonald's you don't need a face, you don't need a brain. You need to have two hands and two legs and move 'em as fast as you can. That's the whole system. I wouldn't go back there again for anything."

JUNE SANDERS

McDonald's french fries are deservedly the pride of their menu; uniformly golden brown all across America and in thirty-one other countries. However, it's difficult to standardize the number of fries per serving. The McDonald's fry scoop, perhaps their greatest technological innovation, helps to control this variable. The unique flat funnel holds the bag open while it aligns a limited number of fries so that they fall into the package with a paradoxically free, overflowing cornucopia look.

Despite the scoop, there's still a spread. The acceptable fry yield is 400 to 420 servings per 100-lb. bag of potatoes. It's one of the few areas of McDonald's cookery in which such a range is possible. The fry yield is therefore one important measure of a manager's efficiency. "Fluffy, not stuffy," they remind the young workers when the fry yield is running low.

No such variation is possible in the browning of the fries. Early in McDonald's history Louis Martino, the husband of the secretary of McDonald's founder Ray Kroc, designed a computer to be submerged in the fry vats. In his autobiography, *Grinding It Out*, Kroc explained the importance of this innovation. "We had a recipe . . . that called for pulling the potatoes out of the oil when they got a certain color and grease bubbles formed in a certain way. It was amazing that we got them as uniform as we did because each kid working the fry vats would have his own interpretation of the proper color and so forth. [The word "kid" was officially replaced by "person" or "crew person" in McDonald's management vocabulary in 1973 in response to union organizing attempts.] Louis's computer took all the guesswork out of it, modifying the frying to suit the balance of water to solids in a given batch of potatoes. He also engineered the dispenser that allowed us to squirt exactly the right amount of catsup and mustard onto our premeasured hamburger patties. . . ."

The fry vat probe is a complex miniature computer. The fry scoop, on the other hand, is as simple and almost as elegant as the wheel. Both eliminate the need for a human being to make "his own interpretation," as Ray Kroc puts it.

Together, these two innovations mean that a new worker can be trained in fifteen minutes and reach maximum efficiency in a half hour. This makes it economically feasible to use a kid for one day and replace him with another kid the next day.

June Sanders worked at McDonald's for one day.

"I needed money, so I went in and the manager told me my hours would be 4 to 10 P.M." This was fine with June, a well-organized black woman in her early twenties who goes to college full time.

"But when I came in the next day the manager said I could work till 10 for that one day. But from then on my hours would be 4 P.M. to 1 A.M. And I really wouldn't get off at 1 because I'd have to stay to clean up after they closed. . . . Yes it was the same manager, a Mr. O'Neil.

"I told him I'd have to check first with my family if I could come home that late. But he told me to put on the uniform and fill out the forms. He would start me out on french fries.

"Then he showed me an orientation film on a TV screen all about fries. . . . No, I still hadn't punched in. This was all in the basement. Then I went upstairs, and *then* I punched in and went to work. . . . No, I was not paid for the training downstairs. Yes, I'm sure."

I asked June if she had had any difficulty with the fries.

"No, it was just like the film. You put the french fries in the grease and you push a button which doesn't go off till the fries are done. Then you take them out and put them in a bin under a light. Then you scoop them into the bags with this thing, this flat, light metal—I can't really describe it—scoop thing that sits right in the package and makes the fries fall in place."

"Did they watch you for a while?" I asked. "Did you need more instruction?"

"Someone leaned over once and showed me how to make sure the fry scooper was set inside the opening of the bag so the fries would fall in right."

"And then?"

"And then, I stood on my feet from twenty after four till the manager took over my station at 10:35 P.M.

"When I left my legs were aching. I knew it wasn't a job for me. But I probably would have tried to last it out—at least more than a day—if it wasn't for the hours. When I got home I talked it over with my mother and my sister and then I phoned and said I couldn't work there. They weren't angry. They just said to bring back the uniform. . . . The people were nice, even the managers. It's just a rushed system."

"June," I said, "does it make any sense to train you and have you work for one day? Why didn't he tell you the real hours in the first place?"

"They take a chance and see if you're desperate. I have my family to stay with. That's why I didn't go back. But if I really needed the money, like if I had a kid and no family, I'd have to make arrangements to work any hours.

"Anyway, they got a full day's work out of me."

DAMITA

I waited on line at my neighborhood McDonald's. It was lunch hour and there were four or five customers at each of the five open cash registers. "May I take your order?" a very thin girl said in a flat tone to the man at the head of my line.

"McNuggets, large fries and a Coke," said the man. The cashier punched in the order. "That will be—".

"Big Mac, large fries and a shake," said the next woman on line. The cashier rang it up.

"Two cheeseburgers, large fries and a coffee," said the third customer. The cashier rang it up.

"How much is a large fries?" asked the woman directly in front of me.

The thin cashier twisted her neck around trying to look up at the menu board.

"Sorry," apologized the customer, "I don't have my glasses."

"Large fries is seventy-nine," a round-faced cashier with glasses interjected from the next register.

"Seventy-nine cents," the thin cashier repeated.

"Well how much is a *small* fries?"

As they talked I leaned over the next register. "Say, can I interview you?" I asked the clerk with glasses, whose line was by then empty.

"Huh?"

"I'm writing a story about jobs at fast-food restaurants."

"O.K. I guess so."

"Can I have your phone number?"

"Well . . . I'll meet you when I get off. Should be sometime between 4 and 4:30."

By then it was my turn.

"Just a large fries," I said.

The thin cashier pressed "lge fries." In place of numbers, the keys on a McDonald's cash register say "lge fries," "reg fries," "med coke," "big mac," and so on. Some registers have pictures on the key caps. The next time the price of fries goes up (or down) the change will be entered in the store's central computer. But the thin cashier will continue to press the same button. I wondered how long she'd worked there and how many hundreds of "lge fries" she'd served without learning the price.

Damita, the cashier with the glasses, came up from the crew room (a room in the basement with lockers, a table and a video player for studying the training disks) at 4:45. She looked older and more serious without her striped uniform.

"Sorry, but they got busy and, you know, here you get off when they let you."

The expandable schedule was her first complaint. "You give them your availability when you sign on. Mine I said 9 to 4. But they scheduled me for 7 o'clock two or three days a week. And I needed the money. So I got to get up 5 in the morning to get here from Queens by 7. And I don't get off till whoever's supposed to get here gets here to take my place. . . . It's hard to study with all the pressures."

Damita had come to the city from a small town outside of Detroit. She lives with her sister in Queens and takes extension courses in psychology at New York University. Depending on the schedule posted each Friday, her McDonald's paycheck for a five-day week has varied from $80 to $114.

"How long have you worked at McDonald's?" I asked.

"Well, see I only know six people in this city, so my manager from Michigan . . . yeah, I worked for McDonald's in high school . . . my manager from Michigan called this guy Brian who's the second assistant manager here. So I didn't have to fill out an application. Well, I mean the first thing I needed was a job," she seemed to apologize, "and I knew I could always work at McDonald's. I always say I'm gonna look for something else, but I don't get out till 4 and that could be 5 or whenever."

The flexible scheduling at McDonald's only seems to work one way. One day Damita had arrived a half hour late because the E train was running on the R track.

"The assistant manager told me not to clock in at all, just to go home. So I said O.K. and I left."

"What did you do the rest of the day?" I asked.

"I went home and studied, and I went to sleep."

"But how did it make you feel?"

"It's like a humiliating feeling 'cause I wasn't given any chance to justify myself. But when I spoke to the Puerto Rican manager he said it was nothing personal against me. Just it was raining that day, and they were really slow and someone who got here on time, it wouldn't be right to send them home."

"Weren't you annoyed to spend four hours traveling and then lose a day's pay?" I suggested.

"I was mad at first that they didn't let me explain. But afterwards I understood and I tried to explain to my sister: 'Time waits for no man.' "

"Since you signed on for 9 to 4," I asked Damita, "and you're going to school, why can't you say, 'Look, I have to study at night, I need regular hours'?"

"Don't work that way. They make up your schedule every week and if you can't work it, you're responsible to replace yourself. If you can't they can always get someone else."

"But Damita," I tried to argue with her low estimate of her own worth, "anyone can see right away that your line moves fast yet you're helpful to people. I mean, you're a valuable employee. And this manager seems to like you."

"Valuable! $3.35 an hour. And I can be replaced by any [pointing across the room] kid off the street." I hadn't noticed. At a small table under the staircase a manager in a light beige shirt was taking an application from a lanky black teenager.

"But you know the register. You know the routine."

"How long you think it takes to learn the six steps? Step 1. Greet the customer, 'Good morning, can I help you?' Step 2. Take his order. Step 3. Repeat the order. They can have someone off the street working my register in five minutes."

"By the way," I asked, "on those cash registers without numbers, how do you change something after you ring it up? I mean if somebody orders a cheeseburger and then they change it to a hamburger, how do you subtract the slice of cheese?"

"I guess that's why you have step 3, repeat the order. One cheeseburger, two Cokes, three . . ."

"Yeah but if you punched a mistake or they don't want it after you get it together?"

"Like if I have a crazy customer, which I do be gettin' 'specially in this city, and they order hamburger, fries and shake, and it's $2.95 and then they just walk away?"

"I once did that here," I said. "About a week ago when I first started my research. All I ordered was some french fries. And I was so busy watching how the computer works that only after she rang it up I discovered that I'd walked out of my house without my wallet. I didn't have a penny. I was so embarrassed."

"Are you that one the other day? Arnetta, this girl next to me, she said, 'Look at that crazy lady going out. She's lookin' and lookin' at everything and then she didn't have no money for a bag of fries.' I saw you leaving, but I guess I didn't recognize you. [I agreed it was probably me.] O.K., so say this crazy lady comes in and orders french fries and leaves. In Michigan I could just zero it out. I'd wait till I start the next order and press zero and large fries. But here you're supposed to call out 'cancel sale' and the manager comes over and does it with his key.

"But I hate to call the manager every time, 'specially if I got a whole line waiting. So I still zero out myself. They can tell I do it by the computer tape, and they tell me not to. Some of them let me, though, because they know I came from another store. But they don't show the girls here how to zero out. Everybody thinks you need the manager's key to do it."

"Maybe they let you because they can tell you're honest," I said. She smiled, pleased, but let it pass. "That's what I mean that you're valuable to them. You know how to use the register. You're good with customers."

"You know there was a man here," Damita said, a little embarrassed about bragging, "when I was transferred off night he asked my manager, 'What happened to that girl from Michigan?' "

"Did your manager tell you that?"

"No, another girl on the night shift told me. The manager said it to her. They don't tell you nothing nice themselves."

"But, see, you are good with people and he appreciates it."

"In my other McDonald's—not the one where they let me zero out but another one I worked in in Michigan—I was almost fired for my attitude. Which was helping customers who had arthritis to open the little packets. And another bad attitude of mine is that you're supposed to suggest to the customer, 'Would you like a drink with that?' or 'Do you want a pie?'—whatever they're pushing. I don't like to do it. And they can look on my tape after my shift and see I didn't push the suggested sell item."

McDonald's computerized cash registers allow managers to determine immediately not only the dollar volume for the store but the amount of each item that was sold at each register for any given period. Two experienced managers, interviewed separately, both insisted that the new electronic cash registers were in fact slower than the old mechanical registers. Clerks who knew the combinations—hamburger, fries, Coke: $2.45—could ring up the total immediately, take the cash and give change in one operation. On the new registers you have to enter each item and may be slowed down by computer response time. The value of the new registers, or at least their main selling point (McDonald's franchisers can choose from several approved registers), is the increasingly sophisticated tracking systems, which monitor all the activity and report with many different statistical breakdowns.

"Look, there," said Damita as the teenage job applicant left and the manager went behind the counter with the application, "If I was to say I can't come in at 7, they'd cut my hours down to one shift a week, and if I never came back they wouldn't call to find out where I was.

"I worked at a hospital once as an X-ray assistant. There if I didn't come in there were things that had to be done that wouldn't be done. I would call there and say, 'Remember to run the EKGs.' Here, if I called and said, 'I just can't come by 7 no more,' they'd have one of these high school kids off the street half an hour later. And they'd do my job just as good."

Damita was silent for a while and then she made a difficult plea. "This might sound stupid, I don't know," she said, "but I feel like, I came here to study and advance myself but I'm not excelling myself in any way. I'm twenty years old but—this sounds terrible to say—I'm twenty but I'd rather have a babysitting job. At least I could help a kid and take care. But I only know six people in this city. So I don't even know how I'd find a babysitting job."

"I'll keep my ears open," I said. "I don't know where I'd hear of one but . . ."

Damita seemed a little relieved. I suppose she realized there wasn't much chance of babysitting full-time, but at least she now knew seven people in the city.

JON DeANGELO

Jon DeAngelo, twenty-two, has been a McDonald's manager for three years. He started in the restaurant business at sixteen as a busboy and planned even then to run a restaurant of his own someday. At nineteen, when he was the night manager of a resort kitchen, he was hired away by McOpCo, the McDonald's Operating Company.

Though McDonald's is primarily a franchise system, the company also owns and operates about 30 percent of the stores directly. These McOpCo stores, including some of the busiest units, are managed via a chain of command including regional supervisors, store managers and first and second assistants who can be moved from unit to unit. In addition, there's a network of inspectors from Hamburger Central who make announced and unannounced checks for QSC (quality, service, cleanliness) at both franchise and McOpCo installations.

Jon was hired at $14,000 a year. At the time I spoke with him his annual pay was $21,000—a very good salary at McDonald's. At first he'd been an assistant manager in one of the highest-volume stores in his region. Then he was deliberately transferred to a store with productivity problems.

"I got there and found it was really a great crew. They hated being hassled, but they loved to work. I started them having fun by putting the men on the women's jobs and vice versa. [At most McDonald's the women tend to work on the registers, the men on the grill. But everyone starts at the same pay.] Oh, sure, they hated it at first, the guys that is. But they liked learning all the stations. I also ran a lot of register races."

Since the computer tape in each register indicates sales per hour, per half hour or for any interval requested, the manager can revv the crew up for a real "on your mark, get set, go!" race with a printout ready as they cross the finish line, showing the dollars taken in at each register during the race.

The computer will also print out a breakdown of sales for any particular menu item. The central office can check, therefore, how many Egg McMuffins were sold on Friday from 9 to 9:30 two weeks or two years ago, either in the entire store or at any particular register.

This makes it possible to run a register race limited to Cokes for instance, or Big Macs. Cashiers are instructed to try suggestive selling ("Would you like a drink with that?") at all times. But there are periods when a particular item is being pushed. The manager may then offer a prize for the most danish sold.

A typical prize for either type of cash register race might be a Snoopy mug (if that's the current promotion) or even a $5 cash bonus.

"This crew loved to race as individuals," says Jon of his troubled store, "but even more as a team. They'd love to get on a production mode, like a chicken-pull-drop or a burger-turn-lay and kill themselves for a big rush.

"One Saturday after a rock concert we did a $1,900 hour with ten people on crew. We killed ourselves but when the rush was over everyone said it was the most fun they ever had in a McDonald's."

I asked Jon how managers made up their weekly schedule. How would he decide who and how many to assign?

"It comes out of the computer," Jon explained. "It's a bar graph with the business you're going to do that week already printed in."

"The business you're *going* to do, already printed in?"

"It's based on the last week's sales, like maybe you did a $300 hour on Thursday at 3 P.M. Then it automatically adds a certain percent, say 15 percent, which is the projected annual increase for your particular store. . . . No, the person scheduling doesn't have to do any of this calculation. I just happen to know how it's arrived at. Really, it's simple, it's just a graph with the numbers already in it. $400 hour, $500 hour. According to Hamburger Central you schedule two crew members per $100 hour. So if you're projected for a $600 hour on Friday between 1 and 2, you know you need twelve crew for that lunch hour and the schedule sheet leaves space for their names."

"You mean you just fill in the blanks on the chart?"

"It's pretty automatic except in the case of a special event like the concert. Then you have to guess the dollar volume. Scheduling under could be a problem, but over would be a disaster to your crew labor productivity."

"Crew labor productivity?"

"Everything at McDonald's is based on the numbers. But crew labor productivity is pretty much *the* number a manager is judged by."

"Crew labor productivity? You have to be an economist."

"It's really simple to calculate. You take the total crew labor dollars paid out, divide that into the total food dollars taken in. That gives you your crew labor productivity. The more food you sell and the less people you use to do it, the better your percentage. It's pretty simple."

Apparently, I still looked confused.

"For example, if you take an $800 hour and you run it with ten crew you get a very high crew labor percent."

"That's good?"

"Yes that's good. Then the manager in the next store hears Jon ran a 12 percent labor this week, I'll run a 10 percent labor. Of course you burn people out that way. But . . ."

"But Jon," I asked, "if the number of crew you need is set in advance and printed by the computer, why do so many managers keep changing hours and putting pressure on kids to work more?"

"They advertise McDonald's as a flexible work schedule for high school and college kids," he said, "but the truth is it's a high-pressure job, and we have so much trouble keeping help, especially in fast stores like my first one (it grossed $1.8 million last year), that 50 percent never make it past two weeks. And a lot walk out within two days.

"When I was a first assistant, scheduling and hiring was my responsibility and I had to fill the spots one way or another. There were so many times I covered the shifts myself. Times I worked 100 hours a week. A manager has to fill the spaces on his chart somehow. So if a crew person is manipulable they manipulate him."

"What do you mean?"

"When you first sign on, you give your availability. Let's say a person's schedule is weeknights, 4 to 10. But after a week the manager schedules him as a closer Friday night. He calls in upset, 'Hey, my availability isn't Friday night.' The manager says 'Well the schedule is already done. And you know the rule. If you can't work it's up to you to replace yourself.' At that point the person might quit, or he might not show up or he might have a fight with the manager."

"So he's fired?"

"No. You don't fire. You would only fire for cause like drugs or stealing. But what happens is he signed up for thirty hours a week and suddenly he's only scheduled for four. So either he starts being more available or he quits."

"Aren't you worried that the most qualified people will quit?"

"The only qualification to be able to do the job is to be able physically to do the job. I believe it says that in almost those words in my regional manual. And being there is the main part of being physically able to do the job."

"But what about your great crew at the second store? Don't you want to keep a team together?"

"Let me qualify that qualification. It takes a special kind of person to be able to move before he can think. We find people like that and use them till they quit."

"But as a manager don't you look bad if too many people are quitting?"

"As a manager I am judged by the statistical reports which come off the computer. Which basically means my crew labor productivity. What else can I really distinguish myself by? I could have a good fry yield, a low M&R [Maintenance and Repair budget]. But these are minor."

As it happens, Jon is distinguished among McDonald's managers in his area as an expert on the computerized equipment. Other managers call on him for cash register repairs. "They say, 'Jon, could you look at my register? I just can't afford the M&R this month.' So I come and fix it and they'll buy me a beer."

"So keeping M&R low is a real feather in a manager's cap," I deduced.

"O.K., it's true, you can over spend your M&R budget; you can have a low fry yield; you can run a dirty store; you can be fired for bothering the high school girls. But basically, every Coke spigot is monitored. [At most McDonald's Coke doesn't flow from taps that turn on and off. Instead the clerk pushes the button "sm," "med" or "lge," which then dispenses the premeasured amount into the appropriate-size cup. This makes the syrup yield fairly consistent.] Every ketchup squirt is measured. My costs for every item are set. So my crew labor productivity is my main flexibility."

I was beginning to understand the pressures toward pettiness. I had by then heard many complaints about slight pilferage of time. For instance, as a safety measure no one was allowed to stay in a store alone. There was a common complaint that a closer would be clocked out when he finished cleaning the store for the night, even though he might be required to wait around unpaid till the manager finished his own nightly statistical reports. An another times kids clocked out and then waited hours (unpaid) for a crew chief training course (unpaid).

Overtime is an absolute taboo at McDonald's. Managers practice every kind of scheduling gymnastic to see that no one works over forty hours a week. If a crew member approaching forty hours is needed to close the store, he or she might be asked to check out for a long lunch. I had heard of a couple of occasions when, in desperation, a manager scheduled someone to stay an hour or two over forty hours. Instead of paying time-and-a-half, he compensated at straight time listing the extra hours as miscellaneous and paying through a fund reserved for things like register race bonuses. All of this of course to make his statistics look good.

"There must be some other way to raise your productivity," I suggested, "besides squeezing it out of the kids."

"I try to make it fun," Jon pleaded earnestly. "I know that people like to work on my shifts. I have the highest crew labor productivity in the area. But I get that from burning people out. Look, you can't squeeze a McDonald's hamburger any flatter. If you want to improve your productivity there is nothing for a manger to squeeze but the crew."

"But if it's crew dollars paid out divided by food dollars taken in, maybe you can bring in more dollars instead of using less crew."

"O.K., let me tell you about sausage sandwiches."

"Sausage sandwiches?" (Sounded awful.)

"My crew was crazy about sausage sandwiches. [Crew members are entitled to one meal a day at reduced prices. The meal are deducted from wages through a computerized link to the time clocks.] They made it from a buttered English muffin, a slice of sausage and a slice of cheese. I understand this had actually been a menu item in some parts of the country but never here. But the crew would make it for themselves and then all their friends came in and wanted them.

"So, I decided to go ahead and sell it. It costs about 9¢ to make and I sold it for $1.40. It went like hotcakes. My supervisor even liked the idea because it made so much money. You could see the little dollar signs in his eyes when he first came into the store. And he said nothing. So we kept selling it.

"Then someone came from Oak Brook and they made us stop it.

"Just look how ridiculous that is. A slice of sausage is 60¢ as a regular menu item, and an English muffin is 45¢. So if you come in and ask for a sausage and an English muffin I can still sell them to you today for $1.05. But there's no way I can add the slice of cheese and put it in the box and get that $1.40.

"Basically, I can't be any more creative than a crew person. I can't take any more initiative then the person on the register."

"Speaking of cash registers and initiative," I said . . . and told him about Damita. I explained that she was honest, bright and had learned how to zero out at another store. "Do you let cashiers zero out?" I asked.

"I might let her in this case," Jon said. "The store she learned it at was probably a franchise and they were looser. But basically we don't need people like her. Thinking generally slows this operation down.

"When I first came to McDonald's, I said, 'How mechanical! These kids don't even know how to cook.' But the pace is so fast that if they didn't have all the systems, you couldn't handle it. It takes ninety seconds to cook a hamburger. In those seconds you have to toast the buns, dress it, sear it, turn it, take it off the grill and serve it. Meanwhile you've got maybe twenty-four burgers, plus your chicken, your fish. You haven't got time to pick up a rack of fillet and see if it's done. You have to press the timer, drop the fish and know, without looking, that when it buzzes it's done.

"It's the same thing with management. You have to record the money each night before you close and get it to the bank the next day by 11 A.M. So you have to trust the computer to do a lot of the job. These computers also calculate the payrolls, because they're hooked into the time clocks.

My payroll is paid out of a bank in Chicago. The computers also tell you how many people you're going to need each hour. It's so fast that the manager hasn't got time to think about it. He has to follow the procedures like the crew. And if he follows the procedures everything is going to come out more or less as it's supposed to. So basically the computer manages the store."

Listening to Jon made me remember what Ray Kroc had written about his own job (head of the corporation) and computers:

> We have a computer in Oak Brook that is designed to make real estate surveys. But those printouts are of no use to me. After we find a promising location, I drive around it in a car, go into the corner saloon and the neighborhood supermarket. I mingle with the people and observe their comings and goings. That tells me what I need to know about how a McDonald's store would do there.[2]

By combining twentieth-century computer technology with nineteenth-century time-and-motion studies, the McDonald's corporation has broken the jobs of griddleman, waitress, cashier and even manager down into small, simple steps. Historically these have been service jobs involving a lot of flexibility and personal flare. But the corporation has systematically extracted the decision-making elements from filling french fry boxes or scheduling staff. They've siphoned the know-how from the employees into the programs. They relentlessly weed out all variables that might make it necessary to make a decision at the store level, whether on pickles or on cleaning procedures.

It's interesting and understandable that Ray Kroc refused to work that way. The real estate computer may be as reliable as the fry vat probe. But as head of the company Kroc didn't have to surrender to it. He'd let the computer juggle all the demographic variables, but in the end Ray Kroc would decide, intuitively, where to put the next store.

Jon DeAngelo, would like to work that way, too. So would Jason, June and Damita. If they had a chance to use some skill or intuition at their own levels, they'd not only feel more alive, they'd also be treated with more consideration. It's job organization, not malice, that allows (almost requires) McDonald's workers to be handled like paper plates. They feel disposable because they are.

I was beginning to wonder why Jon stayed on at McDonald's. He still

2. Ray Kroc and Robert Anderson, *Grinding It Out* (Chicago: Contemporary Books, 1977), p. 176.

yearned to open a restaurant. "The one thing I'd take from McDonald's to a French restaurant of my own is the fry vat computer. It really works." He seemed to have both the diligence and the style to run a personalized restaurant. Of course he may not have had the capital.

"So basically I would tell that girl [bringing me back to Damita] to find a different job. She's thinking too much and it slows things down. The way the system is set up, I don't need that in a register person, and they don't need it in me."

"Jon," I said, trying to be tactful, "I don't exactly know why you stay at McDonald's."

"As a matter of fact, I have already turned in my resignation."

"You mean you're not a McDonald's manager any more?" I was dismayed.

"I quit once before and they asked me to stay."

"I have had such a hard time getting a full-fledged manager to talk to me and now I don't know whether you count."

"They haven't actually accepted my resignation yet. You know I heard of this guy in another region who said he was going to leave and they didn't believe him. They just wouldn't accept his resignation. And you know what he did? One day, at noon, he just emptied the store, walked out, and locked the door behind him."

For a second Jon seemed to drift away on that beautiful image. It was like the kids telling me about Jason, the crewman who just walked out the back door.

"You know what that means to close a McDonald's at noon, to do a zero hour at lunch?"

"Jon," I said. "This has been fantastic. You are fantastic. I don't think anyone could explain the computers to me the way you do. But I want to talk to someone who's happy and moving up in the McDonald's system. Do you think you could introduce me to a manager who . . ."

"You won't be able to."

"How come?"

"First of all, there's the media hotline. If any press comes around or anyone is writing a book I'm supposed to call the regional office immediately and they will provide someone to talk to you. So you can't speak to a real corporation person except by arrangement with the corporation.

"Second, you can't talk to a happy McDonald's manager because 98 percent are miserable.

"Third of all, there is no such thing as a McDonald's manager. The computer manages the store."

ACTIVE READING

1. Garson's interviewees often focus on McDonald's demand for "productivity." Locate passages that mention "productivity," and determine what this concept means for the corporation. Then, for each passage, show how the meaning of productivity might change if it were defined from the perspective of a worker or consumer. Use your response to Before Reading #3 to help you explore how the values of each group differ.

2. As you reread Garson's essay, describe some of the relationships the essay suggests could exist between knowing something and acting on what one knows. How are these relationships different for each of the parties in the essay (the workers, the management, the corporation, Garson herself)? Speculate about what these differences might mean.

3. How does each interview in this essay relate to the one that comes before it? Looking closely at the main points of each interview, discuss why you think Garson might have put these interviews in the order that she did.

READING IN NEW CONTEXTS

1. Garson's essay is a combination of interviews, research, and analysis. Looking at another *Literacies* essay that includes interviews with informants (either Bellah or Kozol is a possibility), try to figure out how each writer uses interviews to support, complicate, and / or extend her or his own analysis. How do their methods of quoting compare with those that you find in one of your own essays? How can you account for the differences you see?

2. What makes the exploitation of McDonald's workers possible? After exploring the reasons that the essay and your own work experience suggest, find some ideas or terms from another *Literacies* text (such as Bettelheim or Ewen) that help you say more about the causes of this exploitation.

3. Are Garson's theories about the oppression of McDonald's workers sufficient to explain the problems faced by Rosaura in Heker or the Mexican-American laborers in Rodriguez? Working closely with one of these texts (or another that addresses workers' problems), show how you might adapt a couple of Garson's ideas to apply them to this new context.

DRAFT ONE / DRAFT TWO

1. *Draft One:* Of all the jobs you have held, which one have you enjoyed the most (or disliked the least)? Which one was least enjoyable? After reading Garson's essay and reflecting on your own experience, comment on the factors that contribute to what you might call "job satisfaction." How do different aspects of your social identity (for instance, as worker or boss, female or male, unemployed or employed) affect the definition you give?

   Draft Two: For Draft Two, look at MacLeod, Angelou, or another *Literacies* text that focuses on work. Use this new text's insights about a social category such as race or gender to help you rethink the responses you offered in your Draft One. Which of your earlier ideas are supported by the new text, and which ones need to be revised?

2. *Draft One:* Compare Garson's essay to another *Literacies* text (such as Lorde's address or the public conversation between hooks & West) that is a written record of spoken words. What do you notice about the interaction between the main parties in each text? What can you tell about the place of writing in their conversations? Use your observations to compose a theory about possible relationships between speech and writing.

   Draft Two: Working with Heath's or Fishman's studies of literacy, revise the theory you developed in Draft One to include relationships between speech and writing in some other social contexts, including one of your own (for example, you might think about oral presentations you have made or religious services you participate in). How do you account for the differences between your original theory and your revised one?

BEFORE READING DAVID GILMORE

1. In your experience, what are some good sources of information about what it means to be a man? What sources of information seem less accurate or useful to you? Why?

2. How would you expect the idea of "masculinity" to fit into a discussion of "community"? Where do you think "community" might fit into discussions of "masculinity"? Explain how your own cultural tradition influences your responses to these questions.

3. Using a college dictionary, look up the etymologies (roots or sources) of words such as *gender, virtue, woman,* and *barbarian.* What differences do you notice between the sources of these words and their everyday meanings in English? What do those differences say to you?

DAVID GILMORE

PERFORMATIVE EXCELLENCE: CIRCUM-MEDITERRANEAN

In Glendiot idiom, there is less focus on "being a good man" than on "being *good at* being a man"—a stance that stresses *performative excellence*, the ability to foreground manhood by means of deeds that strikingly "speak for themselves."

—MICHAEL HERZFELD,
The Poetics of Manhood

The lands of the Mediterranean Basin have for centuries been in close contact through trade, intermarriage, intellectual and cultural exchange, mutual colonization, and the pursuit of common regional interests (Braudel 1972; Peristiany 1965; Davis 1977). The use of terms such as *Mediterranean* or *Circum-Mediterranean* (Pitt-Rivers 1963; Giovannini 1987) to categorize these lands is not meant to imply a "culture area" as that term has been used in American ecological anthropology—for Mediterranean societies are as diverse and varied as anywhere else in the world—but rather to serve as a concept of heuristic convenience in ethnographic analysis and comparison (Pitt-Rivers 1977:viii). Although not representing a unity in the sense of cultural homogeneity (Herzfeld 1980), many Mediterranean societies place importance on "certain institutions"

From *Manhood in the Making* (1990).

(Pitt-Rivers 1977:ix) that invite comparison. Aside from obvious resemblances in ecology, settlement patterns, and economic adaptations, what seems to provide a basis of comparison more than anything else is, in fact, a shared image of manhood. In his magisterial survey, *People of the Mediterranean*, John Davis (1977:22) writes,

> Many observers assert the unity of the Mediterranean on various grounds, some of them more plausible than others. At a straightforward, noncausal level, anthropologists, tourists, even Mediterranean people themselves notice some common cultural features: attitudes, elements of culture that are recognizably similar in a large proportion of Mediterranean societies, and that are readily intelligible to other Mediterranean people. "I also have a moustache," is the phrase happily recorded by J. G. Peristiany. . . . In an emblematic way, it serves to denote not only manliness, which is so common a concern around the Mediterranean, but also a style of anthropological argument.

This invocation of the mustache, of course, is shorthand for saying I am a man, too, the equal of any, so afford me the respect of the hirsute sex. By appealing to this common denominator, the statement is both a warning and an evocation of the fiercely egalitarian (and competitive) values shared by many otherwise diverse peoples of the region.

In the Mediterranean area, most men are deeply committed to an image of manliness because it is part of their personal honor or reputation. But this image not only brings respect to the bearer; it also brings security to his family, lineage, or village, as these groups, sharing a collective identity, reflect the man's reputation and are protected by it. Because of its competitive, sexually aggressive aspects, Mediterranean male imagery has been perceived, at least in some of the Latin countries, as self-serving, disruptive, and isolating, a matter of "personal vice" and a "social evil" (Pitt-Rivers 1961:118). This is part of a distancing stereotype shared by many northern visitors who for their own reasons assume the south to be "different" (Herzfeld 1987). But this overlooks the very important and often constructive group implications of the male image as it exists in many Mediterranean societies and which is not so different in effect from masculine imagery elsewhere. I want to explore the implications of these male ideals as the first step in our quest for the meaning of manhood.

We begin our discussion of masculine imagery in the Mediterranean societies by taking a negative example. This is the man who is not "good at being a man," in Michael Herzfeld's felicitous phrase above. What does he lack? Let me start by describing such a case from my own fieldwork in the Andalusian pueblo of Fuenmayor (a pseudonym). Although the following discussion is geared to southern Spain and to other areas in the northern littoral of the Mediterranean, much of what I say here relates to parts of the Islamic Middle East as well.

LORENZO

Like many other men in the Mediterranean area with whom they share the common sensibilities alluded to by Davis, the Andalusians of Spain's deep south are dedicated to proving their manliness publicly. Even more than other Iberians, they are fervent followers of what the Spanish critic Enrique Tierno Galván (1961:74–76) has called a quasi-religious Hispanic "faith in manhood." If you measure up in this regard, you are "very much a man" (*muy hombre*), "very virile" (*muy macho*), or "lots of man" (*mucho hombre*). If not, you are *flojo*, a weak and pathetic impostor. The polysemous term *flojo* literally means empty, lazy, or flaccid; it is used also to describe a dead battery, a flat tire, or some other hopeless tool that does not work. It connotes flabby inadequacy, uselessness, or inefficiency.

Our example, Lorenzo, was a callow fellow in his late twenties, a perennial student and bachelor. A gentle character of outstanding native intelligence, Lorenzo was the only person from Fuenmayor ever to have attended graduate school to pursue a doctorate, in this case in classic Castilian literature. But he was unable for various reasons ever to complete his dissertation, so he remained in a kind of occupational limbo, unable to find suitable work, indecisive and feckless. Because of his erudition, unusual in such backwater towns, Lorenzo was generally acknowledged as a sort of locally grown genius. Many people had high hopes for him. But the more traditionally minded people in town were not among his admirers. They found him reprehensible for their own curmudgeonly reasons, for in the important matter of gender appropriateness, Lorenzo was considered highly eccentric, even deviant. "A grave case," one townsman put it.

People pointed first to his living arrangements. Oddly, even perversely, Lorenzo stayed indoors with his widowed mother, studying, reading books, contemplating things, rarely leaving his cramped scholar's cloister. He had no discernible job, and as he earned no money, he contributed nothing concrete to his family's impoverished larder, a fact that made him appear parasitic to many. He lived off his uncomplaining old mother, herself hardworking but poor. Withdrawn and secretive, Lorenzo made no visible efforts to change this state of affairs; nor did he often, as other men are wont to do, enter the masculine world of the bars to drink with cronies, palaver, debate, or engage in the usual convivial banter. When he did, he drank little. Rarely did he enter into the aggressively competitive card games or the drunken bluster that men enjoy and expect from their fellows.

Perhaps most bizarre, Lorenzo avoided young women, claiming not to have time for romance. Along with his other faults, Lorenzo was actually intensely shy with girls. This is a very unusual dereliction indeed, one that is always greeted with real dismay by both men and women in Spain. Sexual shyness is more than a casual flaw in an Andalusian youth; it is a serious, even tragic inadequacy. The entire village bemoans shyness as a personal calamity and collective disgrace. People said that Lorenzo was afraid of girls, afraid to try his luck, afraid to gamble in the game of love. They believe that a real man must break down the wall of female resistance that separates the sexes; otherwise, God forbid, he will never marry and will sire no heirs. If that happens, everyone suffers, for children are God's gift to family, village, and nation.

Being a sensitive soul, Lorenzo was quite aware of the demands made upon him by importuning kith and kin. He felt the pressure to go out and run after women. He knew he was supposed to target a likely wife, get a paying job, and start a family. A cultural rebel by default or disinclination, he felt himself to be a man of modern, "European" sensibilities. Above all, he wanted to remain beyond that "stupid rigmarole" of traditional southern expectations, as he called it. He was clearly an agnostic in regards to Tierno Galván's Spanish faith in manhood.

One evening, after we had spent a pleasant hour talking about such things as the place of Cervantes in world literature, he looked up at me with his great, sad brown eyes, and confessed his cultural transgressions. He began by confiding his anxieties about the aggressive courting that is a man's presumed function. "I know you have to throw yourself violently at women," he said glumly, "but I prefer not to," adding, "It's just not me." Taking up his book, he shook his head and cast his mournful eyes to the ground with a shrug, awaiting a comforting word from a sympathetic and, he believed, enlightened foreigner. It was obvious he was pathologically afraid of rejection.

Because he was a decent and honest man, Lorenzo had his small circle of friends in the town. Like Lorenzo, they were all educated people. Given to introspective brooding, he was the subject of much concern among them. They feared he would never marry, bachelorhood being accounted the most lamentable fate outside of blatant homosexuality, which is truly disgusting to them. With the best intentions in mind, these people often took me aside to ask me if I did not think it was sad that Lorenzo was so withdrawn, and what should be done about him? Finally, one perceptive friend, discussing Lorenzo's case at length as we often did, summed up the problem in an unforgettable phrase that caused me to ponder. He expressed admiration for Lorenzo's brains, but he noted his friend's debilitating unhappiness, his social estrangement; he told me in all seriousness and as a matter obviously much considered that Lorenzo's problem was his failure "as a man." I asked him what he meant by this, and he explained that, although Lorenzo had pursued knowledge with a modicum of success, he had "forgotten" how to be a man, and this forgetting was the cause of his troubles. This friend laid the blame for Lorenzo's alienation squarely on a characterological defect of role-playing, a kind of stage fright. Shaking his head sadly, he uttered an aphoristic diagnosis: "Como hombre, no sirve" (literally, as a man he just doesn't serve, or work). He added, "Pobrecito, no sirve pa' na'" (poor guy, he's totally useless).

Spoken by a concerned friend in a tone of commiseration rather than reproach, this phrase, "no sirve," has much meaning. Loosely translated, it means that as a man Lorenzo fails muster in some practical way, the Spanish verb *servir* meaning to get things done, to work in the sense of proficiency or serviceability. There is a sense of the measurable quantity here—visible results. But what are these practical accomplishments of Andalusian manliness? Let me digress briefly in order to place Lorenzo and his apostasy from Tierno's "faith" in the broader context of the Circum-Mediterranean area by offering some comparisons from across the sea.

MANLY SERVICES

Lorenzo's friends made a connection between manhood and some code of effective or "serviceable" behavior. This echoes Chandos's (1984:346) description of the British public-school elite, the English locution connoting utility being both etymologically and conceptually cognate to the Spanish *sirve*. But more than simply serving, this behavior in Lorenzo's community had to be public, on the community stage, as it were. A man's effectiveness is measured as others see him in action, where they can evaluate his performance. This conflation of masculinity and efficaciousness into a theatrical image of performing finds powerful echoes in other Mediterranean lands. Let us take, for example, Greece. Luckily we have excellent data for that country, thanks to the untiring efforts of Michael Herzfeld. There, too, the manly man is one who performs, as Herzfeld has it, center stage. His role-playing is manifested in "fore-grounded" deeds, in actions that are seen by everyone and therefore have the potential to be judged collectively. As Herzfeld says of the Greeks he studied, the excellent man, the admired man, is not necessarily a "good" man in some abstract moral sense. Rather he is *good at being a man*. This means not only adequate performance within set patterns (the male script); it also means publicity, being on view and having the courage to expose oneself to risk. In addition, it means decisive action that works or serves a purpose, action that meets tests and solves real problems consensually perceived as important.

A subtle and perceptive fieldworker, Herzfeld (1985a) describes for the village of Glendi in Crete—an island of Mediterranean cultural synthesis—the archetype of social acceptance that is most relevant to the present case. To be a man in Crete and Andalusia means a pragmatic, agential modality, an involvement in the public arena of acts and deeds and visible, concrete accomplishments. This showy modality has nothing to do with the security or domestic pleasures of the home or with introspection. These things are associated with self-doubt, hesitancy, with-drawal into the wings, that is, with passivity. It is here that Lorenzo, back in Spain, has been deficient. He is, above all else, a recessive man, staying demurely at home, avoiding life's challenges and opportunities. Manhood at both ends of the sea seems to imply a nexus of gregarious engagement, a male praxis endlessly conjoined on the stage of community life.

If we go back in time we find some intriguing echoes. The ancient Greeks also admired an outgoing, risk-taking manliness of effective action. They also judged a man not for being good but for whether or not he was useful in the role he played on the communal stage—an "efficient or defective working part of the communal mechanism" (Dover 1978:108). Their agonistic view of life is the ethos that informs the restless heroism of the Homeric sagas with a call to dramatic, even grandiose, gestures (Gouldner 1965). But this image is also associated with ideals of manly virtue that the ancient Greeks, like some of their modern descendants, held and still hold dear in it vulgar manifestation as *filotimo*, masculine pride or self-esteem (Herzfeld 1980:342–45). The Spaniards or Italians might call this right to pride by some cognate of "honor," *honra* or *onore*, or perhaps respect. It conveys a self-image deeply involved with the endless search for worldly success and fame, for approbation and admiration in the judgmental eyes of others. This emphasis on the dramatic gesture appears early in Greek culture. It shows up in Homer, in the *Iliad* most visibly: in Achilles' willingness to trade a long, uneventful life for a brief one filled with honor and glory, and in Agamemnon's willingness to trade several months of his life for an honorable death on the battlefield at Troy (Slater 1968:35).

This quest for fame and for the glorious deed as a measure of masculine virtue took on a life of its own in the ancient eastern Mediterranean world. Indeed, in the flourishing Athens of the fifth century B.C., male life seems to have been an unremitting struggle for personal aggrandizement—for "fame and honor, or for such goals as could lead to these (wealth, power, and so forth)" (ibid.:38). Despite the Greek emphasis on moderation that we cherish today, this obsessive glory-seeking grew more and more a part of Greek masculine ideals, to the point where the chronicler Thucydides was motivated to chastise his countrymen: "Reckless audacity came to be considered the courage of a loyal ally; prudent hesitation specious cowardice; moderation was held to be a cloak for unmanliness" (1951, iii:82). One mythological model of this manly man covered in glory, the embodiment of this Greek ideal, is the intrepid and wily traveller Odysseus.

The *Odyssey* is a parable of this kind of dramatized manliness uniting practical effect and moral vision. Its hero sets forth, engaging in countless struggles, surviving through physical strength and clever stratagems fair and foul. After innumerable encounters with the dangers and monsters of the world, he returns triumphantly in the final act to succor wife and kin, the ultimate heroic Greek male. Odysseus is no saint; he is portrayed as a trickster and manipulator. But his tricks "work." They have the desired end: the rescue of the endangered wife left at home, Penelope, and the restoration of the family's honor, threatened by the opportunistic suitors. The Homeric epic captures in legend the thrust of this peripatetic, pragmatic, and serviceable Mediterranean manhood.

From a psychological point of view, it is clear that this ancient morality of man-acting has something to do with the cultural encoding of impulse sublimation. An inspirational model of right action, it directs energies away from self-absorption and introspection toward a strategy of practical problem-solving and worldly concerns. The manly image in ancient Greece as well as in modern Andalusia is an inducement toward ceaseless enterprise judged by measurable ends. In an important sense, it is more than simply the sublimation of libido and aggression into culturally-approved channels of practical achievement; it is also the encouragement to resist their opposites: indolence, self-doubt, squeamishness, hesitancy, the impulse to withdraw or surrender, the "sleepiness" of quietude (symbolized in Greek legend by death by drowning—a universal metaphor for returning to the womb). As well as a commitment to commanding action in an agonistic context, an aggressive stance in service to proximate goals—what Gouldner has called the Greek contest system—manliness in much of the Mediterranean world can be called a social agoraphilia, a love for the sunlit public places, for crowds, for the proscenium of life. Such open contexts are associated not only with exposure and sociability but also with risk and opportunity, with the possibility of the grand exploit and the conspicuous deed. We can thus describe Lorenzo's first failure as a man as a refusal to sally forth into the fray.

• • •

SEX AND MARRIAGE

It is, of course, a commonplace version of this kind of mighty inner struggle against self-withdrawal that Lorenzo had become embroiled in and that he seemed to be losing in Spain. But there is more at stake here than a show of self-mastery and competitive fitness. There is also sex; or rather, an aggressive role in courtship. Lorenzo's friends bemoaned his failure to go out and capture a wife. "As a man he does not serve" refers explicitly to wife-capture and phallic predation.

In some Muslim areas, for example, rural Turkey (Bates 1974) and the southern Balkans (Lockwood 1974), this predation often takes the form of actual bride theft or prenuptial rape, often involving kidnapping or violence. Such things used to occur also in parts of southern Italy, where some men first raped and then married reluctant brides. Wife-by-capture is still common in parts of rural Greece (Herzfeld 1985b). This assertive courting, minus the violence, is an important, even essential requirement of manhood in Spain as well. It is a recurrent aspect of the male image in many parts of southern Europe, whereas it seems less critical in the northern countries.

Most of what we know about Mediterranean ideas of manhood, in fact, concerns their more expressive components—more precisely, their sexual assertiveness (Pitt-Rivers 1977): the *machismo* of Spain and the *maschio* of Sicily (Giovannini 1987) are examples. There is also the *rajula* (virility) complex of Morocco (Geertz 1979:364), which has been likened specifically to Hispanic *machismo* by a female anthropologist (Mernissi 1975:4–5). There are parallels in the Balkans, which anthropological observers Simic (1969, 1983) and Denich (1974), male and female scholars respectively, independently identify with the *machismo* of Hispanic culture. A real man in these countries is forceful in courtship as well as a fearless man of action. Both sex and economic enterprise are competitive and risky, because they place a man against his fellows in the quest for the most prized resource of all—women. Defeat and humiliation are always possible.

In Sicily, for instance, masculine honor is always bound up with aggression and potency. A real man in Sicily is "a man with big testicles" (Blok 1981:432–33); his potency is firmly established. Among the Sarakatsani of Greece, also, an adult male must be "well endowed with testicles" (J. K. Campbell 1964:269), quick to arousal, insatiable in the act. Such beliefs also hold true for much of Spain, especially the south (Pitt-Rivers 1965, 1977; Brandes 1980, 1981; Mitchell 1988), where a real man is said to have much *cojones,* or balls. Such big-balled men, naturally, tower over and dominate their less well-endowed and more phlegmatic fellows.

Yet there is more to this than competitive lechery (which, incidentally, is not as highly regarded in the Muslim countries, for in Islam unbridled lust is held to be socially disruptive and immoral for both sexes [Bates and Rassam 1983:215]). This extra dimension is important for a deeper understanding of the social matrix of Circum-Mediterranean ideas of manhood that I mentioned above. Even in those parts of southern Europe where the Don Juan model of sexual assertiveness is highly valued, a man's assigned task is not just to make endless conquests but to spread his seed. Beyond mere promiscuity, the ultimate test is that of competence in reproduction, that is, impregnating one's wife. For example, in Italy, "only a wife's pregnancy could sustain her husband's masculinity" (Bell 1979:105). Most importantly, therefore, the Mediterranean emphasis on manliness means results; it means procreating offspring (preferably boys). At the level of community endorsement, it is legitimate reproductive success, more than simply erotic acrobatics—a critical fact often overlooked by experts on Mediterranean honor who stress its disruptive or competitive elements (Pitt-Rivers 1977:11). Simply stated, it means creating a large and vigorous family. Promiscuous adventurism represents a prior (youthful) testing ground to a more serious (adult) purpose. Sexuality and economic self-sufficiency work in parallel ways.

In southern Spain, for example, people will heap scorn upon a married man without children, no matter how sexually active he may have been prior to marriage. What counts is results, not the preliminaries. Although both husband and wife suffer in prestige, the blame of barrenness is placed squarely on him, not his wife, for it is always the man who is expected to initiate (and accomplish) things. "Is he a man?" the people sneer. Scurrilous gossip circulates about his physiological defects. He is said to be incompetent, a sexual bungler, a clown. His mother-in-law becomes outraged. His loins are useless, she says, "no sirven," they don't work. Solutions are sought in both medical and magical means. People say that he has failed in his husbandly duty. In being sexually ineffectual, he has failed at being a man.

BEYOND SEX: PROVISIONING

Aside from potency, men must seek to provision dependents by contributing mightily to the family patrimony. This, too, is measured by the efficiency quotient, by results (Davis 1977:77). What counts, again, is performance in the work role, measured in sacrifice or service to family needs. What has to be emphasized here is the sense of social sacrifice that this masculine work-duty entails. The worker in the fields often despises manual labor of any sort, because it rarely benefits him personally. For example, the rural Andalusians say that work is a "curse" (D. Gilmore 1980:55), because it can never make a man rich. For the poor man, working means contracting under humiliating conditions for a day-wage, battling with his fellows for fleeting opportunities in the work place, and laboring in the fields picking cotton and weeding sunflowers from dawn to dusk. Synonymous with suffering, work is something that most men will freely admit they hate and would avoid if they could.

Yet for the worker, the peasant, or any man who must earn his bread, work is also a responsibility—never questioned—of feeding dependents. And here, as in matters of sex and fatherly duty, the worker's reputation as a citizen and a man is closely bound up with clearly defined service to family. A man who shirks these obligations renounces his claim to both respectability and manhood; he becomes a despised less-than-man, a wastrel, a *gamberro*. The latter term means an irresponsible reprobate who acts like a carefree child or who lives parasitically off women. Although it is true that women in Andalusia are often wage-earners too, the husband, to be a real man, must contribute the lion's share of income to support wife and family like a pillar and to keep the feminine machine of domestic production running smoothly. A man works hard, sometimes desperately, because, as they say, *se obliga*, you are bound to your family, not because you like it. In this sense, Spanish men are, as Brandes notes (1980:210), like men everywhere, actively pursuing the breadwinning role as a measure of their manhood. The only difference is that they rarely get pleasure or personal satisfaction from the miserable work available to them.

In southern Italy, much the same attitude is found. John Davis (1973:94–95) writes of the town of Pisticci: "Work is also justified in terms of the family of the man who works: 'If it were not for my family, I'd not be wearing myself out' (*non mi sacrifico*). The ability of a husband to support his wife and children is as important a component of his honour as his control of his wife's sexuality. Independence of others, in this context, thus implies both his economic and sexual honour. . . . Work, then, is not regarded as having any intrinsic rewards. Men work to produce food and some cash for their families."

This sacrifice in the service of family, this contribution to household and kin, is, in fact, what Mediterranean notions of honor are all about. Honor is about being good *at being a man*, which means building up and buttressing the family or kindred—the basic building blocks of society— no matter what the personal cost: "[Mediterranean] honor as ideology helps shore up the identity of a group (a family or a lineage) and commit to it the loyalties of otherwise doubtful members. Honor defines the group's social boundaries, contributing to its defense against the claims of equivalent competing groups" (Schneider 1971:17).

The emphasis on male honor as a domestic duty is widespread in the Mediterranean. In his seminal survey of the literature, John Davis, like Jane Schneider in the quote above, finds confirmation for his view of masculine honor as deriving from work and economic industry as much as from sexual success: "It should be said at the outset that honour is not primarily to do with sexual intercourse . . . but with performance of roles and is related to economic resources because feeding a family, looking after women, maintaining a following, can be done more easily when the family is not poor" (1977:77).

Sometimes this kind of economic service can be quantified in terms of money or other objects of value, or it can be expressed in material accumulations that are passed on to women and children, such as dowries. For example, Ernestine Friedl (1962), writing about a Greek peasant village in contemporary Boeotia, describes the honor of fathers as grounded in their ability to provide large dowries in cash and valuables to their daughters. This success assures them of the best in-laws, contributes to family prestige, and consequently enhances their image as provider. Manhood is measured at least partly in money, a man's only direct way of nourishing children. Manhood, then, as call to action, can be interpreted as a kind of moral compunction to provision kith and kin.

MAN-THE-PROTECTOR

After impregnating and provisioning comes bravery. Being a man in Andalusia, for example, is also based on what the people call *hombría*. Technically this simply means manliness, but it differs from the expressly virile or economic performances described above. Rather, hombría is physical and moral courage. Having no specific behavioral correlatives, it forms an intransitive component: it means standing up for yourself as an independent and proud actor, holding your own when challenged. Spaniards also call this *dignidad* (dignity). It is not based on threatening people or on violence, for Andalusians despise bullies and deplore physical roughness, which to them is mere buffoonery. Generalized as to context, hombría means a courageous and stoic demeanor in the face of any threat; most important, it means defending one's honor and that of one's family. It shows not aggressiveness in a physical sense but an unshakable loyalty to social group that signals the ultimate deterrent to challenge. The restraint on violence is always based on the capacity for violence, so that reputation is vital here.

As a form of masculine self-control and courage, hombría is shown multitudinously. For example, in Fuenmayor, a group of young men may wander down to the municipal cemetery late at night after a few drinks to display their disdain for ghosts. They take with them a hammer and a nail or spike. Posturing drunkenly together, they pound the nail into the cemetery's stucco wall. Challenging all manner of goblins and ghouls, they recite in unison the following formula to the rhythm of the hammer blows:

Aquí hinco clavo	I here drive a spike
del tío monero	before goblin or sprite
venga quién venga,	and whatever appear,
aquí lo espero!	I remain without fear!

The last man to run away wins the laurels as the bravest, the most manly. Sometimes adolescents will challenge each other to spend a night in the cemetery in a manner of competitive testing, but otherwise hombría is nonconfrontational, as the defiance is displaced onto a supernatural (nonsocial) adversary. Nevertheless, as the above example shows, it is competitive and, like virility and economic performance, needs proof in visible symbols and accomplishments. Hombría judges a man's fitness to defend his family. Pitt-Rivers (1961:89) has depicted it best: "The quintessence of manliness is fearlessness, readiness to defend one's own pride and that of one's family." Beyond this, hombría also has a specifically political connotation that enlarges its role in Spain.

For the past century, Spain, and Andalusia in particular, has been a land of political struggle. Class consciousness is strong as a result of deep antagonism between landowners and laborers (Martinez-Alier 1971). Hombría among the embattled workers and peasants has taken on a strongly political coloration from this class opposition: loyalty to social class. Among peasants and workers, manliness is expressed not only by loyalty to kindred but also by loyalty to the laboring class and by an active participation in the struggle for workers' rights. For example, workers are very manly who uphold laborers' rights by refusing to back down in labor disputes. This was an especially courageous act under the Franco dictatorship but is still admired today among the committed. Charismatic labor leaders—especially those jailed and beaten by the Franco police, as was Marcelino Camacho, the head of the underground Workers' Commissions—are highly admired as being very virile. In their group they are men with "lots of balls," envied by men, attractive to women. In the eyes of their political enemies they may be hated, but they are also respected and feared.

A concrete example: there was in Fuenmayor the famous case of the militant agitator nicknamed "Robustiano" (the Robust One), so called for his athletic build and his formidable courage. After the Civil War, when his left-leaning family was decimated by the Nationalists in the postwar persecutions, he had openly defied the Franco police by continuing his revolutionary activities. Beatings, threats, and blackballing had no effect. After each return from jail he took up the struggle anew, winning admiration from all sides, including his jailers. Despite torture, he never betrayed his comrades, always taking police abuse stoically as a matter of course. Robustiano developed a huge and loyal following; today he is remembered as one of the martyrs who kept up the workers' spirits during the dark days of the dictatorship. Beyond this, people remember Robustiano as a real man, an apotheosis of the Andalusian ideal of manhood.

Apart from politics, this call to dramatic action in defense of one's comrades finds echoes throughout the Mediterranean region where social class is less important than other primordial ties, as among patrilineal peoples of the African littoral. For example, among the Kabyles of Algeria, according to Bourdieu (1965, 1979a), the main attribute of the real man is that he stands up to other men and fiercely defends his agnates. "All informants give as the essential characteristic of the man of honour the fact that he *faces* others," Bourdieu remarks (1979a:128). A real man suffers no slights to self or, more importantly, to family or lineage. Nearby, in eastern Morocco, true men are those who stand ever ready to defend their families against outside threats; they "unite in defense of their livelihoods and collective identity" (Marcus 1987:50).

Likewise, among the Sarakatsani shepherds of modern-day Greece (J. K. Campbell 1964:269–70), the true man is described as *varvatos*, clearly cognate to the Italian *barbato*, bearded or hairy. Aside from indicating strength and virility (the facial hair again), this also "describes a certain ruthless ability in any form of endeavour" in defense of his kindred. Virile Sarakatsani shepherds are those who meet the demands of pastoral life in which " 'reputation' is impossible without strength" (ibid.:317). In this way the Sarakatsani man gains the respect of competitors and fends off threats to his domain. Thus he maintains his kindred's delicate position in a tough environment. "The reputation for manliness of the men of the family is a deterrent against external outrage" (ibid.:271). Campbell sees this stress on manliness in essentially functional terms. "Here again," he writes (ibid.:270), "we see the *'efficient'* aspect of manliness" (emphasis added).

Man-the-protector is everywhere encountered in the Mediterranean area. Throughout, bureaucratic protections are weakly developed, states are unstable, feuding is endemic, and political alignments, like patronage, are shifting and unreliable. Because of the capriciousness of fortunes and the scarcity of resources, a man ekes out a living and sustains his family through toughness and maneuvering. For example, in Sicily, *"un vero uomo"* (a real man) is defined by "strength, power, and cunning necessary to protect his women" (Giovannini 1987:68). At the same time, of course, the successfully protective man in Sicily or Andalusia garners praise through courageous feats and gains renown for himself as an individual. This inseparable functional linkage of personal and group benefit is one of the most ancient moral notions found in the Mediterranean civilizations. One finds it already in ancient seafaring Greece in the voyager Odysseus. His very name, from *odyne* (the ability to cause pain and the readiness to do so), implies a willingness to expose oneself to conflict, risk, and trouble and to strive against overwhelming odds in order to achieve great exploits. "To be Odysseus, then, is to adopt the attitude of the hunter of dangerous game: to deliberately expose one's self, but thereafter to take every advantage that the exposed position admits; the immediate purpose is injury, but the ultimate purpose is recognition and the sense of a great exploit" (Dimrock 1967:57).

But Odysseus's ultimate goal is not simply one vainglorious exploit after another. All his wayfaring heroism is directed at a higher purpose: to rescue wife and child and to disperse the sinister suitors who threaten them both. The real man gains renown by standing between his family and destruction, absorbing the blows of fate with equanimity. Mediterranean manhood is the reward given to the man who is an efficient protector of the web of primordial ties, the guardian of his society's moral and material integuments.

AUTONOMOUS WAYFARERS

The ideals of manliness found in these places in the Mediterranean seem to have three moral imperatives: first, impregnating one's wife; second, provisioning dependents; third, protecting the family. These criteria demand assertiveness and resolve. All must be performed relentlessly in the loyal service of the "collective identities" of the self.

One other element needs mention. The above depend upon something deeper: a mobility of action, a personal autonomy. A man can do nothing if his hands are tied. If he is going to hunt dangerous game and, like Odysseus, save his family, he needs absolute freedom of movement. Equally important as sex and economic resourcefulness is the underlying appeal to independent action as the starting point of manly self-identity. To enter upon the road to manhood, a man must travel light and be free to improvise and to respond, unencumbered, to challenge. He must have a moral captaincy. In southern Spain, as reported by Brandes (1980:210), dependency for an Andalusian peasant is not just shameful; it is also a negation of his manly image. Personal autonomy is the goal for each and every man; without it, his defensive posture collapses. His strategic mobility is lost, exposing his family to ruin. This theme, too, has political implications in Spain.

An example comes from George Collier's account of the Spanish Civil War in an Andalusian village. Collier (1987–90) points out the role played by masculine pride in the labor movements of workers and peasants in western Andalusia. He describes the critical political connotations of what he calls the "cultural terms in which Andalusians relate autonomy to masculine honor" and the virtues attached to asserting this masculinity (ibid.:96). Collier's discussion of the violent conflicts between landowners and laborers during the Second Republic (1931–36) in the pueblo of Los Olivos (Huelva Province) shows that a driving force behind their confrontations was this issue of personal autonomy. The peasants and workers were defending not only their political rights but also their self-image as men from the domineering tactics of the rich and powerful. Autonomy permitted them to defend their family's honor. Encumbered or dependent, they could not perform their manly heroics. Their revolutionism, as Collier brilliantly shows, was as much a product of a manhood image as their political and economic demands. This was particularly true of southern Spain, but Collier sees this mixture of political ideology and masculine self-image as something more widely Mediterranean:

> Villagers in Los Olivos held to the ideal of masculine autonomy characteristic of property relations and the system of honor in the agrarian societies of the Mediterranean. . . . The prepotent male discouraged challenges by continually reasserting this masculinity and potential for physical aggression while he guarded against assaults on the virtue of his women and stood up to others to protect his family's honor. . . . The ideal of masculine autonomy thus charged employer-employee relations with special tension. In having to accept someone else's orders, the employee implicitly acknowledged his lack of full autonomy and his vulnerability to potential dishonor. (Ibid.:96–97)

To be dependent upon another man is bad enough, but to acknowledge dependence upon a woman is worse. The reason, of course, is that this inverts the normal order of family ties, which in turn destroys the formal basis for manhood. For instance, in Morocco, as reported by Hildred Geertz (1979:369), the major values of *rajula*, or manly pride, are "personal autonomy and force," which imply dominating and provisioning rather than being dominated and provisioned by women. There is indeed no greater fear among men than the loss of this personal autonomy to a dominant woman.

In Morocco there is in fact a recurrent anxiety that a man will fall under the magical spell of a powerful woman, a demonic seductress who will entrap him forever, as Venus entrapped Tannhaüser, or as Circe attempted to enslave Odysseus, causing him to forget his masculine role (Dwyer 1978). The psychological anthropologist Vincent Crapanzano has written an entire book about a Moroccan man who lived in terror of such a demonic female *jinn*. He tells us that this anxiety is widespread: "This theme of enslavement by a woman—the inverse of the articulated standards of male-female relations, of sex and marriage—pervades Moroccan folklore" (1980:102). There, as in Spain, a man must gain full and total independence from women as a necessary criterion of manhood. How can he provide for dependents and protect them when he himself is dependent like a child? This inversion of sex roles, because it turns wife into mother, subverts both the man and the family unit, sending both down to corruption and defeat.

SEXUAL SEGREGATION

Many of these themes—activity versus passivity, extroversion versus introversion, autonomy versus dependence—are expressed in the physical context of Mediterranean rural community life. The requirement that the male separate conclusively from women could be no more clearly expressed than in the prohibitions against domesticity that pervade the ethnographic literature. In many Mediterranean societies (D. Gilmore 1982:194–96), the worlds of men and women are strictly demarcated. Male and female realms are, as Duvignaud says of Tunisia, "two separate worlds that pass without touching" (1977:16). Men are forced by this moral convention of spatial segregation to leave home during the day and to venture forth into the risky world outside. Like Lorenzo, a man hiding in the shadows of home during the daytime is immediately suspect. His masculinity is out of place and thus questionable. A real man must be out-of-doors among men, facing others, staring them down. In Cyprus, for example, a man who lingers at home with wife and children will have his manhood questioned: "What sort of man is he? He prefers hanging about the house with women" (Loizos 1975:92). And among the Algerian Kabyle described by Bourdieu (1979b:141), his fellows will malign a homebody for much the same reason: "A man who spends too much time at home in the daytime is suspect or ridiculous: he is 'a house man,' who 'broods at home like a hen at roost.' A self-respecting man must offer himself to be seen, constantly put himself in the gaze of others, confront them, face up to them (qabel). He is a man among men." So we can see the manly image working to catapult men out of the refuge of the house into the cockpit of enterprise.

ANOTHER ECCENTRIC

To conclude, I will describe another negative case from Andalusia that illustrates these last points. There was a man in Fuenmayor who was a notorious homebody and whose family suffered the consequences.

Alfredo was a rubicund little merchant with the non-Castilian surname Tissot (his ancestors had emigrated from Catalonia generations earlier). A sedentary man of middle age, he operated a small grocery establishment from out of his home—nothing unusual for men with small retail businesses. But Alfredo was unusual in that he rarely ventured out from his home, where he lived with his wife and two pretty grown daughters.

In Andalusia, as in Cyprus or Algeria, a man is expected to spend his free time outdoors, backslapping and glad-handing. This world is the street, the bar, the fields—public places where a man is seen. He must not give the impression of being under the spell of the home, a clinger to wife or mother. While out, men are also expected to become involved in standard masculine rivalries: games of cards and dominoes, competitive drinking and spending, and contests of braggadocio and song. Although aware of such expectations, Alfredo resisted them, because, as he confided to me one day, such socializing was a waste of time and money—you have to spend money in the bars; you have to buy rounds of drinks for the company of fellows, and you have to tipple and make merry. You have to boast and puff yourself up before your cronies. All this conviviality was expensive and boring, so the chubby grocer stayed at home with his family. He read books and watched television at night or went over his accounts.

Like all other townsmen, Alfredo was under the scrutiny of public opinion and was accountable as a man. Although grudgingly admitting his modest business acumen (said however to be based on his wife's capital), the townspeople did not accept his lame excuses for inappropriate comportment. As a descendant of distrusted ethnic outsiders (Catalans are known as a race of workaholics and misers), he was expected to display strange attitudes, but his refusal to enter the public world of men in favor of home was greeted with outrage and indignation. Especially vilified was his stinginess with both time and money, which was felt as an insult to the other men of the pueblo, a calculated withdrawal from the male role, which demands not just familiar provisioning but a certain degree of generosity in the wider society. A man of means is expected to spend freely and thus to support his community. People say such a man owes something to the town. Alfredo's withdrawal damaged both his own prestige and that of his family, which suffered equally in the public spotlight.

One hot afternoon, as I was walking past the Tissot house with a group of friends, my companions made passing comments on Alfredo's strangeness. "What kind of man is he," they muttered, pointing at his sealed and cloistered house, "spending his time at home?" Glowering ominously, they likened him to a mother hen. They offered colorful explanations for his contemptible secretiveness, alluding to certain despicable character traits such as cheapness and egoism. But beyond these picayune moral defects, my informants found something truly repulsive in the merchant's domesticity, furtiveness, and sedentariness. They suggested a basic failure at a deeper level in the most important thing of all: man-acting. Carrying this character assassination further, my informants left the realm of observable fact and ventured into gossipy speculation, which is common in such matters of serious deviance. Unequivocal explanations are deemed necessary when deeply-felt customs are violated.

The men then told me their suspicions about Alfredo. In the telling I could feel a palpable relaxation of their anxiety about him, for they had reduced the deviance to root causes that they could scapegoat and consensually reject in a way that corroborated their own self-image. It all boiled down to Alfredo's failure as a man. This was shown incontrovertibly, as in the case of Lorenzo, by his shadowy introversion. As a consequence of his withdrawn uxoriousness, in the minds of his fellows, the Tissot household, bereft of sexual respectability, was held necessarily to be abnormal in terms of sexual functioning. Its very existence was, therefore, by local standards, attributable to aberrant practices. Since Alfredo was not a real man, as his community had decided, then his daughters, by logical extension, could not be the product of his own seed. The explanation that tied all together (since the eccentric Catalan was also known as a moderately wealthy man) was that he was a panderer and a pimp for his wife, and his daughters and his wealth were the result of her secret whoring. The villagers had thus conceptually, if inaccurately, reversed provider and dependent roles in this ugly and ridiculous slander. The associated success of insemination was stolen by a hostile act of imagination. Poor Alfredo was utterly incapable of combatting this malicious attack because he had cut himself off from male communication, so he and his family suffered from the slights and contempt reserved for deviants.

Hypothetically classified as unnatural, then, Alfredo's inexplicable character traits fell into a kind of preordained order of the man-who-is-no-man. For example, there was the matter of his cooking. He was known to help wife and daughters in the kitchen, cutting, chopping, and so on, performing tasks absolutely unnatural to the male physiology and musculature. Andalusians recognize that there are professional chefs, but they are men who have learned a trade to earn a living, and so they retain their claim to manhood. At home, even chefs do not cook; their wives do. But

Alfredo was said to help eagerly out of his own perverted volition. "Is he a man?" people scoffed, "cooking, hanging about in the kitchen like that?" The Andalusians believe fervidly that male and female anatomy provide for different, complementary skills. It was true that Alfredo helped in the kitchen. Since he invited me into his home (in itself an act of unusual, even deviant hospitality), I saw him. He never hid this indictable bit of information from me. I came to know him fairly well on these occasions. Being a didactic and helpful sort of man in a fussy way, he instructed my wife and myself in the proper preparation of certain specialties of Spanish cuisine, providing precise, often compulsive directions for grinding ingredients to make a tasty gazpacho. I learned how to whip up a savory, if smelly, garlic soup in the gleaming Tissot kitchen. He always watched that everything was done in the proper order. For example, the bread always went in the pot after you added the vinegar: no improvising here. Beaming maternally, the homebody took pride in his knowledge of local recipes and in my vocal appreciation of his culinary skills.

But his fellows in the streets laughed at him, scorning his hurried excuses, grimacing disgustedly when I spoke of him, holding both him and his superfluous wife in contempt. The placid pleasure Alfredo took in his own odd domesticity hastened his withdrawal from manly assemblages and activities. The introverted grocer failed to make it as a man by local standards. This failure in turn robbed his family of respectability, plunging them all into disrepute, so that, for example, his two daughters had to find fiancés in other towns. Alfredo's fatal flaw was that he failed even to present himself for the test of manhood. He failed, most decisively, to separate: his public identity was blurred by the proximity of women. He had withdrawn into a sheltered cocoon of domesticity, self-indulgently satisfied with good food and easeful luxury, unwilling or afraid to enter the risky ring of manhood. This withdrawal made the other men uncomfortable, so they conceptually emasculated him and stole his family's honor, placing them all beyond the pale and obviating the threat they represented.

And yet, Alfredo was for other men a subject of endless discussion and debate. Perhaps, despite their protestations, there was something about him that, though also repellent, attracted these tough, virile men? Or possibly he represented to them some contumacious principle—living well without visibly working, perhaps—that caused ambivalent feelings that had to be expunged through projection and denial?

BIBLIOGRAPHY

Bates, Daniel G. 1974. Normative and alternative systems of marriage among the Yörük of southeastern Turkey. *Anthropological Quarterly* 47:270–87.

Bates, Daniel G., and Amal Rassam. 1983. *Peoples and Cultures of the Middle East.* Englewood Cliffs, N.J.: Prentice-Hall.

Bell, Rudolf M. 1979. *Fate and Honor, Family and Village: Demographic and Cultural Change in Rural Italy Since 1800.* Chicago: University of Chicago Press.

Blok, Anton. 1981. Rams and billy-goats: a key to the Mediterranean code of honour. *Man* 16:427–40.

Bourdieu, Pierre. 1965. The sentiment of honour in Kabyle society. In *Honour and Shame: The Values of Mediterranean Society,* ed. J.-G. Peristiany, pp. 191–241. Chicago: University of Chicago Press.

———. 1979a. The sense of honour. In *Algeria 1960: Essays by Pierre Bourdieu.* Cambridge: Cambridge University Press.

———. 1979b. The Kabyle house, or the world reversed. In *Algeria 1960: Essays by Pierre Bourdieu.* Cambridge: Cambridge University Press.

Brandes, Stanley H. 1980. *Metaphors of Masculinity: Sex and Status in Andalusian Folklore.* Philadelphia: University of Pennsylvania Press.

———. 1981. Like wounded stages: male sexual ideology in an Andalusian town. In *Sexual Meanings,* ed. Sherry B. Ortner and Harriet Whitehead, pp. 216–39. Cambridge: Cambridge University Press.

Braudel, Fernand. 1972. *The Mediterranean and the Mediterranean World in the Age of Philip II.* 2 vols. Trans. Siân Reynolds. New York: Harper and Row.

Campbell, J. K. 1964. *Honour, Family, and Patronage.* Oxford: Clarendon Press.

Chandos, John. 1984. *Boys Together: English Public Schools, 1800–1864.* New Haven: Yale University Press.

Collier, George A. 1987. *The Socialists of Rural Andalusia: Unacknowledged Revolutionaries.* Stanford: Stanford University Press.

Crapanzano, Vincent. 1980. *Tuhami: Portrait of a Moroccan.* Chicago: University of Chicago Press.

Davis, John. 1977. *People of the Mediterranean.* London: Routledge and Kegan Paul.

Denich, Bette. 1974. Sex and power in the Balkans. In *Women, Culture, and Society,* ed. Michelle Rosaldo and Louise Lamphere, pp. 243–62. Stanford: Stanford University Press.

Dimrock, George E., Jr. 1967. The name of Odysseus. In *Essays on the Odyssey: Selected Modern Criticism,* ed. Charles H. Taylor, Jr., pp. 54–72. Bloomington, Ind.: Indiana University Press.

Dover, Kenneth J. 1978. *Greek Homosexuality*. Cambridge, Mass.: Harvard University Press.

Duvignaud, Jean. 1977. *Change at Shebika: Report from a North African Village*, trans. F. Frenaye. New York: Pantheon.

Dwyer, Daisy. 1978. *Images and Self-Images: Male and Female in Morocco*. New York: Columbia University Press.

Friedl, Ernestine. 1962. *Vasilika: Village in Modern Greece*. New York: Holt, Rinehart and Winston.

Geertz, Hildred. 1979. The meanings of family ties. In *Meaning and Order in Moroccan Society*, ed. Clifford Geertz, H. Geertz, and L. Rosen, pp. 315–86. New York: Cambridge University Press.

Gilmore, David D. 1980. *The People of the Plain*. New York: Columbia University Press.

——. 1982. Anthropology of the Mediterranean area. *Annual Review of Anthropology* 11:175–205.

Giovannini, Maureen. 1987. Female chastity codes in the Circum-Mediterranean: comparative perspectives. In *Honor and Shame and the Unity of the Mediterranean*, ed. David D. Gilmore, pp. 61–74. Washington, D.C.: American Anthropological Association, Special Pub. no. 22.

Gouldner, Alvin W. 1965. *Enter Plato: Classical Greece and the Origins of Social Theory*. New York: Basic Books.

Herzfeld, Michael. 1980. Honour and shame: some problems in the comparative analysis of moral systems. *Man* 15:339–51.

——. 1985a. *The Poetics of Manhood: Contest and Identity in a Cretan Mountain Village*. Princeton: Princeton University Press.

——. 1985b. Gender pragmatics: Agency, speech and bride-theft in a Cretan mountain village. *Anthropology* 9:25–44.

——. 1987. *Anthropology Through the Looking-Glass: Critical Ethnography in the Margins of Europe*. Cambridge: Cambridge University Press.

Lockwood, William G. 1974. Bride theft and social maneuverability in western Bosnia. *Anthropological Quarterly* 47:253–69.

Loizos, Peter. 1975. *The Greek Gift*. New York: St. Martin's Press.

Marcus, Michael. 1987. "Horsemen are the fence of the land": Honor and history among the Ghiyata of eastern Morocco. In *Honor and Shame and the Unity of the Mediterranean*, ed. David D. Gilmore, pp. 49–60. Washington, D.C.: American Anthropological Association, Special Pub. no. 22.

Martinez-Alier, Juan. 1971. *Labourers and Landowners in Southern Spain*. London: St. Martin's Press.

Mernissi, Fatima. 1975. *Beyond the Veil*. New York: Schenckman.

Mitchell, Timothy J. 1988. *Violence and Piety in Spanish Folklore*. Philadelphia: University of Pennsylvania Press.

Peristiany, J.-G., ed. 1965. *Honour and Shame: The Values of Mediterranean Society.* London: Weidenfeld and Nicolson.

Pitt-Rivers, Julian. 1961. *The People of the Sierra.* Chicago: University of Chicago Press.

———. 1965. Honour and social status. In *Honour and Shame*, ed. J.-G. Peristiany, pp. 19–77. London: Weidenfeld and Nicolson.

———. 1977. *The Fate of Shechem.* Cambridge: Cambridge University Press.

———, ed. 1963. *Mediterranean Countrymen.* Paris: Mouton.

Schneider, Jane. 1971. Of vigilance and virgins. *Ethnology* 9:1–24.

Simic, Andrei. 1969. Management of the male image in Yugoslavia. *Anthropological Quarterly* 42:89–101.

———. 1983. Machismo and cryptomatriarchy: power, affect, and authority in the contemporary Yugoslav family. *Ethos* 11:66–86.

Slater, Philip E. 1968. *The Glory of Hera.* Boston: Beacon Press.

Thucydides. 1951. *The Complete Writings: The Peloponnesian Wars*, ed. J. H. Finley, Jr., trans. Richard Crawley. New York: Modern Library.

Tierno Galván, Enrique. 1961. Los toros, acontecimiento nacional. In *Desde el Espectáculo a la Trivilización*, pp. 53–77. Madrid: Taurus.

ACTIVE READING

1. How can you tell the difference between Gilmore's opinions about Mediterranean gender roles, on the one hand, and his descriptions of his subjects' own attitudes, on the other? Mark passages that fit each category, and point to some differences between them. Why might it be important to distinguish between Gilmore's assumptions and his subjects'?

2. Gilmore presents his theories about Mediterranean manhood in part by offering examples of men who do not fit the mold. Looking closely at his discussions of Lorenzo and Alfredo, explain what you think he gains by focusing on "the exceptions that prove the rule." What does his strategy highlight about the relationship between the community and individual men in the Mediterranean world?

3. Gilmore refers at one point to "the male script" (278). Rereading his essay, find several instances of what you think is "scripted behavior."

How does such behavior relate to "performative excellence" (273)?

READING IN NEW CONTEXTS

1. Gilmore describes a "moral convention of spatial segregation" (289) for men and women in Mediterranean cultures. Based on your reading, what is the purpose of such segregation and how do ideas of morality figure into it? Use your understanding of segregation in Gilmore's text to examine some kind of separation between social groups in another *Literacies* text (Angelou, Clifford, and el-Saadawi are possibilities). How well do Gilmore's theories fit this new context?

2. Gilmore's text includes a number of words (like *hombría* or *filotimo*) which express traits associated with manhood in various Mediterranean communities. How useful are these terms for discussing the role of masculinity in Rodriguez or Rosaldo? Which terms or concepts in those essays most closely match the meanings of the words Gilmore introduces?

3. Gilmore uses the notion of "performative excellence" to show how Mediterranean men live up to their communities' expectations about manliness. Show how you might use and adapt this idea to discuss another *Literacies* text in which someone's social role involves a good deal of performance.

DRAFT ONE / DRAFT TWO

1. *Draft One:* The villagers of Fuenmayor tell stories about Alfredo which conflict with what Gilmore himself learns about him. Use Fienup-Riordan's or Kingston's text to help you discuss how and why the villagers invent their own version of Alfredo's history.

   Draft Two: Pick some terms from Scholes's essay that help you say more about how Alfredo's story is created and understood by his fellow villagers. What do the myths about Alfredo have to do with what Scholes calls "ideology"?

2. *Draft One:* Gilmore distinguishes between the roles of competition and confrontation in Mediterranean life. How does this distinction help to explain the relationships that men have with each other in this text?

What about relationships between men and women?

Draft Two: Expand your discussion of the distinction between competition and confrontation to include relationships between women in texts by Rich, Brody, or Walker. What are the social functions of such competitions and confrontations?

3. *Draft One:* What images and ideas about manhood are prevalent in your own cultural tradition? How might such images be misunderstood by observers from another social group? Think of some arguments you might use to help an outsider understand your culture's notions of masculinity.

Draft Two: Extend Draft One by considering a *Literacies* essay that deals with gender roles for women (look at Kingston, Rich, or Shanley). What experiences and feelings might men and women share as they go through the process of learning their gender identities? Explain how Gilmore and the second text influence your conclusions.

BEFORE READING SHIRLEY BRICE HEATH

1. Think of someone you know who uses his or her reading and writing skills very differently than you use yours. Describe the ways each of you uses your literacy, and then speculate on the meaning of the differences.

2. What contexts give urgency and meaning to reading, in your experience? Outside school, when have you read something very carefully, and why?

3. Under what circumstances do you read alone? with others? Describe any significant differences you see between reading alone and reading with others.

SHIRLEY   BRICE   HEATH

LITERATE TRADITIONS

IN TRACKTON[1]

Concepts of print

Newspapers, car brochures, advertisements, church materials, and home-work and official information from school come into Trackton every day. In addition, there are numerous other rather more permanent reading materials in the community: boxes and cans of food products, house num-bers, car names and license numbers, calendars and telephone dials, writ-ten messages on television, and name brands which are part of refrigerators, stoves, bicycles, and tools. There are few magazines, except those borrowed from the church, no books except school books, the Bible, and Sunday School lesson books, and a photograph album. Just as Trackton parents do not buy special toys for their young children, they do not buy books for them either; adults do not create reading and writing

From *Ways with Words: Language, Life, and Work in Communities and Class-rooms* (1983).

1. "Trackton" is Heath's fictional name for one of the Appalachian towns in which she carried out her research on literacy [Editors].

tasks for the young, nor do they consciously model or demonstrate reading and writing behaviors for them. In the home, on the plaza, and in the neighborhood, children are left to find their own reading and writing tasks: distinguishing one television channel from another, knowing the name brands of cars, motorcycles and bicycles, choosing one or another can of soup or cereal, reading price tags at Mr. Dogan's store to be sure they do not pay more than they would at the supermarket. The receipt of mail in Trackton is a big event, and since several houses are residences for transients the postman does not know, the children sometimes take the mail and give it to the appropriate person. Reading names and addresses and return addresses becomes a game-like challenge among all the children, as the school-age try to show the preschoolers how they know "what dat says."

Preschool and school-age children alike frequently ask what something "says," or how it "goes," and adults respond to their queries, making their instructions fit the requirements of the tasks. Sometimes they help with especially hard or unexpected items, and they always correct errors of fact if they hear them. When Lem, Teegie, and other children in Trackton were about two years of age, I initiated the game of reading traffic signs when we were out in the car. Lillie Mae seemed to pay little attention to this game, until one of the children made an error. If Lem termed a "Yield" sign "Stop," she corrected him, saying, "Dat ain't no stop, dat say yield; you have to give the other fellow the right of way." Often the children would read names of fastfood chains as we drove by. Once when one had changed name, and Teegie read the old name, Tony corrected him: "It ain't Chicken Delight no more; it Famous Recipe now." When the children were preparing to go to school, they chose book bags, tee shirts, and stickers for their notebooks which carried messages. Almost all the older boys and girls in the community wore tee shirts with writings scrawled across the front, and the children talked about what these said and vied to have the most original and sometimes the most suggestive.

Reading was a public group affair for almost all members of Trackton from the youngest to the oldest. Miss Lula sometimes read her Bible alone, and Annie Mae would sometimes quietly read magazines she brought home, but to read alone was frowned upon, and individuals who did so were accused of being antisocial. Aunt Berta had a son who as a child used to slip away from the cotton field and read under a tree. He is now a grown man with children, and he has obtained a college degree, but the community still tells tales about his peculiar boyhood habits of wanting to go off and read alone. In general, reading alone, unless one is very old and religious, marks an individual as someone who cannot make it socially.

Jointly or in group affairs, the children of Trackton *read to learn* before they go to school to *learn to read*. The modification of old or broken toys and their incorporation with other items to create a new toy is a common event. One mastermind, usually Tony, announces the idea, and all the children help collect items and contribute ideas. On some of these occasions, such as when one of the boys wants to modify his bicycle for a unique effect, he has to read selectively portions of brochures on bicycles and instructions for tool sets. Reading is almost always set within a context of immediate action: one needs to read a letter's address to prove to the mailman that one should be given the envelope; one must read the price of a bag of coal at Mr. Dogan's store to make the decision to purchase or not. Trackton children are sent to the store almost as soon as they can walk, and since they are told to "watch out for Mr. Dogan's prices," they must learn to read price changes there from week to week for commonly purchased items and remember them for comparisons with prices in the supermarket. As early as age four, Teegie, Lem, Gary, and Gary B. could scan the price tag, which might contain several separate pieces of information, on familiar items and pick out the price. The decimal point and the predictability of the number of numerals which would be included in the price were clues which helped the children search each tag for only those portions meaningful to their decision-making.

Children remember and reassociate the contexts of print. When they see a brand name, particular sets of numbers, or a particular logo, they often recall when and with whom they first saw it, or they call attention to how the occasion for this new appearance is not like the previous one. Slight shifts in print styles, and decorations of mascots used to advertise products, or alterations of written slogans are noticed by Trackton children. Once they have been in a supermarket to buy a loaf of bread, they remember on subsequent trips the location of the bread section and the placement of the kind of "light bread" their family eats. They seem to remember the scene and staging of print, so that upon recalling print they visualize the physical context in which it occurred and the reasons for reading it: that is, what it was they wanted to learn from reading a certain item or series of items. They are not tutored in these skills by adults of the community, but they are given numerous graded tasks from a very early age and are provided with older children who have learned to read to perform the tasks their daily life requires. Young children watch others read and write for a variety of purposes, and they have numerous opportunities for practice under the indirect supervision of older children, so that they come to use print independently and to be able to model appropriate behaviors for younger children coming up behind them.

The dependence on a strong sense of visual imagery often prevented efficient transfer of skills learned in one context to another. All of the toddlers knew the name brands and names of cereals as they appeared on the boxes or in advertisements. Kellogg's was always written in script— the name of the cereal (raisin bran, etc.) in all capital letters. On Nabisco products, Nabisco was written in small capitals and the cereal name in capital letters as well. I was curious to know whether or not the children "read" the names or whether they recognized the shapes of the boxes and the artwork on the boxes when they correctly identified the cereals. I cut out the name brands and cereal names and put them on plain cardboard of different sizes, and asked the children to read the names. After an initial period of hesitation, most of the children could read the newly placed names. All of the children could do so by age three. When they were between three and four, I cut out the printed letters from the cereal names to spell Kellogg's in small capitals and otherwise arranged the information on the plain cardboard as it appeared on the cereal boxes. The children volunteered the name of the cereal, but did not immediately read Kellogg's now that it was no longer in the familiar script. When I asked them to read it, they looked puzzled, said it looked "funny," and they were not sure what it was. When I pointed out to them that the print small-capital K was another way of writing the script K, they watched with interest as I did the same for the rest of the letters. They were dubious about the script e and the print E being "the same," but they became willing to accept that what configured on the box also configured on the paper, though in some different ways.

Gradually we developed a game of "rewriting" the words they could read, shifting from script to all capitals, and from all capitals to initial capitals and subsequent small letters for individual words. It was always necessary to do this by moving from the known mental picture and "reading" of the terms (i.e. the script Kellogg's) to the unknown or unfamiliar (rendering of Kellogg's in small print capitals). Once shown they already "knew" the item, they accepted that they could "know" these items in new contexts and shapes. We continued this type of game with many of the items from their daily life they already knew how to read. When I first wrote house numbers just as they appeared on the house on a piece of notebook paper, the three- and four-year-olds said they could not read it; if I varied slightly the shape of the numerals on the notebook paper, they also did not read the numbers. Once comparisons and differences were pointed out, they recognized that they already "knew" how to read what had seemed like strange information to them on the notebook paper. Using the "real" print and my re-created print in a metaphorical way provided a bridge from the known to the unknown which allowed the children to use their familiar rules for recognition of print. They transferred their own daily operations as successful readers in an interactive way to pencil-and-paper tasks which were not immediately relevant in the community context.[2]

Their strong tendency to visualize how print looked in its surrounding

2. These game-like tasks under natural conditions carried purposes similar to those of experimental psychologists who have investigated the effects of the perceived context on children's referential description. It seems clear that the script Kellogg's was easily distinguished or highly encodable on the cereal box, in part, because it differed in both position and style from the printed words on the box. (Cf. Watson's [1977] discussion of the influence of context on referential description by children.) What is much less clear is how and why the Trackton children's apparent strong tendency to remember what I call the "scene and staging" of *print* was also manifest in their linkage of text *illustrations* to a story—either that of the printed text or one they made up. When we went to the library together, the children preferred books with photographs or realistic color pictures to books with flat-line drawings. Often before they heard the book read to them or they had read the book themselves, they could "read" the illustrations. In doing so, their stories were much longer, and more inclusive of fine details given in the illustrations, than the actual text of the book. They would also often use the occasion to branch off into another story, making up stories about themselves on the basis of hints from the book's illustrations. Once they heard the printed text's version, they often voluntarily identified pieces of the illustration which related to details of the story. Samuels 1970 and Concannon 1975 report that there is little evidence that pictures aid reading comprehension or that children can take the integrated simultaneous information of pictures and relate it to the sequential presentation in the written text. Schallert 1980 reports, however, that pictures aid both comprehension and recall of stories. Trackton preschoolers and primary-level children seemed to extend and integrate the text best when its story was staged and set in a scene they could visualize either through illustration in the book or dramatization. For example, often in the community when children were doing homework and asked what a portion of printed text meant, I would suggest an imaginary scene and drama to play out the text. They entered into this "play" eagerly and often extended the text's interpretation in ways similar to Trackton adults' group reading habits. Paley 1981 gives numerous examples of the effects of dramatization by children of their stories on extended discourse around the text. Much careful research is needed to enable scholars to link levels of comprehension with different types of illustrations and dramatizations. Answers must be sought in the perceptual antecedents that contexts, such as graphic design and layout, illustrations, and dramatizations, have for preschoolers from different communities and cultural backgrounds. Chipman 1977 and Chipman and Mendelson 1979 summarize the debate in psychology over the memorial representations of visually perceived patterns.

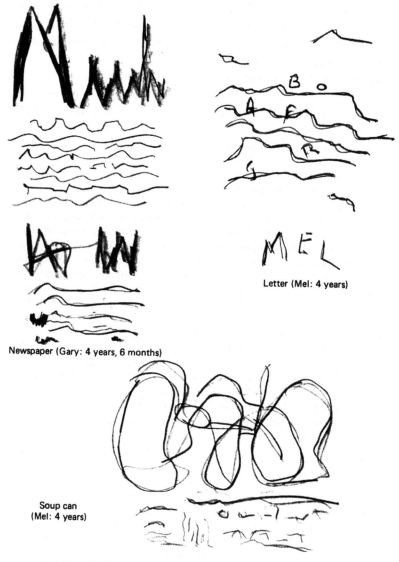

FIGURE 1. Preschool concepts of print.

context was revealed when I asked the three- and four-year-old children to "draw" house doors, newspapers, soup cans, and a letter they would write to someone. Figure 1 illustrates how Gary's representation of a newspaper shows that he knew the letters of headlines were bigger than what came below, and that what was below was organized in straight lines. Moreover, the "headline" near the bottom of the page is smaller than that at the top. Mel writes a "letter" which includes the date, salutation, body, closing, and signature. His "letter" is somewhat atypical, but, since Mel's mother, a transient, wrote frequently to her family up-North, he had numerous opportunities to see letters. None of the other preschoolers provided any of the components of a letter other than body and signature. Mel, however, not only indicates several parts, but also scatters some alphabet letters through the body, and signs his name. Mel also "drew" a soup can, making its name brand biggest, and schematically representing the product information and even what I take to be the vertical pricing and inventory information for computerized checking at the bottom of the can. When asked to "read" what they had written, some giggled, others asked older brothers and sisters to do it and some "read" their writing, explaining its context. Mel's reading of his letter was prefaced by "Now I send you dis letter." Then he read "Dear Miz Hea, bring me a truck we go to Hardee's, Mel." Everyone giggled with Mel who enjoyed the joke of having written what he so often said orally to me. His rendering contained only the primary message, not the date or his letter's closing. It is doubtful that Mel knew what went in these slots, since when I asked him if he had read those parts to me, he shrugged his shoulders and said "I dunno." Trackton children had learned before school that they could read to learn, and they had developed expectancies of print. The graphic and everyday-life contexts of writing were often critical to their interpretation of the meaning of print, for print to them was not isolated bits and pieces of lines and circles, but messages with varying internal structures, purposes, and uses. For most of these, oral communication surrounded the print.

"Talk is the thing"

In almost every situation in Trackton in which a piece of writing is integral to the nature of the participants' interactions and their interpretations of meaning, talk is a necessary component.[3] Knowing which box of cereal

3. Those occasions in which the talk revolves around a piece of writing have been termed *literacy events*. Anderson, Teale, and Estrada 1980 defines a literacy event as "any action sequence, involving one or more persons, in which the production and/ or comprehension of print plays a role" (p. 59). They break literacy events into two types. The first are reading events in which an individual either comprehends or attempts to comprehend a message which is encoded graphically. The second are writing events in which an individual attempts to produce these graphic signs. Heath 1982a suggests that literacy events have social interactional rules which regulate the

is Kellogg's raisin bran does little good without announcing that choice to older brothers and sisters helping pour the cereal. Knowing the kind of bicycle tire and tube on one's old bike is translated into action only at Mr. Green's bicycle shop or with a friend who has an old bike he is not using. Certain types of talk describe, repeat, reinforce, frame, expand, and even contradict written materials, and children in Trackton learn not only how to read print, but also when and how to surround the print in their lives with appropriate talk. For them there are far more occasions in the community which call for appropriate knowledge of forms and uses of talk around or about writing, than there are actual occasions for reading and writing extended connected discourse.

For Trackton adults, reading is a social activity; when something is read in Trackton, it almost always provokes narratives, jokes, sidetracking talk, and active negotiation of the meaning of written texts among the listeners. Authority in the written word does not rest in the words themselves, but in the meanings which are negotiated through the experiences of the group. The evening newspaper is read on the front porch for most months of the year. The obituaries on the back page are usually read first, followed by employment listings, advertisements for grocery and department store sales, and captions beneath pictures and headlines. An obitu-

---

type and amount of *talk* about what is written, and define ways in which *oral language* reinforces, denies, extends, or sets aside the written material. Just as speech events occur in certain speech situations and contain speech acts (Hymes 1972a,b), so literacy events are rule-governed, and their different situations of occurrence determine their internal rules for talking—and interpreting and interacting—around the piece of writing. Jenny Cook-Gumperz, in her proposal of the "situated meaning" (1977) of any verbal message, was perhaps the first to recognize the importance of knowing the rules for talking around written materials in school:

> After the achievement of literacy, the child's communicative ability is judged not only by criteria of effectiveness—do the requisite actions get performed?— but by whether the communication meets adult criteria of contextually relevant and appropriate speech. We suggest that the acquisition and use of these appropriate and relevant speech strategies depend not only on acquiring the strategies, but also on acquiring the adults' rules (perhaps we should call these meta-rules) for the recognition of speech contexts. Contextualizing rules chunk the stream of events into speech activities, which then provide the context for choice of appropriate strategies from the range of known or possible speech acts. (1977: 110)

The child must know not only how to read but also how and when to talk about what he or someone else has read. Compare this description with Philips' (1972) discussion of participant structures.

ary is read for some trace of acquaintance with either the deceased, his relatives, place of birth, church, or school; active discussion follows about who the individual was and who he might have known. Circulars or letters to individuals regarding the neighborhood center and its recreational or medical services are read aloud and their meanings jointly negotiated by those who have had experience with such activities or know about the forms to be filled out to be eligible for such services. Neighbors share stories of what they did or what happened to them in similar circumstances. One day when Lillie Mae had received a letter about a daycare program, several neighbors were sitting on porches, working on cars nearby, or sweeping their front yards. Lillie Mae came out on her front porch, read the first paragraph of a letter, and announced:

TRACKTON TEXT X

Lillie Mae:	You hear this, it says Lem [then two years old] might can get into Ridgeway [a local neighborhood center daycare program], but I hafta have the papers ready and apply by next Friday.
Visiting friend:	You ever been to Kent to get his birth certificate? [friend is mother of three children already in school]
Mattie Crawford:	But what hours that program gonna be? You may not can get him there.
Lillie Mae:	They want the birth certificate? I got his vaccination papers.
Annie Mae:	Sometimes they take that, 'cause they can 'bout tell the age from those early shots.
Visiting friend:	But you better get it, 'cause you gotta have it when he go to school anyway.
Lillie Mae:	But it says here they don't know what hours yet. How am I gonna get over to Kent? How much does it cost? Lemme see if the program costs anything. (She reads aloud part of the letter.)

Conversation on various parts of the letter continued for nearly an hour, while neighbors and Lillie Mae pooled their knowledge of the pros and cons of such programs. They discussed ways of getting rides to Kent, the county seat thirty miles away, to which all mothers had to go to get their children's birth certificates to prove their age at school entrance. The question "What does this mean?" was answered not only from the information in print, but from the group's joint bringing of experience to the text. Lillie Mae, reading aloud, decoded the written text, but her friends and neighbors interpreted the text's meaning through their own experiences. The experience of any one individual had to become common to the group, however, and that was done through the recounting of members' experiences. Such recounting re-created scenes, embellished the truth, illustrated the character of the individuals involved, and to the greatest extent possible brought the audience into the experience itself. Beyond these recountings of episodes (such as one mother's efforts to get her doctor to give her "papers" to verify her son's age), there was a reintegration of these now commonly shared experiences with the text itself. After the reading episode, Lillie Mae had to relate the text's meaning to the experiences she had heard shared, and she checked out this final synthesis of meaning for her with some of the group. Some members did not care about this final synthesis and had wandered off, satisfied to have told their stories, but others commented that they thought her chosen course of action the right one, and her understanding of the letter to fit their interpretations.[4]

About the only material not delivered for group negotiation is that which involves private finances or information which members feel might somehow give them an opportunity their neighbors do not have. A postcard from a local mill announcing days on which the mill will be accepting new employment applications will not be shared aloud, but kept secret because of the competition for jobs. On the other hand, a newspaper story about the expansion of the mill will be read aloud, and all will pool information in general terms.

4. Current research in reading suggests three ways or levels of extracting meaning from print: attending to the text itself, bringing in experiences or knowledge related to the text, and interpreting beyond the text into a creative/imaginative realm or to achieve a new synthesis of information from the text and reader experience (Rumelhart and Ortony 1977; Adams 1980; Fillmore 1981). Trackton residents *as a group* use these methods of extracting meaning from print on some occasions. In the case illustrated here, Lillie Mae decodes the letter, and that information is taken as the basis for the move to the next level in which the group members relate the text's meaning to their own experiences. The third level is achieved by Lillie Mae, after her own text decoding and sharing of experiences from the group. Though these levels match those described in the research literature for school-successful readers, there are some important differences. First, Trackton individuals have relatively few occasions to focus on specific decoding skills such as letter-sound relationships. Weak readers can always find someone else to read aloud, so that the negotiation of text meaning can take place in the group. Second, since reading is a social activity of the group, there are few opportunities when individuals practice extracting meaning and achieving the final synthesis or reintegration of meaning on the basis of only their own experiences.

Tables 1 and 2 show that the uses of writing and reading in the community are multiple, though there are few occasions for reading of extended connected discourse and almost no occasions for writing such material, except by those school children who diligently try to complete their homework assignments. Foremost among the types of uses of reading and writing are those which are *instrumental*. Adults and children read what they have to read to solve practical problems of daily life: price tags, traffic signs, house numbers, bills, checks. Other uses are perhaps not as critical to problem-solving, but *social-interactional* uses give information relevant to social relations and contacts with persons not in Trackton's primary group. Some write letters; many send greeting cards; almost all read bumper stickers, newspaper obituaries and features, and church news bulletins. Other types of reading and writing are *news-related*. From the local newspaper, political flyers, memos from the city offices, and circulars from the neighborhood center, Trackton residents learn information about local and distant events. They rarely read much more than headlines about distant events, since the evening news programs on television give them the same national or metropolitan news. Stories about the local towns are, however, read, because there is often no other source of information on happenings there. Some individuals in Trackton read for

TABLE 1 *TYPES OF USES OF READING IN TRACKTON*

INSTRUMENTAL:	Reading to accomplish practical goals of daily life (price tags, checks, bills, telephone dials, clocks, street signs, house numbers).
SOCIAL-INTERACTIONAL/ RECREATIONAL:	Reading to maintain social relationships, make plans, and introduce topics for discussion and story-telling (greeting cards, cartoons, letters, newspaper features, political flyers, announcements of community meetings).
NEWS-RELATED:	Reading to learn about third parties or distant events (local news items, circulars from the community center or school).
CONFIRMATIONAL:	Reading to gain support for attitudes or beliefs already held (Bible, brochures on cars, loan notes, bills).

Note: Listed in relative order of frequency of occasions when time on these types of tasks exceeded five minutes per day.

TABLE 2 *TYPES OF USES OF WRITING IN TRACKTON*

MEMORY AIDS: (PRIMARILY USED BY WOMEN)	Writing to serve as a reminder for the writer and, only occasionally, others (telephone numbers, notes on calendars).
SUBSTITUTES FOR ORAL MESSAGES: (PRIMARILY USED BY WOMEN)	Writing used when direct oral communication was not possible or would prove embarrassing (notes for tardiness or absence from school, greeting cards, letters).
FINANCIAL:	Writing to record numerals and to write out amounts and accompanying notes (signatures on checks and public forms, figures and notes for income tax preparation).
PUBLIC RECORDS: (CHURCH ONLY)	Writing to announce the order of the church services and forthcoming events and to record financial and policy decisions (church bulletins, reports of the church building fund committee).

Note. Listed in relative order of frequency of occasions when time on these types of tasks exceeded five minutes per day.

confirmation—to seek support for beliefs or ideas they already hold. Miss Lula reads the Bible. When the mayor maintains that one kind of car gets better mileage than another, and others disagree, he has to produce a brochure from a car dealer to prove his point. Children who become involved in boasts often call on written proof to confirm their lofty accounts of themselves or others. Every home has some permanent records—loan notes, tax forms, birth certificates—which families keep, but can rarely find when they are needed. However, if they can be found and are read, they can confirm an oral statement.

The most frequent occasions for writing are those when Trackton family members say they cannot trust their memory (*memory-supportive*), or they have to write to *substitute for an oral message*. Beside the telephone, women write frequently called numbers and addresses; they tack calendars on the kitchen wall and add notes reminding them of dates for their children's vaccinations and the school holidays, etc. Some few women in the community write letters. Lillie Mae often writes relatives up-North to invite them to come home and to thank them for bringing presents. Women sometimes have to write notes to school about children's absences or tardiness or to request a local merchant to extend credit a few weeks longer. Men almost never write except to sign their paychecks, public forms, and to collect information for income tax preparation. One exception in Trackton is the mayor, who meets once a month with a group of other church members to prepare Sunday church bulletins as well as to handle business related to the building fund or to plan for revival meetings. These written materials are negotiated cooperatively at the meetings; no individual takes sole responsibility.[5]

5. A detailed social historical analysis of the Mt. Zion A.M.E. Church at Promised Land, South Carolina (Bethel 1979) chronicles the history of this Piedmont "back country" church from its establishment in 1868 to the present. In the rural countryside, in the midst of a white-dominated region, the church created a firm identity for the black community which emerged during Reconstruction. Bethel writes: "Readily apparent are a distinct level of bureaucratization and rationalization in church structure, a governing body maintained through the principles of participatory democracy, a commitment to the principles and fact of education, and an articulated social responsibility to those in the community unable to meet their own needs" (p. 2). Bethel drew these conclusions on the basis of a content analysis of the ledger books containing church records. For example, in the ledger book covering the period from September 1, 1889 through March 13, 1898, of 177 entries, she found 111 entries recording Sunday School proceedings, 34 recording meetings of the Sunday School Board, 8 detailing special church services, 7 giving financial reports, 3 stating formal resolutions of church policy, and 4 miscellaneous reports. Bethel's analysis of these records illustrates the formality and authoritative chain of command with which the elected church officials kept records and implemented policies. In 1894, the church received a gift of religious books from their minister. The Sunday School Board's resolution thanking the minister read as follows:

> . . . wher as we have received through the agency of our pastor Rev. N. Chiles Such a beautiful lot of Bibles, Testemon & other periodical to the amt of Twenty five ($25.00) wish, for the small sum of $3 25 / 100 to cover the cost of packing & Transportation. . . . And whereas the School wer greatly in need of said Bibles etc, And is herby greatly bennefitted by the reception of them. Resolved 1st That we do herby tender to Rev. N. Chiles for those most highly appreciated from a rising vote of thanks . . .
>
> Signed Respectfully For the fishers of men
R. H. Marshall Teacher

As Bethel points out, both the content and form of Marshall's oratorical excesses illustrate the extent to which the congregation held education and formality in writing for such occasions in esteem. The library's holdings of nineteen volumes included books about the Bible, the standard hymnal catechism, and "how to talk books." Bethel's linguistic analysis of the records indicated that the most distinguishable features of their written language were not those commonly associated with Black English syntax or morphology. Though lacking the careful and precise analysis of documents of Bethel's research, earlier studies of the central role of the black church in building a black community cohesiveness (Kiser 1932; Hunter 1953) also provide evidence of the group cooperation these churches depended on in tasks ranging from maintaining the church building to keeping official records.

Community literacy activities are public and social. Written information almost never stands alone in Trackton. It is reshaped and reworded into an oral mode by adults and children who incorporate chunks of the written text in their talk. They often reflect their own awareness that print imposes a different kind of organization on written materials than talk does. Literacy events in Trackton which bring the written word into a central focus in interactions and interpretations have their rules of occurrence and appropriateness, just as talking junk, fussing, or performing a playsong do. The group activities of reading the newspaper across porches, debating the power of a new car, or discussing the city's plans to bring in earthmoving equipment to clear lots behind the community, produce more speaking than reading, more group than individual effort. There are repeated metaphors, comparisons, and fast-paced, overlapping language as Trackton residents move from print to what it means in their lives. On some occasions, they attend to the text itself; on others, they use it only as a starting point for wide-ranging talk. On all occasions, they bring in knowledge related to the text and interpret beyond the text for their own context; in so doing, they achieve a new synthesis of information from the text and the joint experiences of community members.

BIBLIOGRAPHY

Adams, M. J. 1980. Failures to Comprehend and Levels of Processing in Reading. In *Theoretical Issues in Reading Comprehension.* R. J. Spiro, B. C. Bruce, and W. F. Brever (eds.). Hillsdale, NJ: Erlbaum.

Anderson, A. B., W. B. Teale, and E. Estrada. 1980. Low-income Children's Preschool Literacy Experience: Some naturalistic observations. *The Quarterly Newsletter of the Laboratory of Comparative Human Cognition* 2(3): 59–65.

Bethel, E. 1979. *Social and Linguistic Trends in a Black Community.* Department of Sociology, Lander College, Greenwood, SC.

Chipman, S. 1977. Complexity and Structure in Visual Patterns. *Journal of Experimental Psychology* 106(3): 269–301.

Chipman, S. and M. J. Mendelson. 1979. Influence of Six Types of Visual Structure on Complexity Judgments in Children and Adults. *Journal of Experimental Psychology* 5(2): 365–78.

Concannon, S. J. 1975. Illustrations in Books for Children: Review of research. *The Reading Teacher* 29: 254–6.

Cook-Gumperz, J. 1977. Situated Instructions: Language socialization of school-age children. In *Child Discourse.* S. Ervin-Tripp and C. Mitchell-Kernan (eds.). New York: Academic Press.

Fillmore, C. J. 1981. Ideal Readers and Real Readers. In *Georgetown University Round Table on Languages and Linguistics*. Washington, DC: Georgetown University Press.

Heath, S. B. 1982. Protean Shapes in Literacy Events: Ever-shifting oral and literate traditions. In *Spoken and Written Language: Exploring orality and literacy*. D. Tannen (ed.). Norwood, NJ: Ablex.

Hunter, F. 1953. *Community Power Structure*. Chapel Hill, NC: University of North Carolina Press.

Hymes, D. H. 1972a. Models of the Interactions of Language and Social Life. In *Directions in Sociolinguistics: The ethnography of communication*. J. J. Gumperz and D. H. Hymes (eds.). New York: Holt, Rinehart.

Hymes, D. H. 1972b. Speech and Language: On the origins and foundations of inequality among speakers. In *Directions in Sociolinguistics: The ethnography of communication*. J. J. Gumperz and D. H. Hymes (eds.). New York: Holt, Rinehart.

Kiser, C. V. 1932. *From Sea Island to City*. New York: Columbia University Press.

Paley, V. G. 1981. *Wally's Stories*. Cambridge, MA: Harvard University Press.

Philips, S. 1972. Participation Structures and Communicative Competence: Warm Springs children in community and classroom. In *Functions of Language in the Classroom*. C. Cazden, V. P. John, and D. H. Hymes (eds.). New York: Teachers College Press.

Rumelhart, D. E. and A. Ortony. 1977. The Representation of Knowledge in Memory. In *Schooling and the Acquisition of Knowledge*. R. C. Anderson, R. J. Spiro, and W. E. Montague (eds.). Hillsdale, NJ: Lawrence Erlbaum.

Samuels, S. J. 1970. Effects of Pictures on Learning to Read, Comprehension, and Attitudes. *Review of Educational Research* 40: 397–407.

Schallert, D. L. 1980. The Role of Illustrations in Reading Comprehension. In *Theoretical Issues in Reading Comprehension*. R. J. Spiro, B. C. Bruce, and W. F. Brewer (eds.). Hillsdale, NJ: Lawrence Erlbaum.

Watson, J. M. 1977. The Influence of Context on Referential Description in Children. *British Journal of Educational Psychology* 47: 33–9.

ACTIVE READING

1. List the differences Heath cites between the reading and writing practices of young people and old people and between the reading and writing practices of men and women. What relationship do you see

between literacy practices and the different social roles performed by each of these groups?

2. Heath mentions a number of reading and writing activities that the residents of Trackton do not do, or rarely do, or even disapprove of. List some of these activities, and explore their importance for the community.

3. How does the training provided to Trackton children prepare them for the adult uses of literacy in Trackton? In what ways does this training enable them to move into new social situations, both within and outside Trackton?

READING IN NEW CONTEXTS

1. Heath describes a social process of "talk around writing" that includes "negotiation" and "reintegration." Explain how this process works, and then use it to discuss some portrayal of reading and writing in Christian's, Scheper-Hughes's, or another *Literacies* writer's essay. Consider ways that the process might apply to both individual readers and groups of readers.

2. Consider a text by Anzaldúa, Atwood, Walker, or another *Literacies* writer who explores the difficulties some people face in reading and writing. What do Heath's discoveries about the social aspects of literacy help you say about the difficulties these other readers encounter?

3. What evidence can you find in the essay that there are some links between interpretation, literacy practices, and social class? Summarize your findings and test them on another *Literacies* text.

DRAFT ONE / DRAFT TWO

1. *Draft One:* How do you interpret Heath's use of the word "traditions" in her title? Which of the literate practices you discussed in your responses to the Before Reading questions could be called "traditions," in Heath's sense of the term?

Draft Two: Working with your Draft One and your response to Black Elk, Fienup-Riordan, or Rosaldo, develop a theory about the uses and limitations of "traditional" behavior.

2. *Draft One*: Use the ideas about negotiation and reintegration you generated for Reading in New Contexts #1 to describe the social processes that have occurred in your class's discussion of Heath's essay. What processes have you seen that Heath's essay cannot help you account for? Invent some new terms to cover those aspects of your group's reading practices.

Draft Two: Keeping in mind the processes you wrote about in Draft One, compose a set of specific guidelines and questions that might help your class "negotiate" its way through an essay by Ewen, Sontag, or another *Literacies* writer. Share your list with the class or a peer group. Once the class has discussed the essay, revise your set of guidelines to show which suggestions helped, which didn't, and why.

BEFORE READING LILIANA HEKER

1. Do you expect any particular complications when people of different social classes spend time together? If so, what causes these complications and what can be done about them? If not, what does happen when people of different social classes spend time together?

2. What does "work" mean to you? How do you distinguish work from other activities? What attitudes toward work do you expect from members of the working class, the middle class, and the upper class? Where does your information about these attitudes come from?

3. Think of some stories you have encountered recently in books or movies. How did the conclusions of the stories help you understand the characters or events? Based on this evidence, what kind of information might you expect to find in the conclusion to a story called "The Stolen Party"?

THE STOLEN PARTY

As soon as she arrived she went straight to the kitchen to see if the monkey was there. It was: what a relief! She wouldn't have liked to admit that her mother had been right. *Monkeys at a birthday?* her mother had sneered. *Get away with you, believing any nonsense you're told!* She was cross, but not because of the monkey, the girl thought; it's just because of the party.

"I don't like you going," she told her. "It's a rich people's party."

"Rich people go to Heaven too," said the girl, who studied religion at school.

"Get away with Heaven," said the mother. "The problem with you, young lady, is that you like to fart higher than your ass."

The girl didn't approve of the way her mother spoke. She was barely nine, and one of the best in her class.

"I'm going because I've been invited," she said. "And I've been invited because Luciana is my friend. So there."

"Ah yes, your friend," her mother grumbled. She paused. "Listen, Rosaura," she said at last. "That one's not your friend. You know what you are to them? The maid's daughter, that's what."

From *Other Fires: Short Fiction by Latin American Women,* edited and translated by Alberto Manguel (1986).

Rosaura blinked hard: she wasn't going to cry. Then she yelled: "Shut up! You know nothing about being friends!"

Every afternoon she used to go to Luciana's house and they would both finish their homework while Rosaura's mother did the cleaning. They had their tea in the kitchen and they told each other secrets. Rosaura loved everything in the big house, and she also loved the people who lived there.

"I'm going because it will be the most lovely party in the whole world, Luciana told me it would. There will be a magician, and he will bring a monkey and everything."

The mother swung around to take a good look at her child, and pompously put her hands on her hips.

"Monkeys at a birthday?" she said. "Get away with you, believing any nonsense you're told!"

Rosaura was deeply offended. She thought it unfair of her mother to accuse other people of being liars simply because they were rich. Rosaura too wanted to be rich, of course. If one day she managed to live in a beautiful palace, would her mother stop loving her? She felt very sad. She wanted to go to that party more than anything else in the world.

"I'll die if I don't go," she whispered, almost without moving her lips.

And she wasn't sure whether she had been heard, but on the morning of the party she discovered that her mother had starched her Christmas dress. And in the afternoon, after washing her hair, her mother rinsed it in apple vinegar so that it would be all nice and shiny. Before going out, Rosaura admired herself in the mirror, with her white dress and glossy hair, and thought she looked terribly pretty.

Señora Ines also seemed to notice. As soon as she saw her, she said: "How lovely you look today, Rosaura."

Rosaura gave her starched skirt a slight toss with her hands and walked into the party with a firm step. She said hello to Luciana and asked about the monkey. Luciana put on a secretive look and whispered into Rosaura's ear: "He's in the kitchen. But don't tell anyone, because it's a surprise."

Rosaura wanted to make sure. Carefully she entered the kitchen and there she saw it: deep in thought, inside its cage. It looked so funny that the girl stood there for a while, watching it, and later, every so often, she would slip out of the party unseen and go and admire it. Rosaura was the only one allowed into the kitchen. Señora Ines had said: "You yes, but not the others, they're much too boisterous, they might break something." Rosaura had never broken anything. She even managed the jug of orange juice, carrying it from the kitchen into the dining-room. She held it carefully and didn't spill a single drop. And Señora Ines had said: "Are you sure you can manage a jug as big as that?" Of course she could manage. She wasn't a butterfingers, like the others. Like that blonde girl with the bow in her hair. As soon as she saw Rosaura, the girl with the bow had said:

"And you? Who are you?"

"I'm a friend of Luciana," said Rosaura.

"No," said the girl with the bow, "you are not a friend of Luciana because I'm her cousin and I know all her friends. And I don't know you."

"So what," said Rosaura. "I come here every afternoon with my mother and we do our homework together."

"You and your mother do your homework together?" asked the girl, laughing.

"I and Luciana do our homework together," said Rosaura, very seriously.

The girl with the bow shrugged her shoulders.

"That's not being friends," she said. "Do you go to school together?"

"No."

"So where do you know her from?" said the girl, getting impatient.

Rosaura remembered her mother's words perfectly. She took a deep breath.

"I'm the daughter of the employee," she said.

Her mother had said very clearly: "If someone asks, you say you're the daughter of the employee; that's all." She also told her to add: "And proud of it." But Rosaura thought that never in her life would she dare say something of the sort.

"What employee?" said the girl with the bow. "Employee in a shop?"

"No," said Rosaura angrily. "My mother doesn't sell anything in any shop, so there."

"So how come she's an employee?" said the girl with the bow.

Just then Señora Ines arrived saying *shh shh*, and asked Rosaura if she wouldn't mind helping serve out the hot-dogs, as she knew the house so much better than the others.

"See?" said Rosaura to the girl with the bow, and when no one was looking she kicked her in the shin.

Apart from the girl with the bow, all the others were delightful. The one she liked best was Luciana, with her golden birthday crown; and then the boys. Rosaura won the sack race, and nobody managed to catch her when they played tag. When they split into two teams to play charades, all the boys wanted her for their side. Rosaura felt she had never been so happy in all her life.

But the best was still to come. The best came after Luciana blew out the candles. First the cake. Señora Ines had asked her to help pass the cake around, and Rosaura had enjoyed the task immensely, because everyone called out to her, shouting "Me, me!" Rosaura remembered a story in which there was a queen who had the power of life or death over her subjects. She had always loved that, having the power of life or death. To Luciana and the boys she gave the largest pieces, and to the girl with the bow she gave a slice so thin one could see through it.

After the cake came the magician, tall and bony, with a fine red cape. A true magician: he could untie handkerchiefs by blowing on them and make a chain with links that had no openings. He could guess what cards were pulled out from a pack, and the monkey was his assistant. He called the monkey "partner." "Let's see here, partner," he would say, "Turn over a card." And, "Don't run away, partner: time to work now."

The final trick was wonderful. One of the children had to hold the monkey in his arms and the magician said he would make him disappear.

"What, the boy?" they all shouted.

"No, the monkey!" shouted back the magician.

Rosaura thought that this was truly the most amusing party in the whole world.

The magician asked a small fat boy to come and help, but the small fat boy got frightened almost at once and dropped the monkey on the floor. The magician picked him up carefully, whispered something in his ear, and the monkey nodded almost as if he understood.

"You mustn't be so unmanly, my friend," the magician said to the fat boy.

"What's unmanly?" said the fat boy.

The magician turned around as if to look for spies.

"A sissy," said the magician. "Go sit down."

Then he stared at all the faces, one by one. Rosaura felt her heart tremble.

"You, with the Spanish eyes," said the magician. And everyone saw that he was pointing at her.

She wasn't afraid. Neither holding the monkey, nor when the magician made him vanish; not even when, at the end, the magician flung his red cape over Rosaura's head and uttered a few magic words . . . and the monkey reappeared, chattering happily, in her arms. The children clapped furiously. And before Rosaura returned to her seat, the magician said:

"Thank you very much, my little countess."

She was so pleased with the compliment that a while later, when her mother came to fetch her, that was the first thing she told her.

"I helped the magician and he said to me, 'Thank you very much, my little countess.' "

It was strange because up to then Rosaura had thought that she was angry with her mother. All along Rosaura had imagined that she would say to her: "See that the monkey wasn't a lie?" But instead she was so thrilled that she told her mother all about the wonderful magician.

Her mother tapped her on the head and said: "So now we're a countess!"

But one could see that she was beaming.

And now they both stood in the entrance, because a moment ago Señora Ines, smiling, had said: "Please wait here a second."

Her mother suddenly seemed worried.

"What is it?" she asked Rosaura.

"What is what?" said Rosaura. "It's nothing; she just wants to get the presents for those who are leaving, see?"

She pointed at the fat boy and at a girl with pigtails who were also waiting there, next to their mothers. And she explained about the presents. She knew, because she had been watching those who left before her. When one of the girls was about to leave, Señora Ines would give her a bracelet. When a boy left, Señora Ines gave him a yo-yo. Rosaura preferred the yo-yo because it sparkled, but she didn't mention that to her mother. Her mother might have said: "So why don't you ask for one, you blockhead?" That's what her mother was like. Rosaura didn't feel like explaining that she'd be horribly ashamed to be the odd one out. Instead she said:

"I was the best-behaved at the party."

And she said no more because Señora Ines came out into the hall with two bags, one pink and one blue.

First she went up to the fat boy, gave him a yo-yo out of the blue bag, and the fat boy left with his mother. Then she went up to the girl and gave her a bracelet out of the pink bag, and the girl with the pigtails left as well.

Finally she came up to Rosaura and her mother. She had a big smile on her face and Rosaura liked that. Señora Ines looked down at her, then looked up at her mother, and then said something that made Rosaura proud:

"What a marvellous daughter you have, Herminia."

For an instant, Rosaura thought that she'd give her two presents: the bracelet and the yo-yo. Señora Ines bent down as if about to look for something. Rosaura also leaned forward, stretching out her arm. But she never completed the movement.

Señora Ines didn't look in the pink bag. Nor did she look in the blue bag. Instead she rummaged in her purse. In her hand appeared two bills.

"You really and truly earned this," she said handing them over. "Thank you for all your help, my pet."

Rosaura felt her arms stiffen, stick close to her body, and then she noticed her mother's hand on her shoulder. Instinctively she pressed herself against her mother's body. That was all. Except her eyes. Rosaura's eyes had a cold, clear look that fixed itself on Señora Ines's face.

Señora Ines, motionless, stood there with her hand outstretched. As if she didn't dare draw it back. As if the slightest change might shatter an infinitely delicate balance.

ACTIVE READING

1. Locate several passages where the narrator describes Rosaura's values or opinions. Write informally about how each passage helps you explain Rosaura's actions throughout the story. How are these passages important to your understanding of the text?

2. What do the physical actions of the last few paragraphs say that the characters themselves do not say? Retrace the story's earlier events, and locate other passages where something is said without words. What is your theory about the role of unspoken understandings in situations like these?

3. List as many meanings as you can find for the title of Heker's story: Who steals the party, and from whom? Working with two or three of the meanings you found, explain how your different interpretations of the title affect your thoughts about the story.

READING IN NEW CONTEXTS

1. Use your thoughts about "The Stolen Party" to revise your response to Before Reading #1. Then examine how your ideas about crossing class

boundaries might give you insight into the crossing of racial or ethnic lines in a reading by Baldwin, Clifford, or de Saint Victor. How does the role of class in "The Stolen Party" relate to the role of race or ethnicity in the second text?

2. Look over the essay by Barnlund or Brody, and choose a term or concept that helps you understand the ways people from different backgrounds relate to each other. Use this term to explain Señora Ines's actions during the party. How adequately do these explanations account for Señora Ines's role in the story? How would you revise the term you chose so that the explanations it provides are more satisfying?

3. Reread the conclusion to "The Stolen Party." How does it fulfill or frustrate the expectations about story endings you discussed in Before Reading #3? Based on your reading of Heker's conclusion, revise one or two terms that Scholes uses in his discussion of how narratives operate.

DRAFT ONE / DRAFT TWO

1. *Draft One:* Look up "class" in a college dictionary, and note two or three definitions that apply to this story. Write about two things: the aspects of the story the dictionary definitions help explain; and the aspects of the story that the dictionary definitions do not adequately address. Compose and explain a fuller definition of "class," based on this story and on your analysis of the dictionary definitions.

   Draft Two: Test your fuller definition of "class" from Draft One by applying it to some of the events in another *Literacies* text you have read this semester, perhaps Kozol or Garson. How does this other reading help you extend or qualify your concept of class?

2. *Draft One:* List the people, values, or ideals Rosaura has faith in at the beginning of "The Stolen Party." Why does she have this faith? How does her level of faith in these things change by the end of the story? Use your consideration of the story to develop your own theory of how people use or rely on faith.

   Draft Two: Work with a reading by hooks & West or another *Literacies* author who writes about the uses of faith. How does your theory of faith from Draft One revise your understanding of the role faith plays in the second text?

BEFORE READING BELL HOOKS & CORNEL WEST

1. List some different kinds of partnerships. Why do people form partnerships? How do partnerships differ from other kinds of social bonds? What responsibilities do people in partnerships have toward each other?

2. Would you expect partnerships that cross racial or gender lines to have certain advantages or face certain problems? If so, what kind of advantages or problems would you expect? If not, why not?

3. What relationship do you see between spirituality and the Civil Rights Movement?

4. What kinds of competition do you see in your family, among your friends, or in your community? Why do people become competitive, and what do they compete for? What do you think the advantages or disadvantages of competition are?

BLACK WOMEN AND MEN: PARTNERSHIP IN THE 1990S

a dialogue between bell hooks
and Cornel West presented at
Yale University's African American
Cultural Center

Give gifts to those who should know love.

—NTOZAKE SHANGE,
Sassafrass, Cypress, and Indigo

The history of the period has been written and will continue to be written without us. The imperative is clear: Either we will make history or remain the victims of it.

—MICHELE WALLACE

bh I requested that Charles sing "Precious Lord" because the conditions that led Thomas Dorsey to write this song always make me think about gender issues, issues of Black masculinity. Mr. Dorsey wrote this song after his wife died in childbirth. That experience caused him to have a crisis of faith. He did not think he would be able to go on living without her. That sense of unbearable crisis truly expresses the contemporary dilemma of faith. Mr. Dorsey talked about the way he tried to cope with this "crisis of faith." He prayed and prayed for a healing and received the

From *Breaking Bread: Insurgent Black Intellectual Life,* edited by Gloria Watkins and Cornel West (1991).

words to this song. This song has helped so many folk when they are feeling low, feeling as if they can't go on. It was my grandmother's favorite song. I remember how we sang it at her funeral. She died when she was almost ninety. And I am moved now as I was then by the knowledge that we can take our pain, work with it, recycle it, and transform it so that it becomes a source of power.

Let me introduce to you my "brother," my comrade Cornel West.

CW First I need to just acknowledge the fact that we as Black people have come together to reflect on our past, present, and future. That, in and of itself, is a sign of hope. I'd like to thank the Yale African American Cultural Center for bringing us together. bell and I thought it would be best to present in dialogical form a series of reflections on the crisis of Black males and females. There is a state of siege raging now in Black communities across this nation linked not only to drug addiction but also to consolidation of corporate power as we know it, and redistribution of wealth from the bottom to the top, coupled with the ways with which a culture and society centered on the market, preoccupied with consumption, erode structures of feeling, community, tradition. Reclaiming our heritage and sense of history are prerequisites to any serious talk about Black freedom and Black liberation in the 21st century. We want to try to create that kind of community here today, a community that we hope will be a place to promote understanding. Critical understanding is a prerequisite for any serious talk about coming together, sharing, participating, creating bonds of solidarity so that Black people and other progressive people can continue to hold up the blood-stained banners that were raised when that song was sung in the civil rights movement. It was one of Dr. Martin Luther King's favorite songs, reaffirming his own struggle and that of many others who have tried to link some sense of faith, religious faith, political faith, to the struggle for freedom. We thought it would be best to have a dialogue to put forth analysis and provide a sense of what form a praxis would take. That praxis will be necessary for us to talk seriously about Black power, Black liberation in the 21st century.

bh Let us say a little bit about ourselves. Both Cornel and I come to you as individuals who believe in God. That belief informs our message.

CW One of the reasons we believe in God is due to the long tradition of religious faith in the Black community. I think, that as a people who have had to deal with the absurdity of being Black in America, for many of us it is a question of God and sanity, or God and suicide. And, if you are serious about Black struggle, you know that in many instances you will be stepping out on nothing, hoping to land on something. That is the history of Black folks in the past and present, and it continually concerns those of us who are willing to speak out with boldness and a sense of the importance of history and struggle. You speak, knowing that you won't be able to do that for too long because America is such a violent culture. Given those conditions, you have to ask yourself what links to a tradition will sustain you, given the absurdity and insanity we are bombarded with daily. And so the belief in God itself is not to be understood in a noncontextual manner. It is understood in relation to a particular context, to specific circumstances.

bh We also come to you as two progressive Black people on the Left.

CW Very much so.

bh I will read a few paragraphs to provide a critical framework for our discussion of Black power, just in case some of you may not know what Black power means. We are gathered to speak with one another about Black power in the 21st century. In James Boggs's essay, "Black Power: A Scientific Concept Whose Time Has Come," first published in 1968, he called attention to the radical political significance of the Black power movement, asserting: "Today the concept of Black power expresses the revolutionary social force which must not only struggle against the capitalist but against the workers and all who benefit by and support the system which has oppressed us." We speak of Black power in this very different context to remember, reclaim, re-vision, and renew. We remember first that the historical struggle for Black liberation was forged by Black women and men who were concerned about the collective welfare of Black people. Renewing our commitment to this collective struggle should provide a grounding for new direction in contemporary political practice. We speak today of political partnership between Black men and women. The late James Baldwin wrote in his autobiographical preface to *Notes of a Native Son:* "I think that the past is all that makes the present coherent and further that the past will remain horrible for as long as we refuse to accept it honestly." Accepting the challenge of this prophetic statement as we look at our contemporary past as Black people, the space between the sixties and the nineties, we see a weakening of political solidarity between Black men and women. It is crucial for the future of Black liberation struggle that we remain ever mindful that ours is a shared struggle, that we are each other's fate.

CW I think we can even begin by talking about the kind of existentialist chaos that exists in our own lives and our inability to overcome the sense of alienation and frustration we experience when we try to create bonds of intimacy and solidarity with one another. Now part of this frustration is to be understood again in relation to structures and institutions. In the way in which our culture of consumption has promoted an addiction to stimulation—one that puts a premium on packaged and commodified stimulation. The market does this in order to convince us that our consumption keeps oiling the economy in order for it to reproduce itself. But the effect of this addiction to stimulation is an undermining, a waning of our ability for qualitatively rich relationships. It's no accident that crack is the postmodern drug, that it is the highest form of addiction known to humankind, that it provides a feeling ten times more pleasurable than orgasm.

bh Addiction is not about relatedness, about relationships. So it comes as no surprise that, as addiction becomes more pervasive in Black life, it undermines our capacity to experience community. Just recently, I was telling someone that I would like to buy a little house next door to my parent's house. This house used to be Mr. Johnson's house but he recently passed away. And they could not understand why I would want to live near my parents. My explanation that my parents were aging did not satisfy. Their inability to understand or appreciate the value of sharing family life intergenerationally was a sign to me of the crisis facing our communities. It's as though as Black people we have lost our understanding of the importance of mutual interdependency, of communal living. That we no longer recognize as valuable the notion that we collectively shape the terms of our survival is a sign of crisis.

CW And when there is crisis in those communities and institutions that have played a fundamental role in transmitting to younger generations our values and sensibility, our ways of life and our ways of struggle, we find ourselves distanced, not simply from our predecessors but from the critical project of Black liberation. And so, more and more, we seem to have young Black people who are very difficult to understand, because it seems as though they live in two very different worlds. We don't really understand their music. Black adults may not be listening to NWA (Niggers With Attitude) straight out of Compton, California. They may not understand why they are doing what Stetsasonic is doing, what Public Enemy is all about, because most young Black people have been fundamentally shaped by the brutal side of American society. Their sense of reality is shaped on the one hand by a sense of coldness and callousness, and on the other hand by a sense of passion for justice, contradictory impulses which surface simultaneously. Mothers may find it difficult to understand their children. Grandparents may find it difficult to understand us—and it's this slow breakage that has to be restored.

bh That sense of breakage, or rupture, is often tragically expressed in gender relations. When I told folks that Cornel West and I were talking about partnership between Black women and men, they thought I meant romantic relationships. I replied that it was important for us to examine the multi-relationships between Black women and men, how we deal with fathers, with brothers, with sons. We are talking about all our relationships across gender because it is not just the heterosexual love relationships between Black women and men that are in trouble. Many of us can't communicate with parents, siblings, etc. I've talked with many of you and asked, "What is it you feel should be addressed?" And many of you responded that you wanted us to talk about Black men and how they need to "get it together."

Let's talk about why we see the struggle to assert agency—that is, the ability to act in one's best interest—as a male thing. I mean, Black men are not the only ones among us who need to "get it together." And if Black men collectively refuse to educate themselves for critical consciousness, to acquire the means to be self-determined, should our communities suffer, or should we not recognize that both Black women and men must struggle for self-actualization, must learn to "get it together"? Since the culture we live in continues to equate Blackness with maleness, Black awareness of the extent to which our survival depends on mutual partnership between Black women and men is undermined. In renewed Black liberation struggle, we recognize the position of Black men and women, the tremendous role Black women played in every freedom struggle.

Certainly, Septima Clark's book *Ready from Within* is necessary reading for those of us who want to understand the historical development of sexual politics in Black liberation struggle. Clark describes her father's insistence that she not fully engage herself in civil rights struggle because of her gender. Later, she found the source of her defiance in religion. It was the belief in spiritual community, that no difference must be made between the role of women and that of men, that enabled her to be "ready within." To Septima Clark, the call to participate in Black liberation struggle was a call from God. Remembering and recovering the stories of how Black women learned to assert historical agency in the struggle for self-determination in the context of community and collectivity is important for those of us who struggle to promote Black liberation, a movement that has at its core a commitment to free our communities of sexist domination, exploitation, and oppression. We need to develop a political terminology that will enable Black folks to talk deeply about what we mean when we urge Black women and men to "get it together."

CW I think again that we have to keep in mind the larger context of American society, which has historically expressed contempt for Black men and Black women. The very notion that Black people are human beings is a new notion in Western Civilization and is still not widely accepted in practice. And one of the consequences of this pernicious idea is that it is very difficult for Black men and women to remain attuned to each other's humanity, so when bell talks about Black women's agency and some of the problems Black men have when asked to acknowledge Black women's humanity, it must be remembered that this refusal to acknowledge one another's humanity is a reflection of the way we are seen and treated in the larger society. And it's certainly not true that White folks have a monopoly on human relationships. When we talk about a crisis in Western Civilization, Black people are a part of that civilization, even though we have been beneath it, our backs serving as a foundation for the building of that civilization, and we have to understand how it affects us so that we may remain attuned to each other's humanity, so that the partnership that bell talks about can take on real substance and content. I think partnerships between Black men and Black women can be made when we learn how to be supportive and think in terms of critical affirmation.

bh Certainly, Black people have not talked enough about the importance of constructing patterns of interaction that strengthen our capacity to be affirming.

CW We need to affirm one another, support one another, help, enable, equip, and empower one another to deal with the present crisis, but it can't be uncritical, because if it's uncritical, then we are again refusing to acknowledge other people's humanity. If we are serious about acknowledging and affirming other people's humanity, then we are committed to trusting and believing that they are forever in process. Growth, development, maturation happens in stages. People grow, develop, and mature along the lines in which they are taught. Disenabling critique and contemptuous feedback hinders.

bh We need to examine the function of critique in traditional Black communities. Often it does not serve as a constructive force. Like we have that popular slang word "dissin'," and we know that "dissin'" refers to a kind of disenabling contempt—when we "read" each other in ways that are so painful, so cruel, that the person can't get up from where you have knocked them down. Other destructive forces in our lives are envy and jealousy. These undermine our efforts to work for a collective good. Let me give a minor example. When I came in this morning I saw Cornel's latest book on the table. I immediately wondered why my book was not there and caught myself worrying about whether he was receiving some gesture of respect or recognition denied me. When he heard me say, "Where's my book?" he pointed to another table.

Often when people are suffering a legacy of deprivation, there is a sense that there are never enough goodies to go around, so that we must viciously compete with one another. Again this spirit of competition creates conflict and divisiveness. In a larger social context, competition between Black women and men has surfaced around the issue of whether Black female writers are receiving more attention than Black male writers. Rarely does anyone point to the reality that only a small minority of Black women writers are receiving public accolades. Yet the myth that Black women who succeed are taking something away from Black men continues to permeate Black psyches and inform how we as Black women and men respond to one another. Since capitalism is rooted in unequal distribution of resources, it is not surprising that we as Black women and men find ourselves in situations of competition and conflict.

CW I think part of the problem is deep down in our psyche we recognize that we live in such a conservative society, a society disproportionately shaped by business elites, a society in which corporate power influences are assuring that a certain group of people do get up higher.

bh Right, including some of you in this room.

CW And this is true not only between male and female relations but also Black and Brown relations, and Black and Red, and Black and Asian relations. We are struggling over crumbs because we know that the bigger part has been received by elites in corporate America. One half of one percent of America owns twenty-two percent of the wealth, one percent owns thirty-two percent, and the bottom forty-five percent of the population has two percent of the wealth. So, you end up with this kind of crabs-in-the-barrel mentality. When you see someone moving up, you immediately think they'll get a bigger cut in big-loaf corporate America, and you think that's something real because we're still shaped by the corporate ideology of the larger context.

bh Here at Yale, many of us are getting a slice of that miniloaf and yet are despairing. It was discouraging when I came here to teach and found in many Black people a quality of despair which is not unlike what we know is felt in "crack neighborhoods." I wanted to understand the connection between underclass Black despair and that of Black people here who have immediate and / or potential access to so much material privilege. This despair mirrors the spiritual crisis that is happening in our culture as a whole. Nihilism is everywhere. Some of this despair is rooted in a deep sense of loss. Many Black folks who have made it or are making it undergo an identity crisis. This is especially true for individual Black people working to assimilate into the "mainstream." Suddenly, they may feel panicked, alarmed by the knowledge that they do not understand their history, that life is without purpose and meaning. These feelings of alienation and estrangement create suffering. The suffering many Black people experience today is linked to the suffering of the past, to "historical memory." Attempts by Black people to understand that suffering, to come to terms with it, are the conditions which enable a work like Toni Morrison's *Beloved* to receive so much attention. To look back, not just to describe slavery but to try and reconstruct a psycho-social history of its impact has only recently been fully understood as a necessary stage in the process of collective Black self-recovery.

CW The spiritual crisis that has happened, especially among the well-to-do Blacks, has taken the form of the quest for therapeutic release. So that you can get very thin, flat, and one-dimensional forms of spirituality that are simply an attempt to sustain the well-to-do Black folks as they engage in their consumerism and privatism. The kind of spirituality we're talking about is not the kind that serves as an opium to help you justify and rationalize your own cynicism vis-à-vis the disadvantaged folk in our community. We could talk about churches and their present role in the crisis of America, religious faith as the American way of life, the gospel of health and wealth, helping the bruised psyches of the Black middle class make it through America. That's not the form of spirituality that we're talking about. We're talking about something deeper—you used to call it conversion—so that notions of service and risk and sacrifice once again become fundamental. It's very important, for example, that those of you who remember the days in which Black colleges were hegemonic among the Black elite remember them critically but also acknowledge that there was something positive going on there. What was going on was that you were told every Sunday, in chapel, that you had to give service to the race. Now it may have been a petty bourgeois form, but it created a moment of accountability, and with the erosion of the service ethic the very possibility of putting the needs of others alongside of one's own diminishes. In this syndrome, me-ness, selfishness, and egocentricity become more and more prominent, creating a spiritual crisis where you need more psychic opium to get you over.

bh We have experienced such a change in that communal ethic of service that was so necessary for survival in traditional Black communities. That ethic of service has been altered by shifting class relations. And even those Black folks who have little or no class mobility may buy into a bourgeois class sensibility; TV shows like *Dallas* and *Dynasty* teach ruling class ways of thinking and being to underclass poor people. A certain kind of bourgeois individualism of the mind prevails. It does not correspond to actual class reality or circumstances of deprivation. We need to remember the many economic structures and class politics that have led to a shift of priorities for "privileged" Blacks. Many privileged Black folks obsessed with living out a bourgeois dream of liberal individualistic success no longer feel as though they have any accountability in relation to the Black poor and underclass.

CW We're not talking about the narrow sense of guilt privileged Black people can feel, because guilt usually paralyzes action. What we're talking about is how one uses one's time and energy. We're talking about the ways in which the Black middle class, which is relatively privileged vis-à-vis the Black working class, working poor, and underclass, needs to acknowledge that along with that privilege goes responsibility. Somewhere I read that for those to whom much is given, much is required. And the question becomes, "How do we exercise that responsibility, given our privilege?" I don't think it's a credible notion to believe the Black middle class will give up on its material toys. No, the Black middle class will act like any other middle class in human history; it will attempt to maintain its privilege. There is something seductive about comfort and convenience. The Black middle class will not return to the ghetto, especially given the territorial struggles going on with gangs and so forth. Yet, how can we use what power we do have to be sure more resources are available to those who are disadvantaged? So the question becomes "How do we use our responsibility and privilege?" Because, after all, Black privilege is a result of Black struggle.

I think the point to make here is that there is a new day in Black America. It is the best of times and the worst of times in Black America. Political consciousness is escalating in Black America, among Black students, among Black workers, organized Black workers and trade unions. Increasingly we are seeing Black local leaders with vision. The Black church is on the move, Black popular music, political themes and motifs are on the move. So don't think in our critique we somehow ask you to succumb to a paralyzing pessimism. There are grounds for hope and when that corner is turned—and we don't know what particular catalytic event will serve as the take-off for it (just like we didn't know December

1955 would be the take-off) — but when it occurs we have got to be ready. The privileged Black folks can play a rather crucial role if we have a service ethic, if we want to get on board, if we want to be part of the progressive, prophetic bandwagon. And that is the question we will have to ask ourselves and each other.

bh We also need to remember that there is a joy in struggle. Recently, I was speaking on a panel at a conference with another Black woman from a privileged background. She mocked the notion of struggle. When she expressed, "I'm just tired of hearing about the importance of struggle; it doesn't interest me," the audience clapped. She saw struggle solely in negative terms, a perspective which led me to question whether she had ever taken part in any organized resistance movement. For if you have, you know that there is joy in struggle. Those of us who are old enough to remember segregated schools, the kind of political effort and sacrifice folks were making to ensure we would have full access to educational opportunities, surely remember the sense of fulfillment when goals that we struggled for were achieved. When we sang together "We shall overcome," there was a sense of victory, a sense of power that comes when we strive to be self-determining. When Malcolm X spoke about his journey to Mecca, the awareness he achieved, he gives expression to that joy that comes from struggling to grow. When Martin Luther King talked about having been to the mountain top, he was sharing with us that he arrived at a peak of critical awareness, and it gave him great joy. In our liberatory pedagogy we must teach young Black folks to understand that struggle is process, that one moves from circumstances of difficulty and pain to awareness, joy, fulfillment. That the struggle to be critically conscious can be that movement which takes you to another level, that lifts you up, that makes you feel better. You feel good, you feel your life has meaning and purpose.

CW A rich life is fundamentally a life of serving others, a life of trying to leave the world a little better than you found it. That rich life comes into being in human relationships. This is true at the personal level. Those of you who have been in love know what I am talking about. It is also true at the organizational and communal level. It's difficult to find joy by yourself even if you have all the right toys. It's difficult. Just ask somebody who has got a lot of material possessions but doesn't have anybody to share them with. Now that's at the personal level. There is a political version of this. It has to do with what you see when you get up in the morning and look in the mirror and ask yourself whether you are simply wasting time on the planet or spending time in an enriching manner. We are talking fundamentally about the meaning of life and the place of struggle. bell talks about the significance of struggle and service. For those of us who are Christians there are certain theological foundations on which our commitment to serve is based. Christian life is understood to be a life of service. Even so, Christians have no monopoly on the joys that come from service and those of you who are part of secular culture can also enjoy this sense of enrichment. Islamic brothers and sisters share in a religious practice which also places emphasis on the importance of service. When we speak of commitment to a life of service we must also talk about the fact that such a commitment goes against the grain, especially the foundations of our society. To talk this way about service and struggle, we must also talk about strategies that will enable us to sustain this sensibility, this commitment.

bh When we talk about that which will sustain and nurture our spiritual growth as a people, we must once again talk about the importance of community. For one of the most vital ways we sustain ourselves is by building communities of resistance, places where we know we are not alone. In *Prophetic Fragments*, Cornel began his essay on Martin Luther King by quoting the lines of the spiritual, "He promised never to leave me, never to leave me alone." In Black spiritual tradition, the promise that we will not be alone cannot be heard as an affirmation of passivity. It does not mean we can sit around and wait for God to take care of business. We are not alone when we build community together. Certainly, there is a great feeling of community in this room today. And yet when I was here at Yale I felt that my labor was not appreciated. It was not clear that my work was having meaningful impact. Yet I feel that impact today. When I walked into the room a Black woman sister let me know how much my teaching and writing had helped her. There's more of the critical affirmation Cornel spoke of. That critical affirmation says, "Sister, what you're doing is uplifting me in some way." Often folk think that those folks who are spreading the message are so "together" that we do not need affirmation, critical dialogue about the impact of all that we teach and write about and how we live in the world.

CW It is important to note the degree to which Black people in particular, and progressive people in general, are alienated and estranged from communities that would sustain and support us. We are often homeless. Our struggles against a sense of nothingness and attempts to reduce us to nothing are ongoing. We confront regularly the question: "Where can I find a sense of home?" That sense of home can only be found in our construction of those communities of resistance bell talks about and the solidarity we can experience within them. Renewal comes through participating in community. That is the reason so many folks continue to go to church. In religious experience they find a sense of renewal, a sense of home. In community one can feel that we are moving forward, that struggle can be sustained. As we go forward as Black progressives, we must remember that community is not about homogeneity. Homogeneity is dogmatic imposition, pushing your way of life, your way of doing things onto somebody else. That is not what we mean by community. Dogmatic insistence that everybody think and act alike causes rifts among us, destroying the possibility of community. That sense of home that we are talking about and searching for is a place where we can find compassion, recognition of difference, of the importance of diversity, of our individual uniqueness.

bh When we evoke a sense of home as a place where we can renew ourselves, where we can know love and the sweet communion of shared spirit, I think it's important for us to remember that this location of well-being cannot exist in a context of sexist domination, in a setting where children are the objects of parental domination and abuse. On a fundamental level, when we talk about home, we must speak about the need to transform the African American home, so that there, in that domestic space, we can experience the renewal of political commitment to the Black liberation struggle. So that there in that domestic space we learn to serve and honor one another. If we look again at the civil rights movement, at the Black power movement, folks organized so much in homes. They were the places where folks got together to educate themselves for critical consciousness. That sense of community, cultivated and developed in the home, extended outward into a larger, more public context. As we talk about Black power in the 21st century, about political partnership between Black women and men, we must talk about transforming our notions of how and why we bond. In *Beloved*, Toni Morrison offers a paradigm for relationships between Black men and women. Sixo describes his love for Thirty-Mile Woman, declaring, "She is a friend of mind. She gather me, man. The pieces I am, she gather them and give them back to me in all the right order. It's good, you know, when you got a woman who is a friend of your mind." In this passage, Morrison evokes a notion of bonding that may be rooted in passion, desire, even romantic love, but the point of connection between Black women and men is that space of recognition and understanding, where we know one another so well, our histories, that we can take the bits and pieces, the fragments of who we are, and put them back together, re-member them. It is this joy of intellectual bonding, of working together to create liberatory theory and analysis that Black women and men can give one another, that Cornel and I give to each other. We are friends of one another's mind. We find a home with one another. It is that joy in community we celebrate and share with you this morning.

ACTIVE READING

1. Trace the claims hooks & West make "as individuals who believe in God" and those they make as "progressive Black people on the Left" (326–27). How do hooks & West work both sets of claims into their overall arguments?

2. List some meanings for the words "struggle" and "competition." In what ways might these meanings overlap? Look at the passages in which hooks & West explain their ideas about these terms. What distinctions do hooks & West want to make between them? Why?

3. What emotions do hooks & West mention or experience during their conversation? How do they react to or use these emotions? Based on your observations, develop a theory for the role emotions play in the kind of partnership hooks & West describe.

READING IN NEW CONTEXTS

1. What use do hooks & West want to make of Black tradition and heritage? Examine the use of tradition or heritage in a text by Walker, Fienup-Riordan, or another *Literacies* author. What challenges arise when people try to "use" their heritage in the text you chose? How might hooks's & West's ideas about tradition help overcome those challenges?

2. What do hooks & West mean by "critical affirmation" (330)? How does it differ from other forms of affirmation and from "dissin' "? Discuss the role critical affirmation plays in a text by Anzaldúa, Christian, or Rich. How does this concept alter your view of the second essay?

3. According to hooks, people who are not middle class sometimes "buy into a bourgeois class sensibility" (333). What does this mean to you? How can you use hooks's idea to understand the beliefs of someone in Heker's, MacLeod's, or Rodriguez's texts?

DRAFT ONE / DRAFT TWO

1. *Draft One:* List some of the images or ideas you associate with "home." What roles does the idea of home play in hooks & West's discussion? How do their views compare with your own? Show how you might use their perceptions to see your own thoughts about home in a new way.

   Draft Two: Locate images of "home" in another reading, perhaps one by Angelou, Kingston, or Gilmore. How closely do these images live up to the ideals established by hooks & West? What do you think the people in the second text would gain or lose by adopting ideas from hooks & West's discussion?

2. *Draft One:* What do hooks & West mean by "agency"? List some of the ways you try to assert agency in your own life. What kinds of obstacles limit your agency?

   Draft Two: Write about someone in another *Literacies* essay who attempts to exert agency. How does that person's gender help or hinder his or her attempt? Develop your own theory about the relationship between gender and agency.

BEFORE READING MAXINE HONG KINGSTON

1. Think of a relative or an acquaintance who has been the topic of your family's conversations from time to time. What draws their attention to this particular person? What issues or values do they address in these conversations?

2. Recall a time when an elder told you a cautionary story. What was the story? How did the point you took away from the story resemble or differ from the one the elder intended?

3. Choose a well-known story from literature or the movies, and sketch another plausible way that it might have turned out. How does the change alter the meaning of the story for a reader or viewer?

4. Talk about the role strategic silence—that is, not talking about something important—plays in a social group you know well.

MAXINE HONG KINGSTON

NO NAME WOMAN

"You must not tell anyone," my mother said, "what I am about to tell you. In China your father had a sister who killed herself. She jumped into the family well. We say that your father has all brothers because it is as if she had never been born.

"In 1924 just a few days after our village celebrated seventeen hurry-up weddings—to make sure that every young man who went 'out on the road' would responsibly come home—your father and his brothers and your grandfather and his brothers and your aunt's new husband sailed for America, the Gold Mountain. It was your grandfather's last trip. Those lucky enough to get contracts waved good-bye from the decks. They fed and guarded the stowaways and helped them off in Cuba, New York, Bali, Hawaii. 'We'll meet in California next year,' they said. All of them sent money home.

"I remember looking at your aunt one day when she and I were dressing; I had not noticed before that she had such a protruding melon of a stomach. But I did not think, 'She's pregnant,' until she began to look like other pregnant women, her shirt pulling and the white tops of her black pants showing. She could not have been pregnant, you see, because

From *The Woman Warrior* (1975).

341

her husband had been gone for years. No one said anything. We did not discuss it. In early summer she was ready to have the child, long after the time when it could have been possible.

"The village had also been counting. On the night the baby was to be born the villagers raided our house. Some were crying. Like a great saw, teeth strung with lights, files of people walked zigzig across our land, tearing the rice. Their lanterns doubled in the disturbed black water, which drained away through the broken bunds. As the villagers closed in, we could see that some of them, probably men and women we knew well, wore white masks. The people with long hair hung it over their faces. Women with short hair made it stand up on end. Some had tied white bands around their foreheads, arms, and legs.

"At first they threw mud and rocks at the house. Then they threw eggs and began slaughtering our stock. We could hear the animals scream their deaths—the roosters, the pigs, a last great roar from the ox. Familiar wild heads flared in our night windows; the villagers encircled us. Some of the faces stopped to peer at us, their eyes rushing like searchlights. The hands flattened against the panes, framed heads, and left red prints.

"The villagers broke in the front and the back doors at the same time, even though we had not locked the doors against them. Their knives dripped with the blood of our animals. They smeared blood on the doors and walls. One woman swung a chicken, whose throat she had slit, splattering blood in red arcs about her. We stood together in the middle of our house, in the family hall with the pictures and tables of the ancestors around us, and looked straight ahead.

"At that time the house had only two wings. When the men came back, we would build two more to enclose our courtyard and a third one to begin a second courtyard. The villagers rushed through both wings, even your grandparents' rooms, to find your aunt's, which was also mine until the men returned. From this room a new wing for one of the younger families would grow. They ripped up her clothes and shoes and broke her combs, grinding them underfoot. They tore her work from the loom. They scattered the cooking fire and rolled the new weaving in it. We could hear them in the kitchen breaking our bowls and banging the pots. They overturned the great waisthigh earthenware jugs; duck eggs, pickled fruits, vegetables burst out and mixed in acrid torrents. The old woman from the next field swept a broom through the air and loosed the spirits-of-the-broom over our heads. 'Pig.' 'Ghost.' 'Pig,' they sobbed and scolded while they ruined our house.

"When they left, they took sugar and oranges to bless themselves.

They cut pieces from the dead animals. Some of them took bowls that were not broken and clothes that were not torn. Afterward we swept up the rice and sewed it back up into sacks. But the smells from the spilled preserves lasted. Your aunt gave birth in the pigsty that night. The next morning when I went for the water, I found her and the baby plugging up the family well.

"Don't let your father know that I told you. He denies her. Now that you have started to menstruate, what happened to her could happen to you. Don't humiliate us. You wouldn't like to be forgotten as if you had never been born. The villagers are watchful."

Whenever she had to warn us about life, my mother told stories that ran like this one, a story to grow up on. She tested our strength to establish realities. Those in the emigrant generations who could not reassert brute survival died young and far from home. Those of us in the first American generations have had to figure out how the invisible world the emigrants built around our childhoods fit in solid America.

The emigrants confused the gods by diverting their curses, misleading them with crooked streets and false names. They must try to confuse their offspring as well, who, I suppose, threaten them in similar ways—always trying to get things straight, always trying to name the unspeakable. The Chinese I know hide their names; sojourners take new names when their lives change and guard their real names with silence.

Chinese-Americans, when you try to understand what things in you are Chinese, how do you separate what is peculiar to childhood, to poverty, insanities, one family, your mother who marked your growing with stories, from what is Chinese? What is Chinese tradition and what is the movies?

If I want to learn what clothes my aunt wore, whether flashy or ordinary, I would have to begin, "Remember Father's drowned-in-the-well sister?" I cannot ask that. My mother has told me once and for all the useful parts. She will add nothing unless powered by Necessity, a riverbank that guides her life. She plants vegetable gardens rather than lawns; she carries the odd-shaped tomatoes home from the fields and eats food left for the gods.

Whenever we did frivolous things, we used up energy; we flew high kites. We children came up off the ground over the melting cones our parents brought home from work and the American movie on New Year's Day—*Oh, You Beautiful Doll* with Betty Grable one year, and *She Wore a Yellow Ribbon* with John Wayne another year. After the one carnival ride each, we paid in guilt; our tired father counted his change on the dark walk home.

Adultery is extravagance. Could people who hatch their own chicks and eat the embryos and the heads for delicacies and boil the feet in vinegar for party food, leaving only the gravel, eating even the gizzard lining—could such people engender a prodigal aunt? To be a woman, to have a daughter in starvation time was a waste enough. My aunt could not have been the lone romantic who gave up everything for sex. Women in the old China did not choose. Some man had commanded her to lie with him and be his secret evil. I wonder whether he masked himself when he joined the raid on her family.

Perhaps she encountered him in the fields or on the mountain where the daughters-in-law collected fuel. Or perhaps he first noticed her in the marketplace. He was not a stranger because the village housed no strangers. She had to have dealings with him other than sex. Perhaps he worked an adjoining field, or he sold her the cloth for the dress she sewed and wore. His demand must have surprised, then terrified her. She obeyed him; she always did as she was told.

When the family found a young man in the next village to be her husband, she stood tractably beside the best rooster, his proxy, and promised before they met that she would be his forever. She was lucky that he was her age and she would be the first wife, an advantage secure now. The night she first saw him, he had sex with her. Then he left for America. She had almost forgotten what he looked like. When she tried to envision him, she only saw the black and white face in the group photograph the men had taken before leaving.

The other man was not, after all, much different from her husband. They both gave orders: she followed. "If you tell your family, I'll beat you. I'll kill you. Be here again next week." No one talked sex, ever. And she might have separated the rapes from the rest of living if only she did not have to buy her oil from him or gather wood in the same forest. I want her fear to have lasted just as long as rape lasted so that the fear could have been contained. No drawn-out fear. But women at sex hazarded birth and hence lifetimes. The fear did not stop but permeated everywhere. She told the man, "I think I'm pregnant." He organized the raid against her.

On nights when my mother and father talked about their life back home, sometimes they mentioned an "outcast table" whose business they still seemed to be settling, their voices tight. In a commensal tradition, where food is precious, the powerful older people made wrongdoers eat alone. Instead of letting them start separate new lives like the Japanese, who could become samurais and geishas, the Chinese family, faces averted but eyes glowering sideways, hung on to the offenders and fed them leftovers. My aunt must have lived in the same house as my parents and eaten at an outcast table. My mother spoke about the raid as if she had seen it, when she and my aunt, a daughter-in-law to a different household, should not have been living together at all. Daughters-in-law lived with their husbands' parents, not their own; a synonym for marriage in Chinese is "taking a daughter-in-law." Her husband's parents could have sold her, mortgaged her, stoned her. But they had sent her back to her own mother and father, a mysterious act hinting at disgraces not told me. Perhaps they had thrown her out to deflect the avengers.

She was the only daughter; her four brothers went with her father, husband, and uncles "out on the road" and for some years became western men. When the goods were divided among the family, three of the brothers took land, and the youngest, my father, chose an education. After my grandparents gave their daughter away to her husband's family, they had dispensed all the adventure and all the property. They expected her alone to keep the traditional ways, which her brothers, now among the barbarians, could fumble without detection. The heavy, deep-rooted women were to maintain the past against the flood, safe for returning. But the rare urge west had fixed upon our family, and so my aunt crossed boundaries not delineated in space.

The work of preservation demands that the feelings playing about in one's guts not be turned into action. Just watch their passing like cherry blossoms. But perhaps my aunt, my forerunner, caught in a slow life, let dreams grow and fade and after some months or years went toward what persisted. Fear at the enormities of the forbidden kept her desires delicate, wire and bone. She looked at a man because she liked the way the hair was tucked behind his ears, or she liked the question-mark line of a long torso curving at the shoulder and straight at the hip. For warm eyes or a soft voice or a slow walk—that's all—a few hairs, a line, a brightness, a sound, a pace, she gave up family. She offered us up for a charm that vanished with tiredness, a pigtail that didn't toss when the wind died. Why, the wrong lighting could erase the dearest thing about him.

It could very well have been, however, that my aunt did not take subtle enjoyment of her friend, but, a wild woman, kept rollicking company. Imagining her free with sex doesn't fit, though. I don't know any women like that, or men either. Unless I see her life branching into mine, she gives me no ancestral help.

To sustain her being in love, she often worked at herself in the mirror, guessing at the colors and shapes that would interest him, changing them frequently in order to hit on the right combination. She wanted him to look back.

On a farm near the sea, a woman who tended her appearance reaped a reputation for eccentricity. All the married women blunt-cut their hair in flaps about their ears or pulled it back in tight buns. No nonsense. Neither style blew easily into heart-catching tangles. And at their weddings they displayed themselves in their long hair for the last time. "It brushed the backs of my knees," my mother tells me. "It was braided, and even so, it brushed the backs of my knees."

At the mirror my aunt combed individuality into her bob. A bun could have been contrived to escape into black streamers blowing in the wind or in quiet wisps about her face, but only the older women in our picture album wear buns. She brushed her hair back from her forehead, tucking the flaps behind her ears. She looped a piece of thread, knotted into a circle between her index fingers and thumbs, and ran the double strand across her forehead. When she closed her fingers as if she were making a pair of shadow geese bite, the string twisted together catching the little hairs. Then she pulled the thread away from her skin, ripping the hairs out neatly, her eyes watering from the needles of pain. Opening her fingers, she cleaned the thread, then rolled it along her hairline and the tops of her eyebrows. My mother did the same to me and my sisters and herself. I used to believe that the expression "caught by the short hairs" meant a captive held with a depilatory string. It especially hurt at the temples, but my mother said we were lucky we didn't have to have our feet bound when we were seven. Sisters used to sit on their beds and cry together, she said, as their mothers or their slave removed the bandages for a few minutes each night and let the blood gush back into their veins. I hope that the man my aunt loved appreciated a smooth brow, that he wasn't just a tits-and-ass man.

Once my aunt found a freckle on her chin, at a spot that the almanac said predestined her for unhappiness. She dug it out with a hot needle and washed the wound with peroxide.

More attention to her looks than these pullings of hairs and pickings at spots would have caused gossip among the villagers. They owned work clothes and good clothes, and they wore good clothes for feasting the new seasons. But since a woman combing her hair hexes beginnings, my aunt rarely found an occasion to look her best. Women looked like great sea snails—the corded wood, babies, and laundry they carried were the whorls on their backs. The Chinese did not admire a bent back; goddesses and warriors stood straight. Still there must have been a marvelous freeing of beauty when a worker laid down her burden and stretched and arched.

Such commonplace loveliness, however, was not enough for my aunt. She dreamed of a lover for the fifteen days of New Year's, the time for families to exchange visits, money, and food. She plied her secret comb. And sure enough she cursed the year, the family, the village, and herself.

Even as her hair lured her imminent lover, many other men looked at her. Uncles, cousins, nephews, brothers would have looked, too, had they been home between journeys. Perhaps they had already been restraining their curiosity, and they left, fearful that their glances, like a field of nesting birds, might be startled and caught. Poverty hurt, and that was their first reason for leaving. But another, final reason for leaving the crowded house was the never-said.

She may have been unusually beloved, the precious only daughter, spoiled and mirror gazing because of the affection the family lavished on her. When her husband left, they welcomed the chance to take her back from the in-laws; she could live like the little daughter for just a while longer. There are stories that my grandfather was different from other people, "crazy ever since the little Jap bayoneted him in the head." He used to put his naked penis on the dinner table, laughing. And one day he brought home a baby girl, wrapped up inside his brown western-style greatcoat. He had traded one of his sons, probably my father, the youngest, for her. My grandmother made him trade back. When he finally got a daughter of his own, he doted on her. They must have all loved her, except perhaps my father, the only brother who never went back to China, having once been traded for a girl.

Brothers and sisters, newly men and women, had to efface their sexual color and present plain miens. Disturbing hair and eyes, a smile like no other, threatened the ideal of five generations living under one roof. To focus blurs, people shouted face to face and yelled from room to room. The immigrants I know have loud voices, unmodulated to American tones even after years away from the village where they called their friendships out across the fields. I have not been able to stop my mother's screams in public libraries or over telephones. Walking erect (knees straight, toes pointed forward, not pigeon-toed, which is Chinese-feminine) and speaking in an inaudible voice, I have tried to turn myself American-feminine. Chinese communication was loud, public. Only sick people had to whisper. But at the dinner table, where the family members came nearest one another, no one could talk, not the outcasts nor any eaters. Every word that falls from the mouth is a coin lost. Silently they gave and accepted food with both hands. A preoccupied child who took his bowl with one hand got a sideways glare. A complete moment of total attention is due everyone alike. Children and lovers have no singularity here, but my aunt used a secret voice, a separate attentiveness.

She kept the man's name to herself throughout her labor and dying; she did not accuse him that he be punished with her. To save her inseminator's name she gave silent birth.

He may have been somebody in her own household, but intercourse with a man outside the family would have been no less abhorrent. All the village were kinsmen, and the titles shouted in loud country voices never let kinship be forgotten. Any man within visiting distance would have been neutralized as a lover—"brother," "younger brother," "older brother"—one hundred and fifteen relationship titles. Parents researched birth charts probably not so much to assure good fortune as to circumvent incest in a population that has but one hundred surnames. Everybody has eight million relatives. How useless then sexual mannerisms, how dangerous.

As if it came from an atavism deeper than fear, I used to add "brother" silently to boys' names. It hexed the boys, who would or would not ask me to dance; and made them less scary and as familiar and deserving of benevolence as girls.

But, of course, I hexed myself also—no dates. I should have stood up, both arms waving, and shouted out across libraries, "Hey, you! Love me back." I had no idea, though, how to make attraction selective, how to control its direction and magnitude. If I made myself American-pretty so that the five or six Chinese boys in the class fell in love with me, everyone else—the Caucasian, Negro, and Japanese boys—would too. Sisterliness, dignified and honorable, made much more sense.

Attraction eludes control so stubbornly that whole societies designed to organize relationships among people cannot keep order, not even when they bind people to one another from childhood and raise them together. Among the very poor and the wealthy, brothers married their adopted sisters, like doves. Our family allowed some romance, paying adult brides' prices and providing dowries so that their sons and daughters could marry strangers. Marriage promises to turn strangers into friendly relatives—a nation of siblings.

In the village structure, spirits shimmered among the live creatures, balanced and held in equilibrium by time and land. But one human being flaring up into violence could open up a black hole, a maelstrom that pulled in the sky. The frightened villagers, who depended on one another to maintain the real, went to my aunt to show her a personal, physical representation of the break she had made in the "roundness." Misallying couples snapped off the future, which was to be embodied in true offspring. The villagers punished her for acting as if she could have a private life, secret and apart from them.

If my aunt had betrayed the family at a time of large grain yields and peace, when many boys were born, and wings were being built on many houses, perhaps she might have escaped such severe punishment. But the men—hungry, greedy, tired of planting in dry soil, cuckolded—had had to leave the village in order to send food-money home. There were ghost plagues, bandit plagues, wars with the Japanese, floods. My Chinese brother and sister had died of an unknown sickness. Adultery, perhaps only a mistake during good times, became a crime when the village needed food.

The round moon cakes and round doorways, the round tables of graduated size that fit one roundness inside another, round windows and rice bowls—these talismans had lost their power to warn this family of the law: a family must be whole, faithfully keeping the descent line by having sons to feed the old and the dead, who in turn look after the family. The villagers came to show my aunt and her lover-in-hiding a broken house. The villagers were speeding up the circling of events because she was too shortsighted to see that her infidelity had already harmed the village, that waves of consequences would return unpredictably, sometimes in disguise, as now, to hurt her. This roundness had to be made coin-sized so that she would see its circumference: punish her at the birth of her baby. Awaken her to the inexorable. People who refused fatalism because they could invent small resources insisted on culpability. Deny accidents and wrest fault from the stars.

After the villagers left, their lanterns now scattering in various directions toward home, the family broke their silence and cursed her. "Aiaa, we're going to die. Death is coming. Death is coming. Look what you've done. You've killed us. Ghost! Dead ghost! Ghost! You've never been born." She ran out into the fields, far enough from the house so that she could no longer hear their voices, and pressed herself against the earth, her own land no more. When she felt the birth coming, she thought that she had been hurt. Her body seized together. "They've hurt me too much," she thought. "This is gall, and it will kill me." With forehead and knees against the earth, her body convulsed and then relaxed. She turned on her back, lay on the ground. The black well of sky and stars went out and out and out forever; her body and her complexity seemed to disappear, without home, without a companion, in eternal cold and silence. An agoraphobia rose in her, speeding higher and higher, bigger and bigger; she would not be able to contain it; there would be no end to fear.

Flayed, unprotected against space, she felt pain return, focusing her body. This pain chilled her—a cold, steady kind of surface pain. Inside, spasmodically, the other pain, the pain of the child, heated her. For hours she lay on the ground, alternately body and space. Sometimes a vision of normal comfort obliterated reality: she saw the family in the evening gambling at the dinner table, the young people massaging their elders' backs. She saw them congratulating one another, high joy on the mornings the rice shoots came up. When these pictures burst, the stars drew yet further apart. Black space opened.

She got to her feet to fight better and remembered that old-fashioned women gave birth in their pigsties to fool the jealous, pain-dealing gods, who do not snatch piglets. Before the next spasms could stop her, she ran to the pigsty, each step a rushing out into emptiness. She climbed over the fence and knelt in the dirt. It was good to have a fence enclosing her, a tribal person alone.

Laboring, this woman who had carried her child as a foreign growth that sickened her every day, expelled it at last. She reached down to touch the hot, wet, moving mass, surely smaller than anything human, and could feel that it was human after all—fingers, toes, nails, nose. She pulled it up on to her belly, and it lay curled there, butt in the air, feet precisely tucked one under the other. She opened her loose shirt and buttoned the child inside. After resting, it squirmed and thrashed and she pushed it up to her breast. It turned its head this way and that until it found her nipple. There, it made little snuffling noises. She clenched her teeth at its preciousness, lovely as a young calf, a piglet, a little dog.

She may have gone to the pigsty as a last act of responsibility: she would protect this child as she had protected its father. It would look after her soul, leaving supplies on her grave. But how would this tiny child without family find her grave when there would be no marker for her anywhere, neither in the earth nor the family hall? No one would give her a family hall name. She had taken the child with her into the wastes. At its birth the two of them had felt the same raw pain of separation, a wound that only the family pressing tight could close. A child with no descent line would not soften her life but only trail after her, ghost-like, begging her to give it purpose. At dawn the villagers on their way to the fields would stand around the fence and look.

Full of milk, the little ghost slept. When it awoke, she hardened her breasts against the milk that crying loosens. Toward morning she picked up the baby and walked to the well.

Carrying the baby to the well shows loving. Otherwise abandon it. Turn its face into the mud. Mothers who love their children take them along. It was probably a girl; there is some hope of forgiveness for boys.

"Don't tell anyone you had an aunt. Your father does not want to hear her name. She has never been born." I have believed that sex was unspeakable and words so strong and fathers so frail that "aunt" would do my father mysterious harm. I have thought that my family, having settled among immigrants who had also been their neighbors in the ancestral land, needed to clean their name, and a wrong word would incite the kinspeople even here. But there is more to this silence: they want me to participate in her punishment. And I have.

In the twenty years since I heard this story I have not asked for details nor said my aunt's name; I do not know it. People who can comfort the dead can also chase after them to hurt them further—a reverse ancestor worship. The real punishment was not the raid swiftly inflicted by the villagers, but the family's deliberately forgetting her. Her betrayal so maddened them, they saw to it that she would suffer forever, even after death. Always hungry, always needing, she would have to beg food from other ghosts, snatch and steal it from those whose living descendants give them gifts. She would have to fight the ghosts massed at crossroads for the buns a few thoughtful citizens leave to decoy her away from village and home so that the ancestral spirits could feast unharassed. At peace, they could act like gods, not ghosts, their descent lines providing them with paper suits and dresses, spirit money, paper houses, paper automobiles, chicken, meat, and rice into eternity—essences delivered up in smoke and flames, steam and incense rising from each rice bowl. In an attempt to make the Chinese care for people outside the family, Chairman Mao encourages us now to give our paper replicas to the spirits of outstanding soldiers and workers, no matter whose ancestors they may be. My aunt remains forever hungry. Goods are not distributed evenly among the dead.

My aunt haunts me—her ghost drawn to me because now, after fifty years of neglect, I alone devote pages of paper to her, though not origamied into houses and clothes. I do not think she always means me well. I am telling on her, and she was a spite suicide, drowning herself in the drinking water. The Chinese are always very frightened of the drowned one, whose weeping ghost, wet hair hanging and skin bloated, waits silently by the water to pull down a substitute.

ACTIVE READING

1. "Unless I see her life branching into mine," Kingston said of her aunt, "she gives me no ancestral help" (345). Locate passages where the lives of aunt and niece do branch into one another. What personal matters concern Kingston in these passages?

2. How many different versions of the aunt's story does Kingston provide? Identify the starting and stopping place of each version, and point out the major differences between the accounts. What does each version contribute to Kingston's sense of herself and of her family history?

3. Find places where Kingston's essay moves from the "facts" of the aunt's story to "reflection," "speculation," or even "fiction" about it. What do each of these forms of writing offer Kingston as she examines the family history?

4. "Societies," says Kingston, are "designed to organize relationships among people" (348). Discuss the ways the village uses silence and other social practices to organize gender roles.

READING IN NEW CONTEXTS

1. What does Kingston mean by "the invisible world"? Compare the invisible world Kingston describes with the experience of another tight-knit family or community, such as the ones described in Fishman or Baldwin. How are these "worlds" built or maintained, and what do they accomplish?

2. Use this essay and another *Literacies* text, such as Heath or Gilmore, to talk about some of the factors that shape a culture's views of individuality.

3. Review your comments about silence in Before Reading #4 and Active Reading #4, and then examine another *Literacies* text, such as Scheper-Hughes or Heker, where some important cultural truth remains unspoken. Compose a theory relating silence and culture.

DRAFT ONE / DRAFT TWO

1. *Draft One:* Explain what Kingston means when she says that her mother "tested [Kingston's] strength to establish realities" (343). Where in her essay do you see Kingston "establish[ing] realities" that are different from those approved by her Chinese and American cultures? What does that process have to do with writing?

   Draft Two: Discuss the strategies that Kingston, as an essayist, and you, as a college writer, can use to "establish realities." What obstacles do the two of you face as you try to present a perspective faithful to personal experience? Try to distinguish between obstacles that come from "inside" and "outside" the writer.

2. *Draft One:* Use your own experience and the events of this essay to define and discuss discipline and self-discipline. What relations do you see between the two?

   Draft Two: Draw on your earlier writings about silence (Before Reading #4, Active Reading #4, Reading in New Contexts #3) to extend your discussion of discipline and self-discipline from Draft One. If possible, speculate about the social implications of your findings.

BEFORE READING JONATHAN KOZOL

1. What factors contribute to the way a person understands homelessness? Where have your opinions about homelessness come from?

2. What relationships do you see between "family" and "homelessness," as you understand these terms? How has your experience helped you to answer this question?

3. In your experience, what does it mean to have "control" over your life? Talk about some parts of your life over which you have control and some parts where you may lack control. Where does control come from?

JONATHAN KOZOL

RACHEL AND
HER CHILDREN

Mr. Allesandro is too shaken to attempt to hide his frailties from me. He tells me: "When you're running scared you do some things you'd rather not . . ." He does not regard himself as saint or martyr. There are virtues, feelings and commitments he has forfeited during this long ordeal. Love is not one of them. His desperation for his son and daughters and his adoration of his mother are as solid and authentic as the marble pillars of the Martinique Hotel. The authenticity of love deserves some mention in discussion of the homeless.

Houses can be built without a number of ingredients that other ages viewed as indispensable. Acrylics, plastics and aluminum may substitute for every substance known to nature. Parental love cannot be synthesized. Even the most earnest and methodical foster care demonstrates the limits of synthetic tenderness and surrogate emotion. So it seems of keen importance to consider any ways, and *every* way, by which a family, splintered, jolted and imperiled though it be by loss of home and subsequent detention in a building like the Martinique, may nonetheless be given every possible incentive to remain together.

The inclination to judge harshly the behavior of a parent under for-

From *Rachel and Her Children* (1988).

midable stress seems to be much stronger than the willingness to castigate the policies that undermine the competence and ingenuity of many of these people in the first place.

"Men can be unequal in their needs, in their honor, in their possessions," writes historian Michael Ignatieff, "but also in their rights to judge others." The king's ultimate inequality, he says, "is that he is never judged." An entire industry of scholarship and public policy exists to judge the failing or defective parent; if we listen to some of these parents carefully we may be no less concerned by their impaired abilities, but we may be less judgmental or, if we remain compelled to judge, we may redirect our energies in more appropriate directions.

New Year's Eve.

She stalks into the room. Her eyes are reddened and her clothes in disarray. She wears a wrinkled and translucent nightgown. On her feet: red woolen stockings. At her throat: a crucifix. Over her shoulders is a dark and heavy robe. Nothing I have learned in the past week prepares me for this apparition.

She cries. She weeps. She paces left and right and back and forth. Pivoting and turning suddenly to face me. Glaring straight into my eyes. A sudden halt. She looks up toward the cracked and yellowish ceiling of the room. Her children stand around her in a circle. Two little girls. A frightened boy. They stare at her, as I do, as her arms reach out—for what? They snap like snakes and coil back. Her hair is gray—a stiff and brushlike Afro.

Angelina is twelve years old, Stephen is eleven, Erica is nine. The youngest child, eleven months, is sitting on the floor. A neighbor's child, six years old, sits in my lap and leans her head against my chest; she holds her arms around my neck. Her name or nickname (I do not know which) is Raisin. When she likes she puts her fingers on my mouth and interrupts the conversation with a tremolo of rapid words. There are two rooms. Rachel disappears into the second room, then returns and stands, uneasy, by the door.

Angie: "Ever since August we been livin' here. The room is either very hot or freezin' cold. When it be hot outside it's hot in here. When it be cold outside we have no heat. We used to live with my aunt but then it got too crowded there so we moved out. We went to welfare and they sent us to the shelter. Then they shipped us to Manhattan. I'm scared of the elevators. 'Fraid they be stuck. I take the stairs."

Raisin: "Elevator might fall down and you would die."

Rachel: "It's unfair for them to be here in this room. They be yellin'. Lots of times I'm goin' to walk out. Walk out on the street and give it up. No, I don't do it. BCW [Bureau of Child Welfare] come to take the children. So I make them stay inside. Once they walk outside that door they are in danger."

Angie: "I had a friend Yoki. They was tryin' to beat her. I said: 'Leave her.' They began to chase me. We was runnin' to the door. So we was runnin'. I get to the door. The door was stuck. I hit my eye and it began to bleed. So I came home and washed the blood. Me and my friends sat up all night and prayed. Prayin' for me. 'Dear Lord, can you please help me with my eye? If you do I promise to behave.' I was askin' God why did this happen. I wish someone in New York could help us. Put all of the money that we have together and we buy a building. Two or three rooms for every family. Everybody have a kitchen. Way it is, you frightened all the time. I think this world is coming to the end."

Stephen: "This city is rich."

Angie: "Surely is!"

Erica: "City and welfare, they got something goin'. Pay $3,000 every month to stay in these here rooms . . ."

Rachel: "I believe the City Hall got something goin' here. Gettin' a cut. They got to be. My children, they be treated like chess pieces. Send all of that money off to Africa? You hear that song? They're not thinking about people starvin' here in the United States. I was thinkin': Get my kids and all the other children here to sing, 'We are the world. We live here too.' How come do you care so much for people you can't see? Ain't we the world? Ain't we a piece of it? We are so close they be afraid to see. Give us a shot at something. We are something! Ain't we *something*? I'm depressed. But we are *something*! People in America don't want to see."

Angie: "Christmas is sad for everyone. We have our toys. That's not the reason why. They givin' you toys and that do help. I would rather that we have a place to be."

Erica: "I wrote a letter to Santa Claus. Santa say that he don't have the change."

Raisin: "I saw Santa on the street. Then I saw Santa on another street. I pulled his beard and he said something nasty."

Angie: "There's one thing I ask: a home to be in with my mother. That was my only wish for Christmas. But it could not be."

Raisin: "I saw Mr. Water Bug under my mother's bed. Mr. Rat be livin' with us too."

Angie: "It's so cold right now you got to use the hot plate. Plug it in so you be warm. You need to have a hot plate. Are you goin' to live on cold bologna all your life?"

Raisin: "Mr. Rat came in my baby sister's crib and bit her. Nobody felt sorry for my sister. Then I couldn't go to sleep. I started crying. All of a sudden I pray and went to sleep and then I woke up in the mornin', make my bed, and took a bath, and ate, and went to school. So I came back and did my homework. And all of a sudden there was something *irritatin'* at my hand. I looked out the window and the moon was goin' up. And then—I had a dream. I went to sleep and I was dreamin' and I dreamed about a witch that bit me. I felt *dead.* When I woke back up I had a headache."

Angie: "School is bad for me. I feel ashamed. They know we're not the same. My teacher do not treat us all the same. They know which children live in the hotel."

Erica: "My teacher isn't like that. She treats all of us the same. We all get smacked. We all get punished the same way."

Stephen: "I'm in sixth grade. When I am a grown-up I be a computer."

Erica: "You're in the fifth. You lie."

Raisin: "When I grow up I want to be multiplication and subtraction and division."

Angie: "Last week a drug addict tried to stab me. With an ice pick. Tried to stab my mother too. Older girls was botherin' us. They try to make us fight. We don't fight. We don't start fires. They just pickin' on us. We ran home and got our mother. They ran home and got their mother."

Raisin: "Those girls upstairs on the ninth floor, they be bad. They sellin' crack."

Erica: "Upstairs, ninth floor, nine-o-five, they sellin' crack."

Raisin: "A man was selling something on the street. He had some reefers on him and the po-lice caught him and they took him to the jail. You know where the junkies put the crack? Put the crack inside the pipe. Smoke it like that. They take a torch and burn the pipe and put it in their mouth. They go like this." [Puffs.]

I ask: "Why do they do it?"

Erica: "Feel good! Hey! Make you feel fine!"

Angie: "This girl I know lives in a room where they sell drugs. One day she asks us do we want a puff. So we said: 'No. My mother doesn't let us do it.' One day I was walkin' in the hall. This man asked me do I want some stuff. He said: 'Do you want some?' I said no and I ran home."

Raisin: "One day my brother found these two big plastic bags inside his teddy bear. Po-lice came up to my room and took that teddy bear." She's interrupted. "I ain't finished! And they took it. One day we was by my uncle's car and this man came and he said: 'Do you want some?' We said no. We told my uncle and he went and found the man and he ran to the bar and went into the women's bathroom in the bar. And so we left."

Angie: "I think this world is ending. Yes. Ending. Everybody in this city killin' on each other. Countries killin' on each other. Why can't people learn to stick together? It's no use to fightin'. Fightin' over nothin'. What they fightin' for? A flag! I don't know what we are fightin' for. President Reagan wants to put the rockets on the moon. What's he doin' messin' with the moon? If God wanted man and woman on the moon He would of put us there. They should send a camera to the moon and feed the people here on earth. Don't go messin' there with human beings. Use that money to build houses. Grow food! Buy seeds! Weave cloth! Give it to the people in America!"

Erica: "When we hungry and don't have no food we borrow from each other. Her mother [Raisin's] give us food. Or else we go to Crisis. In the mornin' when we wake up we have a banana or a cookie. If the bus ain't late we have our breakfast in the school. What I say to President Reagan: Give someone a chance! I believe he be a selfish man. Can't imagine how long he been president."

Raisin: "Be too long."

Angie: "Teacher tell us this be a democracy. I don't know. I doubt it. Rich people, couldn't they at least give us a refund?"

Raisin: "This man say his son be gettin' on his nerves. He beat his little son 'bout two years old. A wooden bat. He beat him half to death. They took him to the hospital and at five-thirty he was dead. A little boy. [Interrupted.] Let me talk!"

Erica: "The little boy. He locked himself into the bathroom. He was scared. After he died police came and his father went to jail. His mother, she went to the store."

Raisin, in a tiny voice: "People fight in here and I don't like it. Why do they do it? 'Cause they're sad. They fight over the world. I ain't finished!"

Erica: "One time they was two cops in the hall. One cop pulled his gun and he was goin' shoot me. He said did I live there? I said no. So I came home."

Raisin: "I was in this lady room. She be cryin' because her baby died. He had [mispronounced] pneumonia. He was unconscious and he died." Soft voice: "Tomorrow is my birthday."

The children are tended by a friend. In the other bedroom, Rachel, who is quieter now, paces about and finally sits down.

"Do you know why there's no carpet in the hall? If there was a carpet it would be on fire. Desperate people don't have no control. You have to sleep with one eye open. Tell the truth, I do not sleep at night.

"Before we lived here we were at the Forbell shelter [barracks shelter on Forbell Street in Brooklyn]. People sleep together in one room. You sleep across. You have to dress in front of everybody. Men and women. When you wake, some man lookin' at you puttin' on your clothes. Lookin' at your children too. Angelina, she be only twelve years old . . .

"There's one thing. My children still are pure. They have a concept of life. Respect for life. But if you don't get 'em out of here they won't have anything for long. If you get 'em out right now. But if you don't . . . My girls are innocent still. They are unspoiled. Will they be that way for long? Try to keep 'em in the room. But you can't lock 'em up for long.

"When we moved here I was forced to sign a paper. Everybody has to do it. It's a promise that you will not cook inside your room. So we lived on cold bologna. Can you feed a child on that? God forgive me but nobody shouldn't have to live like this. I can't even go downstairs and get back on the elevator. Half the time it doesn't work. Since I came into this place my kids begun to get away from me."

There's a crucifix on the wall. I ask her: "Do you pray?"

"I don't pray! Pray for what? I been prayin' all my life and I'm still here. When I came to this hotel I still believed in God. I said: 'Maybe God can help us to survive.' I lost my faith. My hopes. And everything. Ain't nobody—no God, no Jesus—gonna help us in no way.

"God forgive me. I'm emotional. I'm black. I'm in a blackness. Blackness is around me. In the night I'm scared to sleep. In the mornin' I'm worn out. I don't eat no breakfast. I don't drink no coffee. If I eat, I eat one meal a day. My stomach won't allow me. I have ulcers. I stay in this room. I hide. This room is safe to me. I am afraid to go outside.

"If I go out, what do I do? People drink. Why do they drink? A person gets worn out. They usin' drugs. Why they use drugs? They say: 'Well, I won't think about it now.' Why not? You ain't got nothin' else to do, no place to go. 'Where I'm gonna be tomorrow or the next day?' They don't know. All they know is that they don't have nothin'. So they drink. And some of them would rather not wake up. Rather be dead. That's right.

"Most of us are black. Some Puerto Rican. Some be white. They suffer too. Can you get the government to know that we exist? I know that my children have potential. They're intelligent. They're smart. They need a chance. There's nothin' wrong with them for now. But not for long. My daughter watches junkies usin' needles. People smokin' crack in front a them. Screwin' in front a them. They see it all. They see it everywhere. What is a man and woman gonna do when they are all in the same room?

"I met a girl the other day. She's twelve years old. Lives on the four-teenth floor. She got a baby the same age as mine. Her mother got five children of her own. I don't want my daughter havin' any baby. She's a child. Innocent. Innocent. No violence. She isn't bitter. But she's scared. You understand? This is America. These children growin' up too fast. We have no hope. And you know why? Because we all feel just the same way deep down in our hearts. Nowhere to go . . . I'm not a killer. My kids ain't no killers. But if they don't learn to kill they know they're goin' to die.

"They didn't go to school last week. They didn't have clean clothes. Why? Because the welfare messed my check. It's supposed to come a week ago. It didn't come. I get my check today. I want my kids to go to school. They shouldn't miss a day. How they gonna go to school if they don't got some clothes? I couldn't wash. I didn't have the money to buy food.

"Twice the welfare closed my case. When they do it you are s'posed to go for a fair hearing. Take some papers, birth certificates. So I went out there in the snow. Welfare worker wasn't there. They told me to come back. Mister, it ain't easy to be beggin'. I went to the Crisis. And I asked her, I said, 'Give me somethin' for the kids to eat. Give me *somethin'!* Don't turn me away when I am sittin' here in front of you and askin' for your help!' She said she had nothin'. So my kids went out into the street. That's right! Whole night long they was in Herald Square panhandlin'. Made five dollars. So we bought bologna. My kids is good to me. We had bread and bologna.

"Welfare, they are not polite. They're personal. 'Did you do this? Did you do that? Where your husband at?' Understand me? 'Cause they sittin' on the other side of this here desk, they think we're stupid and we do not understand when we're insulted. 'Oh, you had another baby?' Yeah! I had another baby! What about it? Are you goin' to kill that baby? I don't say it, but that's what I feel like sayin'. You learn to be humble.

"I'm here five miserable months. So I wonder: Where I'm goin'? Can't the mayor give us a house? A part-time job? I am capable of doin' *somethin'*.

"You go in the store with food stamps. You need Pampers. You're not s'posed to use the stamps for Pampers. Stores will accept them. They don't care about the law. What they do is make you pay a little extra. They know you don't have no choice. So they let you buy the Pampers for two dollars extra.

"Plenty of children livin' here on nothin' but bread and bologna. Peanut butter. Jelly. Drinkin' water. You buy milk. I bought one gallon yesterday. Got *this* much left. They drink it fast. Orange juice, they drink it fast. End up drinkin' Kool Aid.

"Children that are poor are used like cattle. Cattle or horses. They are owned by welfare. They know they are bein' used—for what? Don't *use* them! Give 'em somethin'!

"In this bedroom I'm not sleepin' on a bed. They won't give me one. You can see I'm sleepin' on a box spring. I said to the manager: 'I need a bed instead of sleepin' on a spring.' Maid give me some blankets. Try to make it softer."

The Bible by her bed is opened to the Twenty-third Psalm.

"I do believe. God forgive me. I believe He's there. But when He sees us like this, I am wonderin' where is He? I am askin': Where the hell He gone?

"Before they shipped us here we lived for five years in a basement. Five years in a basement with no bathroom. One small room. You had to go upstairs two floors to use the toilet. No kitchen. It was fifteen people in five rooms. Sewer kept backing up into the place we slept. Every time it flooded I would have to pay one hundred dollars just to get the thing unstuck. There were all my children sleepin' in the sewage. So you try to get them out and try to get them somethin' better. But it didn't get no better. I came from one bad place into another. But the difference is this is a place where I cannot get out.

"If I can't get out of here I'll give them up. I have asked them: 'Do you want to go away?' I love my kids and, if I did that, they would feel betrayed. They love me. They don't want to go. If I did it, I would only do it to protect them. They'll live anywhere with me. They're innocent. Their minds are clean. They ain't corrupt. They have a heart. All my kids love people. They love life. If they got a dime, a piece of bread, they'll share it. Letting them panhandle made me cry. I had been to welfare, told the lady that my baby ain't got Pampers, ain't got nothin' left to eat. I got rude and noisy and it's not my style to do that but you learn that patience and politeness get you nowhere.

"When they went out on the street I cried. I said: 'I'm scared. What's gonna happen to them?' But if they're hungry they are goin' to do *something*. They are gonna find their food from somewhere. Where I came from I was fightin' for my children. In this place here I am fightin' for my children. I am tired of fightin'. I don't want to fight. I want my kids to live in peace.

"I was thinkin' about this. If there was a place where you could sell part of your body, where they buy an arm or somethin' for a thousand dollars, I would do it. I would do it for my children. I would give my life if I could get a thousand dollars. What would I lose? I lived my life. I want to see my children grow up to live theirs.

"A lot of women do not want to sell their bodies. This is something that good women do not want to do. I will sell mine. I *will*. I will solicit. I will prostitute if it will feed them."

I ask: "Would you do it?"

"Ain't no 'would I?' I would do it." Long pause . . . "Yes. I *did*.

"I had to do it when the check ain't come. Wasn't no one gonna buy my arm for any thousand dollars. But they's plenty gonna pay me twenty dollars for my body. What was my choice? Leave them out there on the street, a child like Angelina, to panhandle? I would take my life if someone found her dead somewhere. I would go crazy. After she did it that one time I was ashamed. I cried that night. All night I cried and cried. So I decided I had one thing left. In the mornin' I got up out of this bed. I told them I was goin' out. Out in the street. Stand by the curb. It was a cold day. Freezin'! And my chest is bad. I'm thirty-eight years old. Cop come by. He see me there. I'm standin' out there cryin'. Tells me I should go inside. Gives me three dollars. 'It's too cold to be outside.' Ain't many cops like that. Not many people either . . .

"After he's gone a man come by. Get in his car. Go with him where he want. Takin' a chance he crazy and he kill me. Wishin' somehow that he would.

"So he stop his car. And I get in. I say a price. That's it. Go to a room. It's some hotel. He had a lot of money so he rented a deluxe. Asked me would I stay with him all night. I tell him no I can't 'cause I have kids. So, after he done . . . whatever he did . . . I told him that I had to leave. Took out a knife at me and held it at my face. He made me stay. When I woke up next day I was depressed. Feel so guilty what I did. I feel real scared. I can understand why prostitutes shoot drugs. They take the drugs so they don't be afraid.

"When he put that knife up to my throat, I'm thinkin' this: What is there left to lose? I'm not goin' to do any better in this life. If I be dead at least my kids won't ever have to say that I betrayed them. I don't like to think like that. But when things pile up on you, you do. 'I'm better if I'm dead.'

"So I got me twenty dollars and I go and buy the Pampers for the baby and three dollars of bologna and a loaf of bread and everyone is fed.

"That cross of Jesus on the wall I had for seven years. I don't know if I believe or not. Bible say that Jesus was God's son. He died for us to live here on this earth. See, I believe—Jesus was innocent. But, when He died, what was it for? He died for nothin'. Died in vain. He should a let us die like we be doin'—we be dyin' all the time. We dyin' every day.

"God forgive me. I don't mean the things I say. God had one son and He gave His son. He gave him up. I couldn't do it. I got four. I could not give any one of them. I couldn't do it. God could do it. Is it wrong to say it? I don't know if Jesus died in vain."

She holds the Bible in her hands. Crying softly. Sitting on the box spring in her tangled robe.

"They laid him in a manger. Right? Listen to me. I didn't say that God forsaken us. I am confused about religion. I'm just sayin' evil overrules the good. So many bad things goin' on. Lot of bad things right here in this buildin'. It's not easy to believe. I don't read the Bible no more 'cause I don't find no more hope in it. I don't believe. But yet and still . . . I know these words." She reads aloud: " 'Lie down in green pastures . . . leadeth me beside still waters . . . restores my soul . . . I shall not want.'

"All that I want is somethin' that's my own. I got four kids. I need four plates, four glasses, and four spoons. Is that a lot? I know I'm poor. Don't have no bank account, no money, or no job. Don't have no nothin'. No foundation. Then and yet my children have a shot in life. They're innocent. They're pure. They have a chance." She reads: " 'I shall not fear . . .' I fear! A long, long time ago I didn't fear. Didn't fear for nothin'. I said God's protectin' me and would protect my children. Did He do it?

"Yeah. I'm walkin'. I am walkin' in the wilderness. That's what it is. I'm walkin'. Did I tell you that I am an ex-drug addict? Yeah. My children know it. They know and they understand. I'm walkin'. Yeah!"

The room is like a chilled cathedral in which people who do not believe in God ask God's forgiveness. "How I picture God is like an old man who speaks different languages. His beard is white and He has angels and the instruments they play are white and everything around is white and there is no more sickness, no more hunger for nobody. No panhandlin'. No prostitutes. No drugs. I had a dream like that.

"There's no beauty in my life except two things. My children and"—

she hesitates—"I write these poems. How come, when I write it down, it don't come out my pencil like I feel? I don't know. I got no dictionary. Every time I read it over I am finding these mistakes.

> Deep down in my heart
> I do not mean these things I said.
> Forgive me. Try to understand me.
> I love all of you the same.
> Help me to be a better mother.

"When I cry I let 'em know. I tell 'em I was a drug addict. They know and they try to help me to hold on. They helpin' me. My children is what's holdin' me together. I'm not makin' it. I'm reachin'. And they see me reachin' out. Angelina take my hand. They come around. They ask me what is wrong. I do let them know when I am scared. But certain things I keep inside. I try to solve it. If it's my department, I don't want them to be sad. If it be too bad, if I be scared of gettin' back on drugs, I'll go to the clinic. They have sessions every other night.

"Hardest time for me is night. Nightmares. Somethin's grabbin' at me. Like a hand. Some spirit's after me. It's somethin' that I don't forget. I wake up in a sweat. I'm wonderin' why I dream these dreams. So I get up, turn on the light. I don't go back to sleep until the day is breakin'. I look up an' I be sayin': 'Sun is up. Now I can go to sleep.'

"After the kids are up and they are dressed and go to school, then I lay down. I go to sleep. But I can't sleep at night. After the sun go down makes me depressed. I want to turn the light on, move around.

"Know that song—'Those Monday Blues'? I had that album once."

I say the title: " 'Monday Blues'?"

"I got 'em every day. Lots of times, when I'm in pain, I think I'm goin' to die. That's why I take a drink sometimes. I'm 'fraid to die. I'm wonderin': Am I dying?"

ACTIVE READING

1. Kozol quotes the historian Michael Ignatieff, who argues that people can be unequal in "their rights to judge others" (356). Find some exam-

ples of judgment in this essay, and try to determine which kinds carry special weight for Kozol. Working with the examples you find, try to explain what Ignatieff means.

2. What relationship do you see between what happens to Rachel and her children, on the one hand, and their understanding of those events, on the other? At what points does the relationship between "experience" and "belief" become confusing for them? What does this confusion say to you?

3. As a parent, Rachel is concerned with keeping her children free from various kinds of contamination. Find examples of this concern in Kozol's essay. What do these examples suggest about Rachel's values? about the experience of homelessness? What relationship do you see between Rachel's experience and her values?

READING IN NEW CONTEXTS

1. Rachel says that her children are treated like "cattle" who are "owned by welfare" (362). Once you have collected a few passages that clarify Rachel's meaning, look at Baldwin's, Brody's, and / or Ewen's discussions of "ownership." Based on your reading of these texts, discuss some kinds of ownership that might improve the situation of Rachel and her family, as well as some kinds that might make their situation worse.

2. What does Kozol accomplish by making Rachel's words—her "voice"—the focus of his essay? Study another *Literacies* text that is structured around people's "voices" (try MacLeod or de Saint Victor). How does each writer's use of "voice" contribute to your understanding of his or her text?

3. Rachel professes a religious faith that is complicated by her experiences of poverty and homelessness. How do hooks & West, Baldwin, or Rosaldo help you to talk about the role of faith in Rachel's life?

DRAFT ONE/DRAFT TWO

1. *Draft One:* In the beginning of this text, Kozol insists that "parental love cannot be synthesized" (355). List passages in which Rachel's words or actions express her love for her children. How do Rachel's

expressions of parental love compare with those you received as a child, or now give as a parent? Use your comparison to compose your own theory of what counts as "authentic" love and what counts as "synthetic" love. With this theory, assess Rachel's love for her children and evaluate Kozol's claim that parental love cannot be synthesized.

Draft Two: What is familiar about the discussions of parenthood you find in el-Saadawi, Sanders, or Shanley? What seems strange? Use your ideas about parenthood from Draft One and your responses to a second *Literacies* text to explore the social factors that contribute to people's beliefs about appropriate parenting.

2. *Draft One:* Kozol mentions "policies that undermine the competence and ingenuity" of people in Rachel's position (356). Find examples from his text that help you define what it might mean to be competent as well as what it might mean to be undermined. Based on your reading of Kozol's essay, suggest some policies that would support, rather than undermine, the competence of people like Rachel.

Draft Two: How well do the policies you developed in your first draft apply to the subjects of Bettelheim's, Brody's, or Garson's essays? For those policies that do apply, explain how the issues of competence in Kozol's and the other essay are similar. For those that do not apply, develop additional policies and explain why you think they are appropriate. What can you conclude about the difficulties and satisfactions of policy-making?

BEFORE READING AUDRE LORDE

1. Recall a time when you saw someone being treated unfairly. What did you do? If you chose not to intervene, how did you feel later?

2. What are some social factors that make it difficult to express anger? Discuss some possible consequences of expressing anger and of holding it back.

3. How might being in the audience for a lecture be different from reading a transcript of the speaker's words? Explain some positive and negative aspects of each option.

AUDRE LORDE

THE USES OF ANGER: WOMEN RESPONDING TO RACISM

Racism. The belief in the inherent superiority of one race over all others and thereby the right to dominance, manifest and implied.

Women respond to racism. My response to racism is anger. I have lived with that anger, ignoring it, feeding upon it, learning to use it before it laid my visions to waste, for most of my life. Once I did it in silence, afraid of the weight. My fear of anger taught me nothing. Your fear of that anger will teach you nothing, also.

Women responding to racism means women responding to anger; the anger of exclusion, of unquestioned privilege, of racial distortions, of silence, ill-use, stereotyping, defensiveness, misnaming, betrayal, and co-optation.

My anger is a response to racist attitudes and to the actions and presumptions that arise out of those attitudes. If your dealings with other women reflect those attitudes, then my anger and your attendant fears are spotlights that can be used for growth in the same way I have used learning to express anger for my growth. But for corrective surgery, not guilt. Guilt and defensiveness are bricks in a wall against which we all flounder; they serve none of our futures.

From *Sister Outsider* (1984).

369

Because I do not want this to become a theoretical discussion, I am going to give a few examples of interchanges between women that illustrate these points. In the interest of time, I am going to cut them short. I want you to know there were many more.

For example:

- I speak out of direct and particular anger at an academic conference, and a white woman says, "Tell me how you feel but don't say it too harshly or I cannot hear you." But is it my manner that keeps her from hearing, or the threat of a message that her life may change?
- The Women's Studies Program of a southern university invites a Black woman to read following a week-long forum on Black and white women. "What has this week given to you?" I ask. The most vocal white woman says, "I think I've gotten a lot. I feel Black women really understand me a lot better now; they have a better idea of where I'm coming from." As if understanding her lay at the core of the racist problem.
- After fifteen years of a women's movement which professes to address the life concerns and possible futures of all women, I still hear, on campus after campus, "How can we address the issues of racism? No women of Color attended." Or, the other side of that statement, "We have no one in our department equipped to teach their work." In other words, racism is a Black women's problem, a problem of women of Color, and only we can discuss it.
- After I read from my work entitled "Poems for Women in Rage,"* a white woman asks me: "Are you going to do anything with how we can deal directly with *our* anger? I feel it's so important." I ask, "How do you use *your* rage?" And then I have to turn away from the blank look in her eyes, before she can invite me to participate in her own annihilation. I do not exist to feel her anger for her.
- White women are beginning to examine their relationships to Black women, yet often I hear them wanting only to deal with little colored children across the roads of childhood, the beloved nursemaid, the occasional second-grade classmate—those tender memories of what was once mysterious and intriguing or neutral. You avoid the childhood assumptions formed by the raucous laughter at Rastus and Alfalfa, the acute message of your mommy's handkerchief spread upon the park

---

*One poem from this series is included in *Chosen Poems: Old and New* (W. W. Norton and Company, New York, 1978), pp. 105–108.

bench because I had just been sitting there, the indelible and dehu-manizing portraits of Amos 'n' Andy and your daddy's humorous bed-time stories.

- I wheel my two-year-old daughter in a shopping cart through a super-market in Eastchester in 1967, and a little white girl riding past in her mother's cart calls out excitedly, "Oh look, Mommy, a baby maid!" And your mother shushes you, but she does not correct you. And so fifteen years later, at a conference on racism, you can still find that story humorous. But I hear your laughter is full of terror and dis-ease.
- A white academic welcomes the appearance of a collection by non-Black women of Color.* "It allows me to deal with racism without dealing with the harshness of Black women," she says to me.
- At an international cultural gathering of women, a well-known white american woman poet interrupts the reading of the work of women of Color to read her own poem, and then dashes off to an "important panel."

If women in the academy truly want a dialogue about racism, it will require recognizing the needs and the living contexts of other women. When an academic woman says, "I can't afford it," she may mean she is making a choice about how to spend her available money. But when a woman on welfare says, "I can't afford it," she means she is surviving on an amount of money that was barely subsistence in 1972, and she often does not have enough to eat. Yet the National Women's Studies Association here in 1981 holds a conference in which it commits itself to responding to racism, yet refuses to waive the registration fee for poor women and women of Color who wished to be present and conduct workshops. This has made it impossible for many women of Color—for instance, Wilmette Brown, of Black Women for Wages for Housework—to participate in this conference. Is this to be merely another case of the academy discussing life within the closed circuits of the academy?

To the white women present who recognize these attitudes as famil-iar, but most of all, to all my sisters of Color who live and survive thou-sands of such encounters—to my sisters of Color who like me still tremble their rage under harness, or who sometimes question the expression of our rage as useless and disruptive (the two most popular accusations)—I

---

* This Bridge Called My Back: Writings by Radical Women of Color, edited by Cherríe Moraga and Gloria Anzaldúa (Kitchen Table: Women of Color Press, New York, 1984), first published in 1981.

want to speak about anger, my anger, and what I have learned from my travels through its dominions.

Everything can be used / except what is wasteful / (you will need / to remember this when you are accused of destruction.) *

Every woman has a well-stocked arsenal of anger potentially useful against those oppressions, personal and institutional, which brought that anger into being. Focused with precision it can become a powerful source of energy serving progress and change. And when I speak of change, I do not mean a simple switch of positions or a temporary lessening of tensions, nor the ability to smile or feel good. I am speaking of a basic and radical alteration in those assumptions underlying our lives.

I have seen situations where white women hear a racist remark, resent what has been said, become filled with fury, and remain silent because they are afraid. That unexpressed anger lies within them like an undetonated device, usually to be hurled at the first woman of Color who talks about racism.

But anger expressed and translated into action in the service of our vision and our future is a liberating and strengthening act of clarification, for it is in the painful process of this translation that we identify who are our allies with whom we have grave differences, and who are our genuine enemies.

Anger is loaded with information and energy. When I speak of women of Color, I do not only mean Black women. The woman of Color who is not Black and who charges me with rendering her invisible by assuming that her struggles with racism are identical with my own has something to tell me that I had better learn from, lest we both waste ourselves fighting the truths between us. If I participate, knowingly or otherwise, in my sister's oppression and she calls me on it, to answer her anger with my own only blankets the substance of our exchange with reaction. It wastes energy. And yes, it is very difficult to stand still and to listen to another woman's voice delineate an agony I do not share, or one to which I myself have contributed.

In this place we speak removed from the more blatant reminders of our embattlement as women. This need not blind us to the size and complexities of the forces mounting against us and all that is most human within our environment. We are not here as women examining racism in

---

* From "For Each of You," first published in *From a Land Where Other People Live* (Broadside Press, Detroit, 1973), and collected in *Chosen Poems: Old and New* (W. W. Norton and Company, New York, 1982), p. 42.

a political and social vacuum. We operate in the teeth of a system for which racism and sexism are primary, established, and necessary props of profit. Women responding to racism is a topic so dangerous that when the local media attempt to discredit this conference they choose to focus upon the provision of lesbian housing as a diversionary device—as if the Hartford *Courant* dare not mention the topic chosen for discussion here, racism, lest it become apparent that women are in fact attempting to examine and to alter all the repressive conditions of our lives.

Mainstream communication does not want women, particularly white women, responding to racism. It wants racism to be accepted as an immutable given in the fabric of your existence, like eveningtime or the common cold.

So we are working in a context of opposition and threat, the cause of which is certainly not the angers which lie between us, but rather that virulent hatred leveled against all women, people of Color, lesbians and gay men, poor people—against all of us who are seeking to examine the particulars of our lives as we resist our oppressions, moving toward coalition and effective action.

Any discussion among women about racism must include the recognition and the use of anger. This discussion must be direct and creative because it is crucial. We cannot allow our fear of anger to deflect us nor seduce us into settling for anything less than the hard work of excavating honesty; we must be quite serious about the choice of this topic and the angers entwined within it because, rest assured, our opponents are quite serious about their hatred of us and of what we are trying to do here.

And while we scrutinize the often painful face of each other's anger, please remember that it is not our anger which makes me caution you to lock your doors at night and not to wander the streets of Hartford alone. It is the hatred which lurks in those streets, that urge to destroy us all if we truly work for change rather than merely indulge in academic rhetoric.

This hatred and our anger are very different. Hatred is the fury of those who do not share our goals, and its object is death and destruction. Anger is a grief of distortions between peers, and its object is change. But our time is getting shorter. We have been raised to view any difference other than sex as a reason for destruction, and for Black women and white women to face each other's angers without denial or immobility or silence or guilt is in itself a heretical and generative idea. It implies peers meeting upon a common basis to examine difference, and to alter those distortions which history has created around our difference. For it is those distortions which separate us. And we must ask ourselves: Who profits from all this?

Women of Color in america have grown up within a symphony of anger, at being silenced, at being unchosen, at knowing that when we survive, it is in spite of a world that takes for granted our lack of humanness, and which hates our very existence outside of its service. And I say *symphony* rather than *cacophony* because we have had to learn to orchestrate those furies so that they do not tear us apart. We have had to learn to move through them and use them for strength and force and insight within our daily lives. Those of us who did not learn this difficult lesson did not survive. And part of my anger is always libation for my fallen sisters.

Anger is an appropriate reaction to racist attitudes, as is fury when the actions arising from those attitudes do not change. To those women here who fear the anger of women of Color more than their own unscrutinized racist attitudes, I ask: Is the anger of women of Color more threatening than the woman-hatred that tinges all aspects of our lives?

It is not the anger of other women that will destroy us but our refusals to stand still, to listen to its rhythms, to learn within it, to move beyond the manner of presentation to the substance, to tap that anger as an important source of empowerment.

I cannot hide my anger to spare you guilt, nor hurt feelings, nor answering anger; for to do so insults and trivializes all our efforts. Guilt is not a response to anger; it is a response to one's own actions or lack of action. If it leads to change then it can be useful, since it is then no longer guilt but the beginning of knowledge. Yet all too often, guilt is just another name for impotence, for defensiveness destructive of communication; it becomes a device to protect ignorance and the continuation of things the way they are, the ultimate protection for changelessness.

Most women have not developed tools for facing anger constructively. CR groups in the past, largely white, dealt with how to express anger, usually at the world of men. And these groups were made up of white women who shared the terms of their oppressions. There was usually little attempt to articulate the genuine differences between women, such as those of race, color, age, class, and sexual identity. There was no apparent need at that time to examine the contradictions of self, woman as oppressor. There was work on expressing anger, but very little on anger directed against each other. No tools were developed to deal with other women's anger except to avoid it, deflect it, or flee from it under a blanket of guilt.

I have no creative use for guilt, yours or my own. Guilt is only another way of avoiding informed action, of buying time out of the pressing need to make clear choices, out of the approaching storm that can feed the earth as well as bend the trees. If I speak to you in anger, at least I have spoken to you: I have not put a gun to your head and shot you down in the street; I have not looked at your bleeding sister's body and asked, "What did she do to deserve it?" This was the reaction of two white women to Mary Church Terrell's telling of the lynching of a pregnant Black woman whose baby was then torn from her body. That was in 1921, and Alice Paul had just refused to publicly endorse the enforcement of the Nineteenth Amendment for all women—by refusing to endorse the inclusion of women of Color, although we had worked to help bring about that amendment.

The angers between women will not kill us if we can articulate them with precision, if we listen to the content of what is said with at least as much intensity as we defend ourselves against the manner of saying. When we turn from anger we turn from insight, saying we will accept only the designs already known, deadly and safely familiar. I have tried to learn my anger's usefulness to me, as well as its limitations.

For women raised to fear, too often anger threatens annihilation. In the male construct of brute force, we were taught that our lives depended upon the good will of patriarchal power. The anger of others was to be avoided at all costs because there was nothing to be learned from it but pain, a judgment that we had been bad girls, come up lacking, not done what we were supposed to do. And if we accept our powerlessness, then of course any anger can destroy us.

But the strength of women lies in recognizing differences between us as creative, and in standing to those distortions which we inherited without blame, but which are now ours to alter. The angers of women can transform difference through insight into power. For anger between peers births change, not destruction, and the discomfort and sense of loss it often causes is not fatal, but a sign of growth.

My response to racism is anger. That anger has eaten clefts into my living only when it remained unspoken, useless to anyone. It has also served me in classrooms without light or learning, where the work and history of Black women was less than a vapor. It has served me as fire in the ice zone of uncomprehending eyes of white women who see in my experience and the experience of my people only new reasons for fear or guilt. And my anger is no excuse for not dealing with your blindness, no reason to withdraw from the results of your own actions.

When women of Color speak out of the anger that laces so many of our contacts with white women, we are often told that we are "creating a mood of hopelessness," "preventing white women from getting past guilt," or "standing in the way of trusting communication and action." All these quotes come directly from letters to me from members of this organization within the last two years. One woman wrote, "Because you are Black and Lesbian, you seem to speak with the moral authority of suffering." Yes, I am Black and Lesbian, and what you hear in my voice is fury, not suffering. Anger, not moral authority. There is a difference.

To turn aside from the anger of Black women with excuses or the pretexts of intimidation is to award no one power—it is merely another way of preserving racial blindness, the power of unaddressed privilege, unbreached, intact. Guilt is only another form of objectification. Oppressed peoples are always being asked to stretch a little more, to bridge the gap between blindness and humanity. Black women are expected to use our anger only in the service of other people's salvation or learning. But that time is over. My anger has meant pain to me but it has also meant survival, and before I give it up I'm going to be sure that there is something at least as powerful to replace it on the road to clarity.

What woman here is so enamoured of her own oppression that she cannot see her heelprint upon another woman's face? What woman's terms of oppression have become precious and necessary to her as a ticket into the fold of the righteous, away from the cold winds of self-scrutiny?

I am a lesbian woman of Color whose children eat regularly because I work in a university. If their full bellies make me fail to recognize my commonality with a woman of Color whose children do not eat because she cannot find work, or who has no children because her insides are rotted from home abortions and sterilization; if I fail to recognize the lesbian who chooses not to have children, the woman who remains closeted because her homophobic community is her only life support, the woman who chooses silence instead of another death, the woman who is terrified lest my anger trigger the explosion of hers; if I fail to recognize them as other faces of myself, then I am contributing not only to each of their oppressions but also to my own, and the anger which stands between us then must be used for clarity and mutual empowerment, not for evasion by guilt or for further separation. I am not free while any woman is unfree, even when her shackles are very different from my own. And I am not free as long as one person of Color remains chained. Nor is any one of you.

I speak here as a woman of Color who is bent not upon destruction but upon survival. No woman is responsible for altering the psyche of her oppressor, even when that psyche is embodied in another woman. I have suckled the wolf's lip of anger and I have used it for illumination, laughter, protection, fire in places where there was no light, no food, no sisters, no quarter. We are not goddesses or matriarchs or edifices of divine forgiveness; we are not fiery fingers of judgment or instruments of flagellation; we are women forced back always upon our woman's power. We have learned to use anger as we have learned to use the dead flesh of animals, and bruised, battered, and changing, we have survived and grown and, in Angela Wilson's words, we *are* moving on. With or without uncolored women. We use whatever strengths we have fought for, including anger, to help define and fashion a world where all our sisters can grow, where our children can love, and where the power of touching and meeting another woman's difference and wonder will eventually transcend the need for destruction.

For it is not the anger of Black women which is dripping down over this globe like a diseased liquid. It is not my anger that launches rockets, spends over sixty thousand dollars a second on missiles and other agents of war and death, slaughters children in cities, stockpiles nerve gas and chemical bombs, sodomizes our daughters and our earth. It is not the anger of Black women which corrodes into blind, dehumanizing power, bent upon the annihilation of us all unless we meet it with what we have, our power to examine and to redefine the terms upon which we will live and work; our power to envision and to reconstruct, anger by painful anger, stone upon heavy stone, a future of pollinating difference and the earth to support our choices.

We welcome all women who can meet us, face to face, beyond objectification and beyond guilt.

ACTIVE READING

1. In her first sentence, Lorde mentions "manifest and implied" forms of "dominance." Which passages from her essay help you to distinguish between these two kinds of dominance? In terms of Lorde's arguments, why might it be important to note the difference?

2. Lorde speaks of the importance of acknowledging the sources of one's anger. In your reading of her essay, where do you feel anger? Discuss

some moments where your anger pushes you away from the points Lorde is making and some places where your anger brings you closer to her perspectives. Based on what you discover, explain what you think are the "uses of anger" in Lorde's essay.

3. Lorde, who may be best known as a poet, frequently uses images of startling intensity in her writing. Find several of these images and "translate" them, first into more everyday language, then into an intense image of your own. What does this kind of translation teach you about Lorde's strategies as a writer?

READING IN NEW CONTEXTS

1. How does Lorde's call for "excavating honesty" (373) relate to Scheper-Hughes's or Seidler's attempts to create honesty in their own lives? Explain how each writer's personal and professional social position shapes the kinds of honesty they strive for in their relationships with others.

2. Lorde states that she does "not want this to become a theoretical discussion" (370). Why not? Look at a more explicitly "theoretical" discussion of women's experience, like el-Saadawi's or Shanley's, and determine how much and what kind of common ground this "theoretical" writer shares with Lorde.

3. Like other writers, Lorde often clarifies her ideas by using anecdotes. Examine the ways that Lorde and another writer (perhaps Atwood, Bettelheim, or Tan) use anecdotal evidence. Working with your readings of these essays, generate a theory about the benefits and limitations of this kind of evidence.

DRAFT ONE / DRAFT TWO

1. *Draft One:* Lorde claims that universities frequently exclude members of certain groups from activities and processes that could benefit the community as a whole. Based on your roles as a student and community member, describe what you think is the appropriate relationship between the university and the community within which it exists.

Draft Two: What resources do nonacademics have for understanding academic writing? How can they use such writing for their own purposes? Compose your answers to these questions with your observations from Draft One and some ideas from Anzaldúa, Durham, or Scheper-Hughes.

2. *Draft One:* Lorde emphasizes the need to distinguish between "allies with whom we have grave differences" and "genuine enemies" (372). Who are some "allies with whom [you] have grave differences," both in your personal life and in your understanding of current events and social trends? What goals could these differences keep you and your "allies" from achieving?

Draft Two: Look at Sanders, Sontag, or another *Literacies* writer who sorts "allies" from "enemies." Use this writer's ideas to help you explain why, when it comes to the experiences you describe in Draft One, an ally can sometimes appear to be an enemy.

BEFORE READING ALISTAIR MACLEOD

1. Talk about some of the issues that you expect to encounter in stories or films about young adults. What kinds of issues would you *not* expect to see explored in such narratives? Why not?

2. Why do you think young people choose to leave or remain in their family homes? How much of this decision can be traced to individual personality traits (timidness, love of adventure, etc.)? How much is related to social factors like gender, class, or geography?

3. Explain how your view of your grandparents (or other older relatives) contributes to the way you look at your own parents. What are some of the important continuities you see between your grandparents' and parents' lives? between their lives and your own?

ALISTAIR MACLEOD

THE VASTNESS OF THE DARK

On the twenty-eighth day of June, 1960, which is the planned day of my deliverance, I awake at exactly six A.M. to find myself on my eighteenth birthday, listening to the ringing of the bells from the Catholic church which I now attend only reluctantly on Sundays. "Well," I say to the bells and to myself, "at least tomorrow I will be free of you." And yet I do not move but lie quietly for a while looking up and through the window at the green poplar leaves rustling softly and easily in the Nova Scotian dawn.

The reason that I do not arise immediately on such a momentous day is partially due, at least, to a second sound that is very unlike the regular, majestic booming of the bells. It is the irregular and moistly rat-tling-rasping sound of my father's snoring which comes from the adjoining room. And although I can only hear him I can see very vividly in my mind how he must be: lying there on his back with his thinning iron-grey hair tousled upon the pillow and with his hollow cheeks and even his jet-black eyebrows rising and falling slightly with the erratic pattern of his breathing. His mouth is slightly open and there are little bubbles of saliva forming and breaking at its corners, and his left arm and perhaps even his

From *The Lost Salt Gift of Blood* (1976).

left leg are hanging over the bed's edge and resting upon the floor. It seems, with his arm and leg like that, as if he were prepared within his sleeping consciousness for any kind of unexpected emergency that might arise; so that if and when it does he will only have to roll slightly to his left and straighten and be immediately standing. Half of his body already touches the floor in readiness.

In our home no one gets up before he does; but in a little while, I think, that too will happen. He will sort of gasp in a strangled way and the snoring will cease. Then there will be a few stealthy movements and the ill-fitting door will open and close and he will come walking through my room carrying his shoes in his left hand while at the same time trying to support his trousers and also to button and buckle them with his right. As long as I can remember he has finished dressing while walking but he does not handle buttons nor buckles so well since the dynamite stick at the little mine where he used to work ripped the first two fingers from his scarred right hand. Now the remaining fingers try to do what is expected of them: to hold, to button, to buckle, to adjust, but they do so with what seems a sort of groping uncertainty bordering on despair. As if they realized that there is now just too much for them to do even though they try as best they can.

When he comes through this room he will be walking softly so as not to awaken me and I will close my eyes and do my imitation of sleep so that he will think himself successful. After he has gone downstairs to start the fire there will be a pause and perhaps a few exploratory coughs exchanged between my mother and me in an unworded attempt to decide who is going to make the next move. If I cough it will indicate that I am awake and usually that means I will get up next and follow the route of my father downstairs. If, on the other hand, I make no sound, in a few minutes my mother also will come walking through my room. As she passes I will close my eyes a second time but I have always the feeling that it does not work for her; that unlike my father she can tell the difference between sleep which is real and that which is feigned. And I feel always dishonest about my deception. But today, I think, it will be the last time, and I want both of them down the stairs before I myself descend. For today I have private things to do which can only be done in the brief interval between the descent of my parents and the rising of my seven younger brothers and sisters.

Those brothers and sisters are now sleeping in a very different world across the hallway in two large rooms called generally "the girls' room" and "the boys' room." In the former there are my sisters and their names and ages are: Mary, 15, Judy, 14, Catherine, 12, and Bernadette, 3. In the other there are Daniel, 9, Harvey, 7, and David, 5. They live there, across the hall, in an alien but sociable world of half-suppressed giggles, impromptu pantomimes and muffled-silent pillow fights and fall to sleep in beds filled with oft-exchanged comic books and the crumbs of smuggled cookies. On "our" side of the hall it is very different. There is only one door for the two rooms and my parents, as I have said, have always to walk through my room to get to theirs. It is not a very good arrangement and at one time my father intended to cut another door from the hallway into their room and to close off the inadequate connecting door between their room and mine. But at one time he also probably planned to seal and cover the wooden beams and ribs that support the roof in all our rooms and he has not done that either. On the very coldest winter mornings you can look up and see the frost on the icy heads of the silver nails and see your breath in the coldly crystal air.

Sleeping over here on this side of the hall I have always felt very adult and separated from my younger brothers and sisters and their muffled worlds of laughter. I suppose it has something to do with the fact that I am the oldest by three years and circumstances have made me more alone. At one time each of us has slept in a crib in my parents' room and as I was the first I was not moved very far—only into the next room. Perhaps they kept me close because they were more nervous about me, and for a longer time, as they had not had much experience at that time with babies or younger children. So I have been here in this bed all by myself for as long as I can remember. The next three in our family are girls and I am separated from Daniel, the nearest boy, by an unbridgeable abyss of nine years. And by that time it seems my parents felt there was no point in either moving him in with me or me across the hall with him, as if they had somehow gotten used to hearing me breathing in the room so close to theirs and knew that I knew a great deal about them and about their habits and had been kind of backed into trusting me as if I were, perhaps, a younger brother or perhaps more intimately a friend. It is a strange and lonely thing to lie awake at night and listen to your parents making love in the next room and to be able even to count the strokes. And to know that they really do not know how much you know, but to know that they do know that you know; and not to know when the knowledge of your knowing came to them any more than they know when it came to you. And during these last four or five years lying here while the waves of embarrassed horniness roll over me, I have developed, apart from the problems of my own tumescent flesh, a sort of sympathy for the problem that must be theirs and for the awful violation of privacy that all of us represent. For it must be a very difficult thing for two people to try to have a sex life together when they know that the first product of that life is lying listening to them only a few feet away. Also, I know something else that I do not think they know I know.

I was told it by my paternal grandfather seven years ago when I was ten and he was eighty, on a spring day when, warmed by the sun, he had gone downtown and sat in a tavern most of the afternoon, drinking beer and spitting on the floor and slapping the table and his knee with the palm of his hand, his head wreathed in the pipe smoke of the mine-mutilated old men who were his friends. And as I passed the tavern's open door with my bag of papers he had hailed me as if I were some miniature taxi-cab and had said that he wished to go home. And so we had wended our way through the side streets and the back alleys, a small slightly embarrassed boy and a staggering but surprisingly erect old man who wanted me beside him but not to physically support him as that would hurt his pride.

"I am perfectly capable of walking home by myself, James," he said, looking down at me off the tip of his nose and over his walrus moustache, "no one is taking me home, I only want company. So you stay over on your side and I will stay on mine and we will just be friends going for a walk as indeed we are."

But then we had turned into an alley where he had placed his left arm against a building's brick wall and leaned, half-resting, his forehead against it while his right hand fumbled at his fly. And standing there with his head against the wall and with his shoes two feet from its base he had seemed like some strange, speaking hypotenuse from the geometry books at school and standing in the steam of his urine he had mumbled into the wall that he loved me, although he didn't often say so, and that he had loved me even before I was born.

"You know," he said, "when I learned that your mother was knocked up I was so happy I was just ashamed. And my wife was in a rage and your mother's parents were weeping and wringing their silly hands and whenever I was near them I would walk around looking at my shoes. But I think that, God forgive me, I may have even prayed for something like that and when I heard it I said, 'Well he will have to stay now and marry her because that's the kind of man he is, and he will work in my place now just as I've always wanted.' "

Then his forehead seemed to slide off his resting arm and he lurched unsteadily, almost bumping into me and seeming to see me for the first time. "Oh God," he said with a startled, frightened expression, "what a selfish old fool! What have I done now? Forget everything I said!" And he had squeezed my shoulder too tightly at first but then relaxed his grip and let his gigantic hand lie there limply all the way to his home. As soon as he entered his door, he flopped into the nearest chair and said almost on the verge of tears, "I think I told him. I think I told him." And my grandmother who was ten years younger turned on him in alarm but only asked, "What?" and he, raising both hands off his lap and letting them fall back in a sort of helpless gesture of despair said, "Oh you know, you know," as if he were very much afraid.

"Go on home James," she said to me evenly and kindly although I knew she was very angry, "and pay no attention to this old fool. He has never in all his life known when to open and close his pants or his mouth." As I turned to leave, I noticed for the first time that he had not redone his trousers after urinating in the alley and that his underwear was awry.

No one has ever mentioned it since but because one of my grandparents was so frightened and the other so angry I know that it is true because they do not react that strongly to anything that is not real. And knowing so I have never checked it further. And it is strange too with this added knowledge to lie in bed at night and to hear the actual beginnings of your brother and sisters, to almost share in it in an odd way and to know that you did not begin really in that same way or at least not in that bed. And I have imagined the back seats of the old cars I've seen in pictures, or the grassy hills behind the now torn-down dance halls or the beaches of sand beside the sea. I like to think somehow that it had been different for them at my conception and that there had been joy instead of grim release. But I suppose we, all of us, like to think of ourselves as children of love rather than of necessity. That we have come about because there was a feeling of peace and well-being before the erection rather than its being the other way around. But of course I may be as wrong about that as I am about many things and perhaps I do not know what they feel now anymore than what they might have felt then.

But after today, I will probably not have to think about it anymore. For today I leave behind this grimy Cape Breton coal-mining town whose prisoner I have been for all of my life. And I have decided that almost any place must be better than this one with its worn-out mines and smoke-black houses; and the feeling has been building within me for the last few years. It seems to have come almost with the first waves of sexual desire and with it to have grown stronger and stronger with the passing months and years. For I must not become as my father whom I now hear banging the stove-lids below me as if there were some desperate rush about it all and some place that he must be in a very short time. Only to go nowhere. And I must not be as my grandfather who is now an almost senile old man, nearing ninety, who sits by the window all day saying his prayers and who in his moments of clarity remembers mostly his conquests over coal, and recounts tales of how straight were the timbers he and my father erected in the now caved-in underground drifts of twenty-five years ago when he was sixty-two and my father twenty-five and I not yet conceived.

It is a long, long time since my grandfather has worked and all the big mines he worked in and which he so romanticizes now are closed. And my father has not worked since early March, and his presence in a house where he does not want to be breeds a tension in us all that is heightened now since school is closed and we are all home and forced in upon ourselves. And as he moves about on this morning, banging stove-lids, pretending it is important that he does so, that he is wanted some-where soon and therefore must make this noisy rush, I feel myself sepa-rated from him by a wide and variegated gulf and very far away from the man, who, shortly after he became my father, would take me for rides upon his shoulders to buy ice-cream at the drugstore, to see the baseball games I did not understand, or into the open fields to pat the pit-horses and be placed upon their broad and gentle backs. As we would approach the horses he would speak softly to them so that they might know where we were and be unafraid when he finally placed his hand upon them, for all of them were blind. They had been so long in the darkness of the mine that their eyes did not know the light, and the darkness of their labour had become that of their lives.

But now my father does not do such things with his younger children even as he no longer works. And he is older and greyer and apart from the missing fingers on his right hand, there is a scar from a broken bit that begins at his hairline and runs like violent lightning down the right side of his face and at night I can hear him coughing and wheezing from the rock dust on his lungs. And perhaps that coughing means that because he has worked in bad mines with bad air these last few years he will not live so very much longer. And perhaps my brothers and sisters across the hall will never hear him, when they are eighteen, rattling the stove-lids as I do now.

And as I lie here now on my back for the last time, I think of when I lay on my stomach in the underground for the first time with him there beside me in the small bootleg mine which ran beneath the sea and in which he had been working since the previous January. I had joined him at the end of the school year for a few short weeks before the little mine finally closed and I had been rather surprisingly proud to work there and my grandfather in one of his clearer moments said, "Once you start it takes a hold of you, once you drink underground water, you will always come back to drink some more. The water gets in your blood. It is in all of our blood. We have been working in the mines here since 1873."

The little mine paid very low wages and was poorly equipped and ventilated and since it was itself illegal there were no safety regulations. And I had thought, that first day, that I might die as we lay on our stomachs on the broken shale and on the lumps of coal while the water seeped around us and into us and chilled us with unflagging constancy whenever we ceased our mole-like movements. It was a very narrow little seam that we attacked, first with our drilling steels and bits, and then with our dynamite, and finally with our picks and shovels. And there was scarcely thirty-six inches of headroom where we sprawled, my father shovelling over his shoulders like the machine he had almost become while I tried to do what I was told and to be unafraid of the roof coming in or of the rats that brushed my face, or of the water that numbed my legs, my stomach and my testicles or of the fact that at times I could not breathe because the powder-heavy air was so foul and had been breathed before.

And I was aware once of the whistling wind of movement beside me and over me and saw by the light of my lamp the gigantic pipe-wrench of my father describing an arc over me and landing with a squealing crunch an arm's length before me; and then I saw the rat, lying on its back and inches from my eyes. Its head was splattered on the coal and on the wrench and it was still squeaking while a dying stream of yellow urine trickled down between its convulsively jerking legs. And then my father released the wrench and seizing the not quite dead rat by the tail hurled it savagely back over his shoulder so that the thud of its body could be heard behind us as it bounced off the wall and then splashed into the water. "You dirty son of a bitch," he said between clenched teeth and wiped the back of the wrench against the rocky wall. And we lay there then for a while without moving, chilled together in the dampness and the dark.

And now, strangely enough, I do not know if that is what I hate and so must leave, or if it is the fact that now there is not even that mine, awful as it was, to go to, and perhaps it is better to have a place to go to that you hate than to have no place at all. And it is the latter which makes my father now increasingly tense and nervous because he has always used his body as if it were a car with its accelerator always to the floor and now as it becomes more scarred and wasted, he can only use it for sex or taut too-rapid walks along the seashore or back into the hills; and when everything else fails he will try to numb himself with rum and his friends will bring him home in the evenings and dump him with his legs buckling beneath him, inside his kitchen door. And my mother and I will half carry and half drag him through the dining room to the base of the stairs and up the fourteen steps, counting them to ourselves, one by one. We do not always get that far; once he drove his left fist through the glass of the dining room window and I wrestled with him back and forth across the floor while the wildly swinging and still-clenched fist flashed and flecked its scarlet blood upon the floor and the wallpaper and the curtains and the dishes and the foolish sad dolls and colouring books and *Great Expectations* which lay upon the table. And when he was subdued and the fist became a hand we had to ask him politely to clench it again so that the wounds would reopen while the screaming iodine was poured over and into them and the tweezers probed for the flashing slivers of glass. And we had prayed then, he included, that no tendons were damaged and that no infection would set in because it was the only good hand that he had and all of us rode upon it as perilous passengers on an unpredictably violent sea.

Sometimes when he drinks so heavily my mother and I cannot always get him to his bed and leave him instead on mine, trying to undress him as best we can, amidst his flailing arms and legs and shouted obscenities, hoping at least to get his shoes, and loosen his collar and belt and trousers. And during the nights that follow such days I lie rigid beside him, trying to overcome the nausea caused by the sticky, sweet stench of the rum and listening to the sleep-talker's mumbled, incoherent words, his uneven snoring, and the frightening catches in his breathing caused by the phlegm within his throat. Sometimes he will swing out unexpectedly with either hand and once his forearm landed across my nose with such force that the blood and tears welled to the surface simultaneously and I had to stuff the bedclothes into my mouth to stifle the cry that rose upon my lips.

But yet it seems that all storms subside first into gusts and then into calm and perhaps without storms and gusts we might never have any calm, or perhaps having it we would not recognize it for what it is; and so when he awakens at one or two A.M. and lies there quietly in the dark it is the most peaceful of all times, like the quiet of the sea, and it is only then that I catch glimpses of the man who took me for the rides upon his

shoulders. And I arise and go down the stairs as silently as I can, through
the sleeping house, and fetch the milk which soothes the thickness of his
tongue and the parched and fevered dryness of his throat and he says
"Thank you," and that he is sorry, and I say that it is all right and that
there is really nothing to be sorry for. And he says that he is sorry that he
has acted the way he has and that he is sorry he has been able to give me
so little but if he cannot give he will try very hard not to take. And that I
am free and owe my parents nothing. That in itself is perhaps quite a lot
to give, for many people like myself go to work very young here or did
when there was work to go to and not everyone gets into high school or
out of it. And perhaps even the completion of high school is the gift that
he has given me along with that of life.

But that is also now ended, I think, the life here and the high school
and the thought jolts me into the realization that I have somehow been
half-dozing, for although I think I clearly remember everything, my
mother has obviously already passed through this room for now I hear her
moving about downstairs preparing breakfast. I am rather grateful that at
least I have not had to pretend to be asleep on this the last of all these
days.

Moving now as quickly as I can, I remove from beneath the mattress
the battered old packsack that was my father's in earlier, younger days.
"Would it be all right if I use that old packsack sometime?" I had asked
as casually as possible some months before, trying to make my plans for
it sound like some weary camping expedition. "Sure," he had said in an
even non-committal fashion.

Now I pack it quietly, checking with my ball-point pen the items that
I have listed on the back of the envelope kept beneath my pillow. Four
pairs of underwear, five pairs of socks, two pairs of pants, four shirts, one
towel, some handkerchiefs, a gabardine jacket, a plastic raincoat and a
shaving set. The latter is the only item that is new and unused and is the
cheapest that Gillette manufactures. Up until this time I have always used
my father's razor which is battered and verdigris green from years of use.
I have used it for some years now—more often, at times, than my questionable beard demanded.

As I move down the stairs there is still no movement from the two
larger rooms across the hall and for this I am most grateful. I do not really
know how to say good-bye as I have never before said it to anyone and
because I am uncertain I wish to say it now to as few as possible. Who
knows, though, perhaps I may even be rather good at it. I lay the packsack
down on the second stair from the bottom where it is not awfully visible

and walk into the kitchen. My mother is busy at her stove and my father is standing with his back to the room looking through the window over a view of slate-grey slag heaps and ruined skeletal mine tipples and out toward the rolling sea. They are not greatly surprised to see me as it is often like this, just the three of us in the quiet early morning. But today I cannot afford to be casual and I must say what must be said in the short space of time occupied by only the three of us. "I think I'll go away today," I say, trying to sound as offhand as possible. Only a slight change in the rhythm of my mother's poking at the stove indicates that she has heard me, and my father still stands looking through the window out to sea. "I think I'll go right now," I add, my voice sort of trailing off, "before the others get up it will be easier that way."

My mother moves the kettle, which has started to boil, toward the back of the stove, as if stalling for time, then she turns and says, "Where will you go? To Blind River?"

Her response is so little like that which I anticipated that I feel strangely numb. For I had somehow expected her to be greatly surprised, astounded, astonished, and she is none of these. And her mention of Blind River, the centre of Northern Ontario's uranium mines, is something and someplace that I had never even thought of. It is as if my mother had not only known that I was to leave but had even planned my route and final destination. I am reminded of my reading in school of the way Charles Dickens felt about the blacking factory and his mother's being so fully in favour of it. In favour of a life for him which he considered so terrible and so far beneath his imagined destiny.

My father turns from the window and says, "You are only eighteen today, perhaps you could wait awhile. Something might turn up." But within his eyes I see no strong commitment to his words and I know he feels that waiting is at best weary and at worst hopeless. This also makes me somehow rather disappointed and angry as I had thought somehow my parents would cling to me in a kind of desperate fashion and I would have to be very firm and strong.

"What is there to wait for?" I say, asking a question that is useless and to which I know the all too obvious answer. "Why do you want me to stay here?"

"You misunderstand," says my father, "you are free to go if you want to. We are not forcing you or asking you to do anything. I am only saying that you do not *have* to go now."

But suddenly it becomes very important that I *do* go now, because it seems things cannot help but get worse. So I say, "Good-bye. I will write

but it will not be from Blind River." I add the last as an almost unconscious little gibe at my mother.

I go and retrieve my packsack and then pass back through the house,
out the door and even through the little gate. My parents follow me to
the gate. My mother says, "I was planning a cake for today . . ." and then
stops uncertainly, her sentence left hanging in the early morning air. She
is trying to make amends for her earlier statement and rather desperately
gropes her way back to the fact of my birthday. My father says, "Perhaps
you should go over home. They may not be there if and when you come
again."

It is but a half block to "over home," the house of my father's parents,
who have always been there as long as I can remember and who have
always provided a sort of haven for all of us through all our little storms
and my father's statement that they will not be there forever is an intima-
tion of something that I have never really considered before. So now I
move with a sort of apprehension over the ashes and cinder-filled pot-
holes of the tired street toward the old house blackened with the coal dust
of generations. It is as yet hardly seven A.M. and it is as if I am some early
morning milkman moving from one house to another to leave good-byes
instead of bottles beside such quiet doors.

Inside my grandparents' house, my grandfather sits puffing his pipe
by the window, while passing the beads of his rosary through fingers
which are gnarled and have been broken more times than he can remember. He has been going deaf for some time and he does not turn his head
when the door closes behind me. I decide that I will not start with him
because it will mean shouting and repetition and I am not sure I will be
able to handle that. My grandmother, like my mother, is busy at her stove.
She is tall and white-haired and although approaching eighty she is still
physically imposing. She has powerful, almost masculine hands and has
always been a big-boned person without ever having been heavy or ever
having any difficulty with her legs. She still moves swiftly and easily and
her eyesight and hearing are perfect.

"I am going away today," I say as simply as I can.

She pokes with renewed energy at her stove and then answers: "It is
just as well. There is nothing for one to do here anyway. There was never
anything for one to do here."

She has always spoken with the Gaelic inflection of her youth and
in that detached third-person form which I had long ago suggested that
she modernize.

"Come here James," she says and takes me into her pantry, where with surprising agility she climbs up on a chair and takes from the cupboard's top shelf a huge cracked and ancient sugar bowl. Within it there are dusty picture postcards, some faded yellow payslips which seem ready to disintegrate at the touch, and two yellowed letters tied together with a shoelace. The locations on the payslips and on the postcards leap at me across a gulf of dust and years: Springhill, Scranton, Wilkes-Barre, Yellowknife, Britannia Beach, Butte, Virginia City, Escanaba, Sudbury, Whitehorse, Drumheller, Harlan, Ky., Elkins, W. Va., Fernie, B.C., Trinidad, Colo.—coal and gold, copper and lead, gold and iron, nickel and gold and coal. East and West and North and South. Mementoes and messages from places that I so young and my grandmother so old have never seen.

"Your father was under the ground in all those places," she says half-angrily, "the same way he was under the ground here before he left and under it after he came back. It seems we will be underground long enough when we are dead without seeking it out while we are still alive."

"But still," she says after a quiet pause and in a sober tone, "it was what he was good at and wanted to do. It was just not what I wanted him to do, or at least I did not want him to do it here."

She unties the shoelace and shows me the two letters. The first is dated March 12, 1938, and addressed General Delivery, Kellogg, Idaho: "I am getting old now and I would like very much if you would come back and take my working place at the mine. The seam is good for years yet. No one has been killed for some time now. It is getting better. The weather is mild and we are all fine. Don't bother writing. Just come. We will be waiting for you. Your fond father."

The second bears the same date and is also addressed General Delivery, Kellogg, Idaho: "Don't listen to him. If you return here you will never get out and this is no place to lead one's life. They say the seam will be finished in another few years. Love, Mother."

I have never seen my grandfather's handwriting before and for some reason, although I knew he read, I had always thought him unable to write. Perhaps, I think now, it is because his hands have been so broken and misshapen; and with increasing age, hard to control for such a fine task as writing.

The letters are written with the same broad-nibbed pen in an ink which is of a blackness that I have never seen and somehow these letters now seem like a strangely old and incompatible married couple, each cancelling out the other's desires while bound together by a single worn and dusty lace.

I go out of the pantry and to the window where my grandfather sits. "I am going away today," I shout, leaning over him.

"Oh yes," he says in a neutral tone of voice, while continuing to look out the window and finger his rosary. He does not move and the pipe smoke curls upward from his pipe which is clenched between his worn and strongly stained teeth. Lately he has taken to saying, "Oh yes," to almost everything as a means of concealing his deafness and now I do not know if he has really heard me or is merely giving what seems a standard and safe response to all of the things he hears but partially if at all. I do not feel that I can say it again without my voice breaking and so I turn away. At the door I find that he has shuffled behind me.

"Don't forget to come back James," he says, "it's the only way you'll be content. Once you drink underground water it becomes a part of you like the blood a man puts into a woman. It changes her forever and never goes away. There's always a part of him running there deep inside her. It's what will wake you up at night and never ever leave you alone."

Because he knows how much my grandmother is opposed to what he says he has tried to whisper to me. But he is so deaf that he can hardly hear his own voice and he has almost shouted in the way deaf people do; his voice seems to echo and bounce off the walls of his house and to escape out into the sunshot morning air. I offer him my hand to shake and find it almost crushed in the crooked broken force of his. I can feel the awful power of his oddly misshapen fingers, his splayed and flattened too broad thumb, the ridges of the toughened, blackened scars and the abnormally large knobs that are his twisted misplaced knuckles. And I have a feeling for a terrible moment that I may never ever get away or be again released. But he finally relaxes and I feel that I am free.

Even pot-holed streets are lonely ones when you think you may not see them again for a very long time or perhaps forever. And I travel now mostly the back streets because I am conspicuous with my packsack and I do not want any more conversations or attempted and failed and futile explanations. At the outskirts of the town a coal truck stops for me and we travel for twenty-five miles along the shoreline of the sea. The truck makes so much noise and rides so roughly that conversation with the driver is impossible and I am very grateful for the noisy silence in which we are encased.

By noon after a succession of short rides in a series of oddly assorted vehicles I am finally across the Strait of Canso, off Cape Breton Island and at last upon my way. It is only when I have left the Island that I can feel free to assume my new identity which I don like carefully preserved new clothes taken from within their pristine wrappings. It assumes that I am from Vancouver which is as far away as I can imagine.

I have been somehow apprehensive about even getting off Cape Breton Island, as if at the last moment it might extend gigantic tentacles, or huge monstrous hands like my grandfather's to seize and hold me back. Now as I finally set foot on the mainland I look across at the heightened mount that is Cape Breton now, rising mistily out of the greenness and the white-capped blueness of the sea.

My first ride on the mainland is offered by three Negroes in a battered blue Dodge pickup truck that bears the information "Rayfield Clyke, Lincolnville, N.S., Light Trucking" on its side. They say they are going the approximately eighty miles to New Glasgow and will take me if I wish. They will not go very fast, they say, because their truck is old and I might get a better ride if I choose to wait. On the other hand, the driver says, I will at least be moving and I will get there sooner or later. Anytime I am sick of it and want to stop I can bang on the roof of the cab. They would take me in the cab but it is illegal to have four men in the cab of a commercial vehicle and they do not want any trouble with the police. I climb into the back and sit on the worn spare tire and the truck moves on. By now the sun is fairly high and when I remove the packsack from my shoulders I can feel although I cannot see the two broad bands of perspiration traced and crossing upon my back. I realize now that I am very hungry and have eaten nothing since last evening's supper.

In New Glasgow I am let off at a small gas station and my Negro benefactors point out the shortest route to the western outskirts of the town. It leads through cluttered back streets where the scent of the greasy hamburgers reeks out of the doors of the little lunch-counters with their overloud juke-boxes; simultaneously pushing Elvis Presley and the rancid odours of the badly cooked food through the half open doors. I would like to stop but somehow there is a desperate sense of urgency now as if each of the cars on the one-way street is bound for a magical destination and I feel that should I stop for even a moment's hamburger I might miss the one ride that is worthwhile. The sweat is running down my forehead now and stings my eyes and I know the two dark patches of perspiration upon my back and beneath the straps are very wide.

The sun seems at its highest when the heavy red car pulls over to the highway's gravelled shoulder and its driver leans over to unlock the door on the passenger side. He is a very heavy man of about fifty with a red perspiring face and a brown cowlick of hair plastered down upon his damply glistening forehead. His coat is thrown across the back of the seat and his shirt pocket contains one of those plastic shields bristling with pens and pencils. The collar of the shirt is open and his tie is loosened and awry; his belt is also undone, as is the button at the waistband of his trousers. His pants are grey and although stretched tautly over his enormous thighs they still appear as damply wrinkled. Through his white shirt the sweat is showing darkly under his armpits and also in large blotches on his back which are visible when he leans forward. His hands seem very white and disproportionately small.

As we move off down the shimmering highway with its mesmerizing white line, he takes a soiled handkerchief that has been lying on the seat beside him and wipes the wet palms of his hands and also the glistening wet blackness of the steering wheel.

"Boy, it sure is hot," he says, "hotter'n a whore in hell."

"Yes," I say, "it sure is. It really is."

"Dirty little town back there," he says, "you can spend a week there just driving through."

"Yes, it isn't much."

"Just travelling through?"

"Yes, I'm going back to Vancouver."

"You got a whole lot of road ahead of you boy, a whole lot of road. I never been to Vancouver, never west of Toronto. Been trying to get my company to send me west for a long while now but they always send me down here. Three or four times a year. Weather's always miserable. Hotter'n hell like this here or in the winter cold enough to freeze the balls off a brass monkey." He beats out a salvo of hornblasts at a teenage girl who is standing uncertainly by the roadside.

Although the windows of the car are open, it is very hot and the redness of the car seems to intensify the feeling and sense of heat. All afternoon the road curves and winds ahead of us like a bucking, shimmering snake with a dirty white streak running down its back. We seem to ride its dips and bends like captive passengers on a roller-coaster, leaning our bodies into the curves, and bracing our feet against the tension of the floorboards. My stomach vanishes as we hurtle into the sudden unexpected troughs and returns as quickly as we emerge to continue our twists and turns. Insects ping and splatter against the windshield and are transformed into yellow splotches. The tires hiss on the superheated asphalt and seem almost to leave tracks. I can feel my clothes sticking to me, to my legs and thighs and back. On my companion's shirt the blotches of sweat are larger and more plentiful. Leaning his neck and shoulders back against the seat he lifts his heavy body from the sweat-stained upholstery and thrusts his right hand through his opened trousers and deep into his crotch. "Let a little air in there," he says, as he manoeuvres his genitals, "must be an Indian made this underwear, it keeps creeping up on me."

All afternoon as we travel we talk or rather he talks and I listen which I really do not mind. I have never really met anyone like him before. The talk is of his business (so much salary, so much commission plus other 'deals' on the side), of his boss (a dumb bastard who is lucky he has good men on the road), of his family (a wife, one son and one daughter, one of each is enough), of sex (he can't get enough of it and will be after it until he dies), of Toronto (it is getting bigger every day and it is not like it used to be), of taxes (they keep getting higher and it doesn't pay a man to keep up his property, also too many Federal giveaways). He goes on and on. I have never listened to anyone like him before. He seems so confident and sure of everything. It is as if he knows that he knows everything and is on top of everything and he seems never to have to hesitate nor stop nor run down nor even to think; as if he were a juke-box fed from some mysterious source by an inexhaustible supply of nickels, dimes and quarters.

The towns and villages and train stations speed by. Fast and hot; Truro, Glenholme and Wentworth and Oxford. We are almost out of Nova Scotia with scarcely thirty miles of it ahead according to my companion. We are almost at the New Brunswick border. I am again in a stage of something like exhausted relief as I approach yet another boundary over which I can escape and leave so much behind. It is the feeling I originally had on leaving Cape Breton only now it has been heavied and dulled by the journey of the day. For it has been long and hot and exhausting.

Suddenly the road veers to the left and no longer hooks and curves but extends up and away from us into a long, long hill, the top of which we can see almost a half mile away. Houses appear on either side as we begin the climb and then there are more and more of them strung out loosely along the road.

My companion blasts out a rhythm of hornblasts at a young girl and her mother who are stretching up on their tiptoes to hang some washing on a clothesline. There is a basket of newly washed clothes on the ground between them and their hands are busy on the line. They have some clothespins in their teeth so they will not have to bend to reach them and lose their handhold on the line.

"If I had my way, they'd have something better'n that in their mouths," he says, "wouldn't mind resting my balls on the young one's chin for the second round."

He has been looking at them quite closely and the car's tires rattle in the roadside gravel before he pulls it back to the quiet of the pavement.

The houses are closer together now and more blackened and the yards are filled with children and bicycles and dogs. As we move toward what seems to be the main intersection I am aware of the hurrying women in their kerchiefs, and the boys with their bags of papers and baseball gloves and the men sitting or squatting on their heels in tight little compact knots. There are other men who neither sit nor squat but lean against the buildings or rest upon canes or crutches or stand awkwardly on artificial limbs. They are the old and the crippled. The faces of all of them are gaunt and sallow as if they had been allowed to see the sun only recently, when it was already too late for it to do them any good.

"Springhill is a hell of a place," says the man beside me, "unless you want to get laid. It's one of the best there is for that. Lots of mine accidents here and the men killed off. Women used to getting it all the time. Mining towns are always like this. Look at all the kids. This here little province of Nova Scotia leads the country in illegitimacy. They don't give a damn."

The mention of the name Springhill and the realization that this is where I have come is more of a shock than I would ever have imagined. As if in spite of signposts and geography and knowing it was "there," I have never thought of it as ever being "here."

And I remember November 1956: the old cars, mud-splattered by the land and rusted by the moisture of the sea, parked outside our house with their motors running. Waiting for the all-night journey to Springhill which seemed to me then, in my fourteenth year, so very far away and more a name than even a place. Waiting for the lunches my mother packed in wax paper and in newspaper and the thermos bottles of coffee and tea, and waiting for my father and the same packsack which now on this sweating day accompanies me. Only then it was filled with the miners' clothes he would need for the rescue that they hoped they might perform. The permanently blackened underwear, the heavy woollen socks, the boots with the steel-reinforced toes, the blackened, sweat-stained miner's belt which sagged on the side that carried his lamp, the crescent wrench, the dried and dustied water-bag, trousers and gloves and the hard hat chipped and dented and broken by the years of falling rock.

And all of that night my grandfather with his best ear held to the tiny radio for news of the buried men and of their rescuers. And at school the teachers taking up collections in all of the class-rooms and writing in large letters on the blackboard, "Springhill Miners' Relief Fund, Springhill, N.S." which was where we were sending the money, and I remember also my sisters' reluctance at giving up their hoarded nickels, dimes and quarters because noble causes and death do not mean very much when you are eleven, ten and eight and it is difficult to comprehend how children you have never known may never see their fathers any more, not walking through the door nor perhaps even being carried through the door in the heavy coffins for the last and final look. Other people's buried fathers are very strange and far away but licorice and movie matinees are very close and real.

"Yeah," says the voice beside me, "I was in here six months ago and got this little, round woman. Really giving it to her, pumping away and all of a sudden she starts kind of crying and calling me by this guy's name I never heard of. Must have been her dead husband or something. Kind of scared the hell out of me. Felt like a goddamn ghost or something. Almost lost my rod. Might have too but I was almost ready to shoot it into her."

We are downtown now and it is late afternoon in the period before the coming of the evening. The sun is no longer as fierce as it was earlier and it slants off the blackened buildings, many of which are shells bleak and firegutted and austere. A Negro woman with two lightskinned little boys crosses the street before us. She is carrying a bag of groceries and the little boys have each an opened sixteen-ounce bottle of Pepsi-Cola. They put their hands over the bottles' mouths and shake them vigorously to make the contents fizz.

"Lots of people around here marry niggers," says the voice. "Guess they're so black underground they can't tell the difference in the light. All the same in the dark as the fellow says. Had an explosion here a few years ago and some guys trapped down there, I dunno how long. Eaten the lunches of the dead guys and the bark off the timbers and drinking one another's piss. Some guy in Georgia offered the ones they got out a trip down there but there was a nigger in the bunch so he said he couldn't take him. Then the rest wouldn't go. Damned if I'd lose a trip to Georgia because of a single nigger that worked for the same company. Like I say, I'm old enough to be your father or even your grandfather and I haven't even been to Vancouver."

It is 1958 that he is talking about now and it is much clearer in my mind than 1956 which is perhaps the difference between being fourteen and sixteen when something happens in your life. A series of facts or near facts that I did not even realize I possessed flash now in succession upon my mind: the explosion in 1958 occurred on a Thursday as did the one in 1956; Cumberland No. 2 at the time of the explosion was the deepest coal mine in North America; in 1891, 125 men were killed in that same mine; that 174 men went down to work that 1958 evening; that most were feared lost; that 18 were found alive after being buried beneath 1,000 tons of rock for more than a week; that Cumberland No. 2 once employed 900 men and now employs none.

And I remember again the cars before our house with their motors running, and the lunches and the equipment and the waiting of the week: the school collections, my grandfather with his radio, this time the added reality of a T.V. at a neighbour's house; and the quietness of our muted lives, our footsteps without sound. And then the return of my father and the haunted greyness of his face and after the younger children were in bed the quiet and hushed conversations of seeping gas and lack of oxygen and the wild and belching smoke and flames of the subterranean fires nourished there by the everlasting seams of the dark and diamond coal. And also of the finding of the remains of men flattened and crushed if they had died beneath the downrushing roofs of rock or if they had been blown apart by the explosion itself, transformed into forever lost and irredeemable pieces of themselves; hands and feet and blown-away faces and reproductive organs and severed ropes of intestines festooning the twisted pipes and spikes like grotesque Christmas-tree loops and chunks of hair-clinging flesh. Men transformed into grisly jig-saw puzzles that could never more be solved.

"I don't know what the people do around here now," says the voice at my side. "They should get out and work like the rest of us. The Government tries to resettle them but they won't stay in a place like Toronto. They always come back to their graveyards like dogs around a bitch in heat. They have no guts."

The red car has stopped now before what I am sure is this small town's only drugstore. "Maybe we'll stop here for a while," he says. "I've just about had it and need something else. All work and no play, you know. I'm going in here for a minute first to try my luck. As the fellow says, an ounce of prevention beats a pound of cure."

As he closes the door he says, "Maybe later you'd like to come along. There's always some left over."

The reality of where I am and of what I think he is going to do seems now to press down upon me as if it were the pressure of the caving-in roof which was so recently within my thoughts. Although it is still hot I roll up the windows of the car. The people on the street regard me casually in this car of too bright red which bears Ontario licence plates. And I recognize now upon their faces a look that I have seen upon my grandfather's face and on the faces of hundreds of the people from my past and even on my own when seeing it reflected from the mirrors and windows of such a car as this. For it is as if I am not part of their lives at all but am only here in a sort of movable red and glass showcase, that has come for a while to their private anguish-ridden streets and will soon roll on and leave them the same as before my coming; part of a movement that passes through their lives but does not really touch them. Like flotsam on yet another uninteresting river which flows through their permanent banks and is bound for some invisible destination around a bend where they have never been and cannot go. Their glances have summed me up and dismissed me as casually as that. "What can he know of our near deaths and pain and who lies buried in our graves?"

And I am overwhelmed now by the awfulness of oversimplification. For I realize that not only have I been guilty of it through this long and burning day but also through most of my yet young life and it is only now that I am doubly its victim that I begin vaguely to understand. For I had somehow thought that "going away" was but a physical thing. And that it had only to do with movement and with labels like the silly "Vancouver" that I had glibly rolled from off my tongue; or with the crossing of bodies of water or with the boundaries of borders. And because my father had told me I was "free" I had foolishly felt that it was really so. Just like that. And I realize now that the older people of my past are more complicated than perhaps I had ever thought. And that there are distinctions between my sentimental, romantic grandfather and his love for coal, and my stern and practical grandmother and her hatred of it; and my quietly strong but passive mother and the soaring extremes of my father's passionate violence and the quiet power of his love. They are all so different. But yet they have somehow endured and given me the only life I know for all these eighteen years. Their lives flowing into mine and mine from out of theirs. Different but somehow more similar than I had ever thought. Perhaps it is possible I think now to be both and yet to see only the one. For the man in whose glassed-in car I now sit sees only similarity. For him the people of this multi-scarred little town are reduced to but a few phrases and the act of sexual intercourse. They are only so many identical goldfish leading identical, incomprehensible lives within the glass prison of their bowl. And the people on the street view me behind my own glass in much the same way and it is the way that I have looked at others in their "foreign licence" cars and it is the kind of judgement that I myself have made.

And yet it seems that neither these people nor this man are in any way unkind and not to understand does not necessarily mean that one is cruel. But one should at least be honest. And perhaps I have tried too hard to be someone else without realizing at first what I presently am. I do not know. I am not sure. But I do know that I cannot follow this man into a house that is so much like the one I have left this morning and go down into the sexual embrace of a woman who might well be my mother. And I do not know what she, my mother, may be like in the years to come when she is deprived of the lightning movement of my father's body and the hammered pounding of his heart. For I do not know when he may die. And I do not know in what darkness she may then cry out his name nor to whom. I do not know very much of anything, it seems, except that I have been wrong and dishonest with others and myself. And perhaps this man has left footprints on a soul I did not even know that I possessed.

It is dark now on the outskirts of Springhill when the car's headlights pick me up in their advancing beams. It pulls over to the side and I get into its back seat. I have trouble closing the door behind me because there is no handle so I pull on the crank that is used for the window. I am afraid that even it may come off in my hand. There are two men in the front seat and I can see only the outlines of the backs of their heads and I cannot tell very much about them. The man in the back seat beside me is not awfully visible either. He is tall and lean but from what I see of his face it is difficult to tell whether he is thirty or fifty. There are two sacks of miner's gear on the floor at his feet and I put my sack there too because there isn't any other place.

"Where are you from?" he asks as the car moves forward. "From Cape Breton," I say and tell him the name of my home.

"We are too," he says, "but we're from the Island's other side. I guess the mines are pretty well finished where you're from. They're the old ones. They're playing out where we're from too. Where are you going now?"

"I don't know," I say, "I don't know."

"We're going to Blind River," he says. "If it doesn't work there we hear they've found uranium in Colorado and are getting ready to start sinking shafts. We might try that, but this is an old car and we don't think it'll make it to Colorado. You're welcome to come along with us though if you want. We'll carry you for a while."

"I don't know," I say, "I don't know. I'll have to think about it. I'll have to make up my mind."

The car moves forward into the night. Its headlights seek out and follow the beckoning white line which seems to lift and draw us forward, upward and inward, forever into the vastness of the dark.

"I guess your people have been on the coal over there for a long time?" asks the voice beside me.

"Yes," I say, "since 1873."

"Son of a bitch," he says, after a pause, "it seems to bust your balls and it's bound to break your heart."

ACTIVE READING

1. Near the beginning of this story, James decides that "we . . . like to think of ourselves as children of love rather than necessity" (385). Find some passages that support his desire to see himself as a child of love and some that point to the role of necessity in his identity. How does MacLeod use the tension between love and necessity in this text? Why do you think this might be an important question?

2. Using your response to the last question as a model, analyze some of the other oppositions—like light/dark, female/male, or ignorance/knowledge—that this story presents. How do such oppositions contribute to the meanings you find in MacLeod's text?

3. On the road, James and the driver of the red car encounter the same people and objects, but they do so through very different eyes. Working closely with some of the driver's comments and with James's reactions (spoken or unspoken), try to determine what each one is "seeing" and why. What do the differences between their perspectives have to do with the ending of the story?

READING IN NEW CONTEXTS

1. Make a catalog of all the places where James mentions reading or writing. With the help of Heath's or Fishman's essays, compose your own theory about the uses of literacy in James's community.

2. Describe your reaction to the ending of MacLeod's story: Do you find it satisfying? surprising? ambiguous? (Your response to Active Reading #3 may help here.) Looking at the conclusions of this story and one or two others—Angelou, Heker, and Walker are possibilities—speculate about how different kinds of endings might affect your interpretation of each text. You might even try rewriting each ending.

3. Several writers in *Literacies*, including Baldwin, Bettelheim, and Kozol, explore the resources people may have for escaping difficult or even life-threatening circumstances. After reading one or two of these texts, use some of their ideas about "escape" to evaluate James's attempt to leave home.

DRAFT ONE / DRAFT TWO

1. *Draft One:* James notes that his father is "increasingly tense and nervous because he has always used his body as if it were a car with its accelerator always to the floor" (387–88). Use MacLeod's story and your memories of your own father or another male relative to explore the specific pressures experienced by men in your culture. How do James's observations about his father, his grandfather, and himself compare with your own understanding of male identity?

   Draft Two: Working with Seidler's essay and your own first draft, write about some social, economic, and cultural changes that you think might improve men's lives. What effects would these changes have on women?

2. *Draft One:* What kinds of boundaries (besides the geographical kind) do you see being crossed in MacLeod's text? Write about as many "boundary crossings" as you can find in this story, and speculate about their significance.

   Draft Two: In "No Name Woman," Maxine Hong Kingston writes that her aunt "crossed boundaries not delineated in space" (345). How do the boundaries you analyzed in your first draft relate to those that Kingston or another writer describes?

BEFORE READING ADRIENNE RICH

1. Page through Rich's "Notes" and observe the unusual features of its format. How will you read an essay presented in this way? Why do you think an author might choose this format?

2. In your experience, under what circumstances do people lie? How do you define a "white lie"? When would you pardon a lie and why?

3. Do men and women tend to talk differently about matters of importance? Describe some examples you have encountered, and explain any patterns you see in them.

4. Describe a situation when someone remained silent instead of telling an unpleasant truth. Who was in control of the situation? How do you evaluate the ethics of that event?

WOMEN AND HONOR:
SOME NOTES ON LYING

(These notes are concerned with relationships between and among women. When "personal relationship" is referred to, I mean a relationship between two women. It will be clear in what follows when I am talking about women's relationships with men.)

The old, male idea of honor. A man's "word" sufficed—to other men—without guarantee.

"Our Land Free, Our Men Honest, Our Women Fruitful"—a popular colonial toast in America.

Male honor also having something to do with killing: *I could not love thee, Dear, so much / Lov'd I not Honour more*, ("To Lucasta, On Going to the Wars"). Male honor as something needing to be avenged: hence, the duel.

Women's honor, something altogether else: virginity, chastity, fidelity to a husband. Honesty in women has not been considered important. We

From *On Lies, Secrets, and Silence: Selected Prose, 1966–1978* (1979).

405

have been depicted as generically whimsical, deceitful, subtle, vacillating. And we have been rewarded for lying.

Men have been expected to tell the truth about facts, not about feelings. They have not been expected to talk about feelings at all.

Yet even about facts they have continually lied.

We assume that politicians are without honor. We read their statements trying to crack the code. The scandals of their politics: not that men in high places lie, only that they do so with such indifference, so endlessly, still expecting to be believed. We are accustomed to the contempt inherent in the political lie.

———————

To discover that one has been lied to in a personal relationship, however, leads one to feel a little crazy.

———————

Lying is done with words, and also with silence.

The woman who tells lies in her personal relationships may or may not plan or invent her lying. She may not even think of what she is doing in a calculated way.

A subject is raised which the liar wishes buried. She has to go downstairs, her parking meter will have run out. Or, there is a telephone call she ought to have made an hour ago.

She is asked, point-blank, a question which may lead into painful talk: "How do you feel about what is happening between us?" Instead of trying to describe her feelings in their ambiguity and confusion, she asks, "How do *you* feel?" The other, because she is trying to establish a ground of openness and trust, begins describing her own feelings. Thus the liar learns more than she tells.

And she may also tell herself a lie: that she is concerned with the other's feelings, not with her own.

But the liar is concerned with her own feelings.

The liar lives in fear of losing control. She cannot even desire a relationship without manipulation, since to be vulnerable to another person means for her the loss of control.

The liar has many friends, and leads an existence of great loneliness.

———————

The liar often suffers from amnesia. Amnesia is the silence of the unconscious.

To lie habitually, as a way of life, is to lose contact with the unconscious. It is like taking sleeping pills, which confer sleep but blot out dreaming. The unconscious wants truth. It ceases to speak to those who want something else more than truth.

In speaking of lies, we come inevitably to the subject of truth. There is nothing simple or easy about this idea. There is no "the truth," "a truth"—truth is not one thing, or even a system. It is an increasing complexity. The pattern of the carpet is a surface. When we look closely, or when we become weavers, we learn of the tiny multiple threads unseen in the overall pattern, the knots on the underside of the carpet.

This is why the effort to speak honestly is so important. Lies are usually attempts to make everything simpler—for the liar—than it really is, or ought to be.

In lying to others we end up lying to ourselves. We deny the importance of an event, or a person, and thus deprive ourselves of a part of our lives. Or we use one piece of the past or present to screen out another. Thus we lose faith even with our own lives.

The unconscious wants truth, as the body does. The complexity and fecundity of dreams come from the complexity and fecundity of the unconscious struggling to fulfill that desire. The complexity and fecundity of poetry come from the same struggle.

———————

An honorable human relationship—that is, one in which two people have the right to use the word "love"—is a process, delicate, violent, often terrifying to both persons involved, a process of refining the truths they can tell each other.

It is important to do this because it breaks down human self-delusion and isolation.

It is important to do this because in so doing we do justice to our own complexity.

It is important to do this because we can count on so few people to go that hard way with us.

———————

I come back to the questions of women's honor. Truthfulness has not been considered important for women, as long as we have remained physically faithful to a man, or chaste.

We have been expected to lie with our bodies: to bleach, redden, unkink or curl our hair, pluck eyebrows, shave armpits, wear padding in various places or lace ourselves, take little steps, glaze finger and toe nails, wear clothes that emphasized our helplessness.

We have been required to tell different lies at different times, depending on what the men of the time needed to hear. The Victorian wife or the white southern lady, who were expected to have no sensuality, to "lie still"; the twentieth-century "free" woman who is expected to fake orgasms.

We have had the truth of our bodies withheld from us or distorted; we have been kept in ignorance of our most intimate places. Our instincts have been punished: clitoridectomies for "lustful" nuns or for "difficult" wives. It has been difficult, too, to know the lies of our complicity from the lies we believed.

The lie of the "happy marriage," of domesticity—we have been complicit, have acted out the fiction of a well-lived life, until the day we testify in court of rapes, beatings, psychic cruelties, public and private humiliations.

Patriarchal lying has manipulated women both through falsehood and through silence. Facts we needed have been withheld from us. False witness has been borne against us.

And so we must take seriously the question of truthfulness between women, truthfulness among women. As we cease to lie with our bodies, as we cease to take on faith what men have said about us, is a truly womanly idea of honor in the making?

———————————

Women have been forced to lie, for survival, to men. How to unlearn this among other women?

"Women have always lied to each other."
"Women have always whispered the truth to each other."
Both of these axioms are true.

"Women have always been divided against each other."
"Women have always been in secret collusion."
Both of these axioms are true.

In the struggle for survival we tell lies. To bosses, to prison guards, the police, men who have power over us, who legally own us and our children, lovers who need us as proof of their manhood.

There is a danger run by all powerless people: that we forget we are lying, or that lying becomes a weapon we carry over into relationships with people who do not have power over us.

———————————

I want to reiterate that when we talk about women and honor, or women and lying, we speak within the context of male lying, the lies of the powerful, the lie as false source of power.

Women have to think whether we want, in our relationships with each other, the kind of power that can be obtained through lying.

Women have been driven mad, "gaslighted," for centuries by the refutation of our experience and our instincts in a culture which validates only male experience. The truth of our bodies and our minds has been mystified to us. We therefore have a primary obligation to each other: not to undermine each others' sense of reality for the sake of expediency; not to gaslight each other.

Women have often felt insane when cleaving to the truth of our experience. Our future depends on the sanity of each of us, and we have a profound stake, beyond the personal, in the project of describing our reality as candidly and fully as we can to each other.

———————————

There are phrases which help us not to admit we are lying: "my privacy," "nobody's business but my own." The choices that underlie these phrases may indeed be justified; but we ought to think about the full meaning and consequences of such language.

Women's love for women has been represented almost entirely through silence and lies. The institution of heterosexuality has forced the lesbian to dissemble, or be labeled a pervert, a criminal, a sick or dangerous woman, etc., etc. The lesbian, then, has often been forced to lie, like the prostitute or the married women.

Does a life "in the closet"—lying, perhaps of necessity, about ourselves to bosses, landlords, clients, colleagues, family, because the law and public opinion are founded on a lie—does this, can it, spread into private life, so that lying (described as *discretion*) becomes an easy way to avoid conflict or complication? can it become a strategy so ingrained that it is used even with close friends and lovers?

Heterosexuality as an institution has also drowned in silence the erotic feelings between women. I myself lived half a lifetime in the lie of that denial. That silence makes us all, to some degree, into liars.

When a woman tells the truth she is creating the possibility for more truth around her.

———————————

The liar leads an existence of unutterable loneliness.

The liar is afraid.

But we are all afraid: without fear we become manic, hubristic, self-destructive. What is this particular fear that possesses the liar?

She is afraid that her own truths are not good enough.

She is afraid, not so much of prison guards or bosses, but of something unnamed within her.

The liar fears the void.

The void is not something created by patriarchy, or racism, or capitalism. It will not fade away with any of them. It is part of every woman.

"The dark core," Virginia Woolf named it, writing of her mother. The dark core. It is beyond personality; beyond who loves us or hates us.

We begin out of the void, out of darkness and emptiness. It is part of the cycle understood by the old pagan religions, that materialism denies. Out of death, rebirth; out of nothing, something.

The void is the creatrix, the matrix. It is not mere hollowness and anarchy. But in women it has been identified with lovelessness, barrenness, sterility. We have been urged to fill our "emptiness" with children. We are not supposed to go down into the darkness of the core.

Yet, if we can risk it, the something born of that nothing is the beginning of our truth.

The liar in her terror wants to fill up the void, with anything. Her lies are a denial of her fear; a way of maintaining control.

———

Why do we feel slightly crazy when we realize we have been lied to in a relationship?

We take so much of the universe on trust. You tell me: "In 1950 I lived on the north side of Beacon Street in Somerville." You tell me: "She and I were lovers, but for months now we have only been good friends." You tell me: "It is seventy degrees outside and the sun is shining." Because I love you, because there is not even a question of lying between us, I take these accounts of the universe on trust: your address twenty-five years ago, your relationship with someone I know only by sight, this morning's weather. I fling unconscious tendrils of belief, like slender green threads, across statements such as these, statements made so unequivocally, which have no tone or shadow of tentativeness. I build them into the mosaic of my world. I allow my universe to change in minute, significant ways, on the basis of things you have said to me, of my trust in you.

I also have faith that you are telling me things it is important I should know; that you do not conceal facts from me in an effort to spare me, or yourself, pain.

Or, at the very least, that you will say, "There are things I am not telling you."

When we discover that someone we trusted can be trusted no longer, it forces us to reexamine the universe, to question the whole instinct and concept of trust. For awhile, we are thrust back onto some bleak, jutting ledge, in a dark pierced by sheets of fire, swept by sheets of rain, in a world before kinship, or naming, or tenderness exist; we are brought close to formlessness.

The liar may resist confrontation, denying that she lied. Or she may use other language: forgetfulness, privacy, the protection of someone else. Or, she may bravely declare herself a coward. This allows her to go on lying, since that is what cowards do. She does not say, *I was afraid*, since this would open the question of other ways of handling her fear. It would open the question of what is actually feared.

She may say, *I didn't want to cause pain*. What she really did not want is to have to deal with the other's pain. The lie is a short-cut through another's personality.

Truthfulness, honor, is not something which springs ablaze of itself; it has to be created between people.

This is true in political situations. The quality and depth of the politics evolving from a group depends in very large part on their understanding of honor.

Much of what is narrowly termed "politics" seems to rest on a longing for certainty even at the cost of honesty, for an analysis which, once given, need not be reexamined. Such is the deadendedness—for women—of Marxism in our time.

Truthfulness anywhere means a heightened complexity. But it is a movement into evolution. Women are only beginning to uncover our own truths; many of us would be grateful for some rest in that struggle, would be glad just to lie down with the sherds we have painfully unearthed, and be satisfied with those. Often I feel this like an exhaustion in my own body.

The politics worth having, the relationships worth having, demand that we delve still deeper.

———————

The possibilities that exist between two people, or among a group of people, are a kind of alchemy. They are the most interesting thing in life. The liar is someone who keeps losing sight of these possibilities.

When relationships are determined by manipulation, by the need for control, they may possess a dreary, bickering kind of drama, but they cease to be interesting. They are repetitious; the shock of human possibilities has ceased to reverberate through them.

When someone tells me a piece of the truth which has been withheld from me, and which I needed in order to see my life more clearly, it may bring acute pain, but it can also flood me with a cold, sea-sharp wash of relief. Often such truths come by accident, or from strangers.

It isn't that to have an honorable relationship with you, I have to understand everything, or tell you everything at once, or that I can know, beforehand, everything I need to tell you.

It means that most of the time I am eager, longing for the possibility of telling you. That these possibilities may seem frightening, but not destructive, to me. That I feel strong enough to hear your tentative and groping words. That we both know we are trying, all the time, to extend the possibilities of truth between us.

The possibility of life between us.

ACTIVE READING

1. What relations do you see between the format of Rich's essay and the issues she explores in her writing? Choose a section where this relationship seems significant, and explain why you think so. Or outline the essay and explain how it is organized and why.

2. Trace Rich's concept of "truth" through several of her examples of lying. What do the different passages contribute to her understanding of the word?

3. Locate passages where Rich discusses some kind of force, control, or power. Explain how she sees these operating in everyday life.

4. After you have responded to Active Reading 1–3, talk about the connections you see among them and among the passages you used in your answers. How does Rich create the connections among her various topics?

READING IN NEW CONTEXTS

1. Rich writes that "it has been difficult . . . to know the lies of our complicity from the lies we believed" (408). Use passages from the essay to define "complicity," and then apply the concept to another *Literacies* text you have read this semester. What kinds of social relations create or support complicity?

2. Near the end of her essay, Rich argues that honor "has to be created between people" (412). Discuss Rich's ideas about honor in light of another *Literacies* text in which honor is an important issue, such as MacLeod or Gilmore. Explore the ways honor is created in different circumstances or cultures.

3. Compare several passages from Rich to a *Literacies* text about gender in another culture or social group, such as Gilmore or Kingston. Which of Rich's ideas adapt to that other culture most readily, and which do

not? What can you conclude about the ways in which cultural context shapes gender?

DRAFT ONE / DRAFT TWO

1. *Draft One:* Does your experience of gender roles support the ideas about truthfulness that Rich describes? Write an essay in which you show where and how you learned what it means for a woman or a man to be "truthful." How have these lessons about gender and honor helped to shape your current relationships with other people (both male and female)?

   Draft Two: Examine the concept of class, ethnicity, or some other social category (besides gender) in another *Literacies* text you have read. Reconsider the experiences you described in Draft One in light of that concept. In Draft Two, explore the ways a body of experience reveals different traits when viewed through the lenses of two social categories at once.

2. *Draft One:* Continue Rich's deliberations by picking a phrase or sentence about lying from her essay. Over the space of several days, compose your own "notes" about your chosen phrase or sentence. Use short daily writings to accumulate a variety of materials and try out the style and form of Rich's essay in an essay of your own.

   Draft Two: Use both your essay and Rich's essay as examples, and examine how you or people you know have or have not been able to accomplish some of the things Rich proposes: to "[break] down human self-delusion and isolation" (408), to "do justice to our own complexity" (408), and to "extend the possibility of truth between us" (413).

BEFORE READING RICHARD RODRIGUEZ

1. Explain some theories you have heard about how racial or ethnic background influences a person's achievements. Which theory (or theories) come closest to your own?

2. Briefly describe three or four strong memories from your childhood. What picture of your childhood do these combined memories create? What important aspects of your early experience are missing from this picture?

3. How did you form your understanding of "private" and "public"? Discuss some reasons why people choose to differentiate between private and public areas of experience, and then speculate about some social problems that this division might cause.

4. How do you define "power"? List as many kinds and examples of power as you can think of, and explain how you think they might relate to each other.

RICHARD RODRIGUEZ

COMPLEXION

Visiting the East Coast or the gray capitals of Europe during the long months of winter, I often meet people at deluxe hotels who comment on my complexion. (In such hotels it appears nowadays a mark of leisure and wealth to have a complexion like mine.) Have I been skiing? In the Swiss Alps? Have I just returned from a Caribbean vacation? No. I say no softly but in a firm voice that intends to explain: My complexion is dark. (My skin is brown. More exactly, terra-cotta in sunlight, tawny in shade. I do not redden in sunlight. Instead, my skin becomes progressively dark; the sun singes the flesh.)

When I was a boy the white summer sun of Sacramento would darken me so, my T-shirt would seem bleached against my slender dark arms. My mother would see me come up the front steps. She'd wait for the screen door to slam at my back. 'You look like a *negrito*,' she'd say, angry, sorry to be angry, frustrated almost to laughing, scorn. 'You know how important looks are in this country. With *los gringos* looks are all that they judge on. But you! Look at you! You're so careless!' Then she'd start in all over again. 'You won't be satisfied till you end up looking like *los pobres* who work in the fields, *los braceros*.'

From *Hunger of Memory* (1982).

417

(*Los braceros:* Those men who work with their *brazos*, their arms; Mexican nationals who were licensed to work for American farmers in the 1950s. They worked very hard for very little money, my father would tell me. And what money they earned they sent back to Mexico to support their families, my mother would add. *Los pobres*—the poor, the pitiful, the powerless ones. But paradoxically also powerful men. They were the men with brown-muscled arms I stared at in awe on Saturday mornings when they showed up downtown like gypsies to shop at Woolworth's or Penney's. On Monday nights they would gather hours early on the steps of the Memorial Auditorium for the wrestling matches. Passing by on my bicycle in summer, I would spy them there, clustered in small groups, talking—frightening and fascinating men—some wearing Texas *sombreros* and T-shirts which shone fluorescent in the twilight. I would sit forward in the back seat of our family's '48 Chevy to see them, working alongside Valley highways: dark men on an even horizon, loading a truck amid rows of straight green. Powerful, powerless men. Their fascinating darkness—like mine—to be feared.)

'You'll end up looking just like them.'

|

Regarding my family, I see faces that do not closely resemble my own. Like some other Mexican families, my family suggests Mexico's confused colonial past. Gathered around a table, we appear to be from separate continents. My father's face recalls faces I have seen in France. His complexion is white—he does not tan; he does not burn. Over the years, his dark wavy hair has grayed handsomely. But with time his face has sagged to a perpetual sigh. My mother, whose surname is inexplicably Irish—Moran—has an olive complexion. People have frequently wondered if, perhaps, she is Italian or Portuguese. And, in fact, she looks as though she could be from southern Europe. My mother's face has not aged as quickly as the rest of her body; it remains smooth and glowing—a cool tan—which her gray hair cleanly accentuates. My older brother has inherited her good looks. When he was a boy people would tell him that he looked like Mario Lanza, and hearing it he would smile with dimpled assurance. He would come home from high school with girl friends who seemed to me glamorous (because they were) blonds. And during those years I envied him his skin that burned red and peeled like the skin of the *gringos*. His complexion never darkened like mine. My youngest sister is exotically pale, almost ashen. She is delicately featured, Near Eastern, people have said. Only my older sister has a complexion as dark as mine, though her facial features are much less harshly defined than my own. To many people meeting her, she seems (they say) Polynesian. I am the only one in the family whose face is severely cut to the line of ancient Indian ancestors. My face is mournfully long, in the classical Indian manner; my profile suggests one of those beak-nosed Mayan sculptures—the eaglelike face upturned, open-mouthed, against the deserted, primitive sky.

'We are Mexicans,' my mother and father would say, and taught their four children to say whenever we (often) were asked about our ancestry. My mother and father scorned those 'white' Mexican-Americans who tried to pass themselves off as Spanish. My parents would never have thought of denying their ancestry. I never denied it: My ancestry is Mexican, I told strangers mechanically. But I never forgot that only my older sister's complexion was as dark as mine.

My older sister never spoke to me about her complexion when she was a girl. But I guessed that she found her dark skin a burden. I knew that she suffered for being a 'nigger.' As she came home from grammar school, little boys came up behind her and pushed her down to the sidewalk. In high school, she struggled in the adolescent competition for boyfriends in a world of football games and proms, a world where her looks were plainly uncommon. In college, she was afraid and scornful when dark-skinned foreign students from countries like Turkey and India found her attractive. She revealed her fear of dark skin to me only in adulthood when, regarding her own three children, she quietly admitted relief that they were all light.

That is the kind of remark women in my family have often made before. As a boy, I'd stay in the kitchen (never seeming to attract any notice), listening while my aunts spoke of their pleasure at having light children. (The men, some of whom were dark-skinned from years of working out of doors, would be in another part of the house.) It was the woman's spoken concern: the fear of having a dark-skinned son or daughter. Remedies were exchanged. One aunt prescribed to her sisters the elixir of large doses of castor oil during the last weeks of pregnancy. (The remedy risked an abortion.) Children born dark grew up to have their faces treated regularly with a mixture of egg white and lemon juice concentrate. (In my case, the solution never would take.) One Mexican-American friend of my mother's, who regarded it a special blessing that she had a measure of English blood, spoke disparagingly of her husband, a construction worker, for being so dark. 'He doesn't take care of himself,' she complained. But the remark, I noticed, annoyed my mother, who sat tracing an invisible design with her finger on the tablecloth.

There was affection too and a kind of humor about these matters. With daring tenderness, one of my uncles would refer to his wife as *mi negra*. An aunt regularly called her dark child *mi feito* (my little ugly one), her smile only partially hidden as she bent down to dig her mouth under his ticklish chin. And at times relatives spoke scornfully of pale, white skin. A *gringo's* skin resembled *masa*—baker's dough—someone remarked. Everyone laughed. Voices chuckled over the fact that the *gringos* spent so many hours in summer sunning themselves. ('They need to get sun because they look like *los muertos*.')

I heard the laughing but remembered what the women had said, with unsmiling voices, concerning dark skin. Nothing I heard outside the house, regarding my skin, was so impressive to me.

In public I occasionally heard racial slurs. Complete strangers would yell out at me. A teenager drove past, shouting, 'Hey, Greaser! Hey, Pancho!' Over his shoulder I saw the giggling face of his girl friend. A boy pedaled by and announced matter-of-factly, 'I pee on dirty Mexicans.' Such remarks would be said so casually that I wouldn't quickly realize that they were being addressed to me. When I did, I would be paralyzed with embarrassment, unable to return the insult. (Those times I happened to be with white grammar school friends, *they* shouted back. Imbued with the mysterious kindness of children, my friends would never ask later why I hadn't yelled out in my own defense.)

In all, there could not have been more than a dozen incidents of name-calling. That there were so few suggests that I was not a primary victim of racial abuse. But that, even today, I can clearly remember particular incidents is proof of their impact. Because of such incidents, I listened when my parents remarked that Mexicans were often mistreated in California border towns. And in Texas. I listened carefully when I heard that two of my cousins had been refused admittance to an 'all-white' swimming pool. And that an uncle had been told by some man to go back to Africa. I followed the progress of the southern black civil rights movement, which was gaining prominent notice in Sacramento's afternoon newspaper. But what most intrigued me was the connection between dark skin and poverty. Because I heard my mother speak so often about the relegation of dark people to menial labor, I considered the great victims of racism to be those who were poor and forced to do menial work. People like the farmworkers whose skin was dark from the sun.

After meeting a black grammar school friend of my sister's, I remember thinking that she wasn't really 'black.' What interested me was the fact that she wasn't poor. (Her well-dressed parents would come by after work to pick her up in a shiny green Oldsmobile.) By contrast, the garbage men who appeared every Friday morning seemed to me unmistakably black. (I didn't bother to ask my parents why Sacramento garbage men always were black. I thought I knew.) One morning I was in the backyard when a man opened the gate. He was an ugly, square-faced black man with popping red eyes, a pail slung over his shoulder. As he approached, I stood up. And in a voice that seemed to me very weak, I piped, 'Hi.' But the man paid me no heed. He strode past to the can by the garage. In a single broad movement, he overturned its contents into his larger pail. Our can came crashing down as he turned and left me watching, in awe.

'*Pobres negros,*' my mother remarked when she'd notice a headline in the paper about a civil rights demonstration in the South. 'How the *gringos* mistreat them.' In the same tone of voice she'd tell me about the mistreatment her brother endured years before. (After my grandfather's death, my grandmother had come to America with her son and five daughters.) 'My sisters, we were still all just teenagers. And since *mi pápa* was dead, my brother had to be the head of the family. He had to support us, to find work. But what skills did he have! Twenty years old. *Pobre.* He was tall, like your grandfather. And strong. He did construction work. "Construction!" The *gringos* kept him digging all day, doing the dirtiest jobs. And they would pay him next to nothing. Sometimes they promised him one salary and paid him less when he finished. But what could he do? Report them? We weren't citizens then. He didn't even know English. And he was dark. What chances could he have? As soon as we sisters got older, he went right back to Mexico. He hated this country. He looked so tired when he left. Already with a hunchback. Still in his twenties. But old-looking. No life for him here. *Pobre.*'

Dark skin was for my mother the most important symbol of a life of oppressive labor and poverty. But both my parents recognized other symbols as well.

My father noticed the feel of every hand he shook. (He'd smile sometimes—marvel more than scorn—remembering a man he'd met who had soft, uncalloused hands.)

My mother would grab a towel in the kitchen and rub my oily face sore when I came in from playing outside. 'Clean the *graza* off of your face!' (Greaser!)

Symbols: When my older sister, then in high school, asked my mother if she could do light housework in the afternoons for a rich lady we knew, my mother was frightened by the idea. For several weeks she troubled over it before granting conditional permission: 'Just remember, you're not a maid. I don't want you wearing a uniform.' My father echoed the same warning. Walking with him past a hotel, I watched as he stared at a doorman dressed like a Beefeater. 'How can anyone let himself be dressed up like that? Like a clown. Don't you ever get a job where you have to put on a uniform.' In summertime neighbors would ask me if I wanted to earn extra money by mowing their lawns. Again and again my mother worried: 'Why did they ask *you*? Can't you find anything better?' Inevitably, she'd relent. She knew I needed the money. But I was instructed to work after dinner. ('When the sun's not so hot.') Even then, I'd have to wear a hat. *Un sombrero de* baseball.

(*Sombrero*. Watching gray cowboy movies, I'd brood over the meaning of the broad-rimmed hat—that troubling symbol—which comically distinguished a Mexican cowboy from real cowboys.)

From my father came no warnings concerning the sun. His fear was of dark factory jobs. He remembered too well his first jobs when he came to this country, not intending to stay, just to earn money enough to sail on to Australia. (In Mexico he had heard too many stories of discrimination in *los Estados Unidos*. So it was Australia, that distant island-continent, that loomed in his imagination as his 'America.') The work my father found in San Francisco was work for the unskilled. A factory job. Then a cannery job. (He'd remember the noise and the heat.) Then a job at a warehouse. (He'd remember the dark stench of old urine.) At one place there were fistfights; at another a supervisor who hated Chinese and Mexicans. Nowhere a union.

His memory of himself in those years is held by those jobs. Never making money enough for passage to Australia; slowly giving up the plan of returning to school to resume his third-grade education—to become an engineer. My memory of him in those years, however, is lifted from photographs in the family album which show him on his honeymoon with my mother—the woman who had convinced him to stay in America. I have studied their photographs often, seeking to find in those figures some clear resemblance to the man and the woman I've known as my parents. But the youthful faces in the photos remain, behind dark glasses, shadowy figures anticipating my mother and father.

They are pictured on the grounds of the Coronado Hotel near San Diego, standing in the pale light of a winter afternoon. She is wearing slacks. Her hair falls seductively over one side of her face. He appears wearing a double-breasted suit, an unneeded raincoat draped over his arm. Another shows them standing together, solemnly staring ahead. Their shoulders barely are touching. There is to their pose an aristocratic formality, an elegant Latin hauteur.

The man in those pictures is the same man who was fascinated by Italian grand opera. I have never known just what my father saw in the spectacle, but he has told me that he would take my mother to the Opera House every Friday night—if he had money enough for orchestra seats. ('Why go to sit in the balcony?') On Sundays he'd don Italian silk scarves and a camel's hair coat to take his new wife to the polo matches in Golden Gate Park. But one weekend my father stopped going to the opera and polo matches. He would blame the change in his life on one job—a warehouse job, working for a large corporation which today advertises its products with the smiling faces of children. 'They made me an old man before my time,' he'd say to me many years later. Afterward, jobs got easier and cleaner. Eventually, in middle age, he got a job making false teeth. But his youth was spent at the warehouse. 'Everything changed,' his wife remembers. The dapper young man in the old photographs yielded to the man I saw after dinner: haggard, asleep on the sofa. During 'The Ed Sullivan Show' on Sunday nights, when Roberta Peters or Licia Albanese would appear on the tiny blue screen, his head would jerk up alert. He'd sit forward while the notes of Puccini sounded before him. ('Un bel dí.')

By the time they had a family, my parents no longer dressed in very fine clothes. Those symbols of great wealth and the reality of their lives too noisily clashed. No longer did they try to fit themselves, like paper-doll figures, behind trappings so foreign to their actual lives. My father no longer wore silk scarves or expensive wool suits. He sold his tuxedo to a second-hand store for five dollars. My mother sold her rabbit fur coat to the wife of a Spanish radio station disc jockey. ('It looks better on you than it does on me,' she kept telling the lady until the sale was completed.) I was six years old at the time, but I recall watching the transaction with complete understanding. The woman I knew as my mother was already physically unlike the woman in her honeymoon photos. My mother's hair was short. Her shoulders were thick from carrying children. Her fingers were swollen red, toughened by housecleaning. Already my mother would admit to foreseeing herself in her own mother, a woman grown old, bald and bowlegged, after a hard lifetime of working.

In their manner, both my parents continued to respect the symbols of what they considered to be upper-class life. Very early, they taught me the *propria* way of eating *como los ricos*. And I was carefully taught elaborate formulas of polite greeting and parting. The dark little boy would be invited by classmates to the rich houses on Forty-fourth and Forty-fifth streets. 'How do you do?' or 'I am very pleased to meet you,' I would say, bowing slightly to the amused mothers of classmates. 'Thank you very much for the dinner; it was very delicious.'

I made an impression. I intended to make an impression, to be invited back. (I soon realized that the trick was to get the mother or father to notice me.) From those early days began my association with rich people, my fascination with their secret. My mother worried. She warned me not to come home expecting to have the things my friends possessed. But she needn't have said anything. When I went to the big houses, I remembered that I was, at best, a visitor to the world I saw there. For that reason, I was an especially watchful guest. I was my parents' child. Things most middle-class children wouldn't trouble to notice, I studied. Remembered to see: the starched black and white uniform worn by the maid who opened the door; the Mexican gardeners—their complexions as dark as my own. (One gardener's face, glassed by sweat, looked up to see me going inside.)

'Take Richard upstairs and show him your electric train,' the mother said. But it was really the vast polished dining room table I'd come to appraise. Those nights when I was invited to stay for dinner, I'd notice that my friend's mother rang a small silver bell to tell the black woman when to bring in the food. The father, at his end of the table, ate while wearing his tie. When I was not required to speak, I'd skate the icy cut of crystal with my eye; my gaze would follow the golden threads etched onto the rim of china. With my mother's eyes I'd see my hostess's manicured nails and judge them to be marks of her leisure. Later, when my schoolmate's father would bid me goodnight, I would feel his soft fingers and palm when we shook hands. And turning to leave, I'd see my dark self, lit by chandelier light, in a tall hallway mirror.

2

Complexion. My first conscious experience of sexual excitement concerns my complexion. One summer weekend, when I was around seven years old, I was at a public swimming pool with the whole family. I remember sitting on the damp pavement next to the pool and seeing my mother, in the spectators' bleachers, holding my younger sister on her lap. My mother, I noticed, was watching my father as he stood on a diving board, waving to her. I watched her wave back. Then saw her radiant, bashful, astonishing smile. In that second I sensed that my mother and father had a relationship I knew nothing about. A nervous excitement encircled my stomach as I saw my mother's eyes follow my father's figure curving into the water. A second or two later, he emerged. I heard him call out. Smiling, his voice sounded, buoyant, calling me to swim to him. But turning to see him, I caught my mother's eye. I heard her shout over to me. In Spanish she called through the crowd: 'Put a towel on over your shoulders.' In public, she didn't want to say why. I knew.

That incident anticipates the shame and sexual inferiority I was to feel in later years because of my dark complexion. I was to grow up an ugly child. Or one who thought himself ugly. *(Feo.)* One night when I was eleven or twelve years old, I locked myself in the bathroom and carefully regarded my reflection in the mirror over the sink. Without any pleasure I studied my skin. I turned on the faucet. (In my mind I heard the swirling voices of aunts, and even my mother's voice, whispering, whispering incessantly about lemon juice solutions and dark, *feo* children.) With a bar of soap, I fashioned a thick ball of lather. I began soaping my arms. I took my father's straight razor out of the medicine cabinet. Slowly, with steady deliberateness, I put the blade against my flesh, pressed it as close as I could without cutting, and moved it up and down across my skin to see if I could get out, somehow lessen, the dark. All I succeeded in doing, however, was in shaving my arms bare of their hair. For as I noted with disappointment, the dark would not come out. It remained. Trapped. Deep in the cells of my skin.

Throughout adolescence, I felt myself mysteriously marked. Nothing else about my appearance would concern me so much as the fact that my complexion was dark. My mother would say how sorry she was that there was not money enough to get braces to straighten my teeth. But I never bothered about my teeth. In three-way mirrors at department stores, I'd see my profile dramatically defined by a long nose, but it was really only the color of my skin that caught my attention.

I wasn't afraid that I would become a menial laborer because of my skin. Nor did my complexion make me feel especially vulnerable to racial abuse. (I didn't really consider my dark skin to be a racial characteristic. I would have been only too happy to look as Mexican as my light-skinned older brother.) Simply, I judged myself ugly. And, since the women in my family had been the ones who discussed it in such worried tones, I felt my dark skin made me unattractive to women.

Thirteen years old. Fourteen. In a grammar school art class, when the assignment was to draw a self-portrait, I tried and I tried but could not bring myself to shade in the face on the paper to anything like my actual tone. With disgust then I would come face to face with myself in mirrors. With disappointment I located myself in class photographs—my dark face undefined by the camera which had clearly described the white faces of classmates. Or I'd see my dark wrist against my long-sleeved white shirt.

I grew divorced from my body. Insecure, overweight, listless. On hot summer days when my rubber-soled shoes soaked up the heat from the sidewalk, I kept my head down. Or walked in the shade. My mother didn't need anymore to tell me to watch out for the sun. I denied myself a sensational life. The normal, extraordinary, animal excitement of feeling my body alive—riding shirtless on a bicycle in the warm wind created by furious self-propelled motion—the sensations that first had excited in me a sense of my maleness, I denied. I was too ashamed of my body. I wanted to forget that I had a body because I had a brown body. I was grateful that none of my classmates ever mentioned the fact.

I continued to see the *braceros*, those men I resembled in one way and, in another way, didn't resemble at all. On the watery horizon of a Valley afternoon, I'd see them. And though I feared looking like them, it was with silent envy that I regarded them still. I envied them their physical lives, their freedom to violate the taboo of the sun. Closer to home I would notice the shirtless construction workers, the roofers, the sweating men tarring the street in front of the house. And I'd see the Mexican gardeners. I was unwilling to admit the attraction of their lives. I tried to deny it by looking away. But what was denied became strongly desired.

In high school physical education classes, I withdrew, in the regular company of five or six classmates, to a distant corner of a football field where we smoked and talked. Our company was composed of bodies too short or too tall, all graceless and all—except mine—pale. Our conversation was usually witty. (In fact we were intelligent.) If we referred to the athletic contests around us, it was with sarcasm. With savage scorn I'd refer to the 'animals' playing football or baseball. It would have been important for me to have joined them. Or for me to have taken off my shirt, to have let the sun burn dark on my skin, and to have run barefoot on the warm wet grass. It would have been very important. Too important. It would have been too telling a gesture—to admit the desire for sensation, the body, my body.

Fifteen, sixteen. I was a teenager shy in the presence of girls. Never dated. Barely could talk to a girl without stammering. In high school I went to several dances, but I never managed to ask a girl to dance. So I stopped going. I cannot remember high school years now with the parade of typical images: bright drive-ins or gliding blue shadows of a Junior Prom. At home most weekend nights, I would pass evenings reading. Like those hidden, precocious adolescents who have no real-life sexual experiences, I read a great deal of romantic fiction. 'You won't find it in your books,' my brother would playfully taunt me as he prepared to go to a party by freezing the crest of the wave in his hair with sticky pomade. Through my reading, however, I developed a fabulous and sophisticated sexual imagination. At seventeen, I may not have known how to engage a girl in small talk, but I had read *Lady Chatterley's Lover*.

It annoyed me to hear my father's teasing: that I would never know what 'real work' is; that my hands were so soft. I think I knew it was his way of admitting pleasure and pride in my academic success. But I didn't smile. My mother said she was glad her children were getting their educations and would not be pushed around like *los pobres*. I heard the remark ironically as a reminder of my separation from *los braceros*. At such times I suspected that education was making me effeminate. The odd thing, however, was that I did not judge my classmates so harshly. Nor did I consider my male teachers in high school effeminate. It was only myself I judged against some shadowy, mythical Mexican laborer—dark like me, yet very different.

Language was crucial. I knew that I had violated the ideal of the *macho* by becoming such a dedicated student of language and literature. *Machismo* was a word never exactly defined by the persons who used it. (It was best described in the 'proper' behavior of men.) Women at home, nevertheless, would repeat the old Mexican dictum that a man should be *feo, fuerte, y formal*. 'The three F's,' my mother called them, smiling slyly. *Feo* I took to mean not literally ugly so much as ruggedly handsome. (When my mother and her sisters spent a loud, laughing afternoon determining ideal male good looks, they finally settled on the actor Gilbert Roland, who was neither too pretty nor ugly but had looks 'like a man.') *Fuerte*, 'strong,' seemed to mean not physical strength as much as inner strength, character. A dependable man is *fuerte*. *Fuerte* for that reason was a characteristic subsumed by the last of the three qualities, and the one I most often considered—*formal*. To be *formal* is to be steady. A man of responsibility, a good provider. Someone *formal* is also constant. A person to be relied upon in adversity. A sober man, a man of high seriousness.

428 / RICHARD RODRIGUEZ

I learned a great deal about being *formal* just by listening to the way my father and other male relatives of his generation spoke. A man was not silent necessarily. Nor was he limited in the tones he could sound. For example, he could tell a long, involved, humorous story and laugh at his own humor with high-pitched giggling. But a man was not talkative the way a woman could be. It was permitted a woman to be gossipy and chatty. (When one heard many voices in a room, it was usually women who were talking.) Men spoke much less rapidly. And often men spoke in monologues. (When one voice sounded in a crowded room, it was most often a man's voice one heard.) More important than any of this was the fact that a man never verbally revealed his emotions. Men did not speak about their unease in moments of crisis or danger. It was the woman who worried aloud when her husband got laid off from work. At times of illness or death in the family, a man was usually quiet, even silent. Women spoke up to voice prayers. In distress, women always sounded quick ejaculations to God or the Virgin; women prayed in clearly audible voices at a wake held in a funeral parlor. And on the subject of love, a woman was verbally expansive. She spoke of her yearning and delight. A married man, if he spoke publicly about love, usually did so with playful, mischievous irony. Younger, unmarried men more often were quiet. (The *macho* is a silent suitor. *Formal.*)

At home I was quiet, so perhaps I seemed *formal* to my relations and other Spanish-speaking visitors to the house. But outside the house—my God!—I talked. Particularly in class or alone with my teachers, I chattered. (Talking seemed to make teachers think I was bright.) I often was proud of my way with words. Though, on other occasions, for example, when I would hear my mother busily speaking to women, it would occur to me that my attachment to words made me like her. Her son. Not *formal* like my father. At such times I even suspected that my nostalgia for sounds—the noisy, intimate Spanish sounds of my past—was nothing more than effeminate yearning.

High school English teachers encouraged me to describe very personal feelings in words. Poems and short stories I wrote, expressing sorrow and loneliness, were awarded high grades. In my bedroom were books by poets and novelists—books that I loved—in which male writers published feelings the men in my family never revealed or acknowledged in words. And it seemed to me that there was something unmanly about my attachment to literature. Even today, when so much about the myth of the *macho* no longer concerns me, I cannot altogether evade such notions. Writing these pages, admitting my embarrassment or my guilt, admitting my sexual anxieties and my physical insecurity, I have not been able to forget that I am not being *formal*.

So be it.

3

I went to college at Stanford, attracted partly by its academic reputation, partly because it was the school rich people went to. I found myself on a campus with golden children of western America's upper middle class. Many were students both ambitious for academic success *and* accustomed to leisured life in the sun. In the afternoon, they lay spread out, sunbathing in front of the library, reading Swift or Engels or Beckett. Others went by in convertibles, off to play tennis or ride horses or sail. Beach boys dressed in tank-tops and shorts were my classmates in undergraduate seminars. Tall tan girls wearing white strapless dresses sat directly in front of me in lecture rooms. I'd study them, their physical confidence. I was still recognizably kin to the boy I had been. Less tortured perhaps. But still kin. At Stanford, it's true, I began to have something like a conventional sexual life. I don't think, however, that I really believed that the women I knew found me physically appealing. I continued to stay out of the sun. I didn't linger in mirrors. And I was the student at Stanford who remembered to notice the Mexican-American janitors and gardeners working on campus.

It was at Stanford, one day near the end of my senior year, that a friend told me about a summer construction job he knew was available. I was quickly alert. Desire uncoiled within me. My friend said that he knew I had been looking for summer employment. He knew I needed some money. Almost apologetically he explained: It was something I probably wouldn't be interested in, but a friend of his, a contractor, needed someone for the summer to do menial jobs. There would be lots of shoveling and raking and sweeping. Nothing too hard. But nothing more interesting either. Still, the pay would be good. Did I want it? Or did I know someone who did?

I did. Yes, I said, surprised to hear myself say it.

In the weeks following, friends cautioned that I had no idea how hard physical labor really is. ('You only *think* you know what it is like to shovel for eight hours straight.') Their objections seemed to me challenges. They resolved the issue. I became happy with my plan. I decided, however, not to tell my parents. I wouldn't tell my mother because I could guess her worried reaction. I would tell my father only after the summer was over, when I could announce that, after all, I did know what 'real work' is like.

The day I met the contractor (a Princeton graduate, it turned out), he asked me whether I had done any physical labor before. 'In high school, during the summer,' I lied. And although he seemed to regard me with skepticism, he decided to give me a try. Several days later, expectant, I arrived at my first construction site. I would take off my shirt to the sun. And at last grasp desired sensation. No longer afraid. At last become like a *bracero*. 'We need those tree stumps out of here by tomorrow,' the contractor said. I started to work.

I labored with excitement that first morning—and all the days after. The work was harder than I could have expected. But it was never as tedious as my friends had warned me it would be. There was too much physical pleasure in the labor. Especially early in the day, I would be most alert to the sensations of movement and straining. Beginning around seven each morning (when the air was still damp but the scent of weeds and dry earth anticipated the heat of the sun), I would feel my body resist the first thrusts of the shovel. My arms, tightened by sleep, would gradually loosen; after only several minutes, sweat would gather in beads on my forehead and then—a short while later—I would feel my chest silky with sweat in the breeze. I would return to my work. A nervous spark of pain would fly up my arm and settle to burn like an ember in the thick of my shoulder. An hour, two passed. Three. My whole body would assume regular movements; my shoveling would be described by identical, even movements. Even later in the day, my enthusiasm for primitive sensation would survive the heat and the dust and the insects pricking my back. I would strain wildly for sensation as the day came to a close. At three-thirty, quitting time, I would stand upright and slowly let my head fall back, luxuriating in the feeling of tightness relieved.

Some of the men working nearby would watch me and laugh. Two or three of the older men took the trouble to teach me the right way to use a pick, the correct way to shovel. 'You're doing it wrong, too fucking hard,' one man scolded. Then proceeded to show me—what persons who work with their bodies all their lives quickly learn—the most economical way to use one's body in labor.

'Don't make your back do so much work,' he instructed. I stood impatiently listening, half listening, vaguely watching, then noticed his work-thickened fingers clutching the shovel. I was annoyed. I wanted to tell him that I enjoyed shoveling the wrong way. And I didn't want to learn the right way. I wasn't afraid of back pain. I liked the way my body felt sore at the end of the day.

I was about to, but, as it turned out, I didn't say a thing. Rather it was at that moment I realized that I was fooling myself if I expected a few weeks of labor to gain me admission to the world of the laborer. I would not learn in three months what my father had meant by 'real work.' I was not bound to this job; I could imagine its rapid conclusion. For me the sensations of exertion and fatigue could be savored. For my father or uncle, working at comparable jobs when they were my age, such sensations were to be feared. Fatigue took a different toll on their bodies—and minds.

It was, I know, a simple insight. But it was with this realization that I took my first step that summer toward realizing something even more important about the 'worker.' In the company of carpenters, electricians, plumbers, and painters at lunch, I would often sit quietly, observant. I was not shy in such company. I felt easy, pleased by the knowledge that I was casually accepted, my presence taken for granted by men (exotics) who worked with their hands. Some days the younger men would talk and talk about sex, and they would howl at women who drove by in cars. Other days the talk at lunchtime was subdued; men gathered in separate groups. It depended on who was around. There were rough, good-natured workers. Others were quiet. The more I remember that summer, the more I realize that there was no single *type* of worker. I am embarrassed to say I had not expected such diversity. I certainly had not expected to meet, for example, a plumber who was an abstract painter in his off hours and admired the work of Mark Rothko. Nor did I expect to meet so many workers with college diplomas. (They were the ones who were not surprised that I intended to enter graduate school in the fall.) I suppose what I really want to say here is painfully obvious, but I must say it nevertheless: The men of that summer were middle-class Americans. They certainly didn't constitute an oppressed society. Carefully completing their work sheets; talking about the fortunes of local football teams; planning Las Vegas vacations; comparing the gas mileage of various makes of campers—they were not *los pobres* my mother had spoken about.

On two occasions, the contractor hired a group of Mexican aliens. They were employed to cut down some trees and haul off debris. In all, there were six men of varying age. The youngest in his late twenties; the oldest (his father?) perhaps sixty years old. They came and they left in a single old truck. Anonymous men. They were never introduced to the other men at the site. Immediately upon their arrival, they would follow the contractor's directions, start working—rarely resting—seemingly driven by a fatalistic sense that work which had to be done was best done as quickly as possible.

I watched them sometimes. Perhaps they watched me. The only time I saw them pay me much notice was one day at lunchtime when I was laughing with the other men. The Mexicans sat apart when they ate, just as they worked by themselves. Quiet. I rarely heard them say much to each other. All I could hear were their voices calling out sharply to one another, giving directions. Otherwise, when they stood briefly resting, they talked among themselves in voices too hard to overhear.

The contractor knew enough Spanish, and the Mexicans—or at least the oldest of them, their spokesman—seemed to know enough English to communicate. But because I was around, the contractor decided one day to make me his translator. (He assumed I could speak Spanish.) I did what I was told. Shyly I went over to tell the Mexicans that the *patrón* wanted them to do something else before they left for the day. As I started to speak, I was afraid with my old fear that I would be unable to pronounce the Spanish words. But it was a simple instruction I had to convey. I could say it in phrases.

The dark sweating faces turned toward me as I spoke. They stopped their work to hear me. Each nodded in response. I stood there. I wanted to say something more. But what could I say in Spanish, even if I could have pronounced the words right? Perhaps I just wanted to engage them in small talk, to be assured of their confidence, our familiarity. I thought for a moment to ask them where in Mexico they were from. Something like that. And maybe I wanted to tell them (a lie, if need be) that my parents were from the same part of Mexico.

I stood there.

Their faces watched me. The eyes of the man directly in front of me moved slowly over my shoulder, and I turned to follow his glance toward *el patrón* some distance away. For a moment I felt swept up by that glance into the Mexicans' company. But then I heard one of them returning to work. And then the others went back to work. I left them without saying anything more.

When they had finished, the contractor went over to pay them in cash. (He later told me that he paid them collectively—'for the job,' though he wouldn't tell me their wages. He said something quickly about the good rate of exchange 'in their own country.') I can still hear the loudly confident voice he used with the Mexicans. It was the sound of the *gringo* I had heard as a very young boy. And I can still hear the quiet, indistinct sounds of the Mexican, the oldest, who replied. At hearing that voice I was sad for the Mexicans. Depressed by their vulnerability. Angry at myself. The adventure of the summer seemed suddenly ludicrous. I would not shorten the distance I felt from *los pobres* with a few weeks of physical labor. I would not become like them. They were different from me.

After that summer, a great deal—and not very much really—changed in my life. The curse of physical shame was broken by the sun; I was no longer ashamed of my body. No longer would I deny myself the pleasing sensations of my maleness. During those years when middle-class black Americans began to assert with pride, 'Black is beautiful,' I was able to regard my complexion without shame. I am today darker than I ever was as a boy. I have taken up the middle-class sport of long-distance running. Nearly every day now I run ten or fifteen miles, barely clothed, my skin exposed to the California winter rain and wind or the summer sun of late afternoon. The torso, the soccer player's calves and thighs, the arms of the twenty-year-old I never was, I possess now in my thirties. I study the youthful parody shape in the mirror: the stomach lipped tight by muscle; the shoulders rounded by chin-ups; the arms veined strong. This man. A man. I meet him. He laughs to see me, what I have become.

The dandy. I wear double-breasted Italian suits and custom-made English shoes. I resemble no one so much as my father—the man pictured in those honeymoon photos. At that point in life when he abandoned the dandy's posture, I assume it. At the point when my parents would not consider going on vacation, I register at the Hotel Carlyle in New York and the Plaza Athenée in Paris. I am as taken by the symbols of leisure and wealth as they were. For my parents, however, those symbols became taunts, reminders of all they could not achieve in one lifetime. For me those same symbols are reassuring reminders of public success. I tempt vulgarity to be reassured. I am filled with the gaudy delight, the monstrous grace of the *nouveau riche*.

In recent years I have had occasion to lecture in ghetto high schools. There I see students of remarkable style and physical grace. (One can see more dandies in such schools than one ever will find in middle-class high schools.) There is not the look of casual assurance I saw students at Stanford display. Ghetto girls mimic high-fashion models. Their dresses are of bold, forceful color; their figures elegant, long; the stance theatrical. Boys wear shirts that grip at their overdeveloped muscular bodies. (Against a powerless future, they engage images of strength.) Bad nutrition does not yet tell. Great disappointment, fatal to youth, awaits them still. For the moment, movements in school hallways are dancelike, a procession of postures in a sexual masque. Watching them, I feel a kind of envy. I wonder how different my adolescence would have been had I been free. . . . But no, it is my parents I see—their optimism during those years when they were entertained by Italian grand opera.

The registration clerk in London wonders if I have just been to Switzerland. And the man who carries my luggage in New York guesses the Caribbean. My complexion becomes a mark of my leisure. Yet no one would regard my complexion the same way if I entered such hotels through the service entrance. That is only to say that my complexion assumes its significance from the context of my life. My skin, in itself, means nothing. I stress the point because I know there are people who would label me 'disadvantaged' because of my color. They make the same mistake I made as a boy, when I thought a disadvantaged life was circumscribed by particular occupations. That summer I worked in the sun may have made me physically indistinguishable from the Mexicans working nearby. (My skin was actually darker because, unlike them, I worked without wearing a shirt. By late August my hands were probably as tough as theirs.) But I was not one of *los pobres*. What made me different from them was an attitude of *mind*, my imagination of myself.

I do not blame my mother for warning me away from the sun when I was young. In a world where her brother had become an old man in his twenties because he was dark, my complexion was something to worry about. 'Don't run in the sun,' she warns me today. I run. In the end, my father was right—though perhaps he did not know how right or why—to say that I would never know what real work is. I will never know what he felt at his last factory job. If tomorrow I worked at some kind of factory, it would go differently for me. My long education would favor me. I could act as a public person—able to defend my interests, to unionize, to petition, to speak up—to challenge and demand. (I will never know what real work is.) I will never know what the Mexicans knew, gathering their shovels and ladders and saws.

Their silence stays with me now. The wages those Mexicans received for their labor were only a measure of their disadvantaged condition. Their silence is more telling. They lack a public identity. They remain profoundly alien. Persons apart. People lacking a union obviously, people without grounds. They depend upon the relative good will or fairness of their employers each day. For such people, lacking a better alternative, it is not such an unreasonable risk.

Their silence stays with me. I have taken these many words to describe its impact. Only: the quiet. Something uncanny about it. Its compliance. Vulnerability. Pathos. As I heard their truck rumbling away, I shuddered, my face mirrored with sweat. I had finally come face to face with *los pobres*.

ACTIVE READING

1. Find several passages that discuss *"los pobres"*; in each one, describe Rodriguez's attitude toward these people. Then, based on what Rodriguez tells you about *los pobres*, try to look at Rodriguez from their perspective. What does this way of looking at Rodriguez tell you that Rodriguez himself does not?

2. How does Rodriguez's insecurity about his dark skin and Indian facial features relate to the Mexican belief that a man should be *feo* (or "ugly")? Use your answer to this question to help you address the place of the other "F's" in Rodriguez's self-image.

3. Which social beliefs does Rodriguez develop from his family, and which ones come from his exposure to what he calls the "public" world? After finding examples of "family" and "public" beliefs, explain how knowing the origin of particular attitudes might help you judge their importance for Rodriguez's development as a Mexican-American man.

READING IN NEW CONTEXTS

1. In what ways does Rodriguez identify with other Mexican-Americans or Mexicans, and in what ways does he distance himself from them? Consider a *Literacies* essay by another writer who straddles two cultural identities (Durham, Kingston, or Tan might be helpful). What does this writer's relationship to his or her group of origin let you say about Rodriguez's feelings?

2. Find several moments at which Rodriguez describes someone as silent. How does Rodriguez interpret these moments or images of silence? With the help of Bettelheim, MacLeod, Rich, or another *Literacies*

writer, develop an alternative interpretation of silence in Rodriguez's essay.

3. How does Rodriguez's understanding of his parents' relationship contribute to his ideas about himself? Once you have made some observations, ask the same question about the parents in Kingston's or MacLeod's texts. Why, in your reading, does each writer focus on relationships between parents?

DRAFT ONE / DRAFT TWO

1. *Draft One:* Who has power in Rodriguez's world? Use the definitions you developed in Before Reading #4 to discuss Rodriguez's theories about personal power.

   Draft Two: Consider an essay by another *Literacies* writer, such as Brody, Ewen, or Gilmore, who is also concerned with visible forms of power. Pick a section of your Draft One, and use the special perspectives of this writer to expand your discussion of a particular kind of power in Rodriguez's essay.

2. *Draft One:* Rodriguez argues that if he worked in a factory, he would "be able to defend [his] interests, to unionize" (434). Explain how you think this claim relates to Rodriguez's other statements about collective activity (you might ask, for instance, whether Rodriguez actually would organize or join a union). Your response to Reading in New Contexts #1 may help here.

   Draft Two: Describe the assumptions behind the group-oriented practices mentioned by Anzaldúa, Fishman, Heath, or another *Literacies* writer. What might one of these writers say about Rodriguez's complicated understanding of collective identity?

BEFORE READING RENATO ROSALDO

1. The title of Rosaldo's essay is "Grief and a Headhunter's Rage." How do you think the concepts of "grief," "rage," and "headhunting" might fit together? Discuss any initial questions you might have about reading an essay with this title.

2. Think of something important that you know about yourself now that you didn't know a few years ago. Describe the process that led you to this knowledge. How has this knowledge changed your day-to-day life and relationships with other people?

3. What barriers are people from different religious traditions likely to encounter when they discuss their beliefs? In these situations, what makes understanding possible?

RENATO ROSALDO

GRIEF AND A
HEADHUNTER'S RAGE

If you ask an older Ilongot man of northern Luzon, Philippines, why he cuts off human heads, his answer is brief, and one on which no anthropologist can readily elaborate: He says that rage, born of grief, impels him to kill his fellow human beings. He claims that he needs a place "to carry his anger." The act of severing and tossing away the victim's head enables him, he says, to vent and, he hopes, throw away the anger of his bereavement. Although the anthropologist's job is to make other cultures intelligible, more questions fail to reveal any further explanation of this man's pithy statement. To him, grief, rage, and headhunting go together in a self-evident manner. Either you understand it or you don't. And, in fact, for the longest time I simply did not.

In what follows, I want to talk about how to talk about the cultural force of emotions.[1] The *emotional force* of a death, for example, derives

From *Culture and Truth: The Remaking of Social Analysis* (1989).

1. In contrasting Moroccan and Javanese forms of mysticism, Clifford Geertz found it necessary to distinguish the "force" of cultural patterning from its "scope" (Clifford Geertz, *Islam Observed* [New Haven, Conn.: Yale University Press, 1968]). He distinguished force from scope in this manner: "By 'force' I mean the thoroughness with which such a pattern is internalized in the personalities of the individuals who adopt it, its centrality or marginality in their lives" (p. 111). "By 'scope,' on the other hand,

less from an abstract brute fact than from a particular intimate relation's permanent rupture. It refers to the kinds of feelings one experiences on learning, for example, that the child just run over by a car is one's own and not a stranger's. Rather than speaking of death in general, one must consider the subject's position within a field of social relations in order to grasp one's emotional experience.[2]

My effort to show the force of a simple statement taken literally goes against anthropology's classic norms, which prefer to explicate culture through the gradual thickening of symbolic webs of meaning. By and large, cultural analysts use not *force* but such terms as *thick description, multi-vocality, polysemy, richness,* and *texture.* The notion of force, among other things, opens to question the common anthropological assumption that the greatest human import resides in the densest forest of symbols and that analytical detail, or "cultural depth," equals enhanced explanation of a culture, or "cultural elaboration." Do people always in fact describe most thickly what matters most to them?

THE RAGE IN ILONGOT GRIEF

Let me pause a moment to introduce the Ilongots, among whom my wife, Michelle Rosaldo, and I lived and conducted field research for thirty months (1967–69, 1974). They number about 3,500 and reside in an upland area some 90 miles northeast of Manila, Philippines.[3] They subsist

I mean the range of social contexts within which religious considerations are regarded as having more or less direct relevance" (p. 112). In his later works, Geertz developed the notion of scope more than that of force. Unlike Geertz, who emphasizes processes of internalization within individual personalities, my use of the term *force* stresses the concept of the positioned subject.

2. Anthropologists have long studied the vocabulary of the emotions in other cultures (see, e.g., Hildred Geertz, "The Vocabulary of Emotion: A Study of Javanese Socialization Processes," *Psychiatry* 22 [1959]: 225–37). For a recent review essay on anthropological writings on emotions, see Catherine Lutz and Geoffrey M. White, "The Anthropology of Emotions," *Annual Review of Anthropology* 15 (1986): 405–36.

3. The two ethnographies on the Ilongots are Michelle Rosaldo, *Knowledge and Passion: Ilongot Notions of Self and Social Life* (New York: Cambridge University Press, 1980), and Renato Rosaldo, *Ilongot Headhunting, 1883–1974: A Study in Society and History* (Stanford, Calif.: Stanford University Press, 1980). Our field research among the Ilongots was financed by a National Science Foundation predoctoral fellowship, National Science Foundation Research Grants GS-1509 and GS-40788, and a Mellon Award for junior faculty from Stanford University. A Fulbright Grant financed a two-month stay in the Philippines during 1981.

by hunting deer and wild pig and by cultivating rain-fed gardens (swiddens) with rice, sweet potatoes, manioc, and vegetables. Their (bilateral) kin relations are reckoned through men and women. After marriage, parents and their married daughters live in the same or adjacent households. The largest unit within the society, a largely territorial descent group called the *bertan*, becomes manifest primarily in the context of feuding. For themselves, their neighbors, and their ethnographers, headhunting stands out as the Ilongots' most salient cultural practice.

When Ilongots told me, as they often did, how the rage in bereavement could impel men to headhunt, I brushed aside their one-line accounts as too simple, thin, opaque, implausible, stereotypical, or otherwise unsatisfying. Probably I naively equated grief with sadness. Certainly no personal experience allowed me to imagine the powerful rage Ilongots claimed to find in bereavement. My own inability to conceive the force of anger in grief led me to seek out another level of analysis that could provide a deeper explanation for older men's desire to headhunt.

Not until some fourteen years after first recording the terse Ilongot statement about grief and a headhunter's rage did I begin to grasp its overwhelming force. For years I thought that more verbal elaboration (which was not forthcoming) or another analytical level (which remained elusive) could better explain older men's motives for headhunting. Only after being repositioned through a devastating loss of my own could I better grasp that Ilongot older men mean precisely what they say when they describe the anger in bereavement as the source of their desire to cut off human heads. Taken at face value and granted its full weight, their statement reveals much about what compels these older men to headhunt.

In my efforts to find a "deeper" explanation for headhunting, I explored exchange theory, perhaps because it had informed so many classic ethnographies. One day in 1974, I explained the anthropologist's exchange model to an older Ilongot man named Insan. What did he think, I asked, of the idea that headhunting resulted from the way that one death (the beheaded victim's) canceled another (the next of kin). He looked puzzled, so I went on to say that the victim of a beheading was exchanged for the death of one's own kin, thereby balancing the books, so to speak. Insan reflected a moment and replied that he imagined somebody could think such a thing (a safe bet, since I just had), but that he and other Ilongots did not think any such thing. Nor was there any indirect evidence for my exchange theory in ritual, boast, song, or casual conversation.[4]

In retrospect, then, these efforts to impose exchange theory on one aspect of Ilongot behavior appear feeble. Suppose I had discovered what I sought? Although the notion of balancing the ledger does have a certain elegant coherence, one wonders how such bookish dogma could inspire any man to take another man's life at the risk of his own.

My life experience had not as yet provided the means to imagine the rage that can come with devastating loss. Nor could I, therefore, fully appreciate the acute problem of meaning that Ilongots faced in 1974. Shortly after Ferdinand Marcos declared martial law in 1972, rumors that firing squads had become the new punishment for headhunting reached the Ilongot hills. The men therefore decided to call a moratorium on taking heads. In past epochs, when headhunting had become impossible, Ilongots had allowed their rage to dissipate, as best it could, in the course of everyday life. In 1974, they had another option; they began to consider conversion to evangelical Christianity as a means of coping with their grief. Accepting the new religion, people said, implied abandoning their old ways, including headhunting. It also made coping with bereavement less agonizing because they could believe that the deceased had departed for a better world. No longer did they have to confront the awful finality of death.

The force of the dilemma faced by the Ilongots eluded me at the time. Even when I correctly recorded their statements about grieving and the need to throw away their anger, I simply did not grasp the weight of their words. In 1974, for example, while Michelle Rosaldo and I were living among the Ilongots, a six-month-old baby died, probably of pneumonia. That afternoon we visited the father and found him terribly stricken. "He was sobbing and staring through glazed and bloodshot eyes at the cotton blanket covering his baby."[5] The man suffered intensely, for this was the seventh child he had lost. Just a few years before, three of his

---

4. Lest the hypothesis Insan rejected appear utterly implausible, one should mention that at least one group does link a version of exchange theory to headhunting. Peter Metcalf reports that, among the Berawan of Borneo, "Death has a chain reaction quality to it. There is a considerable anxiety that, unless something is done to break the chain, death will follow upon death. The logic of this is now plain: The unquiet soul kills, and so creates more unquiet souls" (Peter Metcalf, *A Borneo Journey into Death: Berawan Eschatology from Its Rituals* [Philadelphia: University of Pennsylvania Press, 1982], p. 127).

5. R. Rosaldo, *Ilongot Headhunting, 1883–1974*, p. 286.

children had died, one after the other, in a matter of days. At the time, the situation was murky as people present talked both about evangelical Christianity (the possible renunciation of taking heads) and their grudges against lowlanders (the contemplation of headhunting forays into the surrounding valleys).

Through subsequent days and weeks, the man's grief moved him in a way I had not anticipated. Shortly after the baby's death, the father converted to evangelical Christianity. Altogether too quick on the inference, I immediately concluded that the man believed that the new religion could somehow prevent further deaths in his family. When I spoke my mind to an Ilongot friend, he snapped at me, saying that "I had missed the point: what the man in fact sought in the new religion was not the denial of our inevitable deaths but a means of coping with his grief. With the advent of martial law, headhunting was out of the question as a means of venting his wrath and thereby lessening his grief. Were he to remain in his Ilongot way of life, the pain of his sorrow would simply be too much to bear."[6] My description from 1980 now seems so apt that I wonder how I could have written the words and nonetheless failed to appreciate the force of the grieving man's desire to vent his rage.

Another representative anecdote makes my failure to imagine the rage possible in Ilongot bereavement all the more remarkable. On this occasion, Michelle Rosaldo and I were urged by Ilongot friends to play the tape of a headhunting celebration we had witnessed some five years before. No sooner had we turned on the tape and heard the boast of a man who had died in the intervening years than did people abruptly tell us to shut off the recorder. Michelle Rosaldo reported on the tense conversation that ensued:

As Insan braced himself to speak, the room again became almost uncannily electric. Backs straightened and my anger turned to nervousness and something more like fear as I saw that Insan's eyes were red. Tukbaw, Renato's Ilongot "brother," then broke into what was a brittle silence, saying he could make things clear. He told us that it hurt to listen to a headhunting celebration when people knew that there would never be another. As he put it: "The song pulls at us, drags our hearts, it makes us think of our dead uncle." And again: "It would be better if I had accepted God, but I still am an Ilongot at heart; and when I hear the song, my heart aches as it does when I must look upon unfinished bachelors whom I know that I will never lead to take a head." Then Wagat,

6. Ibid., p. 288.

Tukbaw's wife, said with her eyes that all my questions gave her pain, and told me: "Leave off now, isn't that enough? Even I, a woman, cannot stand the way it feels inside my heart."[7]

From my present position, it is evident that the tape recording of the dead man's boast evoked powerful feelings of bereavement, particularly rage and the impulse to headhunt. At the time I could only feel apprehensive and diffusely sense the force of the emotions experienced by Insan, Tukbaw, Wagat, and the others present.

The dilemma for the Ilongots grew out of a set of cultural practices that, when blocked, were agonizing to live with. The cessation of headhunting called for painful adjustments to other modes of coping with the rage they found in bereavement. One could compare their dilemma with the notion that the failure to perform rituals can create anxiety.[8] In the Ilongot case, the cultural notion that throwing away a human head also casts away the anger creates a problem of meaning when the headhunting ritual cannot be performed. Indeed, Max Weber's classic problem of meaning in *The Protestant Ethic and the Spirit of Capitalism* is precisely of this kind.[9] On a logical plane, the Calvinist doctrine of predestination seems flawless: God has chosen the elect, but his decision can never be known by mortals. Among those whose ultimate concern is salvation, the doctrine of predestination is as easy to grasp conceptually as it is impossible to endure in everyday life (unless one happens to be a "religious virtuoso"). For Calvinists and Ilongots alike, the problem of meaning resides in practice, not theory. The dilemma for both groups involves the practical matter of how to live with one's beliefs, rather than the logical puzzlement produced by abstruse doctrine.

HOW I FOUND THE RAGE IN GRIEF

One burden of this introduction concerns the claim that it took some fourteen years for me to grasp what Ilongots had told me about grief, rage,

7. M. Rosaldo, *Knowledge and Passion*, p. 33.
8. See A. R. Radcliffe-Brown, *Structure and Function in Primitive Society* (London: Cohen and West, Ltd., 1952), pp. 133–52. For a broader debate on the "functions" of ritual, see the essays by Bronislaw Malinowski, A. R. Radcliffe-Brown, and George C. Homans, in *Reader in Comparative Religion: An Anthropological Approach* (4th ed.), ed. William A. Lessa and Evon Z. Vogt (New York: Harper and Row, 1979), pp. 37–62.
9. Max Weber, *The Protestant Ethic and the Spirit of Capitalism* (New York: Charles Scribner's Sons, 1958).

and headhunting. During all those years I was not yet in a position to comprehend the force of anger possible in bereavement, and now I am. Introducing myself into this account requires a certain hesitation both because of the discipline's taboo and because of its increasingly frequent violation by essays laced with trendy amalgams of continental philosophy and autobiographical snippets. If classic ethnography's vice was the slippage from the ideal of detachment to actual indifference, that of present-day reflexivity is the tendency for the self-absorbed Self to lose sight altogether of the culturally different Other. Despite the risks involved, as the ethnographer I must enter the discussion at this point to elucidate certain issues of method.

The key concept in what follows is that of the positioned (and repositioned) subject.[10] In routine interpretive procedure, according to the methodology of hermeneutics, one can say that ethnographers reposition themselves as they go about understanding other cultures. Ethnographers begin research with a set of questions, revise them throughout the course of inquiry, and in the end emerge with different questions than they started with. One's surprise at the answer to a question, in other words, requires one to revise the question until lessening surprises or diminishing returns indicate a stopping point. This interpretive approach has been most influentially articulated within anthropology by Clifford Geertz.[11]

Interpretive method usually rests on the axiom that gifted ethnographers learn their trade by preparing themselves as broadly as possible. To follow the meandering course of ethnographic inquiry, field-workers require wide-ranging theoretical capacities and finely tuned sensibilities. After all, one cannot predict beforehand what one will encounter in the field. One influential anthropologist, Clyde Kluckhohn, even went so far as to recommend a double initiation: first, the ordeal of psychoanalysis, and then that of fieldwork. All too often, however, this view is extended

10. A key antecedent to what I have called the "positioned subject" is Alfred Schutz, *Collected Papers*, vol. 1, *The Problem of Social Reality*, ed. and intro. Maurice Natanson (The Hague: Martinus Nijhoff, 1971). See also, e.g., Aaron Cicourel, *Method and Measurement in Sociology* (Glencoe, Ill.: The Free Press, 1964) and Gerald Berreman, *Behind Many Masks: Ethnography and Impression Management in a Himalayan Village*, Monograph No. 4 (Ithaca, N.Y.: Society for Applied Anthropology, 1962). For an early anthropological article on how differently positioned subjects interpret the "same" culture in different ways, see John W. Bennett, "The Interpretation of Pueblo Culture," *Southwestern Journal of Anthropology* 2 (1946): 361–74.

11. Clifford Geertz, *The Interpretation of Cultures* (New York: Basic Books, 1974) and *Local Knowledge: Further Essays in Interpretive Anthropology* (New York: Basic Books, 1983).

until certain prerequisites of field research appear to guarantee an authoritative ethnography. Eclectic book knowledge and a range of life experiences, along with edifying reading and self-awareness, supposedly
vanquish the twin vices of ignorance and insensitivity.

Although the doctrine of preparation, knowledge, and sensibility
contains much to admire, one should work to undermine the false comfort that it can convey. At what point can people say that they have completed their learning or their life experience? The problem with taking
this mode of preparing the ethnographer too much to heart is that it can
lend a false air of security, an authoritative claim to certitude and finality
that our analyses cannot have. All interpretations are provisional; they are
made by positioned subjects who are prepared to know certain things and
not others. Even when knowledgeable, sensitive, fluent in the language,
and able to move easily in an alien cultural world, good ethnographers
still have their limits, and their analyses always are incomplete. Thus, I
began to fathom the force of what Ilongots had been telling me about
their losses through my own loss, and not through any systematic preparation for field research.

My preparation for understanding serious loss began in 1970 with
the death of my brother, shortly after his twenty-seventh birthday. By experiencing this ordeal with my mother and father, I gained a measure of
insight into the trauma of a parent's losing a child. This insight informed
my account, partially described earlier, of an Ilongot man's reactions to
the death of his seventh child. At the same time, my bereavement was so
much less than that of my parents that I could not then imagine the
overwhelming force of rage possible in such grief. My former position is
probably similar to that of many in the discipline. One should recognize
that ethnographic knowledge tends to have the strengths and limitations
given by the relative youth of field-workers who, for the most part, have
not suffered serious losses and could have, for example, no personal
knowledge of how devastating the loss of a long-term partner can be for
the survivor.

In 1981 Michelle Rosaldo and I began field research among the Ifu-
gaos of northern Luzon, Philippines. On October 11 of that year, she was
walking along a trail with two Ifugao companions when she lost her footing
and fell to her death some 65 feet down a sheer precipice into a swollen
river below. Immediately on finding her body I became enraged. How
could she abandon me? How could she have been so stupid as to fall? I
tried to cry. I sobbed, but rage blocked the tears. Less than a month later I
described this moment in my journal: "I felt like in a nightmare, the whole
world around me expanding and contracting, visually and viscerally heav-

ing. Going down I find a group of men, maybe seven or eight, standing still, silent, and I heave and sob, but no tears." An earlier experience, on the fourth anniversary of my brother's death, had taught me to recognize heaving sobs without tears as a form of anger. This anger, in a number of forms, has swept over me on many occasions since then, lasting hours and even days at a time. Such feelings can be aroused by rituals, but more often they emerge from unexpected reminders (not unlike the Ilongots' unnerving encounter with their dead uncle's voice on the tape recorder).

Lest there be any misunderstanding, bereavement should not be reduced to anger, neither for myself nor for anyone else.[12] Powerful visceral emotional states swept over me, at times separately and at other times together. I experienced the deep cutting pain of sorrow almost beyond endurance, the cadaverous cold of realizing the finality of death, the trembling beginning in my abdomen and spreading through my body, the mournful keening that started without my willing, and frequent tearful sobbing. My present purpose of revising earlier understandings of Ilongot headhunting, and not a general view of bereavement, thus focuses on anger rather than on other emotions in grief.

Writings in English especially need to emphasize the rage in grief. Although grief therapists routinely encourage awareness of anger among the bereaved, upper-middle-class Anglo-American culture tends to ignore the rage devastating losses can bring. Paradoxically, this culture's conventional wisdom usually denies the anger in grief at the same time that therapists encourage members of the invisible community of the bereaved to talk in detail about how angry their losses make them feel. My brother's death in combination with what I learned about anger from Ilongots (for them, an emotional state more publicly celebrated than denied) allowed me immediately to recognize the experience of rage.[13]

Ilongot anger and my own overlap, rather like two circles, partially overlaid and partially separate. They are not identical. Alongside striking

12. Although anger appears so often in bereavement as to be virtually universal, certain notable exceptions do occur. Clifford Geertz, for example, depicts Javanese funerals as follows: "The mood of a Javanese funeral is not one of hysterical bereavement, unrestrained sobbing, or even of formalized cries of grief for the deceased's departure. Rather, it is a calm, undemonstrative, almost languid letting go, a brief ritualized relinquishment of a relationship no longer possible" (Geertz, *The Interpretation of Cultures*, p. 153). In cross-cultural perspective, the anger in grief presents itself in different degrees (including zero), in different forms, and with different consequences.
13. The Ilongot notion of anger (*liget*) is regarded as dangerous in its violent excesses, but also as life-enhancing in that, for example, it provides energy for work. See the extensive discussion in M. Rosaldo, *Knowledge and Passion*.

similarities, significant differences in tone, cultural form, and human consequences distinguish the "anger" animating our respective ways of grieving. My vivid fantasies, for example, about a life insurance agent who refused to recognize Michelle's death as job-related did not lead me to kill him, cut off his head, and celebrate afterward. In so speaking, I am illustrating the discipline's methodological caution against the reckless attribution of one's own categories and experiences to members of another culture. Such warnings against facile notions of universal human nature can, however, be carried too far and harden into the equally pernicious doctrine that, my own group aside, everything human is alien to me. One hopes to achieve a balance between recognizing wide-ranging human differences and the modest truism that any two human groups must have certain things in common.

Only a week before completing the initial draft of an earlier version of this introduction, I rediscovered my journal entry, written some six weeks after Michelle's death, in which I made a vow to myself about how I would return to writing anthropology, if I ever did so, "by writing Grief and a Headhunter's Rage . . ." My journal went on to reflect more broadly on death, rage, and headhunting by speaking of my "wish for the Ilongot solution; they are much more in touch with reality than Christians. So, I need a place to carry my anger—and can we say a solution of the imagination is better than theirs? And can we condemn them when we napalm villages? Is our rationale so much sounder than theirs?" All this was written in despair and rage.

Not until some fifteen months after Michelle's death was I again able to begin writing anthropology. Writing the initial version of "Grief and a Headhunter's Rage" was in fact cathartic, though perhaps not in the way one would imagine. Rather than following after the completed composition, the catharsis occurred beforehand. When the initial version of this introduction was most acutely on my mind, during the month before actually beginning to write, I felt diffusely depressed and ill with a fever. Then one day an almost literal fog lifted and words began to flow. It seemed less as if I were doing the writing than that the words were writing themselves through me.

My use of personal experience serves as a vehicle for making the quality and intensity of the rage in Ilongot grief more readily accessible to readers than certain more detached modes of composition. At the same time, by invoking personal experience as an analytical category one risks easy dismissal. Unsympathetic readers could reduce this introduction to an act of mourning or a mere report on my discovery of the anger possible in bereavement. Frankly, this introduction is both and more. An act of mourning, a personal report, *and* a critical analysis of anthropological method, it simultaneously encompasses a number of distinguishable processes, no one of which cancels out the others. Similarly, I argue in what follows that ritual in general and Ilongot headhunting in particular form the intersection of multiple coexisting social processes. Aside from revising the ethnographic record, the paramount claim made here concerns how my own mourning and consequent reflection on Ilongot bereavement, rage, and headhunting raise methodological issues of general concern in anthropology and the human sciences.

DEATH IN ANTHROPOLOGY

Anthropology favors interpretations that equate analytical "depth" with cultural "elaboration." Many studies focus on visibly bounded arenas where one can observe formal and repetitive events, such as ceremonies, rituals, and games. Similarly, studies of word play are more likely to focus on jokes as programmed monologues than on the less scripted, more freewheeling improvised interchanges of witty banter. Most ethnographers prefer to study events that have definite locations in space with marked centers and outer edges. Temporally, they have middles and endings. Historically, they appear to repeat identical structures by seemingly doing things today as they were done yesterday. Their qualities of fixed definition liberate such events from the untidiness of everyday life so that they can be "read" like articles, books, or, as we now say, *texts*.

Guided by their emphasis on self-contained entities, ethnographies written in accord with classic norms consider death under the rubric of ritual rather than bereavement. Indeed, the subtitles of even recent ethnographies on death make the emphasis on ritual explicit. William Douglass's *Death in Murelaga* is subtitled *Funerary Ritual in a Spanish Basque Village*; Richard Huntington and Peter Metcalf's *Celebrations of Death* is subtitled *The Anthropology of Mortuary Ritual*; Peter Metcalf's *A Borneo Journey into Death* is subtitled *Berawan Eschatology from Its Rituals.*[14] Ritual itself is defined by its formality and routine; under such descriptions, it more nearly resembles a recipe, a fixed program, or a book of etiquette than an open-ended human process.

14. William Douglass, *Death in Murelaga: Funerary Ritual in a Spanish Basque Village* (Seattle: University of Washington Press, 1969); Richard Huntington and Peter Metcalf, *Celebrations of Death: The Anthropology of Mortuary Ritual* (New York: Cambridge University Press, 1979); Metcalf, *A Borneo Journey into Death.*

Ethnographies that in this manner eliminate intense emotions not only distort their descriptions but also remove potentially key variables from their explanations. When anthropologist William Douglass, for example, announces his project in *Death in Murelaga*, he explains that his objective is to use death and funerary ritual "as a heuristic device with which to approach the study of rural Basque society."[15] In other words, the primary object of study is social structure, not death, and certainly not bereavement. The author begins his analysis by saying, "Death is not always fortuitous or unpredictable."[16] He goes on to describe how an old woman, ailing with the infirmities of her age, welcomed her death. The description largely ignores the perspective of the most bereaved survivors, and instead vacillates between those of the old woman and a detached observer.

Undeniably, certain people do live a full life and suffer so greatly in their decrepitude that they embrace the relief death can bring. Yet the problem with making an ethnography's major case study focus on "a very easy death"[17] (I use Simone de Beauvoir's title with irony, as she did) is not only its lack of representativeness but also that it makes death in general appear as routine for the survivors as this particular one apparently was for the deceased. Were the old woman's sons and daughters untouched by her death? The case study shows less about how people cope with death than about how death can be made to appear routine, thereby fitting neatly into the author's view of funerary ritual as a mechanical programmed unfolding of prescribed acts. "To the Basque," says Douglass, "ritual is order and order is ritual."[18]

Douglass captures only one extreme in the range of possible deaths. Putting the accent on the routine aspects of ritual conveniently conceals the agony of such unexpected early deaths as parents losing a grown child or a mother dying in childbirth. Concealed in such descriptions are the agonies of the survivors who muddle through shifting, powerful emotional states. Although Douglass acknowledges the distinction between the bereaved members of the deceased's domestic group and the more public ritualistic group, he writes his account primarily from the viewpoint of the latter. He masks the emotional force of bereavement by reducing funerary ritual to orderly routine.

15. Douglass, *Death in Murelaga*, p. 209.
16. Ibid., p. 19.
17. Simone de Beauvoir, *A Very Easy Death* (Harmondsworth, United Kingdom: Penguin Books, 1969).
18. Douglass, *Death in Murelaga*, p. 209.

Surely, human beings mourn both in ritual settings *and* in the informal settings of everyday life. Consider the evidence that willy-nilly spills over the edges in Godfrey Wilson's classic anthropological account of "conventions of burial" among the Nyakyusa of South Africa:

> That some at least of those who attend a Nyakyusa burial are moved by grief it is easy to establish. I have heard people talking regretfully in ordinary conversation of a man's death; I have seen a man whose sister had just died walk over alone towards her grave and weep quietly by himself without any parade of grief; and I have heard of a man killing himself because of his grief for a dead son.[19]

Note that all the instances Wilson witnesses or hears about happen outside the circumscribed sphere of formal ritual. People converse among themselves, walk alone and silently weep, or more impulsively commit suicide. The work of grieving, probably universally, occurs both within obligatory ritual acts and in more everyday settings where people find themselves alone or with close kin.

In Nyakyusa burial ceremonies, powerful emotional states also become present in the ritual itself, which is more than a series of obligatory acts. Men say they dance the passions of their bereavement, which includes a complex mix of anger, fear, and grief:

> "This war dance (*ukukina*)," said an old man, "is mourning, we are mourning the dead man. We dance because there is war in our hearts. A passion of grief and fear exasperates us (*ilyyojo likutusila*)." . . . *Elyojo* means a passion or grief, anger or fear; *ukusila* means to annoy or exasperate beyond endurance. In explaining *ukusila* one man put it like this: "If a man continually insults me then he exasperates me (*ukusila*) so that I want to fight him." Death is a fearful and grievous event that exasperates those men nearly concerned and makes them want to fight.[20]

Descriptions of the dance and subsequent quarrels, even killings, provide ample evidence of the emotional intensity involved. The articulate testimony by Wilson's informants makes it obvious that even the most intense sentiments can be studied by ethnographers.

19. Godfrey Wilson, *Nyakyusa Conventions of Burial* (Johannesburg: The University of Witwatersrand Press, 1939), pp. 22–23. (Reprinted from *Bantu Studies.*)
20. Ibid., p. 13.

Despite such exceptions as Wilson, the general rule seems to be that one should tidy things up as much as possible by wiping away the tears and ignoring the tantrums. Most anthropological studies of death eliminate emotions by assuming the position of the most detached observer.[21] Such studies usually conflate the ritual process with the process of mourning, equate ritual with the obligatory, and ignore the relation between ritual and everyday life. The bias that favors formal ritual risks assuming the answers to questions that most need to be asked. Do rituals, for example, always reveal cultural depth?

Most analysts who equate death with funerary ritual assume that rituals store encapsulated wisdom as if it were a microcosm of its encompassing cultural macrocosm. One recent study of death and mourning, for example, confidently begins by affirming that rituals embody "the collective wisdom of many cultures."[22] Yet this generalization surely requires case-by-case investigation against a broader range of alternative hypotheses.

At the polar extremes, rituals either display cultural depth or brim over with platitudes. In the former case, rituals indeed encapsulate a culture's wisdom; in the latter instance, they act as catalysts that precipitate processes whose unfolding occurs over subsequent months or even years. Many rituals, of course, do both by combining a measure of wisdom with a comparable dose of platitudes.

My own experience of bereavement and ritual fits the platitudes and catalyst model better than that of microcosmic deep culture. Even a careful analysis of the language and symbolic action during the two funerals for which I was a chief mourner would reveal precious little about the experience of bereavement.[23] This statement, of course, should not lead anyone to derive a universal from somebody else's personal knowledge.

---

21. In his survey of works on death published during the 1960s, for example, Johannes Fabian found that the four major anthropological journals carried only nine papers on the topic, most of which "dealt only with the purely ceremonial aspects of death" (Johannes Fabian, "How Others Die—Reflections on the Anthropology of Death," in *Death in American Experience*, ed. A. Mack [New York: Schocken, 1973], p. 178).
22. Huntington and Metcalf, *Celebrations of Death*, p. 1.
23. Arguably, ritual works differently for those most afflicted by a particular death than for those least so. Funerals may distance the former from overwhelming emotions whereas they may draw the latter closer to strongly felt sentiments (see T. J. Scheff, *Catharsis in Healing, Ritual, and Drama* [Berkeley: University of California Press, 1979]). Such issues can be investigated through the notion of the positioned subject.

Instead, it should encourage ethnographers to ask whether a ritual's wisdom is deep or conventional, and whether its process is immediately transformative or but a single step in a lengthy series of ritual and everyday events.

In attempting to grasp the cultural force of rage and other powerful emotional states, both formal ritual and the informal practices of everyday life provide crucial insight. Thus, cultural descriptions should seek out force as well as thickness, and they should extend from well-defined rituals to myriad less circumscribed practices.

GRIEF, RAGE, AND ILONGOT HEADHUNTING

When applied to Ilongot headhunting, the view of ritual as a storehouse of collective wisdom aligns headhunting with expiatory sacrifice. The raiders call the spirits of the potential victims, bid their ritual farewells, and seek favorable omens along the trail. Ilongot men vividly recall the hunger and deprivation they endure over the days and even weeks it takes to move cautiously toward the place where they set up an ambush and await the first person who happens along. Once the raiders kill their victim, they toss away the head rather than keep it as a trophy. In tossing away the head, they claim by analogy to cast away their life burdens, including the rage in their grief.

Before a raid, men describe their state of being by saying that the burdens of life have made them heavy and entangled, like a tree with vines clinging to it. They say that a successfully completed raid makes them feel light of step and ruddy in complexion. The collective energy of the celebration with its song, music, and dance reportedly gives the participants a sense of well-being. The expiatory ritual process involves cleansing and catharsis.

The analysis just sketched regards ritual as a timeless, self-contained process. Without denying the insight in this approach, its limits must also be considered. Imagine, for example, exorcism rituals described as if they were complete in themselves, rather than being linked with larger processes unfolding before and after the ritual period. Through what processes does the afflicted person recover or continue to be afflicted after the ritual? What are the social consequences of recovery or its absence? Failure to consider such questions diminishes the force of such afflictions and therapies for which the formal ritual is but a phase. Still other questions apply to differently positioned subjects, including the person afflicted, the healer, and the audience. In all cases, the problem involves the delineation of processes that occur before and after, as well as during, the ritual moment.

Let us call the notion of a self-contained sphere of deep cultural activity the *microcosmic view,* and an alternative view *ritual as a busy intersection.* In the latter case, ritual appears as a place where a number of distinct social processes intersect. The crossroads simply provides a space for distinct trajectories to traverse, rather than containing them in complete encapsulated form. From this perspective, Ilongot headhunting stands at the confluence of three analytically separable processes.

The first process concerns whether or not it is an opportune time to raid. Historical conditions determine the possibilities of raiding, which range from frequent to likely to unlikely to impossible. These conditions include American colonial efforts at pacification, the Great Depression, World War II, revolutionary movements in the surrounding lowlands, feuding among Ilongot groups, and the declaration of martial law in 1972. Ilongots use the analogy of hunting to speak of such historical vicissitudes. Much as Ilongot huntsmen say they cannot know when game will cross their path or whether their arrows will strike the target, so certain historical forces that condition their existence, remain beyond their control. My book *Ilongot Headhunting, 1883–1974* explores the impact of historical factors on Ilongot headhunting.

Second, young men coming of age undergo a protracted period of personal turmoil during which they desire nothing so much as to take a head. During this troubled period, they seek a life partner and contemplate the traumatic dislocation of leaving their families of origin and entering their new wife's household as a stranger. Young men weep, sing, and burst out in anger because of their fierce desire to take a head and wear the coveted red hornbill earrings that adorn the ears of men who already have, as Ilongots say, arrived (*tabi*). Volatile, envious, passionate (at least according to their own cultural stereotype of the young unmarried man [*buintaw*]), they constantly lust to take a head. Michelle and I began fieldwork among the Ilongots only a year after abandoning our unmarried youths; hence our ready empathy with youthful turbulence. Her book on Ilongot notions of self explores the passionate anger of young men as they come of age.

Third, older men are differently positioned than their younger counterparts. Because they have already beheaded somebody, they can wear the red hornbill earrings so coveted by youths. Their desire to headhunt grows less from chronic adolescent turmoil than from more intermittent acute agonies of loss. After the death of somebody to whom they are closely attached, older men often inflict on themselves vows of abstinence, not to be lifted until the day they participate in a successful headhunting raid. These deaths can cover a range of instances from literal death, whether through natural causes or beheading, to social death where, for example, a man's wife runs off with another man. In all cases, the rage born of devastating loss animates the older men's desire to raid. This anger at abandonment is irreducible in that nothing at a deeper level explains it. Although certain analysts argue against the dreaded last analysis, the linkage of grief, rage, and headhunting has no other known explanation.

My earlier understandings of Ilongot headhunting missed the fuller significance of how older men experience loss and rage. Older men prove critical in this context because they, not the youths, set the processes of headhunting in motion. Their rage is intermittent, whereas that of youths is continuous. In the equation of headhunting, older men are the variable and younger men are the constant. Culturally speaking, older men are endowed with knowledge and stamina that their juniors have not yet attained, hence they care for (saysay) and lead (bukur) the younger men when they raid.

In a preliminary survey of the literature on headhunting, I found that the lifting of mourning prohibitions frequently occurs after taking a head. The notion that youthful anger and older men's rage lead them to take heads is more plausible than such commonly reported "explanations" of headhunting as the need to acquire mystical "soul stuff" or personal names.[24] Because the discipline correctly rejects stereotypes of the "bloodthirsty savage," it must investigate how headhunters create an intense desire to decapitate their fellow humans. The human sciences must explore the cultural force of emotions with a view to delineating the passions that animate certain forms of human conduct.

24. For a discussion of cultural motives for headhunting, see Robert McKinley, "Human and Proud of It! A Structural Treatment of Headhunting Rites and the Social Definition of Enemies," in Studies in Borneo Societies: Social Process and Anthropological Explanation, ed. G. Appell (DeKalb, Ill.: Center for Southeast Asian Studies, Northern Illinois University, 1976), pp. 92–126; Rodney Needham, "Skulls and Causality," Man 11 (1976): 71–88; Michelle Rosaldo, "Skulls and Causality," Man 12 (1977): 168–70.

SUMMARY

The ethnographer, as a positioned subject, grasps certain human phenomena better than others. He or she occupies a position or structural location and observes with a particular angle of vision. Consider, for example, how age, gender, being an outsider, and association with a neocolonial regime influence what the ethnographer learns. The notion of position also refers to how life experiences both enable and inhibit particular kinds of insight. In the case at hand, nothing in my own experience equipped me even to imagine the anger possible in bereavement until after Michelle Rosaldo's death in 1981. Only then was I in a position to grasp the force of what Ilongots had repeatedly told me about grief, rage, and headhunting. By the same token, so-called natives are also positioned subjects who have a distinctive mix of insight and blindness. Consider the structural positions of older versus younger Ilongot men, or the differing positions of chief mourners versus those less involved during a funeral. My discussion of anthropological writings on death often achieved its effects simply by shifting from the position of those least involved to that of the chief mourners.

Cultural depth does not always equal cultural elaboration. Think simply of the speaker who is filibustering. The language used can sound elaborate as it heaps word on word, but surely it is not deep. Depth should be separated from the presence or absence of elaboration. By the same token, one-line explanations can be vacuous or pithy. The concept of force calls attention to an enduring intensity in human conduct that can occur with or without the dense elaboration conventionally associated with cultural depth. Although relatively without elaboration in speech, song, or ritual, the rage of older Ilongot men who have suffered devastating losses proves enormously consequential in that, foremost among other things, it leads them to behead their fellow humans. Thus, the notion of force involves both affective intensity and significant consequences that unfold over a long period of time.

Similarly, rituals do not always encapsulate deep cultural wisdom. At times they instead contain the wisdom of Polonius. Although certain rituals both reflect and create ultimate values, others simply bring people together and deliver a set of platitudes that enable them to go on with their lives. Rituals serve as vehicles for processes that occur both before and after the period of their performance. Funeral rituals, for example, do not "contain" all the complex processes of bereavement. Ritual and bereavement should not be collapsed into one another because they neither fully encapsulate nor fully explain one another. Instead, rituals are often but points along a number of longer processual trajectories; hence, my image of ritual as a crossroads where distinct life processes intersect.[25]

· · ·

In contrast with the classic view, which posits culture as a self-contained whole made up of coherent patterns, culture can arguably be conceived as a more porous array of intersections where distinct processes crisscross from within and beyond its borders. Such heterogeneous processes often derive from differences of age, gender, class, race, and sexual orientation.

[I argue] that a sea change in cultural studies has eroded once-dominant conceptions of truth and objectivity. The truth of objectivism— absolute, universal, and timeless—has lost its monopoly status. It now competes, on more nearly equal terms, with the truths of case studies that are embedded in local contexts, shaped by local interests, and colored by local perceptions. The agenda for social analysis has shifted to include not only eternal verities and lawlike generalizations but also political processes, social changes, and human differences. Such terms as *objectivity*, *neutrality*, and *impartiality* refer to subject positions once endowed with great institutional authority, but they are arguably neither more nor less valid than those of more engaged, yet equally perceptive, knowledgeable social actors. Social analysis must now grapple with the realization that its objects of analysis are also analyzing subjects who critically interrogate ethnographers—their writings, their ethics, and their politics.

25. Pierre Bourdieu, *Outline of a Theory of Practice* (New York: Cambridge University Press, 1977), p. 1.

ACTIVE READING

1. At the end of his essay, Rosaldo warns anthropologists that the people they study "are also analyzing subjects who critically interrogate ethnographers" (457). Study some passages in which Rosaldo shows himself having conversations with Ilongot people. How might these moments clarify the meaning of Rosaldo's conclusion?

2. Look closely at those places in Rosaldo's essay where he uses quotations from his own earlier writings. Why does Rosaldo choose to quote himself? Consider what his use of these quotations tells you about his process of rereading and revision. In what ways are his and your own revision practices similar?

3. Like many writings in the social sciences, Rosaldo's text ends with what he calls a "summary." Carefully read this section of the essay, and note which passages repeat points that Rosaldo has already made and which ones may introduce new arguments. Why would a writer choose to introduce new ideas at the end of his or her text?

READING IN NEW CONTEXTS

1. Locate as many references to religion in Rosaldo's essay as you can find. Taken together, what do these references tell you about the possible social uses of religion? Apply your new insights to Baldwin, Black Elk, or another *Literacies* text which places religion into a social context.

2. Rosaldo claims that, even with the best professional preparation, all anthropologists' interpretations are necessarily incomplete. How do Brody's theories about professionalism help you understand why even well-trained ethnographers might be, in Rosaldo's words, "prepared to know certain things and not others" (446)?

3. Pick another essay from *Literacies* that uses emotion in an illuminating way (Baldwin, Durham, and Lorde are examples). Which of Rosaldo's theories about "the cultural force of emotions" (439) help you to interpret this new essay? How is your understanding of Rosaldo's text changed by the other writer's use of emotion?

DRAFT ONE / DRAFT TWO

1. *Draft One*: Rosaldo offers two ways of looking at social rituals: the "microcosmic view," and the view of ritual as a "busy intersection" (454). Choose a social ritual that you have witnessed or participated in, and interpret it in terms of each of these theories. In your opinion, which theory applies best to the ritual you have described?

Draft Two: Look at Fienup-Riordan's or Scholes's discussions of ritual. What details from Draft One help you to understand how one of these other writers uses the notion of ritual?

2. *Draft One:* Rosaldo describes the "practical" dilemma of "how to live with one's beliefs" (444), a dilemma that the Ilongots face when they can no longer get rid of their anger by headhunting. Working from your own experience, describe an aspect of your life that conflicts uncomfortably with some belief that you share with your culture. How does the difficulty of living with your beliefs become a "problem of meaning" in your life?

Draft Two: Working with Gilmore, Scheper-Hughes, or el-Saadawi, expand the discussion you began in Draft One by considering the perspectives of the new writer and his or her subjects. Taking your own and these other positions into account, what can you say about the problem of living with one's beliefs?

BEFORE READING NAWAL EL-SAADAWI

1. Describe the freedoms (economic, intellectual, sexual, social, among others) that are most important to you. What relationships do you see among these different freedoms? What do you do when they conflict with each other or when they conflict with other people's freedoms?

2. Recall a story that captured your interest. What was it about the story that drew you in? How did it correspond to your own life experiences?

3. What do you expect when you read history? when you read stories? Explain where and when you learned your expectations about each kind of writing. How are these forms related to each other?

NAWAL EL-SAADAWI

LOVE AND SEX
IN THE LIFE OF
THE ARAB

A famous work of art, A *Thousand and One Nights*, has been used by many Western researchers and authors, who describe themselves as 'orientalists', as a source of material and information for studying the life of the Arab. They consider that these stories, especially those dealing with love and sexual intrigues, afford an insight into the understanding of the Arab character, seeing them as keys with which to open the doors to the 'Arab Soul', and as valuable means towards penetrating the depths, or rather the shallow waters, of the Arab mind and heart.

Yet anyone with the slightest knowledge of Arab literature knows that the stories related in A *Thousand and One Nights* are only a partial and one-sided reflection of a very narrow section of Arab society, as it lived and dreamed, loved and fornicated, intrigued and plundered, more than ten centuries ago. I do not know very much about the level reached by European civilization at the time, the state of human affairs in society there, in the sciences and in the arts, but I at least know enough to be able to say that Arab society had undoubtedly advanced much further. Many are the scholars, writers and researchers who have made compari-

From *The Hidden Face of Eve: Women in the Arab World,* translated by Sherif Hetata (1980).

sons between the West and the Arab World, only drawing their examples from a period in our history, now more than a thousand years old. One would have to have a very bad memory to forget, in one gigantic leap, what is in terms of time half the number of years which have elapsed since the birth of Christ. How can we depict the contrasts between the Arab character at the time when the people of A *Thousand and One Nights* flew on their magic carpets, and the Western mind of the Victorian era when purity floated like a thick veil over the corrupt and bloated features of a hypocritical society?[1] How much more true and scientific would a comparative study have been of the lifestyles of Arab and European men from the same period, or at least from the Middles Ages when the clergy, who were the male intelligentsia of the time, were busy prompting women accused of sorcery to utter the most obscene sexual epithets, and, under insufferable torture, forcing them to admit to the very crimes which they had been taught to describe?[2]

This picture of the sex-mad Arab fawning on an extensive harem is maintained with dubious insistence even today. Without exception the films, magazines and newspapers that roll out from the reels of Western producers and the dark-rooms of Western monopolies, depict Arab men as trotting behind the skirts of women, ogling the ample bosoms of seductive blondes, and squandering their money, or quenching their thirst for alcohol or sex. Arab women, in their turn, are depicted as twisting and turning in snake-like dances, flaunting their naked bellies and quivering hips, seducing men with the promise of dark passion, playful, secretive and intriguing, a picture drawn from the palaces of A *Thousand and One Nights* and the slave women of the Caliph, Haroun El Raschid.

Is it possible to believe that this distorted image of Arab men and women is representative of their true life and character in the Arab world of today? Personally, I am sure that it is not even representative of men and women living at the time of Haroun El Raschid. Perhaps it has some authenticity as a reflection of certain aspects of the life led by palace rulers and their concubines in those bygone days, but these were only an infinitesimal minority compared to the vast mass of Arabs, who led a harsh and difficult existence with no room for, nor possibility of ever experiencing, the silken cushions, soft flesh and fiery liquids of dissipation. The sexual life of kings and princely rulers, whether in the past or

1. P. H. Newby, A *Selection from the Arabian Nights*, translated by Sir Richard Burton, Introduction from p. vii–xvii (Pocket Books, N.T., 1954).
2. Franz G. Alexander and Sheldon T. Selesnick, *The History of Psychiatry*, p. 68.

present, in the modern West or more archaic East, to the South of the Earth's equator or to the North, has maintained the same essential pattern, embroidered with a greater or lesser degree of sophistication or refinement, sadism or depravity.

Sweeping judgements, which depict the nature of Arabs in general, and the men of the Arab world in particular, as being obsessed with sex and more inclined to pursue the pleasures of the body than men from other regions or countries, are therefore unfounded and incorrect. Their aim is to contribute to and maintain a distorted image of the Arabs in the minds of people all over the world, to falsify the true colours of their struggle for independence, progress and control over their destinies, and to facilitate the task of conservative, reactionary and imperialist forces that continue to survive and prosper by such means.

I believe that freedom in all its forms, whether sexual, intellectual, social or economic, is a necessity for every man and woman, and for all societies. Nevertheless, I feel that the sexual freedom that has accompanied the evolution of modern capitalist society has been developed very much in a unilateral direction and has not been linked with, or been related to, a parallel development of social and economic freedoms. This sheds some doubt on the real motives behind the consistent and ever increasing campaign calling upon men and women to throw their sexual inhibitions and beliefs overboard. It also jeopardizes the chances of human progress and fulfilment, since a one-sided development that does not take into consideration the totality of life can only lead to new distortions and monstrosities.

This is why there is a growing realization that sexual freedom, as it is preached today in modern capitalist society, has no valid answers or solutions to many of the problems of personal life and human happiness, and that it is only another and perhaps more ingenuous way of making people pay the price of ever expanding consumption, of accumulating profits and of feeding the appetites of monopolistic giants. Another opium to be inhaled and imbibed so that mobilized energies may be dissipated rather than built up into a force of resistance and revolt against all forms of exploitation.

In this respect, Eastern and Arab societies have not differed from the West. Here again it is mainly economic necessity which governs the direction in which values, human morals and norms of sexual behaviour move. The economic imperatives of Arab society required a wide degree of sexual freedom to ensure the provision of large numbers of offspring. Polygamy, as against polyandry, tends to be more prolific as far as children are concerned. Arab society, still primitive and badly equipped to face the vicissitudes and harshness of desert life, suffered from a very high mortality rate, especially among infants and children, which had to be compensated for by correspondingly high birth rates. The economic and military strength of tribes and clans in a society which possessed neither modern tools or machines, nor modern weapons, depended very much on their numbers. In addition, the simple crude existence of desert life and the extreme poverty of nomadic tribes meant that, while the cost of maintaining a child was minimal, the child could play useful roles in meeting the productive needs of the time, being capable of running errands or looking after the camels and sheep.

Wars and battles were an integral part of tribal life and flared up at frequent intervals, and death took a heavy toll of the men. This was particularly the case after Islam started to establish itself and expand. It was natural that this new threat should meet with the resistance of the neighbouring rulers and the older religions entrenched in the surrounding regions, and that the Muslims should be obliged to fight numerous battles before they could succeed in establishing and stabilizing their new State. The result was heavy losses in men and a marked imbalance characterized by a much higher number of women, accentuated by the throngs of women slave prisoners brought back from victorious battles.

The easiest and most natural solution to such a situation was to allow men to marry more than one woman, and in addition to choose from among the women brought back from the wars, or sold in the markets, those whom they considered suitable to be wives, concubines or slaves in their households. Each man did so according to his means, and these means of course varied widely from one man to another. With a superfluity of women, a man would take pride in the number of women he could maintain, and the bigger this number, the more occasion for him to boast about the extensiveness of his female retinue, and about his powers over women, whether in marriage or in love. On the other hand, women would compete for the favours of men and excel in subtle allurements to attract men towards marriage, love and sex.

This was perhaps an additional factor which tended to make Arab women more forward and positive in love and sex, characteristics in clear contrast to the passive attitudes assumed by the vast majority of women living in our modern era. The other factors, mentioned previously, were the matriarchal vestiges which at the time were still strong in Arab society, and the naturalistic attitudes of Islamic teachings which prevented love and sex from being considered sinful as they were by Christianity. On the contrary, Islam described sexual pleasure as one of the attractions of life, one of the delights for those who go to Paradise after death. As a result, Arab women had no hesitation in being positive towards sex, in expressing their desire for men, in exercising their charms, and weaving their net around whoever might be the object of their attentions. Perhaps they were following in the footsteps of their mother, Eve, who had so ably enticed Adam to comply with her wishes and fall victim to *fitna*,[3] with the result that he dropped from the high heavens in which he was confined and landed with his two feet on the solid, rough, but warm and living earth.

For the Arabs the word 'woman' invariably evokes the word *fitna*. Arab women combined the qualities of a positive personality and *fitna*, or seductiveness, to such an extent that they became an integral part of the Islamic ethos which has, as one of its cornerstones, the sexual powers of women, and which maintains that their seductiveness can lead to a *fitna* within society. Here the word is used in a related but different sense to mean an uprising, rebellion, conspiracy or anarchy which would upset the existing order of things established by Allah (and which, therefore, is not to be changed). From this arose the conception that life could only follow its normal steady and uninterrupted course, and society could only avoid any potential menace to its stability and structure, or any disruption of the social order, if men continued to satisfy the sexual needs of their women, kept them happy, and protected their honour. If this was not ensured a *fitna* could easily be let loose, since the honour of women would be in doubt, and as a result uneasiness and trouble could erupt at any moment. The virtue of women had to be ensured if peace was to reign among men, not an easy task in view of the *fitna* (seductiveness) of women.

Islam's contribution to the understanding of love, sex and the relations between the sexes has never to my knowledge been correctly assessed and given the consideration it deserves. However, the contradictory aspects inherent in Islamic society are reflected in another dramatically opposed tendency which runs through the body of Islamic teaching, and is a continuation of the rigid, reactionary and conservative reasoning that dominated the concepts and practices of Judaism and Christianity in matters related to sex.

Islam inherited the old image of Eve and of women that depicts them as the close followers and instruments of Satan, the body of women

3. *Fitna*, in Arabic, means woman's overpowering seductiveness. It combines the qualities of attraction and mischievousness.

being his abode. A well-known Arab saying maintains that: 'Whenever a man and a woman meet together, their third is always Satan'. Mahomet the Prophet, despite his love for and understanding of women, warns that: 'After I have gone, there will be no greater danger menacing my nation and more liable to create anarchy and trouble than women.'[4]

This attitude towards woman was prominent throughout Islamic thought and she always remained a source of danger to man and to society on account of her power of attraction or *fitna*. Man in the face of such seduction was portrayed as helpless, drained of all his capacities to be positive or to resist. Although this was not a new idea, it assumed big proportions in Islamic theology and was buttressed by many *Ahadith* (proverbs and sayings).

Woman was therefore considered by the Arabs as a menace to man and society, and the only way to avoid the harm she could do was to isolate her in the home, where she could have no contact with either one or the other. If for any reason she had to move outside the walls of her prison, all necessary precautions had to be taken so that no one could get a glimpse of her seductiveness. She was therefore enveloped in veils and flowing robes like explosive material which has to be well packed. In some Arab societies, this concern to conceal the body of women went so far that the split-second uncovering of a finger or a toe was considered a potential source of *fitna* in society which might therefore lead to anarchy, uprisings, rebellions and the total destruction of the established order!

Thus it is that Islam confronted its philosophers and theologians with two contradictory, and in terms of logic, mutually exclusive conceptions: (1) Sex is one of the pleasures and attractions of life; (2) To succumb to sex will lead to *fitna* in society—that is crisis, disruption and anarchy.

The only way out of this dilemma, the only path that could reconcile these two conflicting views, was to lay down a system or framework for sex which on the one hand had to avoid *fitna* while on the other would permit abundant reproduction and a good deal of pleasure within the limits of Allah's prescriptions.

The Imam, El Ghazali, explains how the will of Allah and his wisdom are manifested in the fact that he created sexual desire in both men and women. This is expressed in the words of his Prophet when he said: 'Marry and multiply.' 'Since Allah has revealed his secret to us, and has instructed us clearly what to do, refraining from marriage is like refusing

---

4. Abou Abdallah Mohammed Ismail El Bokhary, *Kitab El Gami El Sahib* (1868), p. 419.

to plough the earth, and wasting the seed. It means leaving the useful tools which Allah has created for us idle, and is a crime against the self-evident reasons and obvious aims of the phenomenon of creation, aims written on the sexual organs in Divine handwriting.'[5]

For El Ghazali, apart from reproduction, marriage aims at immunity from the Devil, breaking the sharp point of desire, avoiding the dangers of passion, keeping our eyes away from what they should not see, safe-guarding the female sexual organs, and following the directives of our Prophet when he said: 'He who marries has ensured for himself the fulfilment of half his religion. Let him therefore fear Allah for the other half.'[6]

Islamic thought admits the strength and power of sexual desire in women, and in men also. Fayad Ibn Nageeh said that, 'if the sexual organ of the man rises up, a third of his religion is lost'. One of the rare explanations given to the Prophet's words by Ibn Abbas, Allah's blessing be upon both of them, is that 'he who enters into a woman is lost in a twilight' and that 'if the male organ rises up, it is an overwhelming catastrophe for once provoked it cannot be resisted by either reason or religion. For this organ is more powerful than all the instruments used by Satan against man.' That is why the Prophet, Allah's peace be upon him, said, 'I have not seen creatures lacking in mind and religion more capable of overcoming men of reason and wisdom than you [women].'[7] He also warned men: 'Do not enter the house of those who have absent ones'—meaning those women whose husbands are away—'for Satan will run out from one of you, like hot blood'. And we said, 'From you also, O Prophet!' He answered, 'And from me also, but Allah has given me his support and so Satan has been subdued.'[8]

From the above, it is clear that the Arabs were accustomed to discuss freely with Mahomet and treated him as an ordinary human being like themselves. If he said that Satan ran in their blood, they would riposte that Satan also ran in his blood. Upon which, Mahomet admitted that he was no different from them except in the fact that Allah has come to his rescue and subdued Satan within him. The Arabic word which has been translated into 'subdued' is *aslam*, which means 'to become a Muslim' (to know peace, to be saved). The meaning of Mahomet's words, therefore, is

5. Abou Hamid El Ghazali, *Ihya Ouloum El Dine*, Dar El Shaab Publishers (Cairo, 1970), p. 689.
6. *Ibid.*, p. 693.
7. *Ibid.*, p. 695.
8. *Ibid.*, p. 696.

that his Satan has become a Muslim. Mahomet emphasized the same point when he said: 'I have been preferred to Adam in two ways. His wife incited him to disobedience, whereas my wives have helped me to obey. His Satan was a heretic, whereas mine was a Muslim inviting me always to do good.'[9]

Islam, therefore, inherited the attitude of Judaism towards Eve, the sinful woman who disobeyed God, and towards sex as related essentially to women, and to Satan. Man, on the other hand, though endowed with an overpowering sexual passion, does not commit sin except if incited to do so by the seductiveness and devilry of woman. He is therefore enjoined to marry and thereby is able to beat back the evils of Satan and the bewitching temptations of women.

Islam encourages men to marry. Mahomet the Prophet of the Muslims, says to them: 'Marriage is my law. He who loves my way of life, let him therefore follow my law.'[10]

Despite the fact that Islam recognized the existence of sexual passion in both women and men, it placed all its constraints on women, thus forgetting that their sexual desire also was extremely strong. Islam never ignored the deep-seated sexual passion that lies in men, and therefore suggested the solutions that would ensure its satisfaction.

Islamic history, therefore, witnessed men who married hundreds of women. In this connection we may once more quote El Ghazali: 'And it was said of Hassan Ibn Ali that he was a great marrier of women, and that he had more than two hundred wives. Sometimes he would marry four at a time, or divorce four at a time and replace them by others. The Prophet Mahomet, Allah's blessings and Peace be upon him, said of Hassan Ibn Ali: 'You resemble me, and my creativity.'[11] The Prophet had once said of himself that he had been given the power of forty men in sex.'[12] Ghazali admits that sexual desire in men is very strong and that: 'Some natures are overwhelmed by passion and cannot be protected by only one woman. Such men should therefore preferably marry more than one woman and may go up to four.'[13]

Some of the close followers of Mahomet (El Sahaba) who led an ascetic life would break their fast by having sexual intercourse before food.

9. *Ibid.*, p. 700.
10. *Ibid.*, p. 683.
11. *Ibid.*, p. 697.
12. Mohammed Ibn Saad, *El Tabakat El Kobra*, Vol. 8, Dar El Tahrir (Cairo, 1970), p. 139.
13. *Ibid.*

At other times they would share a woman's bed before the evening prayer, then do their ablutions and pray. This was in order to empty the heart of everything and so concentrate on the worship of Allah. Thus it was that the secretions of Satan were expelled from the body.

Ghazali carries his thoughts further and says: 'Since among Arabs passion is an overpowering aspect of their nature, they have been allowed to marry women slaves if at some time they should fear that this passion will become too heavy a burden for their belief and lead to its destruction. Though it is true that such a marriage could lead to the birth of a child that will be a slave, yet enslaving the child is a lighter offence than the destruction of religious belief.' Ghazali evidently believes that religion cannot be preserved from destruction unless men are allowed to marry as many women as they wish, even though in so doing they would be harming the interests of the children.

It is clear that Islam has been very lenient with men in so far as the satisfaction of their sexual desires is concerned. This was true even if it led to the enslavement of children and injustice to innocent creatures or if sought at the expense of a woman slave completely deprived of a wife's normal rights and whose children were destined never to enjoy the rights of a free child born of a free mother.

The inevitable question which arises in the face of these facts is: Why has religion been so lenient towards man? Why did it not demand that he control his sexual passions and limit himself to one wife, just as it demanded of the woman that she limit herself to one husband, even though it had recognized that women's sexual desire was just as powerful, if not more so, as that of men? Why is it that religion was so understanding and helpful where men were concerned, to the extent of sacrificing the interests of the family, the women and even the children, in order to satisfy their desires? Why, in contrast, was it so severe with woman that death could be her penalty if she so much as looked at a man other than her husband?

Islam made marriage the only institution within which sexual intercourse could be morally practised between men and women. Sexual relations, if practised outside this framework, were immediately transformed into an act of sin and corruption. A young man whom society had not endowed with the possibilities of getting married, or buying a woman slave from the market, or providing himself with a concubine, had no way of expending or releasing his pent-up sexual energies. Not even masturbation was permissible.

Ibn Abbas was once asked what he thought of masturbation? He exclaimed: 'Ouph, it is indeed bad. I spit on it. To marry a slave woman is better. And to marry a slave woman is preferable to committing adultery.' Thus it is that an unmarried youth is torn between three evils. The least of them is to marry a slave woman and have a slave child. The next is masturbation, and the most sinful of all is adultery.[14]

Of these three evils, only the first two were considered permissible. However, the institution of marriage remained very different for men to what it was for women, and the rights accorded to husbands were distinct from those accorded to wives. In fact, it is probably not accurate to use the term 'rights of the woman' since a woman under the Islamic system of marriage has no human rights unless we consider that a slave has rights under a slave system. Marriage, in so far as women are concerned, is just like slavery to the slave, or the chains of serfdom to the serf. Ghazali expressed this fact clearly and succinctly when speaking of the rights enjoyed by a husband over his wife: 'Perhaps the real answer is that marriage is a form of serfdom. The woman is man's serf and her duty therefore is absolute obedience to the husband in all that he asks of her person.'[15] Mahomet himself said: 'A woman, who at the moment of death enjoys the full approval of her husband, will find her place in Paradise.'[16]

The right enjoyed by a wife in Islam is to receive the same treatment as her husband's other wives. Yet such 'justice' is impossible, as the Koran itself has stated: 'You will not be able to treat your women equally even if you exert much effort.'[17] The Prophet himself preferred some of his wives to others. Some Muslim thinkers opposed polygamous marriage for this reason, and maintained that marriage to more than one woman in Islam was tied to a condition which itself was impossible to fulfil, namely to treat the different wives in exactly the same way and avoid any injustice to one or other of them. A man obviously desires his new wife more than the preceding one(s), otherwise he would not seek to marry her. Justice in this context should mean equality in love, or at least the absence of any tendency to like one wife more and so prefer her to the other(s).[18]

Some Muslim thinkers interpret the two relevant verses of the Koran differently: 'Marry as many women as you like, two, three, or four. If you fear not to treat them equally, then marry only one' and 'You will not

14. Abou Hamid, El Ghazali, *Ihy'a Ouloum El Dine*, Dar El Shaab Publishers (Cairo, 1970), p. 697.
15. *Ibid.*, p. 746.
16. *The Koran: Sourat El Nissa'a*, Verse 129.
17. *Ibid.*
18. *El Zamakhshari*, Vol. I, p. 143 and *El Kourtoubi*, Vol. 5, pp. 407–8.

succeed in being just with your women, no matter how careful you are.'[19] They consider that justice in this context simply implies providing the women with an equal share of material means for the satisfaction of their needs and that it does not refer to equality in the love and affection borne by the husband for his women.[20]

The question, however, is: What is more important to a woman, or to any human being who respects her dignity and her human qualities, justice in the apportioning of a few piastres,[21] or justice in true love and human treatment? Is marriage a mere commercial transaction by which a woman obtains some money from her husband, or is it a profound exchange of feelings and emotions between a man and a woman?

Even if we were to assume the impossible, and arrive at a situation where the man treats his wives equally, it would not be possible to call this a 'right', since the first and foremost criterion of any right is that it should be enjoyed equally by all individuals without distinction or discrimination. If a man marries four wives, even if he treats them equally, it still means that each woman among them has only a quarter of a man, whereas the man has four women. The women here are only equal in the sense that they suffer an equal injustice, just as in bygone days all slaves were 'equal' in that sense under the system of slavery. This can in no way be considered equality or justice or rights for women.

The slave and feudal systems came into being in order to serve the interests of the slave and feudal landowners. In the same way, the system of marriage was created to serve the interests of the man against those of the woman and the children.

El Ghazali when speaking of the benefits of marriage for men expresses himself in these words:

> Marriage relieves the mind and heart of the man from the burden of looking after the home, and of being occupied with cooking, sweeping, cleaning utensils and arranging for the necessities of life. If the human being did not possess a passion for living with a mate, he would find it very difficult to have a home to himself, since if obliged to undertake all the tasks of looking after the home, he would find most of his time wasted and would not be able to devote himself to work and to knowledge. A good woman, capable of setting things to rights in the home, is

19. *The Koran: Sourat El Nissa'a*, Verses 3 and 129.
20. *El Kourtoubi*, Vol. 5, pp. 20–2; *El Galadine*, Vol. I, p. 27; El Hassas, *Ahkam El Koran*.
21. Egyptian unit of money. One hundred piastres equal one Egyptian pound.

an invaluable aid to religious holiness. If however things go wrong in this area, the heart becomes the seat of anxieties and disturbances, and life is seized with things that chase away its calm. For these reasons Soleiman El Darani has said: "A good wife is not a creation of this world, for in fact she permits you to be occupied with the life of the hereafter, and this is so because she looks after the affairs of your home and in addition assuages your passions."[22]

Thus it is that a man cannot devote himself to his religious life, or to knowledge, unless he has a wife who is completely preoccupied with the affairs of his home, with serving him, and feeding him, cleaning his clothes and looking after all his needs. But are we not justified in asking: What about the wife? How can she in turn devote herself to her religious life and the search for knowledge? It is clear that no one has ever thought of the problem from this angle, as if it were a foregone conclusion that women have nothing to do with either religion or knowledge. That their sole function in life is sweeping, cooking, washing clothes and cleaning utensils, and undertaking those tasks that Ghazali has described as a source of trouble and disturbance to the heart, and that chase away the calm of life.

How clear it is that the mind of women and their ambitions, whether in science or in culture, have been completely dropped from all consideration, so that man can consecrate himself completely to such fields of human activity. He furthermore imposes on woman the troubles and disturbances of the heart and mind that result from being occupied with such domestic tasks, after which she is accused of being stupid and lacking in religious conviction. Woman shoulders all these burdens without receiving any remuneration except the food, clothing and shelter required to keep her alive. Man not only exploits her mind for his own ends by abolishing it, or at least preventing it from developing any potential through science, culture and knowledge, not only does he plunge her whole life into working for him without reward, but he also uses her to satisfy his sexual desires to the extent required by him. It is considered one of her duties, and she must respond to his desires at any time. If she fails to do so, falls ill, refuses, or is prevented by her parents, it is his right to divorce her, and in addition deprive her of alimony.

Among the sacred duties of the wife is complete obedience to the husband. She is not allowed to differ with him, to ask questions, or even to argue certain points. The man on the other hand is not expected to

22. Abou Hamid El Ghazali, *Ihya Ouloum El Dine*, p. 699.

obey his wife. On the contrary, it is considered unworthy of a man to do what his wife suggests or asks of him. Omar Ibn El Khattab once said: 'Differ with your women and do not do what they ask. Thus you will be blessed. For it is said: Consult them and then act differently.' The Prophet advises: 'Do not live a slave to your wife.' The Muslim religious leader, El Hassan, goes even further when he maintains that: 'Whenever a man has started to obey the desires and wishes of his woman, it has ended by Allah throwing him into the fires of Purgatory.'[23]

One of the rights of a woman is to be paid a sum of money in the form of a dowry when she is married, and to receive another sum of money as alimony if her husband divorces her. In addition, he is supposed to feed and clothe her, to give her shelter in a home. However, the woman cannot specify any conditions as far as the home she is expected to live in is concerned. It might be a hut made of wood or mud, or a beautiful brick house, depending on the means of the husband. She cannot determine the size of the dowry, or the sum paid to her as alimony, or the food which she is supposed to eat and the clothes she will wear. All these things are decided by the husband according to his assessment of the financial means at his disposal, and how he should spend them.

According to Islamic rules, a woman can ask to be paid for breastfeeding her child.[24] The husband is obliged to pay her for this from his earnings, if the child itself has not some financial resources laid aside for it. If these exist, the payment is made to the mother out of them. The mother is not forced to breastfeed the child if she does not want to, even if pay is offered to her. She can ask to be paid as long as there is no other woman who has voluntarily agreed to breastfeed the child, and to whom the father has no objection. However, if such a woman does exist, the wife no longer has the right to ask for any nursing payment.

Here again it is the husband's will that is crucial, since he can prevent the mother from being paid for nursing her child by finding another woman for this purpose, either on a voluntary basis or for a lower wage.

The mother is also eligible for payment for the rearing of her children, but here again it is the father's prerogative to choose another woman who can offer her services either on a voluntary basis or for less pay.

Such limited rights are almost insignificant, surrounded as they are by impossible conditions, and cannot be considered of any real value. On

23. *Ibid.*, p. 706.
24. Sheikh Mohammed Mahdi Shams El Dine, *Al Islam wa Tanzeem El Waledeya*, Al Ittihad El Aalami Litanzeem El Waledeya. El Maktab El Iklimi Lilshark El Awsat wa Shamal Afrikia 1974, Vol. 2, p. 84.

the contrary, they afford the man a possibility of dispensing with the services of the children's mother immediately after she makes a request to be paid, thereby in fact obliging her to forego her right to payment for nursing or child-rearing. The vast majority of women, unable to be immune to the tendency for society and families to exaggerate and sanctify the functions of motherhood, cannot but sacrifice themselves for their children and give them everything, including their lives. To sacrifice some minor sum of money is therefore a matter of no consequence.

The exploitation to which a wife and a mother is exposed is evident from the fact that she carries out a number of vital functions without being paid. She is cook, sweeper, cleaner, washerwoman, domestic servant, nurse, governess and teacher to the children, in addition to being an instrument of sexual satisfaction and pleasure to her husband. All this she does free of charge, except for the expenses of her upkeep, in the form of food, clothing and shelter. She is therefore the lowest paid labourer in existence.

The exploitation of woman is built upon the fact that man pays her the lowest wage known for any category of human beasts of burden. It is he who decides what she is paid, be it in the form of a few piastres, some food, a dress, or simply a roof over her head. With this meagre compensation, he can justify the authority he exercises over her. Men exercise their tutelage over women because, as stated in the Koran, they provide them with the means of livelihood.

Man's lordship over woman is therefore enforced through the meagre piastres he pays her and also through imposing a single husband upon her to ensure that the piastres he owns are not inherited by the child of another man. Preserving this inheritance is the motive force behind the severe and rigid laws which seek to maintain a woman's loyalty to her husband so that no confusion can affect the line of descent. It is not love between husband and wife which is sought to be nurtured and cherished by these rules. If it were love between the couple that was the basis of this search for loyalty between husband and wife, such loyalty would be required equally from both the woman and the man. However, since loyalty is sought in the woman alone, by imposing monogamy on her, whereas the man is permitted to multiply and diversify his sexual relations, it becomes self-evident that conjugal devotion is not a human moral value, but one of the instruments of social oppression exercised against the woman to make sure that the succession and inheritance is kept intact. The line of descent which is sought to be preserved is, of course, that of the man. Thus adultery on the part of the woman, her betrayal of the nuptial vows sworn to on the day of marriage, means the immediate destruction of patrilineal descent and inheritance.

Money is therefore the foundation of morals, or at least of the morals prevalent where property, exploitation and inheritance are the essence of the economic system. Yet in religion it is assumed that true morals are dependent rather on human values. The Koran clearly says: 'Neither your wealth, nor your children can, even if you tread the path of humiliation, bring you close to me.' 'The highest esteem is given by Allah to those who are the purest.'[25]

We have mentioned before that society realized early on the powerful biological and sexual nature of women, which power it compared to that of Satan. It was therefore inevitable that her loyalty and chastity could only be ensured by preventing her from having relations with any males apart from her husband and the men with whom she was forbidden to have sex such as the father, brother, and paternal or maternal uncles. This is the reason behind the segregation that arose between men and women, and the outlawing of free intermixing between them, a segregation put into effect by imprisoning the women within the four walls of the home. This confinement of women to the home permits the attainment of three inter-related aims: (1) It ensures the loyalty of the woman and prevents her from mixing with strange men; (2) It permits her to devote herself entirely to the care of her home, husband and children and the aged members of the family; and (3) It protects men from the dangers inherent in women and their powers of seduction, which are so potent that when faced by them 'men lose two-thirds of their reason and become incapable of thinking about Allah, science and knowledge.'

The Muslim philosophers who so oft proclaim such opinions borrow most of their ideas from the myth of Adam and Eve, seeing woman as a replica of Eve, endowed with powers that are dangerous and destructive to society, to man, and to religion. They believe that civilization has been gradually built up in the struggle against these 'female powers', in an attempt to control and suppress them, so as to protect the men and to avoid their minds from being preoccupied with women to the detriment of their duties towards Allah and society.

In order to preserve society and religion from such evils, it was essential to segregate the sexes, and subjugate women by fire and steel when necessary for fire and steel alone can force slaves to submit to unjust laws and systems built on exploitation. Woman's status within marriage is even

25. *The Koran: Sourat Sab'a*, Verse 37.

worse than that of the slave, for woman is exploited both economically and sexually. This apart from the moral, religious and social oppression exercised over her to ensure the maintenance of her double exploitation. Slaves, at least, are partially compensated for the efforts they make in the form of some material reward. But a woman is an unpaid servant to the husband, children and elderly people within the home. And a slave may be liberated by his master to become a free man, and thus enjoy the rights of free men, foremost amongst which is the recognition that he has a brain and religious conviction. But a woman, as long as she remains a woman, has no chance or hope of ever possessing the brain and religious conviction of a man. For women are 'lacking in their minds and in their religious faith.'

Since men possess more reason and wisdom than women it has become their right, and not that of women, to occupy the positions of ruler, legislator, governor etc. One of the primary conditions in Islam to become a religious or political leader (Imam) or governor (Wali) is to be a 'male'.[26] Then follow piety, knowledge and competence.

The major ideas on which Islam has based itself in dealing with the question of women and sex can thus be listed as follows:

(1) Men should exercise their tutelage over women because they provide for them economically. They are also superior to women as far as reason, wisdom, piety, knowledge and religious conviction are concerned. Authority is the right of men, and obedience the duty of women.

(2) Men's energies should be expended in worship, religious activities and in the search for knowledge. This is to be attained by making women devote themselves to serving their men in the home, preparing food and drink, washing, cleaning and caring for the children and elderly.

(3) The sexual desires of men should be duly satisfied so that they can concentrate with a clear mind and heart on religious activities, the worship of Allah, the search for knowledge, and the service of society. This also aims to ensure that religion is safeguarded and society preserved from being undermined, or even collapsing. Sexual desire is to be satisfied through marriage, the aims of which are reproduction and also experience of one of the pleasures promised in Paradise, so that men may be motivated to do good and so be rewarded in the after-life. It is men's uncontested right to fully satisfy their sexual needs by marrying several women, or by taking unto themselves women slaves and concubines.

26. *Al Imam Abou Hamid El Ghazali*, Dar El Shaab Publishers (Cairo, 1970), Chapter 3, p. 202.

Masturbation however is an evil, and adultery an even greater sin. 'Let those who cannot marry remain chaste so that Allah may bestow upon them of His riches. Let he who can marry a woman, who has matured without marriage, take her as a wife. If he cannot, then abstinence is the path.'[27]

(4) The seduction of women and their powers of temptation are a danger and a source of destruction. Men must be protected from their seductive powers, and this is ensured by confining them to the home. Man is exposed to annihilation if he succumbs to the temptations of women. In the words of Ibrahim Ebn Adham, 'he who is accustomed to the thighs of women will never be a source of anything.'[28]

(5) Women are forbidden to leave the home and enter the outside world of men except if an urgent necessity to do this arises, as in illness or death. If a woman goes outside her home she must cover her body completely and not expose her attractions or anything that is liable to seduce a man. Her ornaments should be hidden and her external genital organs preserved intact.

Islam encouraged men to marry and went as far as considering it a religious duty. A familiar Arab saying goes as follows: 'Marriage is half of religion.' Men were not only asked to marry, but permitted to take several wives, and to have extramarital sexual relations almost at will, by living with concubines or women slaves. They were thus led to boast of the number of women they owned, and to speak with pride of their sexual powers.

The sexual powers of man became a part of the Arab ethos, and within this ethos, were related to manliness and virility. It became a matter for shame if a man was known to be impotent or sexually weak. Obviously, it could only be a woman who would be able to know, and therefore judge, if a man was sexually deficient, and in this resided another source of woman's hidden strength enhancing the dangers she represented. Men therefore had to be protected from her, and society did this by ensuring that her eyes were prevented from seeing anything outside the home—like an animal that becomes blind from being kept in the dark—by covering her face with the thickest of veils, and by obscuring her mind so she would become incapable of discerning the weak from the strong. This is the origin of the greater value attached to a virgin as compared with a

27. *The Koran: Sourat El Nour,* Verse 33.
28. Abou Hamid El Ghazali, *Ihy'a Ouloum El Dine,* Dar El Shaab Publishers (Cairo, 1970), p. 706.

woman, when the time comes for her to marry. The virgin knows little or nothing about men and sex, whereas a woman has experience drawn from her past relations with men and from her knowledge of the arts of sex. She can easily discern where lie the weaknesses of a man and where lies his strength. Hence the reduced value attached to a widow or a divorced woman.

Mahomet the Prophet, however, did not comply with these general rules of male conduct in Arab society. He was married fourteen times to women who had been divorced or widowed. The only virgin he married was Aisha. In this respect he was also much more progressive, and much more open-minded than most of the men of today, who still prefer to marry a virgin and look for the usual bloodstains on the nuptial sheet or cloth. That is why, especially in rural areas, the custom of defloration by the husband's or *daya*'s finger is still widespread, and is meant to demonstrate the red evidence of virginity on a white cloth symbolic of purity and an intact family honour.

As we have seen, the status of women and the attitudes towards them changed rapidly after the death of Mahomet. In the very essence of Islam, and in its teachings as practised in the life of the Prophet, women occupied a comparatively high position. But once they were segregated from men and made to live within the precincts of the home, the values of honour, self-respect and pride characteristic of Arab tribal society became closely and almost indissolubly linked to virginity, and to preventing the women-folk of the family from moving into the outside world. A popular saying among the Palestinians, very common until the middle of the 20th century, goes: 'My woman never left our home until the day she was carried out.'[29] I remember my mother describing my grandmother and saying that she had only ever moved through the streets on two occasions. The first was when she left her father's house and went to her husband after marriage. And the second when she was carried out of her husband's house to be buried. Both times no part of her body remained uncovered.[30]

---

29. Tewfih Canaan, *Kawaneen Gheir Maktouba Tatahakam fi Makanat El Mara'a El Filistineya (Magalat El Torath, Wal Mogtam'a)* El Takadoum Publishers Al Kouds (Jerusalem), No. 2, 1974, p. 39.

30. My maternal grandmother lived in Cairo (1898–1948). She spent her whole life doing the chores at home and looking after her husband and children. She belonged to a middle class or rather higher middle class family. On the other hand, my paternal grandmother who lived during almost the same period in our village, Kafr Tahla, never knew what it was to wear a veil and used to go out to work in the fields or to buy and sell in the market every day, just as other poor peasant women did.

Segregation between the world of men and that of women was so strict that a woman who dared to go outside the door of her home was liable to be maltreated at the hands of men. They might limit themselves to a few rude and insolent glances, or resort to coarse sexual remarks and insults, but very often things would go even further. A man or a boy might stretch out his hand and seize her by the arm or the breast. Sometimes young boys would throw stones at her in the lanes and by-roads of cities and towns, and follow in her footsteps with jeering remarks or sexual insults, in which the organs of her body would be vilified in a chorus of loud voices. As a girl I used to be scared of going out into the streets in some of the districts of Cairo during my secondary school days (1943–48). I remember how boys sometimes threw stones at me, or shouted out crude insults as I passed by, such as 'Accursed be the cunt of your mother' or 'Daughter of the bitch fucked by men'. In some Arab countries women have been exposed to physical or moral aggression in the streets simply because their fingers were seen protruding from the sleeves of their dress.[31]

This tendency among males to harm any woman caught crossing the boundaries of her home, and therefore the outer limits of the world prescribed for her by men, or who dares break into and walk through domains reserved for men, proves that they cannot consider her as merely weak and passive. On the contrary, they look upon her as a dangerous aggressor the moment she steps over the frontiers, an aggressor to be punished and made to return immediately to the restrictions of her abode. This attitude bears within itself the proof of woman's strength, a strength from which man seeks to protect himself by all possible means. Not only does he imprison woman within the house, but he also surrounds the male world with all sorts of barricades, stretches of barbed wire, fortifications and even heavy guns.

The female world, on the other hand, is looked upon by men as an area surrounded by, and peopled with, obscure and puzzling secrets, filled with all the dark mystery of sorcery, devilry and the works of Satan. It is a world that a man may only enter with the greatest caution, and a prayer for Allah's help, Allah who alone can give us strength and show us the way. Thus it is that the Arab man in the rural areas of Egypt mutters a string of Allah's names through pursed, fast moving lips, on entering a house in which there are women: *'Ya Hafez, ya Hafes, ya Lateef, ya*

31. Tewfik Canaan, *Kawaneen Gheir Maktouba Tatahakam fi Makanat El Mara'a*, p. 40.

Sattar, ya Rab, ya Satir, ya Karim' ('O great preserver, almighty one, God the compassionate, who art alone shielder from all harm, protector from evil, bountiful and generous'). In some Arab societies the man might add *destour*, which is the same word used by peasants to chase away evil spirits or devils.[32]

Here again we can observe the commonly held idea of a close link between women and devils or evil spirits. It goes back to the story of Eve, and the belief that she was positive and active where evil is concerned, an instrument of Satan's machinations. The development of a Sufi theology in Islam, characterized by renunciation of the world, and meditation and love for Allah—which became a cult of love in general—allowed women to rise to the level of saints. However, the number of women saints remained extremely small as compared with men. On the other hand, where it came to evil spirits 80% of them were popularly considered to be female.[33]

The history of the Arabs shows that the women were undoubtedly much less afraid of the men than the men were of the women. The tragedy of Arab men however, or rather of most men all over the world, is that they fear woman and yet desire her. But I think it can be said that Arab men in some periods, especially in the pre-Islamic and early Islamic eras, were able to overcome their fear of women to a much greater degree than men in the West. Or perhaps, more precisely, the men's desire for their women was stronger than the inhibitions built from fear. This is due to the difference in the objective conditions prevailing in Arab societies as compared to the West, and to the fact, discussed earlier, that Islam (contrary to Christianity) recognized the validity and legitimacy of sexual desire.

As a result, sex and love occupied a much more important place in the life of the Arabs, and in their literature and arts. But parallel to this flowering in the passions which bind men and women together, there

32. I very often heard the word *destour* repeated by villagers, whether men or women, in gatherings for *zar* (exhortational sessions) when mention was made of evil spirits or devils. One of those present would shout *destour* which means 'O God, chase away the evil spirits from our way'. The same word is used to clear the way for a man, especially when women are present, and are required to withdraw or to be warned by him that he is about to come in. The world also means the established order, constitution, or constitutional laws.

33. Tewfik Canaan, *El Yanabi'i El Maskouna Wa Shayatin El Ma'a (fi filistine) Magalat El Torath Wal Mogtama*, El Takadam Press (Jerusalem), No. 2, July 1974, p. 38.

was an opposite and almost equally strong tendency in the teachings of philosophers and men of wisdom, and in the literary works of writers and poets, that warned against indulging in the pleasures of sex. Men were abjured not to become 'impassioned' with women or to fall victims to their seductions. One of the famous injunctions of the prominent Arab thinker, Ibn El Mokafa, says: 'Know well that one of the things that can cause the worst of disasters in religion, the greatest exhaustion to the body, the heaviest strain on the purse, the highest harm to the mind and reason, the deepest fall in man's chivalry, and the fastest dissipation of his majesty and poise, is a passion for women.'[34]

Ibn Mokafa was no doubt directing his remarks exclusively to those men who possessed 'majesty', 'poise', and a well garnished purse, since only those who possessed these trappings could possibly lose them through love of women. Other men, those that constituted the vast major-ity among the people and who possessed neither majesty, nor poise, nor purse of any kind could not benefit from his advice, or even be in the least concerned with it. They were completely, or almost completely, stripped of all worldly possessions and therefore sometimes even of the means to have just one lawful wife, pay her dowry and keep her children. Such men could not be expected to strut back and forth on the scenes of love and passion.

In Arab society, as in all societies governed by a patriarchal class system where enormous differences exist between various social levels, sex and love, sexual freedom and licence and a life of pleasure were only the lot of a very small minority. The vast majority of men and women were destined to toss and turn on a bed of nails, to be consumed by the flames of sacrifice and to be subjugated by a load of traditions, laws and codes which forbid sex to all except those who can pay its price.

The Arabs, exposed as they were to the shortages and harshness of desert life, to the difficulties and perils of obtaining the bare necessities in a backward and rather savage society, and to the burden of exploitation by their own and surrounding ruling classes, were known for their forti-tude, patience, and capacity to stand all kinds of deprivation, whether from food, sex or even water. Yet they were capable, like people in all lands, and at all stages in human development, of finding compensation in other things. This might explain to us why the Arab people were so fond of listening to the stories of A Thousand and One Nights, pulsating

---

34. Ibn El Mokafa, *El Adab El Saghir, Wal Adab El Kebir*, Maktabat El Bayan (Bei-rut, 1960), p. 127.

as they were with the passions of beautiful women and the seductions of sex. This eagerness to listen to, and repeat, what had been told over a thousand nights, aroused a fiery imagination and substituted illusions for what life could not give them in fact.

These stories, as Sadek El Azm describes them, 'have as their theme incidents and happenings that have been built around an intricate web of passion and love, which appeared all the more fascinating in that it did not conform with the moral codes and religious laws that held sway in the life of society, nor with the way in which good and evil, legitimate and illegitimate, permissible and impermissible were conceived of.' Thus it is that wives are made to betray their husbands with lovers and male slaves, virgins to meet with their handsome favourites in secret, and men to abandon their wives and seek out their mistresses in the rapture of soft summer nights. All those with whom these stories deal are engaged in the sole occupation of giving free rein to their voluptuous and hotly flowing desires, with all the means at their disposal, even if this should entail lying, deceiving, betraying people's confidence and running away from facing the consequences of one's acts. The predominance of these themes in the popular stories of this book echoes the yearnings that lie buried in the hidden depths of every man and woman condemned to live through the daily grind of a routine life, and dreaming of a chance to experience the throbbings of a violent passion. Yet where is the way out when everything around them stands like a vigilant sentinel intent on keeping their footsteps away from the exciting, sinuous and dangerous paths? The only door that remains open is that of tales and stories where people can live in imagination what is forbidden to them in fact by custom and tradition.[35]

35. Sadek El Azm, *Fil Houb Wal Houb El Ozri*, Manshourat Nizar El Kabbani (Beirut, 1968), p. 69.

ACTIVE READING

1. How do you see el-Saadawi interpreting Islamic teaching to fit her argument? Find some passages that help you to unravel and understand el-Saadawi's complicated relationship to authority in Islamic teaching.

2. Find some passages where el-Saadawi uses the Arabic word *"fitna"* to discuss general Arab concerns about women and society. Where does (or where could) el-Saadawi use this term to discuss her own concerns? For each passage you find, explain why you think el-Saadawi chooses or avoids this word.

3. What tensions or conflicts does el-Saadawi reveal regarding Arab ideas about economic, intellectual, sexual, or social freedoms? How do her explorations of these conflicts relate to your own response to Before Reading #1?

READING IN NEW CONTEXTS

1. Find passages where el-Saadawi evaluates the uses of stereotypes, and then find passages where she comes close to using stereotypes herself. Turn to a text by Black Elk, Tan, Seidler, or another *Literacies* writer who highlights the dangers and temptations of stereotypes. Comment on how el-Saadawi and the other writer deal with stereotypes about the groups they belong to.

2. El-Saadawi suggests that Arabs and non-Arabs have different uses for *A Thousand and One Nights.* How does Fishman, Fienup-Riordan, or Christian help you to talk about the ways different communities may use the same texts? From what you can tell, how well do the other writer's ideas apply to el-Saadawi's context?

3. How does el-Saadawi's use of and attitude toward sacred texts relate to the uses and attitudes you see in essays by Baldwin, Fishman, or Kozol? How can you account for the differences you find? (Your response to Active Reading #1 may help here.)

4. El-Saadawi claims that "the status of women and the attitudes towards them changed rapidly after the death of Mahomet" (478). Find passages from her essay that explain how this change occurred. Then look at another *Literacies* text—hooks & West, Rich, or Sanders are possibilities—that discusses some change in cultural gender roles. Based on your reading of these two texts, speculate about some effects that such change can have on the individual members of a community.

DRAFT ONE / DRAFT TWO

1. *Draft One:* El-Saadawi suggests that "It is mainly economic necessity which governs the direction in which values, human morals and norms of sexual behaviour move" (463). Examine other passages in el-Saadawi's text that relate to economic necessity. What relationship do you see between economic necessity and the development of moral codes in these passages?

   Draft Two: Turn to a text by Baldwin, Ewen, Heker, or another *Literacies* writer who considers the relationship between economy and morality, and adapt the ideas you developed in Draft One to help you discuss that relationship in this new text. If you find that your earlier ideas are insufficient, explain why. Then develop some new ideas that fit the second essay.

2. *Draft One:* El-Saadawi claims that certain Islamic practices tend to "sanctify the functions of motherhood" (474). What are these practices, and how do they relate to your own idea about the duties associated with motherhood? (You may need to explain where your own understanding of motherhood comes from.)

   Draft Two: Consider some ideas about motherhood from Christian's, Kozol's, or Shanley's texts. Based on your reading of this new essay and your own Draft One response, discuss some ways in which the sanctified "functions of motherhood" may conflict with the individual needs of women who are mothers. What suggestions do you or these other writers have for addressing such conflicts?

BEFORE READING CAROL DE SAINT VICTOR

1. What enjoyment or frustration have you experienced on your first visit to an unfamiliar place (perhaps moving to a new community, leaving for college, or visiting another country)?

2. List as many meanings as you can think of for the phrase "Go slowly and you arrive." What kind of advice does this phrase offer? What kind of reading experience do you expect from an essay with this title?

3. What advantages and drawbacks do you see to traveling alone through another country? How might gender, race, or religious background play a role in the kinds of experiences a solitary traveler might encounter?

4. What ideas do you have about religious beliefs in India? Where does your information come from?

CAROL DE SAINT VICTOR

GO SLOWLY
AND YOU ARRIVE

OLD DELHI

My first morning in India. I wake up at dawn and take a motor rickshaw to Old Delhi: just any street in Old Delhi, I tell the driver. It is as if I walk through familiar photographs and movies: men wash themselves at pumps, brush their teeth with sticks, sleep on rope beds; women prepare tea on open fires, sweeping a little space in front of doors; children run about; the continuous movement of people around carts past cows between rickshaws, seemingly without beginning and without end, contained only by two- and three-storey buildings of ground-level shops, upper-level living quarters and storage areas. I emerge from the narrow street to one that accommodates two lanes of traffic, and a parade is approaching. In front are drummers and horn players, each of whom seems to play his own desultory tune, oblivious to the sounds around him. Behind the musicians are fifty or sixty men with black eyes, black hair, and brown naked bodies. I look around in search of someone who might tell me who these men are, what their march without clothes is intended to signify, but the people behind me appear to be more interested in me, a middle-aged American woman, fully clothed, than about this parade of

Originally published in *The Missouri Review* (1992).

undisguisedly mysterious men. I am in India, and I do not understand much of what I see: that is what this moment comes to mean to me, and it will recur to me like a refrain, like the private tune each musician plays.

KOUKI

Jaisalmer, the oldest of the desert cities of Rajasthan, is my farthest point west into the Thar Desert, part of the expanse of sand that for centuries served as the highway between Africa and Asia. My first morning here I awake before dawn in order to be out in the hilltop village when light first appears. I climb a wall of the fort, the highest point of the village, and look out at the desert as the sun rises high and hot behind me. It is here that the hard sand gives way to rolling plains of loose sand, and the wind shapes dunes sometimes several kilometers long and sixty to eighty meters high. This is the *maroosthali*, the region of death, a large part of which was once submerged under the Indian Ocean. And now, where the annual rainfall averages about ten inches, and temperatures in May rise to 115°F, this great stretch of desert looks like a sea, as if this parched land were remembering it was once covered by tide.

I walk down a narrow cobblestone street that turns in labyrinthine fashion between rows of houses, some of which are five hundred years old, and they are built of stones that are the colors of the desert—yellow, gold, faint green. Their facades are ornamented with open web-like patterns in stone. Women are washing surfaces and clothes, men are washing themselves, white cows and black goats with large seemingly translucent white ears wander about, smelling for food, children are running about. I find a small restaurant on a square, or a triangle rather, where, outside, there is a table and three benches. The sunlight onto the terrace where I sit is broken by a large tree with the heart-shaped leaf of a linden. I order a pot of tea. A plate of tea? the waiter asks. Yes, I reply, not knowing what I will be served. On the other side of the tree I can see, stretching high into the sky, a gold-tinted sandstone house with a terrace mounted across the top storey. The light dances on the carved arches and balustrade of what might have been the home of a merchant who grew wealthy from trade and taxes levied on camel caravans plying the long lucrative route from the Sahara to Delhi and Agra. On one side of the merchant's house there is a newer, plainer house where a little boy, perhaps four years old, swings on a gate, and when a dirty, limping dog appears and settles in the gutter in front of it, the boy yells at the dog and pushes the gate against it. The dog pulls his aching body farther downhill and collapses under some steps. On the terrace of the house on the other side of the merchant's home, a woman in a yellow sari crouches, and holds at arm's length a short broom with which she draws a large arch, over and over again. The sounds: Indian music from a radio somewhere above the cafe; birds; a woman berating someone in the shop next door; footsteps of people and animals on the cobblestone roadway in front of me. The smells: urine and rot (I am sitting next to an open gutter). A little girl walks by carrying on her head a bowl filled with moist cow dung. Somewhere she will sit down and make round flat pies of it which she will spread in the sun to dry. Trishaws, their motors turned off, coast downhill. Two men sit on the bench farthest from me, drinking tea; one of the two men pours some of the tea from his cup into another cup for a third man who arrives and joins their conversation. One wears earrings, and another a turban of coiled red cotton. They all wear embroidered slippers with pointed upturned toes. A boy hangs rectangles of fabric from the second-floor terrace above the General Store. An old man walks by wearing a pink turban and a white *dhoti*. I take a photo of a camel pushing against the cart that is behind him, to prevent his descending the hill too fast; the driver smiles at me. A policeman in a white uniform and a tan cap walks by, yawning. A cow walks by, pauses to drop a pound of dung, moves on. A black dog with a henna tail follows. A plate of tea is a cup of tea on a metal tray.

A woman approaches the tables where I am sitting and asks if she may sit down. Her eyes are on the traffic and so I may look at her. She is perhaps thirty-five, falsely blond, with green eyes. Makeup does not conceal the fatigue around her eyes or the dirt on her neck. She wears large silver earrings, many bracelets, and her nose is pierced to hold a diamond. Her right hand is intricately painted, in black and red filigree. She has her feet on the bench, and she clutches her knees close to her face. She smokes Gold Flake cigarettes. A boy with a cherubic face arrives and sits by her, and they speak Hindi. She takes a cassette from her bag and gives it to him: *Chipmunk Adventure*. The cherub tells me that Kouki speaks Hindi but she is not Indian. He works for the store above the General Store. Am I interested in clothes, wall hangings? Do I want to see? His English is barely comprehensible to me. Kouki helps him out: "Looking is free," she translates for me, and teaches him the phrase. She has a fan which the cherub opens and closes as they talk. Kouki orders an onion omelette, dry toast and tea. A woman trudges uphill, her stomach hanging over her sari, like a goatskin of wine hanging over the edge of a table in a Spanish inn.

I tell Kouki I would guess she is either Greek or Italian.

Nearly. She was born in Paris (with the perfect exaggerated s of a European) but she soon moved to Spain with her mother. She is Spanish but carries a French passport. She studied art history for four years in Perpignan. She has come to India many times. She first came when she was twenty years old, to take photographs, and her camera was stolen. She has been robbed of seven or eight cameras. For five years she was so fed up she did not have a camera, but now she has one which she does not like. It is automatic. It makes noises she does not like and it does what it wants. A camera should do what Kouki tells it to do, not what it chooses to do.

The cherub is interested in my camera. Do I want to sell it? No but he may look at it. He takes a picture of Kouki and then of me. He wants to study photography, Kouki tells me. He touts for a camera shop too. He goes for photos of Rajasthan to show me: only a rupee for small ones, two rupees for big ones. He returns with a stack of photos, many of them studio shots with fake backgrounds. One is of a young woman in sari and jewels lying voluptuously against a perfectly etched dune. He disappears and returns wearing a jeweled vest from the fabric store. "Looking is free," he says, and points to the store.

Kouki looks through the stacks of photos for one of a man of Jaisalmer who had moustaches five meters long which coiled in tight rings on either cheek. He was a musician: he played a flute; he played ancient songs of Rajasthan. He was born in Jaisalmer, and he was killed in Jaisalmer. For many generations there had been a feud between his family and a family in what is now West Pakistan. Every twenty or thirty years someone of one family kills someone of the other family. Thirty years ago his father killed a man of the Pakistani family, and three years ago the son of that man came to Jaisalmer and murdered the man with the long moustaches in his own house, in front of his wife and children. The Pakistani cut off the gloriously mustachioed head of the Rajasthani, put it in a suitcase, took it across the desert in a jeep and then on a camel and into Pakistan. He took the head in a suitcase to Pakistan.

The dust is terrible, Kouki says. Sometimes there is a dust storm, and dust gets into everything. Into your eyes, your ears, your mouth. Her Japanese friend, who came to Jaisalmer to take photos for a travel book, was obliged to clean his camera five or six times a day. The cherub admires one of her necklaces, a gold chain with small colored stones spaced along it. She speaks in Hindi to him and then in English to me. The necklace is for her mother, who had one like it but with diamonds instead of cheap stones like this one. The necklace was in her mother's purse with other jewelry, and the purse was stolen from her in the street. For three nights she could not sleep, and she cried, she did not want to live. And then she said, It is crazy to care about such things. It is crazy to wake up to unhappiness. If I have things okay, if I don't okay too. I have my daughter who loves me, and it does not matter anything else.

I pay my bill, and tell Kouki I want to see the library at the Jain Temple before it closes at one pm. She says she will be at the cafe in the afternoon if I want to come back. She suggests I go to Pushgar. Agra, she says, is nothing. I should not waste my time going to see the Taj Mahal. I am to tell the guy who sells tickets to the Temple that I am Kouki's friend.

I walk up the hill to the Temple area where there are, my book tells me, 6666 images of the Jain gods. The Jains broke away from Hinduism in five hundred BC, and differed from most other sects in their creed of non-violence, in their belief that the Universe is infinite and eternal and therefore there is no Supreme Creator, and in their holding that to achieve the world of spirit one must learn to control one's senses. One branch of Jainism was especially contemptuous of women, considering them to be a curse of humanity. I do not know which branch of Jainism flourished in Rajasthan, this legendary region of violence, art and commerce.

I tell the ticket vendor that I am Kouki's friend. He sells me a ticket and tells me to go into the temple and he will find the key to the library. I look at a few of the 6666 images. The cupolas are as beautiful as the statues and bas-reliefs they protect, and it is cooler here than in the streets. The vendor at last appears. Am I a good friend of Kouki? I just met her at the cafe, I tell him. We walk down the narrow staircase to a door that is no more than five feet high. The library he shows me is a tiny room, four feet square, in which there are four palm-leaf manuscripts on display. The light is poor, and I do not stay long. At the top of the stairs he points to a temple I did not visit. I should see it, he says. I walk up the polished brown sandstone steps to another cupola and more reliefs of dancers, musicians, lovers. The Jains of Jaisalmer were not, it seems, of the more ascetic sect. Do I want to sit down? he asks; it is very hot. In Jaisalmer, he says, we have very good hash. Did you say hash? Yes hash; you want hash? No, I don't think so. Later? No, not later. I get up to continue my walk along the path to the world of spirit with dancers, more musicians, more lovers. He follows me and shows me something black the size of a half a dollar. Just a little bit for nothing, he offers. No, really no, I'm not interested. Just a little bit, he suggests. Very cheap, what you come for, he hazards. I walk on, then stop for a last photograph of a dancer, his feet and legs turn west, his head and torso east, he smiles at me.

I walked beyond the temples, away from Kouki's friend, along a street that follows close to the wall of the fort. A silversmith sits in a tiny shop about three feet above street level. The shop is at most three feet wide. More goats, cows, women beating clothes on a stone terrace beside a pump. Next to them, a calf sits beneath a wall on which cow dung is drying. A little girl, perhaps eight years old, touts. What is my name? Where am I from? Do I like India? Do I want to see her house? Do I want to take her picture? No thank you. *"Je suis belle?"* she asks, holding her skirt in a half circle. I take a picture of the calf beneath the medallions of drying dung and walk on.

Before I leave Jaisalmer I go to the cafe to say goodbye to Kouki, to tell the cherub I'll buy something from the shop above the General Store. Kouki is inside the cafe where, in darkness, she and two men are watching television. They watch a woman cry and a man try to comfort her. Kouki appears to be engrossed in the drama. I say goodbye and wonder if she hears me, and I walk out into the bright desert sunlight.

JAIPUR STREET

I move in jerks along a street barely wider than the motor rickshaw I am riding in. It is night, and on either side of the street vendors sit in the shops that are raised several feet above the street. Vendors and their customers sit on white mattresses and cushions under fluorescent bulbs or beside kerosene lamps, a few beside candles. Vendors weigh their wares with brass balances: chappati, brightly colored powders, silver and jewels. We arrive at a work compound where, on the ground, women and children work by small dim lights. They sort stones by sifting them through round trays with perforations of different sizes. My guide tells me these things, but I see only grey shadows and hear shoosh, shoosh, shoosh.

MR. SANJEE

It is too hard to trek into the desert, Mr. Sanjee tells me. But he will drive me to villages near Jaisalmer this evening, when the worst heat is over. He speaks in a language I do not understand to the young man standing behind him. Always there is a young man standing behind Mr. Sanjee, waiting for orders which are spoken in the same deep soft voice he uses with me. Mr. Sanjee wears white linen pants and a white shirt; he wears cloth slippers with pointed toes that turn up. He smokes Benson and Hedges.

We leave the old city where I am staying in one of Mr. Sanjee's villas. His brother runs Jaisalmer's only deluxe hotel, and I had intended to stay there, having earned myself a deluxe room after spending a night on a train, I told myself, but the rooms were unpleasantly dark, the furnishings gloomily heavy, the air thick with disinfectant. Next to the deluxe hotel, on the other side of a recently built wall, is Mr. Sanjee's simpler place, where I have a room with a ceiling fan, and windows that allow the night air to enter. I imagine the room was part of a very old building, perhaps quarters for workers, or storage rooms, and now its interior walls are white-washed, and there is no telephone, no overstuffed chairs. Only a bed and a table with a mirror, and a bathroom with one tap, for cold water. Mr. Sanjee tells me to look back at Jaisalmer as we drive away. The view I have is what camel caravans centuries ago saw: the old part of the city has not changed, and the new part is hidden from our view. Twentieth-century wars and boundary disputes have changed the world Jaisalmer now inhabits. Now it is a tourist town, and people no longer care about the past. The old part of the city has not changed, but everything else has, Mr. Sanjee says.

Mr. Sanjee does not come out to the dunes very often, but this is the off-season, and so he can take time from his hotel. I am his only guest, and it is the hot season, but in July and August many French and Italians will arrive, the monsoons will have cooled the air, and his twelve rooms will be filled. He loves the desert but he visits it now with a heavy heart. Here, at Bada Bagh, we may walk through cenotaphs with carved ceilings and equestrian statues of former rulers, but I am to notice that stones are missing, statues are damaged: people come and take souvenirs. No one else is here now, and in the distance we can see camels grazing near a clump of trees that are not as tall as the camels. Further west we visit a Jain temple which has been rebuilt, and here one may see some of the loveliest geometrical patterns of carved stone in all of Rajasthan. Only here, Mr. Sanjee says, may one see designs like these: facades that grow wider as they rise, and give one the impression of bird wings opening. He points to abandoned houses on streets leading to the temple. Sand partially covers their facades. There was once a city here, but no longer. Now, there is only the rebuilt temple guarded by an old priest who accepts coins from visitors. On the road once again, we pass three hitchhikers; one is crippled and walks with a crutch. We do not stop.

On to Mool Sagar and Amar Sagar, dried and disintegrating remnants of formal gardens where once there were fountains and pools and enough water to keep trees green and lush with fruit. There is a wall filled with small niches where candles once were placed, and above, running just beneath the top of the wall, is a narrow slit through which water flowed, down and in front of the candles, to a pool beneath. Can I imagine the sight and the sound at night, of candles burning behind a veil of water? Now people come and take stones away, to use as paper weights and lamp bases. Every year there is less of old Rajasthan, and one day there will be nothing left to remind people of earlier times, of better times. A camel with strangely blotched, perhaps diseased, skin wanders about. A bougainvillea waits in a corner of a disintegrating wall. On the road we again pass the three hitchhikers.

It is dark when we return to Jaisalmer, and I have only a little time before my train leaves to take me back to Jodhpur. Mr. Sanjee invites me to have tea with him at a table in the courtyard outside my room. A younger man is with him who may be his son. Mr. Sanjee does not introduce us, but the young man speaks English as well as Mr. Sanjee.

I recognize the eucalyptus tree to one side of us, but what is the other tree, with yellow leaves? It is a *peepul*, a holy tree. This is its autumn, and so its leaves will soon fall, and women will come to worship it. Indians worship all things—the sun, the stars, snakes, all animals, trees—all things of the universe. To an Indian all things are part of God. I ask if it will be all right if I do not drink the glass of water put before me, as is customary, before we are served tea. Of course, he understands; he says something to the young man standing behind him, and the young man takes my glass, puts it on a tray, stumbles, looks quickly at Mr. Sanjee, who speaks to him in his usual soft voice.

Will I go to Varanasi? Then I will see the holy river, where, in spite of corpses and garbage and all other filth thrown into it, the water is pure. I could fill the jar with water from the Ganges and months later it would still be clear, unlike water from any other river. Yes, he would drink water from the Ganges at Varanasi and bathe in it. But people no longer go to Varanasi to die, as they once did. Little by little, the past is chipped away, and maybe someday people will not believe the Ganges is pure, and it will not be pure. Long ago there were a few people who were very wealthy and many who were moderately wealthy, and everybody had enough to eat. Life was good for all. Now no one in Jaisalmer is wealthy, and no one appreciates the culture of the past except as something to show tourists. There are no longer gardens where friends spend evenings listening to water fall over candlelight, watching dancers. Now we watch television and wait for tourists. Now taxes are very high. I should come back to Jaisalmer in October, when there are few tourists and it is cool. Then I could trek, for four days perhaps, and we would take tents, and we would get beyond telephone wires and hotels, and we could imagine how it was centuries ago.

BRAHMIN

"I am not a guide. I am a student. I study biology. I have examinations in two weeks. I came to the fort to borrow a book from my friend. My father is a teacher. He teaches English, Hindi, mathematics, history, biology. He teaches all subjects. We have a large house. My mother is a cook. She cooks for my father and my sister and me. Will you visit my house? It is a Brahmin house. We are Brahmins, the highest caste. Do you see the very large tree? My house is beside the very large tree. My house is very large. My mother and my younger sister will be so happy to meet you."

We take a shortcut to the village of blue houses we could see from the wall of the fort of Jodhpur. We walk over loose stones, scarcely a path, that trace the steep incline of the hill. The student asks me where I am from, if I like India, where is my husband, how many children I have, how old they are. The student's name is Mahesh, and he is the age of my son.

"This is the house of my cousin. She is my cousin and my friend. This is my house. Knock on the door. My mother and my sister will be so happy to meet you."

His sister is twelve and wears glasses and a Western-style dress. His mother wears a green sari and does not speak English. They are watching television in a tiny room where there is a bed and a table on which the television sits. The mother sits on the floor, the sister on the bed next to me, Mahesh on a stool he pulls out from beneath the table. The mother and sister continue to watch television: a woman is angry, another one is crying. Mahesh and his mother and sister speak in Hindi about what is happening on television. Mahesh offers to show me the house while his mother and sister continue to watch television drama. Adjoining the room we are sitting in are two other rooms, one for women and the other the kitchen. The room where the television is is for men. The family sleeps outside, either on the roof or in the courtyard.

When the program is over the sister and mother go to the kitchen to prepare tea. Mahesh says he wants to give me a special gift—a very old coin, a very old and valuable coin, which appears to be made of aluminum and is dated 1967. He also gives me a green rope necklace which he says is very valuable. I should not wear it outside because I will be robbed. Now he would like a gift from me. I give his sister two ballpoint pens and I give Mahesh my pocket knife. I have nothing else I can give except money, which I think I should not offer. I have cigarettes in my suitcase at the train station, I explain, when I see that my gifts to Mahesh and his sister are disappointing. Would his father like American cigarettes? Mahesh would prefer something he could keep to remind him of me, something that is very dear to me. Would I give him my watch? I cannot give him my watch: it was a gift to me, and also I need it. How many cigarettes do I have in my suitcase? He will meet me at 9:30 tonight, but not in the station. I am to meet him in the street beside the station. There will be policemen in the station. I tell him I will not meet him. I give him fifty rupees and leave.

DONALD

Udaipur belies its desert location. It is, I have read, the Venice of the East. Surrounding it in the distance are the Aravalli Mountains and, close by, three lakes, on which palaces and gardens seem to float. I visit the City Palace and walk beneath eighteenth-century marble arches where Maharajahs and Mogul emperors were weighed in silver and gold which, once a year, was distributed to the citizens. Or so my book says. I walk the short distance between shops to the city's seventeenth-century Jagdish temple, where women sit on the floor and sing to the accompaniment of three male instrumentalists. A tout will not be discouraged. He is a student, he says, and he wants to practice his English. Also he wants me to visit the college where he and his fellow students are studying painting and sculpture under their guru. "Why are you so unfriendly?" he charges. "Do you not want to meet people? Why are you alone?" he hazards. "You ask too much," I say to myself, about myself.

My book tells me to go to Sunset Point for a quiet spot from which to gaze on the lake and hill beyond as night falls. To Sunset Point, I tell a rickshaw driver: how much? (I offer half, and we are off, but not before the student-artist finds me, goads me once more: "Oh God, why are you so arrogant?" he yells. I do not look back. I lift an arm to say goodbye.)

We drive through the new commercial area of Udaipur, which is not like Venice, or any city I have seen except in India. Where animals still walk about even as motorized vehicles spew black fumes at them and me. With every turn of the rickshaw wheels, pain stabs my body. The heat and noises are so intense, the sun so bright, the sights so sharply colored that I feel as if my sensory apparatus has been turned up high—as if my eyes are dilated and so everything I look at hurts me, as if my body is diseased and therefore inflamed by the slightest sensation. India imbues me.

As the driver stops to chat with another rickshaw driver, a young man jumps into our rickshaw, sits beside the driver, and turns around to me and smiles. What is my name? Where am I from? How long am I here? Do I like India?

I am tired. I cannot fight another battle. His friends call him Donald, his skin shines like the temple steps in Jaisalmer, and I do not try to get rid of him.

We arrive at Sunset Hill and Donald leads me to a cafe terrace. He leaves me for a moment to talk with the waiter. He returns.

"It is beautiful, is it not? I will teach you useful phrases: *Chola, chola*—go away. That is a useful phrase, but useful tomorrow, not today. Today we must be friends. If we are friends we will feel it from the heart. Do you want to see India? You do not know this country. You are a foreigner, you are a woman, you are alone. Everything is dangerous for a woman who is a foreigner and alone. Life is dangerous, that is true, and we do not get through it without great hurt."

The waiter brings us bottles of sweet red liquid. I ask Donald what the wall is that follows the crest of a hill on the horizon.

It is a wall that separates Moslems from Hindus. Many years ago. Today it is history, the wall. History is not important. What is important? I do not know. Life is not important. Death is not important. A palmist tells me I will die by accident. Seven months ago my father is killed in a bus. My father is a bus driver, and he accidents into a truck. No man is lucky. Now I am alone with my mother. I save all that I earn. My friends give me things. I have many friends all over the world. Sandra from San Francisco gives me the pants, the shirt, the shoes I now wear. I do not buy anything. I make twenty rupees a day at the studio. What I earn depends on the quality of my work and also the size. If I make a small miniature I earn little. Forget it if you cannot do it. Forget it. If I work hard I will have success. I want to be a talented artist. I speak Italian, German, French, and English. I was born just with my mother: no one was there, just my mother and baby Donald. Now I live alone. I am a flower beside the road, someone sees me, sometimes stops, sometimes not. We are alike, Donald and Carol from Iowa. No father for me, no husband for you.

"I do not live with my mother. Our paths are different. Her path is to Jaisalmer and my path is from Jaisalmer. I will not marry. I do not like marriage. Yes I am a Hindu. But I am all religious. There is only one god but with different names. Which one is real god I don't know. But everyone dies. Life may be two days or three days and then finish. Everyone must leave this. We look at the sunset today and then we die. You see, I tell you truth, Carol of Iowa. I never speak a lie in my life.

"I go to Nepal with a German girl. She pays for my ticket, and I am her guide. I am very happy in Nepal. I sit in the mountains at night with a candle burning and I have food to eat and beer to drink: I am very happy. Candles there are very many every night in the mountains. German girl say, 'Donald, I want mineral water.' I say, 'Be quiet or I am angry.' One night, she is asleep, and Donald goes away. And now German girl is at her home. Maybe she will write. If she does not write, I say okay. If she want to forget, I forget: who is this German girl? I forget her. If you want to forget Donald, okay. Then I say, 'Who is this American woman?' I forget her. '*Shanta, Shanta*': quiet, quiet. A useful phrase. I will not marry. Like candles, there are many women every night. I am in this business three years. I am enjoying of my life.

"Where do you go tomorrow? O you must not take bus tomorrow because I want you not to die. Go slowly and you arrive. I will tell you a story. Jenny from California is antique woman. Boys do not want to be in bed with antique. She likes to play. She wants boy like a puppet. My friend tells her, 'No I do not want to make romantic with you.' So Jenny from California find another boy, and she give her boy thousands of rupees. Then she get sick and for one month she is in hospital, and then she go home. And now her boy wear old clothes and he poor and he says he is sorry he make romantic with Jenny. People want to cheat with Donald, I say forget it. I have many experiences. I go with German girl to Nepal. Hotel manager in Nepal does not give me good respect. Hotel manager thinks I am poor Indian. I tell hotel manager I am from England. Hotel manager ask, which place? Birmingham, I say. I know many places—London, Chester, Bolton. I give address: 33 Bolton Road, Manchester. I want good respect. I want to be natural, not like Michael Jackson.

"I will go when I die and be with people. I don't like animals. Camel is love, horse is power, elephant is good luck. I like only elephant. My friend Sandra from San Francisco sends me twenty-five letters, and gives me this shirt and pants. I will visit her some day. You must not travel by bus. If I am your son and I die, then you do not want to live because I am your son. If you die, then your son does not want to live because you are his mother. You die, you bring very great hurt to your son.

"It is dark now. Many birds. They go to sleep now. I like to travel to meet people and see different things. Now we visit my school. Perhaps you buy souvenir to remember your friend Donald in Udaipur. If not, forget it. *Shanta, Shanta.*"

HOTEL MANAGER

The hotel manager is a young man. He started his business three years ago. Friends say he has changed. Before, he was carefree, happy; now, he worries. He wants to create a nice atmosphere at the hotel, but he has little money. He wants to put a fountain in the little courtyard onto which the seven rooms of the hotel open. He does not want to think about the election. It is very divisive. No one is interested in the country, only themselves. With independence there were many fights, and still there are fights. India is a violent country. Businesses should be privatized. With 900 million people there is no shortage of manpower, but nothing is done, nothing happens, no one cares. Politicians talk, and people fight or do nothing. He advises me to watch people in the street if I want to learn about India. It happens in the streets. Watch people, try to understand them. This one is eating, that one is sleeping, this one is being shaved, that one is having a tooth pulled, that one waits—for what? for change, for violence, for nothing.

JODHPUR TEMPLE

In the temple of Jodhpur I deal with yet another tout. He is a student, he says, and he wants only to practice his English. At last he leaves. The temple carvings express meditation, my book says. The carvings I see are of couples touching one another. A row of horses and a row of elephants serve as borders to a series of couples. I sit against a marble column and listen to an old man with a white moustache sitting on the floor singing as he plays a harmonium. Occasionally the dozen or so women in yellow, saffron, mauve, violet, light green, red, royal blue and burgundy saris chant together. A toothless old woman approaches me and asks me something I do not understand. She looks at my notebook with puzzlement in her eyes. An old man enters the temple clapping his hands in time with the music. The women take turns pulling a cord from which hangs a cloth, a punkah, which cools a priest at the little altar in the center of the temple.

SOLDIERS

I am on a train to Jodhpur. The reservation sheet posted on the platform indicates that I will be the only person in this compartment. The reservation sheet indicates, after my name, my gender and my age. After the train begins to move and the conductor has punched my ticket, two soldiers or policemen—they wear tan uniforms and carry batons—enter the compartment. The younger one is remarkably handsome, is aware of it, smiles, touches his cap to me.

"Where are you from? Do you like India? This is dangerous territory. We must close windows and shades," the young man says as he closes them.

They sit on the bench opposite me, the young man still smiling, the older one not. The younger one rests his hands on his baton, which he has positioned on the floor, between his legs.

"You will sleep there," the younger man says to me, pointing to the top berth.

"My reservation is for this berth," I say, indicating the one I am sitting on.

"You will sleep there," the younger man repeats. "I will sleep here and my friend will sleep here." He points to the lower berths as theirs.

"Sorry. I sleep here. Number 16, as my ticket says."

"I order you to sleep there," the younger man says, and now he is not smiling.

I open the shutter and window on my side, and let the warm wind and dust in. "I will sleep here," I tell them, "and you may sleep wherever you like." Eventually the older soldier stretches out on the berth across from me, and the young soldier roams about, returning frequently, sitting either at the end of my berth or on the one where his friend is resting. They talk between themselves. The older man is sleepy, the younger one is enraged. All night the light is left on, and I sit on the berth next to the open window. From another compartment I hear the voice of a woman who does not stop talking. All night I sit, lulled by words I do not understand spoken by a woman I will never see.

EKLINGJI

I take a bus to Eklingji, an ancient town twenty-three kilometers north of Udaipur. There is no empty seat when I get on the bus, but the conductor finds a place for me in the front compartment, where the driver sits.

People are carrying cloth bags filled with clothes and food. No one appears to be taking the bus for the reason I am, to see some of the remains of a time and culture that indulged aristocratic pleasures with artificial lakes, palaces, much decorated temples. Eklingji is a highway town—a series of small shops lining the road on either side—and an older village built against the side of a hill that rises to the east. The temple in the village will not be open for another hour, giving me time to see the Sas Bahu temples a kilometer away. A guide finds me when I step off the bus, a thin, handsome young man who may be eighteen, maybe twenty-five. He speaks and walks fast, and he does not smile. Yes we can see the temples beyond the village, he says, and off we take, up the steep cobble-stone path that runs through the village. Is it far? I ask. Not far, I will see. He wears thongs and is smoking, but the climb and heat appear not to affect him. He stands at the top of the road waiting for me, his neatly pressed white shirt accentuating his dark skin. When I reach him I can see a lake in the distance and a small temple nearby. Are these the Sas Bahu temples? You want to see the Sas Bahu temples? And off we go, down the cobblestone path, back to the main road and across it to a cobblestone road covered with a canopy of large trees. This road lies beneath and along the highway the bus traveled, but I did not see—I could not have seen—this older road. It too follows an incline, but one less steep than the first one, and the shade makes the walk pleasant. Some young men bathing in a large stone reservoir call hello and exchange words with my guide.

We come to the end of the road and tree canopy, and to the edge of a lake, perhaps five acres large. I can see the hard-surfaced road that runs halfway around it, and, on the other side of the lake, beyond the flat green field my guide points to, are the temples. A cliff of bare red rock rises above the road, and along the lower part of it blanket-size pieces of cloth are drying in the morning sun. We walk around the lake. At the foot of wide stairs leading to it are bathers, and at the far end, where we walk, women are washing clothes, beating them on rocks with wooden paddles. The voices and paddles echo like bells and drums against the cliff as we walk along. Water buffalo rest in the water near the women. We circle the lake past the women and water buffalo, and through a grove of trees. A short way to the temples, my guide says. We come to a large open field, and in the middle of it, far from a road or shop or other people, are two temples of red stone built on a marble pavilion, and in front of the pavilion are two columns, which may have supported a lintel and served as entrance to the sacred area. Now, the columns support nothing.

"These temples built by mother-in-law and daughter-in-law for the king, in competition. Do you understand? Mother-in-law and daughter-in-law jealous for the king, and they built temples to make him happy. First we look at daughter-in-law temple. Here is Shiva, the Destroyer, and Brahma, the Creator, and Vishnu the Preserver. This is cobra, this is Shiva's snake. Cobra is respect. This is Parvati, wife of Ganesh. Shiva wants to be wife to Parvati, but Ganesh says no. And Shiva is very angry and cuts off head of Ganesh, and then sorry, and Shiva gives head of elephant to Ganesh. Elephant is good luck. Now Ganesh is god of good luck. This is Sati, wife of Shiva. Sati puts fire to self. This is Shakti, with skulls on her head, and this is Durga, who has ten hands and rides a tiger."

"Are there erotic statues here?" I ask.

"Erotic statues? Madame wants to see fuck statues?"

He leads me to the side of the temple and points to four rectangles of stone reliefs.

"Shiva temple is for everybody. This statue is for dance, for Krishna dance."

My guide sings and dances to help me understand the reliefs. He sings and dances without smiling, seriously. On the pavilion, in the middle of an immense barren field, in front of statues for everybody, my guide sings and dances, his head bent toward the ground, his arms bent, his feet moving back and forth in short quick steps.

> "Come to my heart.
> I'm going to die.
> I know only Hari Krishna.
> Hari Hari Krishna.
> Hari Hari Krishna.
> Hari Hari Krishna
> Hari Krishna.

"This statue is for music. This one for religion, for meditation. And this for erotic. Temple is everybody. What you write? You happy this day? What is your nature? Some like dance, some like religion, meditation, and some like erotic. It is your nature. Have you been to Mt. Ebu? Much erotic at Mt. Ebu. You go there. It is your nature. Do you have a match?"

"No, I'm sorry."

"Why you sorry? *Eklengji* means *one body, respect*. Do you write *Eklengji?* You must have respect. I am clean, I am always clean. I have respect. My friends are jealous. My family kick me. My father kick me, my mother kick me. Do you understand? Kick me out, yes. I am no longer in my family, no longer in the house of my family. I have only myself."

"How did you learn English?"

"How did I learn English? What do you mean how do I learn English? I don't know. I just know. You talk to me and I know. You tell me erotic statue and now I know fuck statue is also erotic statue. I know nothing by myself. Everything happen is like accident. Accident I born. I live one day, one minute, and I die—accident. I don't care. I show you more erotic statue."

We walk to the mother-in-law temple, though my book does not identify either by the family relationships my guide has talked about. On the sun-filled side of the temple he climbs to a ledge to point out the small figures of lovers in various positions, performing actions that time has not made obscure.

"I have no fix nature. I am different. I like too much experience, many things. I want all experience. I will see the world someday. No I do not vote. I have no respect for politics. I go to politician, and he say he will help me, I will get visa to go to America. I see him next month. Who are you? he say. He talk with someone else. I have no family, I have only myself."

He jumps onto a railing of a porch sheltering the temple entrance. He embraces a column with one arm and stretches his other arm to a frieze of lovers.

"One day Moslems come to destroy Hindu temples. Here, Moslems destroy monkey-god Hanuman, and Krishna, who made romantic with many girls. Moslems break statues, and then they see erotic, and they look at them and they stop. In religion no erotic, Moslems say. This is no temple, Moslems say. They do not understand: Hindus make temple with erotic statues to protect it from Moslems."

As we walk back to the lake and then to the village my guide talks further about himself, but only in answer to direct questions I ask.

"I live on floor and little by little I go up. I do not want to live in sky. My father kick me when I am very young. I have no one, no mother, no father, no brother, no sister. I have only myself. Why is that? Life is accident. An accident we meet because I am born poor and you are born rich. I do not know if I have another life. I do not think so. I only know today, not tomorrow, and yesterday does not matter. I sleep everywhere. I sleep by the water, I sleep under a tree. When I have money I sleep in guest house. I have clean clothes. My friend keeps my clothes in his room. I go there, I put on clean clothes. I am not dirty. Do not give pen to that boy. It is nonsense. He does not go to school. See the temple on the hill? It is not just for religion. Indian couple go there. Madame, this is India. You must experience all things. You live long time, you have happiness ten minutes, and after all, sorrow. Do you understand? Life is like accident."

WATCHING

As I walk along a street of shops where people sit outside and watch the crowd go by, on a street that is less congested than most, I look ahead to see how soon I am noticed—how alert the people of this place are to my intrusions. They see me long before I reach them, perhaps half a city block or more before I pass them. Some say hello, or offer to sell me something, but most pretend not to see me, even as they notice me. I am their spectacle and they are mine. More than in any other country I am not allowed here to be only an observer. I am observed, or I am a participant for a little while in the lives of these people. I think I understand better the scenes in A *Passage to India* when Mrs. Moore and Adela experience assault, violation, involuntary engagement—and then I wonder: am I what I seem? There are times when I think I want to leave India early. I have presumed much in having come here. Let me walk around, I have said; let me observe you. Let our exchanges be brief, formal, seemingly immaterial. And then I will pay well for my observations. I expect to be shown respect, deference. You should understand what it means that I am from another country, that I come here alone, that I depend on your civility. I cannot control the desire that you acquiesce to my expectations. My dismay turns inward.

NIGHT SCENE

Always I am early. The train is to leave at 11:30 pm. At 10:45 I am already in my compartment. No one else is in the compartment, no one else is in the car. There are no lights on in the train, not till 11:30, when the train will start. I sit next to the window and watch people on the platform. I sense I am well concealed in darkness. On the platform soldiers are unrolling bedpacks and preparing to go to sleep under the fluorescent lights that hang from the high roofs. A young man sitting on a bench combs his long black hair, twists it and wraps it around his head. He combs his beard. He puts on a red turban and checks his appearance in a small cosmetic mirror he has resting on his suitcase. A soldier who will not sleep but keep watch leans against a pile of chicken crates, holds his rifle between his legs, and smokes a cigarette. A family squats in a circle and shares food the woman takes from a cloth bag. And then I feel something touching my leg. When I look down toward the floor I see nothing but blackness and then, as my eyes adjust, a face—gaunt, immobile—takes form, barely discernible from the surrounding darkness. And then I see that his legs are twisted useless stumps, and I watch his hand reach onto my lap. For what seems a long time, before I can tell him to go away, I sit there, unable to free myself from the unexpected night visitor. Then he turns away, and drags his body out of the compartment into the corridor. I hear his body sweep to the end of the car. The realization comes to me again and again: I am always observed, I am always engaged, I always want to purge myself of part of myself.

BUS RIDE

I sit in the bus station of Jodhpur. I share a stone bench with a couple and their daughter. Behind us are buses that bear no indication of destination. In front of us, four queues in front of four windows. The one on the right is labeled *Inquiry Counter*. I stand there and inquire if I can get a ticket to Udaipur. I am told to go to the fourth window. I stand in line at Window Four waiting for the shade that has been drawn to hide the clerk to be lifted, which happens, periodically and for a few minutes at a time. My obsession with being early serves me now. I ask for a ticket to Udaipur. No tickets to Udaipur will be sold until 11:30; the bus leaves at 12:00. May I reserve a seat? Go to Window Three, *Reservations*. Again I wait for the shade to go up. No reservations for the Udaipur bus. Behind the clerks at the windows there are several other men. They talk, drink tea, and, at well-spaced intervals, sell tickets and sometimes answer questions.

An old woman approaches me. Her eyes are tearful, and her face is deeply lined. She is barefooted and wears silver bracelets around her ankles. Her body is covered in dark colorless fabric. She points to the man on the ground beside her. He has a rope tied around his neck, the end of which she holds in one hand. He crawls about, and his head jerks from side to side. Occasionally he moans, like a cow, but he obeys the commands of the woman who perhaps is his mother, who perhaps maimed him as an infant in order that he become a more effective beggar. His legs are twisted and withered from the knees down. He has a short greying beard and his hair is cut very short. The family next to me refuses to give her money though the old woman asks them several times. A young man walks up and gives the old woman a coin. The old woman walks away, her son crawling beside her.

At 11:30 I stand in line again, but I am told tickets will not be sold until later. The bus has not arrived. I keep my place in line. At 11:45 the woman in front of me gets a ticket. She turns to me and says, "Now ticket to Udaipur," but the vendor closes the window, and I continue my wait. At last the shade goes up. He gives me a ticket and I give him a hundred-rupee note. The ticket costs 65 rupees. Do I have change? He has no change. Stall Two, he says. I take my ticket and go to the bus. I take one of the last seats. On one side are seats for three people and on the other, seats for two. I sit on a seat for three, near the aisle. There is no place for my bags except in the aisle. As the driver starts the motor many people rush onto the bus. The aisle is filled with luggage and people.

We drive to the edge of Jodhpur where we stop while people get off the bus and buy tickets. Eventually we are out of the city and on our way south through flat dry land. Goats graze under groves of delicately leafed trees; they stand with their front legs against the tree trunks and try to reach the leaves. There are goats of many colors, but most are patterned in black and white; some have long hair, some short; some have large ears, some small. Shepherds carry long crooks and sit in the shade wrapped in loose cloth, their heads in turbans. Camels pull carts of wood and grain-filled gunny sacks. The bus is very noisy. The interior is made of rattling metal parts. Through a hole in the floor the size of an apple I see the road roll by under us. The road looks smooth but the ride is very rough. We stop frequently, sometimes for several minutes when we may buy tea or fruit, sometimes ice cream and cold drinks. I am the only Westerner on the bus. People occasionally speak to me, but I do not understand them. The boy behind me gestures for some of my water. I say no, but he insists. I give him my bottle of mineral water and he turns the bottle up and pours water into his mouth without touching his lips.

Across the aisle from me sits a woman with an infant. At first I did not realize that she had a child, it was so concealed in her dark colorful loose attire. She has with her two sacks filled with clothes which she pushes against my feet. She keeps her face covered with a veil. I notice the infant first when the woman uncovers it to nurse it. It is a boy, the lower part of his body is naked. He has bangles on his ankles and wrists, and his face is painted with mascara and powder. He is very small, maybe 20 inches long and weighing 10 pounds. His eyes seem fixed. When he yawns I can see that he has four teeth. His mother offers him her breast often, but he does not seem to want to be nourished. All during the trip, which lasts thirteen hours, I do not think he makes a sound.

We cross many riverbeds, all of them are bone dry. By 5:00 we are in the hills. The ride is rougher now, and I put a motion-sickness patch behind my ear. The landscape reminds me of the south of France: there is much vegetation now, and land is divided into small fields by walls made of stones collected from the earth around. But there is something different about the landscape, which has been, perhaps, more recalcitrant to the human hand. Here the land seems poised, ready to fall back to its untended, its preferred state.

The only middle-class looking family on the bus is a couple with three young daughters. The father and two daughters sit toward the front, and the mother and one daughter sit in the seat in front of me, next to a man at the window who is smoking. The woman asks the man to open the window, and he does. She is polite to him, speaks something further to him, and he responds, apparently pleased that she engages him in conversation. The father notices what is going on and turns to his wife and says something. The wife and the man by the window say nothing more to one another. We stop again, as it is about to get dark.

We stop in a village where there are many stalls and stores. I buy a cup of tea and wander about. A tall older man dressed in a white shirt and *dhoti* approaches. He could be a Rajasthan warrior of the seventeenth century, I think. He offers me a cigarette, like the one hanging from the corner of his mouth. He speaks no English, but he speaks to me nonetheless, and he smiles. Two other men, his friends, joins us. They share the tall warrior's cigarette.

We take off once more, and a few minutes later the bus stops in response to the honking of a jeep behind us. The man who sat by the window earlier gets on the bus. He appears to be drunk. He struggles to a seat in the front of the bus, near the driver, on the command of the conductor.

It is dark as we pass many marble factories. During the long day I have sat next to two men who I presume are brothers. They are dressed in *longhis*, or loin cloths, and yellow turbans. One has a small face, and seems to depend on his brother, who gets off the bus when we stop and brings him some refreshment—a popsicle, a cup of tea. The small-faced man cannot find one of his slippers. People around laugh as the caretaker brother struggles in the darkness, with luggage and people's feet, looking for the slipper. At last he finds it, and he hands it to his brother who quickly puts it on.

We arrive at Udaipur at 1 am. The bus stops at a well-lit square, where there are many motor rickshaws and hotels. A driver says he will take me to the hotel I name, but he wants to show me another, a better and cheaper hotel first. A policeman drags a rickshaw driver to the street and beats him with his baton. The driver does not make a sound, does not resist in any way. People stand about and watch. I cannot tell whether they sympathize with the officer or the driver, or if they just enjoy the spectacle.

EXCHANGE

As I pass a little girl carrying a pan of wet cow dung on her head she wipes her shit-filled hand on my arm. I cannot find water to wash it off. I try to clean myself with a tissue. My arm is quite red, and for days I imagine my skin where she touched me is burning.

BLESSING

I am sitting on the pavilion of a temple in Agra. Three middle-aged men sit on the ground, each surrounded by six or eight women in saris of coral, yellow, green, red. The men appear to be performing rituals. They wear *dhotis* and are barefooted, as are the women. Most of the women are older, some are in their thirties. There is a small wood fire before one priest, and candles in front of the other two. The women come with trays of flowers and fruit and jars of water. The priests sway as they chant over the offerings. The women leave coins for the priests, who put them in purses inside their shirts. There is much talk among the women and the priests, each of whom has a thick layer of red powder caked to his forehead. A woman will occasionally add powder to what the priests are wearing. An old man in white shirt and pants, with long white hair and a beard, and a saffron turban sits across from me, apart from the priests and women. He gestures for me to take his picture, and then he asks for money. I give him two rupees. It is not enough. I give him two rupees more. A young man comes to sit next to me. His bare feet are very wide and thick as are his hands. He appears to be sleepy, perhaps drugged. He asks for my watch. I tell him no. He repeats his request between moments of apparent sleep. He wants my watch. He does not have a watch. He does not know the time. He wants my watch. He lights a cigarette. As a woman leaves her circle she sprinkles water on her friends, the old man, the young man and me.

VARANASI

I get up at 4 am in order to be at the Ganges when the sun rises. My hotel is far from the river. I wait in the darkness for the first taxi that comes along—a cycle rickshaw. The driver wears a scarf around his neck, and he is barefooted. For a while all I can see is the motion of his back as he peddles; he is lean rather than muscular, and very strong. We ride along the street that was overflowing with life eight hours ago. Now, there are few people, few vehicles. At the edge of the road people sleep on carts, on rope and plastic beds, on the ground, next to dogs and cows. A few people are beginning their day. They light fires, they prepare tea, they wash at a pump. I can see inside some rooms: small, with uncovered bulbs hanging from the ceiling or oil lamps on the floor, but no people are visible in those rooms. Most of the houses and shops are dark.

As we approach the river a procession begins to take shape. People are on their way to the Ganges. I pay the driver and join the pilgrims. I can walk faster now than he can drive. There is a crowd now, and as I walk down the steps of the *ghat* I pass a line of beggars: some are lepers, some are limbless, some are just old. The river is very wide, calm, and oil-smooth. On the far side, beneath the barely grey sky, there are a few trees and a sandbar or beach, I cannot tell which; there are no buildings there that I can see.

I walk down the steps and sit near the river, where bathers stand in the water and face the east. They lift water in their hands, and let it slip through their fingers, or they fill small brass pots with water and then pour it out slowly as they murmur prayers. They dip their heads in the water many times. Leaves carrying flowers and burning candles float down the river, toward the rising sun. At the *ghat* next to us there are stacks of wood and in the water in front of it, boats laden with wood. There is one fire I can see. It is there that the dead are cremated, and their ashes thrown into the Ganges to cross India and go to the sea. Hindus come to Varanasi in hopes of not being reborn to another life. They do not want to wake up to unhappiness again. The sacred river, the constantly changing river, promises them stasis. They may stop. No more births, no more lives, no more suffering, no more deaths: that is their prayer. Release their souls from the cycle of rebirth, O Mother: that is their prayer.

My eyes rest on one woman, standing waist-deep in the river. Her face is turned to the sun, to which she offers water held in her hands briefly, before it returns to the river. I have one life, I think, and she has had thousands. I am burdened with the need of experiencing life as fully as I can in the short time I have. She is in no hurry. She has lived fully, many, too many times over. She has come slowly and now she is ready to arrive. Older than I am able to calculate, she has no age, as I do. I cannot escape the noise that surrounds me. She hears only her prayer, listens only for a reply. I focus on the life about me, she on the sun. I sit on a stone step, and she stands in the eternal, ever-changing water that begins in the Himalayas and flows across India collecting the dead, purifying the living, and promising some they need not live again in this world. Answer her prayer, O Mother, and tell me what my prayer should be. Dogs run in the sand between the *ghats*, cows wander about, a priest stands over a corpse covered with a red cloth, and then two men lift the corpse and carry it to the fire as the sun rises over the river.

ACTIVE READING

1. Find two or three passages where de Saint Victor provides the speech of another person without using quotation marks. How do these passages differ from sections where she gives her own thoughts? Based on these differences, what can you say about the relationships between de Saint Victor and the people she meets?

2. Where does de Saint Victor turn for advice during her trip? Find some places where de Saint Victor follows advice and some where she rejects it. Why do you think she makes these choices? Using the passages you found, develop your own theory about what she hopes to experience on her trip.

3. Locate several passages in which the idea of history seems important. What do de Saint Victor and the people she is with think about history in each passage? What do you learn about people in the essay from the way they look at history?

READING IN NEW CONTEXTS

1. How do de Saint Victor's comments about the role of the observer (in the "Watching" section and elsewhere) relate to the ideas about

observation you found in Scheper-Hughes, Fienup-Riordan, or Clifford? Use the ideas from one or more of these writers to extend your understanding of the observer's role in de Saint Victor's essay.

2. Find three or four sections in which money is used or mentioned. What social functions does the use of money serve in these passages? Use your ideas to examine the social function of money in a reading by another author, perhaps Garson, Kozol, or Rodriguez.

3. List as many occurrences of reading, interpreting, or writing as you can find in de Saint Victor's essay. What kind of power or authority do people seem to have when they are involved in these activities? Use ideas about language and authority from Heath, Fishman, or Anzaldúa to examine your observations.

DRAFT ONE / DRAFT TWO

1. *Draft One:* Make a list of several memories you have about a past experience. Then write an informal narrative telling the full story of that experience. What impressions of your experience would readers get from your narrative that they would not get from your list of memories? Why?

   Draft Two: How do de Saint Victor's subtitles call attention to specific aspects (mood, details, images, etc.) of each section? Using your examination of two or three passages from her essay and your insights from Draft One, develop a theory about how writers use specific memories or images to shape the way readers respond to the writer's experience.

2. *Draft One:* Locate three or four places where de Saint Victor hears about or visits a religious or holy site. What is her attitude toward these sites? What kind of interest, if any, does she show in them? In an essay, try to account for any changes you see between her responses to these places.

   Draft Two: What claims does a second *Literacies* writer, perhaps Black Elk or el-Saadawi, make about the purpose of his or her spirituality? How can you adapt these claims to explain how people use forms of spirituality that are not part of their own religious beliefs? Use your response to these questions to revise Draft One.

BEFORE READING SCOTT RUSSELL SANDERS

1. How do you respond to generalizations about men or women? Why, in your opinion, do people tend to make such generalizations? Using your own experience, explain how generalizations might affect individuals.

2. Think about a man who plays a significant role in your life. What kind of social status, power, and authority does he have in his relationship with you? How do his status, power, and authority change when you look at his place in some broader social context (such as his school, workplace, or community)?

3. What are some advantages and disadvantages of using personal experience to talk about gender relationships or gender identity?

S C O T T   R U S S E L L   S A N D E R S

THE MEN WE CARRY
IN OUR MINDS

"This must be a hard time for women," I say to my friend Anneke. "They have so many paths to choose from, and so many voices calling them."

"I think it's a lot harder for men," she replies.

"How do you figure that?"

"The women I know feel excited, innocent, like crusaders in a just cause. The men I know are eaten up with guilt."

We are sitting at the kitchen table drinking sassafras tea, our hands wrapped around the mugs because this April morning is cool and drizzly. "Like a Dutch morning," Anneke told me earlier. She is Dutch herself, a writer and midwife and peacemaker, with the round face and sad eyes of a woman in a Vermeer painting who might be waiting for the rain to stop, for a door to open. She leans over to sniff a sprig of lilac, pale lavender, that rises from a vase of cobalt blue.

"Women feel such pressure to be everything, do everything," I say. "Career, kids, art, politics. Have their babies and get back to the office a week later. It's as if they're trying to overcome a million years' worth of evolution in one lifetime."

From *The Paradise of Bombs* (1987). Originally published in *Milkweed Chronicle* (1984).

"But we help one another. We don't try to lumber on alone, like so many wounded grizzly bears, the way men do." Anneke sips her tea. I gave her the mug with owls on it, for wisdom. "And we have this deep-down sense that we're in the *right*—we've been held back, passed over, used—while men feel they're in the wrong. Men are the ones who've been discredited, who have to search their souls."

I search my soul. I discover guilty feelings aplenty—toward the poor, the Vietnamese, Native Americans, the whales, an endless list of debts— a guilt in each case that is as bright and unambiguous as a neon sign. But toward women I feel something more confused, a snarl of shame, envy, wary tenderness, and amazement. This muddle troubles me. To hide my unease I say, "You're right, it's tough being a man these days."

"Don't laugh." Anneke frowns at me, mournful-eyed, through the sassafras steam. "I wouldn't be a man for anything. It's much easier being the victim. All the victim has to do is break free. The persecutor has to live with his past."

How deep is that past? I find myself wondering after Anneke has left. How much of an inheritance do I have to throw off? Is it just the beliefs I breathed in as a child? Do I have to scour memory back through father and grandfather? Through St. Paul? Beyond Stonehenge and into the twilit caves? I'm convinced the past we must contend with is deeper even than speech. When I think back on my childhood, on how I learned to see men and women, I have a sense of ancient, dizzying depths. The back roads of Tennessee and Ohio where I grew up were probably closer, in their sexual patterns, to the campsites of Stone Age hunters than to the genderless cities of the future into which we are rushing.

The first men, besides my father, I remember seeing were black convicts and white guards, in the cottonfield across the road from our farm on the outskirts of Memphis. I must have been three or four. The prisoners wore dingy gray-and-black zebra suits, heavy as canvas, sodden with sweat. Hatless, stooped, they chopped weeds in the fierce heat, row after row, breathing the acrid dust of boll-weevil poison. The overseers wore dazzling white shirts and broad shadowy hats. The oiled barrels of their shotguns flashed in the sunlight. Their faces in memory are utterly blank. Of course those men, white and black, have become for me an emblem of racial hatred. But they have also come to stand for the twin poles of my early vision of manhood—the brute toiling animal and the boss.

When I was a boy, the men I knew labored with their bodies. They were marginal farmers, just scraping by, or welders, steelworkers, carpenters; they swept floors, dug ditches, mined coal, or drove trucks, their forearms ropy with muscle; they trained horses, stoked furnaces, built tires, stood on assembly lines wrestling parts onto cars and refrigerators. They got up before light, worked all day long whatever the weather, and when they came home at night they looked as though somebody had been whipping them. In the evenings and on weekends they worked on their own places, tilling gardens that were lumpy with clay, fixing broken-down cars, hammering on houses that were always too drafty, too leaky, too small.

The bodies of the men I knew were twisted and maimed in ways visible and invisible. The nails of their hands were black and split, the hands tattooed with scars. Some had lost fingers. Heavy lifting had given many of them finicky backs and guts weak from hernias. Racing against conveyor belts had given them ulcers. Their ankles and knees ached from years of standing on concrete. Anyone who had worked for long around machines was hard of hearing. They squinted, and the skin of their faces was creased like the leather of old work gloves. There were times, studying them, when I dreaded growing up. Most of them coughed, from dust or cigarettes, and most of them drank cheap wine or whiskey, so their eyes looked bloodshot and bruised. The fathers of my friends always seemed older than the mothers. Men wore out sooner. Only women lived into old age.

As a boy I also knew another sort of men, who did not sweat and break down like mules. They were soldiers, and so far as I could tell they scarcely worked at all. During my early school years we lived on a military base, an arsenal in Ohio, and every day I saw GIs in the guardshacks, on the stoops of barracks, at the wheels of olive drab Chevrolets. The chief fact of their lives was boredom. Long after I left the Arsenal I came to recognize the sour smell the soldiers gave off as that of souls in limbo. They were all waiting—for wars, for transfers, for leaves, for promotions, for the end of their hitch—like so many braves waiting for the hunt to begin. Unlike the warriors of older tribes, however, they would have no say about when the battle would start or how it would be waged. Their waiting was broken only when they practiced for war. They fired guns at targets, drove tanks across the churned-up fields of the military reservation, set off bombs in the wrecks of old fighter planes. I knew this was all play. But I also felt certain that when the hour for killing arrived, they would kill. When the real shooting started, many of them would die. This was what soldiers were *for*, just as a hammer was for driving nails.

Warriors and toilers: those seemed, in my boyhood vision, to be the chief destinies for men. They weren't the only destinies, as I learned from having a few male teachers, from reading books, and from watching television. But the men on television—the politicians, the astronauts, the generals, the savvy lawyers, the philosophical doctors, the bosses who gave orders to both soldiers and laborers—seemed as remote and unreal to me as the figures in tapestries. I could no more imagine growing up to become one of these cool, potent creatures than I could imagine becoming a prince.

A nearer and more hopeful example was that of my father, who had escaped from a red-dirt farm to a tire factory, and from the assembly line to the front office. Eventually he dressed in a white shirt and tie. He carried himself as if he had been born to work with his mind. But his body, remembering the earlier years of slogging work, began to give out on him in his fifties, and it quit on him entirely before he turned sixty-five. Even such a partial escape from man's fate as he had accomplished did not seem possible for most of the boys I knew. They joined the Army, stood in line for jobs in the smoky plants, helped build highways. They were bound to work as their fathers had worked, killing themselves or preparing to kill others.

A scholarship enabled me not only to attend college, a rare enough feat in my circle, but even to study in a university meant for the children of the rich. Here I met for the first time young men who had assumed from birth that they would lead lives of comfort and power. And for the first time I met women who told me that men were guilty of having kept all the joys and privileges of the earth for themselves. I was baffled. What privileges? What joys? I thought about the maimed, dismal lives of most of the men back home. What had they stolen from their wives and daughters? The right to go five days a week, twelve months a year, for thirty or forty years to a steel mill or a coal mine? The right to drop bombs and die in war? The right to feel every leak in the roof, every gap in the fence, every cough in the engine, as a wound they must mend? The right to feel, when the lay-off comes or the plant shuts down, not only afraid but ashamed?

I was slow to understand the deep grievances of women. This was because, as a boy, I had envied them. Before college, the only people I had ever known who were interested in art or music or literature, the only ones who read books, the only ones who ever seemed to enjoy a sense of ease and grace were the mothers and daughters. Like the menfolk, they fretted about money, they scrimped and made-do. But, when the pay stopped coming in, they were not the ones who had failed. Nor did they have to go to war, and that seemed to me a blessed fact. By comparison with the narrow, ironclad days of fathers, there was an expansiveness, I thought, in the days of mothers. They went to see neighbors, to shop in town, to run errands at school, at the library, at church. No doubt, had I looked harder at their lives, I would have envied them less. It was not my fate to become a woman, so it was easier for me to see the graces. Few of them held jobs outside the home, and those who did filled thankless roles as clerks and waitresses. I didn't see, then, what a prison a house could be, since houses seemed to me brighter, handsomer places than any factory. I did not realize—because such things were never spoken of—how often women suffered from men's bullying. I did learn about the wretchedness of abandoned wives, single mothers, widows; but I also learned about the wretchedness of lone men. Even then I could see how exhausting it was for a mother to cater all day to the needs of young children. But if I had been asked, as a boy, to choose between tending a baby and tending a machine, I think I would have chosen the baby. (Having now tended both, I know I would choose the baby.)

So I was baffled when the women at college accused me and my sex of having cornered the world's pleasures. I think something like my bafflement has been felt by other boys (and by girls as well) who grew up in dirt-poor farm country, in mining country, in black ghettos, in Hispanic barrios, in the shadows of factories, in Third World nations—any place where the fate of men is as grim and bleak as the fate of women. Toilers and warriors. I realize now how ancient these identities are, how deep the tug they exert on men, the undertow of a thousand generations. The miseries I saw, as a boy, in the lives of nearly all men I continue to see in the lives of many—the body-breaking toil, the tedium, the call to be tough, the humiliating powerlessness, the battle for a living and for territory.

When the women I met at college thought about the joys and privileges of men, they did not carry in their minds the sort of men I had known in my childhood. They thought of their fathers, who were bankers, physicians, architects, stockbrokers, the big wheels of the big cities. These fathers rode the train to work or drove cars that cost more than any of my childhood houses. They were attended from morning to night by female helpers, wives and nurses and secretaries. They were never laid off, never short of cash at month's end, never lined up for welfare. These fathers made decisions that mattered. They ran the world.

The daughters of such men wanted to share in this power, this glory. So did I. They yearned for a say over their future, for jobs worthy of their abilities, for the right to live at peace, unmolested, whole. Yes, I thought, yes yes. The difference between me and these daughters was that they saw me, because of my sex, as destined from birth to become like their fathers, and therefore as an enemy to their desires. But I knew better. I wasn't an enemy, in fact or in feeling. I was an ally. If I had known, then, how to tell them so, would they have believed me? Would they now?

ACTIVE READING

1. When it comes to the women he knew in college, Sanders claims that he "wasn't an enemy, in fact or in feeling," but an "ally" (518). On what similarities could Sanders and his female classmates have built an "alliance"? What conflicts made such an "alliance" difficult to achieve?

2. Sanders raises and then returns to concepts such as "guilt," "persecution," "inheritance," and "shame." How do his initial understandings of these concepts relate to your own? How and why does his understanding of them change as his argument develops?

3. What social pressures, besides sexism, affect Sanders's understanding of himself? Find some passages that describe these other pressures, and show how they intensify or hide problems caused by sexism.

READING IN NEW CONTEXTS

1. Look at MacLeod, Rodriguez, Shanley, or another *Literacies* writer who links ideas about work to ideas about the body. Pick two or three of Sanders's ideas about this relationship, and apply them to this second text. What do Sanders's ideas tell you about the role of social class in this other text? What do they tell you about gender?

2. Why might Sanders have left his closing questions unanswered? Working closely with some unanswered questions in another *Literacies* text (try the essays by Rich or Tan), develop a theory about when, how, and why writers choose to raise questions without answering them. What are some advantages and drawbacks of this technique? How well does your theory apply to your own writing?

3. What might relationships between generations be able to tell you about the customs and history of a particular cultural group? Describe what you learn when you ask this question of Sanders's and Baldwin's or Scheper-Hughes's texts.

DRAFT ONE / DRAFT TWO

1. *Draft One:* What does Sanders learn from his conversation with Anneke? Explore both the obvious and the unspoken lessons he learns. How does this conversation contribute to Sanders's ultimate conclusions about gender and social class?

   Draft Two: Use your ideas from Draft One to consider the role of conversation in Christian's, Kozol's, or de Saint Victor's essays. As a reader, what do you gain when writers use conversation in their texts? What, if anything, might you lose?

2. *Draft One:* As a boy, Sanders learned that "soldiers were *for*" dying, "just as a hammer was for driving nails" (515). Describe your response to this statement. What made this realization possible or even necessary for Sanders? How do Sanders's adult observations about gender change his understanding of what soldiers and other men are "for"?

   Draft Two: What happens to individuals and society when groups of people are viewed in "instrumental" terms (in other words, as though they are made "for" certain purposes). Expand upon the ideas you developed in Draft One by discussing some examples of "instrumentalism" from Garson's or Shanley's essays.

BEFORE READING NANCY SCHEPER-HUGHES

1. What are some common barriers between specialists (from whatever field) and the people they study or serve? Speculate about how those barriers might be crossed.

2. What do you think might be the primary challenges to an anthropologist as she prepares a written description of a society? (Consult a dictionary or college course catalog if you're unfamiliar with anthropology.)

3. Think of some social problems that your family or community avoids talking about. What consequences follow for those (either inside or outside the group) who openly discuss these social secrets? What consequences follow for the group when these problems are made public?

NANCY SCHEPER-HUGHES

THE ANTHROPOLOGICAL LOOKING GLASS

PREFACE[1]

> Description is revelation. It is neither
> The thing described, nor false facsimile.
>
> It is an artificial thing that exists,
> In its own seeming, plainly visible,
>
> Yet not too closely the double of our lives
> Intenser than any actual life could be.
>
> —WALLACE STEVENS

One source of ethnographic data frequently absent in anthropological analysis is the response of the people studied to the ethnographer's description and interpretation of the meaning of their lives.[2] For the most

From *Saints, Scholars, and Schizophrenics: Mental Illness in Rural Ireland* (1979).

1. In this preface to the second (paperback) edition (1982), Scheper-Hughes discusses the response to the first edition of the book.
2. One notable exception is the volume recently edited by Jay Ruby, *A Crack in the Mirror: Reflexive Perspectives in Anthropology* (Philadelphia: University of Pennsylvania Press, 1982). See especially Eric Michael's contribution to the above volume, "How to Look at Us Looking at the Yanomami": pp. 133–148.

part anthropologists (as well as the communities studied) have been shielded from any local repercussions and aftershocks resulting from publication because we have traditionally worked in what were until recently "exotic" cultures and among preliterate peoples. In most cases the "natives" never knew what had been said about them, their patterns of kinship and marriage, their sexual practices, their beliefs and values or— God help us!—their basic personality structures. The anthropologist might, as a professional courtesy, send a village headman or a mestizo *mayordomo* a copy of the published ethnography which was often proudly displayed in the village. Its contents, however, normally remained as mysterious as the private life of the "masked" white man, that professional lone stranger, who would periodically reappear (sometimes bearing gifts) and then just as inexplicably vanish (not infrequently at the start of the rainy season). Within this traditional fieldwork paradigm our once colonized subjects remain disempowered and mute.

Such local invisibility (and hence invulnerability) has not been the fate of those who have studied "modern" cultures, and in particular that most literate and self-reflexive people, the rural Irish. Irish reaction to, analysis of, and commentary on anthropological writing generally has been swift, frequently harsh, and (at least for the ethnographer) most unsettling.[3] Although, for example, Conrad Arensberg's *The Irish Countryman* (1937) was well received in the Republic as a sympathetic portrait of rural lives, the Irish did *not* like the image of themselves as an appropriate subject for anthropological inquiry. Hence, it was not too long before an enormously popular book appeared by the Anglo-Irish novelist Honor Tracy (*The Straight and Narrow Path*, 1956) which parodied the anthropologist protagonist in an Irish village as a naive, bumbling and pompous fool of uncertain moral principles, given to inept interpretations of local custom, and prone to the perpetration of malicious gossip. Fair enough: the anthropological looking glass reflected back on ourselves. And very reminiscent of the rather blunt warning offered by one resident of "Ballybran": "Ye'll only know how it feels to have your whole family history spilled out for the whole world to see when it's been done to yourselves."

At an early stage in the writing of this book I was tempted to entitle it *The Confessional Conscience*, so struck was I by the rigorously self-

---

3. See, for example, John Messenger's biting reply to his Irish critics in his paper "When the 'Natives' Can Read and Respond: A New Projective Test," *American Anthropological Association Meetings*, Los Angeles 12/5/81.

critical mode of the Irish villager. I trust that a touch of that same reflexivity and introspection has rubbed off on myself as, over the past three years, I have had ample time and opportunities to observe the impact of publication on the lives of those who "so kindly took us in" as total strangers on that stormy day in 1974 and who, during the ensuing months, entrusted to my keeping a few of the "darkest secrets" of their souls.

The ethical dilemma that has gradually emerged through an exchange of letters, a series of review articles and replies in the Irish press,[4] and through a brief return to Ballybran, was most succinctly stated by the village schoolmaster:

> It's not your science [i.e., your accuracy] I'm questioning, but this: don't we have the right to lead unexamined lives, the right *not* to be analyzed? Don't we have a right to hold on to an image of ourselves as 'different' to be sure, but as innocent and unblemished all the same?

If our anthropological code of ethics can be said, minimally, to reflect the medical profession's proscription to "do no harm," then it would be fitting on this occasion of a second edition to reflect on the fundamental question raised by Sir Raymond Firth[5]—*Cui Bonum?* To whose advantage or for whose good do we cast what is so often a critical gaze on the contradictions and paradoxes implicit in the character of human relations, institutions and organizations?

What have they lost, what have they gained in "Ballybran" as a result of the publication of *Saints, Scholars and Schizophrenics*, a book that clearly departs from the traditional anthropological stance of cultural relativism in order to examine the social and cultural contributions to psychological suffering? I will relay here what I have learned by a moving and often painful return to "Ballybran" during the spring of 1981, our first visit since 1976.

They have lost a hitherto unchallenged native interpretation of the meaning of their lives as ones based on the implicitly cherished values of

4. In chronological order: David Nowland, "Death by Suppression," *Irish Times* 8/4/79; Eileen Kane, "Is Rural Ireland Blighted?," *The Irish Press* 12/13/79: 1; Michael Viney, "Geared For a Gale," *Viney's Irish Journey*, *The Irish Times* 9/24/80: 12; Nancy Scheper-Hughes, "Reply to Ballybran," *The Irish Times* (*Weekend* supplement) 2/21/81: 9–10.
5. Sir Raymond Firth, 1981, "Engagement and Detachment: Reflections on Applying Social Anthropology to Public Affairs," *Human Organization* 40(3): 193–201. Originally presented as the Malinowski Award Address at the 41st Annual Meeting of the Society for Applied Anthropology, Edinburgh, Scotland.

familistic loyalty, obedience and sacrifice. I was told that one village lass has not been the same since identifying herself in the following pages. Until that time she herself (and the parish at large) viewed her decision to give up a disapproved "love match" in order to stay at home and care for her widowed father and unmarried brothers as the good, moral, "Christian" thing to do. As was said: "her father and brothers 'had right' to claim her." But now there is an alternative view, and a hint of pity has been introduced: "Oh, what a shame, the poor creature." Worse, a suggestion of something subliminal: "Could she be overly attached to them?"

I intruded into their "commonsense world" with an alternative and sometimes shattering vision—that provided by psychological anthropology. And they are angry at me, not so much for exposing their lives to the larger world outside, but rather for exposing their hurt and pain to each other. So, I was scolded: "Why couldn't you have left it a dusty dissertation on a library shelf that no one would read, or a scholarly book that only the 'experts' would read? Why did you have to write it in a way that *we* could read it and understand exactly what you were saying?"

There is an irony here and a "double-bind." The irony is that my colleagues in the Society for Applied Anthropology honored me in 1981 with the Margaret Mead Award in recognition of a work that "interprets anthropological data and principles in ways that make them meaningful to a broadly concerned public." Probably the most immediately concerned part of that "public," the villagers of Ballybran, rather wish I had kept my mouth shut or else had said what I did in a jargon so confounding that *they* would not have had to deal with it. Committed as I am, however, to writing for "the public" rather than for a scientific elite, the mandate from "the people," so to speak, to render myself inaccessible and unintelligible posed a real paradox.

While it would be implausible to expect that the members of a community would wholeheartedly agree with the outsider's perspective, with his or her rendition of their social, cultural and psychological situation, that same rendition should not be *so* foreign or removed from their commonsense interpretation of the meaning of their lives as to do violence to it. Any ethnography ultimately stands or falls on the basis of whether or not it *resonates*: it should ring true, strike a familiar (even if occasionally painful) chord. It should not leave the "native" reader cold and confused. Angry and hurt, perhaps, but not confused or perplexed.

When I protested in Ballybran during my return visit that there should have been no surprises in the book, that I revealed no "personal" secrets, but only commonly known and widely shared "community" secrets (such as the questionable status of the community as an Irish-speaking or *Gaeltacht* parish, the depressions and drinking associated with the lonely winter months, the difficulty of keeping an heir on the land, and the distance and alienation between the sexes), I was told pointedly:

> There is quite a difference between whispering something beside a fire or across a counter and seeing it printed for the world to see. It becomes a public shame.

There were other objections and responses to what I had written, among them:

> She should be shot.
>
> There's a lot of truth in what she said, you can't deny that. But did she have the right to say it, so?
>
> 'Bad 'Cess to anyone from here who throws good Irish pounds after a copy of that Yankee work.

To be accurate there was also the quite predictable praise from the young emigrés of Ballybran, reporting back from their new homes in America or from University College in Cork or Dublin. As one young scholar wrote to his distraught mother, already fearful for the loss of his soul at University College, Dublin:

> . . . and you can tell Da that '*that* book' is the first one to speak the truth about this secret Ireland of ours.

And there was also the silence—the traditional Irish cut-off—from many of those closest to us and, hence, most stunned by my candor.

I never did learn exactly how many villagers had "thrown away good Irish pounds" after the book since one of the best kept secrets in Ballybran today is just *who* owns a copy, and after that, who has actually read it. Most deny both. *Irish Times* correspondent Michael Viney reported after his investigations in Ballybran that "two or three copies of the book have been passing from house to house, [with] hurt and anger flaring up like a gunpowder trail" (*Irish Times*, 9/24/80). My village friends, however, tell me that there are a good forty or fifty copies in private circulation through the parish:

Everyone is curious, of course, to see if they are in it, and everyone is ashamed to *look* curious by borrowing it. So most have their own copy. It is difficult to say what the 'public consensus' is because '*it*' is never discussed openly and in public, but only privately and among kin.

"How do they get '*it*'?" I asked, falling into the local term of reference.

Oh, they're cute, mind you. They won't go walking into a Tralee [in County Kerry] bookseller and ask for it. They'll get it through contacts going to Cork or Dublin. Or they'll have relatives send it from America the same way we did.

When I argued, somewhat lamely, that it would be pointless for individuals to try to identify themselves since I carefully constructed *composite* characters that would defy any attempts at labeling or identification, I was silenced:

Nonsense! You know us for better than that. You think we didn't, each of us, sit down poring over every page until we had recognized the bits and pieces of ourselves strewn about here and there. You turned us into amputees with hooks for fingers and some other blackguard's heart beating inside our own chest. How do you think I felt reading my words come out of some Tom-O or Pat-O or some publican's mouth? Recognize ourselves, indeed! I've gone on to memorize some of my best lines.

Sensing a possible wedge, I asked my friends whether they could not at least see through to my affection for them and for their way of life. I was brought up short with the answer:

Affection, appreciation, we could see that all right. But wasn't it a case of 'Look, I can love you warts and all'? Isn't love more generous than that? Couldn't you have overlooked the warts?

Cui Bonum? For whose good? What, if anything, has been gained? The "problem of the aged," discussed in the following pages, is being actively debated and a local village association has been formed to look after the solitary elderly to prevent their premature hospitalization. One villager confided that for the first time in their years of friendship she and another wife and mother have been able to discuss family and marital problems they share in common:

A kind of great burden has been lifted. There's no need to hide it and worry over it alone—it's part of the public record, now, anyway.

My suggestion that the *Gaeltacht* status of the community is debatable wounded deeply, and has been met by an even fiercer attempt to revive and restore Irish usage. The new curate, who takes a rather dim view of the Irish revival and who has refused to celebrate the Mass in Irish, has been firmly ignored by the once docile parishioners who have weekly attempted to shout down his English liturgy with their bold Irish responses and Séan O'Riada hymns. "Now, make sure you record *that* next time," I was told. And so I have.

Finally, a new (I will not say better) insight into themselves has been gained. "We are less naive now," said a village teacher,

> We can see more clearly what our problems are, and how deep the roots of them go. Your book made me very sad. After all, it isn't a very pretty picture. But I have said to myself, 'Let's stop grieving over it, and let's get on with what has to be done.' *Quod scriptum est, scriptum est.* There are old lives that need caring for, and new ones still in formation. And I was wondering what might be done for some of our young bachelors, before it's too late. A small, informal marriage information bureau, do you think that might work?

Quod Scriptum est, scriptum est. Therefore, as advised, I leave the original work intact, although the impulse to cut and paste, to excise this phrase or that section, to erase those few words now known by me to have caused pain to one individual or another in Ballybran, is strong. I had already in the original Prologue asked villagers' forgiveness for "exposing the darker and weaker side of their venerable culture." I now understand that this forgiveness is not forthcoming. And while I can never ask my fellow travelers in Ballybran to "bless the work" in the characteristically Kerryman fashion, I can pass on to them what I was told upon leaving Ballybran by a "village elder" when I asked whether it would be at all right for me to accept the Mead award in Scotland for a book that had caused so much local controversy. He thought long and hard about it.

> "Take it," he said finally, "but take it for Ballybran, and for what you have learned from us. For better or for worse our lives are inextricably linked."

And he cited the Celtic proverb: *Ar scáth a chéile a mhaireas na daoine* — In the shadows of each other we must build our lives.

MENTAL ILLNESS AND IRISH CULTURE

Introduction to the First Edition

> Things fall apart;
> The center cannot hold;
> Mere anarchy is loosed upon the world.
>
> — W. B. YEATS, Collected Poems

Each time I have been asked to give a lecture to a university audience on my research, I have approached it with some amount of trepidation. Usually I begin by asking the group (often a lecture hall of two hundred to four hundred people) how many of them are at least partly of Irish descent. Depending on geographical region, from one-quarter to one-third will normally raise their hands. My next response is some version of the theme "*You're* the reason why western Ireland is underpopulated and in distress!" If there is a certain amount of discomfort engendered in the process of addressing an audience about problematic themes from their own cultural background, there is also some satisfaction in demonstrating that anthropologists can bring the exotic home to roost. In learning about the plight of a small Irish village, trapped by circumstances into a state of cultural decline and widespread anomie, we can learn something about ourselves. For it was from such isolated little communities of the western coast that has come a succession of our statesmen and leaders, our local police and our teachers, our clergy and our bartenders — in short, many of those who have guided public and private morality.

The high morale and stunning accomplishments of the Irish abroad are, ironically and sadly, often contrasted to the demoralization of the Irish at home (see Brody 1973; Healy 1968; R. Kennedy 1973; Lynn 1968). There is little doubt from available statistics (*WHO Statistics Reports*, 1961: 221–245; 1968: 529–551) that the Republic of Ireland has the highest hospitalization treatment rate for mental illness in the world. A recent census of the Irish psychiatric hospital population (O'Hare and Walsh 1974) indicates that schizophrenia is the core problem — more than half of the patients are so diagnosed.

The association between Irish ethnicity and mental illness has perplexed the Irish medical profession (see Walsh and Walsh 1968) and social scientists at large (Lynn 1971; Malzberg and Lee 1956; H. B. M. Murphy 1975) for nearly half a century, and they remain divided on the basic issue of etiology: genetic, biochemical, or environmental. In this book, based on a year of fieldwork in a representatively small, isolated rural community of the Kerry Gaeltacht* I attempt a broad *cultural* diagnosis of those pathogenic stresses that surround the coming of age in rural Ireland today. I explore the particularly high vulnerability of young and middle-aged bachelor farmers to schizophrenic episodes in light of such social and cultural problems as the current disintegration of village social life and institutions; the remarkable separation and alienation of the sexes; a guilt- and shame-oriented socialization process that guarantees the loyalty of at least one male child to parents, home, and village through the systematic scapegoating of this (usually the youngest) son; and, finally, cultural attitudes toward the resolution of stress *outside* of family life and through patterns of dependency upon "total" institutions.

This work can be placed within the tradition of earlier "culture and personality" studies (e.g., Benedict 1928, 1934; Erikson 1950; M. Mead 1928, 1935; Powdermaker 1953), which attempted to delineate the cultural parameters of personality development and adult behavior. In addition, it falls into that relatively newer field called transcultural (or ethno-) psychiatry, which explores the interplay of culture and social structure upon the form, frequency, severity, diagnosis, and treatment of mental disorders (e.g., Aberle 1952; Benedict 1935; Boyer 1964; DeVos 1965; Hallowell 1934; H. B. M. Murphy 1965; Opler 1959).

My orientation is both psychological and social structural, insofar as I shall examine the interplay of historical circumstance and economic determinants with the largely symbolic spheres of beliefs, values, and behavior. Throughout the book I shall emphasize the importance of the antithetical social spheres of the sexes to the quality of the emotional life, as well as the oppositional role of older to younger siblings—both grounded in the basic economic strategy of rural farm families. It is a major hypothesis that these preordained age and sex statuses are pivotal in defining parental expectations for their children, and result in entirely different socialization and later life experiences—weighted in favor of the mental health of girls and earlier-born sons, and against the chances for healthy ego-integration of later-born male children.

I share with other recent ethnographers, among them Hugh Brody (1973) and Robert Cresswell (1969), the belief that rural Ireland is dying

---

*One of several small enclaves within the Republic where Irish is still the spoken language in many homes.

and its people are consequently infused with a spirit of anomie and despair. This anomie is expressed most markedly in the decline of the traditional agricultural, sheep grazing, and fishing industries and in the virtual dependence of the small communities of the west upon welfare schemes and the ubiquitous "dole"—this despite marketing improvements through membership in the Common Market and government inducements to production through cattle, dairy, and wool subsidies. The flight of young people—especially women—from the desolate parishes of the western coast, drinking patterns among the stay-at-home class of bachelor farmers, and the general disinterest of the local populace in sexuality, marriage, and procreation are further signs of cultural stagnation. Finally, the relative ease with which a growing proportion of the young, single, male farmers are able to accept voluntary incarceration in the mental hospital as a panacea for their troubles is a final indication that western Ireland, one of the oldest and most continually settled human communities in Europe, is in a virtual state of psychocultural decline.

In chapter one I set the parish of Ballybran (which like all personal names used is a pseudonym) in space and in time, examining vignettes of its history from the oral tradition of legend, myth, and folktale. This section is, more properly speaking, an ethnohistory insofar as I allow the villagers to select and order the significant events of their past as they themselves perceived and remember them. In this way I introduce the reader not so much to an objectively accurate history of the locality, which can be gotten elsewhere,[1] but to the ways in which villagers attempt to validate themselves in terms of a "corrected" and "rewritten" past. Chapter two looks at the present situation of Ballybran: its demographic and economic patterns, the failure of the initially enthusiastically embraced language-revival movement, and its perhaps irreversible decline as a viable and self-sustaining community.

In chapter three I focus on the most visible effect of cultural disorganization and demoralization as I sketch an epidemiological profile of mental illness in the rural west. I suggest that the high psychiatric hospitalization rates must be discussed within the context of what has been called "labeling theory" (see Scheff 1966)—that is, through an examination of community definitions of normal and abnormal behavior, variations in diagnostic usage, and cultural attitudes toward treatment and

---

1. The interested reader is referred to Cusack (1871); Foley (1907); Hayward (1950); King (1931); O'Sullivan (1931).

institutionalization.

Chapter four discusses the relationship between celibacy and mental illness through an ethnographic description of relations between the sexes both within and outside the institution of marriage. I attempt to answer the oft-raised question concerning the source of the Irish antipathy to sex and marriage, and I offer an explanation grounded as much in current social and economic determinants (e.g., the refusal of women to marry into the small farms of Kerry) as in psychological predispositions (including a regressed adult sexuality seemingly fixated on early brother-sister incestual longings).

In addition to participant observation in the lifestyle of Ballybran, two groups of villagers were singled out for particular study—mothers and children. Twenty-eight village parents representing twenty nuclear or extended households were interviewed and observed on the norms of child rearing, following a modified version of the interview schedule outlined in John Whiting *et al., Field Guide for a Study of Socialization* (1966: 78–82). Like the anthropologists involved in the seminal "six cultures" study of child rearing (see B. Whiting 1963), I was primarily interested in the values and beliefs of the society as revealed through socialization techniques. But beyond that, I was problem oriented, attempting to determine if certain rural Irish child-rearing practices might be contributing factors in the etiology of mental illness.

The "children" interviewed ranged in age from newborns to middle-aged bachelors and spinsters still living under the roof and under the thumb of the "old people." The parents interviewed, consequently, spanned three generations and gave me the opportunity to add a historical dimension and note some dramatic changes in child rearing over the past forty or fifty years. In addition I examined, with the help of Professor Sean O'Sullivan, relevant material on child rearing collected in the form of proverbs, folktales, and "old piseogas" (i.e., superstitions) by the Irish Folklore Commission in Dublin. Likewise, I read with care and with relish all the autobiographical literature to have come from the recently defunct culture of the Blasket Islands—once just a short canoe trip from the little market town of Dingle. From the bitter-sweet and poetic recollections of Peig Sayers (1962), Tomás O'Crohan (1951), and Maurice O'Sullivan (1957), I gleaned a picture of Irish attitudes toward children and the principles of child tending "uncorrupted" by sustained contact with outsiders and prior to the decline of Gaelic culture.

Chapters five and six examine current socialization practice and raise this question: Is there something in the nature of parent-child interactions in Ballybran which might be defined as psychogenic, or more exactly, as schizophrenogenic? A qualified yes is suggested by the data, and in chapter five I discuss the cultural pattern of minimal handling and isolation of the infant, and the absence for the very young of what some psychologists call necessary attachment or maternal bonding behavior (see Bowlby 1969, 1973). The casual aloofness and seeming emotional inadequacy of mothers toward infants observed in some rural homes seem to be related to the austere and puritanical cast of Irish Catholicism with its many restrictions on physical expression, and to the, at times, excessive reliance on corporal punishment both in the home and in the classroom. For the more psychologically fragile, the end product of such a socialization experience, I suggest, may be a tendency for the individual to withdraw from painful interactions into the characteristic delusional state of schizophrenia.

I attempt to distinguish the "vulnerable" children from the "less vulnerable" in terms of the differential treatment of daughters and sons and of later- to earlier-born siblings. The pattern of fixed statuses—pets, leftovers, whiteheaded boys, and black sheep—attendant to sex and birth order is discussed in terms of the economic requirements of farm succession and its ultimate effect on the emotional and mental health of the chosen heir.

As the research progressed, I became directly involved with the rural young adults themselves and with the succession of conflicts, stresses, and ultimate decisions which resulted in emigration, in stoical resignation, or in cyclical maladjustment expressed in mental illness and alcoholism. In order to probe largely repressed attitudes of late adolescents toward marriage, sexuality, achievement, and generativity, I administered a variety of projective tests—among them the Thematic Apperception and Draw-a-Person Tests, and the Values Hierarchy Scale—to a sizable portion of young adults in the parish. In addition I assigned essays and compositions on a number of relevant topics to the students at the parish secondary school. These essays covered a myriad of topics, such as "Why Does a Good God Allow Suffering and Sickness?" "Is Violence and Aggression Natural to Man?" "How Does the Idealized Image of Marriage Presented in Films Differ from a Realistic Approach to Marriage?"

Most fruitful of the instruments, and to be discussed in greatest

2. The Thematic Apperception Test consists of a series of standardized pictures that reflect everyday characters in a variety of moods and human situations. The subject is asked to make up a story for each picture with a definite plot and a final outcome. He

detail, was the Thematic Apperception Test (TAT),[2] which was initially administered to thirty-six average village youths between the ages of fifteen and eighteen (twenty-two young women and fourteen young men). Each was tested individually while I transcribed their responses by hand. Whenever possible, the youths were interviewed following the test, on general topics of life history: schooling, family relations, vocational and other goal orientations. Nine of the fourteen boys tested (ages fifteen to eighteen) were potential, if reluctant, farm heirs, while the remaining five had serious designs for higher education or emigration. By contrast, all but three of the twenty-two girls tested expected to leave the village within the next few years in order to pursue a nursing or teaching career or to work abroad. These differences were not selected for, but were a natural reflection of, demographic patterns in the area.

Finally, one day each week for a period of three months I observed, interviewed, and tested young patients of the district mental hospital in Killarney and at the psychiatric clinic in Dingle. Through intensive interviewing of these young adults, already demonstrating early signs of a basic inability to cope, I hoped to identify the major stresses surrounding the coming of age in rural Kerry today. A total of twenty-two patients—eleven of each sex—were tested and interviewed on their life histories. These patients were selected at the discretion of the clinic and hospital directors. My only stipulations were that the patients be young, come from a rural Kerry background, and volunteer for the testing. The latter stipulation (in order to comply with federal regulations for the protection of human subjects) necessarily resulted in a "natural selection" of the most sociable, outgoing, cooperative, and least disturbed patients. The average length of hospitalization for these patients was short—just under one month—and for most it was their first admission to a psychiatric institution. Ten of the twenty-two were diagnosed as schizophrenic, or paranoid.

There was a decided advantage to using written and verbal projective testing among the rural Irish. Forced to generalize, one could say that Irish villagers are extremely reserved and unused to, as well as uncomfortable with, the task of discussing feelings and attitudes relating to personal

---

is also encouraged to tell what each character is thinking and feeling. This psychological test has proven particularly well adapted to the needs and skills of the anthropologist: it is straightforward, relatively free of cultural bias, and suited to answering the kinds of questions which the anthropologist has in mind regarding basic cognitive and normative orientations, appropriate role behaviors and the quality of emotional life, etc., without having to venture into the deeper waters of technical personality assessment or symbolic analysis.

relationships. If asked directly, for example, how he got along with mother or father, the rural Kerryman will invariably answer with a stylized "Yerra, nothing to complain about," or will reverse the question into a question of his own: "And why would ye be wanting to know that, may I ask?" Needless to say, direct questioning often resulted in stalemate. However, the Kerryman is particularly adept at innuendo, ambiguity, and metaphor. All but two of the fifty-eight respondents *thoroughly* enjoyed the testing, which gave them an opportunity to express, indirectly, their feelings on topics such as family relations and religious beliefs, which would have been socially taboo were they brought up in a direct manner.

The fifty-eight youths told a total of 835 Thematic Apperception Test stories, which were later coded according to the ten basic motivational concerns suggested by George DeVos (1973: 20–21). Five of the dimensions are instrumental (goal-oriented) and five are expressive (directly related to feeling).

Instrumental Concerns

Achievement-Anomie
Competence-Inadequacy
Responsibility-Negligence
Control (Dominance-Submission)
Mutuality (Competitive-Cooperative)

Expressive Concerns

Harmony-Discord
Affiliation-Isolation
Nurturance-Deprivation
Appreciation-Disdain
Pleasure-Suffering

Each story is characterized by one dominant theme, but often contains from two to five additional subthemes, depending on length and complexity of the tale. In coding the stories I avoided themes that were implied and relied only on material that was expressly stated. In addition to thematic coding, I noted the sequences and outcomes of the stories and paid particular attention to the roles played by family figures. The results of the test are used illustratively throughout the book.

In general the Irish records reveal large areas of feeling and motivation locked into conflict. Ambivalence is a dominant psychological mode for all the youth, as village lads vacillate between achievement orientation and anomie, and as village girls and boys debate their responsibility to home and parents versus their own personal drive for escape from home and village. A sense of shame and incompetence blocks male strivings for achievement, and an oppressive guilt often interferes with their need to excel *or* escape. A certain superficiality in interpersonal relations is expressed in the desire of village and hospitalized males to be affably sociable without the pressures of intimacy. And throughout all the records runs a strong current of sexual repression and personal asceticism—one that interferes not only with intimacy between the sexes, but with the nurturant and generative aspects of personality as well. With the exception of the schizophrenic patients, whose stories are readily distinguished on the basis of their more idiosyncratic themes, the greatest statistical differences were found between the sexes, rather than between the "average" and hospitalized villagers. Given the separate social realities occupied by males and females in County Kerry, it is the culture of sex rather than the culture of mental illness that is most recognizable in the TAT records. Most poignantly, the tests illustrate the differential stresses experienced by girls, often forced into premature emigration, and by village boys, frequently the casualties of this same female exodus.

The research team was the family—myself, my husband, and our three children: Jenny, aged five, Sarah, aged two, and Nathanael, five months at the start of fieldwork. We could hardly avoid being *participant* observers in the community as we shared with the hardy villagers day in and out their lifestyle, their celebrations, their ennui and depressions during the seemingly endless winter, their fear of the truly awesome wind storms that rocked the peninsula, and their joy at the coming of spring— the flowing of cow's milk and the birth of the calves and lambs. We worshipped with them on Sundays and holy days; we confessed our sins to the same curate; we visited their old and sick, and mourned with them their dead. My elder daughter attended the local primary school, where she learned bilingual reading, math, her prayers, sewing, Irish dancing and music, and how to duck the bamboo rod. She admired her strict Scottish-highlander-trained teacher and enjoyed her peers. Although for the first few weeks Jenny was able to relate fascinating tidbits of information to me about school and yard activities, before very long she was socialized by her friends to the extent that she adopted their world view and joined the conspiracy of silence that separates Irish children and their parents. From that time on I lost her as a prime "informant." All the children, however, served as "rites of entry" into the normally closed lives of villagers, and remarks and criticisms of the way in which we handled our children, as well as comments on their behavior vis-à-vis their own

children's, were an invaluable source of information with regard to socialization.

My husband was the second member of the team to withdraw somewhat from the research, particularly after he was given the highly sanc-
tioned role of secondary-school teacher. His identification with the school
and the Church and his shared perception with some of the villagers that
there was something a little sacrilegious about the way I took notes at
wakes and enquired about personal and intimate aspects of religious
belief, sexual practice, and emotional life made him a rather reluctant
co-worker and informant—particularly when it concerned sharing with
me the jokes, stories, and opinions exchanged with village men at the
pub. As Jenny was socialized into the children's world, Michael joined
the circle of "round"-drinking and tale-swapping bachelor farmers. And
my presence at the pub, silent though it was (with the exception of singing
an occasional ballad), put his companions ill at ease. So, after a few
months, I resignedly left the pub mates in peace. I had in any case learned
by then all that I wanted to know (and then some) about the "culture" of
Guinness stout. Nonetheless, my husband with the cooperation of the
schoolmistress gave me free access to his secondary school classes and
agreed to assign the essays and compositions on topics which I suggested.
He accompanied me on the long trip each week to the county mental
hospital, where he assisted in interviewing and testing mental patients.
Finally, and most importantly, Michael's natural sensitivity and kindred
spirit with the reserved rural Irish served as a foil and a censor, correcting
me when I delved too far or pushed too hard or too quickly, and constantly reminding me that my primary obligation was not to "science" or
to the academic community at large, but to the community—protecting
the villagers' dignity, reserve, and sensitivities, and guarding them from
embarrassment or emotional injury of any kind. And for these gentle
reminders I am grateful to him beyond words.

There was, at first, some confusion over the nature of my research.
When one village publican learned that I was in Ballybran to conduct an
"anthropological survey," he informed me that this had already been done
some twenty years before, and to come right to the point, he did not want
to have his nose and lips and skull measured again! While at first I
explained to villagers in the broadest of terms that I was a social anthropologist interested in the culture and way of life of the parish, I was soon
pressed by some of the village schoolteachers to give the *exact* nature of
the research and to inform them in advance the title of the book I would
write and its contents. To this just enough demand, I would reply as
honestly as I could at the time: "Interpersonal Relations in a Rural Irish

Community." Like most anthropologists, I began my research with the broad areas of interest mapped out, a "sense of problem," and a rather flexible methodology, which would allow for that fortuitous creative process which some call "serendipity" to take over at will. As it became increasingly apparent that I was concentrating on mothers, children, and adolescents, the village seemed to relax somewhat.

However, there were a few very tense incidents with regard to the research—both occurring in a pub during the summertime, and both taking place under the encouragement of outsiders—specifically Irish tourists from Dublin. In one rather trying experience, a local shepherd made belligerent by alcohol and losses at the local sheep market announced to all and sundry that he had been told by some Dubliners that "the anthropologist" was only interested in the villagers' sex practices and that I would write a book which would convert "people into numbers," and that I would ultimately degrade the Irish way of life. When my attempts at reversing the accusation into jovial banter failed, I promised Brian the shepherd a copy of Arensberg's *The Irish Countryman* (1939), which I thought might be to his liking, and told him that part of my aim in coming to Ballybran was to "modernize" the Yankee's image of Ireland because there had been such vast changes since Arensberg's time. Brian read at least parts of Arensberg, asked to keep the book, and offered magnanimously, "There's lots of truth in that book; the man didn't lie." From that day on, Brian and I were on a first name basis, and the shepherd even offered to recite some political verses and songs into my tape recorder.

The second incident occurred some weeks later when a Dublin tourist himself offered to "introduce" me to my drinking mates of some time by explaining at a pub session the basic thesis of Irish Catholic sexual repression presented in John Messenger's recent ethnography of the Aran Islands, *Inis Beag* (1969)—a book which incurred the wrath of several Irish social scientists and which received a bad press in Dublin papers as well as censorship at libraries in the west. Luckily for me, the villagers were embarrassed by the flamboyant personality of the Dubliner and, as confirmed celibates, could not relate at all to the outsider's brash charges that "anthropologists are 'peeping Toms' who write that the Irish take only the 'missionary position.'"

The perhaps apocryphal days of yesteryear, when the anthropologist was accepted and adopted as "hero" into the local kinship of an innocent and guileless people, are over—for the best, I am certain—as once isolated villages and small communities throughout the world become more enlightened as to the uses and abuses of anthropology. Today each anthropologist must confront the awesome task of slowly proving himself or herself blameless and worthy of acceptance and confidence, despite the increasingly "bad press" accorded the profession. Hence, I became keenly aware of the sensibilities of the people in Ballybran, who were not only suspicious of social science research, but who were still angered over the "stage Irishman" impression given by the films *Playboy of the Western World* and, more recently, *Ryan's Daughter*—both of which were filmed in part on the Dingle Peninsula. I worried about their reaction to a book dealing with the death of the countryside, anomie, and mental illness, topics which were not designed before the research had begun, but which grew naturally out of immersion within the depressed community.

After a particularly revelatory and intimate conversation with a village mother for whom I had a great deal of affection, I returned home one evening in Ballybran to fall into a fitful sleep during which I dreamed that a villager invited me in for tea and insisted upon giving me a suit of armor that had belonged to their family for generations, since the time of the Norman Conquest. I reluctantly accepted the unwieldy present, but as I was walking home through the bog with it, a group of strangers appeared and began to chase me, yelling that I had "stolen" the armor of the village. The dream brought to consciousness my still lingering anxiety over whether it is defensible behavior to befriend and ultimately "disarm" a people and "steal," as it were, their guarded secrets. While I never asked intimate questions of villagers until I felt that they had extended to me the role of "confessor," knowing that what passed their lips to my ears would be considered a sacred trust and used with discretion, yet often even the closest of friends would laugh at the impertinence of a particular enquiry: "What?" demanded the tailor of Ballybran with false gruffness, after I had asked him why he had never chosen to marry, "What, my girleen? Will you even have the darkest secrets of my soul?"

One could hardly discuss data gathering among villagers without mentioning the Irish love of *blas*—skill with words—and the recreational arts of blarney (flattery) and codding (teasing). What about the reliability of my data given that peculiarly Irish form of banter that says one thing and means another? Wouldn't the naive anthropologist, notebook in hand and indiscreet question on the tip of the tongue, be a sitting duck for the tall tale and other useful evasions of the Irish?[3] Without a doubt, communicating with the Irish is tricky for the plodding, literal-minded Saxon, and in many an initial encounter I would think myself to be fol-

---

3. See, for example, the characterization of the English anthropologist in an Irish village from Honor Tracy's *The Straight and Narrow Path* (1956).

lowing a linear path of conversation, only to find myself lost on a forked road, waylaid by shortcuts and switchbacks, and invariably led up a blind alley or cul-de-sac. In short, I was being *had*, Irish style. Well, no matter. Reputation of the Irish aside, I'd also been had in the past by Mexican and Brazilian peasants (and more than once found myself on the wrong bus en route to nowhere), and I had eventually learned to crack *their* code. Yes, the Irish lie, and lie they do with admirable touches of wit and ingenuity. Add to the normal defensiveness of the peasant, a folk Catholic moral code that is quite "soft" on lying, and a lack of tolerance for *overt* acts of aggression, and you have a very strong propensity to "cod" (sometimes rather cruelly) the outsider. Beyond cross-checking information, the only safeguard the fieldworker has against "converting the lies of peasants into scientific data" (as one critic of the participant-observation method commented) is simply getting to know the villagers well enough to read the nonverbal cues that signal evasiveness or lying. Unfortunately, those villagers who are most eager to talk to the outsider from the onset are often the most mischievous informants. Weeding out the "unreliables" from the initially small coterie of "gifted informants" can be a painful procedure. An important point, however, and one that statistically oriented social scientists often miss, is that lies *are* data, and very essential data at that. Once I am able to figure out to what extent villagers lie, when and to whom they are most likely to lie, and who in the community have the dubious reputations of being the greatest liars, I go about systematically analyzing the values of villagers as demonstrated by what they want to believe about themselves; what they want me to believe about them; and what they think I want to believe about them. I compare these findings against my own observations and perceptions of what actually does go on in the village—the way people behave "as if" things were, even though they may define the situation quite differently.

No anthropologist likes to depart from his time-honored conventional stance of "cultural relativity" in order to ask the kinds of questions that come more easily to the clinical psychologist, the medical doctor, and the social worker, such as, What has gone wrong with this organism (or this society)? or, What is so pathogenic about the quality of interpersonal relations in this family (or in this village)? The anthropologist is the product of a historical tradition and a moral commitment dedicated to seeing the "good" in every culture. Few colleagues today would defend a traditional "functionalist" view of human societies, such that whatever exists in the culture is there by virtue of its necessity to the operation of the whole, and hence if it exists it is by definition "good." Yet there is still some calling into question the objectivity of those social scientists, like Oscar Lewis (1951), Edward Banfield (1958), and George Foster (1967), who noted dysfunction as well as function and who, in particular, describe peasant social life as often characterized by suspiciousness, greed, envy, uncooperativeness, and interactions as charged with hostility and aggressiveness.

Even more difficult is it to embark on an ethnographic study of a subject as delicate and normally shielded from the gaze of outsiders as mental illness. In raising such questions as whether there is something in the nature of rural Irish socialization practices which might be diagnosed as schizophrenogenic, some may wonder whether I am looking to assign blame on parents, teachers, priests, and social institutions. They may ask whether I am engaged in a perverse, cultural witch-hunt. It might be wise, therefore, for me to begin with a few caveats regarding my orientation and choice of subject matter. My interest in Irish madness is an outgrowth of an earlier research interest in rituals of racial and sexual pollution (Scheper-Hughes 1973). The following pages should be taken not so much as a thesis on mental illness as a book about rural Irish society seen in part through the eyes of its indigenous outsiders. By this I mean that I am not so much interested in the phenomenon of schizophrenia, the disease, as I am in schizophrenics, the social outcasts or social critics (as the case may be), and in the rituals of definition, inclusion, and exclusion that surround them.

In this regard, I am heir to the insights of Michel Foucault, who has suggested that madness be seen as a projection of cultural themes. In his brilliant work *Madness and Civilization* (1967), Foucault documents Western society's search for a scapegoat—the leper, the criminal, or the madman—whose existence emphasizes, by contrast conception, the "normalcy" of others. Madness, like racial and caste categories, is one of the ways of drawing margins around the psychological reality of a social group. But even as a society refuses to recognize itself in the suffering individuals it rejects or locks up, it gives eloquent testimony to the repressed fears, longings, and insecurities of the group. And that particular configuration of Irish schizophrenia, as revealed through the life histories of young mental patients, expresses the continuing dialogue between the repressed and unfulfilled wishes of childhood, and the miseries of adult life in devitalized rural Ireland.

The "madhouse" of Killarney is not altogether dissimilar from the menstrual hut of Lesu or the "Blacks Only" entrance at the back of the dentist's office in Selma, Alabama. And, just as Black sharecroppers from

Gees Bend taught me more about rural economics than the county exten-sion agent (Scheper and Hunt 1970), I thought that I would learn as much or even more about Irish society from the patients of the district mental hospital than I might from the village curate or schoolmaster. Every culture has its own "normality threshold," and a society reveals itself perhaps most clearly in the phenomena it rejects, excludes, and confines.

Others may question to what degree fieldwork observation and analy-sis are influenced by the personality of the researcher. Ralph Piddington observed in this regard that "a critic once remarked that the Trobriand Islanders are very much like Malinowski and the Tikopia very like Profes-sor Raymond Firth" (1957: 546). Similarly, when Reo Fortune published his *Sorcerers of Dobu* (1963), in which he described a tribal people torn asunder by seemingly paranoid witchcraft fear accusations and counter-accusations, and when Oscar Lewis published his contradictory restudy (1951) of Robert Redfield's original ethnography of Tepotzlan (1930), crit-ics were quick to make reference to the large subjective element in the interpretation of behavior. Redfield defended his original description of an almost idyllic social life in Tepotzlan (1955) by offering that where he was concerned with villagers' enjoyment of life, Lewis was concerned primarily with their woes and sorrows. By implication, Redfield was a romantic optimist and Lewis was an unremitting pessimist in search of the evil and tragedy of human existence. However, the question of subjec-tivity based on the personality dispositions of researchers should not be so simply dismissed. Social scientists, despite their biases and temperaments, should be able to describe with some amount of objectivity the actual nature of social relations in any given community.

Certainly, psychologically oriented anthropologists tend to look with a more studied eye on the unconscious content of interpersonal relations, child rearing, religious institutions, and so forth, and thereby introduce dif-ferent sets of data than does a social structuralist looking at the same com-munity. My own biases—grounded in the experiences of growing up in a New York City slum, community organizing among sugarcane cutters of Northeast Brazil, and civil rights work in rural Alabama—can be summa-rized in the belief that nowhere is the human condition very good for the great number, nor free from pain, either physical or psychological. Yet, I maintain a faith in the possibility for positive change and social healing so long as individuals can be alerted to and moved by the needs of their fellow human beings. To romanticize, ignore, or whitewash the darker side of the life of the peoples we study contributes to the perpetuation of social ills.

Finally, there is the question of the degree to which the remote little parish of Ballybran is representative of the Irish, or even of the rural or western Irish—terms I use interchangeably with the more restrictive terms parishioners and villagers. Are not anthropologists notorious romantics, drawn to the exceptional and exotic in human societies? How peculiar, then, to the rest of Ireland are the Seans and Paddys and Peigs written about here? While not wishing to overextend my expertise on the Irish, my observations, psychological testing, and interviewing went beyond the parish of Ballybran. Through the weekly visits to the mental hospital and psychiatric clinic, I had in-depth exposure to the lives of individuals and their families from villages throughout rural Kerry. In addition, I shared my perceptions on "the rural Irish" with psychiatrists who worked with patients throughout the western counties. In a culture area as small and homogeneous as western Ireland, I feel relatively confident in generalizing, within limits, from the village I know best. Unfortunately, Ballybran is not an exception—there are hundreds of Ballybrans just like it up and down the rugged coast of western Ireland.

In the final analysis, I am less concerned with what my anthropological colleagues and critics will think and say than I am about what my friends in Ballybran will *feel* about what is written here. I trust they realize that although I stress some of the more dismal aspects of their life—the death of the countryside, the seemingly irreversible desertion by young people, the alienation between the sexes, the high rates of anxiety and depression—that they will accept the large measure of my concern for their physical, emotional, and spiritual well-being, and my appreciation of their warmth and double-edged humor. Their children were beautiful—their scrubbed ruddy faces and perpetually muddy Wellington boots, their quixotic smiles and shocks of hair that refused to stay in place, their bread and jam sandwiches—and are engraved permanently in my memory. I only lament that in another decade there will be so many the less of these beautiful children born into Ballybran—a loss not so much for this little community as for the world at large, which has been, for generations, the recipient of some of the best of these lads and lasses as they reached adulthood.

BIBLIOGRAPHY

Aberle, David F.
 1952 Arctic Hysteria and Latah in Mongolia. *Transactions of the New York Academy of Sciences*, ser. 2, 22: 291–297.

Arensberg, Conrad
   1968 (1937)   *The Irish Countryman*. Garden City: National History Press.
Banfield, Edward C.
   1958   *The Moral Basis of a Backward Society*. Glencoe: Free Press.
Benedict, Ruth
   · 1928   Psychological Types in Cultures of the Southwest. *Proceedings of the Twenty-third International Congress of Americanists*, 572–581.
   1934   *Patterns of Culture*. Boston: Houghton Mifflin.
   1935   Culture and the Abnormal. *Journal of Genetic Psychology* 1: 60–64.
Bowlby, John
   1969   *Attachment*. New York: Basic Books.
   1973   *Separation*. New York: Basic Books.
Boyer, Bryce, et al.
   1964   Comparison of the Shamans and Pseudo-Shamans of the Apaches of the Mescalero Indian Reservation: A Rorschach Study. *Journal of Projective Techniques and Personality Development* 28: 173–280.
Brody, Hugh
   1973 *Inishkillane: Change and Decline in the West of Ireland*. Harmondsworth: Penguin.
Cresswell, Robert
   1969   *Une Communauté Rurale de L'Irlande*. Paris: Institute de Ethnographie.
Cusak, M. F.
   1871   *A History of the Kingdom of Kerry*. London: Methuen.
DeVos, George
   1965   Transcultural Diagnosis of Mental Health by Means of Psychological Tests. In De Reuck and Porter (eds.), *Transcultural Psychiatry*. Boston: Little Brown.
   1973   *Socialization for Achievement*. Berkeley and Los Angeles: University of California.
Erikson, Erik
   1963 (1950)   *Childhood and Society*. New York: Norton.
Foley, P.
   1907   *History of the County of Kerry*. Dublin: Sealy, Bryers and Walker.
Fortune, Reo
   1963   *Sorcerers of Dobu*. New York: Dutton.
Foster, George
   1967   *Tzintzuntzan*. Boston: Little, Brown.
Foucault, Michel
   1967   *Madness and Civilization*. New York: Mentor.
Hallowell, A. I.
   1934   Culture and Mental Disorders. *Journal of Abnormal and Social Psychology* 29: 1–9.

Hayward, Richard
1950   *In the Kingdom of Kerry*. Dublin: Dundalgan Press.
Healy, John
1968   *The Death of an Irish Town*. Cork: Mercier.
Kennedy, Robert, Jr.
1973   *The Irish: Emigration, Marriage and Fertility*. Berkeley and Los Angeles: University of California Press.
King, J.
1931   *County Kerry Past and Present*. Dublin: Hodges and Figgis.
Lewis, Oscar
1951   *Life in a Mexican Village: Tepozlan Restudied*. Urbana: University of Illinois Press.
Lynn, Richard
1968   The *Irish Brain Drain*. Dublin: Economic and Social Research Institute.
1971   *National Differences in Anxiety*. Dublin: Economic and Social Research Institute.
Mead, Margaret
1928   *Coming of Age in Samoa*. New York: Morrow.
Messenger, John
1969   *Inis Beag*. New York: Holt, Rinehart and Winston.
Murphy, H. B. M.
1965   The Epidemiological Approach to Transcultural Psychiatric Research. In De Reuck and Porter (eds.), *Transcultural Psychiatry*. Boston: Little, Brown.
1975   Alcoholism and Schizophrenia in the Irish: A Review. *Transcultural Psychiatric Research Review* 9: 116–139.
O'Crohan, Tomás
1951   *The Islandman*. Oxford: Clarendon Press.
O'Hare, Aileen, and Walsh, Dermot
1969   *Activities of Irish Psychiatric Hospitals and Units 1965–1969*. Dublin: Medico-Social Research Board.
Opler, Marvin
1959   Cultural Differences in Mental Disorders: An Italian and Irish Contrast in the Schizophrenias. In M. K. Opler (ed.), *Culture and Mental Health*. New York: Macmillan.
O'Súilleabháin, Seán
1963   *A Handbook of Irish Folklore*. Hartboro: Folklore Association.
1967   *Irish Wake Amusements*. Cork: Mercier.
n.d.   *Nosanna agus Piseoga na nGael*. Dublin: Cultural Relations Committee.
O'Sullivan, Maurice
1957   *Twenty Years A-Growing*. London: Oxford University Press.

O'Sullivan, T. F.
  1931   *Romantic Hidden Kerry.* Tralee: Kerryman.
Piddington, Ralph
  1957   *An Introduction to Social Anthropology.* Edinburgh: Oliver and Boyd.
Powdermaker, Hortense
  1953   The Channeling of Negro Aggression by the Cultural Process. In Kluckhohn, Murray, and Schneider (eds.), *Personality in Nature, Society and Culture.* New York: Alfred Knopf.
Sayers, Peig
  1962   *An Old Woman's Reflections.* London: Oxford University Press.
  1973   *Peig: The Autobiography of Peig Sayers.* Dublin: Talbot Press.
Scheff, Thomas
  1966   *Being Mentally Ill: A Sociological Theory.* Chicago: Aldine.
Scheper-Hughes, Nancy
  1973   Woman as Witch. *Popular Psychology* 1(4): 57–65.
Scheper, Nancy, and Hunt, Linda and Gary
  1970   Hunger in the Welfare State. In Ramparts (ed.), *Divided We Stand.* San Francisco: Canfield Press.
Tracy, Honor
  1956   *The Straight and Narrow Path.* New York: Vintage.
Walsh, Dermot, and Walsh, Brendan
  1968   Some Influences on the Intercounty Variation in Irish Psychiatric Hospitalization Rates. *British Journal of Psychiatry* 114: 15–20.
Whiting, Beatrice (ed.)
  1963   *Six Cultures: Studies of Child Rearing.* New York: John Wiley.
Whiting, John, et al.
  1966   *Field Guide for a Study of Socialization.* New York: Wiley.
World Health Organization
  1961   *Statistics Reports,* 14: 221–245. Geneva: World Health Organization.
  1968   *Statistics Reports,* 21: 529–551. Geneva: World Health Organization.

ACTIVE READING

1. Reread the poem by Wallace Stevens that precedes Scheper-Hughes's Preface. Where does Scheper-Hughes address issues that are raised in

the poem? What relationship do you see between Stevens's text and Scheper-Hughes's?

2. In her closing paragraph, Scheper-Hughes distinguishes between what her professional colleagues "think" and what the villagers of Ballybran "feel" about her findings. By setting these terms in opposition to each other, what does Scheper-Hughes highlight in the work of anthropologists and the actions of the villagers? What does she obscure?

3. Find references in Scheper-Hughes's text to as many kinds of reading (both literal and metaphorical) as you can; be careful to note who does which kinds. How are Scheper-Hughes's ways of reading and of talking about reading different from those of the villagers? Explain how you might account for these differences, as well as for any similarities you notice.

READING IN NEW CONTEXTS

1. Draw up a set of guidelines for anthropologists, based on your understanding of Scheper-Hughes's experience. Test those guidelines on another anthropological text in this book, such as Rosaldo, el-Saadawi, or Fienup-Riordan, or on another text in which an author describes the social customs of a people. What do you find?

2. What kinds of power do Scheper-Hughes and the people of Ballybran have in their relationship with each other? Use some of Brody's theories about the social power of experts to reinterpret Scheper-Hughes's interactions with the villagers. Where does she seem to be aware of her power? Where might Brody's insights be helpful to someone in her position?

3. Scheper-Hughes briefly describes the Thematic Apperception Test in her essay and in note 2 (532–33), but doesn't explain how the test works or what its purpose is. Looking at her list of "motivational concerns," the paragraph that follows it (534), and the note, offer your own theory about the goals of this test. Then use her list and your own observations to discuss the "motivational concerns" of someone in MacLeod, Kozol, or another text that explores an individual's feelings. What are some limitations of this approach to understanding personality?

DRAFT ONE / DRAFT TWO

1. *Draft One:* How do the questions you addressed in Before Reading #3 apply to the community Scheper-Hughes studies? Expand your own response to that question to include the villagers' and Scheper-Hughes's experiences with secrets and truth-telling.

   Draft Two: Look at another *Literacies* text, such as Rich or hooks & West, that explores honesty in relationships. What does this second text help you say about possible connections between truth-telling and community-building in the social groups you have described?

2. *Draft One:* At several points, Scheper-Hughes mentions how her arguments for the book developed, how she thought about potential and actual audiences for the book, and how she might have revised her text after its initial publication. Apply some of her insights to one of your own essays for this class. Quoting where appropriate from her text and from your own, explain how your writing process compares to hers.

   Draft Two: Anzaldúa, Durham, and Rosaldo all pay attention to the writing process in their essays. Bringing one or more of these writers into the conversation you started in Draft One, develop a theory about some significant problems writers face and the resources they may possess to deal with those problems.

BEFORE READING ROBERT SCHOLES

1. What roles do the media play in society? Discuss two or three media forms you know well, such as a particular magazine or TV show, and explain how they carry out their social roles.

2. Many people believe they can see through or resist false or inflated advertising. Interview a few friends about how to do that, and compose a guide to reading advertising critically.

3. What literacy and interpretation skills are important for life in a democratic society? How do people gain these skills?

4. What relations or conflicts do you see between patriotism and being critical of the culture in which you live?

ROBERT SCHOLES

ON READING A
VIDEO TEXT

The moments of surrender proposed to us by video texts come in many forms, but all involve a complex dynamic of power and pleasure. We are, for instance, offered a kind of power through the enhancement of our vision. Close-ups position us where we could never stand. Slow motion allows us an extraordinary penetration into the mechanics of movement, and, combined with music, lends a balletic grace to ordinary forms of locomotion. Filters and other devices cause us to see the world through jaundiced or rose-colored optics, coloring events with emotion more effectively than verbal pathetic fallacy and less obtrusively. These derangements of normal visual processing can be seen as either constraints or extensions of visual power—that is, as power over the viewer or as extensions of the viewer's own optical power, or both. Either way they offer us what is perhaps the greatest single virtue of art: change from the normal, a defense against the ever-present threat of boredom. Video texts, like all except the most utilitarian forms of textuality, are constructed upon a base of boredom, from which they promise us relief.

Visual fascination—and I have mentioned only a few of its obvious forms—is just one of the matrices of power and pleasure that are orga-

From *Protocols of Reading* (1989).

nized by video texts. Others include narrativity and what I should like to call, at least tentatively, cultural reinforcement. By narrativity, of course, I mean the pleasures and powers associated with the reception of stories presented in video texts. By cultural reinforcement, I mean the process through which video texts confirm viewers in their ideological positions and reassure them as to their membership in a collective cultural body. This function, which operates in the ethical-political realm, is an extremely important element of video textuality and, indeed, an extremely important dimension of all the mass media. This is a function performed throughout much of human history by literature and the other arts, but now, as the arts have become more estranged from their own culture and even opposed to it, the mass media have come to perform this role. What the epic poem did for ancient cultures, the romance for feudalism, and the novel for bourgeois society, the media—and especially television—now do for the commodified, bureaucratized world that is our present environment.

It is time, now, to look at these processes as they operate in some specific texts. Let us begin with a well-known Budweiser commercial, which tells—most frequently in a format of twenty-eight seconds, though a longer version also exists—the life story of a black man pursuing a career as a baseball umpire. In this brief period of time, we are given enough information to construct an entire life story—provided we have the cultural knowledge upon which this construction depends. The story we construct is that of a young man from the provinces, who gets his "big break," his chance to make it in the big city, to rise to the top of his profession. We see him working hard in the small-time, small-town atmosphere of the minor leagues, where the pace of events is slower and more relaxed than it is "at the top." He gets his chance for success—the voice-over narrator says, "In the minors you got to make all the calls, and then one day you *get* the call"—after which we see him face his first real test. He must call an important and "close" play correctly and then withstand the pressure of dispute, neither giving ground by changing his mind (which would be fatal) nor reacting too vigorously to the challenge of his call by an offended manager. His passing of this test and being accepted is presented through a later scene in a bar, in which the manager who had staged the protest "toasts" the umpire with a bottle of Budweiser beer, with a chorus in the background singing, "You keep America working. This Bud's for you." From this scene we conclude that the ump has now "made it" and will live happily ever after. From a few scenes, then, aided by the voice-over narration and a music track, we construct an entire life. How do we do this? We draw upon a storehouse of cultural information that extends from fairy tales and other basic narrative structures to knowledge about the game and business of baseball.

In processing a narrative text we actually construct the story, bringing a vast repertory of cultural knowledge to bear upon the text that we are contemplating. Our pleasure in the narrative is to some extent a constructive pleasure, based upon the sense of accomplishment we achieve by successfully completing this task. By "getting" the story, we prove our competence and demonstrate our membership in a cultural community. And what is the story that we "get"? It is the myth of America itself, of the racial melting pot, of upward mobility, of justice done without fear or favor. The corporate structure of baseball, with minor leagues offering a path for the talented to the celebrity and financial rewards of the majors, embodies values that we all possess, we Americans, as one of the deepest parts of our cultural heritage or ideology. It is, of course, on the playing field that talent triumphs most easily over racial or social barriers. Every year in baseball new faces arrive. Young men, having proved themselves in the minors, get their chance to perform at the highest level. Yale graduates and high-school dropouts who speak little or no English are judged equally by how well they hit, run, throw, and react to game situations. If baseball is still the national pastime, it is because in it our cherished myths materialize—or appear to materialize.

The commercial we are considering is especially interesting because it shows us a black man competing not with his body but with his mind, his judgment and his emotions, in a cruelly testing public arena. Americans who attend to sports are aware that black athletes are just beginning to find acceptance at certain "leadership" positions, such as quarterback in professional football, and that there is still an active scandal over the slender representation of blacks at baseball's managerial and corporate levels. The case of the black umpire reminds viewers of these problems, even as it suggests that here, too, talent will finally prevail. The system works, America works. We can take pride in this. The narrative reduces its story to the absolutely bare essentials, making a career turn, or seem to turn, on a single decision. The ump must make a close call, which will be fiercely contested by a manager who is deliberately testing him. This is a story of initiation, in that respect, an ordeal that the ump must meet successfully. The text ensures that we know this is a test, by showing us the manager plotting in his dugout, and it gives us a manager with one of those baseball faces (Irish? German?) that have the history of the game written on them. This is not just partisan versus impartial judge, it is old man against youth, and white against black. We root for the umpire because we want the system to work—not just baseball but the whole thing: America. For the story to work, of course, the ump must make the right call, and we must know it to be right. Here, the close-up and slow motion come into play—just as they would in a real instant replay—to let us see both how close the call is and that the umpire has indeed made the right call. The runner is out. The manager's charge from the dugout is classic baseball protest, and the ump's self-control and slow walk away from the angry manager are gestures in a ritual we all know. That's right, we think, that's the way it's done. We know these moves the way the contemporaries of Aeschylus and Sophocles knew the myths upon which the Greek tragedies were based. Baseball is already a ritual, and a ritual we partake of mostly through the medium of television. The commercial has only to organize these images in a certain way to create a powerful narrative.

At the bar after the game, we are off stage, outside that ritual of baseball, but we are still in the world of myth. The manager salutes the ump with his tilted bottle of beer; the old man acknowledges that youth has passed its test. The sword on the shoulder of knighthood, the laying on of hands, the tilted Bud—all these are ritual gestures in the same narrative structure of initiation. To the extent that we have wanted this to happen we are gratified by this closing scene of the narrative text, and many things, as I have suggested, conspire to make us want this ending. We are dealing with an archetypal narrative that has been adjusted for maximum effect within a particular political and social context, and all this has been deployed with a technical skill in casting, directing, acting, photographing, and editing that is of a high order. It is very hard to resist the pleasure of this text, and we cannot accept the pleasure without, for the bewildering minute at least, also accepting the ideology that is so richly and closely entangled with the story that we construct from the video text. To accept the pleasure of this text is to believe that America works; and this is a comforting belief, itself a pleasure of an even higher order—for as long as we can maintain it. Does the text also sell Budweiser? This is something only market research (if you believe it) can tell. But it surely sells the American way first and then seeks to sell its brand of beer by establishing a metonymic connection between the product and the nation: a national beer for the national pastime.

An audience that can understand this commercial, successfully constructing the ump's story from the scenes represented in the text and the comments of the narrative voice, is an audience that understands narrative structure and has a significant amount of cultural knowledge as well, including both data (how baseball leagues are organized, for instance, and how the game is played) and myth (what constitutes success, for example, and what initiation is). At a time when critics such as William

Bennett and E. D. Hirsch are bewailing our ignorance of culture, it is important to realize that many Americans are not without culture; they simply have a different culture from that of Bennett and Hirsch. What they really lack, for the most part, is any way of analyzing and criticizing the power of a text like the Budweiser commercial—not its power to sell beer, which is easily resisted, especially once you have tasted better beer—but its power to sell America. For the sort of analysis that I am suggesting, it is necessary to recover (as Eliot says) from the surrender to this text, and it is also necessary to have the tools of ideological criticism. Recovery, in fact, may depend upon critical analysis, which is why the analysis of video texts needs to be taught in all our schools.

Before moving on to the consideration of a more complex textual economy, we would do well to pause and consider the necessity of ideological criticism. One dimension of the conservative agenda for this country has been conspicuously anticritical. The proposals of William Bennett and E. D. Hirsch, for instance, different as they are in certain respects, are both recipes for the indoctrination of young people in certain cultural myths. The great books of past ages, in the eyes of Bennett, Hirsch, and Allan Bloom, are to be mythologized, turned into frozen monuments of Greatness in which our "cultural heritage" is embodied. This is precisely what Bloom does to Plato, for instance, turning the dialectical search for truth into a fixed recipe for "greatness of soul." The irony of this is that Plato can only die in this process. Plato's work can better be kept alive in our time by such irreverent critiques as that of Jacques Derrida, who takes Plato seriously as an opponent, which is to say, takes him dialectically. In this age of massive manipulation and disinformation, criticism is the only way we have of taking something seriously. The greatest patriots in our time will be those who explore our ideology critically, with particular attention to the gaps between mythology and practice. Above all, we must start with our most beloved icons, not the ones we profess allegiance to, but those that really have the power to move and shake us.

ACTIVE READING

1. Find several passages where Scholes refers to America or Americans. What relations do you see between those passages and Scholes's ideas about patriotism?

2. Use several of Scholes's examples to discuss how well the process of cultural reinforcement solves the problems of living in a country made up of diverse cultural groups.

3. With the help of a college dictionary, compose a definition of "the dialectical search for truth" (553). Use some passages from this essay to explain how to approach something dialectically.

READING IN NEW CONTEXTS

1. Use the ideas you developed about dialectical criticism in Active Reading #3 to analyze a second *Literacies* text, such as Kingston or hooks & West. What role does dialectic play in the second text?

2. How can someone achieve in writing the effects Scholes claims for video texts in his opening paragraph? Investigate one or two passages in another *Literacies* text, such as Heker or Walker, where you see the author "filtering" or otherwise influencing how you view an event, argument, or idea. How do these moments operate as "constraints" and "extensions" of your power as a reader?

3. What does Scholes mean by "ritual"? Consider one or two events in another *Literacies* text, such as Fishman or Baldwin, as ritual. What do you discover when you view these events as rituals?

DRAFT ONE / DRAFT TWO

1. *Draft One:* Analyze something in American culture that Scholes might call a "beloved icon," using any of the interpretive practices you have learned from Scholes and other *Literacies* writers.

   Draft Two: Use your own and Scholes's ideas about patriotism, surrender, and recovery to explain whether your analysis in Draft One is patriotic. Discuss why or why not.

2. *Draft One:* Scholes says that "we draw upon a storehouse of cultural information" (550) in order to make our interpretations. Locate some important points in his essay where your own "storehouse of cultural information" contributes to your understanding and response. Discuss how the "storehouse" works for you as you read this essay.

Draft Two: Return to a *Literacies* text that challenges your ability to interpret because it draws upon information, assumptions, or narrative forms that lie outside your "cultural storehouse." How were you able to construct your interpretations? What implications does your experience have for the arguments Scholes makes in his essay?

BEFORE READING VICTOR SEIDLER

1. How does the community where you grew up inform young people of their expected gender roles as men or women? What traits are taught in this way? Write about a time when you learned something about your community's expectations of you as a man or woman.

2. Think of people you know who are emotional, rational, analytical, unique, assertive, self-sufficient. In your experience, do men and women possess these traits differently according to their gender? Write about a few examples to support your answer.

3. What relations do you see between language use and gender? Do men and women use language differently?

VICTOR SEIDLER

LANGUAGE AND MASCULINITY

Because rationality is taken to be a universal quality, it becomes difficult to realize how rationality becomes an important basis for male superiority in social life. One of the women's movement's more powerful insights has been the identification of the ways that power relationships can be consolidated and sustained through men's assumption of a stance of over-view of a situation, creating a relationship of communication in which what women have to say is branded with the status of the particular, whilst men offer what they see as an encompassing and objectively-grounded account. To see this is to see that men and women do not have the same relationship to language. In the light of it, it is important to explore men's relationships to language, sensitive to the possibility that men can learn to use language to distance and hold in check their experience. This is an investigation which structuralism leaves little space for, convinced as it is that experience is itself constituted through language. The effect of displacing experience in this way is to close off questions about people's different relationships to language and expression; experience is assimi-lated into language so that qualitative differences in experience cannot

From *Rediscovering Masculinity* (1989).

be recognized, let alone grasped in their full significance. Language remains at some level autonomous of experience.

It is a strength of Wittgenstein's later work to challenge a Cartesian rationalism that has underpinned the identification of masculinity with reason that has been so crucial in a post-Enlightenment culture. Wittgenstein is undercutting the claim to superiority we grow up to assume as men over our feelings and emotions. I want to show that rationalist conceptions of language fail to illuminate, how, as men, we can learn to use language instrumentally to conceal ourselves and in so doing form and shape the kind of personal and sexual relationships we can have with others.

LANGUAGE AND MALE IDENTITY

Within a liberal moral culture, the very notion of personal identity has been made problematic. As individuals we take ourselves to be the embodiment of universal qualities though we acknowledge that some people have more of these qualities than others. Some people are more intelligent than others and some can run faster. This is deeply rooted in the rationalist tradition. We witness it in that aspect of Kant's ethical theory that would argue that we are each deserving of respect since we are equally moral beings, or at least have an equal capacity for morality. But Kant was also careful to identify this capacity with our individual powers to reason. This was a possession which was historically since the Enlightenment more closely identified with masculinity. Our very sense of masculinity was consolidated as an experience of superiority over our wants, desires, emotions and feelings. To prove our masculinity, we had to keep our 'inclinations' in check. We had to learn to dominate our inner natures. But this also meant that our masculinity could be upset or challenged. It was not anything we could take for granted, but had to be constantly proved. We still live in the shadow of this conception. We can experience it for ourselves as men in our constant tendency to push ourselves to the edge of exhaustion as if this is the way we can prove ourselves individually and sustain our self-control.

But reason is essentially impersonal. The more our sense of self is identified with reason, the more we are in a process as men of impersonalizing ourselves. At the same time, we have to recognize that historically this was important for the emancipation of classes and ethnic groups who would otherwise have been discriminated against, excluded and humiliated. But at another level this is emancipation at a price, since it is also a pact with the devil as it makes for instance, your blackness, Jewishness or gayness, essentially *incidental* aspects of yourself. We learn to give up these aspects of our history and culture to be treated as equals by others.[1] It is as if we have to pay the price of the painful and difficult work of deconstructing our identities to be treated fairly and equally with others. This means we have to learn to redefine our interests so that we can articulate them in universal terms. In capitalist society this means we want to be richer and more successful than the next person. Our class and ethnic identity become private matters but no part of the 'official identity' we can assume in the larger society.

In this way we become *estranged* from important aspects of our history and culture. We lose an important source of our own power as we are left divided. It should be hardly surprising if those suffering from class, ethnic or gender oppression find it hard to define themselves clearly in the larger society. I have learnt how subtle but powerful is the way that, in discounting my Jewishness, I have discounted an important source of my power and identity.[2] But people often feel uneasy and embarrassed if you bring these 'emotional considerations' into serious intellectual discussion. Rather we are encouraged within a liberal moral culture to think of our class and ethnicity as 'emotional attachments' we will eventually outgrow. It is clear that emotionality has culturally to do with infancy.

This is an integral part of assuming our masculinity in the larger society. I remember feeling that being a 'real man' meant being taller than I was, stronger than I was. Very far from being a residual category, masculinity was something we had to give our lives aspiring towards, never sure that we would ever really make it. It is no accident that the idea of a 'Jewish man' was experienced by me as a kind of contradiction in terms. Jewishness was related to the emotional, and so with the feminine.[3]

1. The relationship of rationalism to our inherited conceptions of personal identity is illuminated in the early part of Sartre's *Anti-Semite and Jew.* This is also usefully explored in Della Volpe's *Rousseau and Marx.*

2. This awareness of a loss of personal power associated with a denial of Jewish identity is explored by Freud. See the discussion of Freud's relationship to Judaism in David Bakan's *Freud and the Jewish Mystical Tradition.* This is also a theme in Marthe Roberts' *From Oedipus to Moses.*

3. It has taken time for some of these connections to surface, only for me to recognize how they were part of the anti-Semitic writing of Otto Weininger's influential *Sex and Character.* This work seemed to have a lasting influence on Wittgenstein, and part of his own reflections on Jewishness brought together in *Culture and Value* are a response to it. It is more difficult to know what this meant for him later in his life.

Growing up, we had to work hard to reassert a notion of Jewish maleness, often forcing ourselves to react against weakness and vulnerability more harshly. This was a potent source of shame.

I am concerned to understand how our inherited conceptions of masculinity connect to processes through which we learn to *displace* important aspects of ourselves. This seems to weaken and impoverish our individuality, but it also makes it harder for Jewish men to define themselves in their own terms, as they are constantly anxious to compete or prove themselves to others. In some way this can make Jewish men adaptable and understanding in their relationships, though at another level leaving them rigid and unforgiving. I know how subtly I work to get my own way, doing well at concealing my tracks. This can mean taking out particular tensions and frustrations on those closest to us, assuming they understand a predicament we have often never explained to them, since we rarely have the language to explain it ourselves. It is of the essence of the situation that we can never make ourselves acceptable to others, since we are constantly on edge that they might discover a different side of ourselves. This is a no-win situation. What is more, we lose our strength in the process.

We betray our cultural integrity as Jewish men, and in a real sense we emasculate ourselves as we are constantly doing our best to prove ourselves in the eyes of others. They inevitably withhold their final approval, since with this they lose their power over us. It is an exhausting and painful process, though one rendered largely invisible through the success and achievement we may have individually achieved. I have had to fight it through myself. I am left haunted by a sense of weakness, since this is no way to discover my own historical and ethnic grounding. But it is a powerful way of sustaining those who have institutional power in the larger society, since the cost of a particularistic identification seems to be minimal, especially if we no longer have a language in which to illuminate the bargain we have struck. Since they set the terms, they are made invulnerable to criticism. This is an important aspect of the centrality notions of equality of opportunity have assumed in legitimating relations of power and subordination in late capitalist society.

Even though this is a predicament that could illuminate the situation of working-class people, women and ethnic minorities, it also reveals something central about contemporary masculinity: the identification of masculinity with rationality undermines the identity of men. The impersonal character of reason makes it hard for us to appropriate a history and culture of masculinity, especially one in opposition to the dominant culture.[4] What is more, it weakens any sense that this could be important to us individually as men. We learn to ground ourselves in our ideas, in our heads. This is the way we protect ourselves. We do our best to capture the claim to be rational and reasonable, which seems to move our own behaviour and experience beyond criticism. It is always others—usually women—who are emotional, if not hysterical. It is always us who have to wait patiently for them to calm down, before we can add the weight of our arguments to the situation. We learn not to lose our self-control, since this is often the basis for our feeling of superiority in the situation. We hold tight.

As men, we are brought up to identify with our 'rationality' as the very core of our masculinity. We learn to appropriate rationality as if it were an exclusively male quality and we deny it to others, especially women. We also deny it to animals and children. The very possession of reason amounts to a claim to superiority, though this can be difficult to realize, since it is also taken to be a universal quality shared by all human beings. This is one of the sources of ambiguity in the liberal tradition of equality. So it becomes difficult to realize how rationality becomes an important basis for male superiority in social life.

Since we identify 'rationality' with knowledge, we systematically deny knowledge to women and children, who are more closely identified with emotions and feelings. Emotions and feelings are systematically denied as genuine sources of knowledge, though they may illuminate how individuals have responded to situations; but often they are indications of weakness and a lack of self-control. They are antithetical to our very sense of masculinity. Even feelings like anger become indications of a lack of control, which men learn to be wary of. This has powerfully influenced the shape and tone of our language and the relationship men grow up to have with language. Even though we are powerfully influenced by traditions, such as romanticism, which show language to be expressive, helping to articulate and form the nature of the self, these visions have been continually marginalized within a scientific culture which, at least since the seventeenth century, has powerfully identified masculinity with dominant forms of scientific knowledge.

• • •

4. Sociological work that offers some kind of passing illumination into the connections between self-respect, male identity and class is provided by Richard Sennett and Jonathan Cobb in *The Hidden Injuries of Class*. It remains a significant model for qualitative research.

Even though analytical philosophy has done important work in questioning the appropriateness of Cartesian dualism for our understanding of our experience, we continue to live our lives in its hidden grip.[5] We still believe in the autonomy and independence of reason. We deny our bodies as genuine sources of knowledge, and we tend to see them as machines which do the work of carrying our minds around. We marginalize what we could otherwise learn from the knowledge of our hearts, as we continue to think in the dualistic terms of mind and body. This is one reason that Reich has been so despised and misunderstood. He threatens not simply the conceptual terms in which we constitute our identities, but the very organization of our everyday experience as he calls us into a different relationship with ourselves. We find it almost impossible to think clearly of ways we are more open or closed to our experience, even though we can be dimly aware that nothing in our experience seems to touch us.

Reich understood this in terms of the over-bounded character of people who have developed a rigid armouring, but he did not connect this enough to the learning of our masculinity or to the historical identification of reason with masculinity. This helps to estrange us from a deeper understanding of self, as we somehow take up a position beyond our own experience. We lose any sense of *grounding* ourselves in our own embodied experience as we identify our sense of masculinity with being objective and impartial. This involves our discounting our own experience and so denying one of the deepest sources of our identity and knowledge.

Descartes saw the human body as a machine organized according to mechanical laws.[6] The body was to be made a part of the natural world to be investigated using the methods of the new sciences. The person was to be identified with the mind, which was seen as essentially impersonal to the extent that people acted rationally. In its own way this was to give secular expression to a Christian tradition which had often denigrated the body as a source of spiritual knowledge. Our bodies held us to the animal world that we should learn to control and dominate. Our sense of our-

5. The influence of Cartesianism was a significant theme in Richard Rorty's stimulating *Philosophy and the Mirror of Nature*.
6. A useful collection of articles focusing on some of the implications of this conception of the body is provided by Ted Polhemus in *Social Aspects of the Human Body*. See also the useful discussion by Oliver Sachs in *A Leg to Stand On*. For a feminist reading of these issues, see Kim Chernin, *Womansize*.

selves as 'civilized' depended upon us claiming a superiority to the natural world of animal wants and desires. It was as if we were continually trying to free ourselves from the demands of the body, which would inherently undermine our freedom and autonomy as it determined our behaviour externally. Women were taken to be 'unfree', to the extent that they allowed themselves to be moved by their emotions and feelings. This was the way Rousseau and Kant argued that women could only be free if they agreed to subordinate themselves to men; but men could only guarantee their own freedom if they insisted upon identifying themselves with their rational powers. We had to learn to disdain our emotions, feelings, dependence and desires, lest they were to fundamentally compromise our masculinity.

Not only were men to learn to identify themselves with rationality, but this was to be fundamentally separated from any sense of embodied experience. Even our bodies are no part of our identities as men. We had to investigate them as matter, as part of the empirical world. In a very real sense, as men, we are fundamentally estranged from this world which we can only observe from a distance. It is no accident that issues of perception became central to modern philosophy. We become historically obsessed with the truthfulness of our perceptions of a world that is estranged and distant.[7] We are systematically estranged from a world we can only 'observe'. We conceive of the mind, in Richard Rorty's phrase, as the mirror of the world.

This conception of mind has been crucially significant, not only for the form of modern philosophy, but also for the gender experience of masculinity which is so closely identified with this form of rationality. This reveals a much deeper connection between masculinity and the forms of philosophical thought in which they have implicitly found expression. Within the rationalist tradition, men learn automatically to relate to themselves and their social relations in an instrumental way. Of course this is not specific to men, since women come under this pervasive influence within a masculinist culture. This means they are also constantly encouraged to turn their experience into a test in which they have to prove themselves, even if this is not so closely identified with a sense of women's identity.

•   •   •

7. The idea of perception as a source of knowledge within a Western philosophical tradition is usefully explored by M. Merleau-Ponty in *The Phenomenology of Perception*.

The identification of masculinity with reason has left a strong impulse for men to become observers of their own experience. We struggle for a certain form of impartiality and objectivity in assessing a situation fairly. Consequently the difficulties we often have as men to say what we personally feel and experience in a situation has deep cultural and historical roots. As men we often become more adept at assessing the different interests involved in a situation than saying what we want individually and negotiating with others on this basis. Rather the forms of moral rationalism we inherit tend to make us feel uneasy about asserting our own individual wants and desires. Often we think of this as a form of 'selfishness'.

This also has deep roots in our upbringing in a culture in which we learn automatically to discount our individual emotions and feelings as having no part in our 'true rational self'. This is a process which psychoanalytic theory can sometimes illuminate. As boys we often learn to identify emotions and feelings with our mothers, and with the feminine. This is something we are forced to separate from to prove ourselves as men. We also have to separate from what we identify as the feminine within ourselves. Masculinity is such an uneasy inheritance. We have to be prepared to defend it at any moment, even if this means striking down parts of ourselves.

We would need to investigate these processes in a way that is specific to class and historical moment. It has only been with the development of a more egalitarian ethos between the sexes that a man's word has been questioned as law within the home. Since domestic life has often been automatically organized around men's needs, little has had to be said: men had to talk very little. D. H. Lawrence illuminates this in *Sons and Lovers*, when he shares his growing up in a mining community. John Cleese has talked about the lower middle class of Weston Super Mare, 'where emotions were kept as hidden as possible. Making scenes wasn't allowed. Anger wasn't shown. It was wrong for anyone to assert themselves. You had to work out what everyone else wanted. All change was dangerous. "You haven't changed a bit" was a tremendous compliment.' (The *Guardian*, Monday 2 January, 1984).

Class differences are very significant, as are the forms of control men can exert in relationships. But within a supposedly more egalitarian period, issues of control are still central if we are not to experience our masculinity as threatened. Often we use our reason to define 'what would be best in the situation', and so get others to agree. In this way we often assume to take the interests of others into account without really giving others a chance to identify and *define their own* interests. It is in the name of reason that we often, as middle-class men, silence others at the same time as giving them no chance of getting back at us. Often this remains a potent source of power, as we can in all honesty present ourselves as working out the most 'rational' way of doing things. Our rationality is often a hidden weapon, since it allows us to assimilate and control the interests of others. It also puts us beyond reproach.

It is within the context of an instrumental notion of masculinity that we learn our language. Often this is a practical language of action, where we are setting out to prove ourselves to others. Since it is what we think that makes us what we are as men, we find ourselves without any natural connection to our emotions and feelings. These are not experienced as integral aspects of our individuality. Our individuality is defined in relation to our thoughts, and often our emotions and feelings have to be turned into thoughts so that we can deal with them in familiar ways. At best we can learn to talk about emotions and feelings.

In the middle class, men have often grown up to be reticent, even scared, of sharing emotions and feelings, lest they threaten the control which sustains our very sense of masculinity. We can feel apologetic and embarrassed if we are emotional with others. We fear that others will see us as weak and unmasculine. We often prefer to withdraw into a sullen silence, unaware of how controlling this silence can be. Our emotions automatically seem to signal a lack of control. We find it almost impossible to identify our anger, resentment or sadness as a rational response to a situation. Only *in extremis* can we allow ourselves these feelings. Rationality has to do with coolness and control. It seems to have no place in our consideration of our emotional and somatic lives.

LANGUAGE AND EXPERIENCE

Men have often assumed a control of language. Since we automatically assume that language has to do with reason, logic and rationality, we easily treat it as our own. Certainly men have often had power in the larger society to define the reality of others, but we have to be careful not to assume universally that language itself is 'man made', in the sense Dale Spender developed in *Man Made Language*.[8] Women have not simply had to conform to a reality men have created, as long as they have remained within the private and domestic sphere. It has been in the pub-

8. Dale Spender's work on language has been critically discussed by Debbie Cameron in *Feminism and Linguistic Theory* and by Lynne Segal in *Is the Future Female?*

lic realm that men have most clearly created the terms on which women could gain access. But we should not forget, as Gramsci was struggling to show in his *Prison Notebooks*, that even here, language is essentially contested.

Gramsci was developing a tradition in which language is embodied in ongoing social relationships in which people are constantly clarifying and redefining a sense of their individual needs, wants and desires. Language does not constitute individuality in the way structuralism has assumed. Gramsci also realized the tension between what we say and what we do, especially where relationships of power and subordination are involved. Oppressed people are constantly trying to make language their own, as they attempt to discover and redefine their experience. This is an ongoing historical process, in which women are not to be conceived as completely passive. Our common sense remains inherently contradictory as it brings together different elements in men's and women's experience.[9]

•   •   •

As long as we continue to see language as a screen or net to be placed against the social world, we remain trapped by the picture Wittgenstein articulated in the *Tractatus*. Unfortunately this is the conception of language informing Spender's work, which otherwise illuminates central issues of the relationship of language to relations of power and subordination. The view Wittgenstein was developing in his later writings is less aware of relations of power, but has a keen awareness of how we learn to talk in the context of learning social activities.

Language is no longer conceived as a single system, though it remains important to acknowledge our capacities to use language. Wittgenstein remarks that 'Children do not learn that there are books, that there are armchairs, etc., etc., but they learn to fetch books, sit in armchairs, etc.' (*On Certainty*, p. 476). We learn language as an integral aspect of learning to do these things. In some crucial sense our language grows out of and extends these activities.

•   •   •

9. An understanding of Gramsci's insights into the relationships between language and power has been difficult to reach since his writings, initially translated in the late 1960s and 1970s, were often interpreted within a tradition of structuralist Marxism, that was then dominant. His work can be more usefully appropriated as a challenge to this tradition of work. See for instance 'The study of philosophy' in Part 3 of *The Prison Notebooks*.

It is only in the context of our deeds that we can begin to grasp the meaning of our utterances. As soon as we separate language as a system of meanings, we have losts its vital interconnection with the ongoing practices of everyday life. It is as a critique of theories of language as an independent and autonomous system through which we make sense of or organize our social world, that we can possibly think of Wittgenstein as developing a form of 'linguistic materialism'.

Wittgenstein is tacitly subverting the basis upon which we identify masculinity with reason. He is unwittingly and unknowingly undercutting the claim to superiority we grow up to assume as men over our feelings and emotions. Rather he can help us understand how we have hurt ourselves through misunderstanding and misconstruing the place of reason in our lives. We have set up a duality where none should exist. We have failed to realize how our thoughts are nurtured from the same ground of actions and deeds as are our emotions and feelings. To the extent that Kant has encouraged us to identify our morality exclusively with our reason, he has limited and injured our sense of ourselves as moral beings and the nature of our relationships with others.

Rationalism has continually undercut our sense of connection with others, forcing us morally to justify whatever care and help one individual might give another. This is related to our inherited notion of masculinity as independence and self-sufficiency. As soon as we act from feelings, we are accused of being 'soft', as if our masculinity is affirmed in our insistence on finding reasons for each of our actions. There is no way to acknowledge our need to be dependent and vulnerable in our relations with others if we are to give these relations depth and substance. As men, we fear this vulnerability which threatens our very sense of masculinity.

Malcolm realizes how Wittgenstein places our relations with others on a different basis, though he resists drawing the implications for our sense of morality and politics. I think it important to quote this part of his article in full since it helpfully shows how rationalist notions are questioned:

> This conception of certain linguistic expressions as replacements for unlearned reactions, was seen by Wittgenstein to extend to some of the sentences that we use to refer to other persons. Not only 'I'm in pain' but also 'He's in pain', can take the place of instinctive behaviour. In *Zettel* Wittgenstein observes that 'it is a primitive reaction to tend, to treat, the part that hurts when someone else is in pain, and not merely when oneself is' (Z 540). . . . Wittgenstein asks himself what he means by saying that these reactions are 'primitive'; and he answers:

'Surely that this way of behaving is *prelinguistic*: that a language-game is based *on it*, that it is the prototype of a way of thinking and not the result of thinking.' (Z 541).

Wittgenstein is disagreeing with a 'rationalistic' explanation of this behaviour—for example, the explanation that we have a sympathetic reaction to an injured person 'because by analogy with our own case we believe that he too is experiencing pain' (Z 542). The actions of comforting or trying to help, that go with the words 'He's in pain', are no more a product of reasoning from analogy than is the similar behaviour in deer or birds. Wittgenstein goes on to say that

'Being sure that someone is in pain, doubting whether he is, and so on, are so many natural, instinctive, kinds of relationship towards other human beings, and our language is merely an auxiliary to, and further extension of, this behaviour. Our language-game is an extension of primitive behaviour. (For our *language-game* is behaviour.)' (Instinct) (Z 545).

So through our words we find another way of comforting those in grief. We could just as well put our arm on their shoulder. This questions any attempt to privilege our language. But it also challenges crude versions of historical materialism which would seek to relate language as an aspect of ideology to an underlying level of material relationships. When Wittgenstein says that language can replace pre-linguistic behaviour, it is to be understood that it serves as an extension, refinement or elaboration of that behaviour. This is the ground we have to place it back into if we are to recover a sense of its meaning and significance in our lives.

Philosophers have mistakenly interpreted the idea that the meaning of an expression is in its use as meaning words and sentences have to be placed in a larger linguistic context of use. This mistake is common in the appropriation of Wittgenstein's writings in conversational analysis in sociology. This places his writings firmly back in the very 'rationalistic' tradition he was struggling to break with.[10] But it is only when we learn how much of our experience has been shaped within this tradition that we can begin to grasp the difficulties of breaking with it. This also involves breaking with an inherited conception of masculinity.

We limit our understanding of the nature of moral relations in assuming we always need to give reasons to explain why one person

10. See, for instance, David Silverman and Brian Torrode's *The Material Word*, which is otherwise a useful, if difficult, introduction to this kind of work.

should care for another, especially if the person is not a close relation or friend. This assumes egoism is to be identified with self-interest and universally treated as the natural character of our relations with others rather than as encouraged by the social relations of a particular society. Morality begins when we give reasons to extend a sense of fair and equal treatment beyond those for whom we have feelings. It is within an assumed framework of liberal individualism that the moral discussion between egoism and altruism takes place. But Wittgenstein questions the basis upon which this distinction is often drawn. In doing this, not only does he question the priority we give to reason in our moral relations, but he opens up a way for the recognition of our emotions and feelings in the 'natural, instinctive, kinds of relationships towards other human beings'. It is not that our language constitutes our individuality and defines these moral relations, but, as Wittgenstein says, 'our language is merely an auxiliary to, and further extension of, this behaviour'.

This marks a profound challenge to the assumptions of liberal individualism. It is not simply that some people will feel this way towards others and others will not. Rather, what is presented as the 'normal' situation of egoistic self-interest becomes something we need to explain, even if we acknowledge the enormous differences that exist between individuals. Possibly it is at this point that we require a clearer distinction between ends individuals choose for themselves, so indicating the different ways individuals find their happiness, and some sense of shared human needs.

Liberal theory often resists any such distinction, wanting to treat needs as if they are simply an extension of the ends people individually choose for themselves. This reticence may grow out of a healthy suspicion that, before we know it, some people will be claiming to decide the human needs of others. But this only makes it crucially important for people to identify and recognize their needs for themselves. Nor can we ever be sure of the road individuals are going to take. This is an arrogance that has sometimes been shared, in their different ways, by both revolutionaries and psychotherapists.

But what Wittgenstein helps us reinstate is a sense of the core nature of our needs for others. We misconstrue the place of morality in our lives and we misunderstand ourselves if we think we can exist as totally independent and self-sufficient people. It is this very masculine ideal which can damage and hurt men's lives. This is not a matter of placing before ourselves ideals which are unworthy, but of recognizing the harm we do ourselves through attempting to form ourselves in their image. This is not something we can begin to grasp unless we already question the identification of masculinity with reason.

This helps us realize that this is not simply a matter of replacing one ideal of masculinity by another. If we already assume that our emotional, somatic and spiritual lives can have no bearing upon the nature of our moral lives, all this talk of 'hurt' and 'damage' carries little weight. It is simply that we learn tacitly to accept to live up to the ideal of self-sufficiency that we have automatically grown up to accept. As men we grow up to feel good if we do not need anything from others. As I have argued, it is a sign of our strength that we can be supportive for others without needing any support for ourselves. We prove our masculinity through showing we do not need anything from others.

Wittgenstein suggests that if we deny our needs to respond directly towards others we are denying something important in ourselves. This is no longer a contingent issue. This is a direct challenge to Kant's idea that we should gradually weaken our instinctive responses towards others, since not only are they unreliable, but they take away from the moral worth of an action performed purely out of a sense of duty. It is Kant who helps sustain traditional notions of masculinity as he warns us of the help others might offer us since this will lessen the moral worth of our own individual efforts. Even though Kant was centrally concerned to illuminate the nature of human beings as moral beings, his implicit identification of reason, morality and masculinity, especially in his earlier more systematic writings, minimized the importance people can have for each other.[11] Our moral lives are essentially individualistic; we are constantly proving our moral worth as individuals. At some level others are distractions taking us away from our moral tasks, or else occasions to show our moral goodness. Our relationships with others are essentially secondary to our sense of moral identity, even our sexual and personal relationships.

Within a 'rationalist' culture, men learn to use language as a way of asserting themselves individually. We learn to hide our vulnerability since

11. With the dominance of Kant within an Enlightenment vision, it has been harder to appreciate the significance of the counter-Enlightenment which, within a liberal moral culture, is too easily discounted as 'irrational' or 'reactionary'. Wittgenstein's questioning of the Cartesian tradition might come to be seen as placing him closer to the writings of Herder in his challenge to Kant. See for instance the illuminating essay by Isaiah Berlin, 'Herder and the Enlightenment' in *Vico and Herder*. Too narrow a grasp of the philosophy of language has led to minimizing some of the broader implications of his work. This is suggested as much by David Pears in the concluding chapter to his *Wittgenstein* by M. O. L. Drury in *The Danger of Words*.

we know it will be interpreted as weakness. Language itself comes to exist as an independent and autonomous system that has been separated from any ongoing sense of our somatic and emotional selves. In this way language is less likely to betray our masculinity as it shows us to be vulnerable and feeling human beings. In bringing us into a different relationship to our language Wittgenstein is also bringing us back to ourselves. But he is also implicitly questioning the way our male identities are constructed out of our achievements, as if the accumulation of wealth and property necessarily reflects back on the quality of self.

As we learn to discount our needs for others, we also learn to grow up as men to discount our history and culture of masculinity. We are more than our reasons and thoughts. We injure ourselves as men, as our culture leaves us with a distorted sense of the importance of reason in our lives. What is more, it even weakens the quality of our thought, as reason constantly becomes formal and abstract as it is systematically separated from emotions and feelings. But we also impoverish ourselves as we learn to deny our history and culture to become equal citizens in civil society. As Mill realized, we become so anxious to prove we are 'normal' like everyone else, that we develop a real fear of anything that would make us different from others. Mill realized in *On Liberty* that even though people heralded individualism within the moral culture of liberalism, the social relations worked to impoverish people's sense of their own individuality.[12]

When we learn to use language as boys, we very quickly learn how to conceal ourselves through language. We learn to 'master' language so that we can control the world around us. We use language as an instrument that will help show us as independent, strong, self-sufficient and masculine. But as we learn to deny and estrange our individual and collective needs and wants so that we can live up to these ideals of ourselves we form and shape the kind of personal and sexual relationships we can have with others. Even though we learn to blame others for our unhappiness and misery in relationships we also know at some unspoken level how our masculinity has been limited and injured as we touch the hurt and pain of realizing how little we seem to feel about anything, even our friends and close relationships. Often we feel trapped and lost since the culture continually tells us we have the world to inherit. We do not know that the price is often knowledge of and relationship to ourselves.

12. The relationship of freedom to individuality is discussed by Alan Ryan in *J. S. Mill* and Isaiah Berlin in 'John Stuart Mill and the ends of life' in *Four Essays on Liberty*.

BIBLIOGRAPHY

Bakan, David (1958), *Sigmund Freud and The Jewish Mystical Tradition*, New York: Schocken.
Berlin, Isaiah (1968), *Four Essays on Liberty*, Oxford: Oxford University Press.
———— (1976), *Vico and Herder*, New York: Random House.
Cameron, Deborah (1986), *Feminism and Linguistic Theory*, London: Macmillan.
Chernin, Kim (1983), *Womansize: The Tyranny in Slenderness*, London: The Woman's Press.
Cobb, J. S., and Sennett, R., *Hidden Injuries of Class*, Cambridge: Cambridge University Press.
Della Volpe, Galvano (1978), *Rousseau and Marx*, London: Lawrence & Wishart.
Drury, M. O'L. (1973), *The Danger of Words*, London: Routledge & Kegan Paul.
Gramsci, A. (1971), *Selections from the Prison Notebooks*, ed. and trans. by O. Hoare and G. Nowell-Smith, London: Lawrence & Wishart.
Merleau-Ponty, M. (1962), *Phenomenology of Perception*, London: Routledge & Kegan Paul.
Polhemus, Ted (1978), *Sexual Aspects of the Human Body*, London: Penguin Books.
Reich, Wilhelm (1942), *The Function of the Orgasm*, New York: Farrar, Strauss & Giroux.
———— (1970), *The Mass Psychology of Fascism*, New York: Farrar, Strauss & Giroux.
———— (1972), *Reich Speaks of Freud*, London: Souvenir Press.
Roberts, Marthe (1976), *From Oedipus to Moses: Freud's Jewish Identity*, London: Litman Library, Routledge & Kegan Paul.
Rorty, Richard (1979), *Philosophy and the Mirror of Nature*, Oxford: Blackwells.
Ryan, Alan (1984), *J. S. Mill*, London: Routledge & Kegan Paul.
Sachs, Oliver (1984), *A Leg To Stand on*, London: Gerald Duckworth.
Sartre, J.-P. (1948) *Anti-Semite and Jew*, London: Secker & Warburg.
———— (1974), *Between Existentialism and Marxism*, trans. John Mathews, London: New Left Books.
Segal, Lynne (1986), *Is The Future Female?*, London: Virago Books.
Silverman, D. and Torrode, B. (1980), *The Material Word*, London: Routledge & Kegan Paul.
Skynner, Robin and Cleese, John (1983), *Families and How to Survive Them*, London: Methuen.

Weininger, Otto (1906), *Sex and Character*, London: Heinemann.

Wittgenstein, Ludwig (1963), *Philosophical Investigations*, Oxford: Basil Blackwell.

———— (1980), *Culture and Value*, trans. Peter Winch, Oxford: Blackwell.

ACTIVE READING

1. Find passages where Seidler describes identity as a choice, as something a person reshapes or constructs. What terms does Seidler use in these places? What might the idea of a reshapable identity offer some of the groups he writes about?

2. In his essay, Ewen quotes an advertisement which describes "a gesture which speaks volumes" (184). What gestures or other silent acts does Seidler associate with masculinity? What do these gestures speak?

3. Seidler talks about men having the power to "assimilate and control the interests of others" (565). Show how he grapples with this problem in passages where he talks about his own experience or uses "we" to speak of common situations that men face.

READING IN NEW CONTEXTS

1. Find several quotations that show the main differences Seidler sees between men's and women's ways of interpreting experiences, along with the consequences of those differences. Test those ideas against your own observations of men and women or against the descriptions of gendered experience found in another *Literacies* text, such as Gilmore or Rich.

2. Seidler writes that "Oppressed people are constantly trying to make language their own, as they attempt to discover and redefine their experience" (566). Use quotations from another *Literacies* text, such as Kingston or hooks & West, to show how a group or individual discovers and redefines experience. How do these people make language their own?

3. How do Seidler's ideas about the limits of formal or systematic reasoning apply to professional problems other *Literacies* writers, such as Rosaldo and Brody, discuss in their essays?

DRAFT ONE / DRAFT TWO

1. *Draft One:* Seidler tells men that

> "we lose any sense of *grounding* ourselves in our own embodied experience as we identify our sense of masculinity with being objective and impartial. This involves our discounting our own experience and so denying one of the deepest sources of our identity and knowledge." (562)

Using one or two of your own experiences, describe how you (whether you are male or female) have handled the tension between cultural demands for "objectivity" and the desire to make personal experience a part of your thinking process.

Draft Two: Working with your draft, Seidler's essay, and another *Literacies* text, test Seidler's idea that we can use personal experience as an analytic tool to make new forms of social and intellectual understanding.

2. *Draft One:* Draw on your own observations of men as well as your answers to any of the Before Reading questions and Reading in New Contexts #1, and discuss the idea that traditional gender roles damage men's lives. Where do you stand on this matter, and why?

Draft Two: Test the understanding you developed in Draft One against the accounts of men's experience in one or more other *Literacies* readings, such as the short story by MacLeod or the essay by Baldwin.

BEFORE READING MARY LYNDON SHANLEY

1. Look up "liberal" in a college dictionary. Which definitions are familiar to you? Which ones are different from everyday understandings of the word? Discuss any conflicts you see between these familiar and unfamiliar definitions.

2. Describe some current controversies surrounding human reproduction. Based on what you have heard, which groups of people are most likely to be concerned about these questions? What are some of the important issues for each of the groups you know about?

3. What makes someone a "mother" or a "father"? Discuss the social and biological factors that make people into parents.

MARY LYNDON SHANLEY

"SURROGATE MOTHERING" AND WOMEN'S FREEDOM: A CRITIQUE OF CONTRACTS FOR HUMAN REPRODUCTION

Feminist theorists and students of public policy are deeply divided over the question whether the so-called surrogate motherhood contract by which a woman agrees to undergo artificial insemination, bear a child, and relinquish the child at birth to someone else (usually the biological father and his wife) is liberating or oppressive to women. Some supporters of contract pregnancy regard a woman as having a right to enter a contractual arrangement to bear a child and receive money for her service; they view the prohibition or nonenforcement of pregnancy contracts as illegitimate infringements on a woman's autonomy and self-determination.[1] Others focus on the desire for a child that motivates those who hire a woman to bear a child; they argue that to prohibit or fail to enforce pregnancy contracts violates the commissioning party's "right to procreate."[2] Those who oppose pregnancy contracts, by contrast, see such contracts as oppressive to the childbearing woman, particularly if she enters the contract out of dire economic need or is forced to fulfill the contract against her will.[3]

From *Signs: Journal of Women in Culture and Society* (1993).

1. See, e.g., Katz 1986; Andrews 1989; Shalev 1989; Shultz 1990.
2. Hill 1990, 157–59; Robertson 1983, 1986; Shalev 1989.
3. See, e.g., Bartlett 1988; Field 1988, 1990; Pateman 1988, 209–18; Rothman 1989, 229–45; and Okin 1990.

These differing viewpoints are reflected even in a dispute as to what to call such a pregnancy; proponents tend to accept the term surrogate mother-hood, while those with reservations resist calling a woman who bears a child a "surrogate" mother (although some regard her as functioning as a "surrogate wife" to a man who commissions the pregnancy).

While contract pregnancy clearly can be viewed from the perspec-tive of those who commission a pregnancy as well as from that of the woman who bears the child, I put the childbearing woman at the center of my analysis.[4] In doing so I seek to focus discussion directly on the issue of women's freedom, both because differing understandings of whether pregnancy contracts enhance or violate a woman's freedom deeply divide feminists, and because the ways in which proponents and opponents describe the gestational mother reveal important but largely unarticulated differences in their views of two clusters of considerations that extend beyond contract pregnancy. The first is the importance we give to human embodiment in our understandings of the "self" and its freedom, and the second is the tension between promoting freedom through contracts on the one hand, and the recognition and preservation of noncontractual human relationships on the other.

Because they raise issues of individual autonomy, freedom, and con-tract, these considerations are important for liberal feminist theory in gen-eral. Starting our analysis of contract pregnancy from women's experiences and perspectives compels us to see how some forms of lib-eral theory have ignored or misunderstood what it means to be "free" and "autonomous" as physically embodied and gendered beings. Contract pregnancy sheds important light on the necessity for any adequate account of human freedom to attend to the conditions under which we form, sustain, and develop within relationships—including sexual and reproductive relationships—that are central to human existence. Con-tract pregnancy raises issues that are important not only for the chil-dren, mothers, and fathers who are directly touched by them, but also for all those concerned with the meaning of new reproductive practices for the common life we shape together through public discourse and law.

---

4. Defenses of the practice of contract pregnancy that focus on the "right to procreate" sometimes ignore the ethical issues related to the woman who bears the child. Robert-son 1983 and 1986 render the pregnant woman all but invisible. For a critique of Robertson's work, see Ryan 1990.

I. "WOMAN'S BODY, WOMAN'S RIGHT": CONSIDERATIONS IN FAVOR OF PREGNANCY CONTRACTS

It is no wonder that many feminists have welcomed contract pregnancy as a way to illustrate that childbearing and child rearing are two quite distinct human functions and that child rearing need not and should not be assigned exclusively to the woman who bears a child. A woman's agreement to bear and then to relinquish custody of a child offers concrete resistance to the overly close connection that law and social practice have often made between women's childbearing capacity and other aspects of their personalities. Motherhood has often been taken as women's preeminent, even defining, characteristic, and possession of a womb deemed reason enough to disqualify women for most activities of public life.[5] Separating the responsibilities of parenthood from gestational activity allows us to see childbearing as one thing a woman may choose to do, but by no means as the definition of her social role or legal rights. In a somewhat parallel fashion, a man who commissions a pregnancy undertakes "fatherhood" quite consciously, and might be expected to be more involved in caring for the child than men traditionally have been. Marjorie Shultz believes that contract pregnancy is thus a way to make the assumption of parental responsibilities more gender neutral: it can "soften and offset gender imbalances that presently permeate the arena of procreation and parenting" (Shultz 1990, 304).

Just as "surrogacy" emphasizes that not all women who bear children (or who have the capacity to bear children) need be thought of as mothers, it allows women who cannot bear children to assume the responsibilities of parenthood. This can also be done through foster care and adoption, of course, but a contract pregnancy allows a couple to take responsibility for a child even before conception; in a heterosexual couple it enables at least the man and sometimes the woman to have a genetic relationship to the child. The "heightened intentionality" of contract pregnancy makes it possible for any number of persons of either sex to commission a pregnancy. While most known contracts to date have involved married couples, there is no technological reason why anyone, male or female, married or not, could not provide or purchase sperm and, using artificial insemination, impregnate a "surrogate" to obtain a child

---

5. See, e.g., Hoyt v. Florida, 368 U.S. 57 (1961), which held that Florida's automatic exemption of women from jury duty because they might have dependent children at home was not unconstitutionally overbroad. See generally Rhode 1989, 29–50.

by contractual agreement; this would encourage a plurality of family forms in which parents would share a deep commitment to raising children (Shultz 1990, 344).

Carmel Shalev regards the gestational mother's obligation to relinquish the child she bore for the commissioning party as an expression of her freedom to undertake whatever work she chooses. She argues that "the refusal to acknowledge the legal validity of surrogacy agreements implies that women are not competent, by virtue of their biological sex, to act as rational, moral agents regarding their reproductive activity." Like other defenders of contract pregnancy, Shalev places great emphasis on the consent that is at the heart of any valid contract. "If the purpose is to increase the voluntariness of the decision, attention should focus on the parties' negotiations before conception. If conception is intentional and the surrogate mother is an autonomous agent, . . . why should she not be held responsible for the consequences of her autonomous reproductive decision?" (Shalev 1989, 11–12, 96). The same liberty that should protect a woman from any governmental effort to prohibit birth control or abortion or to force sterilization also protects her freedom to agree to carry a child for someone else. The slogan "Woman's body, woman's right" succinctly captures the notion that a woman herself—not a husband, not a doctor, not the state—must make those procreative decisions that affect her.

Those who see contract pregnancy as an exercise of freedom particularly emphasize that consent is given prior to conception: "The surrogate consciously enters into the agreement and voluntarily consents to give up the child even before she becomes pregnant. Rather than being unwanted, the pregnancy is actively sought" (Katz 1986, 21). Or again, "if autonomy is understood as the deliberate exercise of choice with respect to the individual's reproductive capacity, the point at which the parties' intentions should be established is before conception" (Shalev 1989, 103). Defenders of contract pregnancy seek to distinguish it from baby selling, arguing that it is not the child or fetus for whom the woman receives payment, but the woman's gestational services.

But how can one be sure a woman's agreement is really voluntary, her consent truly informed? Advocates of contract pregnancy propose a variety of safeguards to help ensure that pregnancy contracts will be fair and noncoercive. For example, so that women fully understand what kind of physical and emotional experiences to expect from pregnancy, the law could allow only women who have previously given birth to contract to bear a child for someone else. To facilitate adjustment to this new mode of family formation, all parties to a contract pregnancy could be required to undergo counseling before the conception, during the pregnancy, and after the birth. And to avoid financial exploitation of poor or economically vulnerable women, only those with a certain level of financial resources could be allowed to enter a pregnancy contract.[6] The emphasis in all these proposals is on the combination of reason and will that are involved in consent. "In contract law, intent manifested by a promise and subsequent reliance provides the basis for enforceable agreements. Typically, the mental element is the pivotal element in determining legal outcomes" (Stumpf 1986, 195). If the choice is a free one, argues Marjorie Shultz, then "the principle of private intention [should] be given substantial deference and legal force" (Shultz 1990, 398). Attention should focus on whether conditions under which the mind can be held to have freely acceded to the bargain pertained when the contract was made.

Feminist proponents of contract pregnancy argue that those who would allow a "surrogate" to change her mind about relinquishing custody fall into the age-old trap of assuming that women are not as rational as men or that their reason can be overridden by instinct or sentiment. "The paternalistic refusal to force the surrogate mother to keep her word denies the notion of female reproductive agency and reinforces the traditional perception of women as imprisoned in the subjectivity of their wombs" (Shalev 1989, 121). One surrogate mother quoted approvingly by Lori Andrews insisted that "a contract is a contract. . . . It's dangerous to say that we are ruled by our hormones, rather than our brains. You don't have a right to damage other people's lives [i.e., those of the expectant couple deprived of a child when a surrogate reneges] because of your hormones." Robin Bergstrom, a legislative aide in the New York State Senate, is quoted in the same vein, "I truly can't understand the feminists who are now arguing against women's rights [i.e., to prohibit payment to surrogates and to make pregnancy contracts revocable]. . . . Women's rights have been cut back in the past based on male perceptions that women are incompetent to make decisions, but this time women will be putting it on themselves" (Andrews 1989, 92, 223).

6. See, e.g., Andrews 1989, 252–72; Shalev 1989, 144; and Hill 1990, 157–59. In his decision in Orange County (Calif.) Superior Court, Judge Richard N. Parslow awarded custody to the commissioning parents, and "he proposed that all parties to any surrogate agreement undergo psychiatric evaluation, that all agree from the start that the surrogate mother would have no custody rights, that she have previous experience with successful childbirth and that a surrogate be used only in cases where the genetic mother is unable to give birth" (Mydans 1990, A14).

It is important to notice that these arguments about a woman's free consent to bear a child assume, implicitly or explicitly, that the "work" of pregnancy is analogous to other kinds of human labor. What distinguishes allowing a surrogate to renege on her contract from state interference in women's contractual capacity implicated in much protective labor legislation? In the early twentieth century many feminists supported legislation to protect women from oppressive working conditions, although the U.S. Supreme Court had struck down protective labor legislation for men as a violation of freedom of contract (Sklar 1986, 25–35). But by the 1990s most advocates of women's rights had come to argue that women should not receive protections unavailable to men, with the possible exception of maternity leave, so that they, like men, could become parents without forfeiting their jobs (many feminists, of course, advocated gender-neutral parental leave policies; Finley 1986, 118–82; Littleton 1987, 1043–59). Many argued that even when work involved substances that might cause fetal damage, pregnant women should not be barred from such jobs. If, after appropriate medical and psychological counseling, a woman freely consents to a pregnancy contract, then allowing her later to renege on her agreement and keep custody of the child she bears—or to share custody with its biological father—smacks of the legal paternalism that many feminists have long opposed. Is it not antithetical to all that feminists have worked for, ask proponents, to argue that women's reproductive experience should be the grounds for allowing the law to treat their contracts concerning pregnancy as less binding than other contracts; does it not suggest that women are less bound than others by their freely given words?

Defenders of contract pregnancy assume not only that gestation of a fetus is work that is analogous to other forms of wage labor, but also that selling one's labor for a wage is a manifestation of individual freedom. From this perspective, prohibiting a woman from receiving payment for her services bearing a child denies her the full and effective proprietorship of her body. Lisa Newton, director of the Program of Applied Ethics at Fairfield University, has argued that surrogacy is a service that is "simply an extension . . . of baby-sitting and other child-care arrangements which are very widely practiced" and that it is "irrational" to allow payment for the latter services and not for pregnancy (Andrews 1989, 267).[7] Shalev similarly believes that "the transaction under consideration is . . . for the

7. Judge Parslow said that Anna Johnson had served as " 'home' " for the embryo she carried, "much as a foster parent stands in for a parent who is not able to care for a child" (Mydans 1990).

sale of reproductive services. . . . A childless couple is regarded as purchasing the reproductive labor of a birth mother." Banning the sale of procreative services will "reactivate and reinforce the state's power to define what constitutes legitimate and illegitimate reproduction," while allowing payment will "recognize a woman's legal authority to make decisions regarding the exercise of her reproductive capacity" (Shalev 1989, 157, 94).

The consequence of prohibiting pregnancy contracts or banning payment for gestational services is suggested by the question of the surrogate who asked, "Why am I exploited if I am paid, but not if I am not paid?" (Andrews 1989, 259). When the state forbids payment for contract pregnancy it treats reproductive activity as it has traditionally treated women's domestic labor—as unpaid, noneconomic acts of love and nurturing, rather than as work and real economic contributions to family life. Even Margaret Radin, who opposes pregnancy contracts, acknowledges that prohibiting paid pregnancy creates a "double bind." Contract pregnancy could "enable a needy group—poor women—to improve their relatively powerless, oppressed condition, an improvement that would be beneficial to personhood" (Radin 1987, 1916). To forbid people to labor or be paid for using their bodies as they choose when no harm is done to others seems extraordinarily hard for a liberal polity to justify, a point that proponents of the decriminalization of prostitution never tire of repeating.[8] Proponents of contract pregnancy emphasize the value of allowing individuals to determine their activities and life courses as they choose. When the contract between the gestational mother and the commissioning parents reflects the procreative intentions of both parties, enforcement of the contract is the only way both to give force to the desire and commitment of those who seek to raise a child and to recognize the autonomy of the gestational mother.

Although I deeply value self-determination, I believe that pregnancy contracts should not be enforceable. I would not, however, prohibit "gift surrogacy" in which only payment of medical and living expenses would be allowed. Such surrogacy agreements could be treated like preadoption agreements that leave the birth mother free to decide not to relinquish custody at birth. I am ambivalent about whether any further payment

---

8. The debate over whether prostitution should be decriminalized finds feminists on both sides of the issue, sometimes for reasons akin to those that divide them with respect to contract pregnancy. See discussions in Jaggar 1980; Pateman 1983; Tong 1984, 37–64; Shrage 1989; Schwarzenbach 1990–91; and Overall 1992.

should ever be permitted.[9] I take up only the enforceability of contracts in any detail here.

II. "OUR BODIES, OUR SELVES": CONSIDERATIONS AGAINST IRREVOCABLE CONTRACTS

Perhaps the most salient problem with the notion that women's freedom is reflected in and protected by a contract signed prior to the conception of a child is that the woman carries to term a fetus that did not exist at the time the agreement was struck. As we have seen, most advocates of contract pregnancy insist that the payment the gestational mother receives is not for the child, but for gestational services.[10] This distinction, however, seems hard to sustain when the fetus develops from the gestational mother's ovum. In such cases, the woman is contributing more than the labor of her womb; she is also selling her genetic material, and it becomes difficult to see how the exchange escapes the charge of baby selling.[11] In

9. Two strong critics of gift surrogacy, on the ground that it reinforces gender stereotypes of women as altruistic conduits for fulfilling the needs of others, are Sharyn L. Roach Anleu and Janice G. Raymond. Anleu 1990 concludes that commercial surrogacy provides an acceptable and desirable challenge to gender norms, while Raymond 1990 condemns both altruistic and commercial surrogacy. Richard J. Arneson, "Commodification and Commercial Surrogacy," *Philosophy and Public Affairs* 21, no. 2 (Spring 1992): 132–64, presents a thoughtful analysis that leads him to argue "tentatively for the claim that commercial surrogacy should be legally permissible" (133).

10. A few writers propose legalizing commissioned adoption or creating a market in babies, but they are in a minority, and they arrived at their views from considering issues other than contract pregnancy. Richard Posner declares that the objections to the sale of babies for adoption are unpersuasive. Even the poor might do better in a free baby market than under present adoption law because people who did not meet adoption agencies' requirements might, "in a free market with low prices, be able to adopt children, just as poor people are able to buy color television sets" (Posner 1986a, 141–42). See also Landes and Posner 1978; but see Posner 1986b, where he says he "did not advocate a free market in babies" (cited in Radin 1987, 1850, 1863).

11. Men sell their genetic material through artificial insemination by donor programs, a fact advocates of contract pregnancy often mention to argue that contract pregnancy is the analogous activity for women. The analogy between donating sperm and gestating a human fetus for nine months is extremely strained. Even donating an egg is not comparable to donating sperm, as doing so requires surgery. The logic of commercial contract pregnancy allows the eventual commodification of all procreative activity, where individuals of either sex might purchase sperm from one source, ova from another, and hire a third person to gestate the fertilized egg. This total commodification seems undesirable and at least raises the question of whether the sale and purchase (rather than the donation) of human sperm and ova is bad public policy.

addition, as Margaret Radin has pointed out, selling an ovum along with gestational services entails pricing all of a woman's personal attributes—race, height, hair color, intelligence, artistic ability—as well as her reproductive capacity, and, in a society in which women's bodies are already highly commodified by advertisers, pornographers, and promoters of prostitution, the dangers of commodification of women's attributes are palpable and pressing (Radin 1987, 1933).

When the childbearing woman has no genetic relationship with the fetus, the assertion that the commissioning couple is purchasing only gestational services is stronger. To date there are some eighty known cases in which an embryo has been introduced into another woman's womb for gestation after having been fertilized in vitro (*New York Times* 1990, 1). In the recent California case in which Anna Johnson bore a child conceived by in vitro fertilization from the ovum and sperm of Crispina and Mark Calvert and sued to have her contract declared invalid, Judge Richard N. Parslow awarded custody to the genetic parents and commented that the contract was binding: "I see no problem with someone getting paid for her pain and suffering. . . . They [gestational mothers] are not selling a baby; they are selling pain and suffering" (Mydans 1990, A14).[12] To Judge Parslow the contract appeared to be an agreement about work, and his remarks raise the question of how the "pain and suffering" of pregnancy are analogous to the physical and psychological demands of other kinds of labor.

Arguments for contract pregnancy depend, it seems to me, on a strong analogy between the "work" of pregnancy and forms of wage labor with which we are already familiar. The analogy seems to rest on two main considerations: pregnancy involves the body, culminating in the extraordinary physical exertion of "labor" and giving birth; and pregnancy ends with the appearance of something new in the world, a tangible "product" of gestational work.

Human gestation is distinguished from other kinds of productive

12. Judge Parslow makes a false distinction between gestational mothers who have a genetic relationship to the fetus they bear and those who do not. The absence of a genetic relationship need not alter a gestational mother's experience of pregnancy, and that experience is the basis of her custodial rights. A gestational mother undergoes all the extensive hormonal and physiological changes of pregnancy, and her social experience as a pregnant woman will be the same whether she has a genetic tie to the fetus or not. From her perspective, the distinction between "full surrogacy" (in which she donates an ovum) and "partial surrogacy" (in which she bears no genetic relationship to the fetus) may well be immaterial.

work, however, by the ways in which it involves both a woman's physical and psychological being and by the difference between the human being that results from a pregnancy and other kinds of products. I concentrate here on the woman's experience and on how a rich account of pregnancy might inform our judgment about the claim that only enforcing pregnancy contracts properly recognizes women's freedom and autonomy.

Women's accounts of pregnancy point out the complexity of women's childbearing experiences and the ways in which a woman's self, not simply her womb, may be involved in reproductive labor. Iris Young offers one such account in a phenomenological examination of pregnancy and embodiment. She notes that in our culture "pregnancy does not belong to the woman herself. It either is a state of the developing foetus, for which the woman is a container; or it is an objective, observable process coming under scientific scrutiny; or it becomes objectified by the woman herself, as a 'condition' in which she must 'take care of herself.' " Young points out that we almost never see the pregnant woman as Julia Kristeva does, as "the subject, the mother as the site of her proceedings" (Young 1990, 160). The mother's body is the "environment" in which the fetus grows, but most arguments in favor of contract pregnancy seem to posit no more intrinsic relationship between them than there would be between an artificial womb and a fetus that might develop within it. Even our everyday language reflects the distinctness of mother and fetus: pregnant women are said to be "expecting" the babies that doctors "deliver" to them (Rothman 1989, 100; Young 1990, 167).

Mother and fetus, however, are not yet, or are not in every way, distinct entities. Neither are they the same being. In her 1945 poem about abortion, "The Mother," Gwendolyn Brooks cries out against the inability of language to express the relationship between mother and fetus: "you are dead. / Or rather, or instead, / You were never made. / But that too, I am afraid, / Is faulty: oh, what shall I say, how is the truth to be said?" (Brooks [1945] 1989, 2505). In her analysis of "The Mother," Barbara Johnson notes that "the poem continues to struggle to clarify the relation between 'I' [the woman] and 'you' [the fetus]," but in the end "[the language of the] poem can no more distinguish between 'I' and 'you' than it can come up with a proper definition of life" (Johnson 1987, 190). Like Brooks, Adrienne Rich testifies to her experience of the fluidity of the boundary between self and other during pregnancy. "In early pregnancy, the stirring of the foetus felt like ghostly tremors of my own body, later like the movements of a being imprisoned within me; but both sensations were *my* sensations, contributing to my own sense of physical and psychic space" (Rich 1976, 47). Iris Young points out that while for observers pregnancy may appear to be "a time of waiting and watching, when nothing happens," for the pregnant subject "pregnancy has a temporality of movement, growth and change. . . . The pregnant woman experiences herself as a source and participant in a creative process. Though she does not plan and direct it, neither does it merely wash over her; rather, she *is* this process, this change" (Young 1990, 167). Mother and fetus are at one and the same time distinct and interrelated entities, and this fundamental fact of human embodiment means that to speak of the "freedom" of the mother as residing in her intention as an "autonomous" agent misunderstands both the relationship between woman and child and that of the woman to her ongoing self.

The interrelatedness of mother and fetus makes it difficult to specify exactly what gestational labor entails. Unlike other work, gestational labor is not consciously controlled; the bodily labor of pregnancy goes on continuously, even while the pregnant woman is asleep. Whether the "work" is done badly or well is only marginally within the mother's control; she can refrain from smoking, drinking, and drug use; eat properly; and get an appropriate amount of exercise, but whether the fetus grows to term, has a safe birth, and is free of genetic abnormalities is otherwise largely beyond her ability to effect.

In her critique of contract pregnancy, Carole Pateman argues that while all wage labor involves selling some aspect of oneself to some degree, the alienation involved in selling gestational services is so extreme as to make it illegitimate. In Pateman's view, wage labor rests on a fundamentally flawed notion of the proprietary self that assumes that it is possible to separate labor power or capacities from the person of the worker "like pieces of property." But "the worker's capacities are developed over time and they form an integral part of [the worker's] self and self-identity" (Pateman 1988, 150). While this is true of all workers, some forms of labor involve the worker's sense of self more directly and intimately than do others. Labor that leaves no time for other pursuits, deadens the mind through boring and repetitive chores, warps the spirit by requiring unethical behavior, or enfeebles the body by unhealthy practices involves a forfeiture of the self greater than that experienced by more fortunate workers. Contract pregnancy entails a very high degree of self-alienation, because the work of pregnancy involves women's emotional, physical, and sexual experiences and understandings of themselves as women. Pateman argues that the "logic of contract as exhibited in 'surrogate' motherhood" sweeps away "any intrinsic relation between the female owner, her body and reproductive capacities. She stands to her property in exactly the same external relation as the male owner stands to his labour power or sperm" (Pateman 1988, 216). This objectifies women's bodies and their reproductive labor in a manner and to a degree that are wholly unacceptable.

Elizabeth Anderson echoes this point when she argues that any form of paid pregnancy involves "an invasion of the market into a new sphere of conduct, that of specifically women's labor—that is, the labor of carrying children to term in pregnancy." In her view, "treating women's labor as just another kind of commercial production process violates the precious emotional ties which the mother may rightly and properly establish with her 'product,' the child." When a woman is required "to repress whatever parental love she feels for the child, these [economic] norms convert women's labor into a form of alienated labor." The forfeiture of self involved in contract pregnancy is an extreme instance of the diminution of the self involved in many labor contracts. Market norms may be legitimate and useful in their proper sphere, but when "applied to the ways we treat and understand women's reproductive labor, women are reduced . . . to objects of use" (Anderson 1990, 75, 82, 81, 92).[13]

It is also important to take into account that payment for gestational service does not occur in some neutral market environment but in a society in which many of our institutions and interactions are shaped by relationships of domination and subordination between men and women. To talk about the freedom of the self-possessing individual to do what she will with her own body while ignoring gender structures in her society distances such arguments from the world of lived experience. I think it is possible (barely) to imagine conditions in which it would be legitimate for a woman to receive payment for bearing a child to whom she had no genetic relationship, provided always she retained the power to assert custodial rights before or at birth. At a minimum, such conditions would include an economy free from wage labor undertaken in order to survive; rough economic equality between men and women; a culture in which the "ideology of motherhood," which asserts that childbearing is women's natural and preeminent calling, did not contribute to some women's deriving their sense of self-worth from being pregnant; a society free from the objectification and commodification of women's sexuality; and a poli-

13. In recommending the prohibition of payment under any circumstances, Anderson assumes the existence and desirability of mother-fetus bonding; I do not assume that such a bond always develops or that the state should prohibit all payment. When a gestational mother does experience a strong tie with the child she is carrying, however, law and social practice should recognize and protect that bond.

tics uninfluenced by gender hierarchy. Descriptions of contract pregnancy that depict the practice as nothing more than womb rental in a supposedly neutral market fail to take account of the profoundly gendered nature of the structures that surround the transaction. Viewed in its social context, contract pregnancy can as appropriately be described as enabling economically secure men to purchase women's procreative labor and custodial rights as allowing women the freedom to sell procreative labor. And in this context payment should be prohibited.

These reflections lead me to think that pregnancy contracts might as usefully be compared to contracts for consensual slavery as to other kinds of employment contracts. Discussions of slave contracts force us to ask whether certain kinds of contracts are illegitimate, whether people can be held to have agreed to certain stipulations that limit in fundamental ways freedoms essential to human dignity, autonomy, and selfhood, or whether some kinds of freedom are inalienable.

In both contract pregnancy and consensual slavery, fulfilling the agreement, even if it appears to be freely undertaken, violates the ongoing freedom of the individual in a way that does not simply restrict future options (such as whether I may leave my employer) but does violence to the self (my understanding of who I am). Both John Locke and John Stuart Mill asserted that consensual slavery was illegitimate. Locke argued that "a man, not having the power of his own life, *cannot*, by compact, or his own consent, *enslave himself* to any one" (Locke [1690] 1980, sec. 23, p. 17).[14] In a much-quoted passage of *On Liberty*, Mill asserted that to agree to be a slave might look like an exercise of freedom in the present, but that since such a contract removed the possibility of free exercise of freedom in the future, "freely choosing" to be a slave was incoherent. "By selling himself for a slave, [a person] abdicates his liberty; he forgoes any future use of it beyond that single act." But, says Mill, this act "defeats . . . the very purpose which is the justification of allowing him to dispose of himself." One limitation on freedom is that one cannot "be free not to be free. It is not freedom, to be allowed to alienate his freedom" (Mill [1859] 1975a, 126).

The analogy of consensual slavery to enforceable pregnancy contracts may seem flawed because slavery is for a lifetime, while human gestation lasts for about nine months. But the time involved in a preg-

14. Locke only allowed for slavery following capture in a just war, when enslavement was substituted for a death sentence. For an excellent discussion of Locke's views of slavery, see Farr 1986, 263–89.

nancy depends upon how one regards pregnancy and childbirth in relationship to a woman's identity and self-understanding. If the baby is an
extrinsic "product" of her gestational work, then the gestational mother
simultaneously fulfills her contractual obligation and regains her freedom
in turning the baby over to the commissioning parent(s). If, however,
she and the fetus were beings-in-relationship during pregnancy and she
perceives herself as (at least one of) its mother(s), then a law that denies
her all custodial rights will deprive her of any lived expression of her
relationship to that child for her entire lifetime. Writing of the lower
court decision denying the gestational mother custody in the "Baby M"
contract pregnancy case, Patricia Williams noted that "Mary Beth
Whitehead's powerlessness came about as a result of a contract that she
signed at a discrete point of time—yet which, over time, enslaved her by
depriving her of freedom to assert custodial rights" (Williams 1988, 15).

Shifting understandings of divorce are also related to the questions
of whether the freedom to choose at one point in time captures what is
most important about human freedoms in a liberal society. Concern for
what it means for a person to exercise freedom over time have dramatically altered divorce laws in Anglo-American jurisdictions during the past
century. Most American states now permit "no fault" divorce, which
entails releasing people upon their request from the promise to be husband or wife "until death do us part." The views of John Stuart Mill are
again interesting for this discussion. Mill frequently referred to marriage
as "slavery" because nineteenth-century marriage law bound a woman for
life to a man who gained possession of all her property, whose consent
was necessary for her to make any valid contract or will, who decided
where she would live, who had legal custody of their children, and who
could not be prosecuted for rape or sexual assault against her. Mill was
ambivalent about divorce but unequivocally believed that the act of consent with which a woman entered marriage—consent often joyfully and
lovingly given—did not and could not legitimate the terms of such a
marriage contract (Mill [1869] 1975b, 425–548).

Arguments in our own day justifying divorce are somewhat different,
because the law has gotten rid of most of the injustices of coverture
(although, notably, marital rape is not a crime in some jurisdictions). Yet
laws of most Anglo-American jurisdictions allow for divorce, a recognition
that the state will not enforce a person's promise to live intimately with
another person for life, nor will it prohibit the formation of a new relationship through remarriage. Divorce law reflects in part society's determination that the law cannot permit people to be bound to a promise when

they and their relationship have fundamentally changed. Not to allow a woman to revoke her consent during pregnancy or at birth seems to ignore the possibility of a somewhat analogous change that simultaneously affects the self as an individual and as a person-in-relationship. It is possible that persons may also undergo such change, regardless of whether or not they are in relationship with someone else, to justify the judgment that the person's sense of self has changed so significantly that enforcing a contract would do violence to that self.[15]

The arguments prohibiting consensual slavery and justifying divorce are related to the issue of enforcing pregnancy contracts. The potential violation of a woman's self when she has entered a pregnancy contract stems from the months she will spend in relationship with a developing human being. It is this relationship that may change her, and it is this relationship that is severed if a pregnancy contract is enforceable. Defenders of pregnancy contracts argue eloquently, and with much truth, that intentional parents have also been in relationship with their child-to-be, imagining the role the child will play in their lives, planning for its care, and loving it as it develops in utero. Marjorie Shultz argues that it is the relationship between intentional parents and fetus that must be protected by enforcing reproductive contracts. "To ignore the significance of deliberation, purpose and expectation—the capacity to envision and shape the future through intentional choice—is to disregard one of the most distinctive traits that makes us human. It is to disregard crucial differences in moral meaning and responsibility. To disregard such intention with reference to so intimate and significant an activity as procreation and child-rearing is deeply shocking." When a surrogate reneges on her promise to relinquish custody, it is wrong "to say to a disappointed parent, 'go get another child.'" Such a judgment "offends our belief in the uniqueness of each individual. It inappropriately treats the miracle and complexity of

15. For example, we might imagine a student who received a college scholarship from the military discovering as she drew near to graduation that she has become a pacifist, and that the person she is now cannot in conscience enter the armed forces as she had promised. To force her to do so would violate her deepest principles concerning the taking of human life and do violence to the "self" she has become since entering into her agreement with the military. On the very complicated problem of whether promises can bind people who experience profound changes in values, see Parfit 1973, 144–46; and Williams 1976. Charles Fried believes that to respect persons we must respect the persistence of their choices over time, and that to release them from their promises "infantilize[s]" them. See Fried 1981, 20–21. I am grateful to Robert Goodin of the Australian National University for an insightful letter about the problem of "later selves" (personal correspondence, October 1989).

particular individual lives as fungible. By contrast, surrogacy and other reproductive arrangements transfer the life and parental responsibility for a particular unique child." Hence, argues Shultz, "although it may seem counter-intuitive, the extraordinary remedy, specific performance of agreements about parenthood, in some sense confirms core values about the uniqueness of life" (Shultz 1990, 377–78, 364).

The claims on behalf of both the intentional parents and the gestational mother rest, then, on assertions about the relationship between parent and fetus. Defenders of contract pregnancy like Shultz are deeply disturbed by the prospect that allowing a gestational mother to void her contractual agreement "expresses the idea that the biological experience of motherhood 'trumps' all other considerations. . . . It exalts a woman's experience of pregnancy and childbirth over her formation of emotional, intellectual and interpersonal decisions and expectations, as well as over others' reliance on the commitments she has earlier made" (Shultz 1990, 384). Yet even Shultz's eloquent plea and my own commitment to gender-neutral law do not persuade me that promises to relinquish custody should be enforced against the wishes of the gestational mother. Her later judgment based on her experience of the pregnancy does "trump," and what it trumps is her own earlier promise, upon which the intentional parents' claim to sole custody depends. It trumps because enforcement of a pregnancy contract against the gestational mother's wishes would constitute a legal refusal to recognize the reality of the woman and fetus as beings-in-relationship, which the law should protect as it does many other personal relationships. Yet the biological father or the commissioning couple also have parental claims, and these can probably best be recognized by granting and enforcing visitation rights.[16]

16. Even if one accepts my argument that a woman's contract to relinquish all custodial claims should not be enforced against her will, the question of how to deal with the custodial claims of the commissioning parent(s) is enormously difficult. One could argue that these claims should be adjudicated on a case-by-case basis, but that would not serve the goal of stabilizing the child's situation as quickly as possible, nor would it give more weight to actual physical relationship and nurturance than to intentionality alone. Yet the claims of the commissioning parents are real and certainly stronger than those of a biological father who "unintentionally" becomes a parent through unprotected intercourse (and who can claim paternal rights and responsibilities in many jurisdictions). This is a large issue that I cannot address adequately here, other than to note that society might do well to develop forms of acknowledging the existence of "intentional" and biological, as well as nurturing, parents, rather than try to make all families resemble households of two heterosexual parents and their biological offspring. In this regard see Bartlett 1988.

I find my thoughts on the importance of the actual embodied relationships of gestational mother and fetus to be akin (with certain significant exceptions) to those of Robert Goldstein, who argues in *Mother-love and Abortion* that most discussions of abortion, whether put forward by regulationists or prochoice advocates, err in regarding pregnant woman and fetus as distinct individuals with competing rights.[17] As he points out, "rights talk" in this context emphasizes what Ferdinand Schoeman refers to as "the appropriateness of seeing other persons as separate and autonomous agents," whereas "the relationship between parent and infant [or fetus] involves an awareness of a kind of union between people. . . . We *share our selves* with those with whom we are intimate" (Schoeman 1980, 35). A correct approach, says Goldstein, would not "define personhood as if it were a solitary achievement of the fetus and its DNA that precedes rather than presupposes participation in the primary community of woman and fetus." With regard to abortion, respect for this "primary community" requires that the law recognize the pregnant woman as the person who must make decisions about the dyad she and the fetus constitute; she must be accorded "a privileged position as dyadic representative that is superior to that of other would-be dyadic participants," such as the biological father, the state, or potential adoptive parents. In Goldstein's analysis, the privacy and autonomy that the *Roe v. Wade* decision protects, then, "[belong] not only to the woman as an individual but also to the dyadic, indeed symbiotic, unit of woman and fetus. This dyad constitutes the relevant community for understanding the abortion decision" (Goldstein 1988, 35, 65, x). In the case of surrogacy, the embodied relationship of the gestational mother (who may or may not be the genetic mother) is stronger than that between the commissioning parent(s) and fetus, or between her own "intentional self" and the fetus prior to conception. In Kenneth Karst's expressive phrase, a critically important aspect of the right of "privacy" is not to isolate people from one another, but to protect and foster what he calls "the freedom of intimate association" (Karst 1980, 634–83). A legal rule enforcing a pregnancy contract would reinforce notions of human separateness and insularity rather than recognize that the development of individuality and autonomy takes place through sustained and intimate human relationship.

None of these considerations argues against a woman's voluntarily

---

17. See Goldstein 1988. I do not believe all women experience mother-love during pregnancy, and I disagree with Goldstein's assumption that mother-love must continue to privilege a mother's relationship to her child over the father's after birth.

bearing a child for someone else or against adoption. Law in a liberal polity should not force a woman to retain physical custody of her child once it is born, and the woman may decide that placing the child in someone else's care may be best for her, for the child, and for the new custodial parent(s). But adoption and "gift" pregnancy must be distinguished from contract pregnancy: even though gestational mothers may mourn for children they entrust to others to care for and raise, they have made their decision to separate from an existing human being, not from a potential one. Their actions, which may bring relief as well as (or as much as) sorrow, are not the consequence of an agreement that ignores or dismisses the relevance of the experience of pregnancy and of the human and embodied relationship between woman and fetus to our understanding of human freedom and choice.

III. CONTRACTS, HUMAN RELATIONSHIPS, AND FREEDOM

Those who argue that respect for women's autonomy necessarily entails allowing and enforcing pregnancy contracts present contract as the paradigmatic bond linking people to one another in human society. Thinking carefully about pregnancy contracts shows what is wrong not only with contract pregnancy but more broadly with certain efforts to enhance women's freedom in family relationships by replacing legal rules based on notions of men's and women's "natural" roles in families with contractual paradigms and rules.

The impetus behind such efforts is quite understandable given the burdens that ascriptive notions about women's "nature" and proper roles have placed upon women seeking equality in both the family and public life. From the mid-nineteenth to the mid-twentieth centuries, feminists found contractual ideas, which emphasize equality, freedom, and volition, to be extremely effective tools for removing the disabilities married women suffered under traditional family law.[18] In place of the common-law rules of coverture that assumed that when a woman married, her legal personality was subsumed in that of her husband, advocates of women's rights fashioned statutes that rested on notions of spousal equality. Gradually the idea that the family was a natural, hierarchical, unitary, and indissoluble association gave way to understandings of families as voluntaristic and egalitarian associations that people could enter and leave at will,

18. For a discussion of nineteenth-century feminist ideology and marriage law reform campaigns, see Basch 1982 and Shanley 1989.

and in which responsibilities were not prescribed by nature but properly determined by the marriage partners themselves. Without arguing for a return to earlier notions of natural or ascriptive family roles, I maintain that some of the inadequacies of a contractual paradigm for family relations are evident in the proposals for legal recognition and enforcement of pregnancy contracts. Family relationships involve and affect the self in ways that cannot be fully predicted or provided for in advance and are particularly striking in parent-child relationships. In addition, Martha Fineman has criticized the effects of adopting abstract liberal principles in laws dealing with child custody, property division, and spousal support after divorce. When a court assumes that its aim should be to restore divorcing parents to their former autonomy and independence, it frequently produces grave inequalities in the actual social and economic opportunities of divorced men and women (Fineman 1991).

The dilemmas and difficulties that arise in trying to conceptualize the proper bases of family law should stimulate a rethinking not only of these laws but also of certain aspects of liberal political theory. This article certainly takes exception to the libertarian version of liberalism that understands freedom only as the ability to determine and pursue one's goals without interference from government or other individuals and that sees relationships among individuals as the result of specific agreements. This individualistic paradigm ignores the human need to foster the interdependence that is the basis of human development. While some of the human associations that the liberal state should protect can be understood in voluntaristic or contractual terms, some cannot. The fallacies of a view of political—as well as family—life that ignores the noncontractual ties among human beings is well captured in Christine Di Stefano's analysis of some passages from Thomas Hobbes's writings. Di Stefano notes that when Hobbes set out to depict those aspects of the state of nature that he hoped would make his prescriptions for civil society seem "welcome and reasonable," he asked his reader to "consider men as if but even now sprung out of the earth, and suddenly, like mushrooms, come to full maturity, without all kinds of engagement with each other." As Di Stefano argues, Hobbes's picture of "abstract man" altogether ignores women's experience of reproduction and early nurturance and falsely assumes that "characteristically human capacities need no particular social life forms in which to develop."[19]

The attempt to justify the enforceability of contracts for pregnancy

19. Di Stefano 1983, quoting Hobbes (1651) 1972, 205, 638.

similarly rests on a model of the autonomous individual that either ignores or takes too little account of the truth that human beings are constituted in part by relationships with others. Men as well as women do not spring like mushrooms from the earth but begin existence in a state of interdependence with and dependence on another human being. As Virginia Held points out, "Western liberal democratic thought has been built on the concept of the 'individual' seen as a theoretically isolatable entity. This entity can assert interests, have rights, and enter into contractual relationships with other entities. But this individual is not seen as related to other individuals in inextricable or intrinsic ways." As Held has correctly observed, "at some point contracts must be embedded in social relations that are non-contractual" (Held 1987, 124, 125). This is not to argue, as some do, that all liberal theory is antithetical to women's interests.[20] Indeed, liberalism's very respect for the individual and her freedom, as seen among other places in Locke's and Mill's condemnations of consensual slavery, shapes my conviction that enforceable pregnancy contracts are illegitimate.[21] It is those contractarian theories that ignore the limits to the freely willed self that run the risk of confusing broadly conceived human freedom and dignity with a narrow notion of freedom of contract.

Feminists must look elsewhere than contractual paradigms to find the theoretical basis for the human liberation we seek. One error of the feminist arguments for contract pregnancy is that they conflate the freedom of the individual woman prior to conception with the conditions that preserve her freedom as a person-in-relationship. Another is that they conceive of market language and mechanisms as morally neutral, whereas market language invokes a particular notion of the person and her relationship to her body and her labor. Further, market transactions occur within social contexts that affect their meanings. In each instance, feminist arguments defending contract pregnancy attribute freedom to the person only as an isolated individual and fail to recognize that individuals are also ineluctably social creatures. Any liberalism worth its salt must

20. For example, Rothman 1989 condemns contract pregnancy as a manifestation of "liberal philosophy [that] is an articulation of the values of technological society, with its basic themes of order, predictability, rationality, control, rationalization of life, the systematizing and control of things and people as things, the reduction of all to component parts, and ultimately the vision of everything, including our very selves, as resources" (63).
21. Damico 1991 intelligently distinguishes liberal values from arguments for contract pregnancy.

protect both individual rights as such and the associations and relationships that shape us and allow us to be who we are. Outlining such a theory is a task well beyond the scope of this article, but I hope that by showing what is wrong with arguments for contract pregnancy I have also shown that the model upon which it rests—the self-possessing individual linked to others only by contractual agreements—fails to do full justice to the complex interdependencies involved in human procreative activity, family relations, and human social life in general. Attention to women's experience, so long absent from political theory, must provide us with ways of understanding and conceptualizing the individual-in-relationship that will allow us to speak more adequately than has been done so far about the simultaneity of human autonomy and interdependence, of freedom and commitment in social and political life.

REFERENCES

Anderson, Elizabeth S. 1990. "Is Women's Labor a Commodity?" *Philosophy and Public Affairs* 19:71–92.

Andrews, Lori. 1989. *Between Strangers: Surrogate Mothers, Expectant Fathers, and Brave New Babies.* New York: Harper & Row.

Anleu, Sharyn L. Roach. 1990. "Reinforcing Gender Norms: Commercial and Altruistic Surrogacy." *Acta Sociologica* 33:63–74.

Bartlett, Katharine T. 1988. "Re-Expressing Parenthood." *Yale Law Journal* 98(2):293–340.

Basch, Norma. 1982. *In the Eyes of the Law.* Ithaca, N.Y.: Cornell University Press.

Brooks, Gwendolyn. (1945) 1989. "the mother." In *The Norton Anthology of American Literature,* 2:2505. 3d ed. New York and London: Norton.

Damico, Alfonso J. 1991. "Surrogate Motherhood: Contract, Gender and Liberal Politics." In *Public Policy and the Public Good,* ed. Ethan Fishman. Westview, Conn.: Greenwood.

Di Stefano, Christine. 1983. "Masculinity as Ideology in Political Theory: Hobbesian Man Considered." *Women's Studies International Forum* 6(6):33–44.

Farr, James. 1986. " 'So Vile and Miserable an Estate': The Problem of Slavery in Locke's Political Thought." *Political Theory* 14(2):253–89.

Field, Martha A. 1988. *Surrogate Motherhood: The Legal and Human Issues.* Cambridge, Mass.: Harvard University Press.

———. 1990. "The Case against Enforcement of Surrogacy Contracts." *Politics and the Life Sciences* 8(2):199–204.

Fineman, Martha Albertson. 1991. *The Illusion of Equality: The Rhetoric and Reality of Divorce Reform.* Chicago: University of Chicago Press.

Finley, Lucinda. 1986. "Transcending Equality Theory: A Way Out of the Maternity and the Workplace Debate." *Columbia University Law Review* 86:1118–82.

Fried, Charles. 1981. *Contract as Promise: A Theory of Contractual Obligation.* Cambridge, Mass.: Harvard University Press.

Goldstein, Robert D. 1988. *Mother-love and Abortion: A Legal Interpretation.* Berkeley and Los Angeles: University of California Press.

Held, Virginia. 1987. "Non-contractual Society: A Feminist View." In *Science, Morality and Feminist Theory*, ed. Marsha Hanen and Kai Nielson. (*Canadian Journal of Philosophy*, vol. 13, suppl.) Calgary: University of Calgary Press.

Hill, John Lawrence. 1990. "The Case for Enforcement of the Surrogate Contract." *Politics and the Life Sciences* 8(2):147–60.

Hobbes, Thomas. (1651) 1972. *The Citizen.* In *Man and Citizen*, ed. Bernard Geit. Garden City, N.Y.: Doubleday.

Jaggar, Alison. 1980. "Prostitution." In *The Philosophy of Sex: Contemporary Readings*, ed. Alan Soble. Totowa, N.J.: Rowman & Littlefield.

Johnson, Barbara. 1987. "Apostrophe, Animation, and Abortion." In her *A World of Difference.* Baltimore: Johns Hopkins University Press.

Karst, Kenneth. 1980. "The Freedom of Intimate Association." *Yale Law Journal* 89(4):624–93.

Katz, Avi. 1986. "Surrogate Motherhood and the Baby-selling Laws." *Columbia Journal of Law and Social Problems* 20(1):1–52.

Landes, Elizabeth, and Richard A. Posner. 1978. "The Economics of the Baby Shortage" (letter). *Journal of Legal Studies* 7:323.

Littleton, Christine. 1987. "Equality and Feminist Legal Theory." *University of Pittsburgh Law Review* 48:1043–59.

Locke, John. (1690) 1980. *Second Treatise of Government*, ed. C. B. Macpherson. Indianapolis: Hackett Publishers.

Mill, John Stuart. (1859) 1975a. *On Liberty.* In his *Three Essays.* New York: Oxford University Press.

———. (1869) 1975b. *The Subjection of Women.* In his *Three Essays.* New York: Oxford University Press.

Mydans, Seth. 1990. "Surrogate Denied Custody of Child." *New York Times*, metropolitan ed., October 23, A14.

New York Times. 1990. *New York Times*, metropolitan ed., August 12, A1.

Okin, Susan Moller. 1990. "A Critique of Pregnancy Contracts." *Politics and the Life Sciences* 8(2):205–10.

Overall, Christine. 1992. "What's Wrong with Prostitution? Evaluating Sex Work." *Signs: Journal of Women in Culture and Society* 17(4):705–24.

Parfit, Derek. 1973. "Later Selves and Moral Principles." In *Philosophy and*

Personal Relations: An Anglo-French Study, ed. Alan Montefiore. Montreal: McGill-Queens University Press.

Pateman, Carole. 1983. "Defending Prostitution: Charges against Ericsson." *Ethics* 93(3):561–65.

———. 1988. *The Sexual Contract*. Stanford, Calif.: Stanford University Press.

Posner, Richard. 1986a. *Economic Analysis of Law*. 3d ed. Boston: Little Brown.

———. 1986b. "Mischaracterized Views" (letter). *Judicature* 69(6):321.

Radin, Margaret Jane. 1987. "Market-Inalienability." *Harvard Law Review* 100:1849–1937.

Raymond, Janice G. 1990. "Reproductive Gifts and Gift Giving: The Altruistic Woman." *Hastings Center Report* 20(6):7–11.

Rhode, Deborah L. 1989. *Justice and Gender: Sex Discrimination and the Law*. Cambridge, Mass.: Harvard University Press.

Rich, Adrienne. 1976. *Of Woman Born: Motherhood as Experience and as Institution*. Bantam Paperback ed. New York: Norton.

Robertson, John. 1983. "Procreative Liberty and the Control of Contraception, Pregnancy and Childbirth." *Virginia Law Review* 69:405–62.

———. 1989. "Embryos, Families and Procreative Liberty: The Legal Structures of the New Reproduction." *Southern California Law Review* 59:942–1041.

Rothman, Barbara Katz. 1989. *Recreating Motherhood: Ideology and Technology in a Patriarchal Society*. New York: Norton.

Ryan, Maura A. 1990. "The Argument for Unlimited Procreative Liberty: A Feminist Critique." *Hastings Center Report* 20(4):6–12.

Schoeman, Ferdinand. 1980. "Rights of Children, Rights of Parents, and the Moral Basis of the Family." *Ethics* 91(1):6–19.

Schwarzenbach, Sibyl. 1990–91. "Contractarians and Feminists Debate Prostitution." *Review of Law and Social Change* 18:103–30.

Shalev, Carmel. 1989. *Birth Power: The Case for Surrogacy*. New Haven, Conn.: Yale University Press.

Shanley, Mary Lyndon. 1989. *Feminism, Marriage and the Law in Victorian England, 1850–1895*. Princeton, N.J.: Princeton University Press.

Shrage, Laurie. 1989. "Should Feminists Oppose Prostitution?" *Ethics* 99:347–61.

Shultz, Marjorie Maguire. 1990. "Reproductive Technology and Intention-based Parenthood: An Opportunity for Gender Neutrality." *Wisconsin Law Review* 1990(2):297–398.

Sklar, Kathryn Kish. 1986. "Why Were Most Politically Active Women Opposed to the ERA in the 1920s?" In *Rights of Passage: The Past and Future of the ERA*, ed. Joan Hoff-Wilson. Bloomington: Indiana University Press.

Stumpf, Andrea E. 1986. "Redefining Motherhood: A Legal Matrix for New Reproductive Technologies." *Yale Law Journal* 96(1):187–208.

Tong, Rosemarie. 1984. *Women, Sex, and the Law.* Totowa, N.J.: Rowman & Allenheld.

Williams, Bernard. 1976. "Persons, Character and Morality." In *The Identities of Persons*, ed. Amelie O. Rorty. Berkeley: University of California Press.

Williams, Patricia. 1988. "On Being the Object of Property." *Signs: Journal of Women in Culture in Society* 14(1):5–24.

Young, Iris Marion. 1990. "Pregnant Embodiment: Subjectivity and Alienation." In her *"Throwing like a Girl" and Other Essays in Feminist Philosophy and Social Theory.* Bloomington: Indiana University Press.

ACTIVE READING

1. Looking closely at passages in Shanley's text, explain how the meaning of "freedom" changes when it is discussed in terms of "work," "relationships," or other concepts that are important in this essay. What connections do you see between these different kinds of freedom?

2. Examine two or three paragraphs that include quotations from other experts on law and public policy. How would you describe Shanley's role in the "conversation" she presents? What does her use of quotations suggest about the kind of argument she is making?

3. Locate several references to "liberalism" in Shanley's text. Working with your response to Before Reading #1, explain which of the dictionary's definitions most closely match Shanley's own descriptions of liberal theories. What is surprising about your findings?

READING IN NEW CONTEXTS

1. Scheper-Hughes, Heker, and Fienup-Riordan all explore spoken or unspoken agreements between various parties. Working with one or more of these texts, show how Shanley's theories about contracts help you explain what people risk and gain when they make agreements with each other.

2. Shanley looks at analogies, or comparisons, that are commonly made between contract pregnancy and work, marriage, or other human activities. Use Sontag's theories about metaphor (another kind of comparison) to explore the advantages and dangers of making analogies about pregnancy. To what extent is Shanley herself aware of the advantages and dangers you identify?

3. In "Women and Honor," Rich suggests that truth is like the complex knots on the underside of a carpet. What do Rich's theories about truth help you to say about the complexity of Shanley's argument? Discuss some passages or ideas from Shanley's essay that illustrate, in your view, what Rich is talking about.

DRAFT ONE / DRAFT TWO

1. *Draft One:* Shanley examines the "dyad" that is formed by a mother and fetus. How do her ideas about this dyad help you discuss relationships within other pairs you have read about (for instance, the headhunter and his victim in Rosaldo, or the doctor and patient in Brody)?

   Draft Two: Use some of your insights from Draft One to explore the meaning of individualism in Bellah or Kingston. In what ways does Shanley's notion of the dyad challenge or support the ideas about individuality you find in these readings?

2. *Draft One:* What traits does the work of pregnancy and childbirth share with the forms of work described in Christian, Garson, or Sanders? Show how Shanley's theories about labor allow you to interpret the work people do in another *Literacies* text.

   Draft Two: With the help of material from Draft One, compose your own theory about the relationship between productivity, the body, and freedom. Try out your theory on another *Literacies* essay about work, such as Rodriguez or MacLeod.

BEFORE READING SUSAN SONTAG

1. What do you think metaphors are? When do you or other people use metaphors? List some topics you and your friends or family speak about with metaphors. How does this way of speaking affect your thoughts about the subject?

2. List several serious illnesses in addition to AIDS. What are your sources of information about AIDS and these other illnesses? How do your thoughts about AIDS and people with AIDS relate to your thoughts about other serious illnesses and the people who have them?

3. In your view, what kind of training or experience qualifies someone to speak about AIDS or other serious illnesses? Why? Which of your own sources of information meet the qualifications you have noted?

S U S A N   S O N T A G

AIDS AND ITS METAPHORS

1

By metaphor I meant nothing more or less than the earliest and most succinct definition I know, which is Aristotle's, in his *Poetics* (1457b). "Metaphor," Aristotle wrote, "consists in giving the thing a name that belongs to something else." Saying a thing is or is like something-it-is-not is a mental operation as old as philosophy and poetry, and the spawning ground of most kinds of understanding, including scientific understanding, and expressiveness. (To acknowledge which I prefaced the polemic against metaphors of illness I wrote ten years ago with a brief, hectic flourish of metaphor, in mock exorcism of the seductiveness of metaphorical thinking.) Of course, one cannot think without metaphors. But that does not mean there aren't some metaphors we might well abstain from or try to retire. As, of course, all thinking is interpretation. But that does not mean it isn't sometimes correct to be "against" interpretation.

Take, for instance, a tenacious metaphor that has shaped (and obscured the understanding of) so much of the political life of this century, the one that distributes, and polarizes, attitudes and social move-

From *AIDS and Its Metaphors* (1988).

ments according to their relation to a "left" and a "right." The terms are usually traced back to the French Revolution, to the seating arrangements of the National Assembly in 1789, when republicans and radicals sat to the presiding officer's left and monarchists and conservatives sat to the right. But historical memory alone can't account for the startling longevity of this metaphor. It seems more likely that its persistence in discourse about politics to this day comes from a felt aptness to the modern, secular imagination of metaphors drawn from the body's orientation in space— left and right, top and bottom, forward and backward—for describing social conflict, a metaphoric practice that did add something new to the perennial description of society as a kind of body, a well-disciplined body ruled by a "head." This has been the dominant metaphor for the polity since Plato and Aristotle, perhaps because of its usefulness in justifying repression. Even more than comparing society to a family, comparing it to a body makes an authoritarian ordering of society seem inevitable, immutable.

Rudolf Virchow, the founder of cellular pathology, furnishes one of the rare scientifically significant examples of the reverse procedure, using political metaphors to talk about the body. In the biological controversies of the 1850s, it was the metaphor of the liberal state that Virchow found useful in advancing his theory of the cell as the fundamental unit of life. However complex their structures, organisms are, first of all, simply "multicellular"—multicitizened, as it were; the body is a "republic" or "unified commonwealth." Among scientist-rhetoricians Virchow was a maverick, not least because of the politics of his metaphors, which, by mid-nineteenth-century standards, are antiauthoritarian. But likening the body to a society, liberal or not, is less common than comparisons to other complex, integrated systems, such as a machine or an economic enterprise.

At the beginning of Western medicine, in Greece, important metaphors for the unity of the body were adapted from the arts. One such metaphor, harmony, was singled out for scorn several centuries later by Lucretius, who argued that it could not do justice to the fact that the body consists of essential and unessential organs, or even to the body's materiality: that is, to death. Here are the closing lines of Lucretius' dismissal of the musical metaphor—the earliest attack I know on metaphoric thinking about illness and health:

> Not all the organs, you must realize,
> Are equally important nor does health

Depend on all alike, but there are some—
The seeds of breathing, warm vitality—
Whereby we are kept alive; when these are gone
Life leaves our dying members. So, since mind
And spirit are by nature part of man,
Let the musicians keep that term brought down
To them from lofty Helicon—or maybe
They found it somewhere else, made it apply
To something hitherto nameless in their craft—
I speak of *harmony*. Whatever it is,
Give it back to the musicians.
        —*De Rerum Natura*, III, 124–35
                    trans. Rolfe Humphries

A history of metaphoric thinking about the body on this potent level of generality would include many images drawn from other arts and technology, notably architecture. Some metaphors are anti-explanatory, like the sermonizing, and poetic, notion enunciated by Saint Paul of the body as a temple. Some have considerable scientific resonance, such as the notion of the body as a factory, an image of the body's functioning under the sign of health, and of the body as a fortress, an image of the body that features catastrophe.

The fortress image has a long prescientific genealogy, with illness itself a metaphor for mortality, for human frailty and vulnerability. John Donne in his great cycle of prose arias on illness, *Devotions upon Emergent Occasions* (1627), written when he thought he was dying, describes illness as an enemy that invades, that lays siege to the body-fortress:

> We study Health, and we deliberate upon our meats, and drink, and ayre, and exercises, and we hew and wee polish every stone, that goes to that building; and so our Health is a long and a regular work; But in a minute a Canon batters all, overthrowes all, demolishes all; a Sicknes unprevented for all our diligence, unsuspected for all our curiositie. . . .

Some parts are more fragile than others: Donne speaks of the brain and the liver being able to endure the siege of an "unnatural" or "rebellious" fever that "will blow up the heart, like a mine, in a minute." In Donne's images, it is the illness that invades. Modern medical thinking could be said to begin when the gross military metaphor becomes specific, which can only happen with the advent of a new kind of scrutiny, represented in Virchow's cellular pathology, and a more precise under-

standing that illnesses were caused by specific, identifiable, visible (with
the aid of a microscope) organisms. It was when the invader was seen not
as the illness but as the microorganism that causes the illness that medicine really began to be effective, and the military metaphors took on new
credibility and precision. Since then, military metaphors have more and
more come to infuse all aspects of the description of the medical situation. Disease is seen as an invasion of alien organisms, to which the body
responds by its own military operations, such as the mobilizing of immunological "defenses," and medicine is "aggressive," as in the language of
most chemotherapies.

The grosser metaphor survives in public health education, where
disease is regularly described as invading the society, and efforts to reduce
mortality from a given disease are called a fight, a struggle, a war. Military
metaphors became prominent early in the century, in campaigns
mounted during World War I to educate people about syphilis, and after
the war about tuberculosis. One example, from the campaign against
tuberculosis conducted in Italy in the 1920s, is a poster called "*Guerre
alle Mosche*" (War against Flies), which illustrates the lethal effects of fly-
borne diseases. The flies themselves are shown as enemy aircraft dropping
bombs of death on an innocent population. The bombs have inscriptions.
One says "*Microbi*," microbes. Another says "*Germi della tisi*," the germs
of tuberculosis. Another simply says "*Malattia*," illness. A skeleton clad
in a hooded black cloak rides the foremost fly as passenger or pilot. In
another poster, "With These Weapons We Will Conquer Tuberculosis,"
the figure of death is shown pinned to the wall by drawn swords, each of
which bears an inscription that names a measure for combating tuberculosis. "Cleanliness" is written on one blade. "Sun" on another. "Air."
"Rest." "Proper food." "Hygiene." (Of course, none of these weapons was
of any significance. What conquers—that is, cures—tuberculosis is antibi-
otics, which were not discovered until some twenty years later, in the
1940s.)

Where once it was the physician who waged *bellum contra morbum*,
the war against disease, now it's the whole society. Indeed, the transformation of war-making into an occasion for mass ideological mobilization has
made the notion of war useful as a metaphor for all sorts of ameliorative
campaigns whose goals are cast as the defeat of an "enemy." We have had
wars against poverty, now replaced by "the war on drugs," as well as wars
against specific diseases, such as cancer. Abuse of the military metaphor
may be inevitable in a capitalist society, a society that increasingly restricts
the scope and credibility of appeals to ethical principle, in which it is

thought foolish not to subject one's actions to the calculus of self-interest and profitability. War-making is one of the few activities that people are not supposed to view "realistically"; that is, with an eye to expense and practical outcome. In all-out war, expenditure is all-out, unprudent—war being defined as an emergency in which no sacrifice is excessive. But the wars against diseases are not just calls for more zeal, and more money to be spent on research. The metaphor implements the way particularly dreaded diseases are envisaged as an alien "other," as enemies are in modern war; and the move from the demonization of the illness to the attribution of fault to the patient is an inevitable one, no matter if patients are thought of as victims. Victims suggest innocence. And innocence, by the inexorable logic that governs all relational terms, suggests guilt.

Military metaphors contribute to the stigmatizing of certain illnesses and, by extension, of those who are ill. It was the discovery of the stigmatization of people who have cancer that led me to write *Illness as Metaphor.*

Twelve years ago, when I became a cancer patient, what particularly enraged me—and distracted me from my own terror and despair at my doctors' gloomy prognosis—was seeing how much the very reputation of this illness added to the suffering of those who have it. Many fellow patients with whom I talked during my initial hospitalizations, like others I was to meet during the subsequent two and a half years that I received chemotherapy as an outpatient in several hospitals here and in France, evinced disgust at their disease and a kind of shame. They seemed to be in the grip of fantasies about their illness by which I was quite unseduced. And it occurred to me that some of these notions were the converse of now thoroughly discredited beliefs about tuberculosis. As tuberculosis had been often regarded sentimentally, as an enhancement of identity, cancer was regarded with irrational revulsion, as a diminution of the self. There were also similar fictions of responsibility and of a characterological predisposition to the illness: cancer is regarded as a disease to which the psychically defeated, the inexpressive, the repressed—especially those who have repressed anger or sexual feelings—are particularly prone, as tuberculosis was regarded throughout the nineteenth and early twentieth centuries (indeed, until it was discovered how to cure it) as a disease apt to strike the hypersensitive, the talented, the passionate.

These parallels—between myths about tuberculosis to which we can all feel superior now, and superstitions about cancer still given credence by many cancer patients and their families—gave me the main strategy of a little book I decided to write about the mystifications surrounding cancer. I didn't think it would be useful—and I wanted to be useful—to tell yet one more story in the first person of how someone learned that she or he had cancer, wept, struggled, was comforted, suffered, took courage . . . though mine was also that story. A narrative, it seemed to me, would be less useful than an idea. For narrative pleasure I would appeal to other writers; and although more examples from literature immediately came to mind for the glamorous disease, tuberculosis, I found the diagnosis of cancer as a disease of those who have not really lived in such books as Tolstoy's "The Death of Ivan Ilyich," Arnold Bennett's *Riceyman Steps*, and Bernanos's *The Diary of a Country Priest*.

And so I wrote my book, wrote it very quickly, spurred by evangelical zeal as well as anxiety about how much time I had left to do any living or writing in. My aim was to alleviate unnecessary suffering—exactly as Nietzsche formulated it, in a passage in *Daybreak* that I came across recently:

> *Thinking about illness!*—To calm the imagination of the invalid, so that at least he should not, as hitherto, have to suffer more from thinking about his illness than from the illness itself—that, I think, would be something! It would be a great deal!

The purpose of my book was to calm the imagination, not to incite it. Not to confer meaning, which is the traditional purpose of literary endeavor, but to deprive something of meaning: to apply that quixotic, highly polemical strategy, "against interpretation," to the real world this time. To the body. My purpose was, above all, practical. For it was my doleful observation, repeated again and again, that the metaphoric trappings that deform the experience of having cancer have very real consequences: they inhibit people from seeking treatment early enough, or from making a greater effort to get competent treatment. The metaphors and myths, I was convinced, kill. (For instance, they make people irrationally fearful of effective measures such as chemotherapy, and foster credence in thoroughly useless remedies such as diets and psychotherapy.) I wanted to offer other people who were ill and those who care for them an instrument to dissolve these metaphors, these inhibitions. I hoped to persuade terrified people who were ill to consult doctors, or to change their incompetent doctors for competent ones, who would give them proper care. To regard cancer as if it were just a disease—a very serious one, but just a disease. Not a curse, not a punishment, not an embarrassment. Without "meaning." And not necessarily a death sentence (one of the mystifications is that cancer = death). *Illness as Metaphor* is not just a polemic, it is an exhortation. I was saying: Get the doctors to tell you the truth; be an informed, active patient; find yourself good treatment, because good treatment does exist (amid the widespread ineptitude). Although *the* remedy does not exist, more than half of all cases can be cured by existing methods of treatment.

In the decade since I wrote *Illness as Metaphor*—and was cured of my own cancer, confounding my doctors' pessimism—attitudes about cancer have evolved. Getting cancer is not quite as much of a stigma, a creator of "spoiled identity" (to use Erving Goffman's expression). The word cancer is uttered more freely, and people are not often described anymore in obituaries as dying of a "very long illness." Although European and Japanese doctors still regularly impart a cancer diagnosis first to the family, and often counsel concealing it from the patient, American doctors have virtually abandoned this policy; indeed, a brutal announcement to the patient is now common. The new candor about cancer is part of the same obligatory candor (or lack of decorum) that brings us diagrams of the rectal-colon or genito-urinary tract ailments of our national leaders on television and on the front pages of newspapers—more and more it is precisely a virtue in our society to speak of what is supposed *not* to be named. The change can also be explained by the doctors' fear of lawsuits in a litigious society. And not least among the reasons that cancer is now treated less phobically, certainly with less secrecy, than a decade ago is that it is no longer the most feared disease. In recent years some of the onus of cancer has been lifted by the emergence of a disease whose charge of stigmatization, whose capacity to create spoiled identity, is far greater. It seems that societies need to have one illness which becomes identified with evil, and attaches blame to its "victims," but it is hard to be obsessed with more than one.

2

Just as one might predict for a disease that is not yet fully understood as well as extremely recalcitrant to treatment, the advent of this terrifying new disease, new at least in its epidemic form, has provided a large-scale occasion for the metaphorizing of illness.

Strictly speaking, AIDS—acquired immune deficiency syndrome—is not the name of an illness at all. It is the name of a medical condition, whose consequences are a spectrum of illnesses. In contrast to syphilis and cancer, which provide prototypes for most of the images and metaphors attached to AIDS, the very definition of AIDS requires the presence of other illnesses, so-called opportunistic infections and malignancies. But though not in *that* sense a single disease, AIDS lends itself to being regarded as one—in part because, unlike cancer and like syphilis, it is thought to have a single cause.

AIDS has a dual metaphoric genealogy. As a microprocess, it is described as cancer is: an invasion. When the focus is transmission of the disease, an older metaphor, reminiscent of syphilis, is invoked: pollution. (One gets it from the blood or sexual fluids of infected people or from contaminated blood products.) But the military metaphors used to describe AIDS have a somewhat different focus from those used in describing cancer. With cancer, the metaphor scants the issue of causality (still a murky topic in cancer research) and picks up at the point at which rogue cells inside the body mutate, eventually moving out from an original site or organ to overrun other organs or systems—a domestic subversion. In the description of AIDS the enemy is what causes the disease, an infectious agent that comes from the outside:

> The invader is tiny, about one sixteen-thousandth the size of the head of a pin. . . . Scouts of the body's immune system, large cells called macrophages, sense the presence of the diminutive foreigner and promptly alert the immune system. It begins to mobilize an array of cells that, among other things, produce antibodies to deal with the threat. Single-mindedly, the AIDS virus ignores many of the blood cells in its path, evades the rapidly advancing defenders and homes in on the master coordinator of the immune system, a helper T cell. . . .

This is the language of political paranoia, with its characteristic distrust of a pluralistic world. A defense system consisting of cells "that, among other things, produce antibodies to deal with the threat" is, predictably, no match for an invader who advances "single-mindedly." And the science-fiction flavor, already present in cancer talk, is even more pungent in accounts of AIDS—this one comes from *Time* magazine in late 1986— with infection described like the high-tech warfare for which we are being prepared (and inured) by the fantasies of our leaders and by video entertainments. In the era of Star Wars and Space Invaders, AIDS has proved an ideally comprehensible illness:

> On the surface of that cell, it finds a receptor into which one of its envelope proteins fits perfectly, like a key into a lock. Docking with the

cell, the virus penetrates the cell membrane and is stripped of its protective shell in the process. . . .

Next the invader takes up permanent residence, by a form of alien takeover familiar in science-fiction narratives. The body's own cells *become* the invader. With the help of an enzyme the virus carries with it,

> the naked AIDS virus converts its RNA into . . . DNA, the master molecule of life. The molecule then penetrates the cell nucleus, inserts itself into a chromosome and takes over part of the cellular machinery, directing it to produce more AIDS viruses. Eventually, overcome by its alien product, the cell swells and dies, releasing a flood of new viruses to attack other cells. . . .

As viruses attack other cells, runs the metaphor, so "a host of opportunistic diseases, normally warded off by a healthy immune system, attacks the body," whose integrity and vigor have been sapped by the sheer replication of "alien product" that follows the collapse of its immunological defenses. "Gradually weakened by the onslaught, the AIDS victim dies, sometimes in months, but almost always within a few years of the first symptoms." Those who have not already succumbed are described as "under assault, showing the telltale symptoms of the disease," while millions of others "harbor the virus, vulnerable at any time to a final, all-out attack."

Cancer makes cells proliferate; in AIDS, cells die. Even as this original model of AIDS (the mirror image of leukemia) has been altered, descriptions of how the virus does its work continue to echo the way the illness is perceived as infiltrating the society. "AIDS Virus Found to Hide in Cells, Eluding Detection by Normal Tests" was the headline of a recent front-page story in *The New York Times* announcing the discovery that the virus can "lurk" for years in the macrophages—disrupting their disease-fighting function without killing them, "even when the macrophages are filled almost to bursting with virus," and without producing antibodies, the chemicals the body makes in response to "invading agents" and whose presence has been regarded as an infallible marker of the syndrome.* That the virus isn't lethal for *all* the cells where it takes up

---

* The larger role assigned to the macrophages—"to serve as a reservoir for the AIDS virus because the virus multiplies in them but does not kill them, as it kills T-4 cells"—is said to explain the not uncommon difficulty of finding infected T-4 lymphocytes in patients who have antibodies to the virus and symptoms of AIDS. (It is still

residence, as is now thought, only increases the illness-foe's reputation for wiliness and invincibility.

What makes the viral assault so terrifying is that contamination, and therefore vulnerability, is understood as permanent. Even if someone infected were never to develop any symptoms—that is, the infection remained, or could by medical intervention be rendered, inactive—the viral enemy would be forever within. In fact, so it is believed, it is just a matter of time before something awakens ("triggers") it, before the appearance of "the telltale symptoms." Like syphilis, known to generations of doctors as "the great masquerader," AIDS is a clinical construction, an inference. It takes its identity from the presence of *some* among a long, and lengthening, roster of symptoms (no one has everything that AIDS could be), symptoms which "mean" that what the patient has is this illness. The construction of the illness rests on the invention not only of AIDS as a clinical entity but of a kind of junior AIDS, called AIDS-related complex (ARC), to which people are assigned if they show "early" and often intermittent symptoms of immunological deficit such as fevers, weight loss, fungal infections, and swollen lymph glands. AIDS is progressive, a disease of time. Once a certain density of symptoms is attained, the course of the illness can be swift, and brings atrocious suffering. Besides the commonest "presenting" illnesses (some hitherto unusual, at least in a fatal form, such as a rare skin cancer and a rare form of pneumonia), a plethora of disabling, disfiguring, and humiliating symptoms make the AIDS patient steadily more infirm, helpless, and unable to control or take care of basic functions and needs.

The sense in which AIDS is a slow disease makes it more like syphilis, which is characterized in terms of "stages," than like cancer. Thinking in terms of "stages" is essential to discourse about AIDS. Syphilis in its most dreaded form is "tertiary syphilis," syphilis in its third stage. What is called AIDS is generally understood as the last of three stages—the first of which is infection with a human immunodeficiency virus (HIV) and early evidence of inroads on the immune system—with a long latency

---

assumed that antibodies will develop once the virus spreads to these "key target" cells.) Evidence of presently infected populations of cells has been as puzzlingly limited or uneven as the evidence of infection in the populations of human societies—puzzling, because of the conviction that the disease is everywhere, and must spread. "Doctors have estimated that as few as one in a million T-4 cells are infected, which led some to ask where the virus hides. . . ." Another resonant speculation, reported in the same article (*The New York Times*, June 7, 1988): "Infected macrophages can transmit the virus to other cells, possibly by touching the cells."

period between infection and the onset of the "telltale" symptoms. (Apparently not as long as syphilis, in which the latency period between secondary and tertiary illness might be decades. But it is worth noting that when syphilis first appeared in epidemic form in Europe at the end of the fifteenth century, it was a rapid disease, of an unexplained virulence that is unknown today, in which death often occurred in the second stage, sometimes within months or a few years.) Cancer *grows* slowly: it is not thought to be, for a long time, latent. (A convincing account of a process in terms of "stages" seems invariably to include the notion of a normative delay or halt in the process, such as is supplied by the notion of latency.) True, a cancer is "staged." This is a principal tool of diagnosis, which means classifying it according to its gravity, determining how "advanced" it is. But it is mostly a spatial notion: that the cancer advances through the body, traveling or migrating along predictable routes. Cancer is first of all a disease of the body's geography, in contrast to syphilis and AIDS, whose definition depends on constructing a temporal sequence of stages.

Syphilis is an affliction that didn't have to run its ghastly full course, to paresis (as it did for Baudelaire and Maupassant and Jules de Goncourt), and could and often did remain at the stage of nuisance, indignity (as it did for Flaubert). The scourge was also a cliché, as Flaubert himself observed. "SYPHILIS. Everybody has it, more or less" reads one entry in the *Dictionary of Accepted Opinions*, his treasury of mid-nineteenth-century platitudes. And syphilis did manage to acquire a darkly positive association in late-nineteenth- and early-twentieth-century Europe, when a link was made between syphilis and heightened ("feverish") mental activity that parallels the connection made since the era of the Romantic writers between pulmonary tuberculosis and heightened emotional activity. As if in honor of all the notable writers and artists who ended their lives in syphilitic witlessness, it came to be believed that the brain lesions of neurosyphilis might actually inspire original thought or art. Thomas Mann, whose fiction is a storehouse of early-twentieth-century disease myths, makes this notion of syphilis as muse central to his *Doctor Faustus*, with its protagonist a great composer whose voluntarily contracted syphilis — the Devil guarantees that the infection will be limited to the central nervous system — confers on him twenty-four years of incandescent creativity. E. M. Cioran recalls how, in Romania in the late 1920s, syphilis-envy figured in his adolescent expectations of literary glory: he would discover that he had contracted syphilis, be rewarded with several hyperproductive years of genius, then collapse into madness. This romanticizing of the dementia characteristic of neurosyphilis was the forerunner of the much more persistent fantasy in this century about mental illness as a source of artistic creativity or spiritual originality. But with AIDS—though dementia is also a common, late symptom—no compensatory mythology has arisen, or seems likely to arise. AIDS, like cancer, does not allow romanticizing or sentimentalizing, perhaps because its association with death is too powerful. In Krzysztof Zanussi's film *Spiral* (1978), the most truthful account I know of anger at dying, the protagonist's illness is never specified; therefore, it *has* to be cancer. For several generations now, the generic idea of death has been a death from cancer, and a cancer death is experienced as a generic defeat. Now the generic rebuke to life and to hope is AIDS.

ACTIVE READING

1. Find several passages in which Sontag makes an argument "against" interpretation. Based on these passages, what do you think it means to be against interpretation? How does Sontag decide when to be against interpretation and when to be for it?

2. What specific observations does Sontag make about the metaphors she finds in the French Revolution, Virchow, and Lucretius? How does she use these observations when she discusses metaphors of illness? What new light might her discussion of illness metaphors shed on these earlier examples?

READING IN NEW CONTEXTS

1. Reread Sontag's first paragraph. Then list several metaphors from a text by Rosaldo, Shanley, or another writer who you believe works metaphorically. How do these metaphors shape your understanding of the text? What would it mean to be "for" or "against" these metaphors?

2. Apply Sontag's claim that "innocence . . . suggests guilt" (607) to a text by MacLeod, Kozol, or another *Literacies* writer you feel raises important questions about innocence and guilt. How convincing or

sufficient do you find your new interpretations of this reading? Based on your observations, what conclusions can you draw about Sontag's claim?

3. What relationship does Sontag see between historical circumstances and the uses of metaphors about illness? What relationship does Ewen see between historical circumstances and the uses of style? Looking at your responses to these questions, discuss any similarities you notice between style and metaphor.

DRAFT ONE / DRAFT TWO

1. *Draft One:* List some events in your life to which you have assigned some kind of metaphorical meaning. How do you draw these meanings out of the events you describe? What has happened to these meanings over time?

   Draft Two: Select a *Literacies* text that traces how the metaphorical meaning(s) of an event can change (Heker's story or Fienup-Riordan's essay might work well). What do your observations from Draft One help you say about the changes in meaning in the reading you chose? Develop your own theory of how and why metaphorical meaning changes.

2. *Draft One:* Sontag claims that "more and more it is . . . a virtue in our society to speak of what is supposed *not* to be named" (609). List some of the examples Sontag offers to support her claim. Then list some examples of your own (you might look at TV commercials, movies, news programs, conversations with friends). Based on your lists, when does it seem appropriate to speak of "what is supposed *not* to be named"? What is gained or lost by speaking in these situations?

   Draft Two: Select a couple of passages from Atwood, Baldwin, Scheper-Hughes, or another *Literacies* text in which someone speaks about events or issues that are not usually mentioned. Why are these issues named? What effect do these namings have on your interpretation of the text?

BEFORE READING AMY TAN

1. Think about some characteristics (both positive and negative) you associate with a particular cultural background. Where did your familiarity with these characteristics come from? How might these ideas influence your expectations about people from that background?

2. Recall an experience when you felt sure another person was misunderstanding you, even though he or she claimed to understand you. What do you think caused the communication barriers you sensed? At the time, how did you try to lessen them?

3. Describe the "polite" way to act in a particular social situation (at the dinner table, in the supermarket checkout line, when meeting a friend's family . . .). How did you learn the right way to behave in this situation? How do you respond to people who do not observe the same rules of polite behavior?

THE LANGUAGE
OF DISCRETION

At a recent family dinner in San Francisco, my mother whispered to me: "Sau-sau [Brother's Wife] pretends too hard to be polite! Why bother? In the end, she always takes everything."

My mother thinks like a *waixiao*, an expatriate, temporarily away from China since 1949, no longer patient with ritual courtesies. As if to prove her point, she reached across the table to offer my elderly aunt from Beijing the last scallop from the Happy Family seafood dish.

Sau-sau scowled. *"B'yao, zhen b'yao!"* (I don't want it, really I don't!) she cried, patting her plump stomach.

"Take it! Take it!" scolded my mother in Chinese.

"Full, I'm already full," Sau-sau protested weakly, eyeing the beloved scallop.

"Ai!" exclaimed my mother, completely exasperated. "Nobody else wants it. If you don't take it, it will only rot!"

At this point, Sau-sau sighed, acting as if she were doing my mother a big favor by taking the wretched scrap off her hands.

From *The State of the Language,* edited by Christopher Ricks and Leonard Michaels (1989).

My mother turned to her brother, a high-ranking communist official who was visiting her in California for the first time: "In America a Chinese person could starve to death. If you say you don't want it, they won't ask you again forever."

My uncle nodded and said he understood fully: Americans take things quickly because they have no time to be polite.

I thought about this misunderstanding again—of social contexts failing in translation—when a friend sent me an article from the *New York Times Magazine* (24 April 1988). The article, on changes in New York's Chinatown, made passing reference to the inherent ambivalence of the Chinese language.

Chinese people are so "discreet and modest," the article stated, there aren't even words for "yes" and "no."

That's not true, I thought, although I can see why an outsider might think that. I continued reading.

If one is Chinese, the article went on to say, "One compromises, one doesn't hazard a loss of face by an overemphatic response."

My throat seized. Why do people keep saying these things? As if we truly were those little dolls sold in Chinatown tourist shops, heads bobbing up and down in complacent agreement to anything said!

I worry about the effect of one-dimensional statements on the unwary and guileless. When they read about this so-called vocabulary deficit, do they also conclude that Chinese people evolved into a mild-mannered lot because the language only allowed them to hobble forth with minced words?

Something enormous is always lost in translation. Something insidious seeps into the gaps, especially when amateur linguists continue to compare, one-for-one, language differences and then put forth notions wide open to misinterpretation: that Chinese people have no direct linguistic means to make decisions, assert or deny, affirm or negate, just say no to drug dealers, or behave properly on the witness stand when told, "Please answer yes or no."

Yet one can argue, with the help of renowned linguists, that the Chinese are indeed up a creek without "yes" and "no." Take any number of variations on the old language-and-reality theory stated years ago by Edward Sapir: "Human beings . . . are very much at the mercy of the particular language which has become the medium for their society. . . .

The fact of the matter is that the 'real world' is to a large extent built up on the language habits of the group."[1]

This notion was further bolstered by the famous Sapir-Whorf hypothesis, which roughly states that one's perception of the world and how one functions in it depends a great deal on the language used. As Sapir, Whorf, and new carriers of the banner would have us believe, language shapes our thinking, channels us along certain patterns embedded in words, syntactic structures, and intonation patterns. Language has become the peg and the shelf that enables us to sort out and categorize the world. In English, we see "cats" and "dogs"; what if the language had also specified *glatz*, meaning "animals that leave fur on the sofa," and *glotz*, meaning "animals that leave fur and drool on the sofa"? How would language, the enabler, have changed our perceptions with slight vocabulary variations?

And if this were the case—of language being the master of destined thought—think of the opportunities lost from failure to evolve two little words, *yes* and *no*, the simplest of opposites! Ghenghis Khan could have been sent back to Mongolia. Opium wars might have been averted. The Cultural Revolution could have been sidestepped.

There are still many, from serious linguists to pop psychology cultists, who view language and reality as inextricably tied, one being the consequence of the other. We have traversed the range from the Sapir-Whorf hypothesis to est and neurolinguistic programming, which tell us "you are what you say."

I too have been intrigued by the theories. I can summarize, albeit badly, ages-old empirical evidence: of Eskimos and their infinite ways to say "snow," their ability to *see* the differences in snowflake configurations, thanks to the richness of their vocabulary, while non-Eskimo speakers like myself founder in "snow," "more snow," and "lots more where that came from."

I too have experienced dramatic cognitive awakenings via the word. Once I added "mauve" to my vocabulary I began to see it everywhere. When I learned how to pronounce *prix fixe*, I ate French food at prices better than the easier-to-say *à la carte* choices.

But just how seriously are we supposed to take this?

Sapir said something else about language and reality. It is the part that often gets left behind in the dot-dot-dots of quotes: ". . . No two lan-

1. Edward Sapir, *Selected Writings*, ed. D. G. Mandelbaum (Berkeley and Los Angeles, 1949).

guages are ever sufficiently similar to be considered as representing the same social reality. The worlds in which different societies live are distinct worlds, not merely the same world with different labels attached."

When I first read this, I thought, Here at last is validity for the dilemmas I felt growing up in a bicultural, bilingual family! As any child of immigrant parents knows, there's a special kind of double bind attached to knowing two languages. My parents, for example, spoke to me in both Chinese and English; I spoke back to them in English.

"Amy-ah!" they'd call to me.

"What?" I'd mumble back.

"Do not question us when we call," they scolded me in Chinese. "It is not respectful."

"What do you mean?"

"Ai! Didn't we just tell you not to question?"

To this day, I wonder which parts of my behavior were shaped by Chinese, which by English. I am tempted to think, for example, that if I am of two minds on some matter it is due to the richness of my linguistic experiences, not to any personal tendencies toward wishy-washiness. But which mind says what?

Was it perhaps patience—developed through years of deciphering my mother's fractured English—that had me listening politely while a woman announced over the phone that I had won one of five valuable prizes? Was it respect—pounded in by the Chinese imperative to accept convoluted explanations—that had me agreeing that I might find it worthwhile to drive seventy-five miles to view a time-share resort? Could I have been at a loss for words when asked, "Wouldn't you like to win a Hawaiian cruise or perhaps a fabulous Star of India designed exclusively by Carter and Van Arpels?"

And when this same woman called back a week later, this time complaining that I had missed my appointment, obviously it was my type A language that kicked into gear and interrupted her. Certainly, my blunt denial—"Frankly I'm not interested"—was as American as apple pie. And when she said, "But it's in Morgan Hill," and I shouted, "Read my lips. I don't care if it's Timbuktu," you can be sure I said it with the precise intonation expressing both cynicism and disgust.

It's dangerous business, this sorting out of language and behavior. Which one is English? Which is Chinese? The categories manifest themselves: passive and aggressive, tentative and assertive, indirect and direct. And I realize they are just variations of the same theme: that Chinese people are discreet and modest.

Reject them all!

If my reaction is overly strident, it is because I cannot come across as too emphatic. I grew up listening to the same lines over and over again, like so many rote expressions repeated in an English phrasebook. And I too almost came to believe them.

Yet if I consider my upbringing more carefully, I find there was nothing discreet about the Chinese language I grew up with. My parents made everything abundantly clear. Nothing wishy-washy in their demands, no compromises accepted: "Of course you will become a famous neurosurgeon," they told me. "And yes, a concert pianist on the side."

In fact, now that I remember, it seems that the more emphatic outbursts always spilled over into Chinese: "Not that way! You must wash rice so not a single grain spills out."

I do not believe that my parents—both immigrants from mainland China—are an exception to the modest-and-discreet rule. I have only to look at the number of Chinese engineering students skewing minority ratios at Berkeley, MIT, and Yale. Certainly they were not raised by passive mothers and fathers who said, "It is up to you, my daughter. Writer, welfare recipient, masseuse, or molecular engineer—you decide."

And my American mind says, See, those engineering students weren't able to say no to their parents' demands. But then my Chinese mind remembers: Ah, but those parents all wanted their sons and daughters to be *pre-med*.

Having listened to both Chinese and English, I also tend to be suspicious of any comparisons between the two languages. Typically, one language—that of the person doing the comparing—is often used as the standard, the benchmark for a logical form of expression. And so the language being compared is always in danger of being judged deficient or superfluous, simplistic or unnecessarily complex, melodious or cacophonous. English speakers point out that Chinese is extremely difficult because it relies on variations in tone barely discernible to the human ear. By the same token, Chinese speakers tell me English is extremely difficult because it is inconsistent, a language of too many broken rules, of Mickey Mice and Donald Ducks.

Even more dangerous to my mind is the temptation to compare both language and behavior *in translation*. To listen to my mother speak English, one might think she has no concept of past or future tense, that she doesn't see the difference between singular and plural, that she is gender blind because she calls my husband "she." If one were not careful, one might also generalize that, based on the way my mother talks, all

Chinese people take a circumlocutory route to get to the point. It is, in fact, my mother's idiosyncratic behavior to ramble a bit.

Sapir was right about differences between two languages and their realities. I can illustrate why word-for-word translation is not enough to translate meaning and intent. I once received a letter from China which I read to non-Chinese speaking friends. The letter, originally written in Chinese, had been translated by my brother-in law in Beijing. One portion described the time when my uncle at age ten discovered his widowed mother (my grandmother) had remarried—as a number three concubine, the ultimate disgrace for an honorable family. The translated version of my uncle's letter read in part:

> In 1925, I met my mother in Shanghai. When she came to me, I didn't have greeting to her as if seeing nothing. She pull me to a corner secretly and asked me why didn't have greeting to her. I couldn't control myself and cried, "Ma! Why did you leave us? People told me: one day you ate a beancake yourself. Your sister in-law found it and sweared at you, called your names. So . . . is it true?" She clasped my hand and answered immediately, "It's not true, don't say what like this." After this time, there was a few chance to meet her.

"What!" cried my friends. "Was eating a beancake so terrible?"

Of course not. The beancake was simply a euphemism; a ten-year-old boy did not dare question his mother on something as shocking as concubinage. Eating a beancake was his equivalent for committing this selfish act, something inconsiderate of all family members, hence, my grandmother's despairing response to what seemed like a ludicrous charge of gluttony. And sure enough, she was banished from the family, and my uncle saw her only a few times before her death.

While the above may fuel people's argument that Chinese is indeed a language of extreme discretion, it does not mean that Chinese people speak in secrets and riddles. The contexts are fully understood. It is only to those on the *outside* that the language seems cryptic, the behavior inscrutable.

I am, evidently, one of the outsiders. My nephew in Shanghai, who recently started taking English lessons, has been writing me letters in English. I had told him I was a fiction writer, and so in one letter he wrote, "Congratulate to you on your writing. Perhaps one day I should like to read it." I took it in the same vein as "Perhaps one day we can get together for lunch." I sent back a cheery note. A month went by and another letter arrived from Shanghai. "Last one perhaps I hadn't writing distinctly," he said. "In the future, you'll send a copy of your works for me."

I try to explain to my English-speaking friends that Chinese language use is more *strategic* in manner, whereas English tends to be more direct; an American business executive may say, "Let's make a deal," and the Chinese manager may reply, "Is your son interested in learning about your widget business?" Each to his or her own purpose, each with his or her own linguistic path. But I hesitate to add more to the pile of generalizations, because no matter how many examples I provide and explain, I fear that it appears defensive and only reinforces the image: that Chinese people are "discreet and modest"—and it takes an American to explain what they really mean.

Why am I complaining? The description seems harmless enough (after all, the *New York Times Magazine* writer did not say "slippery and evasive"). It is precisely the bland, easy acceptability of the phrase that worries me.

I worry that the dominant society may see Chinese people from a limited—and limiting—perspective. I worry that seemingly benign stereotypes may be part of the reason there are few Chinese in top management positions, in mainstream political roles. I worry about the power of language: that if one says anything enough times—in *any* language—it might become true.

Could this be why Chinese friends of my parents' generation are willing to accept the generalization?

"Why are you complaining?" one of them said to me. "If people think we are modest and polite, let them think that. Wouldn't Americans be pleased to admit they are thought of as polite?"

And I do believe anyone would take the description as a compliment—at first. But after a while, it annoys, as if the only things that people heard one say were phatic remarks: "I'm so pleased to meet you. I've heard many wonderful things about you. For me? You shouldn't have!"

These remarks are not representative of new ideas, honest emotions, or considered thought. They are what is said from the polite distance of social contexts: of greetings, farewells, wedding thank-you notes, convenient excuses, and the like.

It makes me wonder though. How many anthropologists, how many sociologists, how many travel journalists have documented so-called "natural interactions" in foreign lands, all observed with spiral notebook in hand? How many other cases are there of the long-lost primitive tribe, people who turned out to be sophisticated enough to put on the stone-age show that ethnologists had come to see?

And how many tourists fresh off the bus have wandered into Chinatown expecting the self-effacing shopkeeper to admit under duress that the goods are not worth the price asked? I have witnessed it.

"I don't know," the tourist said to the shopkeeper, a Cantonese woman in her fifties. "It doesn't look genuine to me. I'll give you three dollars."

"You don't like my price, go somewhere else," said the shopkeeper.

"You are not a nice person," cried the shocked tourist, "not a nice person at all!"

"Who say I have to be nice," snapped the shopkeeper.

"So how does one say 'yes' and 'no' in Chinese?" ask my friends a bit warily.

And here I do agree in part with the *New York Times Magazine* article. There is no one word for "yes" or "no"—but not out of necessity to be discreet. If anything, I would say the Chinese equivalent of answering "yes" or "no" is dis*crete*, that is, specific to what is asked.

Ask a Chinese person if he or she has eaten, and he or she might say *chrle* (eaten already) or perhaps *meiyou* (have not).

Ask, "So you had insurance at the time of the accident?" and the response would be *dwei* (correct) or *meiyou* (did not have).

Ask, "Have you stopped beating your wife?" and the answer refers directly to the proposition being asserted or denied: stopped already, still have not, never beat, have no wife.

What could be clearer?

As for those who are still wondering how to translate the language of discretion, I offer this personal example.

My aunt and uncle were about to return to Beijing after a three-month visit to the United States. On their last night I announced I wanted to take them out to dinner.

"Are you hungry?" I asked in Chinese.

"Not hungry," said my uncle promptly, the same response he once gave me ten minutes before he suffered a low-blood-sugar attack.

"Not too hungry," said my aunt. "Perhaps you're hungry?"

"A little," I admitted.

"We can eat, we can eat," they both consented.

"What kind of food?" I asked.

"Oh, doesn't matter. Anything will do. Nothing fancy, just some simple food is fine."

"Do you like Japanese food? We haven't had that yet," I suggested.

They looked at each other.

"We can eat it," said my uncle bravely, this survivor of the Long March.

"We have eaten it before," added my aunt. "Raw fish."

"Oh, you don't like it?" I said. "Don't be polite. We can go somewhere else."

"We are not being polite. We can eat it," my aunt insisted.

So I drove them to Japantown and we walked past several restaurants featuring colorful plastic displays of sushi.

"Not this one, not this one either," I continued to say, as if searching for a Japanese restaurant similar to the last. "Here it is," I finally said, turning into a restaurant famous for its Chinese fish dishes from Shandong.

"Oh, Chinese food!" cried my aunt, obviously relieved.

My uncle patted my arm. "You think Chinese."

"It's your last night here in America," I said. "So don't be polite. Act like an American."

And that night we ate a banquet.

ACTIVE READING

1. Look up the terms "discreet" and "discrete" in a college dictionary. Working with passages from her essay, analyze the relationship Tan creates between these words. What ideas does this relationship help her get across?

2. Use your responses to Before Reading #2 and #3 to explore the misunderstanding that Tan describes at the beginning of her essay. In what ways is this anecdote about different ideas of politeness? In what ways is it about miscommunication?

3. Define what you think Tan means when she says she has "experienced dramatic cognitive awakenings via the word" (619). Use your definition of this idea to analyze a time when new vocabulary or a new understanding of a term changed your views or behavior.

READING IN NEW CONTEXTS

1. Tan suggests that the "unwary and guileless" are most vulnerable to the mistakes that are a part of describing other cultures (618). With the help of communication specialist Barnlund or anthropologists Rosaldo and Scheper-Hughes, develop some guidelines that address Tan's concerns about the pitfalls of intercultural communication.

2. Tan often focuses on moments when people's interpretations of events are affected by the different cultural contexts they come from. How do her ideas help to clarify a similar moment in Heker's or Walker's stories? What can you say about the different cultures that come into conflict in those texts?

3. Tan, Black Elk, and el-Saadawi all confront the challenges of living biculturally, but they write about these challenges in different ways. Looking at Tan's and another *Literacies* essay, explain what these differences in approach and writing style might say about the goals of each writer.

DRAFT ONE / DRAFT TWO

1. *Draft One:* Tan addresses what might be called "complimentary" stereotypes about the Chinese. In your response to Before Reading #1, which of the cultural characteristics you described might fall into this category? Using Tan's warnings as your model, explain some problems that such "complimentary" stereotypes might cause for the group you describe.

Draft Two: Fienup-Riordan, MacLeod, and el-Saadawi offer information about different people's strategies (conscious or unconscious) for dealing with stereotypes. Looking closely at one of these texts, speculate about how Tan would respond to this other writer's or group's ways of handling stereotypical images of themselves.

2. *Draft One:* Explore Tan's ideas about translation by examining your own use of different "languages": academic, scientific, vocational, generational, etc. How well do Tan's ideas account for your experience of moving back and forth between these languages within the language?

Draft Two: Use the ideas you developed in Draft One to reconsider a difficult passage from another *Literacies* essay. How might the idea of "translation" help you discover something new about this passage? As you work through the passage from this perspective, discuss what you gain and lose through translation. How does your understanding of Tan change when you look at translation from this perspective?

BEFORE READING ALICE WALKER

1. How and why do people remember their family history? How and why do they lose track of it?

2. Interview someone who left home to be educated. What were some of the consequences? How did the person negotiate between the old life and the new?

3. List some objects and words that you associate with your heritage. Describe your relations to a few of these. What do these relations suggest about your attitude to heritage?

4. The events of this story seem to take place in the 1960s. What public events in those years might have been especially important to its African American characters?

A L I C E   W A L K E R

EVERYDAY USE

for your grandmama

I will wait for her in the yard that Maggie and I made so clean and wavy yesterday afternoon. A yard like this is more comfortable than most people know. It is not just a yard. It is like an extended living room. When the hard clay is swept clean as a floor and the fine sand around the edges lined with tiny, irregular grooves, anyone can come and sit and look up into the elm tree and wait for the breezes that never come inside the house.

Maggie will be nervous until after her sister goes: she will stand hopelessly in corners, homely and ashamed of the burn scars down her arms and legs, eying her sister with a mixture of envy and awe. She thinks her sister has held life always in the palm of one hand, that "no" is a word the world never learned to say to her.

You've no doubt seen those TV shows where the child who has "made it" is confronted, as a surprise, by her own mother and father, tottering in weakly from backstage. (A pleasant surprise, of course: What would they

From *In Love & Trouble* (1973).

629

do if parent and child came on the show only to curse out and insult each other?) On TV mother and child embrace and smile into each other's faces. Sometimes the mother and father weep, the child wraps them in her arms and leans across the table to tell how she would not have made it without their help. I have seen these programs.

Sometimes I dream a dream in which Dee and I are suddenly brought together on a TV program of this sort. Out of a dark and soft-seated limousine I am ushered into a bright room filled with many people. There I meet a smiling, gray, sporty man like Johnny Carson who shakes my hand and tells me what a fine girl I have. Then we are on the stage and Dee is embracing me with tears in her eyes. She pins on my dress a large orchid, even though she has told me once that she thinks orchids are tacky flowers.

In real life I am a large, big-boned woman with rough, man-working hands. In the winter I wear flannel nightgowns to bed and overalls during the day. I can kill and clean a hog as mercilessly as a man. My fat keeps me hot in zero weather. I can work outside all day, breaking ice to get water for washing; I can eat pork liver cooked over the open fire minutes after it comes steaming from the hog. One winter I knocked a bull calf straight in the brain between the eyes with a sledge hammer and had the meat hung up to chill before nightfall. But of course all this does not show on television. I am the way my daughter would want me to be: a hundred pounds lighter, my skin like an uncooked barley pancake. My hair glistens in the hot bright lights. Johnny Carson has much to do to keep up with my quick and witty tongue.

But that is a mistake. I know even before I wake up. Who ever knew a Johnson with a quick tongue? Who can even imagine me looking a strange white man in the eye? It seems to me I have talked to them always with one foot raised in flight, with my head turned in whichever way is farthest from them. Dee, though. She would always look anyone in the eye. Hesitation was no part of her nature.

"How do I look, Mama?" Maggie says, showing just enough of her thin body enveloped in pink skirt and red blouse for me to know she's there, almost hidden by the door.

"Come out into the yard," I say.

Have you ever seen a lame animal, perhaps a dog run over by some careless person rich enough to own a car, sidle up to someone who is ignorant enough to be kind to him? That is the way my Maggie walks.

She has been like this, chin on chest, eyes on ground, feet in shuffle, ever since the fire that burned the other house to the ground.

Dee is lighter than Maggie, with nicer hair and a fuller figure. She's a woman now, though sometimes I forget. How long ago was it that the other house burned? Ten, twelve years? Sometimes I can still hear the flames and feel Maggie's arms sticking to me, her hair smoking and her dress falling off her in little black papery flakes. Her eyes seemed stretched open, blazed open by the flames reflected in them. And Dee. I see her standing off under the sweet gum tree she used to dig gum out of; a look of concentration on her face as she watched the last dingy gray board of the house fall in toward the red-hot brick chimney. Why don't you do a dance around the ashes? I'd wanted to ask her. She had hated the house that much.

I used to think she hated Maggie, too. But that was before we raised the money, the church and me, to send her to Augusta to school. She used to read to us without pity; forcing words, lies, other folks' habits, whole lives upon us two, sitting trapped and ignorant underneath her voice. She washed us in a river of make-believe, burned us with a lot of knowledge we didn't necessarily need to know. Pressed us to her with the serious way she read, to shove us away at just the moment, like dimwits, we seemed about to understand.

Dee wanted nice things. A yellow organdy dress to wear to her graduation from high school; black pumps to match a green suit she'd made from an old suit somebody gave me. She was determined to stare down any disaster in her efforts. Her eyelids would not flicker for minutes at a time. Often I fought off the temptation to shake her. At sixteen she had a style of her own: and knew what style was.

I never had an education myself. After second grade the school was closed down. Don't ask my why: in 1927 colored asked fewer questions than they do now. Sometimes Maggie reads to me. She stumbles along good-naturedly but can't see well. She knows she is not bright. Like good looks and money, quickness passed her by. She will marry John Thomas (who has mossy teeth in an earnest face) and then I'll be free to sit here and I guess just sing church songs to myself. Although I never was a good singer. Never could carry a tune. I was always better at a man's job. I used to love to milk till I was hooked in the side in '49. Cows are soothing and slow and don't bother you, unless you try to milk them the wrong way.

I have deliberately turned my back on the house. It is three rooms, just like the one that burned, except the roof is tin; they don't make shingle roofs any more. There are no real windows, just some holes cut in the sides, like the portholes in a ship, but not round and not square, with rawhide holding the shutters up on the outside. This house is in a pasture, too, like the other one. No doubt when Dee sees it she will want to tear it down. She wrote me once that no matter where we "choose" to live, she will manage to come see us. But she will never bring her friends. Maggie and I thought about this and Maggie asked me, "Mama, when did Dee ever *have* any friends?"

She had a few. Furtive boys in pink shirts hanging about on washday after school. Nervous girls who never laughed. Impressed with her they worshiped the well-turned phrase, the cute shape, the scalding humor that erupted like bubbles in lye. She read to them.

When she was courting Jimmy T she didn't have much time to pay to us, but turned all her faultfinding power on him. He *flew* to marry a cheap city girl from a family of ignorant flashy people. She hardly had time to recompose herself.

When she comes I will meet—but there they are!

Maggie attempts to make a dash for the house, in her shuffling way, but I stay her with my hand. "Come back here," I say. And she stops and tries to dig a well in the sand with her toe.

It is hard to see them clearly through the strong sun. But even the first glimpse of leg out of the car tells me it is Dee. Her feet were always neat-looking, as if God himself had shaped them with a certain style. From the other side of the car comes a short, stocky man. Hair is all over his head a foot long and hanging from his chin like a kinky mule tail. I hear Maggie suck in her breath. "Uhnnnh," is what it sounds like. Like when you see the wriggling end of a snake just in front of your foot on the road. "Uhnnnh."

Dee next. A dress down to the ground, in this hot weather. A dress so loud it hurts my eyes. There are yellows and oranges enough to throw back the light of the sun. I feel my whole face warming from the heat waves it throws out. Earrings gold, too, and hanging down to her shoulders. Bracelets dangling and making noises when she moves her arm up to shake the folds of the dress out of her armpits. The dress is loose and flows, and as she walks closer, I like it. I hear Maggie go "Uhnnnh" again. It is her sister's hair. It stands straight up like the wool on a sheep. It is black as night and around the edges are two long pigtails that rope about like small lizards disappearing behind her ears.

"Wa-su-zo-Tean-o!" she says, coming on in that gliding way the dress makes her move. The short stocky fellow with the hair to his navel is all grinning and he follows up with "Asalamalakim, my mother and sister!" He moves to hug Maggie but she falls back, right up against the back of my chair. I feel her trembling there and when I look up I see the perspiration falling off her chin.

"Don't get up," says Dee. Since I am stout it takes something of a push. You can see me trying to move a second or two before I make it. She turns, showing white heels through her sandals, and goes back to the car. Out she peeks next with a Polaroid. She stoops down quickly and lines up picture after picture of me sitting there in front of the house with Maggie cowering behind me. She never takes a shot without making sure the house is included. When a cow comes nibbling around the edge of the yard she snaps it and me and Maggie *and* the house. Then she puts the Polaroid in the back seat of the car, and comes up and kisses me on the forehead.

Meanwhile Asalamalakim is going through motions with Maggie's hand. Maggie's hand is as limp as a fish, and probably as cold, despite the sweat, and she keeps trying to pull it back. It looks like Asalamalakim wants to shake hands but wants to do it fancy. Or maybe he don't know how people shake hands. Anyhow, he soon gives up on Maggie.

"Well," I say. "Dee."

"No, Mama," she says. "Not 'Dee,' Wangero Leewanika Kemanjo!"

"What happened to 'Dee'?" I wanted to know.

"She's dead," Wangero said. "I couldn't bear it any longer, being named after the people who oppress me."

"You know as well as me you was named after your aunt Dicie," I said. Dicie is my sister. She named Dee. We called her "Big Dee" after Dee was born.

"But who was *she* named after?" asked Wangero.

"I guess after Grandma Dee," I said.

"And who was she named after?" asked Wangero.

"Her mother," I said, and saw Wangero was getting tired. "That's about as far back as I can trace it," I said. Though, in fact, I probably could have carried it back beyond the Civil War through the branches.

"Well," said Asalamalakim, "there you are."

"Uhnnnh," I heard Maggie say.

"There I was not," I said, "before 'Dicie' cropped up in our family, so why should I try to trace it that far back?"

He just stood there grinning, looking down on me like somebody inspecting a Model A car. Every once in a while he and Wangero sent eye signals over my head.

"How do you pronounce this name?" I asked.

"You don't have to call me by it if you don't want to," said Wangero.

"Why shouldn't I?" I asked. "If that's what you want us to call you, we'll call you."

"I know it might sound awkward at first," said Wangero.

"I'll get used to it," I said. "Ream it out again."

Well, soon we got the name out of the way. Asalamalakim had a name twice as long and three times as hard. After I tripped over it two or three times he told me to just call him Hakim-a-barber. I wanted to ask him was he a barber, but I didn't really think he was, so I didn't ask.

"You must belong to those beef-cattle peoples down the road," I said. They said "Asalamalakim" when they met you, too, but they didn't shake hands. Always too busy: feeding the cattle, fixing the fences, putting up salt-lick shelters, throwing down hay. When the white folks poisoned some of the herd the men stayed up all night with rifles in their hands. I walked a mile and a half just to see the sight.

Hakim-a-barber said, "I accept some of their doctrines, but farming and raising cattle is not my style." (They didn't tell me, and I didn't ask, whether Wangero (Dee) had really gone and married him.)

We sat down to eat and right away he said he didn't eat collards and pork was unclean. Wangero, though, went on through the chitlins and corn bread, the greens and everything else. She talked a blue streak over the sweet potatoes. Everything delighted her. Even the fact that we still used the benches her daddy made for the table when we couldn't afford to buy chairs.

"Oh, Mama!" she cried. Then turned to Hakim-a-barber. "I never knew how lovely these benches are. You can feel the rump prints," she said, running her hands underneath her and along the bench. Then she gave a sigh and her hand closed over Grandma Dee's butter dish. "That's it!" she said. "I knew there was something I wanted to ask you if I could have." She jumped up from the table and went over in the corner where the churn stood, the milk in it clabber by now. She looked at the churn and looked at it.

"This churn top is what I need," she said. "Didn't Uncle Buddy whittle it out of a tree you all used to have?"

"Yes," I said.

"Uh huh," she said happily. "And I want the dasher, too."

"Uncle Buddy whittle that, too?" asked the barber.

Dee (Wangero) looked up at me.

"Aunt Dee's first husband whittled the dash," said Maggie so low you almost couldn't hear her. "His name was Henry, but they called him Stash."

"Maggie's brain is like an elephant's," Wangero said, laughing. "I can use the churn top as a centerpiece for the alcove table," she said, sliding a plate over the churn, "and I'll think of something artistic to do with the dasher."

When she finished wrapping the dasher the handle stuck out. I took it for a moment in my hands. You didn't even have to look close to see where hands pushing the dasher up and down to make butter had left a kind of sink in the wood. In fact, there were a lot of small sinks; you could see where thumbs and fingers had sunk into the wood. It was beautiful light yellow wood, from a tree that grew in the yard where Big Dee and Stash had lived.

After dinner Dee (Wangero) went to the trunk at the foot of my bed and started rifling through it. Maggie hung back in the kitchen over the dishpan. Out came Wangero with two quilts. They had been pieced by Grandma Dee and then Big Dee and me had hung them on the quilt frames on the front porch and quilted them. One was in the Lone Star pattern. The other was Walk Around the Mountain. In both of them were scraps of dresses Grandma Dee had worn fifty and more years ago. Bits and pieces of Grandpa Jarrell's Paisley shirts. And one teeny faded blue piece, about the size of a penny matchbox, that was from Great Grandpa Ezra's uniform that he wore in the Civil War.

"Mama," Wangero said sweet as a bird. "Can I have these old quilts?"

I heard something fall in the kitchen, and a minute later the kitchen door slammed.

"Why don't you take one or two of the others?" I asked. "These old things was just done by me and Big Dee from some tops your grandma pieced before she died."

"No," said Wangero. "I don't want those. They are stitched around the borders by machine."

"That'll make them last better," I said.

"That's not the point," said Wangero. "These are all pieces of dresses Grandma used to wear. She did all this stitching by hand. Imagine!" She held the quilts securely in her arms, stroking them.

"Some of the pieces, like those lavender ones, come from old clothes her mother handed down to her," I said, moving up to touch the quilts.

Dee (Wangero) moved back just enough so that I couldn't reach the quilts. They already belonged to her.

"Imagine!" she breathed again, clutching them closely to her bosom.

"The truth is," I said, "I promised to give them quilts to Maggie, for when she marries John Thomas."

She gasped like a bee had stung her.

"Maggie can't appreciate these quilts!" she said. "She'd probably be backward enough to put them to everyday use."

"I reckon she would," I said. "God knows I been saving 'em for long enough with nobody using 'em. I hope she will!" I didn't want to bring up how I had offered Dee (Wangero) a quilt when she went away to college. Then she had told me they were old-fashioned, out of style.

"But they're *priceless!*" she was saying now, furiously; for she has a temper. "Maggie would put them on the bed and in five years they'd be in rags. Less than that!"

"She can always make some more," I said. "Maggie knows how to quilt."

Dee (Wangero) looked at me with hatred. "You just will not understand. The point is these quilts, *these* quilts!"

"Well," I said, stumped. "What would *you* do with them?"

"Hang them," she said. As if that was the only thing you *could* do with quilts.

Maggie by now was standing in the door. I could almost hear the sound her feet made as they scraped over each other.

"She can have them, Mama," she said, like somebody used to never winning anything, or having anything reserved for her. "I can 'member Grandma Dee without the quilts."

I looked at her hard. She had filled her bottom lip with checkerberry snuff and it gave her face a kind of dopey, hangdog look. It was Grandma Dee and Big Dee who taught her how to quilt herself. She stood there with her scarred hands hidden in the folds of her skirt. She looked at her sister with something like fear but she wasn't mad at her. This was Maggie's portion. This was the way she knew God to work.

When I looked at her like that something hit me in the top of my head and ran down to the soles of my feet. Just like when I'm in church and the spirit of God touches me and I get happy and shout. I did something I never had done before: hugged Maggie to me, then dragged her on into the room, snatched the quilts out of Miss Wangero's hands and dumped them into Maggie's lap. Maggie just sat there on my bed with her mouth open.

"Take one or two of the others," I said to Dee.

But she turned without a word and went out to Hakim-a-barber.

"You just don't understand," she said, as Maggie and I came out to the car.

"What don't I understand?" I wanted to know.

"Your heritage," she said. And then she turned to Maggie, kissed her, and said, "You ought to try to make something of yourself, too, Maggie. It's really a new day for us. But from the way you and Mama still live you'd never know it."

She put on some sunglasses that hid everything above the tip of her nose and her chin.

Maggie smiled; maybe at the sunglasses. But a real smile, not scared. After we watched the car dust settle I asked Maggie to bring me a dip of snuff. And then the two of us sat there just enjoying, until it was time to go in the house and go to bed.

ACTIVE READING

1. During the story the narrator mentions several differences between Wangero and her sister, or between Wangero and the narrator. What are these differences, and how much of the story's conflict do they help explain?

2. List several cultural objects and customs that are mentioned in the story. How do Wangero, Maggie, and her mother relate to them? Based on your findings, explain how heritage works in their lives.

3. What words do Wangero, Maggie, and her mother use to describe what they value? What do you make of the argument Wangero and the narrator have about naming? What role does the choice of words play in the battle over heritage?

4. Point out some of the differences between the imaginary TV reunion and the one that actually takes place later in the story. What values are at work for various characters in the two reunions? What does each reunion help you notice about the other?

READING IN NEW CONTEXTS

1. In this story and another *Literacies* text, such as MacLeod, Kingston, or Baldwin, locate several passages where family life is made more complicated by the family's place in society. What social practices or values impinge upon a family's ways? How do family members respond?

2. Ewen talks about members of a particular social class who "assemble" an identity in the "semiotic world of objects" (196). How does that process work in this story? How can Ewen's general theory about American history be applied to particularities of African American experience in the 1960s?

3. Use the stories of several individuals or characters you have read about this semester to evaluate the idea that family and society carry the antidotes to each other's poisons.

4. In how many different ways do characters in this story put elements of their heritage to "everyday use"? Use your answer as a guide for analyzing the uses of heritage described in another *Literacies* reading.

DRAFT ONE / DRAFT TWO

1. *Draft One:* Follow up on Reading in New Contexts #4 by applying your answer to another *Literacies* text, such as Rodriguez or Fienup-Riordan, which presents a cultural conflict. How do people use heritage in the cultural conflict described in that text?

   Draft Two: In Draft Two, consider a *Literacies* text that offers a social criticism, such as Bellah. Use Draft One and the new text to discuss the relations you see between social criticism and the use of heritage.

2. *Draft One:* Recall a significant family story that you have heard over the years. Who tells this story, and under what circumstances? Write a version of the story that is as faithful as possible to the family member's way of telling it. How does the storyteller use heritage in telling this story?

Draft Two: Address the same questions for a family portrayed in another *Literacies* reading, such as MacLeod, Angelou, or Rodriguez. What do the stories from your family and the family from the new reading allow you to say about the ways in which storytellers use heritage?

BEFORE READING JEFFREY WEEKS

1. What are some consequences of social uncertainty? Mention some kinds of uncertainty that commonly affect communities, and discuss the resources community members have for handling the problems this uncertainty raises.

2. What are rights and where do they come from? In your experience, what happens when one person's or group's rights conflict with another's?

3. How is AIDS (Acquired Immune Deficiency Syndrome) affecting your town or city? What does your community's response to AIDS say about its values? Discuss any conflicts you notice.

J E F F R E Y   W E E K S

VALUES IN AN AGE
OF UNCERTAINTY

We live in an age of uncertainty, when firm guarantees seem in short supply and our cultural goals are clouded and indeterminate. Nowhere is this uncertainty more acute than in the domain of sexuality, which has been the focus of so many recent moral panics and controversies. Is it still possible, then, to elaborate a coherent set of values and principles without surrendering to absolutism or fundamentalist beliefs of one sort or another? I believe the answer is yes, but I want to reach this tentative conclusion by first exploring some of the dilemmas that face us. And as an introduction to those dilemmas I shall begin with a particular crisis that confronts us all, a crisis that must dominate our thinking about sexuality today: the health crisis generated by HIV infection, summed up in the powerful and symbolic term "AIDS."

I agree fully with those who refuse to see "AIDS" as a metaphor for anything. It is, as AIDS activists have put it, "a natural disaster," though one helped along by prejudice, discrimination, and less than benign neglect. It is not a judgment from God, not "nature's revenge" on any group of people, not a symbol of a culture gone wrong. HIV disease is an

From *Discourses of Sexuality: From Aristotle to AIDS,* edited by Domna C. Stanton (1992).

illness like any other, and it should be confronted with all the compassion, empathy, and resources that other major health crises demand. But that is not, of course, how it has been seen. As the baroque language and the proliferation of metaphors surrounding it suggest, the response to HIV has not been like the response to any other virus.[1] During the 1980s AIDS became a symbol of a culture at odds with itself, a global issue that evoked a multitude of local passions, moralities, and prejudices, the epitome of a civilization whose values were uncertain. The AIDS crisis throws into relief many contemporary discontents and dilemmas, exposing many a dark and murky corner of our collective unconscious. Any discussion of sexual values as we approach the end of the millennium must therefore confront the challenge of AIDS.[2]

Of course, the person with HIV or AIDS must live with uncertainty all the time: the uncertainty of diagnosis, of prognosis, of reactions of friends, families, loved ones, of anonymous and fearful or hate-filled others. Everyone else must live with uncertainty too: the uncertainty bred of risk, of possible infection, of *not* knowing, of loss. Uncertainty breeds anxiety and fear: about the past and for the present and future. For the impact of AIDS is not predetermined but haphazard. Despite efforts to prove the contrary, there is no straightforward correlation between lifestyle and HIV infection. The virus itself, though potentially devastating in its effects, is relatively weak and is not easily transmitted except through interchange of bodily fluids. People who "do risky things" do not necessarily fall ill. As yet ill-understood cofactors (way of life, general health, incidence of poverty and other diseases) may ease the way; but a high element of chance determines who will get HIV and then who among these will succumb to opportunistic diseases. "Contingency" is a hallmark of the AIDS crisis.

Chance, accident, contingency: these are more than characteristics of a particular set of diseases. They appear as markers of the present, when things happen to us without apparent rationale or justification. The hope of modernity, that we could control nature, become the masters of all we survey, may be brought to naught by a stray assassin's bullet, by the fluttering of a butterfly in the jungles of Asia—or by a microscopic organism unknown until the 1980s.

Yet though the event may be random and unexpected, the ways in

---

1. See, for example, Susan Sontag, *AIDS and Its Metaphors* (London: Allen Lane, 1989).

2. For a more detailed discussion of this theme see Jeffrey Weeks, "Postmodern AIDS?," *Ecstatic Antibodies: Resisting the AIDS Mythology*, ed. Tessa Boffin and Sunil Gupta (London: Rivers Oram Press, 1990) 133–41.

which we respond are not. AIDS may be a modern phenomenon, *the* disease of the *fin de millennium*, but it is already a remarkably historicized phenomenon, framed by histories that burden people living with HIV and AIDS with a weight they should not have to bear. There are histories of previous diseases and response to diseases. There are histories of sexuality, especially the unorthodox sexualities, and histories of the ways in which sexuality has been regulated. There are histories of racial categorization, of development and undevelopment. There are histories of moral panics, of punitive interventions, of various forms of oppression, and of resistance. We are overwhelmed with histories, and with the lessons they could, but usually do not, teach us. But they have one thing in common. They are histories of difference and diversity. So with AIDS. Despite the common viral and immunological factors, HIV and AIDS are experienced differently by different groups of people. The suffering and loss felt by gay men in the urban communities of large Western cities is no less nor greater than the suffering or loss of the poor in the black and Hispanic communities of New York or in the cities and villages of East Africa; but it is different.

AIDS is a syndrome that can threaten catastrophe on an unprecedented scale, but it is experienced, directly or empathetically, as a particular, historically and culturally organized series of diseases. AIDS is both global and local in its impact, and this reveals something vital about the historic present. It reminds us, first of all, about our interdependence. Migrations across countries and continents, from country to town, from "traditional" ways of life to "modern," in flight from persecution, poverty, or sexual repression, made the spread of HIV possible. The modern information society, global programs, international consultations and conferences also make possible a worldwide response to threatening disaster. Yet the very scale and speed of this internationalization of experience force us to seek localized or specialized identities, to resurrect or create particularist traditions, to invent moralities. Part of the shock of AIDS, as Paula A. Treichler has put it, was "the shock of identity."[3] In becoming aware of the global village, we seem to need to affirm and reaffirm our local loyalties, our different identities.

HIV and AIDS have also provided the challenge and opportunities for creating new identities and communities, forged in the furnace of suffering, loss, and survival: a testimony to the possibilities of realizing human bonds across the chasms of an unforgiving culture. One among innumer-

3. Paula A. Treichler, "AIDS, Homophobia and Bio-Medical Discourse," *Cultural Studies* 1 (October 1987): 3.

able examples is this testimony from the historian of homosexuality in the military, the historian Joseph Interrante, who lost his partner to the epidemic:

> Paul's illness and death condensed our life experience, and we grew and changed through it as we would through any experience, albeit at a greatly accelerated pace. But Paul's death, and AIDS generally, was not a good thing. It was not romantic, it was not heroic, it was not kind. We shared it, and I discovered, to quote Gerda Lerner, that it is "like life— untidy, tangled, tormented, transcendent. And we accept it finally because we must. Because we are human."[4]

I thus see in the AIDS crisis, and in the response it has engendered, three elements that cast a sharp light on wider currents and concerns. First, many regard AIDS as reinforcing a general sense of crisis, a "sense of an ending," generated by rapid cultural change. This is the crisis of modernity, the herald of the controversial concept of "postmodernity." Secondly, AIDS exposes the complexities and interdependence of the world, a globalization that produces, as if by a necessary reflex, a burgeoning of new identities, new communities, and conflicting demands and obligations. This is the site of many of the most acute political, social, and cultural debates today. But thirdly, these very changes, which seem to many to illustrate the final collapse of the enlightened hopes of modernity, have produced new solidarities as people grapple with the challenges of "postmodernity" in humane ways. Here, I believe, lie the real possibilities of what I shall call "radical humanism." This is a perspective that rejects the essentialism and limitations of traditional humanism and recognizes the contingency of truth—claiming systems of belief while at the same time reaffirming some of the more enduring values of the Enlightenment tradition. This is a humanism, moreover, that is grounded in people's struggles, experiences, and particular histories.

These three tendencies, illuminated by the AIDS crisis but having a wider significance, provide the unifying strands for the rest of my essay. In exploring them my purpose is to demonstrate that we have the opportunity to reinvent or rediscover values that help us to live with what seems to me the only irreducible truth of the contemporary world: the fact of human and social diversity, including sexual diversity. This is the real challenge of living with uncertainty.

4. Joseph Interrante, "To Have without Holding: Memories of Life with a Person with AIDS," *Radical America* 20, n. 6 (1987): 61.

ON APPROACHES TO SEXUALITY

My work on sexuality has been shaped by a rejection of what have come to be known as essentialist arguments and an attempt to elaborate what has generally, though inadequately, been called "social constructionism." Over the past twenty years theories of sexuality as a purely natural phenomenon, of human drives as fixed and inherent, of our identities as dictated by that nature and those drives, and thus of a history of sexuality merely as an account of reactions to those basic biological givens, have been profoundly challenged, building on a century of challenges to essentialist modes of thought. Through anthropology and social analysis we have strengthened our awareness of the relativity and complexity of sexual norms. From Freud we can derive (though sadly most interpreters have not) insights into the tentative and always provisional nature of gender and sexual identities. From the new social history we have become aware of the multiple narratives of sexual life. Since feminism, lesbian and gay politics, and the theoretical work of Michel Foucault we are increasingly sensitive to the subtle forms of power that invest the body and make us simultaneously subjected to and subjects of sex. And we have recognized that ideology works precisely by making us believe that what is socially created and therefore subjected to change is really natural and therefore immutable. We no longer believe that of all social phenomena sexuality is the least changeable but, on the contrary, that it is probably the most sensitive to social influence, a conductor of the subtlest of changes in social mores and power relations. All these influences in turn feed into the deconstructionist project, which questions the fixities and certainties of post-Enlightenment humanism, rationalism, and progressivism.[5]

As a result we increasingly recognize that sexuality can only be understood in its specific historical and cultural context. There cannot

5. For a discussion of all these themes see Jeffrey Weeks, *Sexuality and Its Discontents: Meanings, Myths and Modern Sexualities* (London: Routledge and Kegan Paul, 1985); and *Against Nature: Essays on History, Sexuality and Identity* (London: Rivers Oram Press, 1991). The attempt to recover the radicalism of Freud, particularly by emphasizing his disruption of identity, is perhaps the most controversial of these themes. On this see Jacqueline Rose, *Sexuality in the Field of Vision* (London: Verso, 1986). For the new social history, particularly as inspired by feminist scholarship, see, as examples, Carroll Smith-Rosenberg, *Disorderly Conduct: Visions of Gender in Victorian America* (Oxford and New York: Oxford University Press, 1985); and John D'Emilio, *Sexual Politics, Sexual Communities: The Making of a Homosexual Minority in the United States, 1940–1970* (Chicago and London: University of Chicago Press, 1983).

be an all-embracing history of sexuality, only local histories, contextual meanings, specific analyses. Instead of universalistic arguments which assume a common experience throughout time and history we need, to use Eve Sedgwick's distinction, particularist arguments that strive to understand the specifics of any sexual phenomenon: the histories that organize it, the power structures that shape it, and the struggles that attempt to define it.[6]

• • •

And yet many people fear that if identities are conceived of as historically contingent, then they will lose all solidity and meaning. This points to a real problem. Social constructionism does not carry with it any obvious political program. It can be used as much by sexual conservatives as by sexual progressives. In the attempt to ban the "promotion" of homosexuality in Britain in 1987–88, culminating in the passing into law of the notorious Clause 28 of the Local Government Act, the bill's proponents explicitly argued that homosexuality could be promoted and learned — hence the bill's justification.[7] Of course, the logical corollary is that heterosexuality could equally well be learned, and is in fact promoted all the time by the institutions of our culture. But by and large heterosexuality has not been subjected to the same vigorous inquiry as homosexuality.[8] Very few people are interested in tracing its social construction. It is still regarded as the natural norm from which all else is an unfortunate perversion.

Against the uncertainties of constructionism, then, many seek the certainty of nature. Isn't it better, the argument seems to go, to define lesbians and gays as a permanent and fixed minority of the population, like a racial minority, and to claim their place as a legitimate minority on that basis? Early campaigners for gay rights used precisely that justifica-

6. Eve Sedgwick has usefully suggested that rather than speak any longer about essentialism versus constructionism, which has led to a tired and repetitive (and perhaps incomprehensible) internal debate among students of sexuality, we should think in terms of universalistic and particularist positions: Eve Kosovsky Sedgwick, *The Epistemology of the Closet* (Berkeley: University of California Press, 1990).
7. Clause 28, passed into law in 1988, sought to outlaw the promotion by local authorities of homosexuality as a "pretended family relationship." For a discussion of its implications see my essay, "Pretended Family Relationships," *Against Nature*.
8. Carole S. Vance, "Social Constructionist Theory: Problems in the History of Sexuality," *Homosexuality, Which Homosexuality?*, ed. Anja van Kooten Niekerk and Theo van der Meer (Amsterdam: Uitgeverij An Dekker/Schorer; London: GMP Publishers, 1989) 13–34.

tion. From pioneers such as Ulrichs and Hirschfeld through to the early Mattachine Society, the idea that homosexuals constituted a third or intermediate sex, or a permanent minority, has shaped sexual politics.[9] But it did not prevent the Nazis from using precisely the same argument to persecute homosexuals and to send them to die in concentration camps.

The reality is that theoretical perspectives alone cannot promote a particular outcome. Their effectiveness is dictated by the meanings they glue together in specific power relations. Sexual identities, as I have suggested, are important not because they are either "natural" or "social," but because they provide a basis of positive social identification. Such an identification is important for the sense of security and belonging that is necessary for a productive social life. It also makes possible the achievement of that sense of common cause with others which is indispensable for political struggle against those who would deny the validity of a chosen way of life. For this reason many writers closely identified with both feminist sexual politics and the deconstructionist approach have recently argued for what they call a "strategic essentialism," based not in nature or truth but the political field of force—in my terms, a necessary fiction.[10]

The crucial factor, then, is not the truthful or mythic nature of sexual identities but their effectiveness and political relevance. Sexuality, as Foucault put it, is not a fatality; it is a possibility for creative life.[11] And in creating that life, we need to be clearer than ever before about the values that motivate us and to be able to affirm and validate them in a convincing way.

IDENTITY AND COMMUNITY AGAIN

The contestation of the narratives of the Enlightenment co-exists with a continuing desire for certainty, for a common value system. The roots

9. Karl Heinrich Ulrichs was a German theorist of homosexuality in the 1860s and 1870s. Magnus Hirschfeld was a giant in the German sexology and sex reform movements from the 1890s onwards. The Mattachine Society was established in the USA in the late 1940s and was the pioneering homophile organization there.
10. See Diana Fuss, *Essentially Speaking: Feminism, Nature and Difference* (New York and London: Routledge, 1990). For a wide-ranging discussion of the complexities of the essentialist/constructionist debates see Jonathan Dollimore, *Sexual Dissidence: Augustine to Wilde, Freud to Foucault* (Oxford: Clarendon Press, 1991).
11. Michel Foucault, "Sex, Power and the Politics of Identity" (interview by Bob Gallagher and Alexander Wilson), *The Advocate* n. 400 (1984): 29.

of that desire may have been undermined, but the desire is constantly reaffirmed, most dramatically in recent times in the revival of fundamentalisms of various sorts. Yet those fundamentalisms are the "truths" of distinct groups, specific traditions, which have little hope of generalizing their belief systems over unbelievers, whatever the depth of their faith, the violence of their rhetoric, or the local effects of their communal or legislative powers. The increasing complexity of the social world, the growing intermingling of experiences—and hence the proliferation of possible social belongings and identities—constantly work to undermine the idea that there can be a single truth that must be revealed, whether this is the truth of the body, of gender, of sexuality, of race or nation, or anything else. There are, it appears, only local and partial truths, relative positions, relational identities. Is it possible, then, to inhabit any identity, sexual, racial, or political, without a feeling of being arbitrarily trapped within contingent and limiting categories, pinned like butterflies to the table? The British feminist writer Denise Riley wonders whether it is even possible to inhabit a gender without a feeling of horror.[12]

The question of identity is made even more problematic because of the existence of conflicting values, both among different communities and within our own heads. Debates over values are particularly fraught and delicate because they are not simply speculations about the world and our place in it. They touch on fundamental and deeply felt issues about who we are and what we want to be or become. They also pose what increasingly can be seen as a key question in late twentieth-century politics: how to reconcile our collective needs as human beings with our specific needs as individuals and members of diverse communities.

As the black British sociologist Paul Gilroy has put it, unable to control the social relations in which they find themselves, people have shrunk the world to the size of their communities and begun to act politically on that basis.[13] The result has been the development of a variety of pseudo-pluralisms, in which difference became a substitute for any wider moral strategy, and a "category politics," which prefers a militant particularism to the finding of a common language. But without a sense of the limits of particularist communities and in the absence of some sense of common purpose, the results have often been politically nugatory, where they were

---

12. Denise Riley, "Am I That Name?": Feminism and the Category of "Women" in History (London: Macmillan, 1988).
13. Paul Gilroy, There Ain't No Black in the Union Jack (London: Hutchinson, 1987) 245.

not disastrous.[14] The danger lies not in commitments to community and difference but in their exclusive nature. Community all too often becomes the focus of retreat from the challenges of modernity, while identity becomes a fixed attribute to hold on to at all costs. Yet, as the political theorist Michael Sandel writes:

> Each of us moves in an indefinite number of communities, some more inclusive than others, each making different claims on our allegiance, and there is no saying in advance which is *the* society or community whose purpose should govern the disposition of any particular set of our attributes and endowments.[15]

Difference can never be absolute nor identities finally fixed in the modern world. In a brilliant essay on "Cultural Identity and Diaspora," Stuart Hall rethinks the positioning and repositioning of Caribbean cultural identities in terms of three presences: *Présence Africaine*, the site of the repressed, apparently silenced by the burden of slavery and colonization but present everywhere in Caribbean life; *Présence Européenne*, the site of power, exclusion, imposition, and expropriation but which has become a constitutive element in Caribbean identities; and finally, the *Présence Américaine*, the ground, place, and territory of identity, the site of diaspora, what makes Afro-Caribbean people a people of difference. The Afro-Caribbean identity cannot be defined as essence or purity but, as Hall puts it, "by the recognition of a necessary heterogeneity and diversity; by a concept of 'identity' which lives with and through, not despite, difference; by *hybridity*."[16]

Hybridity, however, is not simply the characteristic of diaspora peoples, but, it can be argued, a marked feature of all identities in the contemporary world, despite the historically organized differences and inequalities among peoples. For identity is not a finished product but a continuing process, which is never finally achieved or completed, of shaping and reshaping into a viable narrative the fragments and diverse experiences of personal and social life, organized as they are through "violent hierarchies" of power and difference. Essentialist views of identity offer a

14. On this see Kobena Mercer, "Welcome to the Jungle: Identity and Diversity in Postmodern Politics," and other essays in *Identity: Community, Culture, Difference*, ed. Jonathan Rutherford (London: Lawrence and Wishart, 1990).

15. Michael J. Sandel, *Liberalism and the Limits of Justice* (Cambridge: Cambridge University Press, 1982) 146.

16. Stuart Hall, "Cultural Identity and Diaspora," *Identity* 235.

final closure which can never be true to the experience of people living through various communities. Hence the paradox: identities are invented in complex histories but apparently essential in negotiating the hazards of everyday life. They provide the sense of belonging that makes social life possible; but they are constantly subject to reassessment and change. They seem to make us whole, but in their variety they signal our allegiances to diverse communities.

The fluidity of identities, and the diversity they reflect, provides the terrain of modern politics in general and sexual politics in particular. To see identity and community as multiple and open creates a space in which political change becomes possible. Benedict Anderson has argued that communities must be distinguished not by their falsity or genuineness but by the style in which they are imagined.[17] How to achieve a new style of debate about values, and in the context of this essay, sexual values, is the supreme challenge of the recognition of difference.

FOR AN ETHICS OF MORAL PLURALISM

Is it possible, then, to construct a common normative standard by which we can affirm different identities and ways of life? Can we balance relativism and some sense of minimal universal values? For would-be reformers of sexual life in earlier periods the answer lay in science and history. But these provide an inadequate basis for a common standard of values today. We no longer fully trust "Science" with a capital S; and we sense that history lacks a hidden dynamic pressing toward enlightenment.

In the absence of a common language for dealing with the dilemma of difference, two types of arguments have emerged. The first is the "discourse of rights," probably still the most powerful mobilizing force in politics and ethics and the one around which most struggles over sexuality focus. Unfortunately, the claim to right does not easily reveal whose rights are to be respected. The rights of lesbians and gay men are denied as often as they are recognized. "The rights of women" are highly contested, even among women. And in the case of abortion, the conflict between "the rights of the unborn child" and the right of a woman to control her own fertility is unresolvable because two value systems pull in violently different directions. The problem is that rights do not spring fully armed from nature and cannot find a justification simply because they are

17. Benedict Anderson, *Imagined Communities: Reflections on the Origin and Rise of Nationalism* (London: Verso, 1982) 15.

claimed. Rights are products of human association, social organization, historical definitions of needs and obligations, and traditions of struggles. Whatever their assumption of universality, they are limited by the philosophical traditions to which they belong and by the social and political contexts in which they are asserted.

The second major argument, the "discourse of emancipation," assumes that difference will be transcended by "liberation." However, there are conflicts over the meaning of emancipation and the "emancipatory potential" of different social movements. Many feminists regarded the sexual liberationists of the 1960s as having increased the burden of sexual oppression on women. And not many people have been prepared to support the emancipatory potential of the pedophile movement. More often than not, the social movements claiming an emancipatory potential tend to represent the militant particularism of some rather than a social emancipation for all. The politics of emancipation, however appealing, have been no more able than the discourse of rights to provide a common set of values for coping with difference.

Against this uncertainty, it is, I believe, important to develop a language of politics that recognizes the positive value of diversity. The starting point for this is an emphasis on the "good" as a human creation, not a gift from heaven, a revelation from science, or an imposition from without, but something we all are involved in developing and defining. "The good," Foucault said, "is defined by us, it is practised, it is invented. And this is a collective work."[18] This collective work in turn relies on the elaboration, invention even, of traditions of values that provide meaning and context.

One thinks, as Ernesto Laclau has put it, from a tradition.[19] Traditions are the context of any truth. As arguments continue over time, they embody their own principles for demarcating the appropriate from the inappropriate, right from wrong. Which traditions we align ourselves with depends on a host of contingencies of birth and location, as much as on conscious choice. We have no absolute grounds for saying one tradition is better than another. But I personally want to align myself with those traditions that prefer tolerance to intolerance, choice to authoritarianism,

18. Michel Foucault, "Power, Moral Values, and the Intellectual" (interview with Michel Foucault conducted by Michael Bess, 3 November 1980), *History of the Present*, n. 4 (Spring 1988): 13.
19. Ernesto Laclau, *New Reflections on the Revolution of Our Time* (London: Verso, 1990) 219.

individual autonomy to group uniformity, and pluralism to absolutism. This is the terrain of what I call *radical pluralism*. It is a tradition like any other. It has roots and points of departure, drawing on the principles of the democratic revolution, of popular struggles for rights and autonomy, of humanism. It is a tradition still in evolution that does not claim to have "truth" on its side. Indeed, if it became a dominant way of seeing the world, many truths would flourish.

In many ways, of course, radical pluralism draws on central values in the liberal tradition: its commitment to toleration and individual autonomy above all. The argument is not against liberalism *per se* nor, certainly, against the achievements of liberal democracy. The problem lies, rather, in the limitations of those achievements. The aim of a *radical* pluralism is to realize the possibilities of liberalism by identifying and combatting the forces that limit its full potentiality: above all, institutionalized inequalities and structures of domination and subordination. It therefore simultaneously draws on traditions other than the liberal one: traditions of feminist analysis, antiracist struggle, democratic and humanist socialism. To put it another way, the achievement of a radical and plural democracy is a project to be constructed, a set of values to be worked for against the institutional barriers that inhibit the possibilities of its realization. Radical pluralism is an argument for a more open and democratic culture which does not assume any historic inevitability nor any *a priori* justification in "the nature of humankind." Its success will not be measured by the attainment of an ideal society but by its ability to respond to individual and collective needs as these evolve and change over time. Like every other, it is an "invented tradition," whose merits can only be demonstrated pragmatically, in concrete historical circumstances.

The guiding principles of this radical pluralism, and in my view the indispensable starting point for thinking about values in a diverse world, are freedom and life. In their book the *Postmodern Political Condition*, Agnes Heller and Ferenc Feher see these as the two minimum universal values, fundamental to a range of systems of thought and ethics.[20] Social systems and forms of regulation can be regarded as just, they suggest, insofar as they share common institutions, maximize the opportunities for communication and discourse, and are controlled by the conditional value of equality: "equal freedom" and "equal life chances" for all. In a pluralistic cultural universe, writes Heller elsewhere, there are "good lives":

20. Agnes Heller and Ferenc Feher, *The Postmodern Political Condition* (Cambridge: Polity Press, 1988).

Different ways of life can be good, and can be equally good. Yet a life-style good for one person may not be good for another person. The authentic plurality of ways of life is the condition under which the life of each and every person can be good.[21]

It follows that the radically different life goals and cultural patterns of different people should be beyond formal regulation to the extent that they are based on the conditions of equal freedom and equal life chances.

There are clearly problems with this claim to universality. It apparently conflicts with the reality of different, and clashing, value systems. I would argue, however, that the claim to universality lies not in the actual current acceptance of these "minimum common values," but in their potentiality for acceptance. They provide the minimum basis for the elaboration of a universalistic set of values that can tolerate difference. These abstract values, of course, need to be further elaborated; this is precisely the project of what we can best call a radical humanism.

I want now to explore three key ideas, which in my view provide ways of developing values around sexuality in the context of this wider inquiry: the idea of morals as pluralistic, situational, and relative; a commitment to the continuing democratization of everyday life; and the setting out of certain rights of everyday life, the necessary guarantee for the protection of individuals. I want to look at each in turn.

The central idea of radical pluralism involves respect for different ways of life, different ways of being human and of achieving self-determined ends. Since values are relative and context-bound, no act in itself can be either good or bad. We can make judgments only by attempting to understand the internal meanings of any action, the power relations at play, the subtle coercions of daily life that limit autonomy, and the formal structures of domination and subordination. But this simple idea is difficult to apply. Radical pluralism requires a set of values that can make pluralism and choice meaningful.

This suggests, as a second key theme, the application of the principle of democracy to the personal sphere. Our concepts are rightly shaped by a commitment to formal democracy at the level of national government and to vaguer notions of participation in other spheres of life. Democratic values in everyday life would judge acts by the way people deal with one another, the absence of coercion, the degree of pleasure and of needs they can satisfy. This suggests in turn a notion of reciprocity that does not

21. Agnes Heller, *Beyond Justice* (Oxford: Basil Blackwell, 1987) 323.

calculate benefits or costs but is sustained over time and acts as a moral cement of involvement. This is often present in the obligations of family life. It is also a key characteristic of many of the alternative foci of daily life. A sense of moral involvement with others, of common belonging sustained over time without expectation of direct or immediate reward except that of mutual support, is characteristic of what Ann Ferguson has called "chosen families," whether of lesbians and gays or others who choose to live outside conventional domestic arrangements.[22] It is also a marked feature of the support systems built up as a response to the AIDS crisis. The idea of reciprocity assumes a sense of common need and common involvement, a compassion and solidarity based on care and responsibility for others. A situational ethic is necessarily an ethic of responsibility because it is about the responsibility of choice: choice about how to live, with whom, under what circumstances. It is concerned with respect for, and the enhancement of, human dignity.

These values provide a context for asking whether there are any distinctive rights of everyday life. One present throughout this discussion is the right to difference. The recognition of diversity and acceptance of individual differences grow out of and facilitate a solidarity based on mutual respect. Indeed, it has been well argued that the right to equality, under whose banner all modern revolutions have been fought, is being replaced by an appeal to the right to difference.[23]

A second claim hovering over this discussion of personal life is the right to space. I use this idea as a metaphor for freedom for people to determine the needs and conditions of their lives. The space for individual self-determination and autonomy is constrained and limited by a host of factors, from economic deprivation and endemic poverty to the structured inequalities along lines of race, gender, sexuality, age, and culture. Calling for freedom of space does not, therefore, mean that we can take for granted that individuals have the necessary means of attaining autonomy. On the contrary, it is establishing an ethical principle against which the limits of freedom can be measured. It offers an objective to be achieved, against all the barriers that inhibit its attainment.

Freedom and autonomy are of course conditional on the acceptance of the principle that these values do not involve the treatment of another person or group of people as mere means. Radical pluralism can only

22. Ann Ferguson, *Blood at the Root: Motherhood, Sexuality and Male Dominance* (London: Pandora, 1989).
23. Bauman, "From Pillars to Post."

work if individuals and groups are prepared to accept that a condition of freedom or space for their way of life is a tolerance of the space of others. Protection of minorities must be a principle of a plural society on the condition that the minorities themselves guarantee the freedom of individuals and thus variety or autonomy for all their members, including the right of exit. In turn, the freedom of exit must be accompanied by the public freedom of voice, which at bottom is the guarantee of all the freedoms and rights of everyday life.

The new elective communities that have emerged in the past generation, particularly around sexuality, have been described as laboratories of social life. These "experiments in living," as Mill described them over a century ago in his essay on liberty,[24] set forth new ways of seeing and describing everyday life and hence put forward new ways of life. Only through a radical tolerance of experimentation and continuous dialogue can new ways of life be properly tested.

Ernesto Laclau has argued that "the first condition of a radically democratic society is to accept the contingent and radically open character of all its values—and in that sense, to abandon the aspiration to a single foundation."[25] That means that the obligation is simply transferred to us to create, choose, and clarify our values. In the end we must choose where our alignments must lie. My position, which I have described as radical pluralism, is clearly located in a certain tradition of humanist thought, and I am aware of the dubious origins of some of that thinking.[26] But I believe it nonetheless contains elements for understanding and learning how to live with the irreducible and irreversible variety and diversity of modern life. Radical pluralism is not a position to be imposed, but it is one that can be argued for and argued above all in the domain of sexuality.

In an interview in 1980 Foucault offered three principles for his morals:

(1) the refusal to accept as self-evident the things that are proposed to us; (2) the need to analyze and to know, since we can understand nothing without reflection and understanding—thus the principle of curios-

24. John Stuart Mill, "On Liberty," *Three Essays: On Liberty, Representative Government, The Subjection of Women*, intro. Richard Wollheim (Oxford and New York: Oxford University Press, 1975).
25. Laclau 125.
26. On the exclusion of women from the liberal humanist tradition see Carole Pateman, *The Sexual Contract* (Cambridge: Polity Press, 1988).

ity; and (3) the principle of innovation: to seek out in our reflection those things that have never been thought or imagined. Thus: refusal, curiosity, innovation.[27]

Foucault's skepticism about received wisdoms, combined with a willingness to confront the challenges of change, seems to me a good position from which to measure the transformations of personal life in general and sexual life in particular. In my view the arguments for a radical pluralism I have put forward here are rooted in those transformations. That does not mean that we are living in a world that is yet willing to accept the positive merits of diversity. The barriers to the full realization of diversity are still high. But we can measure how far we still have to go only by exploring the spaces of personal life and the conflicts around sexuality within them. That seems an appropriate way for us to learn to live with uncertainty.

27. Foucault, "Power, Moral Values, and the Intellectual" 1.

ACTIVE READING

1. Weeks argues that individuals' sexual identities are "constructed" rather than "essential." Find passages from his essay that help you explain some differences between "constructionist" and "essentialist" understandings of human behavior. Then apply your understanding of these terms to the notions of "community," "rights," or another of Weeks's concepts.

2. To what extent does Weeks's essay address individuals? Where is he more concerned with the beliefs and actions of groups? Based on your responses to these questions, explain how Weeks's ideas might apply differently to individuals and to groups.

3. Weeks uses the phrase "invented tradition" (652) to explain his goal of radical pluralism. Find as many other references to "invention" in Weeks's essay as you can. Try to figure out how invention works, who can use it, what it might be good for, and what its possible drawbacks might be. How important is this idea for Weeks's overall arguments?

READING IN NEW CONTEXTS

1. Look closely at the Indian communities in de Saint Victor's essay, the Chinese village in Kingston's essay, or the Amish family in Fishman's essay. What kinds of uncertainty do these people face, and how do they deal with it? How might Weeks's suggestions about living with uncertainty challenge some of their usual attitudes and actions? (Your response to Before Reading #1 may be helpful here.)

2. Weeks suggests that "hybridity" is a common feature of "all identities in the contemporary world" (649). Try applying Weeks's theory to a text about people who straddle two or more cultural identities (Tan and el-Saadawi are possibilities). Then use his theory to discuss a text whose subjects are more firmly planted in a single cultural tradition (try Mac-Leod or Scheper-Hughes). How does your interpretation of Weeks's theory change when you apply it to different contexts?

3. In "Marxism and Lakota Tradition," Frank Black Elk looks at Western political structures through the lens of Lakota beliefs. Using your understanding of Weeks's ideas, show where Black Elk's perspectives resemble what Weeks calls "radical pluralism," and where they might be more "essentialist."

DRAFT ONE / DRAFT TWO

1. *Draft One:* Weeks claims that the rapid global movement of people and information "force[s] us to seek localized or specialized identities" (643). To what extent does another writer's treatment of travel support Weeks's argument? (Clifford's, Durham's, or Anzaldúa's texts might be helpful here.)

   Draft Two: How much do different *kinds* of travel contribute to the identities that people create for themselves? Explain how your ideas from Draft One change when the travelers in question are migrating workers (as in MacLeod's or Rodriguez's texts) rather than Clifford's tourists or Durham's Cherokees.

2. *Draft One:* In his essay, Weeks questions common definitions of "liberation" and "human rights." Find ideas from another text (like el-Saadawi, Shanley, or Bellah) that help you explore why someone might need or want to redefine these common concepts.

Draft Two: Use the ideas you generated in Draft One to talk about a *Literacies* text (like Angelou, Kozol, or Garson) in which someone's rights are endangered or violated. How do the experiences discussed in the second text fit in with the theories about liberation expressed in the other texts? What does your analysis tell you about the relationship between theory and practice?

ASSIGNMENT SEQUENCES

Whether it's used to describe pieces of music, poems, or even college courses, the word "sequence" suggests a set of interconnected activities, each one building upon and transforming the ones that come before it. In putting together this set of assignment sequences, the editors of *Literacies* started with some fairly broad questions, such as "How do ideas of self-expression fit into our practices as writers?" or "How does 'power' really work in our day-to-day lives?" We then assembled groups of readings that offer perspectives on these questions and suggest new questions in turn. Though the word "sequence" comes from a Latin word meaning "to follow," we don't think of these assignments as maps designed to take you safely from point A to point B. Instead, the more closely you work with these readings and assignments, the more new directions you will find to explore. Like a skillfully constructed series of sonnets or a set of complex jazz improvisations, both of which reward careful rereading or relistening, each assignment will send you back to the texts in *Literacies*, back to class discussion, back to your earlier written responses. You will have many opportunities to trace out new and potentially useful lines of thought. Most important, the answers you develop here will always be open to reconsideration in the face of new information and new experiences.

SEQUENCE 1
THE SOCIAL CONTEXTS OF LITERACY

Andrea R. Fishman, "Becoming Literate: A Lesson from the Amish"
Shirley Brice Heath, "Literate Traditions"
Robert Scholes, "On Reading a Video Text"
Nancy Scheper-Hughes, "The Anthropological Looking Glass"

What is literacy? Strictly speaking, literacy is the ability to read and write, but lessons in literacy seldom stop with the ability to encode and decode the black marks on a page. In this sequence, you will examine different ideas of literacy and the social contexts that animate them. For example, Fishman describes the familiar yet unusual literacy practices of a family belonging to one of North America's most distinctive conservative religious groups, the Old Order Amish, a group that avoids many modern innovations in technology and daily living, while Heath, in an excerpt from an important ethnographic study, catalogs literacy practices of an impoverished and isolated community in North Carolina. Both authors concentrate on how families provide models for the emerging literacy skills of their children. Scholes proposes a way of "reading" a television commercial as if it were in writing, implying that our idea of literacy must include many other forms besides written texts. Scholes also believes that one must question the social order that is passed on in texts. Finally, Scheper-Hughes traces the interpretive practices of a professional anthropologist and shows how her own powers as a specialist were challenged by the people she studied, as they resisted what she wrote. These writers take us through a number of contexts for literacy and indicate useful and diverse perspectives on the concept of literacy itself. They invite us to create a social concept of the many contesting literacies of our intricate world.

Assignment 1 (Fishman, Heath)

In these two essays, Fishman and Heath offer accounts of a number of literacy practices of two seemingly very different communities, yet both communities offer their children models of literacy that some readers have argued are appropriate for the lives they are leading. In addition, Fishman describes a group she calls "mainstream educators." If we assume that Fishman and Heath themselves are "mainstream educators," then we have three major social groups represented here, along with some clues about their conceptions of literacy. In your paper, look at some of the literacy practices and ways of talking about literacy that each group values, and begin to formulate a theory of how literacy reflects its social context.

Assignment 2 (Heath, Scheper-Hughes, Fishman)

In these readings, we have several examples of professional educators or ethnographers studying the members of a social group and preparing a written account of their ways of life. In the case of Scheper-Hughes, we see especially the possibility that the people being studied, that is, the subjects, can resist the accounts that have been written about them, and yet in general the authority seems to go with the professional person rather than the person being studied. In this paper, continue developing your theory of the ways literacy reflects its social context. As you do, be sure to examine the special literacy practices of professionals and the sources and character of their power or authority.

Assignment 3 (Scholes, Scheper-Hughes, Fishman)

With Scholes we have a chance to examine the relationship between print literacy and other forms of "text," such as video advertising, as well as to consider the ways texts may invite or require our resistance if we are to protect ourselves from their designs upon us. In this paper, as you continue to develop your theory of literacy in its social context, consider evidence from the readings to show whether a particular conception of literacy matters as a person seeks to thrive or merely survive in a particular social context.

SEQUENCE 2
WRITING SELVES: DEBATING "SELF-EXPRESSION"

Margaret Atwood, "An End to Audience?"
Barbara Christian, "Black Feminist Process: In the Midst of . . ."
Scott Russell Sanders, "The Men We Carry in Our Minds"
Renato Rosaldo, "Grief and a Headhunter's Rage"

Margaret Atwood suggests that many, perhaps most people think of writing as a form of self-expression. This sequence of assignments raises some questions about the notion of "self-expression." What does self-expression mean? What ideas about the "self" and about "expression" does the notion of self-expression imply? How well do those ideas reflect what you really do when you write? The following assignments give you opportunities to address these questions in the context of writers who draw upon their experiences, the words of other writers, and their memories: the same kinds of things you draw upon when you write. As you work with these assignments, keep in mind their implications for your own perception of yourself as a writer.

Assignment 1 (Atwood)

Margaret Atwood observes that "We like to think of writing as merely personal, merely self-expression . . . because it lets us off the hook. If that's all it is . . . we don't have to pay any serious attention to it" (29). How seriously do you take self-expressive writing? Find several passages in Atwood's essay where you suspect Atwood engages in self-expression and a few more passages where she seems to do something else. How do you respond to these different kinds of passages? Why? How convincing do you find self-expression as a form of evidence? As you consider these questions, develop your own theory of the role of self-expression in writing. Based on your reading of Atwood's essay, why do you think writers choose to use or avoid self-expression?

Assignment 2 (Atwood, Christian, Sanders)

Assignment 1 asked you to work with ideas about self-expression that suggest that "we are all self-enclosed monads, with an inside and an outside, and that nothing from the outside ever gets in" (Atwood 29). In this assignment, you will work with writers who do not necessarily assume that we all are distinct "selves" and that when we express ourselves we reveal something that comes out of or originates within us. While reading and discussing the selections from Christian and Sanders, reflect on how much of their written expression is really self-expression. What sources or experiences from beyond themselves do Christian and Sanders call upon in their essays? What strategies do they use to mold the "voices" of others into their writing? Use your observations to revise the theory of self-expression you developed in Assignment 1.

Assignment 3 (Atwood, Christian, Sanders, Rosaldo)

To what extent do the essays by Christian and Sanders force us to abandon the idea of individual self-expression? Consider this question as you read Rosaldo's essay. What happens when Rosaldo attempts to use or reject the voices of others as he explains his experiences? What happens to Rosaldo's sense of himself as a result of his exposure to other voices? How do his own ideas about self-expression change in his essay? Use these questions to help you explore the ways we perhaps create ourselves—or create our "selves"—when we write.

Note: To an extent, Rosaldo's essay breaks away from the direct attention to gender we find in the readings by Christian and Sanders. To maintain a greater focus on gender throughout the sequence, try substituting Anzaldúa's essay for Rosaldo's. The sequence also takes an interesting new direction when Angelou's text replaces Christian's.

SEQUENCE 3
POWER AND KNOWLEDGE IN EVERYDAY LIFE

Howard Brody, M.D., "The Social Power of Expert Healers"
Barbara Garson, "McDonald's—We Do It All for You"
Maxine Hong Kingston, "No Name Woman"
Liliana Heker, "The Stolen Party"

Sometimes concepts like "power" and "knowledge" can seem alien to the ways people experience their day-to-day lives. It's easy for people to recognize power in those who hold important political office or who manage large corporations, just as they can recognize knowledge in those who have devoted themselves to intensive study in specialized fields like medical research or ancient history. This sequence asks you to consider possible uses for concepts of power and knowledge in areas that are probably more familiar and more meaningful to you, because they are more likely to be aspects of your everyday experience. You will begin by considering these concepts in terms of health care, a specialized field to which most people have been exposed. Once you have worked with notions of power and knowledge in this context, you will have opportunities to consider your ideas within other contexts: the media, the workplace, and the family.

Assignment 1 (Brody)

Brody examines the different agendas of the people involved in caring for Opal and the Bakers, and he considers the role that power relations play in the way decisions about health care are made. In general, where do people's agendas seem to come from? What determines how much power people have to influence or coerce others to follow their agenda? Consider these questions by using a few of Brody's ideas to discuss an episode of a television show, perhaps a sitcom. Identify the problem or problems that need to be resolved in this episode of the show, and explain why the characters approach or avoid the problem in the ways that they do. What interests are at stake? How do power relations help determine the way these competing interests shape whatever resolution the episode offers? Use your insights to assess how useful Brody's ideas are in contexts other than health care.

Assignment 2 (Brody, Garson)

In his discussion of Rabkin's analysis, Brody indicates that sometimes it can be useful to view a nonfiction text as though it were a piece of fiction. Why might this be so? What aspects of Barnard's report is Rabkin able to highlight by approaching it as a fictional text? What insights about the role of knowledge and power in the Bakers' case does he develop by employing this method? Explore the limitations and uses of Rabkin's method by applying it to Garson's essay. How does your understanding of her essay change when you consider her as the "narrator" of a "story" about McDonald's instead of as a reporter? What new insights about the roles of power and knowledge in everyday life at McDonald's do you gain by considering the roles of power and knowledge in Garson's telling of her story?

Assignment 3 (Kingston, Heker)

Kingston and Heker provide accounts of power and knowledge in the context of family dynamics. Locate the sources of power and knowledge in their texts, and identify some of the situations in which people with power are at odds with people who possess knowledge. How are these conflicts between power and knowledge resolved? What do these resolutions suggest to you about the ways power and knowledge work within family dynamics? Use your reading of these texts to examine one or two situations in your own experience of family life.

Note: Assignment 3 is especially flexible. The readings by Rodriguez and MacLeod offer different perspectives about family and could substitute for Kingston and Heker. Or, replacing Kingston and Heker with Bellah and Barnlund could extend the current emphasis on the family community to a wider emphasis on community in general. In that case, it might be worthwhile to replace Garson with hooks & West for the second assignment.

Note: This sequence will work best in the second half of the semester; Assignment 1 can pick up on the students' earlier reading of almost any other text in *Literacies*.

SEQUENCE 4
READERS, WRITERS, AND "AUDIENCES"

Barbara Christian, "Black Feminist Process: In the Midst of . . ."
Jimmie Durham, "Those Dead Guys for a Hundred Years"
Nancy Scheper-Hughes, "The Anthropological Looking Glass"

This sequence asks you to look closely at relationships between readers and writers. Though the situation is usually different in composition classes, much of the time, writers do not know the people they write for, and most readers do not get the chance to respond to writers in person. This doesn't mean, though, that readers and writers are uninterested in each other. Both groups try hard to imagine the assumptions and expectations of the other—in part, of course, by switching from reading to writing (and vice versa). Then, too, as Barbara Christian shows, there is the professional literary critic, the person who studies relationships between readers and writers for a living. In the assignments that follow, you will explore both writing and reading as specifically imaginative acts. You will also consider the limitations of this view of reading and writing.

Assignment 1 (Christian and another *Literacies* essay)

In her essay "Black Feminist Process: In the Midst of . . . ," Barbara Christian writes that the social identities and life experiences of readers make them "reinterpret" texts and "reinvent" themselves whenever they read. For Assignment 1, begin by discussing several passages in which you see Christian reinterpreting texts and reinventing herself as she talks about reading with her daughter. Then use your insights to discuss your experience reading another text from *Literacies*. How do Christian's theories about reinterpretation and reinvention fit into the theories about reading that you have developed thus far in the semester? Where might you revise your own theories?

Assignment 2 (Christian, Durham)

In Assignment 1, you focused on reading as a kind of social interaction between a text and an individual reader. If you choose to define reading in this way, what happens to your ideas about writing? Use your own and Christian's theories about the relationship between reading and writing to help you pose (and answer) some questions about Jimmie Durham's "Those Dead Guys for a Hundred Years." Here are a few questions to start with: What might Durham hope to accomplish by writing his text? What kinds of relationships might different readers have with his text, and why? Where in "Those Dead Guys" does Durham seem to make room for different kinds of readers? As you ask and explore your own questions, be sure to explain how they grow from particular ideas about reading and writing (especially those you discussed in Assignment 1).

Assignment 3 (Christian, Durham, Scheper-Hughes)

The first two assignments in this sequence asked you to think about several different, but perhaps related questions. First, you examined how a reader's experiences in the world shape her interpretations of a text and how those interpretations have the power, in turn, to shape her understanding of herself. Then you asked (among other questions) how a writer's ideas about his audience might influence the direction or form his text takes. For your final essay, bring these questions together to help you discuss what happens between Nancy Scheper-Hughes and the villagers of Ballybran in "The Anthropological Looking Glass." How do the villagers' ideas about reading and Scheper-Hughes's ideas about writing contribute to the conflict that develops between them? What possibilities for reconciliation or growth do their ideas offer?

SEQUENCE 5
COMMUNITY AND INDIVIDUAL AGENCY

> Robert Bellah et al., "Community, Commitment, and Individuality"
> James Baldwin, "Down at the Cross"
> Jonathan Kozol, "Rachel and Her Children"
> bell hooks & Cornel West, "Black Women and Men: Partnership in the 1990s"
> Barbara Garson, "McDonald's—We Do It All for You"

You are probably familiar with many different kinds of communities, from such well-defined groups as families and religious or social organizations to less formal communities like groups of friends, coworkers, or classmates. This assignment sequence encourages you to think analytically about some of these communities, so that you can develop a clearer understanding of communities in general and, perhaps, of some of the specific communities you belong to. In particular, it asks you to consider ways in which community membership empowers you, borrowing bell hooks's words, "to act in [your] best interest" (329).

Assignment 1 (Bellah)

As Bellah writes about his conversations with Les Newman and the other people interviewed for the essay, he frequently draws attention to the "civic contrast between the private person who thinks first of himself alone and the citizen" who fulfills him- or herself by participating in community (86). Discuss how one or two people from Bellah's essay try to balance this contrast between the goals of private individuality and community participation. Based on your discussion, explain how Bellah would like people to balance this contrast. What do Bellah's ideas help you say about your own experience in one or two communities?

Assignment 2 (Bellah, Baldwin)

Baldwin refers to a "labyrinth of attitudes" that are "historical and public" (55). Considering examples from Baldwin's essay, compose your own definition of "labyrinth of attitudes," and explain what it means for someone's attitudes to be "historical and public." How does the notion of a labyrinth of public, historical attitudes help you reexamine the contrast between individuality and community in one or two or your examples from Assignment 1?

Assignment 3 (Baldwin, Kozol)

List some of the communities Rachel belongs to, and describe some of the specific perceptions she has of these communities. How does Baldwin's suggestion that some attitudes are "historical and public" help you discuss Rachel's attitudes about the communities she belongs to? How does Baldwin's suggestion help you examine your own thoughts about Rachel and her participation in various communities?

Assignment 4 (Kozol, hooks & West)

bell hooks claims that "one of the most vital ways we sustain ourselves is by building communities of resistance, places where we know we are not alone" (335). How do you think "communities of resistance" are built? What happens when you apply hooks's notion of "communities of resistance" to one or two of Rachel's communities in Kozol's essay? Consider how you might revise hooks's concept to make it more appropriate to Rachel's experiences.

Assignment 5 (Bellah, hooks & West, Garson)

bell hooks describes individual agency as "the ability to act in one's best interest" (329). Using several examples from the essays by Bellah and Garson, discuss some of the ways that communities can promote or limit people's ability to exert agency. Based on your observations, consider some of the specific ways that two or three communities you belong to affect how much agency you have.

SEQUENCE 6
THE TRAVELER'S GAZE/GAZING ON TRAVEL

Carol de Saint Victor, "Go Slowly and You Arrive"
Robert Scholes, "On Reading a Video Text"

Richard Rodriguez, "Complexion"
James Clifford, "Incidents of Tourism in Chiapas and Yucatan"
Jeffrey Weeks, "Values in an Age of Uncertainty"
Alistair MacLeod, "The Vastness of the Dark"
Gloria Anzaldúa, "Speaking in Tongues: A Letter to 3rd World Women
    Writers"
Alice Walker, "Everyday Use"

In "Values in an Age of Uncertainty," Jeffrey Weeks connects the spread of the HIV virus to "migrations across countries and continents, from country to town, from 'traditional' ways of life to 'modern,' in flight from persecution, poverty, or sexual repression . . ." (643). He goes on to argue that the very speed of modern travel is an important tool for fighting the problems associated with migration. In doing so, he reminds readers that movement within and between cultures presents us with new social responsibilities and opportunities for more self-conscious kinds of community.

This semester-long group of writing assignments invites you to examine travel from a number of vantage points. Some of the readings for the sequence introduce you to different kinds of travelers: "independent" and "expert" tourists, migrating workers, students who return home after leaving for an education, and an artist in search of community. Other readings offer you tools for analyzing how people talk about and value their own travels. Each assignment will ask you to consider how perspective shapes what travelers (and people writing about travel) are able to "see." You will also explore the ethics and morality of looking at travel in particular ways.

Assignment 1 (de Saint Victor)

As an American tourist traveling alone in India, Carol de Saint Victor writes, "I do not understand much of what I see" (488). Write about some of the specific barriers to understanding that de Saint Victor describes in her text, and then comment on the strategies she uses to overcome those barriers. In your opinion, how well do her strategies work? How can you tell?

Assignment 2 (de Saint Victor, Scholes)

In Assignment 1, you examined the problems de Saint Victor faces as she tries to interpret an unfamiliar culture. In this assignment, you will focus on the challenges de Saint Victor's text presents to your own attempts at interpretation. Working with ideas from Scholes's "On Reading a Video Text," discuss some of de Saint Victor's techniques for "framing" what you, as a reader, are able to "see" in her text. Based on your reading of de Saint

Victor and Scholes, what can you say about the difficulties of interpreting other people's intercultural encounters?

Assignment 3 (Rodriguez, Clifford)

Near the end of "Complexion," Richard Rodriguez argues that what separated him from the Mexican migrant workers he encountered as a college student was "an attitude of *mind*, [his] imagination of [him]self" (434). After reading James Clifford's "Incidents of Tourism in Chiapas and Yucatan," explain how you think Clifford would respond to Rodriguez's theory. What might Clifford notice about Rodriguez's relationship to these workers that Rodriguez himself misses?

Assignment 4 (Weeks, MacLeod, Anzaldúa)

In Assignment 3, you explored how various outsiders may interpret the lives of people who move in order to find work. For this assignment, consider some of the ways in which people who migrate interpret their own experiences. Using theories from Jeffrey Weeks's "Values in an Age of Uncertainty," discuss some of the problems and opportunities that such travel presents for James (in MacLeod's "The Vastness of the Dark") and Gloria Anzaldúa (in "Speaking in Tongues").

Assignment 5 (Walker and others)

During this semester, you have examined several different but interrelated questions about the relationship between travel, perspective, and interpretation. What do tourists "see"? How should we interpret what travelers show us? How do travelers come to understand themselves? For this final essay, use Alice Walker's "Everyday Use" and another *Literacies* text that explores a particular experience of travel in order to consider the ways in which travel changes people. Then, thinking back to your work with Scholes, Clifford, or Weeks, describe some interpretive strategies that you believe could help the people you discuss make sense of their own and others' travels.

SEQUENCE 7
GENDER AND "TRUTH"

Mary Lyndon Shanley, " 'Surrogate Mothering' and Women's Freedom"
Jeffrey Weeks, "Values in an Age of Uncertainty"
Victor Seidler, "Language and Masculinity"
Adrienne Rich, "Women and Honor: Some Notes on Lying"

Scott Russell Sanders, "The Men We Carry in Our Minds"
bell hooks & Cornel West, "Black Women and Men: Partnership in the
1990s"

Certainly, there are many useful ways to talk about gender and its influence on our everyday lives: You can look at sexuality, work, family relations, and political power, among other subjects. In a course about writing and interpretation, though, you can also focus on how your ideas about gender shape what you know and how you communicate your knowledge. By looking at connections between gender and knowledge, perhaps you can create even better approaches to issues that concern you.

Personal freedom, social equality, and economic justice are a few of the issues that concern the writers in this sequence. All of these writers challenge traditional understandings of gender. Shanley examines how new reproductive technologies encourage people to rethink their ideas of women as independent beings and as citizens, while Rich asks you to reconsider relationships between women. Seidler and Sanders emphasize the ways in which traditional ideas about manhood have hurt men. Weeks and hooks & West all show how notions of gender shape (and sometimes distort) the kinds of communities people create. Taken together, these writers invite you to use your own experiences and your own knowledge of the world to invent new ways of thinking about women, men, and the problem of "truth."

Assignment 1 (Weeks, Shanley)

In "Values in an Age of Uncertainty," Jeffrey Weeks writes that the "good" is "something we are all involved in developing and defining" (651). From this perspective, we can think of Mary Lyndon Shanley's essay as one attempt to "develop and define" a "good" approach to difficult questions about surrogate mothering and women's independence. Your first assignment for this sequence is to use Weeks's theories about human values to explore some of the conflicts that Shanley presents between different approaches to surrogate mothering. What do you think these conflicts say about the relationship between women and the law in Western culture? Based on your reading of Weeks and Shanley, how are women involved (or how should they be involved) in defining the "good"?

Assignment 2 (Seidler, Rich)

(Before beginning this assignment, it might be helpful to answer the Reading in New Contexts #3 question following Shanley's essay.)

Though their writing styles are very different, Victor Seidler and Adrienne Rich are both concerned with the ways men and women use language to know themselves (or to repress self-knowledge) and to control their relationships with others. How do their ideas apply to your own experiences with language and gender? For Assignment 2, tell a personal story or discuss a problem that you think relates to the issue of gender and language. Once you have told your story or outlined your problem, use it to help you explain the significance of a few ideas from Rich's and Seidler's texts. Thinking about your work here, what can you conclude about the connections among language, gender, and self-knowledge?

Assignment 3 (Sanders, hooks & West, your first two essays)

In your other essays, you considered how gender contributes to our knowledge of ourselves and of what we want for ourselves and our communities. Clearly, Scott Russell Sanders, bell hooks, and Cornel West are interested in those same questions. For Assignment 3, use some of your own new theories to explore the role of dialogue in creating good relationships between men and women. In particular, think about ways in which the dialogues that take place in these two *Literacies* texts are examples of or challenges to the ideas about truth that you encountered in your reading of Weeks, Shanley, Seidler, and/or Rich.

SEQUENCE 8
INTERPRETING "WORK"

Stuart Ewen, "Chosen People"
Richard Rodriguez, "Complexion"
David Gilmore, "Performative Excellence: Circum-Mediterranean"
Mary Lyndon Shanley, " 'Surrogate Mothering' and Women's Freedom"
Bruno Bettelheim, "The Ignored Lesson of Anne Frank"
Barbara Garson, "McDonald's—We Do It All for You"
Howard Brody, M.D., "The Social Power of Expert Healers"
Barbara Christian, "Black Feminist Process: In the Midst of . . ."

This sequence offers you several opportunities to think and write about the social meanings of work. In particular, it asks you to consider how workers' identities are created and often passed on from one generation to the next, or from one worker to another. Your own experiences as a worker may have given you some knowledge about this question; the readings, no doubt, will encourage you to revise and expand upon some of your own observations. The first two assignments ask you to apply a number of theories about social class and gender to Richard Rodriguez's "Complexion." Once you have explored the subtle ways our cultural beliefs affect our self-images as workers, you will have a chance in the third assignment to examine strategies for addressing those beliefs in a more direct way. Finally, this sequence will ask you to use your own developing expertise as an interpreter of work to comment on the differences between "expert" and "nonexpert" workers in a given field.

Assignment 1 (Ewen, Rodriguez)

In "Chosen People," Stuart Ewen remarks that in a consumer society, "judgment about a person is not based on what one *does* within society, but rather upon what one *has*" (194). For your first essay, apply some arguments and insights from Ewen's text to Richard Rodriguez's "Complexion." How well do Ewen's theories clarify the sources of Rodriguez's confusion about work and social class? What aspects of Rodriguez's essay are *not* made clearer by Ewen's theories?

Assignment 2 (Rodriguez, Gilmore, Shanley)

Assignment 1 asked you to speculate about the connections Rodriguez makes between work and social class in terms of Ewen's text. For this essay, you should consider how ideas about gender shape people's experiences of work. To be sure, Gilmore (who studies Mediterranean men's self-images) and Shanley (who looks at pregnancy as a form of work) have very different approaches to this question. Taken together, though, their ideas may help you say something new about Rodriguez. Use a few of their important observations to compose your own theory about the relationship between gender and work in Rodriguez's "Complexion."

Assignment 3 (Bettelheim, Garson)

Up to this point, all of the readings in this sequence have explored beliefs about work that individuals may not consciously recognize, but which nonetheless affect their experiences as workers. In his essay "The Ignored Lesson of Anne Frank," psychologist Bruno Bettelheim suggests some reasons why people choose not to acknowledge their own situations and beliefs and examines some consequences of that refusal. Working closely with Bettelheim's arguments, explain what you see as the main challenges facing workers in Garson's "McDonald's—We Do It All for You."

Assignment 4 (Brody, Christian, and your first three essays)

"Experts," by definition, are believed to be especially knowledgeable and devoted to their work—they exist, in many people's minds, in a class apart from the rest of us. For your final essay in this sequence, begin by discussing the differences that you think Brody and Christian might see between experts and other kinds of workers. Then bring in ideas from your first three essays that help you explore some concerns or responsibilities that are shared by experts and nonexperts alike. How much do various classes of workers have in common? How can you tell?

SEQUENCE 9
FAMILY IN CONTEXT

Alistair MacLeod, "The Vastness of the Dark"
Adrienne Rich, "Women and Honor: Some Notes on Lying"
Bruno Bettelheim, "The Ignored Lesson of Anne Frank"
Maxine Hong Kingston, "No Name Woman"

This sequence asks you to consider the workings of one of the most intimate social systems in any culture: the family. Cultures hold many sacred beliefs about the family's role in molding responsible, morally aware citizens. How are actual families equipped to live up to their culturally defined roles? Rich and Bettelheim suggest that in all relationships—whether between neighbors, close friends, or biologically linked persons—the participants' attitudes toward knowledge and truth are a crucial factor. Rich writes that "an honorable human relationship—that is, one in which two people have the right to use the word 'love'—is . . . a process of refining the truths they can tell each other" (407). In this sequence, you will explore how figures like James (from MacLeod's "The Vastness of the Dark") and the narrator of "No Name Woman" struggle to sort out their own and their families' understandings of truth.

Assignment 1 (MacLeod, Rich)

Rich writes that "The lie is a short-cut through another's personality" (412). Use this insight and others from her essay to explore how James comes to understand his relationship to his family and home at the end of MacLeod's story. In what sense do James's "oversimplifications" resemble Rich's ideas about "lying"? Does James, in Rich's words, try "to extend the possibilities of truth" between himself and his family (413)? How?

Assignment 2 (Bettelheim, Rich, MacLeod)

Like Rich, Bettelheim examines the truths that people do not want to confront and the consequences of avoiding those truths. How does your understanding of MacLeod's story change when you look at it from Bettelheim's perspective instead of Rich's? Using James and his family as a case study, show how Rich's and Bettelheim's theories differ. Then explain how those differences contribute to your understanding of family relationships, both in MacLeod's story and in your own experience.

Assignment 3 (Kingston, MacLeod, your first two essays)

Working with ideas from your first two essays, show how Kingston's response to her mother's story relates to James's realizations about his family. Once you have discussed this relationship, develop a theory about Kingston's use of fiction or fantasy to explain her ancestors' behavior. What does this strategy have to do with truth?

Assignment 4

> If we are certain that we are helpless to protect ourselves against the danger of destruction, we cannot contemplate it. We can consider the danger only as long as we believe that there are ways to protect ourselves, to fight back, to escape.
>
> (BETTELHEIM 98)

> People who refused fatalism because they could invent small resources insisted on culpability. Deny accidents and wrest fault from the stars.
>
> (KINGSTON 349)

Starting with these two passages and then bringing in material from other parts of the texts and from your own experience, evaluate some of the different ways that knowledge gets used in the family setting. What are some factors—inside and outside the family—that influence the ways families use what they know? Why might this be an important question?

SEQUENCE **10**
THINKING CRITICALLY ABOUT HISTORY: USING THE PAST IN THE PRESENT

Robert Bellah et al., "Community, Commitment, and Individuality"
Bruno Bettelheim, "The Ignored Lesson of Anne Frank"

Jimmie Durham, "Those Dead Guys for a Hundred Years"
Ann Fienup-Riordan, "Yup'ik Lives and How We See Them"
Alice Walker, "Everyday Use"

These assignments give you an opportunity to explore some important questions about the meaning of history: What can people gain from thinking critically about the past? What meaning can seemingly distant events in history have for our lives today? You will work with some writers, such as Bettelheim, who very consciously attempt to learn lessons from the past. Other writers pose questions that reveal some of the difficulties of learning from the past: Which past should people work with? Why? In his essay, Durham suggests compelling reasons for his own need to look to the past but also outlines some of the ways the past resists being used. As you discuss these readings, you will develop your own understanding of the promise and limitations of working with the past.

Assignment 1 (Bellah, Bettelheim)

Through interviews with several middle-class Americans, Bellah invites readers to reflect on their own critical awareness and the ways their awareness shapes the everyday choices they make. Discuss the critical practices of one or two individuals from Bellah's essay. What terms or ideas from these examples might help you evaluate the role of criticism in Bettelheim's essay? What value do you see in his critical practice? Consider how his observations about specific events surrounding the Holocaust might become part of your own everyday critical awareness.

Assignment 2 (Bettelheim, Walker)

Bettelheim observes that some victims of the Nazis became passive when they "invest[ed] personal property with life energy," because they stopped "using" their possessions and instead became "captivated by them" (99). Evaluate these observations by applying them to two or three characters from Walker's story. How do these characters invest life energy in their possessions? What relationship do you see between each character's use of—or captivation by—material possessions and the kind of passivity Bettelheim describes? Discuss how your insights about Walker's story might raise new questions about Bettelheim's observations.

Assignment 3 (Walker, Fienup-Riordan)

Fienup-Riordan notes that "In the face of . . . massive and unprecedented inquiry, some Nelson Islanders may view their past as inadequate to vindicate present positions" (216). As you take another look at Walker's story, what do you think about the different ways the characters relate to their cultural and familial history? Why? What critical perspectives about the past help the characters to vindicate the meaningfulness of their present lives? Use your responses to these questions to discuss the Nelson Islanders' efforts to vindicate their past and present experiences.

Assignment 4 (Fienup-Riordan, Durham, Bellah, Bettelheim)

The last assignment in this sequence asked you to consider how thinking critically about the past might be useful for finding meaning in your present life. Now use the ideas you've developed thus far to examine how present meanings shape the way people think about the past. First, explore how the filming of *Winter Warrior* affected the Nelson Islanders' relationship to their history. Then, consider how Durham's present concerns influence him to speak about his past the way he does in his essay. Finally, explore what your observations about Fienup-Riordan and Durham might teach you about the value of thinking critically about history. Use some of your new ideas to revise your conclusions from Assignment 1.

Note: With minor modifications to the assignments, the essay by hooks & West can replace Bellah's text, and MacLeod's story can replace Walker's. If MacLeod's story is used, it might be interesting to substitute Kingston for Durham.

SEQUENCE 11
"PRIVATE WORLDS": TALKING ABOUT COMMUNICATION

> Audre Lorde, "The Uses of Anger: Women Responding to Racism"
> Amy Tan, "The Language of Discretion"
> Maya Angelou, " 'Mary' "
> Adrienne Rich, "Women and Honor: Some Notes on Lying"
> Maxine Hong Kingston, "No Name Woman"
> Dean Barnlund, "Communication in a Global Village"
> Susan Sontag, "AIDS and Its Metaphors"
> Frank Black Elk, "Marxism and Lakota Tradition"

Why do people say the things they say? How do you account for the sometimes surprising choices people make as they express their feelings or ideas? This sequence offers you opportunities to explore how factors such as culture, social standing, and emotion affect the ways in which people communicate with each other. These writers' emotions, their subject matter, and their theories of communication may challenge your usual ways of interpreting texts. As you work your way through this sequence, keep in mind how your ability to communicate about these ideas is being influenced by your encounters with different writing styles and forms of expression.

Assignment 1 (Lorde, Tan)

Select two or three passages from Lorde's essay where she seems to use anger or to offer advice about how her readers might use anger. Explain which uses of anger Tan would consider "discrete" and which she would call "discreet." How might your discussion help you examine your own discrete/discreet uses of strong emotions like anger?

Assignment 2 (Lorde, Tan, Angelou)

Apply your insights about discrete/discreet uses of anger from Assignment 1 to several examples of anger in " 'Mary.' " Who feels anger in this text, and how do they express their anger? How do age, race, social class, or other circumstances affect the way people in Angelou's text use or express their anger?

Assignment 3 (Tan, Rich, Kingston)

One might say that Rich investigates how certain kinds of discretion can become forms of lying. Discuss two or three passages from Rich's essay that help you define the boundary between discretion and lying. What happens when you apply your definition to Kingston's aunt from "No Name Woman"? Consider what your analysis of Rich and Kingston suggests about the relationships between social context and discretion and between social context and lying.

Assignment 4 (Barnlund, Kingston)

In your last two essays, you explored how external circumstances can affect the way people communicate with others. Yet Barnlund claims that communication is shaped by "internal" circumstances: He suggests that each person lives in a "distinctive world, not the same world others occupy," and he believes that "every communication . . . is a transaction between these private worlds" (67). Reconsider your discussion of Kingston in Assignment 3 with Barnlund's ideas in mind. What kinds of "transactions"—between "private worlds," or between internal and external circumstances—do you see in the communication that occurs in Kingston's text?

Assignment 5 (Black Elk, Lorde, Barnlund, Sontag)

Taking your insights from Assignment 4 as your starting point, consider Black Elk's use of anger and other emotions in his essay. How do external factors influence his communicative styles? How does his "private world" shape his use of emotional expression? How well does Black Elk's essay uphold Sontag's claim that it has become "a virtue in our society to speak of what is supposed not to be named" (609)?

SEQUENCE 12
CONSERVING ACTS: PRESERVING SOCIAL VALUES

Ann Fienup-Riordan, "Yup'ik Lives and How We See Them"
Andrea R. Fishman, "Becoming Literate: A Lesson from the Amish"
Robert Bellah et al., "Community, Commitment, and Individuality"
Maxine Hong Kingston, "No Name Woman"
James Baldwin, "Down at the Cross"
Adrienne Rich, "Women and Honor: Some Notes on Lying"

In this sequence of assignments, you will examine the efforts of a number of groups and individuals to protect, abide by, and pass on a body of values that matter deeply to them, sometimes in the face of powerful obstacles. While the people you will read about do not share the same political or social views, they all perform or reflect upon a number of "conserving acts"—attempts to preserve and carry out some of their social values. Their conserving acts will allow you to consider the sources of authority in society and in personal lives, as well as the role of tradition in providing guidance for our actions. You will begin with an account of a people whose culture, founded on a rich web of customs, lore, and spiritual values, was challenged by its encounter with a powerful and contrasting culture. Their strategic responses to the challenge will allow you to consider some of the ways the conservation of culture requires actions. You will then read an account of the literacy practices of the Old Order Amish, a people who refuse to take advantage of many aspects of modern technology and who isolate themselves from much that they find corrupt in modern life, including many things that other conservative individuals gladly accept. Then you will read the work of Robert Bellah and his co-authors, a team of sociologists who examine the ways individuals make meaningful contact with the traditions and values of a community, whether that community is religious, ethnic, political, or of some other kind. After that you will look at the ways a first-generation Chinese-American, Maxine Hong Kingston, grapples with the instructions she receives from her mother in traditional Chinese values. Kingston offers a detailed portrait of her attempt to understand a culture's ways of teaching and enforcing customs. Finally, you will work with two essays in which individuals, in an effort to abide by one set of values, find they must challenge another set of values that comes to them in similar fashion from their cultures. James Baldwin describes distancing himself from the church in order to abide by democratic values, and Adrienne Rich talks about the need to protect herself from "gaslighting"—from having the truth of one's experience undermined by the authority of others. These writers show the ways social customs and individual experiences pull us toward and away from a simple relationship to established values and challenge us to think about our responsibilities, to self and to others, as we choose our own conserving acts.

Assignment 1 (Fienup-Riordan)

Fienup-Riordan describes the cultural crisis caused by the Yup'ik people's ongoing encounter with other groups who have settled in Alaska. In your essay, consider some of the choices that the Yup'ik have made about their traditions as a result of their contacts with other groups. Use some of Fienup-Riordan's terms and ideas of your own to explore the differing ways a people like the Yup'ik can relate, in a time of change, to the traditions and beliefs they inherit from their ancestors. How do you evaluate the choices that the Yup'ik have made and the relations they have established to tradition?

Assignment 2 (Fienup-Riordan, Fishman)

Fishman describes some of the customs of a family belonging to a well-known but isolated group, the Old Order Amish, that carries on a traditional way of life far more restricted than that of most other descendants of European settlers to North America. Continue to develop your thinking about a people's relations to tradition by drawing on the ideas and examples from Fishman's reading. How do the Yup'ik, the Old Order Amish, as seen in the family life of the Fishers, and the mainstream educators described by Fishman each work out their relations to traditions and inherited beliefs? What consequences do you see for these different groups as they carry out their own approaches to traditional knowledge?

Assignment 3 (Fishman, Bellah, Fienup-Riordan)

In this essay Bellah and his collaborators examine the ways a number of individuals have grappled with change and uncertainty and become members of meaningful communities. As in Fienup-Riordan's essays, though, the process has often come in response to some disruption rather than through a simple connection to tradition. Fienup-Riordan speaks of the Yup'ik's relations to traditions in terms of dialogue, negotiation, and invention, and Bellah describes a common need to "invent a second language out of the failing fragments of [one's] usual first language" (81). Fishman's portrait of an Old Order Amish family presents a strong sense of continuity, rather than disruption or discontinuity. Use ideas and examples from these three readings to discuss and evaluate the roles that discontinuity or disruption play in a society's traditions.

Assignment 4 (Kingston, Bellah)

Kingston tells and retells the story of her aunt's ostracism and death, repeatedly speculating to fill in around the sketchy details her mother provided as a lesson in traditional values. Draw on some of Bellah's concepts about how an individual achieves a sense of identity in a community, and discuss the ways Kingston negotiates between her mother's traditional lesson, Kingston's own experiences on the borders between Chinese and American culture, and a number of possible meanings she finds in the story of her aunt. Considering what you know of Kingston, her mother, and her aunt, what important relations do you see between an individual and her society's traditions?

Assignment 5 (Baldwin, Rich)

Rich and Baldwin both describe their encounters with troubling social customs and search for ways to respond to them that satisfy their sense of value and meaning. Extend the work you have done in Assignment 4 by looking at the essays by Rich and Baldwin as accounts of individuals who have found themselves threatened or limited by contradictory values in their society. Use ideas, examples, and events from these two essays and, if you like, from earlier readings in the sequence to discuss the relations of individuals to tradition, the range of choices they have when confronted by a powerful social norm, and the role traditional values play in acts of resistance.

DOCUMENTING SOURCES USING
MLA OR **APA** STYLE

When you include the words and ideas of other writers in your own writing, you must give publication information so that your readers can find the sources you have used. In this way, the written "conversation" that you have participated in can continue and grow. Your readers may wish to know more about the writers whose work you have discussed, or they may have different interpretations of that work. In either case, being able to locate sources increases everyone's opportunities to understand what other people have already written and to produce new ideas in response to those writings. As a result, colleges and universities expect students to learn how to document sources as a basic element of academic integrity. Failure to do so is usually considered a form of academic dishonesty or plagiarism.

Though there are other standard styles for documenting material, the two most frequently used in college courses are MLA and APA. MLA, which stands for Modern Language Association, is used mostly by writers in the humanities, languages, and arts. American Psychological Association style, or APA, is used mostly by writers in the social sciences. This brief guide to MLA and APA styles offers information on documenting some basic kinds of texts: single- and multiple-author books, anthologies, and articles from scholarly journals, newspapers, and magazines. In a first-year writing course, this may be all the citation information you need. As you progress through college, however, you will probably need a more complete guide. Many writing handbooks offer extensive information on documentation; the MLA and APA also publish their own authoritative guides. As you choose a major, find out which style is preferred by teachers in your field and learn it. In the meantime, you may wish to familiarize yourself with some of these frequently encountered patterns for citation.

IN-TEXT CITATIONS

Both MLA and APA styles recommend using in-text, or parenthetical, citations, which refer to a bibliography—a list of Works Cited in MLA style; a list of References in APA style. In MLA style, when you refer to a writer's work in the body of your essay, place the author's last name and the page number in parentheses at the end of the sentence (if you use the author's name in your sentence, you do not need to repeat it in the parenthetical citation). You should not use the word "page" or any abbreviation for it in the citation.

In APA style, include the year of publication and the abbreviation "p." In both styles, the sentence's final punctuation goes after the parenthetical citations. Here is how the same quoted passage would appear in essays using MLA and APA style:

M L A

> Anthropologist Michael Moffatt argues that most of the college students he studied at Rutgers University shared "an ideal: a loosely formulated but very pervasive one concerning collective harmony or friendliness" (73).

If your sentence did not include Moffatt's name, the parenthetical citation would look like this: (Moffatt 73). Also, if you mention more than one source in the sentence, include the author's name in the parentheses to indicate which source you are quoting: (Moffatt 73).

A P A

> Anthropologist Moffatt (1989) argues that most of the college students he studied at Rutgers University shared "an ideal: a loosely formulated but very pervasive one concerning collective harmony or friendliness" (p. 73).

Note that the year in the APA-style quotation is placed immediately after the author's name. Because writers in the social sciences actively seek to build on and improve existing knowledge, the "freshness" of other writers' research is especially important in APA style. If you did not include Moffatt's name in your sentence, the parenthetical citation would look like this: (Moffatt, 1989, p. 73).

QUOTING A LONG PASSAGE

If the passage you are using is more than four typed lines long (or, in APA style, more than forty words long), quote it as a "block" quotation. Start a new line, indent ten spaces (five spaces for APA), and continue to type double-spaced. Block quotations do not require quotation marks—the indentation tells your reader that you are quoting from a source. You should place your parenthetical citation two spaces after the final punctuation of the quotation. Remember to use long quotations sparingly, only when they are really needed to advance your argument. Here is an example of a block quotation incorporated into an essay written in MLA style:

> In their essay "Minority Men, Misery, and the Market-
> place of Ideas," Richard Delgado and Jean Stefancic
> write that
>> The images of African-American women in U.S.
>> culture—the Mammy, the welfare mother, the
>> militant-but-lazy office worker—are bad
>> enough (and the same is true of Mexican seño-
>> ritas, Indian squaws, and Asian temptresses
>> and Mata Haris), but those of males of color
>> are, if anything, worse. (213)
> When James Baldwin writes about the "careers" that
> were open to him (prizefighter, singer, dancer), it is
> clear that he has been affected by the widespread
> images that trouble Delgado and Stefancic (25).

QUOTING PART OF A PASSAGE

Sometimes, for reasons of space or emphasis, writers choose to delete part of a quotation. When you do this, you should use ellipses dots to indicate where you have left something out. If you delete a few words or a phrase from within a sentence, use three dots:

> Delgado and Stefancic conclude that "the predominant
> images of men of color in any era are apt to be
> intensely negative, although the quality or content of
> the images changes from period to period . . . in
> response to social needs" (217).

If you delete a whole sentence, or the last part of a sentence, use four dots (the first one is actually the period that would end the sentence anyway). The following example shows both kinds of deletion:

```
According to Delgado and Stefancic,
            If most European settlers of America knew
            something of blacks and Indians, they had
            far fewer contacts with Asians and Mexi-
            cans. . . . Most Chinamen, as they were
            called, worked in the gold mines, built rail-
            roads, and did the backbreaking work that
            other settlers shunned. . . .    (215)
```

MLA List of Works Cited and APA References

Whether you use MLA or APA style, all of the texts that you refer to should be listed alphabetically by author or editor (or title, if neither author nor editor is known) at the end of your essay. The list of Works Cited in MLA style and References in APA style should start on a new page and, like the rest of your essay, should be typed double-spaced for easy reading. Here is how the Moffatt book would be listed in MLA and APA styles:

MLA

```
Moffatt, Michael. Coming of Age in New Jersey: College
        and American Culture. New Brunswick: Rutgers UP,
        1989.
```

APA*

```
Moffatt, M. (1989). Coming of age in New Jersey: Col-
        lege and American culture. New Brunswick, NJ:
        Rutgers University Press.
```

CITATION GUIDELINES FOR BOOKS

In both MLA and APA styles, book citations require the name of the author, the book's title, and basic publication information (place of publication, publishing company, year of publication). Here are some examples of citations for various types of books.

---

*The latest APA style manual (1994) presents its sample References entries in indented-paragraph style, with a note stating that the typesetter will convert the entries to a hanging-indent format for final copy. In the case of student writers, APA recommends using hanging-indent style, since almost all students prepare their own final copy.

A BOOK BY A SINGLE AUTHOR
M L A

Spellmeyer, Kurt. *Common Ground: Dialogue, Understanding, and the Teaching of Composition.*
Englewood Cliffs: Prentice Hall, 1993.

APA

Spellmeyer, K. (1993). *Common ground: Dialogue, understanding, and the teaching of composition.*
Englewood Cliffs, NJ: Prentice Hall.

TWO OR MORE WORKS BY THE SAME AUTHOR
M L A

In MLA style, the author's name is replaced in the second and subsequent
entries by three hyphens, and the works are listed in alphabetical order by
the first word of the title (excluding *a*, *an*, and *the*).

Gallop, Jane. *The Daughter's Seduction: Feminism and
Psychoanalysis.* Ithaca: Cornell UP, 1982.
---. *Reading Lacan.* Ithaca: Cornell UP, 1985.

APA

In APA style, texts by the same author are arranged by year of publication.
The earliest should come first. References with the same publication date
should be arranged alphabetically by title.

Gallop, J. (1982). *The daughter's seduction: Feminism
and psychoanalysis.* Ithaca, NY: Cornell University Press.
Gallop, J. (1985). *Reading Lacan.* Ithaca, NY: Cornell
University Press.

A BOOK BY TWO OR MORE AUTHORS
M L A

Stallybrass, Peter, and Allon White. *The Politics and
Poetics of Transgression.* Ithaca: Cornell UP,
1986.

A P A

Stallybrass, P., & White, A. (1986). *The politics and
poetics of transgression.* Ithaca, NY: Cornell
University Press.

686 / Documenting Sources Using MLA or APA Style

AN ANTHOLOGY OR COMPILATION
M L A

Gates, Henry Louis, Jr., ed. *Black Literature and Literary Theory.* New York: Routledge, 1984.

A P A

Gates, H. L., Jr. (Ed.). (1984). *Black literature and literary theory.* New York: Routledge.

A WORK IN AN ANTHOLOGY
M L A

Baldwin, James. "Down at the Cross." *Literacies.* Ed. Terence Brunk et al. New York: Norton, 1997. 41–56.

Washburn, S. L. "The Study of Race." *The "Racial" Economy of Science: Toward a Democratic Future.* Ed. Sandra Harding. Bloomington: Indiana UP, 1993. 128–32.

A P A

Baldwin, J. (1997). Down at the cross. In T. Brunk, S. Diamond, P. Perkins, & K. Smith (Eds.), *Literacies* (pp. 41–56). New York: W. W. Norton.

Washburn, S. L. (1993). The study of race. In S. Harding (Ed.), *The "racial" economy of science: Toward a democratic future* (pp. 128–132). Bloomington, IN: Indiana University Press.

THE INTRODUCTION TO A WORK
M L A

Brunk, Terence, et al., eds. Introduction. *Literacies.* New York: Norton, 1997. xv–xxv.

A P A

Brunk, T., Diamond, S., Perkins, P., & Smith, K. (Eds.). (1997). Introduction. *Literacies.* (pp. xv–xxv). New York: W. W. Norton.

AN ARTICLE IN A DICTIONARY OR REFERENCE BOOK
M L A

"Orbicular." *Webster's New Collegiate Dictionary.* 9th ed.

A P A
> Orbicular. (1981). In *Webster's new collegiate
>   dictionary* (p. 800). New York: G. & C. Merriam.

CROSS-REFERENCES

In MLA style, you do not have to retype the entire bibliographic entry when you are using two or more texts that come from the same collection. This format is called "cross-referencing." In APA style, by contrast, you must include complete bibliographic information for all texts, even those that come from the same collection.

M L A
> Ginsberg, Allen. "I Love Old Whitman So." Lewis 69–70.
> Lewis, Joel, ed. *Bluestones and Salt Hay: An
>   Anthology of Contemporary New Jersey Poets.* New
>   Brunswick: Rutgers UP, 1990.
> Ostriker, Alicia. "Surviving." Lewis 160–66.

A TRANSLATION

M L A
> Foucault, Michel. *The Birth of the Clinic.* 1963. Trans.
>   A. M. Sheridan Smith. New York: Vintage, 1973.

A P A
> Foucault, M. (1973). *The birth of the clinic* (A. M.
>   Sheridan Smith, Trans.). New York: Vintage.
>   (Original work published 1963)

CITATION GUIDELINES FOR PERIODICAL ARTICLES

As with a book, the basic information needed for the Works Cited or References list consists of the author's name, the title of the article, the title of the publication, and publication information. Though you will occasionally refer to newspaper and magazine articles in college writing, you will also find yourself consulting scholarly journals, which feature the most up-to-date and specialized research in many disciplines. Publication information generally appears either on the title page or on the cover of the journal. Listed below are some examples of citation formats for articles that appear in journals organized in various ways:

A SCHOLARLY JOURNAL WITH SEPARATELY PAGINATED ISSUES (each issue begins with page 1)

M L A
> Reyes-Matta, Fernando. "Journalism in Latin America

in the '90s: The Challenges of Modernization."
Journal of Communication 42.3 (1992): 74-83.

A P A

Reyes-Matta, F. (1992). Journalism in Latin America
in the '90s: The challenges of modernization.
Journal of Communication, 42(3), 74-83.

A SCHOLARLY JOURNAL WITH CONTINUOUS PAGINATION

(the first issue in a year or volume begins with page 1; subsequent issues for that volume begin counting pages where the previous issues left off)

M L A

Stevens, Jane Ellen. "The Growing Reality of Virtual
Reality." *BioScience* 45 (1995): 435-39.

A P A

Stevens, J. E. (1995). The growing reality of virtual
reality. *BioScience, 45,* 435-439.

A NEWSPAPER ARTICLE

M L A

McNutt, Michael. "OSU Giving Fulbright Scholars
Inside Look at Indian Life." *Daily Oklahoman* 3
Nov. 1995: 12.

A P A

McNutt, M. (1995, November 3). OSU giving Fulbright
scholars inside look at Indian life. *The Daily
Oklahoman,* p. 12.

A MAGAZINE ARTICLE

M L A

Golsan, Richard. "Fashionable Fascism." *Utne Reader*
Nov.-Dec. 1995: 60-61.

A P A

Golsan, R. (1995, November-December). Fashionable
fascism. *The Utne Reader, 72,* 60-61.

BIOGRAPHICAL SKETCHES

Maya Angelou (b. 1928)

American author, playwright, actress, poet, and singer. Born in St. Louis, Angelou attended public schools in Arkansas and California before studying music and dance. In a richly varied career, she has been a cook, streetcar conductor, singer, actress, dancer, and teacher. Author of several volumes of poetry and ten plays (stage, screen, and television), Angelou may be best known for her poem "On the Pulse of Morning," which she read at the inauguration of President Bill Clinton in 1993. *I Know Why the Caged Bird Sings* (1970), the first volume of her autobiography, is one of the fullest accounts in contemporary literature of an African American woman's experience. *All God's Children Need Traveling Shoes* (1986), another autobiographical work, describes Angelou's experiences in Ghana as that nation won its independence. Most recently, she has written a children's book, *My Painted House, My Friendly Chicken, and Me* (1994).

Gloria Anzaldúa (b. 1942)

Self-described "queer Chicana tejana feminist patlache poet and writer." Anzaldúa grew up on a ranch in south Texas, torn between the everyday life she knew there and her intellectual interests. After graduating from the University of Texas, she became a summer-school teacher for migrant families in the Midwest. Since that time, she has taught creative writing at a number of colleges and has been writer-in-residence and artist-in-residence around the country. In her writing, Anzaldúa blends her cultural identities with her academic interests, as she combines Spanish and English poetry, autobiography, and historical analysis. Her book, *Borderlands/La Frontera: The New Mestiza* (1987), was voted one of *Literary Journal's* Best Books of 1987, and she edited the award-winning *Making Face, Making Soul/Haciendo Caras: Creative and Critical Perspectives by Feminists-of-Color* (1990). She is working on both a novel and a short story collection and on a book theorizing about the production of writing, knowledge, and identity.

Margaret Atwood (b. 1939)

Canadian novelist, poet, and critic. Born in Ontario, educated at the University of Toronto, Radcliffe College, and Harvard University, Atwood began writing as a poet in the 1960s; her later fiction builds on many of the themes she first explored in her poetry. Her novels are well-regarded by critics and the general public, an unusual feat for any writer. Atwood has said that many of her characters, and the difficulties with which they must deal, come from the lives of those she knows. Her best-known novels include *The Edible Woman* (1969); *Surfacing* (1972); *Bodily Harm* (1982); *The Handmaid's Tale* (1986), which was made into a movie in 1990; *Cat's Eye* (1988); and *The Robber Bride* (1993). Her most recent book is a collection of poetry, *Morning in the Burned House* (1995).

James Baldwin (1924–1987)

American essayist, novelist, and social activist. Baldwin was born in Harlem, became a minister at fourteen, left the church, and worked as a laborer in New York City until his late twenties. Disgusted with the racism and prejudice in the United States, Baldwin moved to Paris and began to write. Both his first novel, *Go Tell It on the Mountain* (1953), and his first play, *The Amen Corner* (1955), are autobiographical explorations. Although he would write other plays, Baldwin concentrated his energies on novels and essay collections, including *Notes of a Native Son* (1955), *Nobody Knows My Name* (1961), and *The Fire Next Time* (1963). A number of his most important essays and reviews have been gathered in *The Price of the Ticket* (1985).

Dean Barnlund (1920–1992)

American educator. After attending the University of Wisconsin and receiving his doctorate from Northwestern University, Barnlund taught communications at San Francisco State University. While a visiting professor at International Christian University in Tokyo, he conducted a survey on Japanese expression, the results of which led him to write *Communicative Styles of Japanese and Americans: Images and Realities* (1989) and *Public & Private Self in Japan and the United States: Communicative Styles of Two Cultures* (1989). Barnlund has also written and co-written numerous communications textbooks, including *Interpersonal Communication: Survey and Studies* (1968) and *The Dynamic of Discussion* (1960).

Robert Bellah (b. 1927), Richard Madsen (b. 1941), William Sullivan (b. 1945), Ann Swidler (b. 1944), and Steven Tipton (b. 1946)

American sociologists. This team of authors wrote the best-selling, award-winning *Habits of the Heart* (1985), a call for people to value social obligations over individual gains. They followed up with a collection of essays, *Individualism and Commitment in American Life: Readings on the Themes of "Habits of the Heart"* (1987). Four years later, the team published *The Good Society* (1991), which offers suggestions for strengthening community and increasing social responsibility. Bellah and Swidler teach at the University of California at Berkeley, Madsen at the University of California at San Diego, Sullivan at LaSalle University, and Tipton at Emory University.

Bruno Bettelheim (1903–1990)

American child psychologist, teacher, and writer. Born and educated in Vienna, Bettelheim came to the United States in 1939, having spent a year in the concentration camps of Buchenwald and Dachau. He joined the faculty of the University of Chicago in 1944 and spent the rest of his career there. Bettelheim wrote several dozen books, including *Love Is Not Enough: The Treatment of Emotionally Disturbed Children* (1950), *The Informed Heart: Autonomy in a Mass Age* (1960), *The Children of the Dream* (1969), *A Good Enough Parent* (1987), and the posthumous *Art of the Obvious* (1993). His most famous book, *The Uses of Enchantment: The Meaning and Importance of Fairy Tales* (1976), combines psychoanalysis with developmental psychology in the understanding of fairy tales; it won numerous awards.

Frank Black Elk (b. 1951)

Native American activist and writer. Black Elk grew up in Nebraska and now lives and works in Denver. An active member of the Colorado chapter of the American Indian Movement, Black Elk believed that the movement needed to open new doors for Native Americans; consequently, he studied information processing, bookkeeping, and accounting in Denver and Albuquerque and helped found the Western American Indian Chamber of Commerce, which aids Native American entrepreneurs. Black Elk has recently become active in the Democratic Party in Denver and plans to run for the state legislature. He has said that his interest in politics stems from a desire to help and inspire the economically repressed to gain economic independence. Black Elk's recent writing includes a short story based on a continuing dream he has had over the last five years, as well as editorial writing for the Democratic Party.

Howard Brody (b. 1949)

Physician, medical ethicist, and educator. Trained in philosophical ethics and in medicine, Brody has spent much of his career bringing the two together, both in the medical profession and in the public consciousness. To this end, he has written widely on a number of medical and ethical issues, including life-sustaining treatments, physician-assisted death, informed consent, and health care programs. A professor of family practice and philosophy, and the director of the Center for Ethics and Humanities in the Life Sciences at Michigan State University, Brody has written *Ethical Decisions in Medicine* (1976), *Stories of Sickness* (1987), and *The Healer's Power* (1992).

Barbara Christian (b. 1943)

African American educator and critic. Born in the Virgin Islands, Christian was educated at Marquette and Columbia, where she received her doctorate with honors. She now teaches African American Studies at the University of California, Berkeley, where she was the first African American woman to be awarded tenure and the rank of full professor. Christian has long been involved in educational outreach programs for disadvantaged populations, particularly those for women and African Americans. Her scholarship focuses on race issues and literary theory; her books include the award-winning *Black Women Novelists: The Development of a Tradition, 1892–1976* (1980) and *Black Feminist Criticism: Perspectives on Black Women Writers* (1985).

James Clifford (b. 1945)

American sociologist. Now at the University of California, Santa Cruz, in the History of Consciousness program. One of the most prominent cultural theorists in the United States, Clifford and his work have influenced research in a wide variety of disciplines. He has written extensively on ethnography, museums, and the history of missionary language, questioning in particular the ways in which cultures are assigned commodifiable values. His best-known books are *Writing Culture: The Poetics and Politics of Ethnography* (1986) and *The Predicament of Culture: Twentieth-Century Ethnography, Literature, and Art* (1988).

Jimmie Durham (b. 1940)

Native American artist, activist, and writer. Raised in a Cherokee community in the southwest, Durham learned how to read when he joined the navy at age 19. He was an active leader in the American Indian Movement and twice has moved out of the United States, intending not to return. The first move was to the Ecole des Beaux Arts in Geneva, which launched his studio art career and further sensitized him to political injustices. Achieving international prominence with his painting, Durham has been known to give away his work to protest the financial structure of the art industry. He also feels that "multiculturalism is only lip service . . . happening at this point in time because the state has to somehow acknowledge the current reality of the U.S." He now lives in Mexico, where he continues to paint and write. He has published a book of poetry, *Columbus Day* (1983), and is currently editor of the newspaper *Art & Artists*.

Stuart Ewen (b. 1945)

American cultural historian. Born in New York, Ewen has been politically active since his days as a student at the University of Wisconsin, University of Rochester, and State University of New York at Albany. He now teaches history and media studies throughout the City University of New York system, and he remains committed to the idea that the "power of mass produced images in our lives requires a historical understanding, a political analysis, and a radical response." His books include *Captains of Consciousness: Advertising and the Social Roots of the Consumer Culture* (1976), *Channels of Desire: Mass Images and the Shaping of American Consciousness* (1982), and *All Consuming Images: The Politics of Style in Contemporary Culture* (1988).

Ann Fienup-Riordan (b. 1948)

American anthropologist. Educated as a cultural anthropologist at the University of Chicago, Fienup-Riordan now teaches at the University of Alaska in Anchorage. She has studied the Yup'ik Eskimos for years and early on realized that it was not possible to understand their complexities until she lived among them. Fienup-Riordan is particularly good at writing for both scholarly and popular audiences, and her books include *The Nelson Island Eskimo* (1983), *Eskimo Essays: Yup'ik Lives and How We See Them* (1990), *The Real People and the Children of Thunder* (1990), and most recently, *Boundaries and Passages: Rule and Ritual in Yup'ik Eskimo Oral Tradition* (1994).

Andrea R. Fishman (b. 1947)

American educator. Born in New York City, Fishman graduated from Dickinson College and the University of Pennsylvania. Fishman lived on an Amish farm in Pennsylvania while studying the roles of reading and writing in Amish populations; this research informed her book *Amish Literacy: What and How It Means* (1988). Her more recent work has discussed multiculturalism, gender issues, and public schools. Fishman currently teaches in the English department at West Chester University in Pennsylvania, and she remains interested in the broad issues of literacy, writing, and education. She is the founding director of the Pennsylvania Literature Project, which is aimed at improving the ways in which literature is taught throughout the school system.

694 / Biographical Sketches

Barbara Garson (b. 1941)

American labor historian, playwright, and self-described "socialist agitator and educator." Born in Brooklyn, Garson has led a varied and fascinating life. Her earlier paths were in the theater, where her play *MacBird!* (1967) parodied politics and propaganda using the framework of Shakespeare's *Macbeth*, and her children's play, *The Dinosaur Door*, won her an Obie award. From there, Garson's interests turned to the increased automation of both blue- and white-collar workforces, with her books *All the Livelong Day: The Meaning and Demeaning of Routine Work* (1975) and *The Electronic Sweatshop: How Computers Are Transforming the Office of the Future into the Factory of the Past* (1988). Garson says that her goal is to reinsert humanity into work processes by telling the stories of the individuals with whom she works, while sounding an alarm to larger societal issues.

David Gilmore (b. 1943)

American anthropologist. Born in New York, Gilmore was educated at Columbia and the University of Pennsylvania before embarking on his anthropological fieldwork in Spain. While in a small town in southern Spain, Gilmore observed the importance of masculinity, noting that "people there were always talking about 'real men' and about being macho." Further research led Gilmore to write *Manhood in the Making: Cultural Concepts of Masculinity* (1990). In addition, he has published numerous articles on social class and rural revolutionism in nineteenth-century Spain. His other books include *The People of the Plain: Class and Community in Lower Andalusia* (1980) and *Aggression and the Community: Paradoxes of Andalusian Culture* (1987).

Shirley Brice Heath (b. 1939)

American linguist and anthropologist. Now a professor at Stanford University, Heath brought an appreciation of ethnographic research methods to the study of language with her book *Ways with Words: Language, Life and Work in Communities and Classrooms* (1983). Primarily interested in language acquisition, the relations between oral and written language, and thinking across cultural boundaries, Heath has written numerous books, chapters, and articles focusing on language use in different settings, including *Children of Promise: Literate Activity in Linguistically and Culturally Diverse Classrooms* (1991) and *The Braid of Literature: Children's Worlds of Reading* (1993). Most recently, she has been studying inner-city youth groups, analyzing and documenting the organizational structures and communications that surround their everyday learning successes in *Identity and Inner-City Youth: Beyond Ethnicity and Gender* (1993).

Liliana Heker (b. 1943)
Argentinean writer and editor. Born in Buenos Aires, Heker began writing as a teenager. Her first book of short stories, *Those Who Beheld the Burning Bush* (1966), established her as one of Argentina's most promising writers. In addition to her own writing, Heker edited the important literary magazine *(El Ornitorrinco) The Platypus*, which gave writers a national publishing forum during the years of censorship and dictatorship in Argentina. Her more recent publications are *Zone of Cleavage* (1987) and *The Stolen Party* (1994).

bell hooks (b. 1952) and Cornel West (b. 1953)
African American educators and intellectuals. Born in Kentucky, Gloria Watkins chose the pseudonym bell hooks to honor the memory of her grandmother, a quilt-maker. Educated at Stanford University, the University of Wisconsin, and the University of California, Santa Cruz, hooks is best known for her histories and theories of race and gender, particularly the double-bind that holds women of color. Her books include *Ain't I a Woman* (1981), *Talking Back: Thinking Feminist, Thinking Black* (1989), *Yearning: Race, Gender, and Cultural Politics* (1990), and *Killing Rage: Ending Racism* (1995). Cornel West was born in Oklahoma and educated at Harvard, Princeton, and Union Theological Seminary. A professor of religion and director of Afro-American Studies at Princeton, West writes and lectures widely about race relations, religion, and ethics, combining theories of Christianity with Marxist thought. His books include *Prophetic Fragments* (1988), *Keeping Faith* (1993), *Beyond Eurocentrism and Multiculturalism* (1993), and *Race Matters* (1993). West and hooks collaborated on *Breaking Bread: Insurgent Black Intellectual Life* (1991), their dialogue about a variety of issues facing the African American community.

Maxine Hong Kingston (b. 1940)
Asian American autobiographer and novelist. Born in California, the eldest of six children in a Chinese immigrant family, Kingston grew up in a world where English was a distant second language and friends and relatives regularly gathered at her family's laundry to tell stories and reminisce about their native country. After graduating from the University of California, Berkeley, she taught school in California and Hawaii and began publishing poetry, stories, and articles in a number of magazines, including *The New Yorker, New West, The New York Times Magazine, Ms.,* and *Iowa Review.* Her two acclaimed books of reminiscence are *The Woman Warrior: Memoirs of a Girlhood Among Ghosts* (1973) and *China Men* (1980); her most recent work is the novel *Tripmaster Monkey* (1989).

Jonathan Kozol (b. 1936)
American writer and social critic. Born in Boston to a doctor and a social worker and educated at Harvard, Kozol's experiences as a fourth-grade

teacher in an inner-city school led him to write his award-winning first book, *Death at an Early Age: The Destruction of Hearts and Minds of Negro Schoolchildren in the Boston Public Schools* (1967). Since then, he has devoted his research and writing to identifying and publicizing class and racial inequities in our public education system, particularly as these inequities manifest themselves in illiteracy. His other books include *Illiterate America* (1985), *Rachel and Her Children* (1988), *Savage Inequalities* (1991), and most recently *Amazing Grace: The Lives of Children and the Conscience of a Nation* (1995).

Audre Lorde (1934–1992)
African American lesbian poet and activist. The child of parents from Grenada, Lorde grew up in New York City. She taught at various schools throughout the City University of New York system and became poet laureate of New York State after winning the Walt Whitman Citation of Merit. Her poetry is aimed at exposing social injustice and supporting those lost in mainstream American culture. She published many volumes of poetry, most notably *The Cancer Journals* (1980), about her struggles with breast cancer, and *Zami: A New Spelling of My Name* (1982). *A Burst of Light* (1988), a collection of essays, won the American Book Award. Before her death, Lorde took the African name "Gambda Adisa" (meaning "Warrior: She Who Makes Her Meaning Known"), echoing her feeling that "imposed silence about any area of our lives is a tool for separation and powerlessness."

Alistair MacLeod (b. 1936)
Canadian fiction writer and educator. Born in Saskatchewan, MacLeod was educated and has taught in both the United States and Canada. He currently lives in Windsor, Ontario. Lauded as the foremost writer of Canada's Maritimes and Nova Scotia, MacLeod is a master of the short story. Anthologized widely in collections such as *Best American Short Stories* and *Best Canadian Short Stories*, MacLeod's work also helps preserve the history and ethnic identity of the Maritimes by chronicling its people's struggle for survival. He has written a few plays, and his short story collections include *The Lost Salt Gift of Blood* (1976) and *As Birds Bring Forth the Sun and Other Stories* (1986).

Adrienne Rich (b. 1929)
American poet. While she was an undergraduate at Radcliffe, Rich's first book of poetry, *A Change of World*, was chosen by W. H. Auden for the Yale Younger Poet's Prize (1951). Since then, Rich has published nineteen books of poetry and prose, including *Diving into the Wreck* (1973), *Of Woman Born* (1976), and *An Atlas of the Difficult World: Poems 1988–1991* (1991). In 1994 she was awarded a MacArthur fellowship. Her newest work is *Dark Fields of the Republic* (1995).

Richard Rodriguez (b. 1944)

American essayist and teacher. The son of Mexican American immigrants, Rodriguez was a proficient student at his Catholic school in San Francisco. He then received his advanced degrees from Stanford, Columbia, and the University of California, Berkeley. Despite his academic success, including several prestigious fellowships, Rodriguez left the university partly because he was uncomfortable with advantages he felt he received because of his minority status. He now works as a lecturer and educational consultant as well as a freelance writer, often arguing against bilingual education and affirmative action. His books *Hunger of Memory: The Education of Richard Rodriguez* (1982) and *Days of Obligation: An Argument with My Mexican Father* (1992) recount his assimilation into mainstream American society.

Renato Rosaldo (b. 1941)

American anthropologist. Born in Illinois to an academic family, Rosaldo was educated at Harvard University before beginning his teaching career at Stanford. His research has focused particularly on the Philippines and on Mayan and Chicano studies. Rosaldo advocates locating "border narratives" rather than cultural norms—in other words, finding multiple stories and interpretations rather than a single, unifying one. His current interests include examining the role of experience and emotion in cultural interpretation and the status of history in anthropological studies. Rosaldo's books include *Ilongot Headhunting, 1883–1974* (1980) and *Culture and Truth: The Remaking of Social Analysis* (1993).

Nawal el-Saadawi (b. 1931)

Egyptian feminist, psychiatrist, sociologist, and writer. Born in Kafr Tahla, a village in Egypt on the banks of the Nile, el-Saadawi had a highly visible career in public health, both as a practitioner, as editor of *Health* magazine, and as Egypt's director of public health. In 1981, she was arrested by the Egyptian government, stripped of her titles, and imprisoned with other political activists. *Memoirs from the Women's Prison* (1994) catalogs her experiences as a political prisoner. Earlier books, such as *The Hidden Face of Eve* (1977), discuss the oppression of Arab women and their struggles for liberation. Her most recent novel is *Innocence of the Devil* (1994). El-Saadawi currently teaches in the Women's Studies Department at the University of Washington, and she continues to be an activist and writer, saying that "[w]e cannot separate between the oppression of women and the international politics in neocolonialism which increases the gap between nations, classes, [and] sexes."

Carol de Saint Victor (b. 1934)

American educator. Trained in literary studies at Indiana University and in both England and France, de Saint Victor now teaches in the creative nonfiction program at the University of Iowa. Although educated through a traditional literature program, she became increasingly interested in writing about events, insights, and the multiple ways people create their realities, rather than in studying a particular author. Much of her writing now focuses on her personal reflections about her travels. "Go Slowly and You Arrive" was one of the first personal essays she wrote; it grew out of her desire to travel to India, a woman alone. This essay represents for de Saint Victor her realization that she had a calling to write outside the boundaries of traditional academic discourse.

Scott Russell Sanders (b. 1945)

American writer and teacher. Born in Tennessee and educated at Brown and Cambridge, Sanders is now professor of English at Indiana University. He has published fifteen books, including eight works of fiction. Sanders's writing is especially concerned with humanity's relationship to nature, issues of social justice, the character of community, and the effect of science on our lives. *The Paradise of Bombs* (1987), a collection of essays on violence in the United States, won an award for creative nonfiction. Other books include *In Limestone Country* (1985), *Staying Put: Making a Home in a Restless World* (1993), and his most recent, *Writing from the Center* (1995).

Nancy Scheper-Hughes (b. 1944)

American anthropologist. Born in New York City and trained at the University of California, Berkeley, Scheper-Hughes claims that much of her education came from her fieldwork in Ireland and Brazil. She began working as a Peace Corps volunteer in Brazil, teaching basic health care to the squatter peasants. They, in turn, educated her to the cultural and economic pressures which shaped their lives. In her words: "[E]ducation is never a monologue. It is a continuing, critical dialogal encounter between consciousness and unconsciousness, reason and unreason, silence and words, between I and thou, self and others." Her books include the award-winning *Saints, Scholars, and Schizophrenics: Mental Illness in Rural Ireland* (1979) and *Death Without Weeping: The Violence of Everyday Life in Brazil* (1992). Scheper-Hughes is currently studying moral development through anthropological studies, and she teaches at the University of California, Berkeley.

Robert Scholes (b. 1929)

American educator and literary scholar. Born in Brooklyn and educated at Yale and Cornell, Scholes now teaches at Brown University. He considers himself "a teacher first and a writer second, and I have to admit that my writing is of the 'academic' variety." In fact, Scholes has written some of the most influential books in current literary criticism, including *The Fabulators* (1967), *Semiotics and Interpretation* (1982), the award-winning *Textual*

Power: Literary Theory and the Teaching of English (1985), and most recently *Hemingway's Genders: Rereading the Hemingway Text* (1994). In addition to his scholarly books, Scholes has written numerous English textbooks, including *Elements of Literature, Elements of Writing, The Practice of Writing,* and *Textbook: An Introduction to Literary Language.*

Victor Seidler (b. 1945)

British social philosopher. Seidler teaches at the University of London. His aim is to make possible a better social order by breaking down personal and political barriers that further traditional notions of masculinity. He wants men to embrace emotion, feeling, and desire; Seidler advocates borrowing from feminism to create a new image of masculinity. His work began with *Rediscovering Masculinity* (1989), which he followed up with *Recreating Sexual Politics: Men, Feminism, and Politics* (1991) and *Unreasonable Men: Masculinity and Social Theory* (1995). Seidler has also written a biography, *Truer Liberty: Simone Weil and Marxism* (1989).

Mary Lyndon Shanley (b. 1944)

American educator. A professor of political science at Vassar College, Shanley is currently researching ethical issues in contemporary family law. She is also working on a project to reconceptualize traditional Western political theory. She has published numerous books and articles, including *Feminism, Marriage and the Law in Victorian England* (1989) and *Feminist Interpretations and Political Theory* (1990).

Susan Sontag (b. 1933)

American critic, social activist, and filmmaker. Born in New York City, Sontag graduated from high school at the age of fifteen and immediately entered the University of California, Berkeley; after receiving her B.A., she went on to graduate school at the University of Chicago and Harvard. Her collection of essays *Against Interpretation* (1966) established her as a serious intellectual, and *Trip to Hanoi* (1968) established her as a political and cultural critic. After a bout with breast cancer, Sontag wrote *Illness as Metaphor* (1978), followed by *AIDS and Its Metaphors* (1988). She continues to write films, plays, novels, and literary criticism, including her most recent work, *Homo Poeticus* (1995).

Amy Tan (b. 1952)

Asian American novelist. Born in Oakland, California, to immigrant parents, Tan began writing short stories about her family as a form of therapy while working as a technical writer in San Francisco. These pieces became chapters of her first novel, *The Joy Luck Club* (1989), which was later produced as a motion picture. Most of her writing, including her children's books *The*

Moon Lady (1992) and *The Chinese Siamese Cat* (1994), combines elements of her Chinese heritage and her American upbringing, often focusing on the tensions between Chinese-born mothers and their American-born daughters. Tan's other books include *The Kitchen God's Wife* (1991) and *The Hundred Secret Senses* (1995).

Alice Walker (b. 1944)
African American poet, novelist, and essayist. Born and raised by sharecroppers in rural Georgia, Walker was educated at Spelman College and Sarah Lawrence College. Walker then worked as an editor for *Ms.* magazine and became active in the civil rights movement. She received widespread fame for her Pulitzer Prize–winning *The Color Purple* (1982). In addition to her many volumes of poetry, her books include *In Search of Our Mothers' Gardens* (1983), *The Temple of My Familiar* (1989), *Possessing the Secret of Joy* (1992), and *Everyday Use* (1994). Recently, she has written a study of genital mutilation in Africa, *Warrior Marks* (1993). She currently lives in San Francisco and runs her own publishing company, Wild Trees Press.

Jeffrey Weeks (b. 1945)
British sociologist. Born in Wales and educated at the University of London, Weeks is now a professor of social relations at Bristol Polytechnic. Much of his research draws connections between history, sexuality, and identity; he argues that sexuality is a product of social formations, particularly politics. A frequent spokesperson for the homosexual community, Weeks says he is primarily interested in "the social revolution of sexuality and the forms of sexual politics." His books include *Sexuality and Its Discontents: Meanings, Myths, and Modern Sexualities* (1985), *Sex, Politics, and Society: The Regulation of Sexuality since 1800* (1989), *Against Nature: Essays on History, Sexuality, and Identity* (1991), *Between the Acts: Lives of Homosexual Men, 1885–1967* (1991), and most recently *Invented Moralities: Sexual Values in an Age of Uncertainty* (1995).

ACKNOWLEDGMENTS

Angelou: "Mary" from *I Know Why the Caged Bird Sings* by Maya Angelou. Copyright © 1970 by Maya Angelou. Reprinted by permission of Random House, Inc.

Anzaldúa: "Speaking in Tongues: A Letter to 3rd World Women Writers" from *This Bridge Called My Back,* edited by Cherríe Moraga and Gloria Anzaldúa. Copyright © 1983. Reprinted by permission of the author and Kitchen Table: Women of Color Press, Box 40-4920, Brooklyn NY 11240.

Atwood: "An End to Audience?" from *Second Words* by Margaret Atwood. Originally published in *Dalhousie Review* 60.3 (1980). Reprinted by permission of the author and *Dalhousie Review.*

Baldwin: "Down at the Cross" from *The Fire Next Time* by James Baldwin. Copyright © 1962 by James Baldwin. Copyright renewed. Reprinted by permission of the James Baldwin Estate.

Barnlund: "Communication in a Global Village" from *Public and Private Self in Japan and the United States* by Dean C. Barnlund. Copyright © 1975. Reprinted by permission of Intercultural Press, Inc., Yarmouth, ME.

Bellah et al.: "Community, Commitment, and Individuality" from *Habits of the Heart.* Copyright © 1985 by The Regents of the University of California. Reprinted by permission of the University of California Press.

Bettelheim: "The Ignored Lesson of Anne Frank" from *Surviving and Other Essays* by Bruno Bettelheim. Copyright © 1952, 1960, 1962, 1976, 1979 by Bruno Bettelheim and Trude Bettelheim, as Trustees. Reprinted by permission of Alfred A. Knopf, Inc.

Black Elk: "Observations on Marxism and Lakota Tradition" from *Marxism and Native Americans,* ed. Ward Churchill. Copyright © 1983. Reprinted by permission of South End Press.

Brody: "The Social Power of Expert Healers" from *The Healer's Power* by Howard Brody. Copyright © 1992. Reprinted by permission of Yale University Press.

Christian: "Black Feminist Process" from *Black Feminist Criticism: Perspectives on Black Women Writers* by Barbara Christian. Copyright © 1985 by Teachers College, Columbia University. Reprinted by permission of the author and Teachers College Press.

Clifford: "Incidents of Tourism in Chiapas & Yucatan" from *Sulfur* 29 (Fall 1991). Copyright © 1991. Reprinted by permission of *Sulfur.*

Durham: "Those Dead Guys for a Hundred Years" from *I Tell You Now: Autobiographical Essays by Native American Writers*, edited by Brian Swann and Arnold Krupat. Copyright © 1987 by the University of Nebraska Press. Reprinted by permission of the University of Nebraska Press.

Ewen: "Chosen People" from *All Consuming Images* by Stuart Ewen. Copyright © 1988 by Basic Books, Inc. Reprinted by permission of Basic Books, a division of Harper Collins Publishers, Inc.

Fienup-Riordan: "Yup'ik Lives and How We See Them" from *Eskimo Essays* by Ann Fienup-Riordan. Copyright © 1990 by Ann Fienup-Riordan. Reprinted by permission of Rutgers University Press.

Fishman: "Becoming Literate: A Lesson from the Amish" from *The Right to Literacy*, edited by Andrea Lunsford et al. Copyright © 1990. Reprinted by permission of the Modern Language Association of America.

Garson: "McDonald's—We Do It All for You" from *The Electronic Sweatshop* by Barbara Garson. Copyright © 1988 by Barbara Garson. Reprinted by permission of Simon & Schuster.

Gilmore: "Performative Excellence: Circum-Mediterranean" from *Manhood in the Making* by David Gilmore. Copyright © 1990. Reprinted by permission of Yale University Press.

Heath: "Literate Traditions" from *Ways with Words: Language, Life, and Work in Communities and Classrooms* by Shirley Brice Heath. Copyright © 1983 by Cambridge University Press. Reprinted by permission of the author and Cambridge University Press.

Heker: "The Stolen Party" from *Other Fires: Short Fiction by Latin American Women*, translated by Alberto Manguel. Copyright © 1982 by Liliana Heker. Translation copyright © 1985 by Alberto Manguel. Reprinted by permission of Westwood Creative Agents and Crown Publishers, Inc.

hooks & West: "Black Women and Men: Partnership in the 1990s" from *Breaking Bread: Insurgent Black Intellectual Life*. Copyright © 1991 by South End Press. Reprinted by permission of South End Press.

Kingston: "No Name Woman" from *The Woman Warrior* by Maxine Hong Kingston. Copyright © 1975, 1976 by Maxine Hong Kingston. Reprinted by permission of Alfred A. Knopf, Inc.

Kozol: "Rachel and Her Childrren" from *Rachel and Her Children* by Jonathan Kozol. Copyright © 1988 by Jonathan Kozol. Reprinted by permission of Crown Publishers, Inc.

Lorde: "The Uses of Anger" from *Sister Outsider* by Audre Lorde. Copyright © 1984 by Audre Lorde. Reprinted by permission of Crossing Press, Freedom, CA.

MacLeod: "The Vastness of the Dark" from *The Lost Salt Gift of Blood* by Alistair MacLeod. Reprinted by permission of the Canadian Publishers, McClelland & Stewart, Toronto.

Rich: "Women and Honor" from *On Lies, Secrets, and Silence* by Adrienne Rich. Copyright © 1979 by W. W. Norton & Company, Inc. Reprinted by permission of W. W. Norton & Company, Inc.

Rodriguez: "Complexion" from *Hunger of Memory* by Richard Rodriguez. Copyright © 1982 by Richard Rodriguez. Reprinted by permission of David R. Godine, Publisher, Inc.

Rosaldo: "Grief and a Headhunter's Rage" from *Culture and Truth* by Renato Rosaldo. Copyright © 1989, 1993 by Renato Rosaldo. Reprinted by permission of Beacon Press.

el-Saadawi: "Love and Sex in the Life of the Arab" from *The Hidden Face of Eve: Women in the Arab World* by Nawal el-Saadawi. Copyright © 1980 by Nawal el-Saadawi. Reprinted by permission of Zed Books Ltd.

Saint Victor: "Go Slowly and You Arrive" from *Missouri Review* 15.2. Reprinted by permission of the author.

Sanders: "The Men We Carry in Our Minds." First appeared in *Milkweed Chronicle*. Reprinted by permission of the author and Virginia Kidd, Literary Agent.

Scheper-Hughes: "The Anthropological Looking Glass" from *Saints, Scholars, and Schizophrenics: Mental Illness in Rural Ireland* by Nancy Scheper-Hughes. Copyright © 1979 by The Regents of the University of California. Reprinted by permission of the University of California Press.

Scholes: "On Reading a Video Text" from *Protocols of Reading* by Robert Scholes. Copyright © 1989 by Robert Scholes. Reprinted by permission of Yale University Press.

Seidler: "Language and Masculinity" from *Rediscovering Masculinity* by Victor Seidler. Reprinted by permission of Routledge.

Shanley: " 'Surrogate Mothering' and Women's Freedom: A Critique of Contracts for Human Reproduction," *Signs* (Spring 1993). Reprinted by permission of the University of Chicago Press.

Sontag: "AIDS and Its Metaphors" from *Aids and Its Metaphors* by Susan Sontag. Copyright © 1988, 1989 by Susan Sontag. Reprinted by permission of Farrar, Straus, & Giroux, Inc.

Tan: "The Language of Discretion" from *The State of the Language*, edited by Christopher Ricks and Leonard Michaels. Copyright © 1990 by Amy Tan. Reprinted by permission of the author and the Sandra Dijkstra Literary Agency.

Walker: "Everyday Use" from *In Love & Trouble: Stories of Black Women* by Alice Walker. Copyright © 1973 by Alice Walker. Reprinted by permission of Harcourt Brace & Company.

Weeks: "Values in an Age of Uncertainty" from *Discourses of Sexuality: From Aristotle to AIDS*, edited by Domna C. Stanton. Reprinted by permission of the University of Michigan Press.